Building Problem Solvers

Kenneth D. Forbus
Johan de Kleer

Building Problem Solvers

A Bradford Book
The MIT Press
Cambridge, Massachusetts
London, England

This book was composed and typeset in ZzTEX by Paul C. Anagnostopoulos and Joe Snowden. The typeface is Lucida Bright and Lucida New Math created by Charles Bigelow and Kris Holmes specifically for scientific and electronic publishing. The Lucida letterforms have the large x-heights and open interiors that aid legibility in modern printing technology, but also echo some of the rhythms and calligraphic details of lively Renaissance handwriting. Developed in the 1980s and 1990s, the extensive Lucida typeface family includes a wide variety of mathematical and technical symbols designed to harmonize with the text faces.

This book was printed and bound in the United States of America.

Library of Congress Cataloging-in-Publication Data

Forbus, Kenneth D.
Building problem solvers / Kenneth D. Forbus, Johan de Kleer,
p. cm. — (Artificial intelligence)
"A Bradford book."
Includes index.
ISBN 0-262-06157-0
1. System design. 2. Expert systems (Computer science)
3. Artificial intelligence. I. De Kleer, Johan. II. Title.
III. Series: Artificial intelligence (Cambridge, Mass.)
QA76.9.S88F67 1993
004.2'1—dc20 93-20456
CIP

Contents

Series Foreword

Artificial intelligence is the study of intelligence using the ideas and methods of computation. Unfortunately a definition of intelligence seems impossible at the moment because intelligence appears to be an amalgam of so many information-processing and information-representation abilities.

Of course psychology, philosophy, linguistics, and related disciplines offer various perspectives and methodologies for studying intelligence. For the most part, however, the theories proposed in these fields are too incomplete and too vaguely stated to be realized in computational terms. Something more is needed, even though valuable ideas, relationships, and constraints can be gleaned from traditional studies of what are, after all, impressive existence proofs that intelligence is in fact possible.

Artificial intelligence offers a new perspective and a new methodology. Its central goal is to make computers intelligent, both to make them more useful and to understand the principles that make intelligence possible. That intelligent computers will be extremely useful is obvious. The more profound point is that artificial intelligence aims to understand intelligence using the ideas and methods of computation, thus offering a radically new and different basis for theory formation. Most of the people doing work in artificial intelligence believe that these theories will apply to any intelligent information processor, whether biological or solid state.

There are side effects that deserve attention, too. Any program that will successfully model even a small part of intelligence will be inherently massive and complex. Consequently artificial intelligence continually confronts the limits of computer-science technology. The problem encountered have been hard enough and interesting enough to seduce artificial intelligence people into working on them with enthusiasm. It is natural, then, that there has been a steady flow of ideas from artificial intelligence to computer science, and the flow shows no sign of abating.

The purpose of this series in artificial intelligence is to provide people in many areas, both professionals and students, with timely, detailed information about what is happening on the frontiers in research centers all over the world.

J. Michael Brady
Daniel G. Bobrow
Randall Davis

1 Preface

Artificial intelligence has matured. Steady scientific progress has led to intellectual respectability. Commercially, the 1970s saw a trickle of applications, while in the 1980s expert systems technology became an accepted factor in solving information processing problems. Fueled in part by the microelectronics revolution, these trends have led to rapid growth in the field. Compared to the explosive growth of the 1980s, the trend for the 1990s seems to be a continual, quiet propagation of artificial intelligence techniques into mainstream computing.

One consequence of this growth is a substantial rise in the number of people interested in AI research and applications. Unfortunately, the dissemination of AI expertise has not kept pace. Artificial intelligence is an experimental discipline. AI research invariably requires programming. Applying AI as part of a system to perform some large task requires either understanding the strengths and weaknesses of subsystems embodying AI techniques or "rolling your own" to meet your constraints. Although the skills required for successful AI programming are mostly the same as those needed for any other kind of programming, the technology involved is often unfamiliar. Previously these techniques were passed on by apprenticeship, but the explosive growth of the field has caused that system to break down. As progress moves the frontier farther away, it becomes essential to master the fundamentals more quickly. This book is designed to help.

1.1 The role of this book

The goal of this book is to teach the reader how to design and build computer problem solvers. Although there have been several books that describe Lisp and AI programming, this book is unique in several ways:

1. We assume a thorough knowledge of Common Lisp. There are several good Lisp textbooks already in print; we see no reason to add yet another. Assuming familiarity with Common Lisp allows us to explore more advanced topics.
2. We focus on techniques for building reasoning systems, instead of attempting to cover every variety of AI programming. For example, we do not explore the design of natural language systems, vision programs, learning systems, or neural networks. We believe the technology of building problem solvers has advanced enough that a book about it alone seems both necessary and useful. Specifically, we believe we give the reader unparalleled coverage of techniques such as pattern-directed inference systems, truth maintenance systems, and constraint languages.
3. We assume the reader already has some familiarity with basic AI ideas, as one would get from studying a good introductory textbook. We often explore theoretical issues, but always with the goal of how they relate to designing problem solvers.
4. We tie principles of problem-solving techniques to practice. We discuss the underlying principles of each problem-solving technique, then demonstrate the ideas through programs that clearly exhibit their essence. Finally, how these ideas work is illustrated through several examples, often substantial, to provide a deeper understanding.
5. We discuss the engineering issues required to scale up simple programs into "industrial strength" AI systems. There is an overall complexity gradient in the programs we present. The early systems are written to be easily understood by readers with only classroom experience in Common Lisp. Later systems illustrate programming techniques commonly used in "industrial-strength" AI systems, where efficiency is as important as elegance.

6. We include exercises, ranging from simple homework problems to open research questions, to get the reader started exploring these ideas.

The reader who diligently works through the programs and exercises in this book will be rewarded with the ability to apply and develop a variety of useful AI reasoning systems.

This book is designed for two audiences. First, it is designed as a textbook for graduate (or advanced undergraduate) courses in AI programming. The material can be covered in a single semester, often giving new graduate students a head start in the skills they need to complete their theses (or for undergraduates, the skills needed to participate in research, summer jobs, and honors theses). Second, it is designed to be useful for self-study and industrial training, for those with other backgrounds who wish to master AI technology. To this end we have included complete, working programs to simplify experimentation. These programs (and their descendants) have already been used in research projects at Northwestern University, the University of Illinois, Oxford University, the Xerox Corporation, Bolt, Beranek, and Newman, and many other universities, companies and government agencies.

1.1.1 Why use Common Lisp?

Given the tidal wave of enthusiasm for C (and now C++) in mainstream computing and some applied AI circles, why use Lisp? Obviously, one could in principle write every program in this book in C++. Our goals are pedagogical: we choose Lisp because it is the best generally accepted language for easily communicating these ideas. Lisp's treatment of procedures as first-class entities, the provision of automatic storage management, and its simplified syntax which allows programs to easily write and analyze other programs greatly simplifies our systems and minimizes the cognitive load on you, the reader. Developing these facilities in C or C++ would make an already long book burst at the seams.

Logic programming aficionados might argue that Lisp is too "low-level," and that a language such as Prolog would be more appropriate. We believe the goals of logic programming—including providing powerful reasoning mechanisms with solid declarative semantics—are extremely important. However, we do not believe that today's logic programming languages are necessarily the best starting point for developing the logic programming systems of the future. By making fewer a priori commitments to reasoning system design, Common Lisp gives us the ability to craft a variety of quite different systems more easily.

Yet another alternative might have been one of the many commercially available knowledge engineering toolkits or expert system shells. Such systems are inappropriate for our purpose for three reasons:

1. A deep understanding of the principles underlying the tools gives one a better chance of using them successfully. This understanding is best gained by "opening the hood" and looking at how the engine is built.
2. Commercial tools are not appropriate for many purposes. Sometimes the reason is efficiency, sometimes source code access is necessary, and sometimes reasoning must be done by a computer for which an appropriate commercial tool kit is not available. In such cases the ability to build your own reasoning system is crucial.
3. The state of the art in building reasoning engines is far from static. While we believe there is now a stable core, many important ideas remain to be discovered. To develop the next generation of toolkits and AI applications requires exploring new ideas, beyond the capabilities of today's systems.

Finally, why use Common Lisp instead of a simpler dialect of Lisp, such as Scheme? Common Lisp has been called the PL/1 of the Lisp community: large, ungainly, and tough to implement because of the massive libraries it provides. But those massive libraries are precisely the reason it has become so popular in AI work. Anyone who remembers the days when Lisp programmers were faced with several overlapping and incompatible libraries of structure facilities, string manipulation utilities, and print routines is grateful for standardized libraries. Because we rely on the facilities of Common Lisp, our systems are shorter and simpler than they would be otherwise.

We are sympathetic to readers who, due to limited resources, must use Scheme or partial Common Lisp implementations. For such readers there are two options: translate the programs by hand into your dialect of choice, or write a compatibility package that fills in the parts of Common Lisp that are used by the programs you wish to run but that are missing from your implementation. We have ourselves used both strategies at various times to run certain of these programs on small microcomputers (including 8086-based laptops). It does require extra patience and determination, however.

1.2 About the programs

The programs in this book are all written in standard Common Lisp for portability. They are known to run in Symbolics Common Lisp, Lucid Common Lisp on the IBM RT, IBM RS/6000, Sun SPARCStation. At various times we have used the Symbolics CLOE environment for Microsoft Windows, Gold Hill's GCLisp-LM[1] and Apple's Macintosh Common Lisp as well. Information about setting up the programs can be found in Appendix A.

Much of the book can be read without looking at the programs. However, what our students have found most effective is to have both this text and the listings in hand while reading. A companion volume of the listings, with index, is available from the MIT Press, or listings may be generated from the programs themselves.

An important note: Although the programs in this book have been useful in a variety of research settings, they should not be viewed as a substitute for commercial toolkits and systems. We do not provide telephone support, extensive documentation, newsletters, and regular upgrades, as commercial software enterprises do. We do not provide amazing user interfaces. We have not concerned ourselves with foreign function interfaces, report generators, or the wide variety of software issues that any commercial vendor must deal with. We are only trying to improve everyone's grasp of the technology and speed the process of getting you to the frontiers.

1.3 Obtaining the programs

The programs can be obtained in two ways:

1. In one or two cases this requires implementing a missing Common Lisp primitive.

- For readers with internet access, the code can be obtained via anonymous ftp. Since ftp protocols and sites change frequently, please contact us to get detailed information about sites where the code can be found. Ways to reach us are described in the next section.
- For readers who do not have internet access, a floppy disk can be ordered from the MIT Press.

Due to the increasingly litigious nature of American culture, we must make an important disclaimer at this point. The permission to use these programs, and legal restrictions on their use, are described by the notice in the file `legal.txt` which comes with the code. The contents of this file are reproduced below.

1.4 Feedback

We would greatly appreciate any comments or suggestions about the programs or the text. The best way to communicate with us is via electronic mail. We have set up the alias

`bug-bps@ils.nwu.edu`

for electronic mail. All mail to this address is automatically forwarded to both of us. Though we prefer electronic mail, physical mail is also fine. Forbus's address is:

Kenneth D. Forbus
The Institute for the Learning Sciences
Northwestern University
1890 Maple Avenue
Evanston, Illinois, 60201, USA
email: `forbus@ils.nwu.edu`
fax: (708) 491-5258

de Kleer's address is:

Johan de Kleer
Xerox PARC
3333 Coyote Hill Road
Palo Alto, California, 94304, USA
email: `dekleer@parc.xerox.com`
fax: (415) 812-4770

1.5 About the exercises

Mastering any skill takes practice, and AI programming is no exception. To this end we have supplied exercises with each chapter. The problems are starred to indicate their level of difficulty. The rating system is:

⋆ Simple test of comprehension.

⋆⋆ Slightly more subtle problem.

⋆⋆⋆ A much harder problem, usually involving writing a fairly complex program. Solving it could take days or weeks.

⋆⋆⋆⋆ An even harder problem that could take weeks or months. Some of these are topics of active research.

⋆⋆⋆⋆⋆ An open research question. Could be the topic of a great Ph.D. thesis.

We recommend that everyone do the ⋆ and ⋆⋆ exercises. If you really want to grasp the technology, do all of the ⋆⋆⋆ and some of the ⋆⋆⋆⋆ exercises as well. And if you do a good job on one of the ⋆⋆⋆⋆⋆ problems, you might well become famous for it!

1.6 Acknowledgments

This book evolved out of a graduate course developed and taught by Forbus, "Design of Computer Problem Solvers," first at the Department of Computer Science at the University of Illinois at Urbana-Champaign (UIUC) and now in the Electrical Engineering and Computer Science Department at Northwestern University. The first versions of the programs were written during the spring of 1986, and each spring a new set of graduate and undergraduate students cheerfully found new bugs and made helpful suggestions. Despite geographic distance and different institutional affiliations, de Kleer was in the loop almost from the beginning, since we developed the first AAAI tutorial on truth-maintenance together in 1986.

Forbus would like to thank the many students, both graduate and undergraduate, who helped improve these materials over the last seven years. Comments and suggestions from John Collins, Dennis DeCoste, Brian Falkenhainer, Boi Faltings, John Hogge, Chris Lopez, Paul Nielsen, Yusuf Pisan, and Nikitas Sgouros were particularly helpful. The initial offering of the course at UIUC would not have been possible without the equipment provided by IBM through the EXCEL project. At Northwestern University, the rapid approval of C44, "Design of Computer Problem Solvers," was helpful in finishing the book in a (relatively) timely fashion. The Office of Naval Research supplied summer support. IBM also provided additional hardware support, in the form of IBM RTs, for continued development. Donations from Xerox, Boeing, and Hewlett-Packard also provided important development resources. Most importantly, he thanks Dedre Gentner for her unfailing encouragement and patience.

de Kleer would like to thank Brian C. Williams, Gregor Kiczales, Vijay Saraswat, and Daniel G. Bobrow for their assistance. Nora Boettcher provided her steadfast support and helped edit and create the figures for the seemingly endless series of "final drafts." He also appreciates the patience and support of the staff at Xerox PARC's Systems and Practices Laboratory. Most of all he thanks his family Marilyn, Elisabeth, Katherine and Ruth for their love and patience throughout the endless years this book took to finish.

We both thank Peter Andrae for meticulous and copious feedback. We also thank Dan Weld, Hirosi G. Okuno, Bruce Roberts, and Lance Rips for careful reading of drafts and useful comments that helped improve the book.

2 Introduction

What makes an AI program different from other programs? Two key differences are *explicit representation of knowledge* and *increased modularity*. The ability to use explicit representations of knowledge is perhaps the best hallmark of AI programs. Traditional programs, to be sure, have knowledge embedded in their procedures and data structures. But AI programs include structures that can be interpreted declaratively, that is, independently of any single usage, both by the program and the programmer. The program, rather than the programmer, can decide what to do based on this knowledge in particular contexts. Often this allows the process of making improvements to an AI program to take on more of the character of telling it something, rather than of programming.

The increased modularity in AI programs comes from decomposing procedures into small, fine-grained pieces. This extreme decomposition leads some to claim that AI programs necessarily consist of rules, but as we shall see, this need not be the case. Explicit knowledge representations support such fine-grained partitioning of procedures by providing a richer vocabulary for different parts of a program to communicate with each other. This increased flexibility is not without cost: to obtain the information a procedure needs to execute requires more complex reference mechanisms than the simple notion of variable and binding commonly used in programming languages. Often these mechanisms involve some form of *pattern matching*, but not always. The increased modularity and explicit communication between parts of a program increase its ability to make its own decisions, dynamically, rather than forcing the programmer to anticipate all possibilities in advance.

2.1 Comparing AI reasoning systems to conventional programs

How should a problem solver be organized? One way to consider this question is to explore the desiderata for traditional programs and for AI programs. Let us take as an example of a traditional program one that runs the traffic lights in a major city. One may curse any particular instance of the operation of said program, while agreeing that in general it does a reasonably good job. How does this program differ from an AI program?

Our imaginary prototypical traffic control program was probably written in Fortran, has evolved over a decade or two, and was developed by dozens of people, many of whom probably never met. It is quite likely that no single person really understands in detail exactly what the traffic control program does. (Unfortunately, the same can be true of some AI programs.) The fact that it is written in Fortran is not important per se. What is important is that it consists of a large slab of procedural code. We would like our AI programs to be constructed differently, for a variety of reasons.

Any program must satisfy a number of constraints. Such desiderata include (1) *efficiency*, (2) *coherence*, (3) *flexibility*, (4) *additivity*, and (5) *explicitness*. Let us consider how the traffic control program satisfies these desiderata:

Efficiency: Procedural languages excel at saying "how." Much of the development of procedural languages has concerned automatically turning them into machine code that runs extremely efficiently. So, with adequate care, our traffic control program should be extremely efficient.

Coherence: A well-written traffic control program handles routine situations without much dithering around. Like any well-evolved organism, its behaviors are highly tuned to its normal ecological niche.

Flexibility: Human programmers can often perform prodigal feats of planning and design, anticipating an amazing variety of problems and conditions. But anticipating all possible conditions is impossible. The implicit nature of its world model makes the traffic control program difficult to change. In many cities, parades or other special events often cause them to turn the traffic control program off, since it is just too difficult to get the traffic control program to adapt to the new conditions.

Viewed as an organism, the traffic control program can only survive in a tightly constrained niche.

Additivity: Anyone who has dealt with large conventional programs knows that they can be extremely hard to change. A small modification in one routine may have unexpected effects that crop up all over. Besides brittleness, the implicit encoding of knowledge often leads to a dreadful kind of inertia. Since any particular fact of the world may play a role in many design decisions, each decision must be reexamined. This means system-level programmers are often needed for even simple changes. Great job security for programmers, but frustrating for city planners.

Explicitness: The traffic control program works, in that it handles the lights appropriately according to the policies embedded in it by its designers. But it is opaque in its operation: it is hard to find out why one action was taken rather than another. Conventional programmers often make it easy to display the data the system used to make its decision, but rarely provide tools that can give non-programmers insight into the tangled skein of conditionals and subroutine calls underlying that decision.

To summarize, the traffic control program does well on efficiency and coherence, but not very well on flexibility, additivity, and explicitness. This should not be surprising: efficiency and coherence almost always trade off against the others. Consider efficiency first. A program that stores the absolute minimum amount of information required to get a particular job done will always perform faster than one that must consult explicit knowledge and record the rationales for its decisions. And it is a sad reality that the more a program knows, the more storage space it requires. What about coherence? Coherence often demands performing actions in a particular order. The ability to respond to new facts implies the ability to change course, and thus to change when things happen. So coherence trades off against flexibility and additivity.

In this imperfect world we will never succeed at optimizing along all these dimensions simultaneously. Where we choose to optimize in any particular program depends on its purpose, as we discuss below. As a gedanken experiment, suppose we wanted to transform a huge, monolithic conventional program, such as our traffic light program, into an organization more like an AI problem solver, to optimize along the other dimensions. How should we proceed?

We might start by carving up the procedural knowledge in the system into tiny pieces, so that each piece is as small as can be while still making sense as a module. These modular pieces correspond to the problem-solver's rules. When these pieces of procedure lived inside the monolith, the environment they needed was supplied by the program's variables. A different, more sophisticated reference mechanism is needed to provide the context that would allow these procedure fragments to run. Pattern matching provides one such mechanism. Each piece of data needed by the rule must be either an assertion or some piece of an assertion. One can think of the inference engine's job as providing for each rule all possible environments constructible from known assertions for it to execute in. To be useful, the rule's results must be expressed as assertions, so that other rules can execute based on its results.

Consider what happens if we execute the rules obtained by transforming the monolithic program. Everything that happens in the monolithic program will also happen when executing the rules. The actions may take place in a different order, if the logical dependencies between them allow it, since many events in the traditional program are ordered by programmer preference rather than by need. Other actions may take place as well, corresponding to actions that follow from the data but that the programmer optimized out. This new program will be less efficient than the old one. Besides the possibility of performing extra actions, even executing the minimum necessary actions now takes more work, due to the extra overhead of using pattern matching to establish execution environments rather than more compact and efficient stack (or even static) structures. Consequently, any rule-based program will invariably be slower than the corresponding procedural program.

What have we bought with this reconstruction? First, each small procedure fragment (i.e., rule) can be easier to understand on its own, both because of its size and because of the more expressive description of the information it is executing on. (To use a real-life example, `(>> speed propeller frigate32)` is easier to read than `ETTNS`.) By using a *truth maintenance system*, the reasons for taking actions can be recorded for later inspection and contemplation. Thus the increased bandwidth between the procedure fragments provides the infrastructure for increased explicitness. Since the order of execution of pieces of procedure is now governed by some *execution strategy*, rather than the preplanned decisions of a human programmer, the system can be more flexible. And finally, additivity is enhanced because new procedure fragments can be expressed in terms of the kinds of knowledge they use and produce, and thus can be automatically used when relevant.

Depending on the task, these advantages can be substantial. Furthermore, it is often the case that the AI problem solver can come very close to the original system in performance, given careful design and programming—so close, in fact, that the increased flexibility, additivity, and explicitness of the AI system will make it far more valuable.

2.1.1 A design space for problem solvers

In looking at the AI literature it appears that there is a bewildering variety of ways to build problem solvers. We believe that underlying this diversity is a design space that can be characterized, at least in a general way, by a few major distinctions. This belief is based on many years of experience in building and analyzing such systems. Since the science of designing and understanding problem solvers is still developing, any account at this stage is necessarily incomplete. Our map of the terrain is thus sketchy, but it is better than no map at all.

Briefly, the "axes" of this space are:

Knowledge model: How is the system's knowledge represented?

Reference mechanism: How do procedures get the data they need to execute?

Procedure model: How are procedures decomposed and organized?

Execution strategy: How are procedures carried out?

Dependency model: What information is recorded about the relationships between a system's beliefs?

Understanding this design space is important in figuring out when a technique could be useful. For example, in 1980s expert systems technology a common set of choices was:

Knowledge model: object, attribute, value triples.

Reference mechanism: Pattern matching within global or nested context database.

Procedure model: IF-THEN rules.

Execution strategy: Backward-chaining.

Dependency model: Trace of rule executions.

Since this part of the design space has been heavily explored, we in fact ignore it in this book. Instead, we focus on areas in this design space which we believe have seen significant advances and are potentially extremely useful.

2.2 Phases of AI programming

Traditional system design methodologies are rarely appropriate for problems where AI techniques are needed, because solving the problem often requires figuring out what it really is, as opposed to having a complete, formal specification to begin with. Nevertheless, the general outlines of how programs come to be written and how they evolve apply to AI programs as well. The typical life of an AI program can be viewed as having four phases, described roughly as follows:

1. *Conceptualization:* A problem is carefully chosen and analyzed. The literature is combed to see how others have fared on it.[1] After thinking about it a long time, inspiration strikes, and a promising new idea or solution is generated.
2. *Initial exploration:* Rapid exploratory programming provides a program that embodies your ideas so that you can test them to see if they have any merit. Quick development is important so that ideas that look good on paper but fail on further consideration can be weeded out as soon as possible.
3. *Experimentation:* Once the idea has passed through the exploratory phase it is time to give it a really good workout. This means running the program on dozens or even hundreds of examples. Often this leads to a complete rethinking, or even abandoning, of the idea.

   In the early days of AI, "one example wonders" were common. Often, this was due to the poor machine resources available at the

1. A saying among scientists is "Six months in the lab can often save an hour in the library."

time—the micros found on most people's desks today have as much memory as those early 1970s mainframe computers shared by a whole laboratory of scientists. Today, we do not have the same excuse. Serious experimentation is now a central requirement of respectable AI research.

4. *Production:* Once an idea has proven itself, it is time either to apply it or to move on to studying something else. Often this means converting the program embodying your idea into a module that can be used in other projects and by other people. Sometimes, the program becomes a product, part of a product, or is put into daily use. Sometimes this is done by transforming the programs built in previous phases, but sometimes it is better to start over. Here issues of robustness and clean interfaces become paramount, while speed of coding and program simplicity fade into secondary status.

Only experience can teach you the skill of knowing which kind of programming activity you should be doing when. We touch on this issue only peripherally in this book.

It is important to notice that the requirements of each programming phase are very different. In exploratory programming, it is a sin to spend much time optimizing. Spending a day optimizing a program is foolhardy if you are going to throw it away next week. Conversely, not optimizing is a common mistake in experimental programming. It is equally foolhardy to wait hours a day for several weeks (or even months) for a program to solve a problem when spending a day on optimization could turn those run times into minutes or even seconds. In production programming, it is often worth sacrificing some modularity for greatly increased efficiency. Programming techniques often viewed as "evil" in pedagogical settings, such as side-effects on list structure, are often a practical necessity. We do not attempt to shield the reader from these realities. Instead, we illustrate how to do such things, so that you can do them when necessary.

The amount of effort spent on user interfaces differs in each phase. In exploratory programming it is not worth spending much time on the interface. But a good interface for an experimental program can pay great dividends. If, for example, you spend several hours plotting the results of your program, it may be time to consider spending a day or two writing a graphical system that does the plotting automatically for you more rapidly. Making production-quality interfaces is a difficult topic in its own right, so we do not deal with it at all in this book. We do illustrate techniques that are important in exploratory and experimental programming, restricting ourselves to non-graphical interfaces for portability.

In all phases of programming, readability is always important. Programs are a means of communicating ideas, just as prose and mathematics are. Therefore programs should be understandable by human beings as well as by highly organized pieces of beach sand (i.e., our computers). Even if you are the only person using your program, readability is important. After all, you must be able to understand your own program when you come back to it after six months of doing something else.

2.3 Outline of the book

Chapter 3 begins by examining *classical problem solving*. This is a warm-up exercise, since we expect that readers have seen simple search programs in introductory AI or Lisp texts. After briefly reviewing the problem space model of problem solving, we show how a modular program can be used for applying search strategies to several domains. Our sample problems include navigating the Boston subway system and solving simple algebra problems. Our focus is on writing clean, portable, and efficient code, setting the style for the exploratory end of programming.

Chapter 4 describes a specific form of *pattern-directed inference systems*. Pattern-directed inference systems of various forms dominate AI reasoning research today, and there is little sign (save stirrings from connectionism) that they will not continue to do so in the future. We begin by introducing an antecedent rule model, in the form of the *Tiny Rule Engine*, or TRE. We show how aspects of natural deduction can be implemented in this framework. TRE is designed for simplicity, illustrating the kind of system that might be developed in exploratory programming.

Consideration of TRE's limitations lead us to examine extensions of this model in Chapter 5. Problem-solving programs often must manipulate assumptions and retract data. We examine a simple *stack-oriented context mechanism* which allows assumptions and their consequences to be temporarily made and then withdrawn. Pattern matching and rule execution can be inefficient, so we explore how pattern matching may be open coded and how rules may be compiled for better performance.

These ideas are embodied in another version of TRE, called FTRE. We show how FTRE can be used to build a powerful natural deduction system for propositional logic. We also show how search problems, including the classic *N-queens* puzzle, can be solved via chronological search.

The bulk of this book focuses on exploiting *truth maintenance systems* in building reasoning systems. The literature on truth maintenance systems has often been turgid and confusing. We impose a classification scheme on such systems, in hopes of bringing order. Roughly, we break truth maintenance systems into *justification-based*, *logic-based*, and *assumption-based* systems. These basic ideas are developed in Chapter 6, with the next eight chapters devoted to exploring their implications, including how to interface truth maintenance systems to various inference engines, and how to use them effectively as part of a larger problem-solving system.

Justification-based truth maintenance systems are explored in Chapters 7 and 8. Chapter 7 covers the basics, including how they operate and linking their semantics to definite clause logic. Chapter 8 explores how to interface a JTMS to a pattern-directed inference system. The resulting program, JTRE, is used to illustrate the notion of *dependency-directed search*. We also partially reconstruct Slagle's symbolic integration program, `SAINT`, to illustrate how dependencies can be used to record data and control dependencies and produce explanations.

Logic-based truth maintenance systems and their applications are covered in Chapter 9, Chapter 10, Chapter 11, and Chapter 13. Chapter 9 discusses the use of unrestricted clauses as dependencies and describes how *Boolean constraint propagation* (BCP) works. Chapter 10 explores how the LTMS impacts inference engine design and describes a technique for *contradiction handling* that supports powerful reasoning techniques for making closed-world assumptions and more general dependency-directed search facilities. Chapter 11 shows how these inferential facilities can be combined to yield a program, TGIZMO, which uses qualitative physics to interpret observations of simple physical systems. Boolean constraint propagation is efficient but incomplete; Chapter 13 explores the trade-offs in making it more complete. (This chapter uses several ideas from assumption-based truth maintenance, which is why it comes later than the other LTMS-related chapters.)

Assumption-based truth maintenance systems are explored in Chapters 12 and 14. Chapter 12 explores the radical shift in perspective required to use an ATMS efficiently and describes a logical specification for it as well as efficient implementation techniques. Chapter 14 describes two basic execution strategies, *many-worlds* and *focused*, used in ATMS-based problem solvers. Two ATMS-based planners are illustrated, and we outline techniques for using an ATMS to reason about open worlds.

In examining truth maintenance systems we stick with the model of pattern-directed inference systems for simplicity. In the rest of the book we explore a different set of design choices, corresponding to *constraint languages*. Constraint languages sacrifice generality of reference for efficiency. That is, instead of pattern matching, inheritance schemes similar to those found in object-oriented programming are used to provide environments for rules. By restricting rules to work in purely local structures, and by requiring the kinds of assertions to be determined in advance, these systems provide facilities for describing much larger—but more restricted—problems than would be possible in standard rule-based paradigms. These advantages are why constraint languages are commonly used in model-based reasoning systems, for example.

Chapter 15 illustrates the basics of constraint languages by way of the TCON constraint interpreter, showing how to implement diagnosis via *constraint suspension*. The dependency model used in TCON is essentially a JTMS; Chapter 16 explores the issues involved in using an ATMS with the constraint knowledge and procedure model. Chapter 17 illustrates how the *General Diagnostic Engine* (GDE) can be implemented using the ATCON interpreter developed in Chapter 16. The final chapter on constraints (Chapter 18) examines a radically different form of constraint language, one that supports *symbolic relaxation* or *constraint satisfaction*. We outline the basic ideas of constraint satisfaction, and show how they can be embodied in a simple constraint language WALTZER (named in honor of David Waltz). We show how certain scene labeling and temporal reasoning can be cast as constraint satisfaction problems and solved by WALTZER. Finally, Chapter 19 briefly highlights what we believe are some important frontiers in building problem solvers.

3 Classical Problem Solving

In the early days of AI, it was often hoped that a small set of grand principles could be found that provided the basis for understanding the nature of intelligence, much as Newton's laws provided a basis for understanding the interactions of force, matter, and motion. One of the first principles proposed was *search*. Why search? Cognitive science starts with the assumption that human intelligence is a computational process. A natural question to ask is, what kind of computation is it? Intelligence seems utterly unlike simple algorithms, such as sort routines or accounting systems. Such algorithms perform a single task extremely well, but cannot deal with situations where what to do next isn't clear. Intelligence seems to require the ability to try something out, look at how well it did, and try something else until you get something that works. That is search.

While few today hold that search is the single key idea underlying intelligence, most would agree that search has a central role to play in building AI programs. Here we examine how to implement a classical model of problem solving, the *problem space* model[5], in a clean and modular fashion.

3.1 The problem space model

People deal fluently with physical space. Thus it seems natural that abstractions from physical space play a major role in our formalisms. Mathematicians speak of metric spaces and other topologies, physicists use phase space to reason about complex dynamical systems, and self-help books are filled with admonishments to "get your head into a good space." The problem space model of problems and problem solving makes similar use of the ideas of location, shape, and distance that are so useful in physical space.

Suppose we are playing a game of chess, or solving an algebraic equation. The class of problem or domain we are working on is represented as a *problem space.* A problem space is a set of *states* that represent distinct configurations of the objects and relationships of the domain, and a set of *operators* which define how to move between states. If we are playing chess, the states consist of arrangements of chess pieces on the board, the operators are the legal moves between states, and the problem space is the set of all legal configurations and moves. If we are solving an equation, the particular form of the equation we are working on is the state, the operators are the laws of mathematics we can apply to transform one equation into another, and the problem space is all possible equations. Clearly problem spaces are usually large, and often infinite.

Operators typically have parameters. In chess, for instance, the legal moves available in a board position depend on what types of pieces are on the board and where they are. Suppose we decide to include an operator `MOVE-KNIGHT` in creating a problem space for chess. Depending on its position and the position of other pieces on the board, there are up to eight places a knight can move, and thus up to eight *instantiations* of this operator per knight on the chessboard.

Defining a problem in a given problem space requires two things: an *initial state*, and a *goal*. The initial state is a distinguished state that represents the starting point within the space, such as the opening position on a chessboard or the equation you are given to solve. The goal is a specification of the subset of the problem space which could serve as a solution to the problem. In chess the goal is to find a board position that leaves the opponent's king checkmated. In algebra the goal is to transform the given equation into a new equation whose left-hand side consists of the unknown variable and whose right-hand side consists of an expression without the unknown. Notice that while we know exactly what the initial state looks like, we often don't have a single, predetermined goal state. While each algebra word problem typically has a unique numerical answer, for instance, there are many ways to win at chess.

Solving a problem in this model is accomplished by finding a sequence of operators which, when applied to the initial state, allows one to reach a state satisfying the goal criterion. In playing chess a solution is a sequence of moves that leads to checkmate, and in algebra a solution is a sequence of transformations that solves the equation. Sequences of operators are generated by search; for instance, trying different operators on the initial state and recursively on the states that result, until a state satisfying the goal criterion is found.

It is easy to see why this is an attractive model of problem solving. To solve a problem, all we have to do is define the problem space and then unleash a general-purpose search engine on it. A problem space can be defined by developing a representation for states and operators. Formulating a problem consists of defining the initial state and developing the goal criterion. The only issue left for problem-solver design is what search strategy to use.

Implementing simple search strategies is one of the first programming tasks used in AI textbooks and introductory Lisp books. We presume, therefore, that you have seen programs illustrating search before. The program we describe here, CPS, is a warm-up exercise, to highlight some stylistic issues in a familiar setting. We concentrate on making an implementation general yet efficient, showing some techniques for sound "ecological programming" along the way. We illustrate how CPS can be applied to two kinds of problems: subway navigation and solving algebraic equations. By analyzing what is required to implement problem solvers for these domains, we gain insight about why AI practitioners became so concerned with issues of representation and knowledge-intensive reasoning techniques.

3.2 CPS design

Conceptually, CPS consists of two parts: an interface for user-supplied problem spaces, and a search engine. We begin with the problem space interface. Clearly we need the ability to manipulate states and operators. What kinds of manipulations are needed?

There are three things we need to do with states.

1. Goal detection: Ascertain whether a given state satisfies the goal criterion.
2. State identity: Detect when two descriptions of states refer to the same state.
3. State display: Produce a human-readable description of a given state.

The importance of goal detection is obvious. State identity is important because we make no progress by reexploring already examined states. Displaying states is important even if the results of CPS are only intended to be used by another program: such displays are often necessary for debugging.

In many domains goal detection and state identity are simple operations. In chess, for instance, a board position represents a win if the king for the side to move is under attack and cannot escape. Two chess positions are the same if they are described as having exactly the same pieces in exactly the same positions. In other domains carrying out these operations can be substantial tasks in themselves. Consider the problem space consisting of all possible programs, with the goal being transforming a program to ensure that it halts on all inputs. Since detecting that one has achieved this goal requires solving the Halting Problem, which is undecidable, in the worst case goal detection is undecidable. Determining that two arbitrary programs are the same is also undecidable, so recognizing that two descriptions actually refer to the same state is also, in the worst case, undecidable.[1] Intelligence is possible because Nature is kind. However, the ubiquity of exponential problems makes it seem that Nature is not overly generous.

What should the interface for operators look like? Conceptually, there are four distinct manipulations required:

1. Identify what operators are available.
2. Determine whether a given operator is applicable to a particular state.
3. Given a state and an operator applicable to it, ascertain all the ways the operator can be instantiated on that state.
4. Figure out what new state results from applying an instantiated operator to a state.

Collectively these operations are often called *expanding* a state, and a state for which all successive states have been calculated is said to have

1. This is not a fault of the problem space metaphor: Any sufficiently powerful representational system contains such cliffs, if you will, in what it can express. In natural language, for instance, we can easily spend hours pondering "what happens when an irresistible force meets an immovable object."

been *expanded*. They typically are tightly intertwined, which is why it is common to view them as an atomic operation. Figuring out whether an operator is applicable usually requires finding legal instantiations of it, and finding legal instantiations often involves producing the resulting state. For instance, determining whether a knight move is possible requires finding both knights and unblocked destination squares for them. We exploit this intertwining below to simplify our problem space/CPS interface.

Now let us consider the implementation of the problem space/CPS interface. It is tempting to choose a particular representation for states and operators and stipulate that problem spaces must be written with it. But this would restrict CPS unnecessarily—no matter what choice we make, inevitably we will find a problem space that would profit from a different convention. Instead, we make as few assumptions as possible about the implementation of problem spaces by defining generic procedures to perform the necessary tasks on states and operators. Only these generic procedures are used in the search engine.

The first decision is whether we are defining a problem space, a particular problem in that space, or some mixture of the two ideas. A pure problem space should include all the procedures necessary to define states and operators, but leave out the initial state and the goal criterion. If we are defining a specific problem, we would include those last two pieces of information as well. Both extremes have their advantages. A pure problem space description could be shared across many copies of CPS, each solving a different problem in that space. On the other extreme, a complete problem description encapsulates all the information defining a specific problem. Notice, however, that in many problem spaces the goal criterion is always the same. In playing chess, for instance, the goal is to achieve a checkmate (or at least a stalemate). In solving equations, the goal is always to isolate the unknown on one side of the equation. Thus we choose an intermediate course here by including the goal criterion, but not the initial state, in the problem space description.

To define the interface more precisely, we must name the procedures that are included (and specify their arguments and outputs) as well as any other data assumed. With this information in hand, we can proceed to building search engines. We attach a `pr-` prefix to each procedure as a mnemonic. The procedures associated with states are:

`pr-goal-recognizer` Implements the goal criterion for the problem space.

`pr-states-identical?` Detects when two given states are identical.

`pr-display-state` Produces a human-readable description of a state.

Each procedure takes either a single state or, in the case of `pr-states-identical?`, a pair of states as input. What should their output be? Essentially, CPS only needs a Boolean result from these procedures, and presumably only executes `pr-display-state` for its side-effects.

Recall that the interface procedures for operators consisted of several conceptually distinct operations, but that these operations in practice are often intertwined. From the perspective of CPS, it makes sense to use just two operations in the interface:

`pr-operators` Provides a list of operators for the problem space.

`pr-operator-applier` Given a state and an operator, finds all complete instantiations of that operator to that state and the states that result from applying them.

Presumably in implementing problem spaces the representations for operators will provide the data that the operator application procedure needs to do its work.

What about the search engine itself? The design of such programs should be familiar to the reader. Basically, there is a queue, which initially contains just the initial state for the search. Search proceeds via the following steps:

1. Pop a state from the queue.
2. If the state satisfies the goal criterion, halt and signal success by returning the successful path.
3. Otherwise, calculate the operators that can be applied to the current state and the states that will result from each of them. Update the queue accordingly, and begin again.
4. If the queue is empty then return, signaling failure.

The details of how the queue is organized and updated determine which search strategy is being followed. An unordered FIFO queue corresponds to breadth-first search, and an unordered LIFO queue corresponds to depth-first search. Given a heuristic estimate of distance remaining to a goal state, more powerful search strategies are possible. Sorting the queue according to the minimum estimated distance to the goal constitutes best-first search. Beam search is a resource-limited version of best-first search which places a fixed upper bound on the size of the queue. As shown below, all these variations are quite simple to implement given our basic design.

What should elements of the queue be? Clearly the state to be explored must be part of it. For some problems, that would be enough—we may only care about the solution to an equation, for example, not how it was derived. For other problems the path taken to the goal is of paramount importance: a chess program needs the path the search took in order to move towards a win. Consequently, when a search succeeds we stipulate that the search engine must return the path it found between initial and goal states. The path is a list of alternating states and operator instances.

With our design finished, we begin considering how to implement it.

3.3 CPS implementation issues

There are several ways to encode these interface procedures. One good way would be to use the new object-oriented programming features of Common Lisp, CLOS. Using CLOS one would define problem-spaces, operators, and states as objects, and the interface routines would be generic procedures. We have chosen not to use CLOS in this book for two reasons. First, the CLOS specification was not completely standardized when most of this book was written. Second, we want to ensure maximum portability, including the ability to run many of the systems on today's micros. Many Common Lisp subsets available for such machines do not include CLOS, nor would they have enough memory left over for reasonable examples if they did.

Given that we are eschewing CLOS for the present, we must fall back on more traditional techniques. The most obvious approach is to define a set of global variables that hold the required constants and procedures. The only advantage to this time-honored technique is simplicity, and its disadvantages are legion. It is very hard to keep track of exactly what set of variables must be defined before firing up the search engine. Worse, subtle bugs can occur when not every variable is appropriately initialized (or reinitialized when switching from one type of problem to another).

Using global variables prevents several copies of the system from being active at once. This is not problematic when using CPS by itself, but it makes CPS harder to use as a module in a larger system.

The best compromise, given our constraints, is to define a structure that combines the necessary information "under one roof", so to speak. The Common Lisp structure facility provides just what we need. We can provide slots for procedures corresponding to each operation which our search engine will access to get the appropriate procedures.

Now let us further specify the constraints on the interface procedures. Consider the goal recognition procedure. For some problem spaces, like subway navigation, a distinguished goal state can be named in advance. In such cases the test is a straightforward identity check. For others, like chess or design, the goal can only be characterized indirectly, and the test can be more complicated. As noted above, we only need a Boolean result from this procedure and from the test as to whether states are identical. Any other details about how these procedures operate are up to the designer of the problem space.

Similarly, the output for the procedure `pr-operators` must be a list of operators. Any representation whatsoever can be used for operators, as long as the procedure the problem space designer supplies for `pr-operator-applier` can handle it. What should `pr-operator-applier` produce? Since the number of applicable operator instances cannot be predicted in advance, the easiest data structure for it to return is a list. Each element of the list must contain the operator instance and the given state. We stipulate that each entry will be a pair of the form

(⟨*OperatorInstance*⟩ . ⟨*ResultState*⟩)

This gives us all the information needed to extend a path.

At this point we turn to the CPS listings, to explain the code in detail.

3.4 The CPS implementation

The CPS program is contained in three files:

`cps.lisp` System definition.

`search.lisp` Structure definitions and breadth-first search.

`variants.lisp` Other search strategies.

The system definition in `cps.lisp` provides information for compiling and loading CPS. It assumes the utility procedure `load-files`, which, given a list of files and a path, loads each file in turn. (If your environment has a compiler, use `compile-load-files` the first time, and then `load-files`. `compile-load-files`, given a list of files, compiles and loads each in turn.) The variable `*cps-path*` indicates where the code is to be found;[2] when installing it on your computer you should change the value to reflect the directory structure of your system. In the rest of the book we include similar files without comment; for more details, see Appendix A.

3.4.1 The basic search system

Turn now to the first page of the listing `search.lisp`. Notice it is mostly comments. We highly recommend starting your programs out this way, and recommend liberal use of comments throughout your programs. Remember, programs should be read by people as well as computers. Even if you don't have other humans reading your code, you will end up having to read it yourself months or even years later. Unless you document the interfaces, typical procedures to call, intent, and implicit assumptions in the code, you may not understand your own programs six months later. The alert reader may notice that we seem to be violating our own advice in later chapters, since the number of comments in our code drops precipitously. We have done this to save space in the listings, since the text itself provides more documentation than one is likely to receive from even the most prolific commenter.

Another variation from our normal Common Lisp programming practice is that, for simplicity, in this book we do not place our programs into separate packages. In using Common Lisp we normally strongly recommend the use of packages as a tool for enforcing modularity. However, to make it easier for readers with simpler Lisp implementations to benefit from this book, we place all of our code and datastructures in the `user` package.

The program begins by defining the variable `*debug-cps*`, a debugging aid. When non-`nil`, it causes CPS to print extra information about

2. We use a common convention among Lisp programmers: All global variables have `*`'s as their first and last character. This allows globals to be easily recognized as such when reading a program. No Lisp environment enforces this convention, however.

the state of the search. Often programmers include print statements when developing a program and comment them out when it is running properly. Here we prefer to let such print statements remain as a permanent part of the code, and condition their execution on flags. Using debugging flags enhances flexibility in two ways. First, what is traced can be changed without recompiling or reloading the source code. Second, debug flags can be set by other programs, thus providing tighter control over the amount of material printed. The only disadvantage is a slight increase in code size and the overhead for testing the flag. Invariably we have found this overhead to be negligible.

Next, the `problem` struct is defined which implements the design laid out in Section 3.2. Since this is our first use of `defstruct`, it is worth mentioning some useful conventions. `:CONC-NAME` provides an abbreviation for the struct's fields. Generally it is easiest to use the name of the struct itself, since it presumably is chosen for mnemonic value. But sometimes prepending the struct's name to field names would result in long, unwieldy names, and `:CONC-NAME` provides a solution. Here, for instance, we specify `pr-` as the prefix, to enforce the naming convention decided upon previously.

When defining a struct it is almost always worth using the `:print-function` option. Why? In faithful Common Lisp implementations, the default printed form of structures is:

`#s`⟨*StructureContents*⟩

where ⟨*StructureContents*⟩ is a list of the values of the struct's fields. Often these fields will contain other structs, which in turn point to other structs, and so forth. Often this leads to circular chains of pointers, which usually spells disaster for printing.[3]

The `problem` struct contains all the fields mentioned in our design, namely `goal-recognizer`, `operator-applier`, `operators`, `states-`

3. Some dialects of Scheme (such as PC-Scheme) and partial implementations of Common Lisp on small micros adopt the convention of printing a struct's internals without providing an equivalent to the `:PRINT-FUNCTION` option. Alas, this makes such structure facilities virtually useless, since structures involving backpointers cannot be printed without causing infinite loops. For such implementations it is often better to write a separate structure facility. A traditional method is to use the property lists, since symbols have a compact printed representation.

`identical?`, and `state-printer`. It includes several other fields as well, containing information which is so commonplace as not to need mentioning or whose necessity may not be apparent in an initial, high-level design. An example of the former is the `name` field, a string for human consumption which distinguishes a `problem` struct from others. Examples of the other kind are:

`path-filter` Supplies domain-specific guidance to prune search paths that do not make sense. Its use is exhibited in Section 3.5.

`distance-remaining` Optional procedure which provides a numerical estimate of "distance" from a given state to a goal state. This procedure is needed by search engines implementing best-first search or beam search, discussed in Section 3.4.2.

`solution-element-printer` Produces a string which can be printed as part of an explanation of a solution path. This procedure is used by `print-answer`, defined below.

The `path` struct defines queue elements. Each path includes the current state (called `current`) and the sequence of states and operators traversed to arrive at this current state (called `so-far`). `so-far` is implemented as a list of alternating states and operator instances. Some search strategies require the estimated distance to the goal along the path, so we include the `distance` slot to hold this information. Notice that the `pr` slot points back to the problem that generated this search effort. This backpointer provides access to the procedures for expanding states and printing them.

Generally the printed representation of a struct should be short, but contain enough information to distinguish one instance of it from another. In the case of paths, this would be the contents of `so-far`. Since printing the entire path would be too ungainly, we compromise by using the value of `current` to distinguish one path from another. This is not perfect, since the same state could be reached from several different paths and hence different path structs could print identically. However, since paths are loop-free, we count on the context provided by other debugging statements to discriminate in such cases.

Since breadth-first search is simple and finds a shortest path (with respect to the number of operators applied), we implement it as the basic search strategy. Other search strategies are explored in Section 3.4.2. The

```
(defun bsolve (initial)
      (bsolve1 (list (list initial initial))))

(defun bsolve1 (queue)
      (if (goal-recognizer (caar queue))
          (values (caar queue) (cdar queue))
          (bsolve1 (append (cdr queue)
                           (expand-path (car queue))))))
```

Figure 3.1 Elegant but inefficient breadth-first search

procedure `bsolve` implements breadth-first search. The first thing to notice is that it doesn't look much like the versions one sees in introductory textbooks. (The alert reader might have been expecting this, given that we have already defined two structures where most introductory textbooks define none.) There are good engineering reasons for these differences, so let us explore them.

Suppose for a moment that the queue consisted of dotted pairs of the form

(⟨*EndState*⟩ . ⟨*Path*⟩)

instead of structs. Figure 3.1 shows how `bsolve` might be written in an introductory text. This code is short and elegant. However, it is not appropriate for building usable AI problem solvers. Let's examine why.

The first problem is the recursion in `bsolve1`. Of course, it is only recursion in a syntactic sense. Because no operations are performed "on the way out" it is an example of *tail recursion*. A good compiler should turn a tail recursive procedure into an iterative program. Still, there are several reasons to avoid purely syntactic recursion when the description being traversed is large. First, as every seasoned programmer knows, not all compilers are good compilers. Writing code that assumes tail recursion is automatically recognized and dealt with appropriately is a bit like only knowing how to eat when your place setting has fingerbowls—you can do well in high society, but might have difficulty in rougher environments. Second, it is easy while debugging to transform inadvertently a program with merely syntactic recursion into one with true recursion, with dreadful results the next time it is executed on large datastructures. Finally, in tail-recursive procedures with several arguments understanding their functional role can be difficult. A good iteration construct, on

```
(defun bsolve (initial)
       (do ((queue (list (list initial initial))
                   (append (cdr queue) new-paths))
            (new-paths nil nil))
           ((null queue))
         (when (goal-recognizer (caar queue))
              (return (values (caar queue) (cdar queue))))
         (setq new-paths (extend-path (car queue)))))
```

Figure 3.2 A better version of breadth-first search

the other hand, makes functional roles more explicit in its syntax. Common Lisp provides a plethora of iteration constructs, and a careful choice of construct can make the programmer's intent more apparent.

Figure 3.2 illustrates a better version. It requires fewer assumptions about the operating environment and would be implicated in fewer stack overflow errors. However, the translation to a `do` loop has left us without the ability to easily debug the program using `trace`, since most of the work is encapsulated in one procedure. The version in the listing `search.lisp` remedies this oversight by using `*debug-cps*` to determine whether or not internal details are printed.

Let us return to the version of `bsolve` in `search.lisp`. The `do` variable `queue` represents the state of the search. Each element of the queue is a `path` struct, starting with a path consisting solely of the initial state. Each path is examined exactly once, since its `current` is either a goal state, a dead end, or a state that can be extended. In the first two cases there is no need to examine it ever again, and in the last case it is the newly extended paths we are interested in. These extended paths are stored in `new-paths`. `number-examined` keeps track of how many states we have examined for statistical purposes.

Notice that the end test of the `do` only checks for the queue being exhausted. This corresponds to the search failing. Success is noted by the first `when` in the body, which uses `pr-goal-recognizer` to ascertain when the path being examined has reached a goal state. The `return` statement is used to provide a non-local exit from the loop. Some stylists think that such non-local exits are a sin. We disagree. When there is more than one exit condition, the only alternative to using a non-local exit is to use a disjunctive end test in the `do`. If there are several termination conditions the logic of the end test can become quite baroque. Furthermore, care must be taken to ensure that the loop variables are incremented properly in such cases. Worse yet, if the body contains several actions, often they must be conditioned on whether or not one of the exit criteria has been triggered. Using `return`, especially with multiple values, actually provides better modularity in such cases. Here, we immediately return with the successful path and the number of states examined, to indicate how much effort was expended during the search.

If the current state doesn't satisfy the goal criteria, `extend-path` is called to generate new paths from the current one. Each such path is appended to the end of the current queue when the `do` updates `queue`, thus ensuring breadth-first exploration. This essentially completes our search engine. Notice that two debugging statements provide all the details we need to follow the search: The first statement reports any success; the second describes the state being examined currently and how it is being extended.

Now let us turn to `extend-path`. This procedure depends only on the state and the set of potential operators, and is independent of the particular search strategy. This means it makes sense to keep it distinct from `bsolve`. Recall that a problem space typically has several operators, and often each operator can be applied in several different ways to a situation. (For instance in chess one might have several pieces to move, including a knight, and the knight in turn might be able to move to one of several squares.) This suggests organizing the program as a double iteration. The outer loop goes through the list of operators, and the inner loop examines each operator instance and the result of applying it. The information needed by these loops (i.e., `pr-operators` and `pr-operator-applier`) is obtained from the problem struct pointed to by `path-pr`.

(Another stylistic note: We tend to use `&aux` with `setq` instead of `let` when defining parameters which are local to an entire procedure. The reason is aesthetic: The indentation conventions which normally make Common Lisp quite readable can sometimes result in code that clumps on the right-hand side of a page and leaves large amounts of blank space. The combination of `&aux` and `setq` typically leads to less indentation than `let`.)

Recall that `pr-operator-applier` returns a list of pairs whose `car` is an instance of the operator and whose `cdr` is the state that results from applying that instance to the argument state. The extension of the path represented by each pair is encapsulated in a path struct, and the set of these structs is cached in the variable new-path. Recall that the original path was a list whose sole element was the initial state. To update the path correctly, the so-far field of the new path is the contents of the so-far of the path being extended, plus the operator instance and new state. This ensures that we have a complete record for each path explored.

Before this extended path is accepted as part of the search (by pushing it onto the result variable new-paths) two tests are made. The first check is looping; as mentioned before, it is pointless to reexamine a state that we have already seen. path-has-loop? checks for looping by skipping down the path (via cddr) and using the pr-states-identical? procedure to see if any of the states are the same as the current state. The second test is a domain-specific path filter, which the problem space designer may or may not supply (hence the and check). We stipulate that pr-path-filter returns nil if the path is okay, and non-nil otherwise.

The last two procedures in search.lisp concern printing. print-new-paths is used by bsolve to show the operator instances along a path. print-answer assumes that its argument is a path struct corresponding to a legitimate solution. It also assumes pr-solution-element-printer is a procedure that takes an operator instance and a state and produces a string that makes sense to the user. To be understandable we should clearly start with the initial state and end with the goal state, so print-answer begins by reversing the path and caching it in rpath. step produces "line numbers" in the answer for easy reference.

We make two more stylistic notes here. First, notice the use of the optional variable stream. Often programs become modules in yet larger systems. This can involve having the module's results become part of a report generated by the calling system. By using the optional stream variable we provide the flexibility needed to do this. For example, the caller could use with-output-to-string to generate a subsection of a large report. Second, notice that the exact details of printing a state or printing an operator instance applied to a state are supplied by the domain model itself via the procedures pr-state-printer and pr-solution-element-printer. All that print-answer assumes is that the state is printable, that the path takes the form of alternating states and operator instances, and that line numbers are appropriate. These weak assumptions suffice to produce quite readable output. In general, providing such report procedures is a useful thing to do. Far from a frill, they can provide valuable insight into what a program is actually doing and make the results more understandable. The only danger is that, as with graphics, it is easy to waste time fooling around making minor improvements to such facilities.

3.4.2 Alternative search strategies

It is easy to vary `bsolve` to explore different search strategies. The listing `variants.lisp` contains implementations of several alternate strategies. The major source of variation lies in how the queue is managed. In `dsolve`, for instance, depth-first search is implemented simply by placing new elements on the front of the queue rather than the end.

`best-solve` implements best-first search. Recall that best-first search requires that the caller supply a procedure which, given a state, provides an estimate of the distance remaining to the goal. This estimate is provided by assuming a procedure `pr-distance-remaining`. `best-solve` begins by first checking to see that this procedure is actually defined. (After all, the `best-solve` procedure might be called by some innocent user who did not know that this optional procedure was required for this strategy.) Aside from this error management and how the queue is manipulated, `best-solve` is the same as the others.

The secret of `best-solve` is to update the queue so that the "best" path will be the next one tried. This is carried out when `queue` is incremented in the main loop. First, a temporary variable `nqueue` is initialized so that the state we just expanded is no longer available for consideration. Then we use `pr-distance-remaining` to cache the distance estimate for each new path in its `path-distance` field. Finally, we merge the new paths into the queue, preferring those whose estimated distance is smallest. (It is straightforward to prove that this always leaves `queue` properly sorted.)

Our final variation of classical search strategies is beam search, implemented in the `beam-solve` procedure. Notice that `beam-solve` takes an optional argument `n`. `n` is the maximum size of the queue, which corresponds to the "width of the beam" used to search through the space. Updating the queue works almost exactly like `best-solve`. The only difference is that we clip the queue off whenever it gets longer than `n`, using `nthcdr` to access the new end of the list and `setf` to do the clipping.

Again, we note that some stylists would eschew the use of `merge`, which destructively affects the list given as input, and our use of `setf` on a list (also known as `rplacd`). The alternative to such side-effects is to create new list structure instead, but this can lead to gross inefficiencies, such as needless extra garbage collection. Good engineering practice consists in part of knowing when to optimize. Here we know that the queue is not accessible to external routines, and hence it is safe to perform destructive operations on it. In general, destructive operations on datastructures can be crucial in making programs efficient.

With search engines in hand, it is time to develop some problem spaces to try them out on.

3.5 Navigating the Boston subway

Finding routes is a classic search problem. And since subways constrain travel to occur between well-defined stations along particular paths, they are naturally represented by labeled graphs, as in Figure 3.3. Since the graph is small and explicitly known, it is a trivial problem space to define. This trivial example lets us focus on program style; a more complex problem space is explored in Section 3.6.

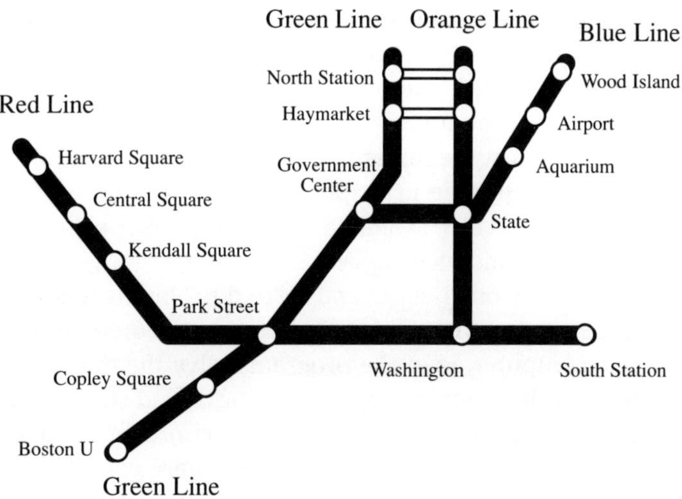

Figure 3.3 A subset of the Boston subway

We begin by implementing a means for representing subways. We store stations and lines in the global variables `*stations*` and `*lines*`. A subway station struct includes the name of the subway station, the lines that station is on, and, optionally, the coordinates of the station. The subway line, in turn, has its name and the list of stations on that line. Notice again that we have used the `:PRINT-FUNCTION` option to define how stations and lines are displayed. We assume the names of stations and lines are represented by symbols instead of strings. This way we can set the value of the associated symbol to the struct representing the station, and thus provide a simple mapping from what users can type in to the internal datastructures.

An engineering note: There are many alternative representations we could use to simplify the mapping from typed input to the program's internal structures. For instance, an alist or hash table could associate strings with structures. However, using symbols is simpler in this case. For example, we use symbols in the `lines` slot of the subway station struct and in the `stations` slot of the subway line struct. These symbols act as placeholders, allowing us to define stations and lines in any order we please. Even if we choose another means to associate names with internals, it still makes sense to use indirection. Otherwise, one must enforce a rigid format on how subways are defined, to avoid referring to a name before it is bound.

The macros `defline` and `defstation` provide readable input. Using these macros, a user can define a map of a subway while knowing very little about the internals of the representation. That is the way it should be. Modularity requires hiding irrelevant details from both programs and people. A guiding principle of AI interface design is that, whenever possible, any facility available to a human user should be available to other programs, and vice-versa.

Typically one has several related problems to solve or additional questions about some scenario. It would be tedious in such cases to sit down at a computer, load the program, solve the first problem, then be forced to boot the machine to solve the next, and so forth. Good ecology in programming requires returning the environment to a usable form when you are finished with it. Ecological issues are especially important when you try to use a program as a module in a larger system. The costs of cleaning up after a computation should always be considered as part of designing the procedures to carry it out.

Good ecology in this case requires removing pointers to the structs from symbols when the subway map is no longer required. This is what the procedure `clear-subway-map` does. It iterates over the list of stations and lines, calling `makunbound` on each. Thus, the symbols are no longer known when irrelevant, and the garbage collector can pick up the contents. We end `clear-subway-map` by resetting the variable `*station*` and `*line*` to `nil`, thus ensuring that we keep no references to these structures so the garbage collector can do its job. In general, the cost of writing such cleanup procedures and determining when to invoke them is an issue that should be considered when making implementation choices. Typically one uses global variables sparingly to avoid such problems.

Finally we must define the interface procedures that CPS expects. Both recognizing goals and recognizing identical states are quite simple. Since the goal of navigating the subway is to reach a particular named station, we can use the procedure that recognizes identical states as the goal recognizer, too. We define the procedure `subway-states-identical?` as an `eq` test. Notice that this works either if the states are both symbols or if the states are both structs, but not if one is a symbol and the other is a struct.

There is only one operator in the subway domain, the act of taking a subway line from one station to another. Consequently, we can simply use a symbol `take-line` as our operator, and put the definition of operator instantiation into the procedure `subway-operator-finder`. We define an instance of an operator in the subway domain to be

(`take-line` ⟨*OldStation*⟩ ⟨*line*⟩ ⟨*NewStation*⟩)

That is, taking the subway line ⟨*line*⟩ from ⟨*OldStation*⟩ to ⟨*NewStation*⟩. A simple double iteration suffices to find operator instances.

By looking at the station we can find what lines it is on. By looking at the list of stations on that line, we can find out what stations can be reached by one trip. Since we are already at a station on the line, namely the current state, the inner loop removes that state from the list of stations considered. (After all, getting on the train and not going anywhere is a pretty silly thing to do.)

We can provide some "street smarts" by including domain-specific filtering information. For example: Suppose CPS proposes that you take the green line from Haymarket to Government Center, get off, get back on the green line at Government Center and go until you hit Park Street. That's silly. While perhaps a scenic route, it's not the most efficient way to get from one place to the other. Therefore, unless we had some other, unstated, goal, heuristically we do not want to take the same subway line two trips in a row. `prune-subway-path?` prevents us from doing that, by ruling out trips that use the same line in two successive operator instances.

Part of good programming ecology is providing easy ways to set up an environment for your work. Consequently, we provide the procedure `setup-subway-problem`, which creates an instance of the `problem` struct that holds the appropriate interface procedures. The goal recognizer is created by using `lambda` to generate a closure, thus encapsulating the goal state available when the problem space was defined. All the other initializations are straightforward, basically "plugging in" the parts defined in this file to the problem interface. The only non-obvious binding is `:OPERATORS`, which includes the symbol `take-line` to provide the outer loop of `extend-path` something to chew on.

The rest of the file contains ancillary definitions. `print-path-element` defines how to print an element of a solution, by producing a string incorporating the subway line and the start and end stations. `subway-distance` uses grid coordinates provided with the station definitions to provide a notion of distance for search strategies that require it.

These definitions are illustrated in the file `boston.lisp`, which provides a map of a subset of the Boston subway.

Now let us look at how various search strategies perform on our subway problem. Suppose we are trying to get to Kendall Square (which is near MIT) from the airport. If we call `bsolve` of `airport` we get back a CPS struct (indicating a successful solution) and note that we examined twenty-two states to find this path (see Figure 3.4). Calling `print-answer` on this struct shows us our route, and indeed that is the best route if you are using the subway.

If we call `dsolve` to try out depth-first search we notice two things (Figure 3.5). First, we only examine seven nodes instead of twenty-two, and thus have an answer more quickly. Unfortunately, the solution is not as good since the trip it recommends is longer. Given the typical delays on the Boston subway, this extra leg is a considerable disadvantage (unless we want to get out at Washington Street and shop at Downtown Cross-

```
>(setq mit (setup-subway-problem 'kendall-square))
<Problem: KENDALL-SQUARE>
> (bsolve 'airport mit)
<path KENDALL-SQUARE>
22
>(print-answer *)

Initial state: AIRPORT.
1.  Take the BLUE-LINE to GOVERNMENT-CENTER.
2.  Take the GREEN-LINE to PARK-STREET.
3.  Take the RED-LINE to KENDALL-SQUARE.
 Done.
NIL
```

Figure 3.4 Getting to MIT from Logan Airport on the Boston subway. In depicting human/machine dialogs, lines typed by the user begin with ">."

```
> (dsolve 'airport mit)
<path KENDALL-SQUARE>
7
> (print-answer *)

Initial state: AIRPORT.
1.  Take the BLUE-LINE to GOVERNMENT-CENTER.
2.  Take the GREEN-LINE to HAYMARKET.
3.  Take the ORANGE-LINE to WASHINGTON.
4.  Take the RED-LINE to KENDALL-SQUARE.
 Done.
NIL
```

Figure 3.5 Depth-first subway navigation

ing). The best mix of computation and result is provided by `best-solve`, which only examines five states and yet provides the optimal answer. We leave it as an exercise for the reader to explore different widths of beam in using `beam-solve` to determine what is a safe setting to allow you to successfully navigate the Boston subway.

3.6 Solving algebra problems

Aristotle once claimed that one could detect intelligence by the ability to do sums. If he were alive today, Aristotle might have modified that statement given the existence of pocket calculators. He might say instead that the ability to do algebra is a better indication that something is smart. The difficulty people have in learning algebra is suggestive evidence for this view. Since algebra is used heavily in engineering and scientific disciplines, and since solving equations can be intellectually challenging, there have been several AI studies of equation solving. Here we use CPS to implement a simple equation solver. This example serves two purposes. First, it shows what is involved in using CPS in a more substantial problem space. Second, it provides a good way to examine some issues in pattern matching that we return to with different perspectives in Chapters 4 and 5.

Our system is based on an elegant theory of mathematical reasoning due to Alan Bundy. Figure 3.6 contains one of Bundy's examples, a typical equation and a derivation of the solution for that equation. The left-hand side of the initial equation contains a complicated expression involving logarithms and sums, but is transformed by a series of small steps into an equation whose left-hand side contains only the unknown x and whose right-hand side is an expression without x. This is the general character of solutions to algebraic equations. (For simplicity, in this chapter we always refer to the unknown by its classical moniker, x.)

Mathematics provides many laws to use in solving equations like this one. Figure 3.7 shows a group of these laws sufficient to solve the problem in Figure 3.6. You can find laws like these, and many more, in any standard mathematics reference work. Already we have what we need to cast equation solving as a problem for CPS. The problem space is simply the set of mathematical equations, and the operators are the laws that

Solve for x, given:

$$log_e(X+1) + log_e(X-1) = C$$

1. $log_e(X+1)(X-1) = C$
2. $log_e(X^2-1) = C$
3. $X^2 - 1 = e^C$
4. $X^2 = e^C + 1$
5. $X = \pm\sqrt{e^C + 1}$

Figure 3.6 A sample algebra problem

$log_U V = W \longleftrightarrow V = U^W$

$U - V = W \longleftrightarrow U = W + V$

$U^2 = V \longleftrightarrow U = \pm\sqrt{V}$

$(U + V)(U - V) \longleftrightarrow U^2 - V^2$

$UV + UW \longleftrightarrow U(V + W)$

$log_W U + log_W V \longleftrightarrow log_W UV$

$(W^U)^V \longleftrightarrow W^{UV}$

Figure 3.7 Some laws of algebra

allow the transformation of one equation into another. The goal criterion is an expression of the form

x = expression not containing x

Unfortunately, this account is too simple to capture the expertise of human mathematicians. As anyone who has done trigonometry knows, applying the wrong law, or even the right law at the wrong time, can make the situation much worse. The sheer number of laws and ways that they might be applied suggests that we face a potentially explosive search problem. Let's do a worst-case analysis. In Figure 3.7 there are seven laws. Each law can be used in at least two distinct ways. For example, if we find some part of the equation we are solving that matches the left-hand side, we may replace that with the right hand side, and vice versa. Thus, seven laws gives us a branching factor of perhaps thirteen per node. Suppose the shortest solution takes five steps. This means it lies in a tree of depth 5. Assuming the search looks like a tree with a branching factor of 14, the worst-case size of the space we must search is 13^5, or 371, 293 states.

This is a horrible prospect. Fortunately, though, this analysis is far too pessimistic. There are several constraints we did not take into account. First, the form of the equation strongly limits the set of laws applicable at each stage, so the branching factor is invariably smaller than 13. Second, many pairs of transformations negate each other, and hence the search space is not actually a tree, but a (much smaller) graph. This still does not mean that equation solving is trivial. Beginning students do indeed seem to start out searching blindly for solutions to problems that experts solve easily. But the problem in Figure 3.6 is one that most mathematicians can solve in their sleep. What do experienced mathematicians have that novices do not?

Bundy [2, 3] has suggested that what expert mathematicians have, and that beginners lack, is a set of *implicit methods* which control how they use algebraic laws. Formalizing these methods requires an explicit vocabulary of control. For centuries mathematicians have discovered, named, and taught certain explicit methods, like Gaussian elimination, as part of mathematics. However, traditional mathematics has rarely codified guidance about when and how to use transformations like those of Figure 3.7 in solving equations. Bundy argues that if we create a vocabulary that allows these implicit methods to be codified, then we could then teach them as efficiently as we teach Gaussian elimination. Telling human learners this control vocabulary, instead of forcing them to induce it, should thus improve mathematics education. And for our purposes, making this vocabulary explicit means we can encode it in CPS.

Bundy divides these implicit methods into three distinct categories. The first kind are called *attraction* methods. Attraction moves occurrences of the unknown "closer together" in some sense. If we have an x in one part of the equation and a hundred terms separating it from the other occurrence of x, it is hard to imagine that we can find a law that directly merges those two x's into one. By bringing them close together, we improve our chances of finding some identity that helps to get rid of them.

Collection methods are the second kind. They reduce the number of occurrences of the unknown in the equation. Thus, if we can get several x's closer together, a collection method would suggest a change that reduces the number of x's. This is useful since it brings us closer to our goal, namely having just one occurrence of x by itself on one side of the equation.

The third kind of methods are *isolation methods*. Isolation methods remove stuff that isn't the unknown from the left-hand side of the equation by moving it to the right-hand side. Essentially, they "strip off" layer after layer of expressions from the left-hand side until the single remaining x stands alone.

Where do these methods come from? Essentially, they are descriptions of the roles that the laws of algebra can play in the equation-solving

Assumptions:

1. The term being rewritten is the least dominating term in x.
2. U and V match terms containing x.
3. No other parts of the expression contain x.

$$WU + WV \longrightarrow W(U + V)$$

$$log_W U + log_W V \longrightarrow log_W UV$$

$$(W^U)^V \longrightarrow W^{UV}$$

$$U^{VW} \longrightarrow (U^V)^W$$

Figure 3.8 Attraction methods. Attraction methods rewrite terms to move occurrences of x closer together.

process. Students learn the ways that algebraic laws can be used by trial and error. Bundy points out that we can perform a syntactic analysis of each law to determine directly what roles it can play.

To see how to assign problem-solving roles to a law, consider an algebraic expression as a tree. An equation is just two trees, one for the left-hand side and one for the right-hand side. Suppose that the tree for the left-hand side contains several occurrences of x but the tree representing the right-hand side contains none. The intuitive role of attraction methods in bringing occurrences of x closer together can be precisely defined as reducing the total distance between occurrences of x in the tree, as measured by the number of steps required to move through the tree from one occurrence to another. Collection methods produce a tree with fewer occurrences of x. Isolation methods reduce the depth of occurrences of x in the left-hand tree. Since the goal is achieved by the left-hand tree becoming a single occurrence of x, each method always brings us closer to that goal. Applying a law that does not perform one of these roles, in this simple theory, does not lead us toward the goal.[4]

Let us arrange the identities in Figure 3.7 into sets of attraction, collection, and isolation methods. Figure 3.8 shows how a subset of these identities can be written as attraction methods. In what follows, U, V,

4. In some equation-solving problems a change of variables is required, which can lead to intermediate expressions that are larger than previous steps. We ignore such cases here.

$$(U + V)(U - V) \longrightarrow U^2 - V^2$$

$$UW + UY \longrightarrow U(W + Y)$$

Figure 3.9 Collection methods. Collection methods reduce the number of occurrences of x. Here we assume U and V contain x, but W and Y do not.

and W are variables which are matched against parts of an expression. (Notice we now have three kinds of variables around—Lisp variables, algebraic variables (such as x), and pattern variables, such as U. Algebraic variables have numbers as values, while pattern variables have structures as values, which could be numbers, algebraic variables, or expressions. It should be clear from context which is which, but it can be confusing initially.) In attraction laws we assume that U and V are terms containing x, and that W does not contain x. Notice that in each case we map the left-hand side of the rule into an expression on the right-hand side of the rule, but not vice versa. For example, if we are looking at the sum of two products, each containing a common term which does not involve x, then by factoring out that common term we have brought the occurrences of x closer together: they are now separated only by a sum. Running this rule in reverse would actually make things worse. Hence we only apply such laws in the given direction.

Bundy notes that attraction laws should not be applied to every part of the expression. A *least dominating term* is a term that contains at least two subterms that contain the unknown. Notice that an expression may have more than one least dominating term. For instance, the expression

$$[log(x) \times x^p] + [(x - 1) \times (x + 1)] + q$$

has three least dominating terms,

$$[log(x) \times x^p] + [(x - 1) \times (x + 1)] + q$$

$$log(x) \times x^p$$

$$(x - 1) \times (x + 1)$$

Both attraction and collection laws are applied only to least dominating terms.

Figure 3.9 shows collection methods based on the identities. Here we stipulate that the subterms U and V contain at least one occurrence of x

$$log_W U = Y \longrightarrow U = W^Y$$

$$U - W = Y \longrightarrow U = Y + W$$

$$U^2 = W \longrightarrow U = \pm\sqrt{W}$$

Figure 3.10 Isolation methods. Isolation methods reduce the depth of occurrences of x. These methods apply to the whole equation, unlike the others.

and the variables W and Y do not. As with attraction methods, collection methods apply only to the least dominating term in x.

Finally, Figure 3.10 shows how a subset of the identities are used as isolation methods. Only the pattern variable U may have occurrences of x. Isolation laws are directed, and apply only to the entire equation. They reduce the depth of occurrences of x by making U be the only term on the left hand side of the equation. In general U may not be x itself, but is some other complicated expression containing a number of occurrences of x. One must then in turn attract the occurrences of x together in these new subexpressions, collect them together, and isolate them again. Unless we get stuck somewhere along the way, applying the laws repeatedly in this fashion must achieve a solution because we are always reducing either the number of occurrences of x or reducing their depth in the equation.

We can implement a simple equation solver in CPS by implementing these methods as operators. To create operators we must encode some set of the attraction, collection, and isolation methods we have already described. Next we consider the design issues and then delve into the code.

3.6.1 CPS algebra system design

The outline of our design is fixed by the structure of CPS: Our job as problem-space designers is to develop a representation for states and operators that will allow the search engine to do its job. If best-first or beam search are to be used, we also must supply a procedure that estimates the distance remaining between a given state and some goal state.

The first choice we must make is how to encode states. A straightforward representation is to use a list to represent an equation. We use

(= < *LeftHandSide* > < *RightHandSide* >)

to represent an equation, and use the standard prefix Lisp notation to represent algebraic expressions. That is, our original example takes the form

```
(= (+ (log (+ x 1) E) (log (- x 1) E)) C)
```

Given this choice of representation, we must now figure out how to represent operators and provide a procedure that uses them to expand a state. We choose a very simple representation here, in keeping with the mode of exploratory programming. An operator will simply be a list of two elements whose form is

(⟨*OperatorName*⟩ ⟨*ExpansionProcedure*⟩)

where ⟨*OperatorName*⟩ is a symbol indicating the operator's name and ⟨*ExpansionProcedure*⟩ is a procedure which, when executed on a state, produces the kind of result CPS expects from an operator applier procedure.

The notion of pattern matching is a natural way to think about algebraic laws and their applications. Our code will be simplest if we incorporate a pattern matcher into it, for then we may simply define operator procedures in terms of pattern-matching operations. What should the matcher do? First, it must provide a representation for pattern variables, and means to bind them to values. Second, we must provide *substitution facilities* for using the results of the match process.

A concrete example will make the constraints on the matcher clearer. Consider again the isolation law

$$log_W U = Y \longrightarrow U = W^Y$$

Suppose we indicate pattern variables by a list whose first element is ? and whose second element is the name of the variable (i.e., `(? foo)`). Then we could write the left-hand side of this rule as

```
(= (log (? arg) (? base)) (? rhs))
```

where `(? arg)` is U, `(? base)` is W, and `(? rhs)` is Y. A successful match of this pattern to a state should yield values for the variables `(? arg)`, `(? base)`, and `(? rhs)`. Since there can be any number of variables in a pattern (including none), we will use a list to serve as a *dictionary* of bindings linking variables to values. Given such a dictionary, the substitution facility should then be able to take a pattern corresponding to the right-hand side of the law, in this case

```
(= (? arg) (expt (? base) (? rhs)))
```

and produce a new state by substituting the values from the dictionary for the pattern variables.

This design is fine so far, but we can add still more features to make our job as domain modelers easier. Recall that there are additional restrictions on what the pattern variables can match. In the isolation law just defined, for instance, `(? arg)` must contain an occurrence of x while `(? base)` `(? rhs)` must not. Such restrictions could easily be stored with pattern variables by adding an extra element to the list that comprises them. If the procedures `contains-x?` and `no-x?` return non-`nil` if their argument does and does not contain an occurrence of x, respectively, then we can encode the value restrictions by modifying the left-hand side to be

```
(= (log (? arg contains-x?) (? base no-x?)) (? rhs no-x?))
```

There is one more complication which may not be apparent at first glance. Some laws of algebra are always worth applying. For example, no matter what the value of U is, the following laws always decrease the complexity of the expression:

$$U + 0 \longrightarrow U$$

$$U \times 0 \longrightarrow 0$$

$$U \times 1 \longrightarrow U$$

Similarly, suppose some subterm consists of an operator such as `+` which has a procedural definition, and all of its arguments have numerical values (e.g., `(+ 2 2)`). Replacing this subterm by the value computed by applying the operator's procedure to its arguments results in replacing a subtree with a leaf, and hence always results in a simpler expression.

We could encode these laws as operators, using our pattern-matching facility. However, since they are always appropriate, we instead provide a separate facility for applying such transformations. This is standard practice in symbolic algebra systems, which call such facilities *simplifiers*. We can use the same pattern-matching abilities used for applying operators to define the *rewrite rules* that comprise a simplifier. The details of this system are explained in Section 3.6.4. The important point to consider right now is that the special properties of algebraic laws suggest designing a slightly more powerful pattern matcher. Rewrite rules typically have a left-hand side, consisting of a pattern which is to be matched, and a right-hand side, consisting of an expression that replaces the pattern just matched. The pattern variables bound when matching the left-hand side are used in the right-hand side. For instance, the law

$$U + 0 \longrightarrow U$$

says that $U + 0$ can be replaced by U, for any U. Of course, this same law holds when there are additional terms besides U involved in the sum as well. What this rule really says is that we can remove all terms of a sum which evaluate to zero. That is,

$$\cdots + 0 + \cdots \longrightarrow \cdots + \cdots$$

Laws like this suggest introducing *segment variables*, which can match several elements of a list. Suppose we agree that `(?? foo)` indicates a segment variable. Then the left-hand side of the law for removing zeros could be written

```
(+ (?? pre) 0 (?? post))
```

and the right-hand side could be written as

```
(+ (?? pre) (?? post))
```

We call the kind of variable that can only match a single item in a list *element variables*, to distinguish them from segment variables.

One complication of segment variables is that they enable a pattern to match an expression in more than one way. For example, the pattern

```
((?? before) Foo (?? after))
```

can match the expression

```
(a b Foo Foo Foo c d)
```

in three different ways, resulting in the following sets of variable bindings:

```
(?? before) = (a b)             (?? before) = (a b Foo)    (?? before) = (a b Foo Foo)
(?? after) = (Foo Foo c d)      (?? after) = (Foo c d)     (?? after) = (c d)
```

To simplify matters, we only require our matcher to return a single set of variable bindings. Furthermore, we presume that the expression we are matching our pattern against is free of pattern variables. (The problems caused by allowing pattern variables in data are described in Chapter 4.)

Let us pin down these design decisions by specifying the data abstraction for pattern variables. Even though we have made assumptions about their structure (e.g., lists with particular first elements) to simplify their use, it is still important to keep the interface clean.

`pattern-variable?` Returns non-`nil` if its argument is a pattern variable, `nil` otherwise.

`element-var?` Returns non-`nil` if its argument is an element variable, `nil` otherwise.

`segment-var?` Returns non-`nil` if its argument is a segment variable, `nil` otherwise.

`var-name` Returns name of a pattern variable.

`var-restriction` Returns procedure of one argument corresponding to a restriction on the binding of the variable if such a restriction is in force, returns `nil` otherwise.

`var-value` Given a dictionary and a variable, returns its value, signaling an error if it isn't bound.

`lookup-var` Takes as input a dictionary and a variable. If the variable is bound in that dictionary, returns a pair whose second element is the value of the variable. Otherwise it returns `nil`.

`bind-element-var` Takes as input a dictionary, an element variable, and a new value. Produces a new dictionary consisting of the old dictionary augmented by the binding of the given variable to the given value.

`bind-segment-var` Like `bind-element-var` for segment variables.

The implementation of this data abstraction is covered in the next section.

Implementing a simplifier by using rewrite rules forces us to extend the substitution facilities of the pattern matcher beyond just plugging in constant values. For instance, one way to simplify a sum is to add up all the numerical terms in it. The pattern that would trigger such a rule might be

```
(+ (? num1 numberp) (? num2 numberp) (?? terms))
```

where what we want to do is plug in the result of evaluating an expression containing the variables in the dictionary. We define a special form :EVAL to be used in such cases, as an instruction to the substitution facility that it should evaluate its argument. Thus the right-hand side of the simplification rule could be written

```
(+ (:eval (+ (? num1) (? num2))) (?? terms))
```

Yet one other special form will be allowed in substitutions. Sometimes it is useful to rearrange the arguments to an operator. Simplifiers often include one or more *canonical forms* to simplify pattern matching. For instance, the rule just suggested for simplifying sums would not trigger on the expression

```
(+ A 2 3)
```

since the first two elements of the sum are not numbers. If we had written the sum instead as

```
(+ 2 3 A)
```

the rule would have triggered. If we define an ordering on terms such that all numerical terms are "less than" all non-numerical terms, and sort the argument lists to + and * accordingly (which is safe since both operations are commutative), then our simplification rules can be less complex than they would be otherwise.

To support this and similar operations, we define :SPLICE to be like :EVAL, except that its results are presumed to be a list that is spliced into the containing list rather than simply being a member of it. The use of :SPLICE is described in Section 3.6.4.

It is important to realize that algebraic simplification is actually an extremely hard problem. In fact, showing that any two arbitrary algebraic expressions are identical is NP-hard. Consequently, our simplifier only handles some easy cases of removing constants, combining numerical subexpressions, and canonicalizing expressions to make finding applicable operators easier.

3.6.2 The CPS algebra implementation

The algebra system consists of the following files:

`match.lisp`:	The pattern matcher.
`algebra.lisp`:	Operator implementations and environmental setup.
`simplify.lisp`:	A simple algebraic simplifier.

We describe each in turn.

3.6.3 Implementing the pattern matcher

Turn to the listing `match.lisp`. The basic routine is `match`, which takes a pattern (`pat`) and an expression (`dat`). It also accepts an optional argument `dict`, a dictionary of bindings. Any match must respect the variables already bound in `dict`. `match` returns a dictionary corresponding to the complete set of bindings required to complete the match. The special value `:FAIL` for a dictionary indicates that the match is impossible. If an initial dictionary was provided through the optional argument `dict`, if the match succeeded then the dictionary returned necessarily includes those bindings as well.

The basic structure of `match` is a recursive tree walk, stepping through the pattern and the expression together looking for mismatches and potential variable bindings. This means that additions to the dictionary made stepping down one part of the structure must be passed down into the other parts as well to ensure consistent bindings. If a substructure fails to match, `match` could be called with a dictionary of `:FAIL`, and hence we check for that possibility first. The next two clauses concern the possibility that `pat` is a constant which matches `dat` directly. The `eq` test comes first, since it will detect identical symbols (and, depending on your implementation, identical small integers). The `equal?` test is used only if `pat` is not a cons, since a piece of list structure might be (or include) a pattern variable, and those take special handling. Notice that `equal?` is simply Common Lisp `equal`, but will return `t` if its arguments are floating-point numbers within a preset tolerance.

The cases where `pat` is a pattern variable are handled next, by the procedures `match-element-var` and `match-segment-var`. It is worth splitting them off for two reasons. First, as described below, each involves several chores. Second, the segment variable must detected while we are still one level above it in the expression, since its binding must potentially be able to range over the entire list, rather than just matching against the corresponding element in `dat`. Once the last two clauses are reached we know that `pat` is a cons. If `dat` is not, then clearly we have a mismatch, and hence return `:FAIL` in the next-to-last clause. The last clause is a classic `car-cdr` tree walk with result passing.

`match-element-var` is straightforward. It uses `lookup-var` to access the value for the variable from the dictionary, if any. If there is an existing value, then unless that value is the same as the datum the match fails. If the variable has not yet been bound, the restriction associated with the variable (if any) is applied to the potential new value, and if successful, a new dictionary is returned which includes the old dictionary plus the binding of the element variable to this piece of the pattern. Otherwise the match fails.

When we defined our dictionary data abstraction we specified that the value of a segment variable must be a list. How this is implemented has a strong impact on how efficiently segment variables are matched, so let us consider now how to do it. In figuring out how we wanted segment variables to behave, we saw that they could typically be bound in more than one way. Even though we only want one match ultimately, we must still allow for backtracking, since several possible bindings for segment variables might have to be tried before a globally consistent match is created. The obvious implementation of segment variables, that is, storing as its value a copy of the piece of the original list, thus could result in many wasted conses since a copy would be made for each guess for a segment variable's binding. A more efficient implementation is to specify the value of a segment variable by two pointers into the original list, one to the start of the segment and the other to the end. Call these pointers `beg` and `end` respectively. With this implementation a fixed-size structure represents a segment of arbitrarily length. Of course, to evaluate variable restrictions or use the binding we must make a copy of that segment of the list (a chore performed by `segment->list`). As it turns out, most segment variables do not have restrictions, so this implementation is actually a very good idea. The procedures `segment-beg` and `segment-end`, defined below, extract these pointers from a dictionary entry.

`match-segment-var` has the same overall structure as `match-element-var`: See if the variable has already been bound, check its value if so, and otherwise bind it. But since we haven't stored the value explicitly, the procedure check-segment walks down the datum and value to perform the identity check. Since there can be several possible bindings for a segment variable, we embody that guessing mechanism in the procedure try-segment-bindings. It iterates through the possible bindings of the segment variable, ranging from nil to the entire list itself. This is accomplished by the do loop, which uses beg and end to point at the beginning and ending of the segment. Initially both beg and end point to the beginning of the list. Since it is the piece of the list between beg and end that will be the current guess at the segment variable's value, in this case the value guessed is nil. If another guess is needed, end is moved down the list. Thus the guess grows by one element each time, reaching its maximum size (i.e., the whole list) when end falls off the end of the list and becomes nil. For each guess, the variable restriction is checked (using segment->list to produce a copy of the list the restriction procedure can execute on), the segment variable is bound (using bind-segment-var) and the rest of the list is tested using match.

Now let us implement the dictionary and variable data abstraction. The procedure pattern-variable? is defined in terms of element-var? and segment-var? for simplicity. Recall that variables are implemented as lists (a choice we made early in the design phase to simplify the task of typing in patterns), with the second element being the variable's name and the third element, if any, representing the value restriction. var-name and var-restriction are just syntactic sugar for cadr and caddr, in this implementation. lookup-var is implemented via assoc, as is var-value. They differ in two ways, though, since lookup-var is intended to be used during the matching process and var-value is intended to be used by the substitution facilities after a match is complete. The first difference is that, as per our specification, var-value signals an error if asked about a variable that isn't bound. The second difference is that var-value constructs a list when asked about the value of a segment variable, while lookup-var does not. A binding corresponding to an element variable is a two-element list whose car is the variable name and whose second element is the value. The binding for a segment variable is a list consisting of the name and the beg and end pointers. This makes it easy for var-value to figure out what kind of variable it is dealing with. bind-element-var and bind-segment-var do the obvious alist updates.

How are the results of a match used? Any program can use `var-value` to access the bindings created by `match`. For our purposes, the most important use of the bindings is to create new expressions containing them, such as the right-hand side of a simplification rule. The procedure `substitute-in` provides a handy facility for doing this. Since dictionaries are alists, one might think that `subst` would suffice for this purpose. However, segment variables demand to be treated differently, and we must support `:EVAL` and `:SPLICE`, as noted in the previous section.

`substitute-in` starts with an expression (`exp`) that may include variables and a dictionary (`dict`). Its output is a new expression with appropriate substitutions made. The basic structure is a recursive tree walk, with element variables being replaced by their values, just as one might implement `subst`. However, there are three critical differences in the code. The first difference is the treatment of segment variables, whose values are spliced into the new expression using `append`. Suppose the dictionary included `(1 2)` as the value for `(?? A)` and `(3 4)` as the value for `(?? B)`. Then calling `substitute-in` on the expression

```
(+ (?? A) (?? B))
```

returns `(+ 1 2 3 4)`.

The second difference is the test for expressions of the form `(:eval` < *form* >`)`, where the value of the expression obtained by applying the dictionary substitutions on < *form* > becomes part of the output expression rather than the newly derived version of < *form* > itself. Assuming the same dictionary as above, the expression

```
(:eval (+ (?? A) (?? B)))
```

yields `10`.

The third difference is the test for subexpressions starting with `:SPLICE`, which indicate that the rest of that subexpression should be spliced into the result expression. Continuing with the same dictionary, calling `substitute-in` on the expression

```
(* (:splice (42 (?? A) (?? B))))
```

would yield `(* 42 1 2 3 4)`.

Notice that we can combine `:EVAL` and `:SPLICE` to do some interesting things. For instance, suppose we want to ensure that the arguments to an operator were sorted in some particular way (as the simplifier must do when canonicalizing expressions). If using the same dictionary we call `substitute-in` with

```
(+ (:splice (:eval (sort (append (quote (? A))
                                 (quote (? B))) #'>))))
```

The subtlety is that when we access the value of a variable, we do not check to see if it is a variable of the same type. That is, we might have treated a particular name as a segment variable when binding it, but in substitution treat it as an element variable. As this example demonstrates, this can be handy when one needs to perform some operation on an entire segment.

3.6.4 Implementing a simplifier

A concrete example helps illustrate the importance of simplification. Suppose we used the collection method

$$UW + UY \longrightarrow U(W + Y)$$

on the expression

```
(+ (* X -2) (* X 2))
```

If we apply this rule literally, the result would be `(* X (+ -2 2))`, which is zero. Simplification gets rid of redundant expressions by performing such "obvious" transformations. The bulk of a simplifier consists of a set of rewrite rules which take the following form:

(⟨*pattern*⟩ ⟨*result*⟩)

where if an expression matches <*pattern*> it is replaced by <*result*>. An example of a rewrite rule is

```
((* (? e) (? e)) (sqr (? e)))
```

which transforms a product of two identical terms into the square of those terms. The knowledge of simplification can be encoded by a set of such rules. This makes the job of maintaining and extending this knowledge easier. We implement such rules as lists, using the procedures `rule-pattern` and `rule-result` to access a rule's parts.

How should such rewrite rules be applied? The recursive nature of algebraic expressions suggests that we should try each rule on every subexpression. Does the order of trying the rules matter? Yes. As it happens, efficiency can change dramatically depending on how they are ordered (more on this later). When should we stop? If the result of simplifying an expression is the expression itself, then further attempts to simplify it will achieve nothing.

With these ideas in mind, examine the listing `simplify.lisp`. The procedure `simplify` is our entry point into the simplifier. It calls `simplify-it` to do the real work. Notice that a hash table (`*simplify-cache*`) is used to cache results of previous calls to `simplify`. Caching the simplification of an expression makes sense because there are many regularities and symmetries in algebraic problems, and hence one sees the same expression repeatedly.

The procedure `simplify-it` begins to simplify an expression (`exp`) by attempting to simplify its subexpressions, if any. `exp` itself is processed by calling `try-match-rules`. `try-match-rules` looks for a rewrite rule that can be applied to `exp`, and if it finds one, returns the instantiated result. In finding out if a rule is applicable, it first uses `match` to attempt to generate a binding list. If `match` succeeds, then `substitute-in` is used to provide the replacement expression.

A few useful utilities come next. The procedure `alg<` provides a partial order on algebraic expressions. Having such an ordering is useful because it allows expressions to be turned into a canonical form, which simplifies further matching operations. A canonical form helps make expressions that mean the same look the same. For instance, the expressions `(+ a b)` and `(+ b a)` would not be considered the same by `match`, even though the commutative nature of addition means they are the same. We use rewrite rules to sort the arguments to commutative operations, and thus make it more likely that `match` will recognize common subexpressions. These reorderings can greatly reduce the complexity of the rewrite rules needed, and hence reduce the computational cost of the simplifier.

The rest of these utilities are all quite simple. `alg=` provides a heuristic equality check for algebraic expressions. The predicate `sorted?` is satisfied if the list it is given is properly ordered by the order procedure `pred`. The predicate `+/*?` recognizes the two commutative operators used in our examples. The predicate `same-constant?` requires strict identity for integers and identity within a tolerance for floating-point numbers. `same-constant?` is used in turn to provide procedures that recognize 0 (`zero?`) and 1 (`one?`), since they play a central role in the simplification laws.

The rules used by `simplify` are stored in the global variable `*algebra-rules*`. The first thirteen rules take care of special case arguments to operators. The next four rules handle equivalences involving multiplication, squaring, and exponentiation. The next nine rules reduce expressions when numerical values are available. The last two rules provide some canonicalization, by using the associative law to sanction "flattening" nested additions and multiplications and by using `alg<` to sort the arguments to commutative operations.

Notice that the simplifier rules are tested in order. Does the order matter? In some systems of rewrite rules order can affect both efficiency and what answer is derived. However, some systems of rewrite rules can be proved to be *commutative*, that is, the answer derived is independent of the order in which the rules are used. We leave it to the reader to figure out whether order matters, and if so how much, in this case.

3.6.5 Implementing operators and the environment

The file `algebra.lisp` completes the algebra problem space implementation for CPS by defining the interface procedures it needs and a collection of operators. The macros `lhs` and `rhs` provide some abstraction for defining our operator-finding procedures, and `occurs-in?` is the predicate we assumed earlier in this discussion.

Most of the interface procedures are very simple. For the algebra system, we define operators as a list of two elements. The first element is the name of the operator, and the second element is the name of the procedure which finds instances of that operator. This means that `pr-operator-applier`, defined here as `find-algebra-operator`, simply calls the associated procedure on the given state. The goal recognizer is provided by the procedure `got-algebra-goal?`. `print-derivation-`

`step` provides the hook `print-answer` needs to show a solution, and `equal` suffices to detect if two states are identical.

Using beam search or best-first search requires an estimate of how far a state is from a goal. For algebraic equations a reasonable heuristic is the sum of the depths of occurrences of x in the expression tree. Why? The value calculated by this procedure is 1 for a solved equation, since the only occurrence of x is one side of the equation. Suppose there is only one occurrence of x, but it is at depth d. Then at least d applications of isolation methods are required to reach a goal state. Furthermore, each additional occurrence of x will require additional applications of attraction and collection methods, so the more occurrences there are, the farther a state is from a solution. The procedure `algebra-distance` implements this heuristic.

The rest of the interface to the search engines is provided by the procedure `setup-algebra-problem`. Notice that the list of operators is fixed by the definition of this procedure, in that `:OPERATORS` is always initialized to the same constant list for each problem. A classic test case is stored in the variable `*bundy*`.

The rest of this file defines the procedures needed to implement a particular set of operators. Given the substantial effort we have already invested in defining a pattern matcher and simplifier, one might expect that this part would be relatively easy. And it is.

The procedures associated with operators all have a common form. First `match` is called to establish whether or not the operator is relevant to the given expression. For isolation methods this expression is the left-hand side of the equation. For attraction and collection methods the matching is done against all least dominating terms, as found by the procedure `find-least-dominating-terms`. Liberal use is made of the ability to filter matches by variable restrictions. The definitions included are a subset of those in the figures above. The only new operator is *canonicalization* which calls `simplify` on the equation to put the terms in an order more conducive to matching.

Some find it hard to see how to implement the notion of least dominating term. A recursive argument shows that the procedure `find-least-dominating-terms` is correct. Suppose the whole expression does not contain an occurrence of the variable x. Then there is no least dominating term in x, and checking its subexpressions is useless. Now suppose there is some subterm which is a least dominating term in x. For any expression, either no subexpression will contain x, one subexpression will contain x, or more than one subexpression will contain x. We have just dealt with the case of no subexpressions. If more than one subterm contains x then the expression itself is a least dominating term. Those subexpressions that contain x must be further searched, but by the argument above, no subexpression not containing x need be examined. If only one subexpression contains x then that term, or some subexpression of it, might itself be a least dominating term. So we repeat the process on that term. Since expressions are trees, this recursion must terminate.

Should the match succeed, an appropriate form is created for further CPS processing. The operator instance is represented by a form consisting of the operator name and the equation it is applied to. The new state is computed by substituting the bindings into the form for the right-hand side of the operator and calling `simplify` on the results.

3.6.6 Analysis of algebra system

If Bundy's theory is right, we will not see large differences between different search strategies because the additional control knowledge in the method formulation heavily constrains each step. Figure 3.11 shows what happens when we try solving his test case, and indeed this prediction seems correct. If we run `bsolve` we find we get the answer we expect, and in fact, if we run `dsolve` we get the same answer with fewer states explored. The total number of states explored in each case (17 and 7) makes our earlier dire worst-case prediction of 13^5 states seem pretty naive. The reason for the difference lies in the applicability constraints: no matter how complicated the expression, each method can apply to at most one expression in an equation. Why? Isolation methods can apply only to the whole equation, and attraction and collection methods can apply only to a least dominating term in the unknown. Each method applies only to a specific operator, hence often only a single method makes sense. In this example, for instance, using `beam-solve` with a beam of one still leads to a solution! What appeared to be a horrible search problem has been tamed, turned into a problem that can be solved straightforwardly.

```
>*bundy*
(= (+ (LOG (+ X 1) E) (LOG (- X 1) E)) C)
> (setq a (setup-algebra-problem))
<Problem: ALGEBRA>
>(bsolve *bundy* a)
<path (= X (SQRT (+ 1 (EXPT E C))))>
17
>(print-answer *)

Initial state: (= (+ (LOG (+ X 1) E) (LOG (- X 1) E)) C).
1.  (= (LOG (* (+ 1 X) (- X 1)) E) C), via ATTRACT-LOG-SUM
2.  (= (LOG (- (SQR X) 1) E) C), via COLLECT-PRODUCT-SUM
3.  (= (- (SQR X) 1) (EXPT E C)), via ISOLATE-LOG-INSTANCES
4.  (= (SQR X) (+ 1 (EXPT E C))), via ISOLATE-DIFFERENCE
5.  (= X (SQRT (+ 1 (EXPT E C)))), via ISOLATE-SQUARE
 Done.
NIL
```

;;; Depth-first version

```
>(dsolve *bundy* a)
<path (= X (SQRT (+ 1 (EXPT E C))))>
7
>(print-answer *)

Initial state: (= (+ (LOG (+ X 1) E) (LOG (- X 1) E)) C).
1.  (= (+ (LOG (+ 1 X) E) (LOG (- X 1) E)) C), via CANONICALIZATION
2.  (= (LOG (* (+ 1 X) (- X 1)) E) C), via ATTRACT-LOG-SUM
3.  (= (LOG (- (SQR X) 1) E) C), via COLLECT-PRODUCT-SUM
4.  (= (- (SQR X) 1) (EXPT E C)), via ISOLATE-LOG-INSTANCES
5.  (= (SQR X) (+ 1 (EXPT E C))), via ISOLATE-DIFFERENCE
6.  (= X (SQRT (+ 1 (EXPT E C)))), via ISOLATE-SQUARE
 Done.
NIL
```

Figure 3.11 Algebra runs on Bundy's example

3.7 Sic transit gloria search?

In CPS we see that a very simple yet general search engine can indeed be usefully employed as part of a problem solver. Is search truly the core idea of building problem solvers, and thus potentially the key computational idea for explaining intelligence? A closer analysis of our CPS examples can shed light on this question.

The real question is this: what percentage of the work in developing problem solvers needs to go into developing search engines? If search really is the key idea, then most of our effort as problem-solver designers should go into building better and cleverer search routines. On the other hand, if the real determinants of performance lie elsewhere, then energy poured into improving and tuning search routines may be misspent. We will get more leverage if we concentrate our energies on those other aspects of problem-solving.

In the Boston subway problem space, the search engines were a substantial fraction of the code. However, this was due to the trivial nature of the domain. Searching a finite, preenumerated graph is a very simple kind of problem. The CPS algebra problem space provides a better test case. In the algebra system we ended up creating two systems of roughly the same complexity as the search engine (i.e., the pattern matcher and simplifier). Search was needed to solve equations, of course, but most of the work went into defining the representations and knowledge of algebra.

This is a well-known AI lesson: knowledge reduces the need to search. Caching the results to specific problems is one kind of speedup, but the more useful efficiencies are gleaned from careful analyses of classes of problems which uncover structure that can be used to guide search. Bundy's identification of attraction, collection, and isolation methods is a splendid example of such an analysis. Indeed, the language of the field has shifted to speaking of *domains* rather than problem spaces (save when thinking about search issues).

In many situations search is unavoidable. But search should be viewed as something you do when you don't have enough domain knowledge to figure out an answer more efficiently. Search is exponential, and embedding an exponential process unnecessarily in a computation is bad design. Faster computers or massive parallelism cannot tame the ravenous computational demands of raw exponential search. Improvements in domain-independent search strategies will not let you beat the exponential. For some problems there are linear algorithms that can provide approximate solutions which are good enough in most cases [4]. But in general, only domain knowledge can tame the exponential.

What are the implications for us, as problem-solver designers? CPS provided no leverage in defining the control knowledge we needed. Many of the interesting concepts ended up embedded in Lisp code: efficient, but hardly perspicuous. How could such a program ever learn to improve its performance, or explain its results to us, or perform its own reality checks to ensure that its reasoning is sound? We have not provided support for building systems where most of the interesting knowledge is embedded in an explicit set of beliefs inside the program's head, so to speak. What is missing from CPS are commitments about representation. In the rest of this book we focus on models that make such commitments, in terms of their *knowledge models* for domain information and *procedure models* for control knowledge, the "how to" of reasoning.

Search by itself is no longer viewed as the essence of intelligence. Clearly search is a part of it, but only a part. A search routine is just like a routine for sorting or taking square roots or printing numbers: simply a component that is used as part of a larger system. Search appears repeatedly, but we will recognize our old friend simply as a subroutine, part of a much larger system in which the interesting work lies elsewhere.

3.8 Backpointers

The pattern matcher and simplifier were inspired by a Scheme version written by Gerald Sussman for research purposes.

3.9 Exercises

1. ⋆ What setting of beam suffices to successfully navigate the Boston subway? That is, what is the smallest value of `n` given to `beam-solve` that results in plotting a successful course from Logan Airport to Kendall Square?

2. ⋆ Show that `algebra-distance` can overestimate the number of steps required to solve an equation.

3. ⋆ Rewrite `bsolve` to detect and discard proposed new paths which have reached a previously explored state. Analyze the time and space complexity of your solution, and decide whether or not this modification is worthwhile.

4. ⋆⋆ Recall that the algebra system includes a fixed set of operators. This has two problems. In experimenting it is often useful to switch between alternate sets of operators. In extending a system it is convenient to be able to add new operators simply by loading additional files of operators, without editing existing code. Rewrite `setup-algebra-problem` to allow this, adding any needed ancillary definitions to `algebra.lisp`.

5. The implementation of operators in the algebra system does not fully exploit their common structure. In particular, it would make adding new operators much easier if there were generic procedures for each class of method. Suppose we had procedures

   ```
   (Use-Attraction-Method ⟨Name⟩ ⟨Before⟩ ⟨After⟩)
   (Use-Collection-Method ⟨Name⟩ ⟨Before⟩ ⟨After⟩)
   (Use-Isolation-Method ⟨Name⟩ ⟨Before⟩ ⟨After⟩)
   ```

   where ⟨*Name*⟩ is a symbol naming the operator, ⟨*Before*⟩ is the pattern representing the left-hand side of the algebraic law and ⟨*After*⟩ is the pattern representing the right-hand side of the law. Thus some of our operators might be implemented internally as follows:

   ```
   (Use-Isolation-Method 'Isolate-Log
    '(= (log (? arg (lambda (term) (occurs-in? 'X term)))
             (? base (lambda (term) (not (occurs-in? 'X term)))))
        (? rhs (lambda (exp) (not (occurs-in? 'X exp)))))
    '(= (? arg) (expt (? base) (? rhs))))

   (Use-Collection-Method 'Collect-Product-Sum
    '(* (+ (? v (lambda (term) (not (occurs-in? 'x term))))
           (? u (lambda (term) (occurs-in? 'x term))))
        (- (? u) (? v)))
    '(- (sqr (? U)) (sqr (? V))))
   ```

```
(Use-Attraction-Method 'Attract-Log-Sum
 '(+ (log (? u (lambda (e) (occurs-in? 'X e)))
          (? w (lambda (e) (not (occurs-in? 'X e)))))
     (log (? v (lambda (e) (occurs-in? 'X e)))
          (? w)))
 '(log (* (? U) (? V)) (? W)))
```

a. ⋆⋆ Define `use-attraction-operator`, `use-collection-operator`, and `use-isolation-operator`.

b. ⋆⋆ The job of maintaining the algebra system could be made even easier by adding a bit of "syntactic sugar." Implement a macro `defAlgebraOperator` that provides a simple interface for defining new operators. It should take as arguments the name of the operator, the kind of method it represents, the pattern before, and the pattern afterward.

c. ⋆⋆ Given that the definition of isolation, attraction, and collection methods is purely syntactic, one can in fact automatically translate a given algebraic identity into an appropriate set of methods. Define such a translation procedure, build a civilized interface macro for it (`defAlgebraLaw`), and test it by adding several new algebraic identities to your system with it.

6. ⋆⋆ Using the programs in `variants.lisp` as a guide, implement A* search.

7. Suppose we wanted to use `match` in a rewrite system that performed more backtracking. This new constraint on `match` means it should be more exhaustive. That is, we now want to find all the ways a pattern might match a given expression, not just one match, as the program does now.

   a. ⋆ One motivation for such a system is the desire to write more complex transformation rules. Explain why the following call to `match` returns `:FAIL`.

   ```
   (match '(+ (* (?? A) x (?? B)) (* (?? A) (- 1 x)))
          '(+ (* 2 x x) (* 2 x (- 1 x))))
   ```

   b. ⋆ Write a new version of `match.lisp` that returns a list of dictionaries, each representing a different way a pattern can legally match an expression.

c. ⋆⋆ Given the large number of potential matches, incremental generation strategies are usually more desirable than exhaustive enumeration. Rewrite `match.lisp` to produce matches incrementally by creating a generator. That is, `match` should now return two values: a dictionary representing the current match, and a procedure of no arguments which, when evaluated, returns the next match (if any) and a new generator.

8. An important wrinkle in search strategies is the idea of *iterative deepening* [6, 4]. Iterative deepening is based on the observation that in an exponentially growing search tree, the number of nodes at depth d is roughly the same as the number of nodes in the entire tree of depth $d - 1$. Therefore it makes sense to exhaustively explore possible solutions at depth $d - 1$ before expanding the search to depth d. Iterative deepening can be implemented by adding a cutoff to a depth-first search algorithm, and using this modified algorithm to explore the search tree with ever-increasing depth bounds.

   a. ⋆⋆ Implement `id-search`, an iterative deepening version of depth-first search.

   b. ⋆⋆ How does `id-search` compare empirically with other search strategies on the subway and algebra domains?

   c. ⋆⋆ Iterative deepening can be applied to A* search as well. Implement a version of A* which uses iterative deepening, and evaluate its performance empirically.

9. The algebra system has two glaring limitations: the use of a fixed unknown and the ability to manipulate only one equation at a time.

   a. ⋆ Change the algebra system so that the variable to be solved for can be specified as part of the problem.

   b. ⋆⋆ Extend the algebra system so that states now consist of a set of algebraic equations, and the goal is to find a state which contains an equation that has only the designated unknown on its left-hand side. (Hint: A useful strategy is to treat the choice of what variables to substitute for as a search problem itself, and call CPS recursively to solve equations for those variables.)

   c. ⋆ Using your new algebra system, come up with an expression for W_e, a person's equilibrium weight, assuming the following equations are valid:

$$\delta W = \frac{7MW - C_f + C_e}{3500}$$

$$C_f = 7C_{f_d}$$
$$C_e = \frac{NW}{150}$$

where

W = Weight at the beginning of a week.

δW = Change in weight at the end of the week.

C_{f_d} = Food calories taken in each day.

N = Number of miles walked that week.

M = Metabolic factor; about 11 for men, 10 for women.

10. ⋆⋆⋆ A classic early use of pattern matching in AI research was Bobrow's STUDENT program [1], which solved algebra word problems. For example, given the following problem

    Bill's father's uncle is twice as old as Bill's father. Two years from now Bill's father will be three times as old as Bill. The sum of their ages is 92. Find Bill's age.

    STUDENT is able to figure out that Bill is eight years old. Reconstruct STUDENT by:

    a. Creating a set of rewrite rules that translate sentence fragments into algebraic expressions.

    b. Extending the CPS algebra system to solve the algebraic expressions so generated.

3.10 Bibliography

[1] Bobrow, D. G., "Natural language input for a computer problem-solving system," in Minsky, M. (Ed.), *Semantic Information Processing*, MIT Press, 1968.

[2] Bundy, A., and Welham, B., "Using meta-level inference for selective application of multiple rewrite rules in algebraic manipulation," *Proceedings of IJCAI-79*, 1979, 1017–1027.

[3] Bundy, A., *The Computer Modeling of Mathematical Reasoning*, Academic Press, 1983.

[4] Korf, R., "Search: A survey of recent results," in Shrobe, H. (ed.), *Exploring Artificial Intelligence*, Morgan-Kaufmann, 1988.

[5] Newell, A., and Simon, H., *Human Problem Solving*, Prentice Hall, 1972.

[6] Slate, D. J., and Atkin, L. R., "CHESS 4.5 - the Northwestern University chess program," in Frey, P. W. (ed.), *Chess Skill in Man and Machine*, Springer-Verlag, 1977.

[7] Steele, G., *COMMON LISP the Language*, 2nd edition, Digital Press, 1990.

4 Pattern-Directed Inference Systems

As we saw previously, the classical problem-space model itself makes no committment to any particular form of representation. This lack of restrictions gave us generality, in that we could encode problem spaces any way we liked. But without some conventions, the inference engine cannot provide us with much leverage. A good compromise is to choose a common underlying "medium" in which particular representations can be encoded. The most common choice is the use of list structure to implement *assertions*. Informally, an assertion is a statement, an encoding of some kind of knowledge into a language that can be used in reasoning. As we shall see, assertions are an extremely powerful medium that can be used to encode a wide variety of representations. By using pattern matching as a reference mechanism, much like the rewrite rules used in the CPS symbolic algebra system, we can achieve far greater modularity. Systems organized around this idea are often called *pattern-directed inference systems* (or PDIS for brevity).

This chapter explores the ideas of pattern-directed inference systems. We begin by outlining the basic ideas underlying such systems. Next, we describe the *Tiny Rule Engine*, or TRE, which implements this model. TRE is an exploratory program, designed to be extremely simple. This allows us to focus on the essentials of pattern-directed inference systems before showing how to make them both more powerful and more efficient in Chapter 5. Designing problem solvers using TRE-like systems is something of an art. To illustrate, we use *natural deduction* as a source of examples. We describe a particular natural deduction scheme, KM*, adapted from the work of Kalish and Montague [7], and show how far TRE goes in allowing us to implement this scheme. The limitations that prevent TRE from providing a full implementation of KM* will be overcome by the extensions presented in Chapter 5.

4.1 The pattern-directed inference system model

We begin with assertions, then describe the format of rules. Then we describe how assertions and rules interact in detail.

4.1.1 Assertions

Data, whether it be raw information, facts about the world, or the consequences of internal deliberations, is encoded in the form of assertions. Assertions take the form of lists, containing symbols, lists, and numbers, such as:

```
(Robot Robbie)
(Implies (Physical-Being Robbie) (Mortal Robbie))
(= (Height Robbie) (6 feet))
(= (Position (House Robbie)) :lattitude (32 degrees)
                             :longitude (45 degrees))
```

Assertions provide a flexible representational medium. The previous examples, for instance, can be interpreted as terms in first-order predicate calculus. But assertions can be used to model many other kinds of data as well. An OPS datum can be modeled as an assertion consisting of alternating indicators and properties, such as:

```
(Name Datum32 Color Red Recency 32)
```

We can also encode knowledge in assertions via English sentences, such as

```
(THE MOON IS MADE OF GREEN CHEESE)
(THIS STATEMENT IS FALSE)
```

Assertions can also provide a declarative expression of procedural knowledge, such as

```
(defun fact (n)
       (if (= n 0) 1 (* n (fact (- n 1)))))
```

Some encodings are more useful than others. The particular conventions for interpreting assertions must be established by the author(s) of a particular system's rules. In these examples, human readers easily ascribe meaning to each assertion. However, assertions have no particular meaning by themselves to the PDIS system. Any meaning they have for the system is entirely determined by how they are used by the system's rules.

Assertions are stored in a database. In some systems the internal representation of an assertion is more complicated than a piece of list structure. For example, as Chapter 6 explains, programs which use truth maintenance systems associate extra structure with each assertion to record whether or not, and why, an assertion is believed. In such cases we use the term assertion to refer to the entire structure, and we use the term *form* to refer to the actual list structure expression of the assertion. For now, we make two simplifications:

1. The assertion is identical to its form.
2. An assertion is believed exactly when it can be found in the system's database.

More complex models of belief are introduced when we discuss truth maintenance systems.

The primary interface between the assertion database and the rest of the system consists of two procedures, `assert!` and `fetch`. `assert!` inserts a form into the database as a new assertion. If the form has already been asserted, `assert!` does nothing. Given a pattern, `fetch` retrieves assertions in the database that match it.

The kind of pattern matching appropriate for pattern-directed inference systems is somewhat different from the form of pattern matching used in the CPS algebra system. Patterns can contain variables, as before, but no value restrictions can be associated with variables. This stipulation forces us to put more of the knowledge into assertions and rules rather than special-purpose procedures. Furthermore, there are no segment variables. Segment variables were motivated by the need to manipulate algebraic expressions, where the added complexity of nondeterministic matching was worthwhile. For most pattern-directed inference systems the extra overhead of considering segment variables is not worthwhile.[1] Instead, we use a form of pattern matching first developed in logic, called *unification.* Two patterns *unify* if there exists a set of values for their variables so that, when substitutions are made, the patterns become identical. Notice that unification can match two expressions when both contain variables, unlike our previous pattern matcher. Detailed treatments of unification can be found in most logic or AI texts (e.g., [7, 3, 8]), so we shall not dwell on it here.

From this point onward we represent pattern variables by symbols with "?" as their first character. Thus `?foo`, `?BAR`, and `?Grumble` are variables, while `Foo`, `bar?`, and `!Grumble` are not. These two patterns unify

```
(Has-Value (gain ?amp) ?beta)
(Has-Value (gain Amplifier32) 10000)
```

assuming the bindings

```
 ?amp = Amplifier32
?beta = 10000
```

whereas these two patterns do not unify

```
(Has-Value (gain ?amp) ?beta)
(Has-Value (Output-Voltage Amplifier32) (5.0 V))
```

There can be some interesting subtleties when both patterns contain variables. For instance, these two patterns unify

```
(Caused-by ?agent Event543)
(?rel ?robot ?event)
```

while these two patterns do not

```
(Mystical ?agent (friend ?x))
(Mystical ?x ?agent)
```

Why? Recall that unification is defined by the existence of a set of substitutions that makes two expressions equal. In the first pair, we can make the second assertion identical to the first by making the following substitutions

1. Simplifiers can always be used as a subroutine by pattern-directed inference systems, as JSAINT in Chapter 8 illustrates.

```
  ?rel = Caused-by
?robot = ?agent
?event = Event543
```

In the second pair, it may look as though we can use the substitutions

```
?agent = (friend ?x)
    ?x = ?agent
```

to make the two expressions identical. This doesn't work because we must apply substitutions uniformly. Attempting to do so reveals that `?x` does not correspond to a finite expression

```
?x = (friend (friend (friend ,⟨ . . . ⟩ )))
```

In defining a unifier we must be careful to ensure that we compute correct substitutions. We return to this issue later.

All of the state in an assertion must be expressed in its structure in order for pattern matching to be sufficient as a reference mechanism. In implementation terms, this means assertions should only be built out of lists, symbols, and numbers. There are cases where assertions must contain complex data structures, as when interfacing a PDIS to another module (such as a spatial reasoning system). Such compound datastructures should be used with great caution. Changes in the value of a struct's slot, for instance, will not show up when matching patterns. This subverts the explicit representation of knowledge via assertions.

Alert readers may have noticed that the database interface does not contain any mechanism for deleting assertions. This is deliberate. The semantics of deletion, given that we identify belief in a fact with the appearance in the database of the assertion corresponding to that fact, would be retracting belief in that fact. Our design so far has just a single global database, with no particular links between beliefs. This means we have no easy method for removing the consequences of a belief, which in turn means we cannot correctly handle deletion. We return to this issue later.

4.1.2 Rules

Procedural knowledge is expressed in rules. Like assertions, rules are stored in a database. Each rule has two parts, a *trigger* and a *body*. The trigger is a pattern that specifies the kinds of assertions to which the rule is intended to respond. In effect, whenever an assertion matching the trigger enters the database, the rule will "wake up" and execute its body on that piece of data. The body consists of Lisp code, evaluated in the environment formed by unifying the pattern with a particular assertion. The syntax we use here for rules is

(rule ⟨*trigger*⟩ . ⟨*body*⟩)

A rule one might use for debugging is

```
(rule (foo ?x) (format t "foo(~A) has been asserted." ?x))
```

which will inform us whenever any instance of (foo ?x) has been asserted.

Typically it is desirable to have rules trigger when a combination of assertions hold. For instance, we might want to create a rule asserting that three blocks sitting one on top of the other comprises a special kind of tower, a "three tower." We can write such a rule by nesting several simpler rules. Rules are lexically scoped. That is, the environment used to execute the body of a rule includes all the variable bindings made by the trigger patterns for the rules that contain it. An example will make this clearer. Here is a rule for spotting towers that are three blocks high:

```
(rule (on ?x table)
 (rule (on ?y ?x)
  (rule (on ?z ?y) (assert! `(3-Tower ,?x ,?y ,?z)))))
```

Suppose the database includes the following set of assertions:

```
(ON D TABLE)
(ON E D)
(ON F E)
```

The first trigger would match (ON D TABLE). The environment for executing the body of the outer rule now has ?x bound to D. This binding will now form part of any environment created for any rule defined within the body of the outer rule. One consequence of this fact is that the trigger of the next rule is effectively (ON ?y D), not (ON ?y ?x). Of course, this only applies for this particular usage of the rule—other new rules may be generated when other assertions are matched. But in each case, when the rule comprising the body of the outermost rule is added to the database, its environment will include whatever binding for ?x was discovered in matching the first pattern.

The same thing happens when the first inner rule is successfully matched against (ON E D). A new rule is added to the database (using the specification of the innermost rule, since it is the body of the rule whose trigger is (ON ?y ?x)), whose environment contains bindings for ?x and for ?y, whose trigger pattern is (ON ?z ?y), subject to the binding for ?y matching its current value, and whose body is the assert! statement. This third rule triggers on (ON F E), and thus causes (3-TOWER D E F) to be asserted.

To summarize: When an assertion is found that matches a rule's trigger pattern, the body of the rule is queued for eventual execution. When the body of a rule includes the specification of other rules (i.e., forms beginning with the symbol rule), one result is the creation of a new rule which is added to the database and treated like any other. Both the trigger and body of this new rule have as their defining environment any bindings introduced by triggers for the sequence of rules that contained the specification.

Rules have indefinite extent: each rule spawned remains in the database forever. This holds for rules created by nested specifications as well as for their progenitors. In this model, rules are never deleted from the system or made inactive: they always trigger on any matching assertion that appears. Returning to our three-tower example, suppose there were some other block, say G, on top of E as well. Then the innermost rule would trigger again on the assertion (On G E), and (3-Tower D E G) would also be asserted. Since traditional procedures don't work this way, this can take some getting used to. One important benefit of the infinite extent of rules is that pattern-directed inference systems can be designed to be *order-independent*. That is, rules and assertions can be put into the system in any order you choose, and eventually the same set of consequences should be produced. A drawback of this property is that it becomes easier to generate combinatorial explosions and can be harder to maintain efficiency. The trade-offs involved in designing problem-solver operations to be order-independent versus exploiting assumptions about ordering to gain efficiency and inferential power show up repeatedly through this book.

4.1.3 Variations on the PDIS theme

The model described so far represents one family of pattern-directed inference systems. All such systems include assertions as their knowledge model and rules as their procedure model, but vary in both the details of these aspects and in their execution strategy. The PDIS model described here uses an antecedent, or forward-chaining strategy. Another choice, found in systems such as MYCIN and its descendants as well as Prolog and other common logic-programming languages, is a consequent, or backward-chaining, strategy. Much has been written about organizing expert systems using backward-chaining rule strategies (see for example [1, 5]), so we do not cover them further here.

Another important class of pattern-directed inference systems comprises those organized around *production rules*. Most production rule systems allow assertions to be deleted and even modified as part of the effects of rules. This enhances storage economy, but makes keeping track of relationships between beliefs more complex (Chapter 6 examines these issues in detail). The execution strategy of such systems is typically designed to select a single best rule to execute during each cycle of the interpreter, rather than executing all applicable rules. Production rule systems have seen wide application both in expert systems and in cognitive simulation research.

A third class of pattern-directed inference systems is made up of *procedural deduction* systems, such as MicroPlanner [12], Conniver [8], and Schemer [14]. Procedural deduction systems sometimes include rules, but generally organize their procedures around traditional programming constructs which include pattern matching and non-deterministic operations to provide more flexible control structures. Procedural deduction systems have received less attention to date than the other forms of pattern-directed inference systems, and have not seen widespread application.

One reason for our focus on the antecedent model for pattern-directed inference systems comes from our observation of how such systems tend to be used. Designers of problem-solving architectures tend to view their systems as all-encompassing. That is, users of their systems—designers of problem solvers for specific classes of problems—should be able to work entirely within their systems. This is natural, given the designer's goal of creating powerful, general-purpose architectures. In our experience, though, a single pattern-directed inference system rarely consititutes a complete architecture by itself. Instead, problem solvers are built from several modules whose interactions are carefully designed to provide an efficient division of labor. Consequently, we tend not to view a problem solver as consisting entirely of an antecedent PDIS. Instead, a PDIS is typically used as a module in a larger system. A problem solver might use one PDIS as its database or several, and may have more or less of its procedures cast as rules. Typically ultimate responsibility for control lies elsewhere, in the rest of the problem solver. Other programs start up a PDIS, examine their output, toss in new assertions when an impasse is reached, and so forth. We explore such organizations in Chapters 5, 8, 11, and 14.

The Tiny Rule Engine, or TRE, provides a simple implementation of our pattern-directed inference system model. We begin by laying out TRE's design, following with its implementation in Section 4.3.

4.2 The design of TRE

We have seen the knowledge model for pattern-directed inference systems (assertions), the reference model (pattern matching, in this case unification), and the procedure model (rules). Here we examine how computation is organized in such systems by looking at their execution strategy and its consequences.

Rules and assertions are added incrementally. The goal of the execution strategy for antecedent inference systems is to ensure that each rule is run on every assertion that matches its pattern. To achieve this, whenever an assertion is added each rule that might trigger on that assertion must be tested to see if it actually matches. Similarly, whenever a new rule is added all assertions that might match its trigger pattern must be retrieved and tested against it. In both cases, a successful match results in a set of bindings which form part of the environment for executing the body of the rule. The body and this environment are then queued for eventual execution.

As we have just seen, when a rule is executed it can in turn create new rules and assertions, which are treated exactly as those added previously. The whole cycle continues until the system attains quiescence, that is,

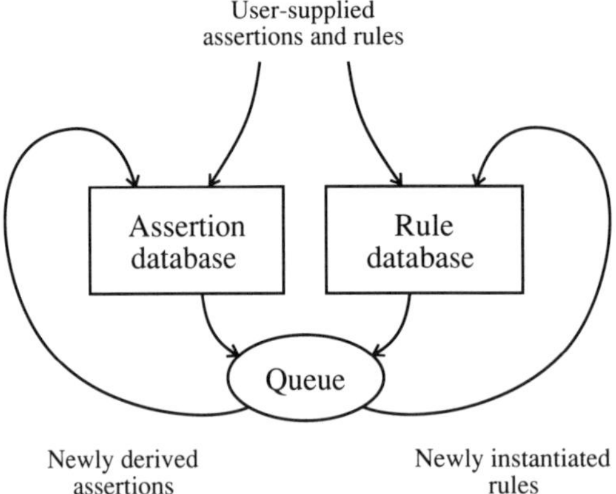

Figure 4.1 Antecedent architecture

when no more rules can be executed. Figure 4.1 depicts this cycle and the its components.

Any system can be viewed from several perspectives, each highlighting a different set of issues. From the perspective of a potential TRE user, one consequence of this organization is that we must be careful when designing a set of rules to ensure that they will reach quiescence. That is, given a starting set of assertions, the operation of the TRE should stop after a finite number of rule executions. This can fail to happen if the system of rules "feeds on itself," producing an infinite number of assertions. Another consequence is that we should not presume that rules will be executed in any particular order. Rules that attempt to interact via setting values of global variables, for instance, may or may not work depending on the order in which matching combinations of rules and assertions are executed. All interactions must be carried out through the databases.

From the perspective of designing TRE, these user expectations are both constraining and liberating. Since the TRE user (who may be an end user, but more commonly will be a problem solver designer using TRE as a tool in creating a problem solver) must worry about quiescence, we as designers are not required to detect infinite loops or to supply mechanisms for bounding resources. Since TRE users are not assuming any particular execution order for triggered rules, we may arrange for the execution of such rules in whatever order is simplest for us. However, the central role of rules in the procedure model and the total reliance on pattern matching as the reference mechanism suggests that we must make the triggering of rules and their subsequent execution as efficient as possible, to keep our users (even if they are ourselves!) happy.

Efficiency is relative, of course. Industrial-strength PDIS efficiency techniques are covered in Chapter 5. TRE is designed for exploratory programming. It is extremely simple, and not terribly efficient, as is proper for exploratory programming.

Several of our design choices are obvious:

Assertions: Implement as list structure.

Pattern matching: Implement as unification

Others are not so obvious:

Databases: How do we store rules and assertions to simplify getting matching ones together?

Rules: What needs to be included in a rule, and how should we implement them? In particular, how should we arrange for the appropriate execution environments?

Queuing rules: What exactly should go on the queue, and how should it be serviced?

Let us consider each in turn.

4.2.1 PDIS database design

There are many ways to organize a pattern-directed database. The easiest way to organize the database would be to use two lists, one for assertions and one for rules. Every time a new assertion is added it would be unified against every trigger pattern in the list of rules. Every time a new rule is added, its trigger would be unified against every item in the list of assertions. Each successful unification would result in the combination of rule and assertion being queued for execution. Unfortunately this scheme is too inefficient even for simple problems. Instead, we use a simple but powerful technique called *class indexing* (also known as `car` *indexing*).

The idea of class indexing is to partition both assertions and rules into *dbclasses* (i.e., *d*ata*b*ase *classes*), corresponding to sets whose elements are likely to match. We define the class of an assertion (or trigger pattern) as its leftmost constant symbol. For example,

DBClass(`(implies foo bar)`) = `implies`

DBClass(`foo`) = `foo`

DBClass(`((grumble mumble) bar)`) = `grumble`

Clearly, unless an assertion and a trigger are in the same database class they cannot match, for we already know they differ in one position. This means that when adding a new assertion we need only test it against rules indexed under its own database class, and when adding a new rule we need only test it against assertions in its own database class. Suppose the leftmost symbol in a pattern is a variable. In that case, we take the database class of that variable's value. We consider it an error if the variable is unbound. Why? Because in that case our only option would be a linear search through the entire database, which is unacceptably inefficient. In practice this restriction is rarely chafing, and more sophisticated schemes are described in Chapter 5 for such circumstances.

Using this scheme, we now have one database, consisting of a set of classes, each containing both facts and rules. Given an assertion or trigger pattern we should be able to easily find its database class, by first extracting the appropriate symbol from its structure and retrieving the associated database class datastructure for that symbol.

An aside: one problem with class indexing is that it is very hard to do certain kinds of queries. For instance `(?X Foo)` is not a legitimate query unless it appears in some scope where `?X` is bound. Is this a serious problem? One can imagine cases where it would be—suppose, for instance, one wanted to know all the two-place predicates that held between `A` and `B`. However, in realistic situations such queries do not arise often and can be handled with special-case procedures anyway. (In the worst case, one could do a linear search of all the assertions in the database.) By optimizing this database for the most common cases, we gain great efficiency without sacrificing simplicity.

Once this implementation choice is made, it does affect how one encodes knowledge in the system. Suppose that in fact one did want to know all the binary relationships that held between `A` and `B`, and that in fact such queries were quite common in the task at hand. Then instead of encoding binary relations as

`(`⟨*Predicate*⟩ ⟨*1st arg*⟩ ⟨*2nd arg*⟩`)`

one might instead choose to encode them as

(⟨*1st arg*⟩ ⟨*Predicate*⟩ ⟨*2nd arg*⟩)

which gives a slightly "frame-ish" flavor.

Why restrict database classes to symbols? After all, one could imagine using floating-point numbers, say, as database classes. The problem with things that are not symbols is that identity testing can become tricky. For instance, is `3.14159292` the same or different database class from `3.14159265`? List structures might at first be a reasonable exception, since one could always use `equal`. But consider the following assertion

```
((distance-between A B) . (3 km))
```

which might say that the distance between `A` and `B` is three kilometers. If we let the database class be the `car` of this expression the database class would be `(distance-between A B)`. This choice disallows queries like

```
((distance-between A ?x) . (?val ?units))
```

where we might want to find all the distances involving some interesting place `A`. By using the leftmost symbol (in this case `distance-between`) this query becomes legitimate. To be sure, we lose the ability to discriminate between

```
((distance-between A B) . (3 km))
(((((((distance-between)))) foo bar)) Grumble))
(distance-between A B)
```

at the level of database classes, but this discrimination can be handled through the unifier.

4.2.2 The design of rules

We have already specified that rules have a *trigger*, a pattern that specifies what form of assertions the *body* will be executed on. Once created, rules have indefinite temporal extent. This means they must be created as distinct computational entities in the TRE database. Furthermore, we must make the bindings found via pattern matching available during the execution of the rule's body. There are several strategies for achieving this. Generally the best strategy is to arrange the system so that the values bound to the pattern variables are bound as the Lisp values of the symbols that serve as pattern variables for the duration of the execution

```
(rule (Transitive ?R)  ;; Rule R1
  (rule (?R ?x ?y)     ;; Rule R2
    (rule (?R ?y ?z)   ;; Rule R3
      (assert! (?R ?x ?z)))))
```

Figure 4.2 Nested rules are lexically scoped. In this nested rule, the outer rule (labeled *R1*) binds `?R`. This binding is in force for the execution of its body, i.e., the definition of the rule labelled *R2*. Whenever *R2* is triggered its body is executed in an environment where `?R`, `?x`, and `?y` are bound, resulting in the definition of a rule as specified by *R3*. Every triggering of rules instantiated from *R3* will also have `?z` bound, in addition to their inherited bindings for `?R`, `?x`, and `?y`.

of the body of the rule. This means we can treat the body simply as a piece of Lisp code.

This *alignment* strategy for implementing rules is not the only possible strategy, of course. A frequently used alternative, a form of *substitution* strategy, instead analyzes the rule's body, replacing all references to pattern variables with forms that access and set the appropriate pattern variables. This strategy is substantially more complicated than the alignment strategy, since it requires the ability to analyze the code in the body in detail. The only situations in which the substitution strategy might be advantageous are when substantial reworking of the rule body is required for other reasons. Otherwise, we believe alignment strategies provide the best combination of simplicity and efficiency.

We also stated that pattern variables in nested rules would be lexically scoped. Suppose we had a nested sequence of rules $R_1, \ldots, R_n$. Consider the trigger of the ith rule, T_i. Any variables appearing in T_i that occurred in $T_1, , \ldots, T_{i-1}$ will be interpreted as bound when matching T_i. When T_i matches an assertion, any variables bound by that match will be part of the environment for the rules $R_{i+1}, , \ldots, R_n$. Figure 4.2 illustrates. Whatever implementation method we choose for aligning rules must enforce this constraint.

Here we pick an extremely simple (but not very efficient) version of the alignment method. Let us stipulate that, in addition to returning a table of bindings, our unifier must also accept a table of bindings as part of its input, and that the match must be made with respect to these previously existing bindings. When each rule is created, we can attach to it an *environment* consisting of the table of bindings in force when it was created. When executing the body of a rule we must align the values of the symbols corresponding to pattern variables with the values in the rule's environment. Furthermore, we must ensure that any rule created during the execution of the body must inherit this environment, so that its triggering will respect the context of its creation. Section 4.3.3 describes the implementation.

4.2.3 The design of the unifier

Our design for TRE rules requires that we allow a list of previously existing bindings to be passed in to the unifier, so that a new match will respect the bindings established by an earlier match. So the inputs to our unifier must be a pattern, an assertion, and a (possibly empty) table of bindings. The simplest implementation of tables of bindings uses an alist, where the key of an entry is the pattern variable and the value of an entry is the binding for that variable. This choice means we cannot simply return the traditional value of `nil` to indicate failure, since we could not then distinguish failure to unify from two patterns matching exactly. One alternative would be to return two values, a success flag and the binding list. But since unifiers tend to be defined recursively this would lead to considerable extra work. Instead, we shall return a special symbol, `:FAIL`, to indicate the failure of a match. This value is always recognizable since no table of bindings can be a non-`nil` symbol.

4.2.4 The design of the queue

We have not specified any particular order of execution for rules, only that all matching rule/assertion pairs must eventually be executed. Any strategy, including last-in, first-out (LIFO) or first-in, first-out (FIFO) satisfies these conditions, and we can make our choice based on simplicity of implementation.

4.3 The implementation of TRE

Now let us see how our design can be implemented. The listing for TRE consists of five files. The first file is `tre.lisp`, which defines where the system resides and what other files are involved. The other four files are:

`tinter.lisp` Interface procedures and basic definitions.

`data.lisp` Creating and manipulating assertions.

`rules.lisp` Creating and executing rules.

`unify.lisp` Defines variables and pattern matching.

We describe each in turn.

4.3.1 TRE definitions and interface (tinter.lisp)

The routines in `tinter.lisp` provide an interface for people or other programs using TRE. As in CPS, we use a structure to encapsulate the variables, flags, and parameters that define the state of a TRE. The `title` contains a string which should allow human users to tell different TREs apart. The `dbclass-table` holds a hash table which is used in retrieving assertions and rules. The `debugging` field controls whether or not extra information about a particular TRE's internal operations are displayed. `rule-counter` provides a unique identifier for telling rules apart, and `rules-run` provides a statistic indicating how much work has been performed within this TRE.

A complex problem solver might use several TREs, each handling a different aspect of a problem. Thus it is important when doing something with a TRE to make sure that we are using the right one. The next set of macros and procedures supports this. It is convenient to provide a mechanism for procedures to refer to the "current TRE,", even when there is only one copy of TRE around. The global variable `*TRE*` provides this. We require any procedure that is intended to be called by external users (be they programs or people)—i.e., any interface procedures—to ensure that `*TRE*` is appropriately bound. Internal TRE procedures can then assume that `*TRE*` is bound correctly.

As a convenience, TRE interface procedures tend to provide `*TRE*` as an optional parameter, bound by default to its current value. This leaves one less thing for humans (or other programs) using the system to take care of, and simplifies bookkeeping within the TRE code as well. The macro `With-TRE` and the procedure `in-TRE` encapsulate this particular implementation choice. `With-TRE` evaluates a list of forms in an environment where a particular TRE is the default, by simply lambda-binding `*TRE*` to the appropriate value during the execution of the forms. `in-TRE` is analogous to `in-package`, changing the dynamic value of `*TRE*` and hence (if evaluated outside of any lambda-bindings for it) providing a global change.

An example of how the *TRE* mechanism can simplify TRE internals is provided by debugging-tre. This macro is used in TRE internals, to control when extra information is printed. As expected, it uses the value of the debugging field (actually tre-debugging, due to the :CONC-NAME) to control printing. The choice of TRE to examine is made by the binding of *TRE*, rather than passing another argument explicitly. If debugging-tre were used indiscriminately this could be trouble, but since it is an internal procedure, by the "contract" specified above, *TRE* will always be appropriately bound.

TREs are created via create-tre. The title is required. A keyword argument provides the option of turning on debugging from the beginning. Because the keys to the database class table will always be symbols, the hash table can be predicated on eq rather than equal, making it a bit faster. The only field of a TRE that a user should be able to change directly is the debugging flag. The procedure debug-tre provides this ability, insulating users from internals.

The next two procedures provide *interface drivers* which take in data and compute its consequences. run is intended for human use, furnishing a modified read-eval-print loop which computes the consequences of any input for the TRE. Stating new assertions or rules, for example, causes rule-data pairs to be queued. run-rules, defined in rules.lisp, runs the queue until quiescence before asking for more input. run-forms is similar, but is designed for batch operation or use by programs. Notice that both drivers ensure that, given a list of additions, all consequences of each new rule and assertion are computed before adding another one. This greatly simplifies debugging.

The final procedure in this file is show, which calls subroutines show-data and show-rules to do the actual work. show is only useful for debugging extremely simple examples.

4.3.2 The TRE database (data.lisp)

Database classes are implemented by the dbclass datastructure. Dbclass structs are stored in the TRE's database class table. Each database class has an associated name (i.e., the symbol it corresponds to), and the assertions and rules that belong to it (facts and rules fields respectively). The dbclass-tre field provides a backpointer to the TRE the database class is part of. show-data illustrates how maphash can be used to get information about all assertions (and even all rules) when necessary.

Recall that the procedure `assert!` must take an assertion and install it in the database. It is important to check whether the assertion is already in the database first, since then we do not have to check what rules might be run—presumably that has already occured. `assert!` thus begins by calling `insert`, which returns non-`nil` if the assertion was not already in the database. In that case `try-rules` (defined in the `rules` module) looks for rules that might be triggered by the new assertion and queues them as appropriate. Otherwise, `assert!` does nothing. `insert` operates by checking the assertion's database class to see if it is already there. If not, it pushes the assertion onto the `dbclass-facts` and returns.

Finding the database class of an assertion or pattern is slightly complicated. The basic operation is to compute the database class of an assertion, use the database class table to retrieve its struct if already created, and build it otherwise. The reason things get complicated is that in operating on rules we must sometimes handle patterns as well as fully ground assertions. Suppose our rule trigger is `(?x ?y ?z)`. Since `?x` is a pattern variable, clearly `?x` is not the intended database class. We have to look at the current binding for `?x` to figure out the right database class. As described below in the implementation of rules, it turns out we will need two notions of binding in TRE, which is why `get-dbclass` looks more complicated than one might at first expect. The first notion is just the traditional Lisp notion of binding, handled by the `boundp` clause. The second notion is used in setting up the appropriate lexical scoping for rules. The variable `*env*` holds the substitution environment for a rule, and it, too, must be checked for possible values. This is carried out in the next `cond` clause.

`fetch` operates in two stages. First it gets a candidate set by retrieving the assertions associated with the database class of the pattern. Then it uses `unify` on each candidate to ascertain if it indeed matches the pattern. `unify` returns a set of bindings (possibly empty) when it succeeds, or the distinguished symbol `:FAIL` to indicate that the match was unsuccessful. If `unify` succeeds, the candidate is included in the set of assertions returned.

An engineering note: If you are confident that the system that used the results of `fetch` never modified these datastructures, it would be more efficient to simply return the candidate rather than using `sublis`.

However, if you don't know how the results of `fetch` are to be used, then you might be allowing external procedures to seriously damage the integrity of the TRE database. Since the `sublis` provides a copy of the datum, it can be passed on to other programs and manipulated without qualm.

4.3.3 The TRE rule system (rules.lisp)

As usual, we implement compound computational entities via `defstruct`-defined datastructures. The `id` field is an integer used to distinguish rules when printing. There are several ways we might choose to provide a unique identity for rules, but this method has several advantages. First, integers are compact, conserving screen (and paper) "real estate." Second, it provides an easy key to use in retrieving rules during debugging. Third, it provides some information about when a rule was created: since we use a parameter of the TRE itself, rule N is the nth rule created by the system, and if M is greater than N, then rule M was created after rule N. And, finally, since we keep the counters local to each TRE and initialize a new TRE's value to zero, if we have two TREs that have been given the same sequence of inputs, the same integer will refer to equivalent rules in the two systems.

This last property of integer structure `id`s can be used in a variety of debugging tricks. Suppose for instance that a particular rule is not triggering when one thinks it should. If one knows the `id` of the rule, one can set traps that turn on extra tracing or breakpoints exactly when this particular rule is being processed. This increased focus can substantially increase one's efficiency when debugging.[2]

The `dbclass` field of a rule points to the database class of the rule's trigger. `trigger` contains the rule's pattern, and `body` contains the lisp code that constitutes the procedural import of the rule. `environment` contains an alist representing the bindings that are inherited from the rule's defining context. This alist is used when matching the trigger to

2. The more traditional Lisp strategy of using an arbitrary symbol as a name does not allow this debugging technique. Even if the prefix and counter of the Lisp environment's `gensym` mechanism are reset, its global nature often precludes repeatable naming.

ensure that nested rules are interpreted correctly. In particular, the rule evaluation mechanism binds the dynamic variable `*ENV*` to this alist when the rule is evaluated. This allows various procedures, such as `get-dbclass` above, to be informed about the current rule's lexical environment.

`show-rules` lists the rules, using `print-rule` to provide a more informative description of each rule. This procedure does not show the body of the rule because in this system that code is generally interpreted, and thus can take a lot of display real estate. Such a modification is not difficult (see Exercise 5).

The macro `rule` simplifies rule definition by supporting the minimal syntax we have defined (so far) for rules. That is, the first element after `rule` is considered to be the trigger and the rest is considered to be the body of the rule. (Later variations of TRE require more syntax to support new facilities.) The real work is done by the procedure `add-rule`, which creates a new rule struct and indexes it under the database class of the trigger. Notice that the `environment` field is initialized to `*ENV*`, thus ensuring the new rule inherits whatever set of lexical bindings was in effect when it was created. Finally, the assertions that might match this rule are retrieved (via `get-candidates`, defined above) and tested to see if it can be executed on them.

Recall that rule-assertion pairs can be created either by adding new rules or by adding new assertions. No matter where the match started, the procedure `try-rule-on` is where it is tested for compatibility. Given an assertion and a rule, `try-rule-on` checks whether the rule's trigger unifies with the assertion, assuming the bindings given by the rule's environment. If it does, then the body and new binding list (which includes any newly bound variables as well as the containing environment) are placed onto the queue for eventual execution.

The procedure `try-rules` is provided for the database system. It uses `get-candidate-rules`, the dual of `get-candidates`, to find the rules in the appropriate database class and tests each one against the new assertion using `try-rule-on`.

The procedure `run-rules` oversees the queue. As noted above, any exhaustive queue-servicing strategy will work, so we choose a last-in/first-out (LIFO) implementation for simplicity. The procedures `enqueue` and `dequeue` implement this abstraction. Aside from keeping statistics (via the local variable counter), run-rules' job is simply to call run-rule until nothing is left to do.

run-rule must do two things. First, it must create a Lisp environment in which the variables bound via pattern matching have the correct values. Otherwise, the body of the rule cannot be properly executed. Second, run-rule must provide a compact representation of the rule's environment to be passed on to any rules created during the execution of the body, in order to enforce lexical scoping. The second task is the easiest: we simply lambda-bind *ENV*, using a let statement, to the current set of bindings. We have arranged for the current value of *ENV* to be packaged up with a rule when it is created, so any rule forms evaluated during the execution of the body will include the correct environment. The first task requires a little more work. Essentially, we build a let on the fly which includes the binding list as its lambda-list and the body of the rule as its body, and evaluate this new piece of code. Thus the newly constructed let creates an environment in which the Lisp value of the pattern variables corresponds to their binding list values. In creating the lambda-list, sublis is used to ensure that all known substitutions are made in the value assigned to a pattern variable. Values in the lambda-list are quoted because they could be arbitrary s-expressions.

The only virtue of this implementation is its simplicity. It is very inefficient, since translating between the two different notions of value requires creating a new piece of code every time a rule is executed. In the next chapter we demonstrate a more efficient way of accomplishing the same task.

4.3.4 Variables and unification (unify.lisp)

Recall that we need to distinguish variables from constant symbols, and that the convention chosen is to prefix variables with "?". The procedure variable? returns non-nil if its argument is in fact a pattern variable.

The procedure unify should actually be called "near-unify" or "sub-unify," since it does not implement full unification. In particular, it assumes that the sets of variables used in the two patterns do not overlap. This assumption is reasonable for the examples we explore here, since the assertions in the database tend to be ground terms, i.e., free of variables (see Exercise 3). As specified earlier, we allow an optional binding list to be passed in to enforce the effects of previous matches and thus ensure consistent binding environments.

`unify` performs a case analysis. If the two forms are equal then they are identical under the current bindings, so `unify` succeeds. `unify-variable` takes care of variables, and we return to it momentarily. If both forms are lists then we unify their `cars`, and if that succeeds, unify their `cdrs`, making sure to pass in any variable bindings made while checking the `cars` (hence the `setq` in the fifth `cond` clause).

When a variable is found, it might have a value already. `unify-variable` starts by looking for such a value on the binding alist. If bound, the unification continues using that value. If not, it might be safe to bind the variable to the corresponding part of the other form. One can't always do this: consider binding `?x` to `(F ?x)`. In cases like this there is no finite set of subsitutions that will produce a form that doesn't contain any bound variables (i.e., we get a pathological expression `(F (F (F ,⟨...⟩))))`). Such bindings are not legal, and we use the procedure `free-in?` to detect such cases. `free-in?` ensures that the given variable doesn't occur in an expression, given the subsitutions available on the binding list.[3] If the expression does in fact contain the variable, `unify-variable` indicates failure.

4.3.5 Testing TRE (treex.lisp)

Before testing a system on a complex example it is always a good strategy to try some simpler examples first. A common and useful engineering tactic is to include a set of procedures that provides a suite of test cases with systems that you develop. There are several reasons for this practice. First, simple cases are easier to debug, and can be designed to stress particular components of the system. Second, the test suite can be used to ensure that new features (or porting to another Lisp environment) have not broken the program. This is especially important when the port is done by someone else, perhaps in some geographically (or temporally) distant location. The test suite can provide an "acceptance check" if the proper answers are included in it. And finally, such routines help others

3. This is an example of an *occurs check*, in logic programming terminology.

learn how to use the system by demonstrating what it is capable of and what the interface procedures are.

Designing good test suites is an art. Ideally the test suite should exhibit all the interesting features and functionality of the system, stressing each critical part independently, while minimizing uninteresting computations. The examples in the listing `TRE-EX1` are not perfect, but they suffice for our present purposes. Notice they all have the same form: a call to `create-tre` builds a TRE to work with, and `run-forms` feeds assertions and rules into it. They differ only in how they display their results. Running these examples with `*debug-tre*` turned on is a good way to get a feeling for how TRE operates.

`ex1` hints at how one can implement natural deduction in TRE, a topic we take up in detail below. `ex2` illustrates one way to use TRE with other systems. Suppose you had a "universal diagnostic system" for homeowners that would help them fix anything they were likely to come in contact with. The ability to depict parts graphically would be essential, since a typical homeowner isn't an expert on every kind of appliance. The display system might use an alist to index the parts of the machine(s) being repaired. This alist needs to be updated to include the parts for any new system being considered. When a new system is asserted (as in the assertions concerning `Ariel` and `Hal-9000`), the TRE rules add the parts of that system into the database, which in turn causes the `has-part` rule to update the graphics alist.[4]

The final example in this file, `ex3`, illustrates one danger associated with antecedent inference systems. You should probably run this example last, and be sure you know what the interrupt keys are for your system. We return to this phenomenon later.

4.4 Natural deduction

Natural deduction provides an interesting domain for testing problem solvers. Systems of natural deduction have been studied by logicians for

4. Notice that we consider "diskless workstation" to be an oxymoron.

decades, and their inferential power is well understood. Of course, automatic generation of proofs via natural deduction was not a concern of logicians. Natural deduction systems tend to use many inference rules, leading to the problem of choosing which inference rule to use when constructing a proof. Since resolution uses only one inference rule, this problem is eliminated, leaving only the problem of choosing which data to try resolving next. This apparent simplicity led many AI practictioners in the 1960s to abandon natural deduction for resolution theorem proving. (We discuss resolution later, in Chapters 10 and 13.) Resolution can be very efficient in many circumstances, especially for propositional databases. However, advocates of natural deduction argue that the process of translating axioms to clause form, required to use resolution, actually makes finding proofs more difficult because it destroys structure in the original axioms that provides important hints. In natural deduction systems, the proof rules and forms of assertions are designed to be more intuitive, offering the possibility of producing understandable explanations in addition to proofs.

For our purposes, the control issues in natural deduction form an excellent laboratory to examine how to write pattern-directed rules that encode knowledge about problem-solving tactics, in order to make reasoning strategies more explicit. In this section we introduce a particular natural deduction system for propositional reasoning. This system will be used as a source of examples in several chapters, to highlight the differences between alternative techniques. We sketch how TRE can be used to partially implement it. As you will discover, this version of TRE lacks an essential ingredient, the ability to manipulate assumptions, necessary for a full implementation of natural deduction. There are several ways to add this missing ingredient, as later chapters illustrate.

4.4.1 The KM* system

The particular system we use is adapted from one invented by Kalish and Montague [7]. It has three advantages over other systems of natural deduction we have seen. First, it is better organized than most. Second, it has a natural (at least for computer scientists) formalism for handling the introduction and discharging of assumptions. And third, it includes at least some control information explicitly in the formalism. This becomes especially handy when we turn to considering how to implement these formal rules in TRE.

4.4.1.1 The format of proofs

A proof consists of a numbered set of lines. Each line contains three parts:

⟨*LineNumber*⟩ ⟨*Statement*⟩ ⟨*Justification*⟩

where ⟨*LineNumber*⟩ is the number of the line, ⟨*Statement*⟩ is what is proven (or to be proven) by that line, and ⟨*Justification*⟩ indicates how that line was derived. The line number is used to refer to this result elsewhere in the proof. Justifications take two forms. The first is a list, whose first element is a tag indicating the inference rule used in the derivation (the *informant* of the justification) and the other elements being the line numbers that this application of the rule relied upon. Thus we might see in a proof

```
453 Made-of(Moon,Green-Cheese) (CE 23 452)
```

meaning that this is line 453 of the proof, demonstrating that the moon is made of green cheese, shown via inference rule CE (a shorthand for CONDITIONAL ELIMINATION, introduced below) on the results of lines 23 and 452. This clear-cut link between a conclusion and the reasons for believing it helps provide an ability to produce good explanations, a goal of natural deduction systems.

The second kind of justification consists of a special tag, either `premise` or `asn`. The tag `premise` indicates that ⟨*Statement*⟩ is a given in the problem, and thus holds without argument. `asn` indicates that we are assuming ⟨*Statement*⟩ as part of an effort to prove something. For a proof to be valid, all assumptions must be *discharged*. Assumptions are introduced and discharged by the inference rules themselves, and so we postpone further discussion of assumptions until then.

Finished proofs are intended to be crystal clear, elegant arguments. Anyone who has constructed proofs knows, however, that the process of achieving the proof is often messy, littered with false starts and blind alleys. Most mathematical and logical formalisms developed before the notion of computation took flower do not include any formal method for recording such information as part of the proof. KM* uses the metalinguistic predicate `show` to indicate intent during the proof process. That is, we write `show P` in a line of a proof we are building to indicate that we want to derive the statement `P`. This line cannot be used as a result elsewhere in the proof until it is justified, of course. When it is justified, by finding a valid proof for `P`, we will say that the `show` is *canceled*, and indicate this by crossing it out. At that point, for purposes of proving other things, the line is now simply a normal line in the proof. (Of course, if we were explaining how we got the result, the crossed-out `show` would help us reconstruct the logic of the argument.) `show` assertions can be introduced at any time, and are both used and introduced by KM* inference rules. Let us turn now to an example.

4.4.1.2 *Proof rules*

The proof rules of KM* are specified by schemata that indicate how an application of that rule looks. Here is the schema for the rule of *indirect proof*:

```
h   s̶h̶o̶w̶ P    (IP i j k)
i  | (not P)  asn  |
   |  .            |
   |  .            |
   |  .            |
j  | Q             |
   |  .            |
   |  .            |
   |  .            |
k  | (not Q)       |
```

The basic idea of indirect proof should is straightforward; if we assume `(not P)` and derive a contradiction (as indicated by lines `j` and `k`) then `P` must be true. However, our use of `show` and the boxes may not be obvious. Presumably line `h` started out as the intent to prove `P`, either because it was the goal of the problem or it is a subgoal that appeared in the course of finding a solution. This proof schema licenses the introduction of the assumption `(not P)`, and indicates that when a contradiction is found, one may cancel the `show` of line `h` and consider the assumption discharged. The box drawn around lines `i-k` indicate that the contents of the box rely on the assumption of line `i`, and must not be used else-

NOT ELIMINATION

```
i        (not (not P))
         P                (NE i)
```

AND ELIMINATION

```
i        (and P Q)
         P                (AE i)
         Q                (AE i)
```

OR ELIMINATION

```
i        (or P Q)
j        (implies P R)
k        (implies Q R)
         R                (OE i j k)
```

CONDITIONAL ELIMINATION

```
i        (implies P Q)
j        P
         Q                (CE i j)
```

BICONDITIONAL ELIMINATION

```
i        (iff P Q)
         (implies P Q)    (BE i)
         (implies Q P)    (BE i)
```

Figure 4.3 Elimination rules for KM*

where in the proof. Think of the box as a fence that other justifications cannot cross. Boxes can be nested, and in fact behave like the contour model for variable semantics in procedural languages.

The rest of the KM* proof rules are organized into two classes: *elimination rules* and *introduction rules*. Elimination rules get rid of a connective in a term, perhaps resulting in several new terms. Introduction rules sanction the construction of terms involving particular connectives. Each connective has an introduction rule and an elimination rule. These rules, plus indirect proof, are sufficient for propositional reasoning. We begin with the elimination rules because they are simpler.

The elimination rules are given in Figure 4.3. NOT ELIMINATION reflects the fact that a double negative is, at least in propositional logic, equivalent to a positive. AND ELIMINATION expresses the fact that if a conjunction is true then each individual conjunct must be true. OR ELIMINATION encodes a form of arguing from cases: since one of the disjuncts must hold, anything that follows from either disjunct must always be true. CONDITIONAL

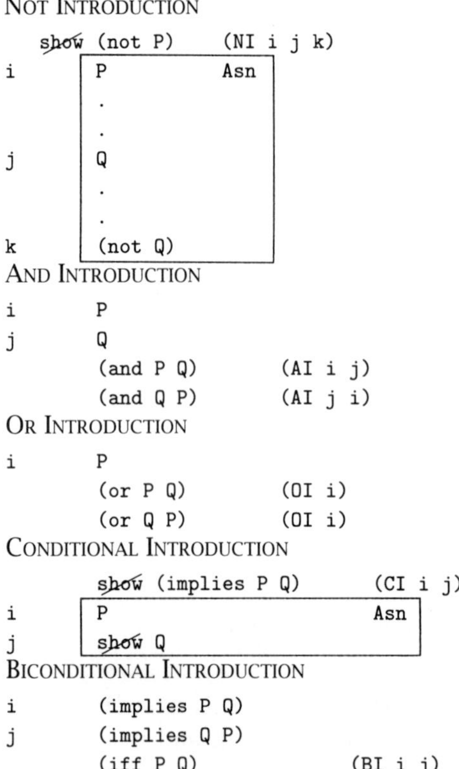

Figure 4.4 Introduction rules for KM*

ELIMINATION is more classically known as *modus ponens*, and BICONDITIONAL ELIMINATION encodes the definition of logical equivalence.

The introduction rules are described in Figure 4.4. NOT INTRODUCTION is actually like indirect proof, but for negative statements. AND INTRODUCTION and OR INTRODUCTION are direct applications of the definition of conjunction and disjunction. CONDITIONAL INTRODUCTION is more interesting: here we see a rule that introduces a `show` assertion as part of its operation. That is, to show an implication, we assume the antecedent and express interest in the consequent. This hint presumably inspires us to apply other KM* inference rules to prove the consequent. BICONDITIONAL INTRODUCTION, like BICONDITIONAL ELIMINATION, simply encodes the definition of logical equivalence, but in the other direction.

4.4.2 Some examples

Here is a simple logic problem adapted from [11]:

Either George and Fred were at the scene of the crime, or George and Bob were. Fred being at the scene of the crime means George wouldn't have been there, of course. Show Bob was at the scene of the crime.

The first step, which lies outside our present discussion, is to translate this problem into its formal equivalent. Here the propositions are:

G = "George was at the scene of the crime"

F = "Fred was at the scene of the crime"

B = "Bob was at the scene of the crime"

If we translate each sentence into propositional statements, we get

```
1. (or (and G F) (and G B))
2. (implies F (not G))
3. show B
```

Think for a moment about how you might attack this proof. Intuitively, the disjunction indicates a case split, so showing that the goal follows from either choice will give us our result. In terms of the KM* system, this corresponds to using the rule of OR ELIMINATION. Indeed, this plan provides a valid proof:

```
1. (or (and G F) (and G B))      premise
2. (implies F (not G))           premise
3. show B                        (OE 1 4 11)
4.  show (implies (and G F) B)   (CI 5 6)
5.     |  (and G F)              asn
6.     |  show B                 (IP 7 8 10)
7.     | |(not B)                asn
8.     | |G                      (AE 5)
9.     | |F                      (AE 5)
10.    | |(not G)                (CE 2 9)
11. show (implies (and G B) B)   (CI 12 13)
12.    |  (and G B)              asn
13.    |  show B                 (AE 12)
```

The use of indirect proof on line 6 may seem unnecessary, since we did not in fact use the assumption in line 7. However, if we stay strictly within the KM* rules that is what we must do.

Let us examine another example:

"If an AI student gets a good job and has access to fast computers, then that student will write neat programs. An AI student will make lots of money and have access to fast computers if and only if that student either writes neat programs or gets a good job. An AI student will get a good job. Prove that an AI student will write neat programs and make lots of money."

Here the propositions can be encoded as:

J = "AI students will get good jobs"

M = "AI students will make lots of money"

P = "AI students will write neat programs"

C = "AI students will have access to fast computers"

By translating the sentences into propositional logic the problem becomes:

```
1. (implies (and J C) P)
2. (iff (and M C) (or P J))
3. J
4. Show (and P M)
```

Again, think about how you might prove this. The goal is a conjunction, so clearly we will use AND INTRODUCTION at some point. This means we have to look for the conjuncts. We can get some useful implications from the biconditional, since disjunctions are easy to introduce. The other byproducts from "cracking" the biconditional is C, which we can then use to crack open premise 1 to get P. Using the KM* system, our proof becomes:

```
1.  (implies (and J C) P)          premise
2.  (iff (and M C) (or P J))       premise
3.  J                              premise
4.  Show (and P M)                 (AI 11 8)
5.  (implies (or P J) (and M C))   (BE 2)
6.  (or P J)                       (OI 3)
7.  (and M C)                      (CE 5 6)
8.  M                              (AE 7)
9.  C                              (AE 7)
10. (and J C)                      (AI 3 9)
11. P                              (CE 1 11)
```

Notice that this proof did not require any assumptions.

Many natural deduction systems allow extending their rules by adding new tautologies. To determine if something is a tautology, however, first requires proving it. Consider how you might prove

```
show (implies (implies P Q) (or (not P) Q))
```

There isn't much to start with here, and that makes it very difficult. It is worth spending five or ten minutes trying to prove this yourself, for it will reward you with a deeper understanding of the KM* system. Here is one proof:

```
1. show (implies (implies P Q) (or (not P) Q))      (CI 2 3)
2.    (implies P Q)                                 asn
3.    show (or (not P) Q)                           (IP 4 4 5)
4.         (not (or (not P) Q))                     asn
5.         show (or (not P) Q)                      (OI 6)
6.              show (not P)                        (NI 7 4 9)
7.                   P                              asn
8.                   show (or (not P) Q)            (OI 9)
9.                        Q                         (CE 2 7)
```

The subtlety of this proof lies in the use of multiple nested assumptions to build a scaffold upon which to work. For the goal of line 3 there simply aren't any premises to play off of, so Or Introduction cannot be used. This leaves us only with Indirect Proof. Showing the negation of an implication looks pretty fruitless, so deriving a contradiction in terms of the newly introduced disjunction seems to be the best bet. To introduce the disjunction requires showing one of the disjuncts. `(not P)` is a better choice because you would need `P` to get `Q` via Conditional Elimination anyway. Since Negation Introduction introduces `P`, we can use that to finally show a contradiction, again using one of our earlier assumptions.

4.4.3 A partial implementation of KM*

To implement the KM* natural deduction system in TRE we must solve three general problems:

1. The *representation problem:* How do we represent KM* statements and rules of inference in TRE?

2. The *control problem:* How do we specify when each rule applies, so that problems are solved efficiently?
3. The *assumption problem:* How do we control the introduction and retraction of assumptions required by several KM* laws of inference?

This version of TRE does not provide any mechanism for solving the assumption problem. Suppose we attempted to model retraction by deleting an assumption from the database. We would still need to find a way to delete all the assertions derived from that assumption. We might try stipulating that each rule that made an assertion required the creation of a complementary rule which, when one of its triggers was deleted, would delete that rule's consequences.[5] This is not a good solution. Often there is more than one way to derive something. In our current version of TRE, multiple derivations have no effect on the database. If an existing assertion is rederived, nothing needs to happen since the rules that should be tested against it already have been. If we extended TRE to include deletion, this property would no longer hold. Before deleting an assertion, we would either have to check for multiple derivations of it (somehow) or attempt to rederive it after deleting it. All such deletion schemes impose critical dependencies between internal events in the database, and making them work correctly is extremely difficult.[6] A better solution is introduced in the next chapter, so we defer further discussion until then.

We solve the representation problem in this context by using TRE assertions to represent propositions in a proof and by using TRE rules to encode KM*'s laws of inference. This solution is only partial, since it does not provide the explanation capabilities found in KM*'s use of line numbers and justifications. We could in principle encode such information as assertions. However, there are other more serious limitations in using TRE to implement KM*, which will be described shortly. Furthermore, the most efficient techniques for encoding such justifications involve truth maintenance systems (Chapter 6).

---

5. Such mechanisms were actually used in some early AI languages, including MicroPlanner and Conniver.

6. The reader may be struck by the analogy between this problem and the problem of reclaiming storage in a dynamically allocated memory. This analogy inspired early truth maintenance systems, which were called "fact garbage collectors" [10].

Here are some TRE encodings of KM* inference rules:

```
(rule (not (not ?p)) (assert! ?p)) ;; Not Elimination

(rule (and . ?conjuncts)  ;; And Elimination
      (dolist (con ?conjuncts) (assert! con)))

(rule (implies ?ante ?cons) ;; Conditional Elimination
      (rule ?ante (assert! ?cons)))

(rule (iff ?arg1 ?arg2)  ;; Biconditional Elimination
      (assert! ?arg1) (assert! ?arg2))
```

Each TRE rule directly implements a single KM* inference rule.

The control problem can be addressed by introducing explicit *control assertions* and adding rules that trigger on control assertions as well as data. We have already seen how `show` assertions are used in the KM* system to indicate to the prover (in this case, a person) interest in a particular proposition. We will carry this technique much farther, using it as a means of encoding the kind of knowledge human reasoners bring to bear when figuring out how to proceed with a proof.

Let us consider the rules in KM* that do not require assumptions, and see how careful application of control knowledge can guide the search for a solution. First, some rules don't need control knowledge. Think of assertions as tree structures. If the effect of a rule is to decompose a large structure into smaller structures, it is generally safe to execute that rule without further thought. The reason is that the smaller pieces might be useful, and since each piece is only finitely large, this rule cannot be reapplied forever to its results (which is one way of losing control, as we saw in the `ex3` example). In the KM* system, the rules we described above (NOT ELIMINATION, AND ELIMINATION, CONDITIONAL ELIMINATION, and BICONDITIONAL ELIMINATION) are safe rules by this criterion.

One use of control assertions is to post advice about what to do, based on current goals and data. There is little advice to give for NOT, AND, and BICONDITIONAL ELIMINATION, since they simply operate whenever they can. There is some strategy associated with CONDITIONAL ELIMINATION, however. Suppose we want to prove a proposition that is the consequent of an implication. If we prove the antecedent, we know that the CONDITIONAL ELIMINATION rule will prove the original proposition. We can express this advice, which is really a form of backward chaining, with the following rule:

```
(rule (show ?q) ;; Back-chaining on CE
      (rule (implies ?p ?q) (assert! '(show ,?p))))
```

This rule of course does not know how to show ?p. It merely express interest in it via a show assertion which brings the rest of our rule-based machinery to bear on the question. A useful optimization is to ensure that we don't offer advice when it isn't needed:

```
(rule (show ?q) ;; Back-chaining on CE
      (unless (fetch ?q)
              (rule (implies ?p ?q) (assert! '(show ,?p)))))
```

It is important to remember that the unless test is performed only once for each binding of ?q. Once the body of the unless is triggered, the rule that seeks implications for deriving ?q will continue to exist. Furthermore, any work started for showing ?p will continue until it dies down of its own accord, whether or not ?q has been successfully proven in the meantime. Combinatorial explosions can happen with control knowledge just as easily as with data.

To further illustrate this point, consider how we might write a backward-chaining rule for Or Elimination. One simple version is

```
(rule (show ?r) ;; Or Elimination
      (rule (or ?p ?q)
            (assert! '(show (implies ,?p ,?r)))
            (assert! '(show (implies ,?q ,?r)))
            (rule (implies ?p ?r)
                  (rule (implies ?q ?r) (assert! ?r)))))
```

The problem with this rule is that the show assertions it produces can match the initial trigger as well, leading to the generation of statements with unbounded depth. It is useful in such cases to restrict the kinds of assertions that are acceptable for ?r, by using a test inside the body of the outermost rule. Finding acceptable restrictions can be difficult, since each restriction eliminates the possibility of solving particular goals.

The only introduction rules that do not require assumptions are those for and, or, and iff. and and or each have the potential for unbounded generation, so we must control them very carefully. In particular, there is no reason to even try using them unless we have a specific reason to do so, as indicated by a show assertion. Once interest is shown, each rule must in turn post show assertions to express interest in its constituents, and then spawn a rule that looks for these constituents and, when it finds them, constructs the desired statement. The following three rules accomplish this.

```
(rule (show (and ?a ?b)) ;; And Introduction
      (assert! '(show ,?a))
      (assert! '(show ,?b))
      (rule ?a (rule ?b (assert! '(and ,?a ,?b)))))

(rule (show (or ?a ?b)) ;; Or Introduction
      (assert! '(show ,?a))
      (assert! '(show ,?b))
      (rule ?a (assert! '(or ,?a ,?b)))
      (rule ?b (assert! '(or ,?a ,?b))))

(rule (show (iff ?a ?b)) ;; Biconditional Introduction
      (assert! '(show (implies ,?a ,?b)))
      (assert! '(show (implies ,?b ,?a)))
      (rule (implies ?a ?b)
            (rule (implies ?b ?a)
                  (assert! '(iff ,?a ,?b)))))
```

The major difference between these rules comes from the nature of the underlying logical constraints. For and and iff, both constituents must be found; for or, either constituent suffices.

The file ND-EX provides both some basic tests of these rules and some sample problems, translated from logic textbooks, which these rules can solve.

4.5 Conclusions

Assertions are a flexible representational medium, providing a powerful reference mechanism via pattern matching. How well does the PDIS model satisfy the desiderata for AI programming set out in Section 2.1?

The PDIS model ranks high on explicitness, because the medium of assertions can express advice as well as data. It ranks high on flexibility, since rules will run whenever their triggers match, rather than within some complex control structure in a traditional system. It also maximizes additivity, since one can always add more rules.

Within the appropriate restrictions, pattern-directed inference systems can be viewed as a mechanism for providing a procedural reading of propositional logic and other formal systems. As in traditional programming, side effects are to be avoided if the program is to be easily understood. That is, ideally the body of a rule should only contain the definitions of more rules or `assert!`. In this way we keep every operation "on the table" and hence potentially subject to reasoned control. The assumption that the operation of the PDIS rules is order-independent, for instance, depends crucially on not allowing rules to fiddle with the internals of the inference engine.

One drawback of the PDIS model is efficiency. As we saw earlier, the extra step of pattern matching increases the cost of reference. In Chapter 5 we see how this inefficiency can be greatly reduced. Another drawback is the lack of coherence, since rules can run in any order. Unlike the pencil and paper version of KM*, this implementation does not have justifications, and this lack of coherence makes explanation generation difficult. This is harder to fix, because coherence generally requires a central mechanism to decide what to do next. We will explore such mechanisms in later chapters.

4.6 Backpointers

There are many variations on the idea of pattern-directed inference system, corresponding to different procedure and knowledge models. A good historical source is [13]. We focus on the antecedent rule model in this book for several reasons. The most important reason is that it is the model we have found the most useful for our purposes. There are already a variety of good books on popular alternatives, such as `prolog`-like systems, `OPS`-like production rule systems and MYCIN-style expert systems. And while there are other variations not well covered in textbooks, such as procedural deduction systems, such systems have not so far been widely used in practice. (In the particular case of procedural deduction systems, we suspect the reason is that they tend to hide too many control decisions from the author of the problem solver.)

We thank Carl Hewitt for introducing us to the Kalish and Montague natural deduction system. The version we use here is adapted from a version he has used in teaching. The control ideas in the implementation of KM* are based on [2].

4.7 Exercises

1. ⋆ Why is order-independence a useful property for a pattern-directed inference system?
2. Select a problem from your favorite logic textbook.
   a. ⋆ Solve the problem by hand, using the KM* system.
   b. ⋆ Encode it in a form suitable for the natural deduction rules, and see if TRE can solve it.
3. We hinted that `unify` wasn't correctly implementing full unification, in particular because it did not properly handle situations where both patterns contain variables.
   a. ⋆ Explain how `unify` fails to operate correctly on the following pattern:

      `(FOO ?x ?x)` and `(FOO ?x ?x)`

   b. ⋆⋆ Implement `full-unify`, which correctly handles this case.
4. ⋆⋆ Write `multi-fetch`, which takes as input a set of patterns and returns a list of sets of assertions which match those patterns.
5. ⋆⋆ Write a procedure `show-rule` that looks up a rule based on the integer stored in its `counter` field and prints a detailed description of its trigger and body. The trigger and environment should be shown separately.
6. The rules for AND INTRODUCTION and BICONDITIONAL INTRODUCTION actually do unnecessary work. If the system cannot prove one conjunct, for

example, there is no reason to waste time on attempting to prove the other.

a. ⋆ Write new versions of AND INTRODUC- TION and BICONDITIONAL INTRODUCTION that only look for the second constituent when the first has been proven.

b. ⋆ These more efficient versions make an important assumption about the set of rules as a whole. What is that assumption? How might it be violated?

7. Blackboard systems are often described as collections of knowledge sources, each of which are potentially problem solvers in their own right. An important feature of blackboard systems is their concern with real-time performance, which requires tight control over the computational resources allocated to each knowledge source, and often entails sophisticated reasoning about control. This problem considers how blackboard systems might be implemented, using TRE-based problem solvers as knowledge sources.

   a. ⋆ Pick out two design decisions in TRE which must be changed before such an implementation is possible, explaining what problems they would cause in this context.

   b. ⋆ ⋆ ⋆ Implement a shell for building blackboard systems, using an appropriately extended TRE as the basis for the facility for building knowledge sources.

4.8 Bibliography

[1] Bratko, I., *Prolog Programming for Artificial Intelligence*, Addison-Wesley, 1986.

[2] Brownston, L., Farrell, R., Kant, E., and Martin, N., *Programming Expert Systems in* OPS5*: An Introduction to Rule-based Programming*, Addison-Wesley, 1985.

[3] Bundy, A., *The Computer Modeling of Mathematical Reasoning*, Academic Press, 1983.

[4] Clocksin, W. F., and Mellish, C. S., *Programming in Prolog*, Springer-Verlag, 1981.

[5] de Kleer, J., Doyle, J., Steele, G. L., and Sussman, G.J., "AMORD: Explicit control of reasoning," *Proceedings of the Symposium on AI and Programming Languages* (*SIGART Newsletter* No. 64), 1977.

[6] Engelmore, R., and Morgan, T. (eds.), *Blackboard Systems*, Addison-Wesley, 1988.

[7] Kalish, D., Montague, R., and Mar, G., *LOGIC: Techniques of Formal Reasoning*, 2nd edition, Harcourt Brace Jovanovich, 1980.

[8] McDermott, D., and Sussman, J., "The CONNIVER reference manual," MIT AI Lab Memo No. 259a, 1973.

[9] Nilsson, N. J., *Principles of Artificial Intelligence*, Morgan-Kaufmann, 1980.

[10] Stallman, R., and Sussman, G., "Forward reasoning and dependency-directed backtracking in a system for computer-aided circuit analysis," *Artificial Intelligence* 9(1977): 135–196.

[11] Suppes, P., *Introduction to Logic*, Van Nostrand, 1957.

[12] Sussman, G., Winograd, T., and Charniak, E., "MICRO-PLANNER Reference Manual," MIT AI Lab Memo No. 203a, 1971.

[13] Waterman, D., and Hayes-Roth, F., (Eds,), *Patten-Directed Inference Systems*, Academic Press, 1978.

[14] Zabih, R., McAllester, D., and Chapman, D., "Non-deterministic Lisp with dependency-directed backtracking," Proceedings of AAAI-87, 1987.

5 Extending Pattern-Directed Inference Systems

The simple pattern-directed inference system model of the previous chapter can be extended in several ways. This chapter explores three of them. First, we show how to support a cleaner syntax to simplify writing rules. Second, we show how to improve efficiency without compromising the flexibility of reference provided by pattern matching. The two methods introduced to do this are *rule compilation* and *open-coded unification*. Third, we address the problem of manipulating assumptions by extending the model to include a stack-oriented *context mechanism*. We embody these ideas in FTRE, a new version of TRE. We use the classic N-queens puzzle to illustrate how FTRE can be used to perform search. Finally, we demonstrate that the combination of these mechanisms allows us to implement a full and efficient version of the natural deduction system KM*.

The structure of FTRE has been kept as close to that of TRE as possible, so that we may focus here on discussing the issues surrounding the extensions. Thus this chapter should not be read without first understanding the previous chapter.

5.1 Designing for convenience, efficiency, and power

We tackle these extensions in order of increasing conceptual complexity.

5.1.1 The fine art of syntax

The art of writing AI programs, like any other kind of programming, involves managing abstractions. Nobody likes to wallow in unimportant details. One important way to manage abstractions is to ensure that one's language allows common patterns of usage to be concisely expressed.[1] Sometimes this is best accomplished by designing a special-purpose language. Our language of pattern-directed inference rules is one example of a special-purpose language, and the chapters to come include several more. Here let us focus on some changes that will make our language of pattern-directed rules more useful.

There is always a trade-off in designing special-purpose languages between fidelity to the class of problems being addressed and closeness to the host language (i.e., what the special-purpose language is written in). Optimizing fidelity to problems and methods maximizes the ability to concisely express our ideas in a manner that is unfettered by implementation details. The cost tends to be expensive, complicated implementations. Optimizing closeness to the host language simplifies implementations, but often at the cost of making the special-purpose language less useful. Since here we (1) are already starting with a fairly high-level language (i.e. Common Lisp), (2) assume that the users of the system are familiar with that language, and (3) wish to avoid needless complications, we lean here toward solutions that are very close to the host language.

In designing a language, stylistic issues play a central role. Taste in such matters varies, and thus there is some scope for disagreement. However, there are some basic properties of languages which everyone can agree upon. For our purposes we focus on three such properties:

1. *Support common usage:* Every language has idioms, patterns of constructs and operations that are used over and over again. Such patterns should be simple, if not atomic operations, in a good syntax.
2. *Support conciseness:* Generally the easier it is to do something, the fewer chances there are for mistakes. Shorter programs are often easier to read and understand than equivalent, longer programs.
3. *Remain close to the host language:* It is all too easy to squander time and treasure trying to make the "optimal" syntax. Outside of production programming, it is far better to pick conventions that are

1. It is no accident that in natural languages common words tend to be shorter than less common words.

easy to implement and provide reasonable leverage, than to try for complete insulation from the underlying language.

Let us examine a typical TRE rule and see how it might be improved. Here is the rule for back-chaining on CONDITIONAL ELIMINATION, from the previous chapter:

```
(rule (show ?q) ;; Back-chaining on CE
      (rule (implies ?p ?q) (assert! `(show ,?p))))
```

Notice that we have one rule nested inside another, indicating that the trigger `(implies ?p ?q)` depends on having matched `(show ?q)` first. This pattern of nested rules occurs over and over again, and consequently we should enshrine it in the syntax of our rule language. The simplest way to do so is to change rules to take a list of triggers, such as:

```
(rule ((show ?q) (implies ?p ?q)) (assert! `(show ,?p)))
```

This rule also satisfies our other two principles, since we now have less to type and the list manipulations to "parse" these triggers are likely to be easy. Notice that we now *must* make triggers be lists. We can no longer say:

```
(rule (not (not ?p)) (assert! ?p))
```

but instead must say:

```
(rule ((not (not ?p))) (assert! ?p))
```

Our change has actually made this rule a bit more complex, but our supposition is that nested triggers are more frequent than single triggers so that, overall, complexity is reduced.

There are several similar improvements that are well worth making at this stage. For example, since binding variables through pattern matching is our primary reference mechanism, it is extremely common for rules to generate new assertions that use the bindings of these variables. The statement `(assert! `(show ,?p))` above is one example. Conceptually, this is something of a pun: we are treating pattern variables as Lisp variables. When viewing `?p` as a pattern variable we have substitution, not evaluation, in mind. Thus our implementation is showing through more than it really needs to.

Recall that we do not allow (or, more precisely, do not guarantee always to interpret appropriately) variables in database assertions. Consequently, whenever we assert a pattern, we almost always want to substitute in the bindings of its pattern variables for the variables themselves. Using backquote and commas certainly is better than explicitly using QUOTE and LIST, but we can do even better. We can define `rassert!` (for rule `assert!`) to be like `assert!`, except that all pattern variables (i.e., those beginning with "?") are evaluated. Thus our back-chaining rule for Conditional Elimination can be written as:

```
(rule ((show ?q)(implies ?p ?q)) (rassert! (show ?p)))
```

Although visually this is a small change, anyone who has tried to track down a missing comma in a backquoted expression will appreciate the convenience. Better yet, we can now more easily indicate when we are thinking of variables in terms of substitution versus when we are thinking of them as Lisp variables.

We can carry this alignment between pattern variables and Lisp variables even farther. Intuitively, if we compute a value for a new pattern variable within the body of a rule, any rules spawned within this environment should respect the binding of this pattern variable. The macro `rlet`, analogous to `let`, does this. Consider for instance the following rule:

```
(rule ((project ?project)
       (needed (cost-estimate-for ?project)))
 (rlet ((?cost (expensive-estimation-method ?project)))
  (rassert! (Cost-of ?project ?cost :1st-cut))
  (rule ((improve-on (Cost-of ?project ?cost :1st-cut)))
   (rlet ((?new-cost (even-more-expensive-method ?project)))
    (rassert! (Cost-of ?project ?new-cost :2nd-cut))))))
```

The intent of this rule is clear: a first-pass cost is computed when need for it is expressed (via the `needed` assertion appearing in the database), and if this estimate is not accurate enough, an even more expensive cost estimation method is used to give a more accurate answer. A simple `let` would bind `?cost` as a Lisp variable, but the rule system would not know that `?cost` is, when viewed as a pattern variable, already bound.

We can support two other common patterns of programming by allowing our syntax for triggers to be slightly more complicated. So far we have moved from a rule having a single trigger to a list of triggers. Suppose we also allow optional keywords in the list of triggers. That is, we will allow the keywords `:VAR` and `:TEST` to appear after any trigger pattern. Their meanings are as follows:

`:VAR`: The next element of the trigger list is a variable which will be given the value of the entire preceding trigger pattern.

`:TEST`: The next element of the trigger list is a Lisp expression which provides an additional matching test. That is, unless the expression returns non-`nil` when evaluated with respect to the pattern variables bound so far, the match will be considered to have failed.

Here is an example of how these options can be used:

```
(rule ((show ?q) :test (not (fetch ?r))
       (implies ?p ?q) :var ?imp)
 (debug-nd "~%  BC-CE: Looking for ~A to use ~A.."
           ?p ?imp)
 (rassert! (show ?p)))
```

The `:VAR` lets us use the trigger pattern freely inside the body of the rule without retyping it. This is only a minor convenience for FTRE, but this facility will become very useful when we interface the descendant of this pattern-directed inference system to various truth maintenance systems. The `:TEST` ensures that we won't waste effort trying to prove something that we already know. We could always achieve the same effect by using `when` or `unless` in the body of the rule, of course. However, such tests are often conceptually part of the pattern-matching process, so writing them via `:TEST` expresses our intent more clearly.

5.1.2 Increasing efficiency

How can we speed up a pattern-directed inference system? There are several aspects that can be optimized. First, we can speed up the process of figuring out which rules are runnable. Second, we can speed up the execution of rules themselves, by turning them into procedures which can be compiled like any other. Third, we can do some of the pattern-matching work when a rule is defined, and thereby reduce the effort required whenever the rule is triggered. We examine each aspect in turn.

5.1.2.1 Speeding up rule retrieval

Recall that when a new assertion is added we must find all the rules that match it. Similarly, when each new rule is added we must find all assertions that could trigger it. The access scheme we used in TRE was to sort both rules and assertions into *classes*, according to the leftmost symbol in the pattern. Each rule or assertion need only be checked against those in its class, since if two forms don't match in one constituent they cannot match at all. How can this technique be improved? Considering how the class organization can break down provides some insight into possible improvements. Suppose we had many assertions of the same database class. For instance, we might be building spatial reasoning system which could have thousands of assertions of the form:

```
(Left-Of ?A ?B)
```

If we add a rule whose trigger is `(Left-Of CORNER-BAR32 ?X)`, we could waste much effort matching against other kinds of buildings.

This problem has intrigued many PDIS designers, and many fancy indexing schemes have been created to address it. We outline some of these alternatives next. However, our conclusion will be that the indexing scheme used in TRE is, for most purposes, the best.

Discrimination trees provide one indexing scheme. The idea of discrimination trees is that the database can be viewed as a tree whose leaves are the assertions and rules. Each vertex of the tree represents a choice involving some aspect of the structure. For instance, the first node of the vertex might discriminate based on the `car` of the assertion, the second level of the tree might discriminate on the `cadr`, and so forth. Adding a new rule or assertion requires traversing the tree to find the appropriate leaf, and the other items at that leaf are the candidate rules or assertions to try unifying against. There are several ways to design discrimination trees; for instance, if done carefully the unification can be interleaved with the indexing, so that no further pattern matching is needed.

By exploiting more of the structure of the pattern than simply one symbol, discrimination trees keep the set of candidates for unification small. The cost is the extra overhead involved in indexing each trigger and assertion. The database class technique can be viewed as a one-level discrimination tree, so the question of relative performance boils down to whether extra levels of indexing (versus unification) are worthwhile. If a database class has many triggers and facts, few of which matched, then additional levels of discrimination are more likely to become useful. The technique of discrimination trees and its tradeoffs are described clearly in [1], so we will not dwell further upon it.

Another indexing strategy is *generalized hashing*. If we didn't have variables in either assertions or trigger patterns, then we could retrieve assertions and rules by simply using a hash table. To use variables, we have to "carve up" the pattern somehow so we can index based on the parts of it we know. Consider again the query (Left-Of CORNER-BAR32 ?X). We might describe this pattern as:

```
car = Left-Of
cadr = CORNER-BAR32
cdddr = NIL
```

Each feature (car, cadr, cdddr) has a value which describes a known aspect of the pattern's structure. (Since ?x is a variable, we have no value for the CADDR feature for this pattern.) Each pair of feature and value is hashed such that given a particular feature-value pair we can retrieve the set of all assertions and triggers including this substructure. All assertions and triggers matching a given pattern can be retrieved by computing the features of the pattern, fetching the sets associated with each feature, and intersecting them to find the candidates for unification. In our example there are three such sets. The first set contains all assertions whose car is Left-Of, the second contains all assertions whose cadr is CORNER-BAR32, and the third contains all assertions of length three.[2] Several tricks can be used to optimize retrieval. For instance, if any of the sets is empty then clearly nothing matches. Furthermore, one can order the sets based on size to speed the intersection process (the sizes can be cached with the set, and updated whenever a new item is added).

The advantage of generalized hashing is that it is very flexible. For instance, we could fetch all Left-Of and Right-Of assertions about

2. Assuming, of course, that the process of describing the assertion stopped computing features at the first null result in a chain of cdrs—otherwise, any piece of list structure would have an infinite set of features!

CORNER-BAR32 by the pattern (?rel CORNER-BAR32 ?other). This query would be disallowed in the class scheme used in TRE unless we bound ?rel. However, generalized hashing has significant drawbacks. It is very complicated and can be very expensive. Why? First, notice that unification is still required to complete the process, since it does not enforce consistent variable bindings throughout the structure. For instance, both (FOO 3 4) and (FOO 6 6) would both be retrieved with the query (FOO ?x ?x), but only one of them would unify with it. One could in principle compute indices like "patterns whose third element is the same as their fourth and eighth elements," but the combinatorics are stunningly bad, since one doesn't know which, if any, of these indices will ever be used. So now we have to ask if the extra cost of generating and maintaining extra indices saves us enough extra unifications to be cost-effective. There is no good analytic model of this choice, given that it depends on the statistical properties of the assertions, the triggers, and the queries. Empirically, however, these schemes have been poor performers. Such databases were popular in the 1970s, being the basis for CONNIVER and early versions of EL [4]. Users of these systems estimated that 90% of the systems' time was spent riffling through the database. To our knowledge, this technique was virtually abandoned in the 1980s and has never been used in serious practice.

Since most PDIS systems seem to use either discrimination nets or class indexes, we will stick with class indexes. A variant of the class index, used in some Prolog implementations, is to subindex on the cadr of an assertion when a class gets "too large." We will eschew this and other modifications here, although they can be useful in real systems. Instead we recommend reorganizing classes and introducing redundant classes to overcome retrieval problems. Consider again the problem of CORNER-BAR32. If we really want to fetch all the facts about CORNER-BAR32, we would be better off if the classes in our database corresponded to objects. For instance, we might express CORNER-BAR32's location as:

```
(CORNER-BAR32 Left-Of CHURCH12)
(CORNER-BAR32 Right-Of CAR-WASH18)
```

While better for our desired queries, this format makes writing many spatial rules difficult. For instance, if all our incoming information were in terms of Left-Of assertions and we wanted to install the symmetric Right-Of assertions, we would write in the old format:

```
(rule ((Left-Of ?A ?B)) (rassert! (Right-Of ?B ?A)))
```

But this won't work in the new format. Our trigger would have to be (?A Left-Of ?B), which cannot work since we do not know the class of ?A. If we know that we will have many Left-Of statements, and will be doing many queries with the first argument fixed (corresponding to finding the object on the query object's right), then it is worth adding the extra assertions to make this fetch easy. The following rule does the trick:

```
(rule ((Left-Of ?A ?B))
      (rassert! (?A Left-Of ?B))
      (rassert! (?B Right-Of ?A)))
```

If we never care about the set of all Left-Of or Right-Of assertions, this format makes much more sense. True, we are storing three times as much information as if we had just used the original Left-Of assertions. But now each fetch takes time proportional to the number of facts known about the object, rather than the total number of facts involving that predicate in the database. Assuming that fetching object properties and completions of relational patterns are very common, this organization best exploits the simplicity of the class indexing.[3] So we continue using class indexing for retrieval, albeit allowing clever organization of assertional format to reduce the size of the candidate set.

5.1.2.2 Compiling rules

Ideally the body of a PDIS rule is simple, mainly consisting of rassert! and rule statements. But these statements are implemented as Common Lisp procedures, of course. Furthermore, we rely on the host language for control primitives and other computational needs, so arbitrary Lisp code is allowed in the body of a rule. The implementation strategy for executing rules used in TRE, of creating at rule execution time a Lisp expression to be evaled, is not very efficient. It does not exploit the fact that, except for the values of the pattern variables, the code comprising the body of a rule is the same across every instance of that rule. We can execute rules much more efficiently if we arrange for the body of a rule to be a separate procedure.

3. This is the same intuition underlying some aspects of frame languages.

Arranging for the creation of a procedure for each rule body has two significant advantages. First, consing up an expression at rule execution time is no longer required: the body procedure can simply be called with the current values of the pattern variables as arguments. Second, the body procedure can itself be compiled, ensuring that its execution is as efficient as possible.

5.1.2.3 Open-coding unification

Another aspect of rules we can optimize is pattern matching. Consider what `unify` does in the context of triggering PDIS rules. It walks down the expressions given as its arguments, analyzing them component by component to see if the constant aspects match and if the variables in the trigger pattern can be consistently bound. The structure of both patterns is unknown, so `unify` must scrutinize them both carefully at run time. However, since we know when defining a rule what the trigger pattern is, we could analyze the trigger when the rule is defined. Based on this analysis, we can write a special-purpose matcher that will perform just those tests that `unify` would perform on the second pattern and for checking properties of both patterns.

An example will make this clearer. Suppose we have

```
(Foo ?A ?B (Bar ?B))
```

as the trigger of a rule, where `?A` is bound and `?B` is not. We will need some name for the other pattern, so let us call it `P`. If we think about what tests are needed on `P` to ensure that it unifies with our trigger under the stated conditions, it is easy to see that the following tests suffice:

```
(consp p)                              ;Ensure it is a cons
(equal 'foo (car p))                   ; whose CAR is FOO
(consp (cdr p))                        ; which continues to be a list
(equal ?a (cadr p))                    ; whose 2nd element matches ?A
(consp (cddr p))                       ; and which continues for
(consp (cdddr P))                      ; at least four elements.
(consp (fourth P))                     ;The 4th element is a cons
(equal 'bar (car (fourth P)))          ;  whose CAR is BAR
(consp (cdr (fourth P)))               ;  and is a list not a pair.
(null (cddr (fourth p)))               ;  and is two elements long.
(null (cddddr P))                      ;There is no fifth element.
(equal (cadr (fourth P)) (third P))    ;?B is used consistently.
```

The binding for ?B is then given by either (caddr P) or (cadar (cdddr P)), with the former being slightly more efficient.

This analysis can be automated. By doing so we *open-code* unification. That is, our new system will create for each trigger pattern a *match procedure* that does what a unifier would do, but more efficiently. In addition to the trigger pattern itself, to perform this analysis we must know what variables are already bound by earlier matches. This information provides the equivalent of the list of bindings that can be passed into the unifier. Since this information is fixed by the lexical scoping of the rules, we can figure all this out at rule definition time. By creating a special-purpose matching procedure we also gain one of the same advantages we did for creating procedures for the body of a rule: we can arrange for files of rules to be compiled, so they will execute as quickly as possible.

The decisions to open-code unification and to create procedures for rule bodies (as outlined above) interact, so we must establish conventions for communications between these two new kinds of procedures. Each match procedure must return two things: a flag indicating whether or not it succeeded, and any new bindings for the pattern variables imposed by the match. Since we define the bound pattern variables to be the arguments of the body procedure, the inclusion of these new bindings with the rest of the bindings established so far will provide the correct environment for executing the body. Since rules can be nested, this means that when defining a rule we must carefully analyze what pattern variables will be bound when. As Section 5.2.3 illustrates, this analysis has its subtleties.

5.1.3 A stack-oriented context mechanism

Many forms of reasoning involve making assumptions. To carry out an indirect proof, for example, one assumes the negation of that which is to be shown and attempts to derive a contradiction. In exploring the consequences of a chess move, one imagines what the board would look like after it was made. These assumptions are temporary, in that one presumes when they are made that they will soon be retracted. The *assumption problem*, introduced in Chapter 4, consists of correctly managing the introduction and retraction of such assumptions. Here we explore a simple mechanism that solves this problem.

It is helpful to consider an analogous but simpler problem in computer programming. Think about how the value of a variable is determined. The

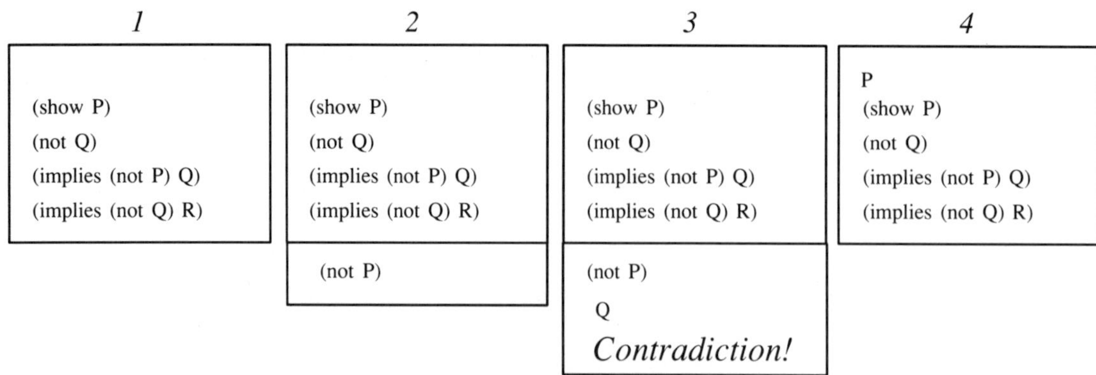

Figure 5.1 How stacks allow manipulations of logical environments

value of a variable depends on the *environment* in which it is evaluated. Different variable binding disciplines correspond to different environment structures and means of manipulating them. The simplest environment is a global environment, where changing the value associated with a variable changes it everywhere. The TRE data model is analogous to this global environment, with ground patterns corresponding to variables and whether or not they are in the database corresponding to their possible values (i.e., "believed" or "not believed"). Thus it makes sense to speak of the *logical environment* of a TRE computation, defined by the set of assertions in the database. Just as one cannot tell how to evaluate an expression containing variables in a standard programming language without knowing the environment in which it is to be evaluated, one cannot always tell what effects a TRE program will have without knowing what is already in the database.

Of course, in standard computer languages one also finds more complex environment structures. For instance, to define recursive procedures it is essential to be able to reuse variable names, and stacks are introduced to provide this functionality. The stack provides a local context in which variables can take on distinct values for a time, and then can revert to their old values when the computation is finished. Stacks, too, are useful for controlling logical environments. Consider the first database in the sequence of databases shown in Figure 5.1. Suppose that in addition to these assertions we have loaded the set of KM* rules described in Chapter 4. In order to prove P we might try an indirect proof. To try an indirect proof we need a temporary environment, a *context* in which we can assume `(not P)` to see if we can derive a contradiction. The context plays the role of the box in KM*. Snapshot 2 in Figure 5.1 depicts this context as a new database extended below the original (global) database, depicted in shapshot 1. In this newly "pushed" context we assert `(not P)` and execute all the rules to determine its consequences. All new assertions and rule instantiations are placed in the new context. Assuming we have a rule that detects contradictions (how this works is explained in Section 5.3.2), we then discover (snapshot 3) that the combination of the beliefs in the new context and the global database are contradictory. Detecting this contradiction allows us to conclude `P` in the global database. Since our indirect proof is finished, we "pop" the context used to explore `(not P)`, which throws away all the consequences derived under that assumption. This is the analog of drawing a box around part of a proof in KM* when the assumption has been discharged.

Now that the behavior we want to achieve is clear, how can we actually do it? We can think of each context as an additional database into which assertions can be made. The procedures for asking whether or not something holds must then look at all the active contexts. There are three slightly subtle constraints that we must respect for our system to be both correct and efficient:

1. Whenever we make an assumption we must push a new context. We could push a new context and make several assumptions in it, but then if we decide that we wanted to change only one assumption we would have to throw all our work away and start over again. If a new context is pushed for each assumption, then popping that context only discards work based on that assumption and any assumptions made after it.
2. Whenever an assertion is made it must be stored in the most recently created context. The reason is that the computation that created it may have depended on the most recent assumption, and so it should be discarded if that assumption is.
3. The execution of rules should be arranged so that conclusions are drawn in the simplest logical environments (i.e., fewest number of assumptions) as possible. In Figure 5.1, for instance, we could conclude `R` holds via CONDITIONAL ELIMINATION. Suppose we only got around to asserting this conclusion after we had assumed `(not Q)`. Then `R`

would hold only in the pushed context, and when we retracted `(not Q)` it would be incorrectly lost. Worse, we would never derive it again in that way. (Can you explain why?)

What do these constraints imply about how we should organize our rules and their interpreter? First, we need to distinguish between rules that make assumptions and those that do not. All rules that do not make assumptions should be executed before any rules that do. This ensures that conclusions are drawn in the smallest logical environment. Second, we have to reorganize our database so that we can correctly push and pop both assertions and rule instances. Just as we do not wish to retain the consequences of an assumption once that assumption is retracted, we also must not retain a rule instance that triggered on a now-departed assertion, since it could pollute later contexts.

By choosing a stack model for logical environments we have also (implicitly) chosen our search strategy for manipulating assumptions. In particular, we will be carrying out a depth-first search in the space of assumptions. One potential problem of depth-first search—looping—is easily avoided by looking to see if we already believe something before assuming it. Another potential problem is that depth-first search can waste an enormous amount of time searching intricate blind alleys before coming upon a simpler solution. The only good way to solve this problem is to introduce resource bounds. There are two kinds of bounds that are easy to impose in this model. First, we can impose a bound on the depth of the assumption stack. Notice that this is not the same as bounding the number of conclusions that can be drawn from each assumption; each assumption could still spawn an arbitrary number of conclusions. Second, we can impose an absolute bound on the number of assumptions made in the whole computation (i.e., a limit on the number of "stack frames" we are willing to generate). In FTRE we implement only resource bounds on depth (but see Exercise 12).

It is possible to view FTRE as a logical system, in the following sense. Given a set of rules, the triggers of the rules correspond to the premises of an inference rule, and any assertions produced correspond to its conclusions. Our goal is to ensure that the stack discipline we use is sound, in the sense that if the inference rules are also sound, then all conclusions we draw are sound. It is asking too much of a logical system to be sound, complete, and efficient. Having finite life spans and the desire to not be too inconsistent, we generally choose soundness and efficiency and let completeness suffer. In Chapter 4 we saw how completeness and efficiency trade off in designing rules for KM*. Here we are seeing another instance of this tradeoff. Resource bounds guarentee that the system won't waste too much time trying to prove something it cannot, but unfortunately also ensure that there are conclusions it could in principle prove but in actuality will not.

5.2 Implementing FTRE

With the design of FTRE in mind, let us examine how it is implemented. FTRE consists of the following files:

`finter.lisp` Organizing datastructure and context mechanism.

`fdata.lisp` Database system.

`frules.lisp` Rule system.

`unify.lisp` Unifier.

`funify.lisp` Open-coding for unification.

The file `unify.lisp` is the same as TRE. We describe each of the others in turn.

5.2.1 The FTRE interface (finter.lisp)

The `ftre` struct organizes the information about a particular FTRE, and in fact is a superset of the `tre` struct. When non-`nil`, the `debugging-contexts` field causes extra information to be printed when making or retracting an assumption. Since we need to derive facts in the logically minimal environments we must execute rules that do not make assumptions before rules that do. This is accomplished by using two queues. `asn-queue` holds triggered rules that make assumptions and `normal-queue` holds triggered rules that do not make assumptions. The field `depth` indicates the current stack depth. It is incremented every time a context is pushed and decremented every time a context is popped. When the depth is zero, all assertions and rules are placed in the global database. Otherwise they are placed in `local-rules` and `local-data`, which will be maintained appropriately by the procedures `seek-in-context` and `try-in-context`, the interfaces to the context mechanism. (These procedures are defined later in this file and are explained below.) The `max-depth` field is used by these procedures to establish the maximum depth of assumptions allowed.

The incorporation of the context mechanism means we must provide a few extra arguments to our constructor `create-ftre`, in order to set the maximum depth bounds and to control whether or not debugging information is printed about context manipulations. Otherwise, the rest of this part of the file is analogous to the definitions in `inter.lisp` in TRE.

The remainder of the file defines the interface to the context mechanism, `try-in-context` and `seek-in-context`. `try-in-context` executes a given piece of code (the argument `form`) in the logical environment created by adding the argument `assumption` to the current logical environment. `seek-in-context` is designed for doing proofs. The structures of these routines are very similar, since their main concern is enforcing the abstraction of an assumption stack. Since `try-in-context` is simpler we begin with it.

`try-in-context` begins by checking the current depth against the maximum depth, to see if the resource bound has been exceeded. If it has, `try-in-context` immediately returns. Otherwise, it begins pushing a new context by lambda-binding the local state information (i.e., `local-rules`, `local-data`, `normal-queue` and `asn-queue`) so they may be reinstated when the work in the new context is finished. The current values of `local-data` and `local-rules` remain in force since assertions and rules from containing environments are inherited by new environments. The queues are cleared, since the triggered rules of the containing environment should be explored in that environment, not in the new one. The `depth` field is incremented to indicate that another assumption has been added. (The current value of `depth` is pushed onto `local-data` so that it will be easy to determine which facts were introduced in each context while debugging.)

Now the stage is set for the next phase, namely making the new assumption and working with it. `with-ftre` is used to ensure that the assumption is made in the current FTRE. After calling `assert!`, `run-rules` is executed to derive its consequences. Finally, the piece of code provided by the `form` argument is evaluated to construct the result to be returned from the procedure. Before `try-in-context` returns, it undoes the effects of making the assumption—that is, it pops the context. This is accomplished by resetting the local state information using the values saved earlier.

`seek-in-context` encapsulates the operations needed to prove something within a context. There are three things that must be done, in addition to the work that `try-in-context` does. First, interest in the goal must be expressed. Asserting `show` of the goal does this, assuming that the FTRE rules use the convention of `show` control assertions. Second, `seek-in-context` must return a result that indicates whether or not the goal was proven. This is accomplished by setting `result` to the result of calling `fetch` on the goal before popping the context. The third requirement is that if we succeed in proving the goal we want to return immediately, rather than allowing the current context to run to quiescensce. This is especially important given FTRE's ability to create new contexts—otherwise every assumption-making rule will be tried, up to the depth bound, even though the goal may have been proven already. To do this, a rule is created to detect when the goal has been found. It uses a `throw` to prevent doing extra work once the result has been found. The reason for the explicit test of depth in the goal detection rule is somewhat subtle. Recall that a subcontext inherits all rules in the context(s) above it (using the spatial metaphors "push" and "pop" to be "push down" and "pop up"). Furthermore, since we are running the queue to exhaustion, we could run new `a-rules`, which in turn would cause `seek-in-context` to be called recursively. Consequently, this rule could be triggered in some deeper context, where the goal was derived using several additional assumptions. Counting such derivations as success would render our mechanism unsound, since the derivation relied on extra assumptions. The depth test ensures that the rule triggers only when the goal is asserted in the appropriate context, and hence protects the soundness of the system.

Notice that both `seek-in-context` and `try-in-context` are bristling with debugging probes. This kind of information can be essential in debugging complex programs. For example, by keeping track of the lengths of the stack one can see just how much effort is invested in each assumption as it occurs. Predicating these probes on a different switch than the usual debugging flag is useful because this information is most valuable in the later stages of debugging a set of rules.

5.2.2 The FTRE database (fdata.lisp)

The database system has been changed in four ways:

1. `show-data` now displays both the global database and the current context.
2. `rassert!` is implemented as a macro which calls a new procedure, `quotize`, to convert its argument into an appropriate set of calls to `QUOTE` and `LIST`. Since `quotize` is concerned with manipulations of pattern variables, it is defined in `funify.lisp` (see Section 5.2.4).
3. Since `*env*` is no longer required to accumulate the lexical environment of rules, `get-class` has been simplified accordingly.
4. The procedures `get-candidates` and `insert` have been changed to take the context mechanism into account. `get-candidates` now includes all the data on the stack as candidates for matching, in addition to facts of the given class from the global database. `insert` now uses the `depth` field of the FTRE to ensure that it adds data in the appropriate place.

Notice that this implementation will work best when most assertions are made in the global environment and relatively few assertions are made in contexts, since a linear search through the elements of the context stack is required for each fetch of data or rules. Exercise 4 explores an alternate implementation.

5.2.3 The FTRE rule system (frules.lisp)

Our design for FTRE strives for efficiency by eliminating run-time work, at the cost of doing more work when a rule is defined. Consequently, the implementation of the rule system is substantially more complex than the rule system in TRE.

Let us begin with the `rule` struct. Like TRE, the `counter` field of a rule provides a unique identifier and the `dbclass` field points to its database class. The `environment` field is gone; we exploit instead the ability of Common Lisp to make closures to package up environments. The `matcher` and `body` fields hold the rule's match procedure and the rule's body procedure, respectively. The field `assumption?` is non-`nil` if the rule makes an assumption, and `nil` otherwise.

The procedures show-rules, print-rule, and fetch-rule provide an interface to the rule system. show-rules, like the new version of show-data, ensures that both the local and global rules are displayed. print-rule provides a concise way of displaying a rule, while fetch-rule uses the counter field to access a rule via its unique identifier.

The macros rule and a-rule serve as the constructors for rules. The constraint that we must run all rules that don't make assumptions before any rules that do make assumptions means that we need the ability to classify rules accordingly. That is the purpose of the distinction between rule and a-rule. A non-nil third argument to do-rule indicates that the rule makes an assumption. This information is propagated through to its ultimate destination, insert-rule, which sets the corresponding rule-assumption? field of the struct implementing the instance of that rule. Notice that we are counting on the rule author to correctly indicate whether or not the body of the rule pushes the assumption stack. This is necessary because we allow arbitrary Lisp code in rule bodies, and so cannot guarantee that an automatic analysis would make this decision correctly. This is a disadvantage, of course. An alternative is to tightly restrict the contents of rules, so that we could perform a simple case analysis on them to set this flag itself. Since we are opting for simplicity in this system, we stick with making the rule author do the work.

Conceptually, nested triggers are implemented by creating a nested sequence of single-trigger calls to rule, which are then analyzed as before. In frules.lisp this is accomplished by the combination of the macro internal-rule and the procedure make-nested-rule. The mechanics of "unwinding" a list of triggers into a sequence of nested rules is handled by make-nested-rule. We say that a rule is a *top-level* rule if it is not defined within the scope of any other rule, i.e., is not itself a nested rule. The indexing form for nested rules must be treated differently than for top-level rules. The reason is that nested rules must only be added to the database whenever the rule that contains them is triggered. Furthermore, where they are indexed often depends on the bindings provided by the containing triggers, since the class of an internal trigger might be a variable which is bound by some enclosing pattern. So the "trace" left behind when defining a nested rule is just an indexing form, which appears in the body procedure of the containing rule. On the other hand, the indexing form for the top-level rule should actually be executed as soon as it is evaluated, since it doesn't depend on anything else. This distinction is why `internal-rule` is substituted for `rule` inside the body.

The procedure `do-rule` orchestrates the process of creating a rule. Recall that every rule now includes a body procedure and a match procedure. Furthermore, we must arrange for the rule to be created and indexed appropriately, even if the file of rules is compiled. Correctly enforcing the semantics of nested rules makes this process a bit tricky. To make a file of rules compilable, we must ensure that all the body and match procedures are visible to the compiler, and that the outermost rule will be indexed appropriately. Knowing the form of the answer is often a great help in understanding how to derive it, so Figure 5.2 shows a simple rule and the code produced for it by FTRE.

Let us examine the structure of `do-rule`. The global variable `*rule-procedures*` accumulates the `defuns` generated in the course of analyzing a rule. The global variable `*bound-vars*` represents the run-time environment of a rule. In analyzing any nested rule, if a pattern variable appears as a member of `*bound-vars*`, then that variable will be bound before that rule is executed and will be free otherwise.

Where do we put the definitions for each rule's match and body procedures? We want these definitions to be processed as top-level forms by Lisp, so that they can be compiled. Furthermore, we want to ensure that all procedures are defined before the indexing form for the top-level rule is evaluated, since executing the indexing form may result in these procedures being called. After all, there may already be assertions that trigger them in the database. As mentioned above, we accomplish this by using the global variable `*rule-procedures*` to accumulate procedure definitions. The form returned by `do-rule` is a `progn`, so that its contents will be compiled, and the procedures are included before the indexing form to ensure a correct order of evaluation.

The actual creation of the indexing form and the match and body procedures is arranged by `build-rule`. The process of building the match and body procedures is described later. Its final result, the indexing form, is an expression consisting of a call to `insert-rule`. `insert-rule` creates a new rule under the class of the rule's trigger. The complications in this form stem from the need to maintain the proper lexical environment for rules. Think of the process of evaluating a rule definition as repeated macro-expansion (which it is). When `build-rule` is executed, it will be within the scope of the definition of any rules that contain the rule cur-

Before expansion:

```
(rule ((Foo ?X) (Bar ?X ?Y)) (rassert! (Mumble ?X ?Y)))
```

After expansion:

```
(PROGN
  (DEFUN |(FOO ?X)474| (?X)
    (INSERT-RULE (GET-CLASS 'BAR *FTRE*)
                 #'(LAMBDA (P) (|(BAR ?X ?Y)453| P ?X))
                 #'(LAMBDA (?Y)
                     (|(BAR ?X ?Y)459| ?Y ?X)) NIL))
  (DEFUN |(FOO ?X)452| (P)
    (IF
     (AND (CONSP P) (EQUAL 'FOO (CAR P))
                   (CONSP (CDR P)) (NULL (CDR (CDR P))))
     (VALUES T (LIST (CAR (CDR P))))))
  (DEFUN |(BAR ?X ?Y)459| (?Y ?X)
    (ASSERT! (LIST 'MUMBLE ?X ?Y)))
  (DEFUN |(BAR ?X ?Y)453| (P ?X)
    (IF
     (AND (CONSP P) (EQUAL 'BAR (CAR P)) (CONSP (CDR P))
          (EQUAL ?X (CAR (CDR P))) (CONSP (CDR (CDR P)))
          (NULL (CDR (CDR (CDR P)))))
     (VALUES T (LIST (CAR (CDR (CDR P)))))))
  (INSERT-RULE (GET-CLASS 'FOO *FTRE*)
               #'|(FOO ?X)452| #'|(FOO ?X)474| NIL))
```

Figure 5.2 Rules can be made efficient by open-coding unification

rently being processed. Therefore if, as noted above, we use the variable `*bound-vars*` to indicate what pattern variables have been bound by the enclosing rules, we can know exactly which pattern variables will already be bound at run time. This information allows us to set up the correct arguments to the match and body procedures. This assumes of course that `generate-match-procedure` and `generate-body-procedure` also use `*bound-vars*` to define the arguments they take.

What arguments should the match and body procedures take? A match procedure must take as an argument at least the assertion to be matched against. This argument is called `p` here, for no particular reason. It may also need the values of any pattern variables bound so far, to ensure that the constraints imposed by earlier bindings are respected. Rather than analyze exactly what subset of the previously bound variables are required, it is easier to just provide them all as inputs. That is why `*bound-`

vars* is incorporated into the argument list for the match procedure, if there will be pattern variables bound in the enclosing pattern environment at run time. Uniformity is attained by creating a closure (e.g., the use of function) so that only p needs to be supplied when calling a match procedure.

The argument list for the body procedure is a bit more complex, since it must include any variables bound by the trigger. These are computed by pattern-free-variables (in funify.lisp and described below), which uses *bound-vars* to figure out what variables are still free in the trigger. Each such variable will be newly bound as a consequence of executing that rule's match procedure, and these new bindings are combined with the previous bindings to provide the body procedure's full environment.

In general the class of a nested rule can only be determined at run time, since the leftmost symbol could well be a variable. get-trigger-dbclass creates a form that extracts this class, mirroring the logic of get-dbclass. If the leftmost symbol is a variable, get-trigger-dbclass ensures it will be bound at run time, by checking *bound-vars*. If the trigger's database class is a constant known at definition time, then that quoted symbol is used in the call to get-dbclass that is constructed. Otherwise, a form that evaluates the variable at run time is produced, so that the appropriate database class will be calculated.

More happens in generate-body-procedure than first meets the eye. Its result is a defun form which defines the body procedure. As we saw in build-rule, the arguments for this procedure include the variables just bound by the current trigger (i.e., newly-bound) and those bound by containing rules (i.e., *bound-vars*), and generate-body-procedure ensures that the procedure's arguments are defined in a corresponding fashion. Creating the body of the procedure takes more work. This work is performed by fully-expand-body. It is called within the scope of the macro with-pushed-variable-bindings, so that *bound-vars* is updated appropriately. fully-expand-body walks through the body of a procedure, recursively macro-expanding it. Why? That is the only way to ensure that the procedures corresponding to each nested rule are created and defined in the correct order. Nested rules, remember, show up as calls to the macro add-internal-rule, which calls build-rule, which ultimately calls fully-expand-body, which in turn may call add-internal-rule, and so on. Throughout this activity new procedures are being accumulated on *rule-procedures*. So no matter how deeply nested rules are, every nested rule is guaranteed to be completely defined before it is triggered.

The procedure generate-match-procedure is defined in funify .lisp, and so we postpone describing how it works until later.

An engineering note: Notice that the procedure generate-rule-procedure-name creates a symbol which is used as the name of rule and body procedures. The purpose of the format statement is to produce a prefix string from the pattern, thus giving the rule names some mnemonic value. This is a good practice in general, since authors of rule systems will often be forced to track down bugs based on these names.

As mentioned above, fully-expand-body recursively macro-expands an expression. One way to implement this procedure is to simply expand every subexpression. This method is fraught with peril, because Common Lisp is syntactically rich and contains many special forms, which are often implemented via macros. Since implementations vary in how they implement their primitives, writing such a code analyzer is tricky, as anyone who has written compilers or interpreters can attest. A better way to implement this procedure is based on the observation that we only need to expand macros when they will yield new rules or new bindings to pattern variables. By noting such macros in a list (called here *macros-to-expand*), fully-expand-body can operate by walking recursively through an expression, calling macroexpand only when it recognizes a situation where expansion is required. Notice that systems which extend FTRE must update *macros-to-expand* if they include new macros that can appear inside rules and themselves either write new rules or bind pattern variables.

Like insert, the procedure insert-rule uses the depth field to determine where to put a newly created rule. Like get-candidates, the procedure get-candidate-rules includes the rules on the stack as well as the rules for the appropriate class in the global database.

The procedure try-rule-on, which evaluates whether a rule should be triggered on an assertion, follows our design in assuming that the match procedure returns a flag signaling whether or not the match is good and a list of bindings it requires. This list of bindings is provided to the body procedure as its argument and queued for eventual execution. Instead of the complicated consing of an expression, run-rules now simply applies the body procedure to the bindings supplied.

The queuing of rules has been changed to reflect the assumption/non-assumption distinction. Recall that an FTRE contains two queues, the normal-queue for rules that don't make assumptions and the asn-queue for those that do. enqueue is passed the flag from the rule struct in order to figure out which queue to place it in, and dequeue empties the queue of standard rules before returning rules that introduce assumptions.

5.2.4 The FTRE unification system (funify.lisp)

The code in this file does two things: it implements several features for making rule-writing more convenient, and it implements the open-coding of unification.

The first feature for convenience is quotize, which was used in fdata.lisp by rassert!. quotize recurses down an expression, creating a new expression which, when evaluated, will reproduce the constant parts of the input expression while replacing pattern variables with their bindings. Thus if we call quotize with

```
(foo ?a (Mumble ?b))
```

the result will be

```
(cons 'foo
      (cons ?a
            (cons (cons 'Mumble
                        (cons ?b nil))
                  nil)))
```

As noted above, this allows us to avoid a lot of backquoting. The :EVAL option allows more complex results to be computed at run time.

The macro rlet provides a means of binding pattern variables within the scope of a rule. This is yet another aspect of how FTRE ensures that Lisp variables and pattern variables are closely aligned. The form returned by rlet is in fact a let expression, but with the value expressions in the let's variable list appropriately quotized. Furthermore, the body of the new let has been fully expanded, during which time *bound-vars* was augmented to ensure that the appropriate information about bound pattern variables is available.

The rest of the code to implement match procedures starts with pattern-free-variables. This procedure does a car/cdr recursion through the expression, accumulating all pattern variables not already appearing on *bound-vars*. These are exactly the pattern variables which must be newly bound by the match procedure. The order in which this procedure returns the free variables is very important, since it determines in part the order of arguments given for body procedures. In defining the rest of the system we must take care to ensure that the variable bindings returned by the match procedure are in this order so that rules will execute correctly.

generate-match-procedure assembles match procedures from tests and binding specifications provided by generate-match-body. The name of the match procedure is created by generate-rule-procedure-name. Recall that p is the canonical variable we are using for the pattern, so p and the already-bound trigger variables (i.e., *bound-vars*) provide the arguments for the match procedure. The logic of the procedure is that if all the tests hold (the and test in the if), then the first value returned is the flag indicating that the match is okay and the other argument is the list of values that the free variables in the trigger should be bound to. The list of expressions that compute these values was the value of binding-specs returned from generate-match-body, which we describe next.

We already know the output of generate-match-body: a list of the tests on the structure of the candidate assertion and a list of expressions which specify where in the assertion the bindings for the trigger's free variables can be found. Both of these values must be generated by a recursive analysis of the trigger pattern. Consequently, it makes sense to use the same recursive analysis to calculate both lists and then sort them afterwards. The procedure generate-unify-tests does the recursive analysis of the trigger. The elements in its output which specify locations for variable bindings are those which have a pattern variable as their first element. The dolist sorts the output, stashing normal tests on the local variable structure-tests.

The locations for variables bound in matching the trigger are used in three ways. First, one expression is selected to be used in extracting the value if the pattern matches. Since generate-unify-tests accumulates results "on the way down" and visits cars before cdrs, in general the expressions at the front of the list of places where a specific variable can occur will be more complex than those at the back of the list. By picking the last element of this list, we are thus more likely to have a cheaper expression to evaluate. The second use of these expressions is to ensure that the same value appears everywhere the variable is used in the assertion. If it isn't, then in fact the pattern does not match. The procedure `generate-pairwise-tests` creates an appropriate list of such tests. The third use of these expressions is implementing the `:TEST` option. Notice that the test, if any, is passed as the argument `extra-test` to `generate-match-body`. The code of the `:TEST` is transformed into an executable expression by the call to `sublis`. For increased robustness we ensure that no free pattern variables appear in the test, signaling an error if any are found. The resulting code is then appended to the end of the unification tests, thus ensuring the pattern is correct before attempting the final check.

After sorting out the results of the analysis, `generate-match-body` finally returns the combination of the tests on the structure and the equality tests as the list of tests that must be peformed on any assertion to determine if it matches, and `binding-specs` as the expressions that will access the new bindings for the trigger's free variables. Notice again that order is important: tests that ensure a particular piece of list structure exist must be carried out before others that presume that list structure is there. That is why the equality checks are placed after every other structural test. This procedure and `generate-unify-tests` were written together, to ensure that the order of the lists involved would come out correctly with minimal consing. Similar orchestration occurred with the order provided by `pattern-free-variables`, as noted earlier, to ensure that the arguments provided by the binding specifications would be in the same order as the pattern variables given as the arguments for body procedures.

We already know what `generate-unify-tests` produces. What it takes as input is the pattern it is analyzing (`pattern`), a list of free variables for the trigger (`vars`), the set of tests accumulated so far (`tests`), and a specification in terms of `cars` and `cdrs` about how to arrive at the piece of the structure being analyzed (`path`). Initially `pattern` is the whole trigger and `path` is `P`. Each recursive step of the analysis causes `path` to be incremented appropriately. Thus the first clause of the main `cond` in `generate-unify-tests` detects that the current path has led to nothing, so a `null` test is included in the list of tests. Notice that each test result will be considered successful at run time if the result is non-`nil`. Similarly, the `numberp` and `atom` tests detect constants in the trigger. The final clause is the recursive descent, which goes down the `car` first and passes back those tests to add to those for the `cdr`.[4] The `consp` test is added to ensure that `car` and `cdr` make sense.

What happens when a variable is encountered in `generate-unify-tests` depends on whether or not it was previously bound. If this trigger is what binds it (as indicated by its appearance in `vars`) then the current path is pushed onto the list of specifications of where that variable has appeared. If the variable is bound, an equality test is added to ensure that the value in the run-time environment is the same as that to which unifying the pattern with this assertion would bind it.

5.3 Examples

Let us now put our context mechanism to work. We first look at a toy example, the *N*-queens puzzle, for two reasons. First, it provides a very simple illustration of some basic ideas about organizing searches, such as *choice sets* and *chronological backtracking*. Second, the performance of this system is used as a baseline in evaluating the efficiency of dependency-directed search in Chapter 8. Section 5.3.2 contains the major example for this chapter: A full implementation of KM* that is capable of performing a variety of natural deduction proofs.

5.3.1 Example: The *N*-queens puzzle

They are queens
Reckless
Blasting forth
Insatiable
They need more
Ever more
Dimension
To conquer
When they stop
Panting
They rest
Like drowsy cows
—Locomotives, by R. de L. Furtado (in *The Centre* 1955)

4. We do a `car/cdr` walk to allow "rest" variables, i.e., `(Foo . ?x)` can match `(Foo 1 2)` and `(Foo 1 2 3)` with `?x = (1 2)` and `?x = (1 2 3)` respectively.

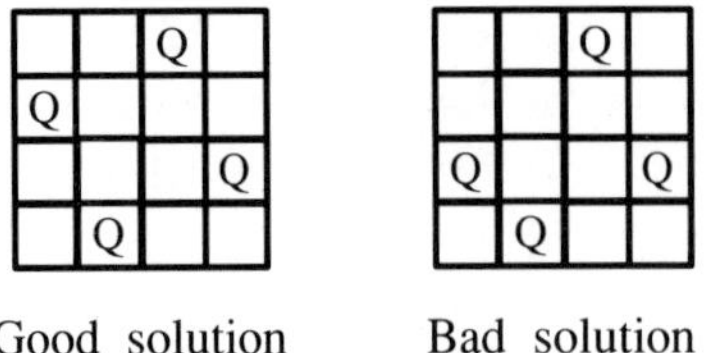

Figure 5.3 The N-queens puzzle. This simple puzzle is commonly used to illustrate issues in combinatorial searches.

A classic example of combinatorial search is the N-queens puzzle. The question is simple: Given an $N \times N$ chessboard and N queens, how many ways can you place the queens on the board so that none of them can capture any other? For $N < 4$ the answer is zero, that is, it cannot be done. For $N = 4$ there are two ways (see Figure 5.3), and the number of legal combinations rapidly goes up with N. The rapid growth in solutions combined with its simplicity of statement makes this an ever-popular toy example for programming.

The files `fqueens.lisp` and `fqrule.lisp` provide one encoding of this puzzle for FTRE. A chessboard is encoded as a two-dimensional grid, with zero as the starting coordinate for both rows and columns. Since we know that placing two queens in the same row cannot be a legal solution, we simply identify each queen with a row. The problem becomes finding consistent column placements for each queen. Conceptually, we can view the set of alternative placements for the queen as a *choice set*, and each legal placement as a consistent combination of choices from each choice set.

The idea of choice sets as a method of organizing searches in problem solving is very powerful and is widely used in practice. The general principles are:

1. Each choice set represents some factor or aspect which must appear in any complete solution.
2. Within each choice set, the choices are mutually exclusive and collectively exhaustive.
3. The collection of choice sets must span the set of possible solutions: that is, every solution can be found by a consistent set of selections, one from each choice set.

4. The converse is also true: Every consistent set of selections, one from each choice set, is a solution to the problem. Said another way, the span of the choice sets must be no larger than the space of solutions.

Understanding a problem well enough to carve it up into a collection of choice sets is a key step in formulating it. In puzzles (like N-queens) the decomposition is often obvious. For more complex problems, such as planning and design, figuring out the right set of constraints to narrow the problem down to one whose choice sets are obvious is a major part of their difficulty.

Once we have broken a problem down into a collection of choice sets, one way to solve it is by *chronological search*. Abstractly, we can describe chronological search as follows:

```
(defun Chrono (choice-sets)
 (if (null choice-sets) (record-solution)
     (dolist (choice (first choice-sets))
      (while-assuming choice
         (if (consistent?)
             (Chrono (rest choice-sets)))))))
```

where

- `record-solution` is executed whenever a consistent set of choices has been made, to store the results before trying another combination.
- `while-assuming` makes the particular choice, retracting it when its body is finished executing.
- `consistent?` tests the choices so far for consistency.

The first step in instantiating this abstract procedure is to choose a representation for the queens. The assertion `(Queen ?I ?J)` indicates that the queen of row `?I` is placed in column `?J`. The routine `queens-okay?` uses this encoding to determine whether the coordinates of two queens imply the potential for capture. This routine is used by the FTRE rule in `fqrule.lisp` to assert the symbol `Contradiction` if two queens are ever discovered to be in mutual peril.

Given N, the routine `n-queens` finds all consistent solutions. It begins by calling `setup-queens-puzzle`, which creates an FTRE and initializes `*n-assumptions*` to keep statistics and `*placements*` to store solu-

Table 5.1
Performance of FTRE on N-queens. Times are for an IBM RT model 125, running Lucid Common Lisp.

N	# Soln's	# Asns	Time
4	2	60	0.55
5	10	220	1.33
6	4	894	5.13
7	40	3,584	20.23
8	92	15,720	95.13

tions. `setup-queens-puzzle` then loads the capture rule. The procedure `make-queens-choice-sets` is called to create the choice sets which are then passed to `solve-queens-puzzle`. `make-queens-choice-sets` is straightforward, computing a list of choice sets, each encoded by a list of patterns involving a row's queen.

`solve-queens-puzzle` does the real work. It begins by checking if the last placement led to a capture by seeing if `contradiction` is believed. (Notice that on the first call to `solve-queens` we start with an empty board and so this can't occur, but no harm is done, either.) If the last placement led to a capture, we simply return without doing any further work. Otherwise, `solve-queens` checks to see if any choice sets remain. If there are more choices to be made, the first choice set is selected and each alternative is tried in turn (via the `dolist` over `(car choice-sets)`). Notice that the form we ask `try-in-context` to execute is another call to `solve-queens`, with the rest of the choice sets. This is the heart of the search. Finally, when no more choice sets remain to be explored, we have a consistent solution to the puzzle, and all currently believed `Queen` assertions are pushed onto `*placements*` to record this fact.

The strategy used by this system is known as *chronological backtracking*. It is called that because when an inconsistency is found the program backs up to the very last choice that was made. We were careful in this system to ensure that contradictions would be detected as soon as possible, so in fact the last choice was indeed relevant. As we see later, this is not always easy to do.

How well does this system perform? Running times of course depend on the specific combination of hardware and software used. But the number of capture tests and assumptions made are a property of the algorithm itself, and thus give us a machine-independent way to characterize its behavior. The variable `*n-assumptions*` records this information for each FTRE run. (For concreteness, some sample run times are included in Table 5.1 as well.) Clearly, exploring each assumption takes time, both to compute its consequences and to test the result for consistency. So these figures will give us some estimate of how run time changes as N grows.

Figure 5.4 plots how run time and assumptions explored grows with N. The curve is clearly an exponential, as one might expect from a combinatorial search problem. Even in this simple puzzle lurks the nemesis of all problem-solvers: combinatorial explosion. In later chapters we see how dependency-directed search allows one to ameliorate this problem.

In N-queens, the exponential is inherent in the problem: there are simply an exponential number of solutions. In other problems, even when there is a single solution it can take exponential work to find it. No code optimization, no faster clock rate, no increment of parallel processing will overcome the computational demands of an exponential procedure in the long run. The best you can do is figure out how to formulate your problem so that you either eliminate the exponential (perhaps by settling for approximate solutions) or keep its growth as small as possible.

5.3.2 Example: A full implementation of KM*

In Chapter 4 we saw that the inference rules of a natural deduction system could be easily mapped into the rules of a pattern-directed inference system. However, we could not completely implement KM*, since we had no mechanism for manipulating assumptions. Our new context mechanism allows us to complete the implementation of KM*.

Recall that three inference rules require temporary assumptions: Indirect Proof, Not Introduction, and Conditional Introduction. Let us begin with Indirect Proof. Its form is:

```
     show P   (IP i j k)
   +------------------+
i  | (not P)  asn     |
   | .                |
   | .                |
   | .                |
j  | Q                |
   | .                |
   | .                |
   | .                |
k  | (not Q)          |
   +------------------+
```

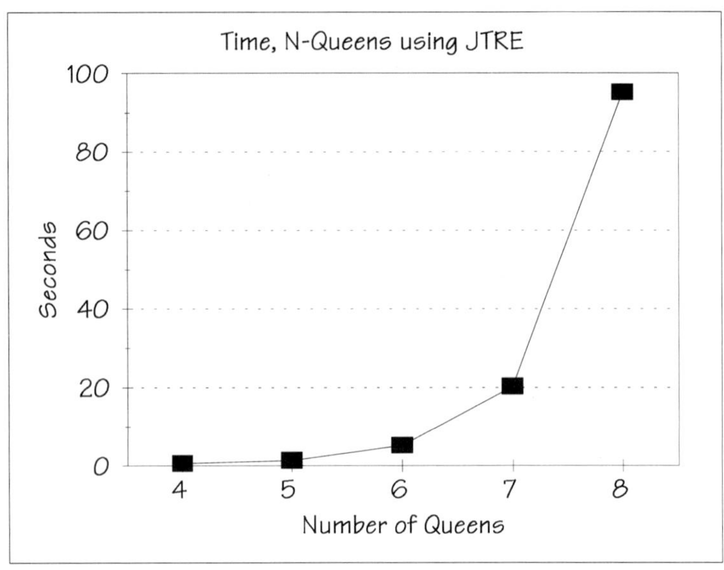

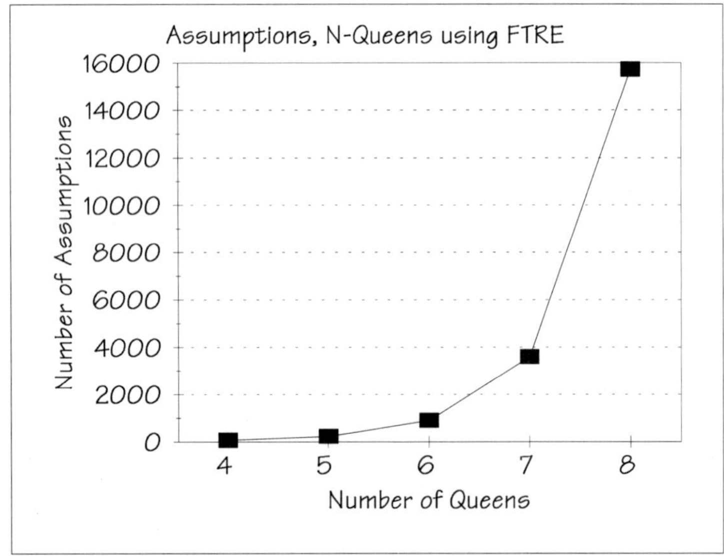

Figure 5.4 Performance as *N* increases

where P is what is to be proven and Q is some arbitrary fact embroiled in a contradiction, presumably as a consequence of assuming (not P). Since the notion of a contradiction is generally interesting, it is worth encoding contradiction detection as a distinct rule. In this case we will predicate its operation on the desire to show a contradiction. This desire is expressed by asserting (show contradiction). (In many other circumstances, it is advantageous to have contradiction detection occurring antecedently. One example is checking consistency of data from multiple sources.) The following rule suffices:

```
(rule ((show contradiction)          ;; When trying to detect contradictions
       (not ?p)                      ;;  and you find a negative term
       ?p)                           ;;  and you believe the positive term, too
      (rassert! contradiction))      ;;  Then you have a contradiction
```

Notice that we must put the trigger for (not ?p) before the trigger for ?p in order for the class of ?p to be bound when spawning the (implicit) innermost rule. Actually this is a good idea in any case: typically there will be many more positive terms than negative ones. Control assertions, for instance, are positive terms whose negations make little sense, so spawning rules to look for their negations is a gross waste of resources. (Amusingly, at least one early pattern-directed inference system did exactly this!)

The contradiction rule gives us a means of detecting when an indirect proof succeeds. Now we have to define a rule which (1) detects when indirect proof is an appropriate technique to try and (2) sets up a temporary context in which to try it. The latter is easy; we can simply call seek-in-context with the negation of the fact to be shown as the assumption and contradiction as our goal. Figuring out just when we want to do indirect proof is a little harder.

Let ?p be the proposition to be proven. One obvious intuition is that we should not attempt an indirect proof if we already believe ?p. The discipline of show assertions isn't quite enough to guarantee this, since even if we succeed in proving something the show assertion remains in force. All we have to do is try fetching ?p, and if it is already in the database, abort the attempt to use indirect proof. This tactic is also useful for implementing other intuitions about when not to use indirect proof. For example, indirect proof doesn't make sense for some kinds of assertions. Suppose, for example, that ?p is an implication. Trying indirect proof on an implication probably won't do much good. Why? There generally isn't much one can conclude in KM* from the negation of an implication. No proof rules mention them, for example. Could it be used for getting a contradiction directly? This is unlikely, unless you already believed ?p itself, in which case we shouldn't be doing an indirect proof.

We can take this argument farther. Each connective already has an associated introduction rule for demonstrating propositions using that connective. Thus we might as well restrict indirect proof to simple propositions, namely those not involving connectives. (This is not the same as restricting it to atomic terms, of course: (Left-Of X Y) for instance is a simple proposition, since its functor is not a connective.)

There is yet one more restriction to make. Viewed syntactically, contradiction is itself a simple proposition. But using indirect proof to show contradiction doesn't make sense, since it is part of the mechanism of indirect proof itself. With these restrictions, the rule for INDIRECT PROOF becomes:

```
(a-rule ((show ?p))
   (unless (or (fetch ?p)
               (eq ?p 'contradiction)
               (not (simple-proposition? ?p)))
        (when (seek-in-context `(not ,?p) 'contradiction)
              (rassert! ?p))))
```

The fact that INDIRECT PROOF is encoded with a-rule means it will be tried only if other rules failed to prove it. The rule for NEGATION INTRODUCTION is very similar:

```
(a-rule ((show (not ?p)))
   (unless (or (fetch `(not ,?p))
               (eq ?p 'contradiction))
      (when (seek-in-context ?p 'contradiction)
            (rassert! (not ?p)))))
```

Here restricting ?p to simple propositions doesn't make sense, since the assumption will (presumably) be a positive term which might indeed be proven by some other rule.

Conditional Introduction is very similar to Indirect Proof and Negation Introduction. The intent is to demonstrate that by assuming the antecedent one can derive the consequent. Given `(implies ?p ?q)`, clearly assuming `?p` and looking for `?q` will do the trick. However, there is an important optimization we can make. Suppose in the context of `?p` we derive `contradiction`. Then we should claim success in this case as well. After all, we could in principle use Indirect Proof (or Negation Introduction, depending on `?q`'s form) to show `?q` in one more step. This gives us the following rule for Conditional Introduction:

```
(a-rule ((show (implies ?p ?q)))         ;; Conditional Introduction
   (unless (fetch '(implies ,?p ,?q)) ;; Punt if already known
      (when (seek-in-context ?p          ;;  o.w. assume the antecedent
               '(or ,?q contradiction)) ;;  And look for consequent
            (rassert! (implies ?p ?q)))))
```

This rule relies on our rule for Or Introduction, defined in Chapter 4, to decompose the disjunctive goal and express interest in its parts.

These rules, combined with the KM* rules from Chapter 4, provide an implementation of KM* with considerable power. For good engineering, we need two more things. First, we need to instrument our rules. That is, we should add statements that can be switched on when debugging to provide more information, and switched off when operating normally. We can do this by including `format` statements, conditionalized by a global variable such as `*debug-nd*`. The macro `debug-nd` provides a civilized interface. Second, we need to develop a suite of test cases designed to give each rule a workout. The instrumented rules can be found in the file `fnd.lisp`, while the file `fnd-ex.lisp` provides a suite of test cases. The test cases all have a common form: `setup-ftre` creates a new FTRE and loads the rule set, and then the assertions that define the problem are evaluated by `run-forms`, which unleashes the rules on them. Examples `ex1` through `ex5` provide simple checks of the basic rules. Examples `ex6` through `ex9` provide more substantial fare, with all but `ex6` being examples from Chapter 4. By studying FTRE's behavior on these examples, one can gain useful insights into the construction of pattern-directed inference systems.

5.4 Reprise

This chapter carries the simple antecedent pattern-directed inference system model about as far as it can go. We have seen that by using some simple macros it is possible to provide "syntactic sugar" which simplifies the rule author's work. We also saw techniques for speeding up such rules, by turning them into compilable procedures and open-coding pattern matching. Finally, we saw how temporary assumptions could be introduced and manipulated via a stack discipline. This simple context mechanism provided the basis for searching through board placements in the N-queens problem and searching through possible assumptions in finding natural deduction proofs.

One of the key ideas of this chapter is the notion of *logical environment*. Recall that we defined a logical environment as the set of assertions believed at some particular point in a computation. The stack-based context mechanism used in FTRE provides the simplest mechanism for controlled introduction and retraction of temporary assumptions and their consequences, and thus for manipulating logical environments. However, it has certain important disadvantages. First, the choice of a stack limits us to depth-first search. Often other search strategies would be more appropriate. Implementing any other search strategy would require substantial changes to the system. Another disadvantage of the stack mechanism is that it provides no means for caching the results of rule firings. This means the system must rederive what follows from an assumption each time it is reintroduced.

One obvious method that overcomes part of these problems would be to generalize the assumption stack into a tree. Switching between contexts then would only require changing pointers into a different logical environment.[5] Many inefficiencies would remain, however. For example, the same logical environment could show up in many different branches, due to assumptions being introduced in different orders. In each case the same rules would be run over and over again, rederiving the same consequences. Truth maintenance systems, which we begin to explore in the next chapter, provide better ways to manipulate logical environments, as

5. This is essentially the strategy used in the CONNIVER language of the 1970s.

well as providing other advantages. Consequently, we turn our attention to them.

5.5 Backpointers

The idea of open-coding unification was invented by David Warren, in the DEC-10 Prolog compiler [5]. Our discipline of `show` assertions to provide more explicit control of reasoning derives from [2].

5.6 Exercises

1. ⋆ Consider the first two tests in the match procedures in Figure 5.2, i.e., `(consp p)` and the equality check for the `car`. Are these tests really necessary, given the class structure?

2. ⋆ Notice that `do-rule` signals an error if an assumption-making rule has multiple triggers. Why is this a good idea?

3. ⋆ Explain why the following two rules are not equivalent, and explain the advantages and disadvantages of each.

   Indirect Proof, Version 1:

   ```
   (a-rule ((show ?p))
      (unless (or (fetch ?p)
                  (eq ?p 'contradiction)
                  (not (simple-proposition? ?p)))
           (when (seek-in-context `(not ,?p) 'contradiction)
                 (rassert! ?p))))
   ```

   Indirect Proof, Version 2:

   ```
   (a-rule ((show ?p)
             :test (and (not (fetch ?p))
                        (not (eq ?p 'contradiction))
                        (simple-proposition? ?p)))
           (when (seek-in-context `(not ,?p) 'contradiction)
                 (rassert! ?p)))
   ```

4. ⋆⋆ Suppose we wanted to avoid the linear search through the rule and data stacks when matching. One way to do this is to make the `facts` and `rules` field of each `dbclass` into stacks. Implement this scheme, analyze its complexity, and determine experimentally whether it is more efficient than centralized stacks.

5. ⋆⋆ A purist might argue that the use of any task-specific Lisp code is not appropriate in building problem solvers on top of a good PDIS system. Explore this claim by implementing an *N*-queens puzzle solver entirely within FTRE rules. That is, the FTRE database should be used for all side effects and intermediate results, and the amount of non-FTRE primitves used in the bodies of rules should be minimized. How does this system compare with the system of Section 5.3.1?

6. ⋆ Suppose someone wished to add a new kind of rule which would be executed only when no assertion in the database matched its trigger pattern. What could such a rule be used for, and how hard would it be to implement?

7. ⋆ Show a case where the heuristic for choosing the most efficient expression for computing the value of a newly bound variable in `generate-match-body` will fail. How could we guarantee that the most efficient choice is always made? Is it worth it?

8. ⋆ `rlet` does not check to ensure that the variables it binds are actually FTRE variables. Is this a problem?

9. ⋆⋆ The implementation of rules in FTRE requires problem-solver designers to define not just what triggers a rule should have, but also what order they will be tested in. Implement a rule system which automatically reorders rule triggers to maximize efficiency, and explain the trade-offs involved in manual versus automatic ordering of trigger conditions.

10. Consider the use of `*bound-vars*` in `build-rule`. The match procedure doesn't need the value of every pattern variable bound so far, it really only requires variables mentioned in the trigger. So in some cases we are building procedures with unused arguments, and passing around more information than we need to.

a. ⋆ Can passing around this extra information ever lead to incorrect results?

b. ⋆⋆ Modify the code so that match procedures expect and receive only the information they strictly need.

c. ⋆ Is this optimization worthwhile?

d. ⋆ Can a similar optimization be performed for the body procedure? Why or why not?

11. The current method for open-coding unification only supports assertions consisting of symbols, conses, and integers.

a. ⋆⋆ Extend `generate-unify-tests` to handle comparisons between floating-point numbers.

b. ⋆⋆ Extend `generate-unify-tests` to allow user-defined types and identity tests. Your extension should allow someone else to define strings, arrays, or even structs, as constituents of patterns.

c. ⋆ What danger(s) is there in extending the constituents of assertions to be arbitrary datastructures?

12. As mentioned in Section 5.1.3, other kinds of resource bounds could be imposed on FTRE. One such resource bound is limiting the total number of assumptions an FTRE can explore.

a. ⋆⋆ Implement a limit on the total number of assumptions that can be introduced in an FTRE.

b. ⋆ How does the bound on the total number of assumptions interact with the existing bound on assumption depth?

13. ⋆⋆ Implement iterative deepening (see Exercise 8 of Chapter 3) in FTRE, and evaluate its performance on solving KM* problems.

14. ⋆⋆ The match procedures produced by FTRE are suboptimal, in the sense that many `cars` and `cdrs` they execute are redundant. A more clever scheme would be to use internal variables which are reset as the program walks through the structure. Write a new version of the rule code that does this.

15. ⋆⋆ One problem with choosing to use named procedures as the implementation of rules is that the function cell of symbols in Common Lisp has infinite extent. Thus if one throws away an FTRE, not

all of the memory it used is recovered because the match and body procedures remain defined. Build a version of FTRE that avoids this problem.

16. ⋆ Consider the goal-detection rule defined in `seek-in-context`. What is the purpose of the test `(= *context* ,*context*)`? Construct an example where removing this test leads to a problem.

17. *(Premises and goals)* The control predicate `show` allows us to encode advice and strategy in rules, thus enabling more explicit control of reasoning. Other control predicates can be useful, too. Let us define `premise` as follows:

    `premise`*(⟨x⟩) is true just in case ⟨x⟩ is believed as an assumption of the problem.*

    Thus instead of simply assuming `P`, we wouid assume `premise(P)`. Similarly, `goal` can be defined as:

    `goal`*(⟨x⟩) is true just in case ⟨x⟩ is the proposition whose proof is the goal of the problem.*

    Thus instead of asserting `show(P)` in our problem statement to indicate our goal, we would instead assert `goal(P)`. As this problem illustrates, adding these control predicates can enhance our problem solver's performance.

    a. ⋆⋆ Implement the semantics of these new control predicates. For each predicate, write a single FTRE rule that does this.

    b. ⋆⋆ One advantage these predicates confer is the ability to automatically tell whether or not you have succeeded in solving the user's problem. Write a procedure `solved?` which takes an FTRE and returns non-`nil` if the user's problem has been solved.

18. *(Tuning up the rule set)* The `fnd` rules do a reasonable job on our test cases. However, there is room for considerable improvement. In this problem you will build an improved set of rules.

    a. ⋆⋆ Begin by making a new version of `fnd-ex.lisp`, called `myfnd-ex.lsp`, which extends `fnd.lisp` with the `premise` and `goal` control predicates you developed in solving Exercise 17. Test your rules on our standard examples, indicating (1) which examples are solved and (2) how many rules are run and how many assertions are created for each example.

b. ⋆ For those examples that don't work, figure out why. Describe your reasons in a brief paragraph or two.

c. ⋆⋆ Change your rule set so that it solves all of the examples. (Hint: it doesn't take much to do this. An ounce of analysis is worth a pound of hacking.) As always, strive for elegance and generality in your solution.

19. The choice of a stack organization for logical environments forces a control strategy of depth-first search. Sometimes other search strategies are desirable, such as best-first search or beam search.

    a. ⋆ What parts of FTRE would have to be changed to implement a context tree?

    b. ⋆⋆⋆ Design and implement a version of FTRE that supports context trees. That is, given a particular context, (1) each a-rule that can trigger in it gives rise to a new subcontext and (2) the system chooses which "fringe" context to explore next by some user-provided criteria.

    c. ⋆⋆ Compare the performance of the tree-based FTRE with that of the stack-based FTRE on a suite of natural deduction problems. Which works more efficiently?

20. KM* is a purely propositional system.

    a. ⋆⋆⋆ Extend KM* to handle full first-order predicate calculus by adding inference rules for quantifiers. Your extension should follow the existing structure of KM*; that is, each quantifier should have its own introduction and elimination rules. For instance, the universal quantifier `for-all` requires two rules, UNIVERSAL INTRODUCTION and UNIVERSAL ELIMINATION, and the existential quantifier `there-is` requires EXISTENTIAL INTRODUCTION and EXISTENTIAL ELIMINATION.

    b. ⋆⋆⋆ Implement your extended KM* system, and test it on a variety of examples.

5.7 Bibliography

[1] Charniak, E., Riesbeck, C., McDermott, D., and Meehan, J., *Artificial Intelligence Programming*, 2nd edition, Erlbaum, 1987.

[2] de Kleer, J., Doyle, J., Steele, G. L., and Sussman, G.J., "AMORD: Explicit control of reasoning," *Proceedings of the Symposium on AI and Programming Languages* (*SIGART Newsletter* No. 64), 1977.

[3] McAllester, D. "Reasoning Utility Package user's manual—Version one," MIT AI Lab Memo No. 667, 1982.

[4] McDermott, D., "Very large PLANNER-type data bases," MIT AI Lab Memo No. 339, 1975.

[5] Warren, D., "Implementing Prolog," Res. Rep. 39, 40, Department of AI, University of Edinburgh, 1977.

6 Introduction to Truth Maintenance Systems

In the previous chapters we explored two pattern-directed inference systems. We saw how context mechanisms play an important role in problem solvers and illustrated a stack-oriented context mechanism using FTRE. We studied how this stack-oriented context mechanism is used to solve the *N*-queens problem as well as to implement KM*. The stack-oriented context mechanism allows the problem solver to introduce assumptions, i.e., to add facts to the database which could later be retracted when the context was popped.

The ability to hypothetically add facts to the database which may later be retracted is fundamentally important in problem solving. The core reason for this is that most AI tasks cannot be solved in the simple antecedent-driven way that TRE uses. Sophisticated problem solvers are often faced with having to choose among mutually incompatible choices with no immediate reason to choose one over the other. To make progress, some choice must be made which may later have to be retracted. The context mechanism of FTRE achieves some of the desired functionality, and schemes like it were used in many early AI problem solvers. Unfortunately, the context mechanisms also suffer from many shortcomings. *Truth maintenance systems* are a general problem-solving facility to help inference engines such as TRE and FTRE conveniently and efficiently manipulate assumptions.

This chapter is a general introduction to truth maintenance systems and is divided into two major parts. First, we analyze the shortcomings faced by systems such as FTRE. Second, we provide a general introduction to TMSs. The reason for the general introduction is that there are several families of truth maintenance systems, each providing somewhat different functionality. In this chapter we give the fundamentals for the three main ones, and subsequent chapters deal with each family individually.

6.1 Why use a TMS?

In this section we discuss five general shortcomings in conventional problem solvers which are addressed by a TMS.

6.1.1 Identifying responsibility for conclusions

A problem solver must to identify responsibility for its conclusions by providing rational explanations of how its conclusions follow from the premises. Generally, just providing the answer is not enough. A medical diagnosis program that suggests cutting a patient's heart out would not be listened to unless it explained why. If, for instance, radical bypass surgery is necessary for a particular set of reasons, then the user can look at those reasons and see if they make sense. Similarly, if you are an engineer who has finished a new design for an airplane and your boss says only that the design will not work, not only will you be disappointed and distressed, but you will not know what to do next. If, however, your boss points out that no material will stand the projected stresses imposed by your design, then you have a way of going back and perhaps modifying your design so that it will work. By providing explanations, the problem solver enables the user (or itself) to figure out what to change when things go wrong.

6.1.2 Recovering from inconsistencies

In an ideal world all the data would be valid and every constraint imposed would be perfectly satisfied. Neither we nor our programs live in such a world. For example, the data we give our programs can be wrong. If a data entry person or machine mistypes the patient's temperature as 986 degrees, then our diagnosis program should not call the fire department. Constraints imposed by the real world can often be unsatisfiable. For instance, a venture capitalist funding a start-up company might insist that a new computer product run on batteries, fit in a shirt pocket and work faster than a Cray: an unsatisfiable constraint given today's technology. If you have a way of generating an explanation about why it is impossible, then you might be able to make your backer see reason.

6.1.3 Maintaining a cache of inferences

As we have seen in preceding chapters, most AI problem solvers search. Since they search, they often go over parts of the search space again and again. If a problem solver cached its inferences, then it would not need to rederive conclusions that it had already derived earlier in the search. By not rederiving conclusions, the problem solver avoids throwing away useful results and avoids wasting effort rediscovering the same things over and over again. The stack-oriented context mechanism of FTRE is a classic example of the problem. For example, when an assumption is introduced and then later retracted, the effects of all rules executed since the assumption was introduced are completely discarded. If that same assumption is reintroduced later in the problem-solving process, all this work must be repeated.

These problems are subtle, so an example is worth examining. Consider the graph of potential choices shown in Figure 6.1 which depicts a "God's Eye" view of the entire space of alternatives. This is not what the problem solver sees, of course. We assume there are three sets of choices and that we must pick a choice from each set to form a total solution which is then checked for consistency by problem solver. Furthermore, each choice set is mutually exclusive. We can choose either A or B, then we must choose one of C or D, and then we must choose one of E or F. For instance, the choice set A or B might represent a strategy to be taken in the design, the choice set C or D might represent the materials out of which to build the object, and the choice set E or F might represent heuristics for sizing the parts in the design. Suppose that A and C are contradictory when taken together, and that B and E are contradictory when taken together.

Given these constraints, the search space contains eight potential solutions, only four of which are consistent. These are also shown in Figure 6.1. A common technique (used by FTRE, for example) for finding consistent solutions is chronological backtracking. Chronological backtracking, however, suffers from several problems. Let's assume that the combination of choices D and F causes a lot of work (involving, for instance, running a finite element analysis program).

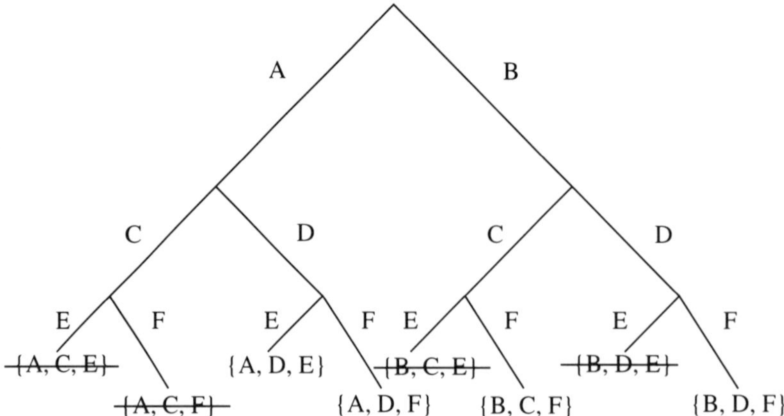

Figure 6.1 The search space is characterized by a sequence of three choices —*A* or *B*, *C* or *D*, *E* or *F*. *A* and *C* cannot hold together, neither can *B* and *E*.

Suppose search through the set of alternatives of Figure 6.1 proceeds depth first from left to right. When the search explores the solution $\{A, D, F\}$ it will perform the expensive computation which depends on D and F. Later (see Figure 6.2), the search backtracks to $\{B, D, F\}$ and the same computation is redone. The problem is that when chronological backtracking leaves a context, all information in that context is lost. Even though the work that follows from D and F does not depend on the choice of A or B, chronological backtracking has no way of recording this. We need some way of caching the result, and, more importantly, some way of recognizing that the result of the expensive computation does not depend on the choice of A or B.

Chronological backtracking also wastes effort by rediscovering contradictions. Suppose (see Figure 6.3) that the search has reached $\{B, C, E\}$ and noticed that it is inconsistent. Later the search tries $\{B, D, E\}$ even though it is futile. It is important to notice that it is futile because we see that B together with E is inconsistent. However, pure chronological search can neither recognize this fact nor cache it. If it could, then a lot of wasted effort would be saved by never descending in the tree without first checking whether the new state would violate a previously encountered inconsistency. However, to do this the search needs to recognize what choices an inconsistency depends on and cache that information for later checking.

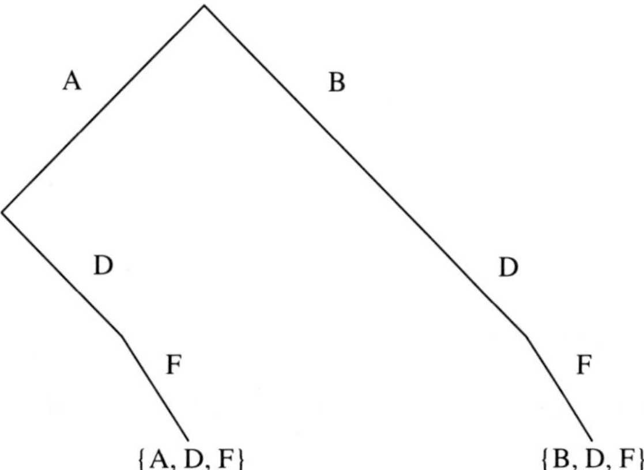

Figure 6.2 Chronological backtracking leads to wasted computation. Suppose *D* and *F* taken together cause a lot of work (e.g., start up a finite element analysis program). All this work will be lost when the context is popped.

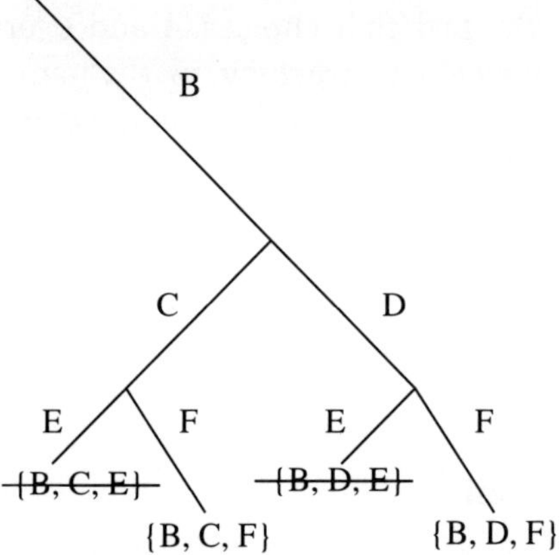

Figure 6.3 Chronological backtracking leads to rediscovering contradictions. Trying *B* with *E* is always a waste of effort, since *B* and *E* taken together are contradictory.

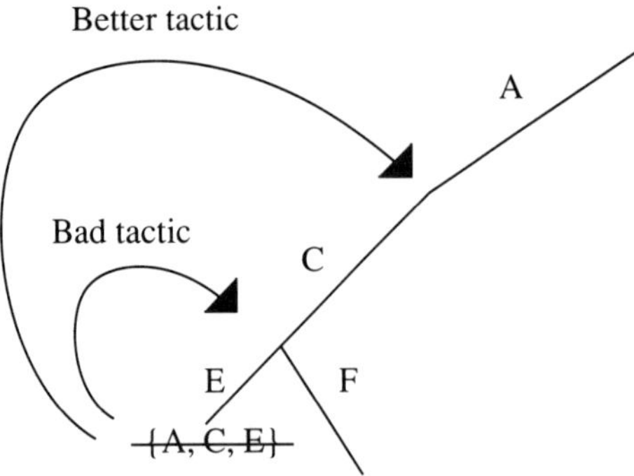

Figure 6.4 Guiding backtracking. Recall that A and C are contradictory.

6.1.4 Guiding backtracking

Historically, futile backtracking was the catalyst for the invention of truth maintenance systems. Suppose the search (see Figure 6.4) detected an inconsistency while exploring the solution $\{A, C, E\}$. This inconsistency is caused by the fact that choices A and C are incompatible with each other. Chronological backtracking, as the name implies, backtracks to the most recent choice the search has made and explores the next alternative, namely F. Exploring $\{A, C, F\}$ is futile because it too contains the contradictory pair A and C. If somehow we could detect the choices an inconsistency depended on, then the backtracker could backtrack to the most recent choice contributing to the contradiction. This strategy, called *dependency-directed backtracking*, is made possible by truth maintenance systems.

6.1.5 Default reasoning

Many AI applications require the problem solver to make conclusions based on insufficient information. The generic solution is to assume x unless there is some evidence to the contrary. The classic example in AI is to assume that since Tweety is a bird, Tweety can fly. Tweety can, of course, unless Tweety is a penguin or is broiled, stir-fried, baked, a statue, dead, stuffed, or in any of a number of unfortunate conditions. Therefore to prove Tweety can fly requires the problem solver to show that Tweety is not a penguin, etc. This may be difficult or impossible to show and in most cases the problem solver should simply assume

Tweety can fly at the outset, but if any one of these conditions is discovered, the problem solver must be able to retract the inference gracefully.

Default reasoning occurs in a wide variety of applications aside from reasoning about mythical birds. For instance, we often make "closed-world assumptions" to help constrain our choices. For instance, someone designing a computer might decide to use either NMOS or CMOS technologies to implement the design. There exist, in fact, a much larger variety of technologies, including ECL and so forth, but the designer may choose to not consider those at first just to make his search space more manageable. Similarly, someone might assume when debugging a car that the only possible faults are in the fuel pump or carburetor, even though there may be a leak in the engine block. After all, if the leak is in the engine block there is little the person can do directly unless he or she is a mechanic with access to a lot of spare parts.

6.2 What is a TMS?

The motivations analyzed in the previous section guided invention of truth maintenance systems in the mid-1970s [1, 5]. Since then TMSs have become a common and very widely used piece of AI technology. For example, they are used in qualitative simulation, analog circuit design and analysis systems, temporal reasoning, diagnosis, ITS systems, knowledge representation languages, rule-based deduction systems, and constraint languages, as well as in many commercially available expert system shells such as KEE and ART.

The fundamental architectural observation is that the problem solver can be decomposed into two parts: an inference engine and a TMS (see Figure 6.5). This natural partitioning of concerns allows the inference engine to focus on drawing inferences within the task domain and the TMS to focus on beliefs, assumptions, and contexts (Section 6.3.6 lists the possible transactions). The result is a much simpler and more efficient problem solver.

6.2.1 How do TMSs help?

During problem solving, the inference engine and the TMS continuously interact in a well-defined protocol which is described in the following

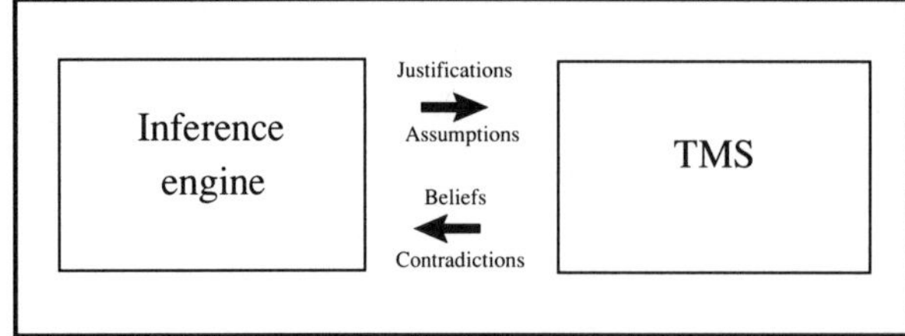

Figure 6.5 Problem solver = inference engine + TMS

sections and chapters. Every important inference made by the inference engine is communicated to the TMS as a justification (defined more precisely later). The justifications recorded by the TMS allow the problem solver to cope with five issues raised in Section 6.1.

1. The problem solver generates explanations by tracing the justifications for a belief.
2. To recover from inconsistencies, the problem solver traces backward through the justifications to identify the source of a bad conclusion.
3. The justifications cache information about what doesn't work as well as what does work, thus providing a cache that helps control the search.
4. The justifications pinpoint the assumptions underlying contradictions, and therefore identify the optimal backtrack point.
5. Since justifications can include explicit assumptions that, for instance, nothing is abnormal about Tweety, the problem solver can use the TMS to manipulate assumptions and to do default reasoning.

6.2.2 When are TMSs useful?

TMSs make three kinds of contributions to problem solving: (1) they provide a general framework which makes it easier to build many kinds of problem solvers, (2) they enable additional functionality such as explanation generation, and (3) they can improve the overall efficiency. Although a TMS provides an extremely useful problem-solving facility, it is not always appropriate to use one. There are many cases in which a TMS reduces the overall efficiency of the problem solver. Here are two such cases.

A fundamental assumption of a TMS is that consulting a set of cached inferences is more efficient than rerunning the inference rules that generated them in the first place. If, however, the inference rules are very inexpensive and the task does not require an exponential number of them, then a TMS is probably inappropriate. For example, connecting a TMS to a PROLOG interpreter is a bad idea for most applications. All the advantages of a TMS notwithstanding, on average it will substantially degrade PROLOG performance. Of course, one can find PROLOG programs that would perform better with a TMS, but such examples are rare.

The second area in which TMSs can hurt arises because they enforce a very rigid form of rationality: a fact cannot be removed from a context if it has a perfectly good justification for being there. TMSs only remove belief in facts that no longer have a good justification. Therefore, to retract a fact, one must somehow defeat its justifications. This discipline makes it relatively difficult to implement systems written in an OPS5-like fashion which frequently and arbitrarily retract facts. Although OPS5-like retraction can be implemented indirectly using a TMS, the result is relatively inefficient because TMSs keep all old inactive justifications around in case their antecedents become believed again. Thus the problem solver's database becomes filled with justifications and facts which have become irrelevant.

6.3 The basics of truth maintenance systems

In this section we define many of the concepts and terminology required to understand all the different kinds of TMSs presented in later chapters.

6.3.1 Establishing a common vocabulary between the inference engine and the TMS

In order for the inference engine and the TMS to communicate, a common ground must be established. Every important problem-solver *datum* (which may include assertions, facts, inference rules, and procedures) must be assigned a TMS *node*. Thus, in the implementation, the datastructure for a datum points to the associated TMS node, and the datastructure for a node points to the associated problem solver datum. The responsibility for establishing this connection rests with the inference engine.

All communication between the inference engine and the TMS is in terms of these nodes. It is important to note that the TMS and the inference engine interpret the nodes quite differently. To the problem solver the nodes represent data from which it can draw inferences. For example, suppose node N0001 has as its datum the inference engine rule,

```
N0001:
(rule (Graduate-Student ?x)
      (assert (and (Underpaid ?x) (Overworked ?x))))
```

and node N0002 has as its datum the assertion,

```
N0002:
(Graduate-Student Robbie).
```

The inference engine can now deduce (let's say it is the datum of node N0003),

```
N0003:
(and (Underpaid Robbie) (Overworked Robbie)).
```

The TMS cannot directly make these deductions as it may not examine the datum of a node. However, if the inference engine informs the TMS that N0003 follows from the conjunction of N0001 and N0002, then it can. We see how in a moment.

6.3.2 Node properties

The different TMSs allow various kinds of nodes. The space of possible node types is best understood by considering three properties (note that no matter what properties a node has, it can always have justifications).

- A node is a *premise* if the inference engine has explicitly indicated that it holds universally.
- A node is a *contradiction* if the inference engine has indicated that it can never hold. Contradictions can never be changed. In most TMSs, when a contradiction is discovered, the inference engine is interrupted.
- An *assumption* is a node which the problem solver has, for the mo-

ment, chosen to believe whether or not it has any supporting justification. Assumption nodes are typically used to represent data which the inference engine prefers to believe but which it may want to retract later. For example, "the federal budget is unbalanced" is an assumption that may change with time.

Although at first blush these properties seem mutually exclusive, they need not be. As there are three possible properties, there are conceivably eight different types of nodes—some combinations are more useful than others. The typical node has none of the three properties—it will become believed only when it receives a valid justification. All TMS implementations allow one to select the properties of a node when it is first created, and most restrict subsequent changes.

6.3.3 Justifications

The deductions the inference engine makes are communicated to the TMS as constraints or conditions on the nodes. The simplest such constraint is the *justification.* For example, the preceding deduction of

```
(and (Underpaid Robbie) (Overworked Robbie))
```

must be communicated to the TMS as a justification. A justification consists of three parts:

- The *consequent* is the node of the inference engine datum which was inferred.
- The *antecedents* are the nodes of the data used as antecedents to the inference rule.
- The *informant* is supplied by the inference engine to explain the inference in more detail. The informant has no effect on TMS algorithms, but the TMS must record it and supply it to the inference engine when requested.

Justifications are typically written as

(⟨*consequent*⟩ ⟨*informant*⟩ . ⟨*antecedents*⟩)

Thus, the preceding inference about Robbie might be represented as:

```
(N0003 MODUS-PONENS N0002 N0001).
```

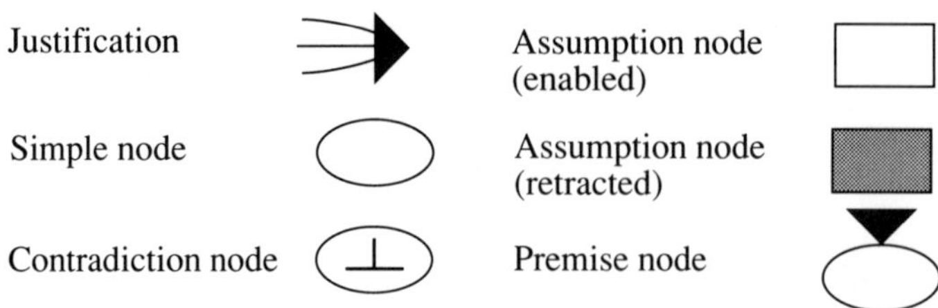

Figure 6.6 Dependency networks: Graphical notation. The node properties allow for eight distinct types of nodes, however, it is hard to notate all these possibilities. We adopt the convention that an assumption node which also is a premise or a contradiction, is notated as a premise or a contradiction. Nodes which are both premises and contradictions (admittedly rare) are represented by superimposing their icons.

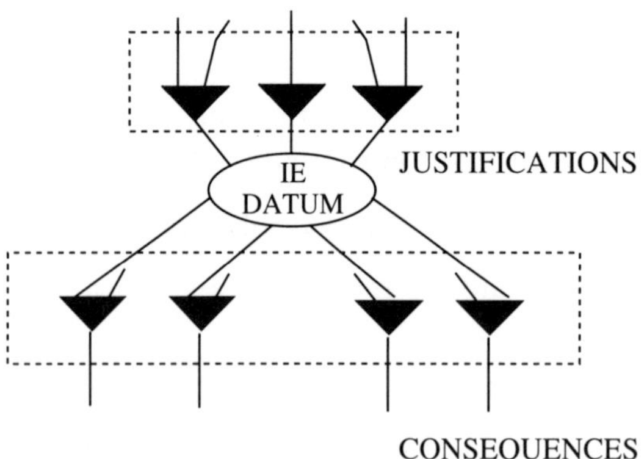

Figure 6.7 Dependency network structure

A set of nodes and justifications form a dependency network. Figure 6.6 outlines the graphical notation we use to represent dependency graphs.

Figure 6.7 illustrates a fragment of a dependency network. The node IE DATUM has three distinct justifications and appears as an antecedent in four justifications.

6.3.4 Labels

All the TMS implementations presented in this book associate a *label* with each node (most TMS implementations in the research literature use labels also). The TMS uses the label to store its representation of the current belief in this node. There is no hard and fast rule about what this label looks like—each TMS family represents labels differently. For example, in the simplest TMS (a JTMS) this label is either `:IN` or `:OUT`. A node is labeled `:OUT` unless one can construct an argument using the dependency network starting from premises and assumptions leading to belief in the node.

6.3.5 Representing TMS data

The TMS permanently stores every justification it is provided. Each TMS has a complex datastructure for representing nodes which allows it to represent the dependency network as well as the important node properties. For most TMS implementations we see the following properties:

datum Supplied by the inference engine.

label Represents current belief status of the node.

justifications The set of justifications which could provide support for this node.

consequences The set of justifications which use this node as an antecedent.

contradictory? If non-`nil`, this field indicates that belief in this node represents a contradiction.

assumption? If non-`nil`, this field indicates that this node should be treated as an assumption whose belief can be explicitly enabled and retracted by the inference engine.

premise? If non-`nil`, this field indicates that this node is a premise.

Some TMSs do not explicitly represent all node properties, so these fields may be absent. Also, some TMSs (e.g., the LTMS) combine consequences and justifications.

6.3.6 Basic TMS-inference engine transactions

All TMSs support the following four basic actions (see Figure 6.5):

1. Upon request, the TMS creates a node with the specified properties.
2. The TMS accepts records of inference engine deductions (usually the justifications).
3. The TMS maintains the correct labels for nodes and supplies them on request.
4. When a contradiction is detected, the inference engine is signaled.
5. The TMS accepts rules from the inference engine to be scheduled for execution when particular belief conditions are met.

6.4 How justifications help

One should note that the elementary justification structures just outlined are sufficient to address two of the issues raised in Section 6.1. First, the convention of recording justifications for deductions allows a problem solver incorporating a TMS to generate explanations for its conclusions (see Section 6.1.1). Second, building a dependency structure is enough to avoid the backtracking problems discussed in Section 6.1.4. The justifications are also important to achieve the other three goals, but we discuss those in the context of specific TMSs.

6.4.1 Identifying responsibility for conclusions

Suppose a problem solver constructed a dependency network for the facts associated with Socrates' death (Figure 6.8).

By just tracing through the dependency structure the problem solver can construct the following explanation: "Socrates died because he was mortal and drank poison, and all mortals die when they drink poison. Socrates was mortal because he was a man and all men are mortal. Socrates drank poison because he held dissident beliefs, the government was conservative, and those holding dissident beliefs under conservative governments must drink poison."

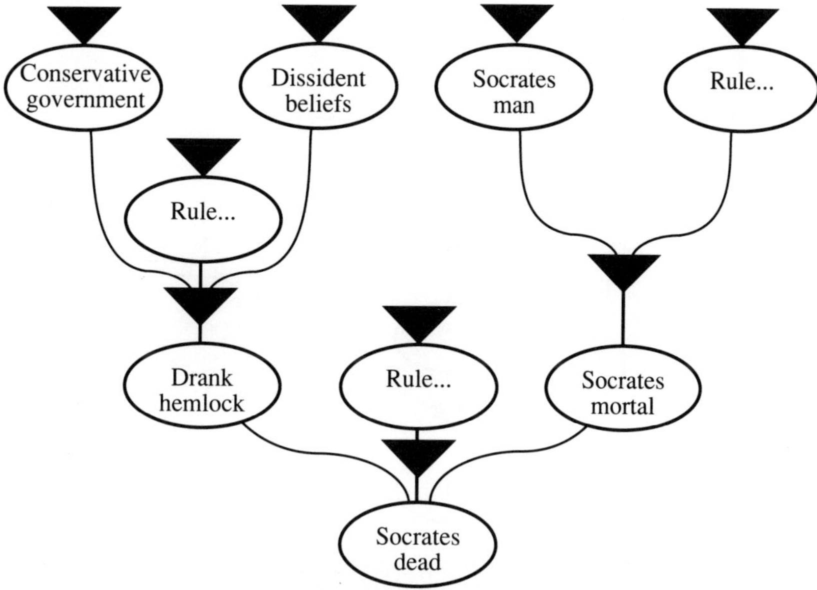

Figure 6.8 Constructing explanations for conclusions

6.4.2 Guiding backtracking with a TMS

Consider a simple backtracking problem solver which has introduced assumptions and drawn inferences as illustrated in Figure 6.9. The vertical axis indicates the time at which assumptions and nodes become believed: First assumption A is introduced, then assumption C is introduced, then assumption E is introduced, then node g is concluded, then node h is concluded, and then a contradiction is detected. Chronological backtracking would retract E, the most recent assumption. However, by consulting the dependency structure of Figure 6.9 the problem solver can recognize that the most recent assumption upon which the contradiction depends is C and therefore C should be retracted. This is an example of dependency-directed backtracking, mentioned earlier.

A common argument raised against dependency-directed backtracking is that futile backtracking in chronological search can be avoided by reorganizing the search. In our previous example, for instance, the search program could have detected the contradiction before introducing

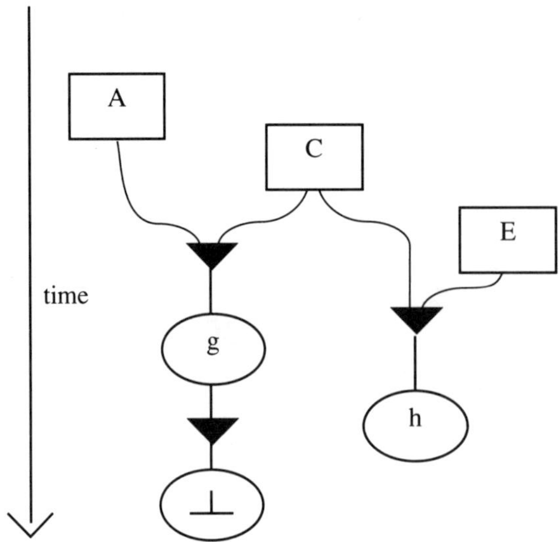

Figure 6.9 Guiding backtracking with a TMS

E. Clearly such reorganizations should be done if at all possible. However, there are many cases where such reorganizations are not feasible. Even when they are feasible, it may not always be efficient to run every rule to completion: the addition of new data or new rules, for instance, may completely invalidate existing rules. In general, dependency-directed search provides a relatively efficient means for searching complex problem spaces whose structure is poorly understood.

6.5 The propositional specification of a TMS

The inferential import of all the TMSs presented in this book can be specified to a large degree using the propositional calculus. This section provides basic underpinnings for such specifications, and we elaborate on this basic model for each specific TMS in subsequent chapters. Every TMS node can be interpreted as a propositional symbol. Every justification can be interpreted as a simple propositional definite clause. If nodes $x_1, \ldots, x_m$ justify node n, then this is represented by the clause:

$$\neg x_1 \vee \cdots \vee \neg x_m \vee n,$$

which is equivalent to the material implication:

$$x_1 \wedge \cdots \wedge x_m \Rightarrow n.$$

In addition, the inference engine has specified that some nodes are premises, assumptions, and contradictions. These specifications can be logically viewed as additional clauses. The premise n is specified by the unit clause n. The contradiction n can be (but isn't in all TMSs) specified by the negative clause $\neg n$.

Every TMS answers a variety of different queries about the current set of justifications, premises, and assumptions, but all can be formulated within (or within a version of) the propositional calculus. The most fundamental query is whether a node logically follows from the current TMS database state. For the simple TMSs where justifications are only definite clauses, it is relatively easy to design efficient algorithms. However, if justifications are extended to arbitrary clauses, it can be very expensive to design correct algorithms. Therefore, as we shall see, many TMS implementations forgo logical completeness.

6.6 Families of TMSs

There are several different families of truth maintenance systems. Each type partitions problem-solving concerns somewhat differently, and hence supports different types of problem solver-inference engine interactions. Within each family there remain a large number of design alternatives. As a result there are many unexplored combinations of options.

Nevertheless it is possible to lay out the different families of TMSs along two dimensions (Figure 6.10). The vertial dimension concerns the type of constraint that the inference engine is permitted to express among the nodes. So far we have only seen the definite clause justification, but we can see logically that many other types of constraints are possible. The three basic possibilities are: (1) Horn or definite clauses (e.g., justifications), (2) non-monotonic justifications, and (3) arbitrary clauses. The horizontal dimension is the kind of query the TMS is expected to answer efficiently. For example, the simple label TMSs are

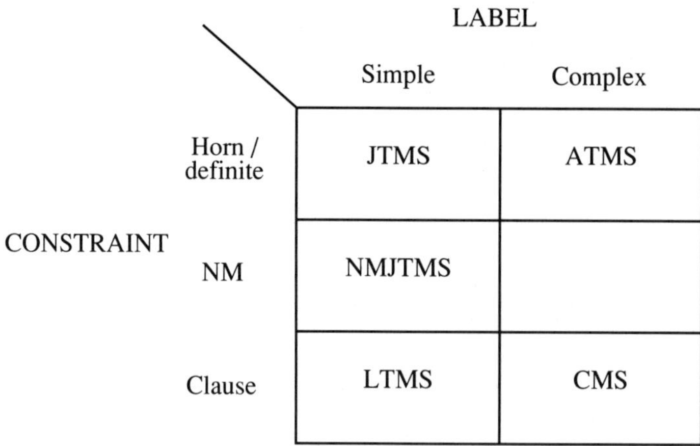

LABEL
Simple
Complex
CONSTRAINT
Horn / definite
NM
Clause
JTMS
ATMS
NMJTMS
LTMS
CMS

Figure 6.10 Families of TMSs

designed to efficiently answer the query of whether a node follows from the current TMS database state.

The main families of TMS are as follows:

- *Justification-based truth maintenance systems* (abbreviated JTMS). These systems are the very simplest type of TMS upon which all others are based. A typical JTMS can only represent definite clauses supplied by the inference engine.
- *Logic-based truth maintenance systems* (abbreviated LTMS). Unlike the JTMS, the LTMS allows negation to be expressed explicitly and therefore can represent any propositional calculus formula. Otherwise, the JTMS and LTMS are very similar.
- *Assumption-based truth maintenance systems* (abbreviated ATMS). The ATMS is like a JTMS but allows the problem solver to make inferences in multiple contexts at once. The typical ATMS can only represent Horn clauses supplied by the inference engine.
- *Non-monotonic justification-based truth maintenance systems* (abbreviated NMJTMS). An NMJTMS is much like a JTMS except that it accepts non-monotonic justifications. These systems are surprisingly hard to use and therefore have limited utility. Historically they were the first systems actually called "truth maintenance systems," although the capability was evident in some earlier systems [2, 5].

- *Clause management systems* (abbreviated CMS) . A CMS is much like an ATMS but can represent any propositional calculus formula.

In this book we focus on the JTMS, LTMS, and ATMS. For this introductory book, the complexity of the NMJTMS and CMS outweighs their utility. In choosing a TMS it should be noted that, in principle, every type of TMS is logically powerful enough to simulate the other kinds (see [3, 4]). For example, a JTMS can be used to simulate an ATMS. This observation, although logically correct, is pointless in practical terms because each TMS is designed to answer a certain pattern of queries more directly and efficiently than others.

The selection of which TMS is most appropriate to a task remains an art. We hope this book provides the reader some insights about which kind of TMS to choose. The first principle is that one should use the simplest TMS that naturally matches the task. The reason for this is that the more complex TMSs are likely to spend a great deal of computation on aspects irrelevant to the task. The list of TMSs above is organized roughly in order of complexity.

We can also see two fundamental criteria directly in Figure 6.10. Often the task will specify what kinds of constraints the TMS must be able to represent. In most cases we've found that the justification (and hence the JTMS or ATMS) is adequate. Choosing the horizontal dimension is much more difficult. Two considerations which indicate that a complex-label TMS would be preferable are: (1) whether the task requires finding most or all solutions, and (2) whether the number of context changes is far greater than the number of queries about node labels.

6.7 Exercises

1. ⋆ Even multiplication can be viewed as inference. For example, a problem-solving task might require multiplying x and y to produce z. Describe how a TMS would be used to record this multiplication. Describe a task where using a TMS to record multiplications produces a 10^{10} speedup. On average, do you think treating multiplication as inference is a good idea?

2. ⋆⋆ The simplest kind of TMS only accepts justifications as inputs and does not use premises, contradictions, or assumptions. Write a simple TMS with these properties. When would such a TMS be useful?

6.8 Bibliography

[1] Doyle, J., "A truth maintenance system," *Artificial Intelligence* 12 (1979): 231-272.

[2] London, P.E., "Dependency networks as a representation for modeling in general problem solvers," Technical Report No. 698, Department of Computer Science, University of Maryland, 1978.

[3] McAllester, D., "Truth Maintenance," in *Proceedings of AAAI-90*, 1990, 1109–1116.

[4] McDermott, D., "A general framework for reason maintenance," *Artificial Intelligence* 50 (1991): 289–329.

[5] Stallman, R., and Sussman, G. J., "Forward reasoning and dependency-directed backtracking in a system for computer-aided circuit analysis," *Artificial Intelligence* 9 (1977): 135–196.

7 Justification-Based Truth Maintenance Systems

In this chapter we discuss the JTMS family of TMSs and present one particular implementation of the JTMS. The "justification" in the name comes from the fact that the only logical constraint this type of TMS allows is the justification, i.e., a definite clause as defined in Section 6.5. The JTMS is the simplest and most commonly used family of TMSs.

7.1 JTMS node properties

Our JTMS architecture represents the three generic TMS node properties as follows:

- A node is a premise if the inference engine has provided it with a justification with no antecedents. Premises are therefore not distinguished from other nodes in the architecture.
- A node is a contradiction if the inference engine has explicitly designated it so. Believing a contradiction has no effect on the JTMS operations. It is the inference engine's job to ensure that contradictions are not believed. The JTMS will simply inform the inference engine when a contradictory node becomes believed.
- A node is an assumption if the inference engine has explicitly designated it so. An assumption is *enabled* if the inference engine has signaled the TMS that it chooses to believe it. Otherwise the assumption is *retracted* and treated as any other node—i.e., it will be believed only if it has a valid justification. Note that a node which is both an assumption and a premise is retracted and believed.

It would be possible to make a single contradiction node which is then implicated in all contradictions. For simple systems, this strategy is fine. But for complicated systems, knowing where the contradiction occurred is of value. Introducing several contradictory nodes can be very useful for debugging and explanations. Suppose one is building a diagnosis system. It could invoke contradictions involving different kinds of knowledge and the contradiction handling may do different things according to the type of contradiction discovered. Having separate nodes for each kind of contradiction simplifies this decomposition. For example, there might be contradictions involving numerical relationships, relationships between symptoms and fault models, and qualitative descriptions. Furthermore, a common step in debugging a system that uses a TMS is to look at the justifications for a node, including contradictory nodes. If every such justification points to the same node, one must wade through far more information than if the contradictions were distinguished by their type.

7.2 The propositional specification of a JTMS

Before presenting JTMS examples and algorithms we must first be very clear as to what exactly the JTMS is computing. The basic JTMS specification can be given in terms of two sets: the set of justifications and the set of enabled assumptions. These sets evolve as problem solving progresses, and the JTMS algorithms must answer queries correctly with respect to the contents of these two sets at the moment the query is made. The set of justifications grows monotonically as we do not allow justifications to be removed. However, the set of enabled assumptions is always in flux. It is the fact that assumptions might be retracted that introduces most of the complexity in the JTMS algorithms.

By formulating the JTMS within the propositional calculus we can be precise about what it is expected to compute. Every JTMS node is a propositional symbol. A subset $\mathcal{A}$ of those symbols is designated as enabled assumptions. Every justification can be interpreted as a simple propositional (definite) clause. Let $\mathcal{J}$ be the set of such clauses.

A fundamental task of the JTMS is to answer queries about whether a particular node holds given the current set of enabled assumptions and justifications. The JTMS replies that a node n is *in* exactly when node

n follows from the union of $\mathcal{A}$ and $\mathcal{J}$ under the rules of propositional calculus. Otherwise the JTMS replies that n is *out*.

Since the justifications are all definite clauses, the JTMS can be implemented efficiently by simple forward propagation. Contradictions do not play a role in this logical specification of a JTMS. As far as the JTMS is concerned, a contradictory node is simply a node with the property that if it becomes in, the inference engine must be signaled (discussed later). It is the inference engine's job to retract assumptions so that these justifications no longer support the contradiction. A JTMS cannot represent the contradiction n as simply as $\neg n$ because $\neg n$ is a non-definite singleton clause. Extending JTMS to handle these would require a more complex propagation algorithm that propagated labels backward as well as forward through justifications.

7.3 Well-founded support

Not only must a JTMS determine which nodes are in and which are out, but it must also provide good explanations, or *well-founded supports* for why nodes are believed. A well-founded support for node n is a sequence of justifications $J_1, \ldots, J_k$ which has the following properties:

- J_k justifies node n.
- All the antecedents of J_i are justified earlier in the sequence or are enabled assumptions.
- No node has more than one justification in the sequence.

A node has a well-founded support exactly when it is propositionally derivable from the current JTMS state.

As nodes can have multiple justifications, there might be an exponential number of well-founded explanations for any particular node. The JTMS is obligated to find only one of them. All JTMSs achieve this specification by identifying a single *supporting justification* for each node. The set of supporting justifications forms a directed acyclic graph. A well-founded explanation for any node can then be found by traversing backward from consequences to antecedents.

The JTMS, and in fact all TMSs, operate incrementally. More precisely, every JTMS algorithm is designed to take maximum advantage of the current database state: when presented with a new justification, assumption, etc., the JTMS converts the previously correct data base to a new one. It never starts from scratch. This incrementality sometimes produces some odd effects which are important to know about because they might otherwise be viewed as bugs. The order in which the justifications are supplied to the JTMS has no effect on whether a node is in or out. However, as there are usually many possible well-founded explanations for the nodes, the order in which the justifications are introduced to the JTMS will affect which of those well-founded explanations the JTMS finds. Moreover, as these well-founded justifications are consulted in backtracking, the search might backtrack to a different state if the justifications were reordered. Of course, any correctly designed backtracker should take this into account.

7.4 In and out versus true and false

The JTMS is logically very weak as it only allows definite clauses. Consequently, a JTMS can never deduce the negation of any node. A node being out can mean either that its negation is propositionally derivable from $\mathcal{A}$ and $\mathcal{J}$ or that neither it nor its negation is derivable.

Many inference engines need to reason about the negations of data. This is achieved by creating two nodes for a datum: a node representing the datum and a node representing its negation. Since a node can be in or out, this gives four possible combinations for believing in the datum, as shown in Figure 7.1. Consider some datum P and its negation $\neg P$. By encoding these as two nodes the inference engine is essentially functioning with a four-valued logic: (1) P and $\neg P$ can both be in, allowing the inference engine to reason with contradictory data, (2) P is in and $\neg P$ is out, which can be interpreted as P being true, (3) P is out and $\neg P$ is in, which can be interpreted as P being false, (4) both P and $\neg P$ are out, indicating that nothing is known about P.

7.5 How justifications save inference engine work

In Section 6.1.3 and Figure 6.2 we saw how a chronological search repeated expensive computations. The JTMS justification cache avoids this.

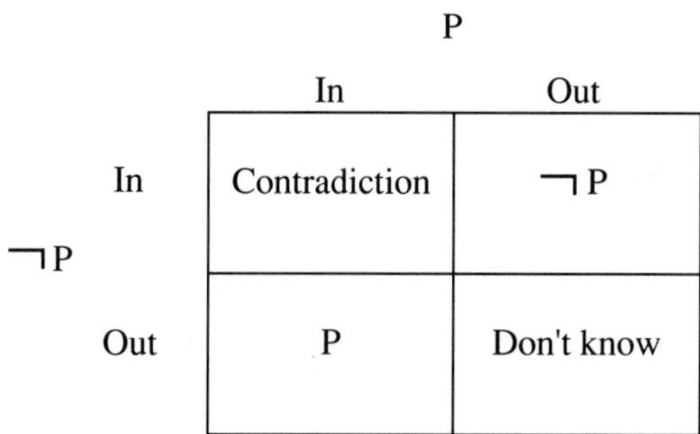

Figure 7.1 Representing a node and its negation

Figure 7.2 illustrates three snapshots of JTMS dependency network fragments. In network (a) the problem solver runs the finite element analysis program (FEA) to deduce g and records as this justification; in network (b) the problem solver has moved the search into some intermediate state where B holds but neither D nor F do (i.e., assumption B is enabled, and assumptions D and F are retracted); in network (c) the search has reached the state where B, D, and F hold. The problem solver need not recompute g at this point because it can now simply ask the JTMS whether g is now in and thus avoid the expensive recomputation. (Of course, the inference engine needs to know enough to ask. This issue is discussed later.)

There are two ways to view what the justification cache is achieving here. Whenever the inference engine changes the JTMS state (by adding justifications and adding or retracting assumptions), the JTMS carefully analyzes the difference between the states and carries as much of the problem-solving work forward as is logically possible. Another way to view it is that under this problem-solving architecture, no inference engine deduction (of which the JTMS is informed) will be performed more than once.

To achieve the full benefit of a TMS requires a closer coordination between the inference engine and the JTMS than is explained in this chapter. Consider the following issues in the preceding example of Figure 7.2. The FEA program computes a complex result; how could the problem solver check for g without knowing that it was g that the FEA program would produce? In a later chapter we discuss how to design a problem solver that avoids this and associated difficulties.

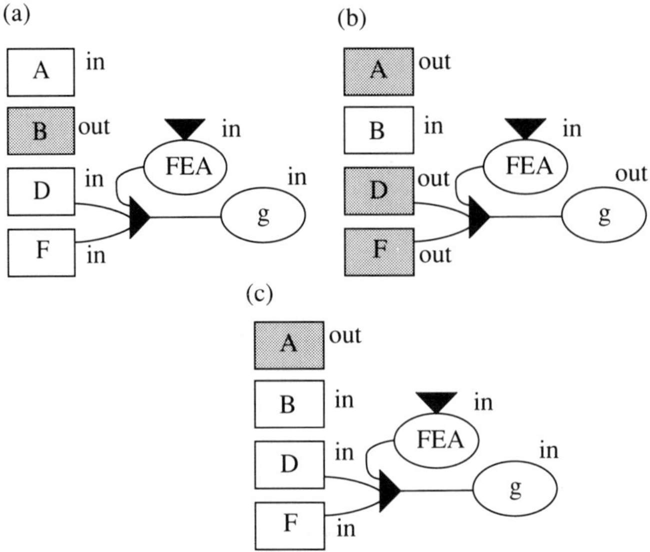

Figure 7.2 Maintaining a cache

7.6 How justifications enable default reasoning

According to the semantics of defaults, a default node should be in unless labeling it in would produce a contradiction. Although the JTMS itself is based on straightforward propositional logic, it can easily be used to implement defaults. Every assertion the inference engine wants to default should be marked as an enabled assumption. Thus all defaults are initially in. When a contradiction occurs, the inference engine should retract enough assumptions to remove all contradictions. At this point additional processing is required to ensure that the semantics of default are met. An attempt should be made to bring every default node back in. If no contradiction is introduced by bringing a default in, it should be enabled; otherwise it should be retracted.

Consider the dependency networks illustrated in Figure 7.3. Suppose A, B, and C are defaults, and the inference engine adds the justification for a contradiction node as indicated in (a). Then the inference engine retracts A to remove the contradiction and subsequent problem solving introduces a new justification for a contradiction node based on B and

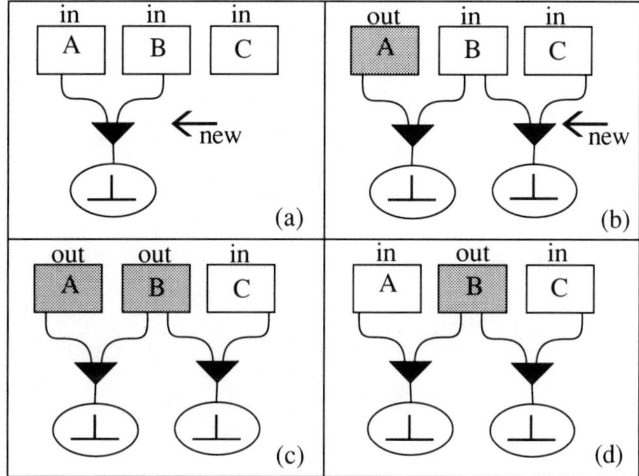

Figure 7.3 Maintaining the semantics of default

C, producing the dependency structure shown in (b). The dependency structure that results from retracting assumption *B* is shown in (c). At this point assumption *A* fails to obey the semantics of default because it can be brought in without introducing a contradiction, as shown in (d). The basic JTMS presented in the next sections includes a simple helping procedure to maintain defaults. However, this issue is discussed in far greater detail in subsequent chapters.

7.7 The JTMS interface

The preceding sections provide an elegant formulation of the JTMS, but when we get down the nuts and bolts we always find that a large number of auxiliary procedures and hooks of various kinds are needed. The inference engine needs a fairly rich interface allowing many types of queries. The following specifies the interface through which the JTMS and the inference engine communicate. After analyzing this interface we will return to a conceptual analysis of the JTMS algorithms before delving into the Common Lisp code which implements this particular interface.

assume-node	just-antecedent	retract-assumption
assumptions-of-node	just-consequence	supporting-justification-for-node
change-jtms	just-informant	tms-create-node
create-jtms	justify-node	tms-node-datum
enable-assumption	make-contradiction	tms-node-in-rules
in-node?	out-node?	tms-node-out-rules

```
(create-jtms title &key (node-string 'default-node-string)
                        (debugging nil)
                        (checking-contradictions t)
                        (contradiction-handler 'ask-user-handler)
                        (enqueue-procedure nil))
```

Any real problem solver is likely to incorporate more than one TMS, and perhaps many instances of the same JTMS. Therefore the JTMS supplies this procedure to create a new JTMS. `create-jtms` returns a datastructure which contains the entire state of the JTMS. Two subsequent calls to `create-jtms` will return two different JTMSs which do not interact in any way. Hence, it is never necessary to initialize or clear the JTMS database: Common Lisp garbage collects all the cached JTMS datastructures when the inference engine drops the pointers to them. The five keyword arguments are as follows:

`node-string` The JTMS user should provide a procedure of one argument which, when supplied a node, returns a string describing the node. The JTMS supplies the default:

```
(defun default-node-string (n)
      (format nil "~A" (tms-node-datum n)))
```

`debugging` If non-`nil`, then the JTMS traces all basic JTMS operations.

`checking-contradictions` If non-`nil`, then the JTMS signals the inference engine (we see how later) when a contradiction becomes in.

`contradiction-handler` This specifies the procedure the JTMS calls when it detects a contradiction. We discuss this in detail later.

`enqueue-procedure` This is a procedure which is called when a node becomes in. This procedure should not do any JTMS operations itself because it may be called when the JTMS database is inconsistent.

```
(change-jtms jtms &key node-string
                       debugging
                       checking-contradictions
                       contradiction-handler
                       enqueue-procedure)
```

This procedure allows the inference engine to change the initial settings provided in the original call to `create-jtms`. Don't be tempted to change these settings directly by simple `setf`s—more sophisticated JTMS implementations have to invoke more complex operations when some of these flags are changed.

```
(tms-create-node jtms datum &key assumptionp contradictoryp)
```

The inference engine creates a TMS node with this procedure call specifying the initial properties of the node to be created. The inference engine must indicate to which JTMS the node is to be added. Premises are indicated by providing the node with a justification with no antecedents using `justify-node`. A node can be in only one JTMS, and every node keeps track of the JTMS it belongs to. Hence, most subsequent JTMS procedures need not be supplied with the explicit JTMS argument. The inference engine can access and modify the node slots `tms-node-datum`, `tms-node-in-rules`, and `tms-node-out-rules` as any other defstruct slot.

```
(enable-assumption node)
(retract-assumption node)
```

If a node is created with the assumption property, then the assumption is initially retracted. These two procedures allow the inference engine to enable and retract an assumption are.

```
(make-contradiction node)
```

A node can be marked as contradictory at any time by calling this procedure.

```
(assume-node node)
```

This gives the node the assumption property and enables it.

```
(in-node? node)
(out-node? node)
```

Checks whether a node is in or out (these return `t` or `nil`).

```
(justify-node informant consequent antecedents)
```

This justifies a node.

To access the fields of a justification, the inference engine should use the procedures `just-consequence`, `just-informant`, and `just-antecedents`.

The next three procedures support the exploration of the dependency network.

```
(supporting-justification-for-node node)
```

This procedure returns one of three values, according to the belief status of the node. If the node is an enabled assumption it returns `:ENABLED-ASSUMPTION`. If the node is in, then it returns the justification currently providing support. Otherwise it returns `nil`. The well-founded explanation can be constructed by recursively calling `supporting-justification-for-node` on the antecedents of the justification returned by this procedure.

```
(assumptions-of-node node)
```

This procedure returns the set of enabled assumptions underlying the well-founded support for a node. The most common reason for exploring the well-founded explanation for a node is to identify the enabled assumptions which underlie it. This is very important for handling contradictions, where the inference engine needs to find an assumption to retract in order to remove the current inconsistency. It is crucial to note that the JTMS only finds the set of assumptions underlying the current well-founded explanation for the node. There may be an exponential number of such explanations. Therefore there may be exponentially many sets of assumptions potentially underlying the node. Consequently, a contradiction cannot always be removed by simply retracting one of its underlying assumptions—there might be another well-founded explanation for the node with a different set of underlying assumptions. To retract a contradiction requires that all of the sets of assumptions that can be used to derive it be retracted, which in turn requires an auxiliary search. (Retracting all the assumptions usually removes the contradictions, but then the problem solver is back to its initial state.)

When the JTMS detects that the current database state contains contradictions, it calls the inference engine-supplied contradiction-handling procedure with two arguments: the particular instance of the JTMS involved and the current set of contradictory nodes. The JTMS checks for contradictions as the very last thing it does. Therefore, it is acceptable (and usual) for the contradiction handler to simply do a `throw`. Also, the contradiction handler can perform any JTMS operations it likes. (If the contradiction handler does nothing, the JTMS procedure originally invoked by the inference engine just returns, leaving contradictions believed in the database.)

7.8 Simple example of JTMS usage

The following simple sequence of top-level Common Lisp procedure calls produces the dependency structure illustrated in Figure 6.9. First we must create a fresh JTMS for our example (recall that we distinguish user input by prefixing the expressions with >):

```
>   (setq *jtms* (create-jtms "Simple Example"))
```

Then we must create the initial three assumptions and enable them:

```
>     (setq assumption-a (tms-create-node *jtms* "A" :ASSUMPTIONP t)
            assumption-c (tms-create-node *jtms* "C" :ASSUMPTIONP t)
            assumption-e (tms-create-node *jtms* "E" :ASSUMPTIONP t))
>     (enable-assumption assumption-a)
>     (enable-assumption assumption-c)
>     (enable-assumption assumption-e)
```

Then we introduce the node `h` and justify it:

```
>   (setq node-h (tms-create-node *jtms* "h"))
>   (justify-node "R1" node-h (list assumption-c assumption-e))
```

Then we introduce node g, justify it, and then contradict it:

```
>  (setq node-g (tms-create-node *jtms* "g"))
>  (justify-node "R2" node-g (list assumption-a assumption-c))
>  (setq contradiction
         (tms-create-node *jtms* 'CONTRA :CONTRADICTORYP t))
>  (justify-node "R3" contradiction (list node-g))
```

This last interaction introduces a contradiction and invokes the default contradiction handler supplied with the JTMS. As the contradiction depends on A and C it asks which one of the assumptions we want to retract:

```
Contradiction found: CONTRADICTION
1 C
2 A
Call (TMS-ANSWER <number>) to retract assumption.
Break: JTMS contradiction break
```

Any real problem solver will incorporate a much more sophisticated contradiction handler. This merely serves to illustrate that the JTMS has detected the contradiction and uncovered its underlying assumptions.

7.9 The JTMS algorithms

Here are three basic designs for a JTMS which meet the specifications of Section 7.2:

- The *context* approach. The JTMS maintains an explicit set of nodes currently believed with their supporting justifications.
- The *lazy* approach. The JTMS computes the belief status of a node when it is requested by the inference engine.
- The *labeling* approach. The JTMS augments the node datastructure with two fields indicating its belief status and supporting justification.

Most JTMS implementations take the last approach. An example of the context approach is the stack-oriented context mechanism of FTRE. It has the disadvantage of potentially having to manipulate large sets of nodes. The advantage of the labeling approach over the lazy approach is less clear. The labeling approach is based on the observation of the typical patterns of interactions with inference engines. Usually the ratio of queries to assumption retractions is extremely high. If this were not the case, the lazy approach would be better because it does not have to update the belief status of every node after every change. The node datastructure field allocated to the belief status is called the node's *label*.

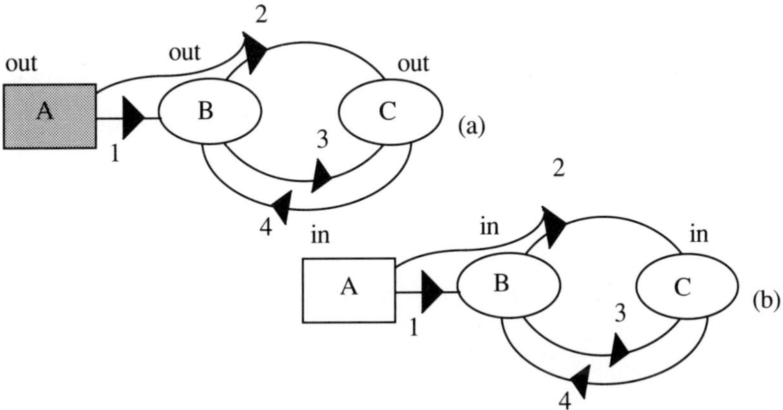

Figure 7.4 Dependency network just before and after enabling assumption A

Historically, the use of the terms in and out for node labels originates from context approaches where a node is said to be either in or out of the current context.

7.9.1 Enabling an assumption

Enabling an assumption is the simplest core JTMS operation. Note that assumptions which have become premises will not be enabled. First, the JTMS marks the assumption as enabled, removes its current supporting justification (if any), and marks it as supported by virtue of being an enabled assumption. Second, it checks whether the assumption was already in; if so, it does nothing more. Third, it looks to see whether any justification in which it appears as an antecedent is *satisfied*, i.e., that all the antecedents of the justification are labeled in. If any such justification is satisfied, it labels the consequence in and makes the justification be the supporting justification for the consequence. If any node becomes labeled in by this procedure, its consequences are recursively checked. As this algorithm only changes node labels from out to in, and as there are a finite number of nodes, it must terminate.

Suppose the inference engine has accumulated the dependency network illustrated in Figure 7.4(a).

When assumption A is enabled, node B is labeled in with the supporting justification 1. Node B appears in two justifications for C. The JTMS arbitrarily picks supporting justification 3 for node C. Notice that the justifications 2 and 4 are both satisfied but do not contribute to any well-founded support.

7.9.2 Adding a justification

When the inference engine adds a justification, the following JTMS steps are performed. First, the JTMS adds the new justification to the dependency network. Second, the JTMS checks whether the consequence of the justification is already labeled in. If so, the JTMS returns control to the inference engine. Otherwise, it checks whether the justification is satisfied. If so, then it labels the consequence in, and makes the new justification the supporting justification for the consequence. As does the assumption-enabling procedure, this continues recursively for any nodes which become in.

7.9.3 Retracting an assumption

Retracting an assumption is the most complex JTMS operation. Consider the dependency network illustrated in Figure 7.4. There is a strong temptation to write the assumption retraction algorithm as follows: If the supporting justification for a node ceases to be satisfied, then immediately look for an alternative satisfied justification. If one is found, then do not retract the node. If we apply this simple approach to Figure 7.4(b) when we retract node A, then node B will remain labeled in because the alternative justification C holds for it. This is incorrect because B is not logically derivable. Equivalently, belief in B is not well founded (in the dependency network, violations of well-foundedness show up as circularities).

The correct algorithm for retracting an assumption without creating meaningless circularities proceeds in two phases. In the first phase all nodes whose well-founded explanation contains the retracted assumption are labeled out. This is done by looking at all the supporting justifications in which the retracted assumption appears, labeling those nodes out, and continuing recursively. Only when this first phase is complete is every node that was labeled out in the first phase analyzed to see if an alternative support can be found for it. If an alternative support is found, then its consequences are checked to see if they can be brought in as well, exactly as in the assumption enabling and justification-addition algorithms.

7.10 JTMS code

The code in `jtms.lisp` is a simple justification-based truth maintenance system. In reading the code you will notice a few additional hooks to allow systems like TRE to interface with it. Otherwise the algorithms are precisely as presented so far. The end of the file `jtms.lisp` contains some auxiliary procedures to allow the JTMS to be used by itself.

This JTMS makes certain assumptions about its processing environment. JTMS operations cannot be safely aborted, nor can one JTMS operation be safely invoked before another is finished (except as specified in the interface), nor can multiple processes safely access the same JTMS simultaneously. A truly bulletproof JTMS would use `unwind-protects` and proper process locking primitives. But these are concerns beyond our scope.

7.10.1 Overview

In building a problem solver there is always the temptation to directly invoke internal TMS procedures not specified in the interface (Section 7.7). To an extent this is unavoidable, but you should be warned that: (1) the internal procedures may not do what you think they do, and (2) the JTMS implementor is only obligated to maintain the interface, not the internal procedures. So, for example, if we design an entirely new JTMS, say on the Connection Machine, then most of the internal procedures disappear.

The program is divided into 7 parts:

1. *Definitions.* The datastructures, and initialization procedures.
2. *Basic interface.* Interfaces for programs that use the JTMS.
3. *Adding justifications.* Computing the results of adding a new justification or ground support.
4. *Retraction.* Making sure all the consequences of a retracted assumption are removed, and looking for alternative support for such nodes.

5. *Contradiction-handling interface.* For signaling contradictions to the inference engine.
6. *Well-founded support.* Procedures for inquiring about the well-founded support of nodes and their underlying assumptions.
7. *Inference engine stub.* Some basic procedures which allow the JTMS to be used alone. Any serious problem solver will replace all these, or encapsulate them within more sophisticated procedures.

7.10.2 Definitions

To make it possible for multiple JTMS instances to be used within a single problem solver, the JTMS algorithms do not use any global variables. Instead a single top-level datastructure `jtms` describes all the important variables of an instance of the JTMS. It contains the following fields:

`title` Ignored by the JTMS but useful for debugging.

`node-counter` Provides a "unique name" for nodes. This is a common trick for making defstructs that print compactly, yet are still distinguishable.

`just-counter` Provides a "unique name" for justifications. Another advantage of this technique is that it provides a simple ordering predicate when needed.

`nodes` List of all nodes created. Used only for debugging. Useful for printing out the state of the JTMS database.

`justs` List of all justifications. Combined with the unique integer id, this list provides a handy way to access datastructures during debugging that otherwise might be difficult.

`debugging` A debugging flag to trace the internals of JTMS operation.

`contradictions` A list of nodes which have been declared contradictory. When such a node becomes in, a contradiction will be signaled.

`assumptions` A list of nodes which have been declared assumptions.

`checking-contradictions` This flag defaults to `t`. It allows advanced programs to turn off contradiction checking temporarily.

`node-string` An inference engine-supplied procedure which should return a descriptive string for a node. The JTMS supplies a default.

`contradiction-handler` An inference engine-supplied procedure which is called on two arguments: the set of contradictions currently in, and the current JTMS. The file `jtms.lisp` supplies a default contradiction handler for stand-alone operation. Any real problem solver should supply a better one.

`enqueue-procedure` An inference engine-supplied procedure which should be called if some node with in-rules becomes in. Its use is explained later in the TRE interface.

Two defstructs are introduced to implement TMS nodes and justifications. The fields of the `tms-node` defstruct have the following interpretation:

`index` Integer serving as unique name for this node.

`datum` Supplied by the inference engine. For simple demonstration systems one should put something printable in here. For TRE-like system, a pointer to the assertion object goes here, as we will see later.

`label` Represents current belief status of the node. `:IN` indicates the node is believed, and `:OUT` indicates that the node is not believed. Any other value indicates a bug.

`support` This field is `nil` if the node is labeled `:OUT`. If the node is derived, then it contains the justification currently providing support. If the node is an enabled assumption, this field contains the symbol `:ENABLED-ASSUMPTION`.

`justifications` The set of justifications that could provide support for this node.

`consequences` The justifications that use this node as an antecedent.

`mark` Holds a marker for the sweep algorithm used in finding the assumptions underlying a node.

`contradictory?` If non-`nil`, this field indicates that belief in this node represents a contradiction. These nodes are handled specially in the JTMS.

`assumption?` If non-`nil`, this field indicates that this node should be treated as an assumption whose belief can be explicitly enabled and retracted by the inference engine. If the value is `:DEFAULT`, the auxiliary procedure `enable-defaults` maintains the semantics of default for such nodes.

`in-rules` Rules which should be run when the node is believed. If this JTMS is being used without an external system, this field should be `nil`. The JTMS enqueue procedure is called on each element of this field if it is non-`nil`. This queue is then cleared.

`out-rules` Like `in-rules`, but these rules are queued when the node is disbelieved.

`jtms` The JTMS instance to which this node belongs.

The `just` defstruct encodes justifications. The fields are:

`index` Integer for unique name.

`informant` An inference engine-supplied description of the justification. This is usually only supplied for generating explanations; however, some problem solvers which explicitly reason about justifications can cache whatever information they want here. While this information is preserved within the JTMS, it is not used by any of the algorithms.

`consequence` The node which this justification can support.

`antecedents` The nodes which must be believed in order for this justification to provide support for its consequence.

`node-string`, `debugging-jtms`, and `tms-error` are three very simple utilities for printing out explanations and unusual conditions, and are used throughout the JTMS code. The procedure `default-node-string` is the default procedure to construct a string describing a node. Usually the inference engine will override this default and supply a procedure that will make a printable version of whatever is found in the `datum` field of the node.

The procedure `create-jtms` creates a new JTMS instance. It initializes all the necessary states of the JTMS. It permits a number of keyword arguments for initializing many of the fields of the JTMS datastructure. The procedure `change-jtms` allows the caller to change the externally settable fields of the JTMS.

7.10.3 Basic JTMS interface procedures

The procedures `in-node?` and `out-node?` are used to query the state of a node. The procedure `tms-create-node` creates a JTMS node. The caller must specify to which JTMS instance this node belongs. The procedure takes keyword arguments to specify whether the node is a contradiction or an assumption. If the node is an assumption, then it is initially retracted. The value of `:ASSUMPTIONP` can be the keyword `:DEFAULT`, which has no effect on the core JTMS algorithms (i.e., the node is treated as any other assumption). By using the auxiliary procedure `default-assumptions`, the inference engine can force all such nodes to be treated as defaults.

The procedure `assume-node` converts a non-assumption node to an assumption node and then enables it.

The procedure `make-contradiction` converts a non-contradiction node to a contradiction node. It adds the node to the contradiction list for the JTMS, which is always checked at the conclusion of any operation that might cause new contradictions. As `make-contradiction` can be called on a node that may already have justifications, this may provoke a contradiction.

The procedure `justify-node` adds a justification to a node. If the node is out but the justification is satisfied, it initiates the labeling algorithm and finally checks whether any contradictions have come in. Notice that calling `justify-node` twice with the same arguments will result in the creation of distinct datastructures that represent the same justification. No errors will result, but duplicate justifications decrease efficiency. While it is straightforward to look for an existing justification that would make a new one redundant, well-designed problem solvers will prevent this from happening anyway. Consequently, it is rare to find such tests in TMS implementations.

The canonical sequence of internal events when belief in a new fact is established is:

1. Make this particular node be believed (`make-node-in`).
2. Compute what other nodes must be believed as a consequence of believing this node (`propagate-inness`).
3. See if any contradictions result (`check-for-contradictions`).

For `justify-node` these first two steps are accomplished in the procedure `install-support`. A justification of no antecedents is indicative of a premise. Therefore, if the JTMS is provided a premise justification, this justification becomes the consequence's current support. Once a node is a premise it always remains a premise. Thus one can always tell whether a node is a premise by checking whether its support is a justification with no antecedents. If an assumption becomes a premise, then it can no longer be enabled.

7.10.4 Adding justifications

The code in this subsection figures out whether or not a justification can supply support, and computes the consequences of new support from whatever source.

The procedure `check-justification` returns non-`nil` when the given justification can supply new support for its consequent node. This occurs exactly when the node is not already known and the justification is satisfied.

The procedure `justification-satisfied?` checks whether a justification is satisfied. A justification is satisfied when all of its antecedent nodes are `:IN`.

The next few procedures figure out what other nodes are believed as a consequence of new beliefs.

The procedure `install-support` makes a particular node `:IN`, and calls `propagate-inness` to determine the consequences.

The procedure `propagate-inness` works by checking the justifications that use the newly believed node, checking each to see if they can lend new support. When they can, these new nodes are queued for subsequent processing. Notice that `check-justification` will only return non-`nil` when a node is out, and this procedure can only make nodes `:IN`.

The actual bookkeeping required for making a node believed is carried out by `make-node-in`. The label of the node is changed to `:IN`, the justification or `:ENABLED-ASSUMPTION` marker is installed as the support, and the enqueue procedure is called on anything in the `in-rules` field of the node. Notice that the enqueue procedure should not do any JTMS operations, since it is called in the middle of JTMS processing. In most problem solvers the enqueue procedure just queues the node for future processing when the JTMS operation finishes. Importantly, the list of rules is cleared out once these rules have been queued. Since justifications serve as a cache for the results of running a rule, one rarely wants to run a rule twice.

7.10.5 Assumption manipulation

Retraction is the inverse of supporting a node. The basic sequence of operations is similar:

1. Make the particular node to be disbelieved (i.e., :OUT) (make-node-out).
2. Forget all nodes that depend on this particular node (propagate-outness).
3. Attempt to find alternative support for nodes which have been retracted (find-alternative-support).

The process for clearing the status of a particular node (make-node-out) is parallel to make-node-in. propagate-outness works by recursively retracting all justifications which relied on the given node. The search starts with the justifications that mention the node being forgotten as antecedents. Each justification in the queue is tested to see if it was the source of support for its own consequence. If it was, then that node in turn is labeled :OUT and each justification that uses it as an antecedent is queued for examination.

As each node is forgotten it is placed on the out-queue. The procedure find-alternative-support attempts to find alternative support for everything on this queue. Each justification for a particular node (the contents of the node's justifications field) is tested to see if it can supply support. If so, install-support is used to provide that new support. Recall that this new support can propagate, and so some nodes on the out-queue may have received alternative support before being examined by find-alternative-support. That is why in-node? is used to filter queue entries.

The procedure enable-assumption overrides whatever support the node currently has (if the node is a premise, enabling the assumption has no effect). The current supporting justification of the node becomes :ENABLED-ASSUMPTION. Otherwise, the procedure is very similar to that of justify-node.

7.10.6 Contradiction processing

JTMS contradiction processing is affected by two fields of the JTMS datastructure (contradiction-handler and checking-contradictions) which are initially set by the procedure `create-jtms` and can later be changed by `change-jtms`. At the conclusion of every JTMS operation that can cause new contradictions, the JTMS invokes the procedure `check-for-contradictions`. If contradiction checking is not enabled, `check-for-contradictions` returns immediately. Otherwise, `check-for-contradictions` finds all the contradictions currently in and calls the inference engine-supplied contradiction handler with this set.

For some types of problem solvers it is necessary to temporarily disable contradiction checking and change the way contradictions are handled. Doing so is always dangerous, and so great care must be taken. To facilitate such operations the JTMS supplies three macros. The macro `without-contradiction-check` turns off contradiction checking completely within its body. Analogously, the macro `with-contradiction-check` turns on contradiction checking within its body. The macro `with-contradiction-handler` temporarily changes the contradiction handler within its body. The style of these macros may be unfamiliar. First, new uninterned variable names are created to distinguish them from variables that might occur freely (such as in `body`). Second, when the body finishes execution, normally or abnormally, the `unwind-protect` clause guarantees that the contradiction-handler procedure and contradiction-checking flag will be returned to their original state.

The procedure `default-assumptions` is a simple auxiliary procedure which achieves the semantics of default. It should be called by the inference engine (usually right after contradiction handling). It uses the macros just defined to bring in all defaults unless they introduce a contradiction.

7.10.7 Inquiring about well-founded support

The two procedures `supporting-justification-for-node` and `assumptions-of-node` allow the inference engine to explore the well-founded explanations for nodes.

The procedure `supporting-justification-for-node` returns the supporting justification for a node if there is one. The procedure `assumptions-of-node` finds the enabled assumptions of the current well-founded explanation for the node. It operates by searching backward through the antecedents of justifications until enabled assumptions are found. Consider the directed acyclic graph of justifications involved in supporting a particular conclusion. The root is the node being supported, and the leaves are the enabled assumptions and premises. A single node may be reached through more than one path. Thus a marker is used to record what parts of the graph have been visited already. This marker allows the search to avoid examining any part of the graph more than once.[1]

The procedure `enabled-assumptions` returns a list of all the enabled assumptions.

7.10.8 Procedures for stand-alone operation

The remaining set of procedures in `jtms.lisp` allows the JTMS to be used in a stand-alone mode without any inference engine. Any serious inference engine will include much more sophisticated, task-specific versions of these procedures for debugging.

The interrogatives are straightforward: `why-node` shows the status and source of support for a node, and `why-nodes` uses `why-node` to show the state of the entire JTMS database. `why-nodes` is useful for debugging small examples, but typically will not be used in more complex systems. `why-node` itself, however, is designed for use with external systems.

The final procedures in `jtms.lisp` provide an extremely simple-minded contradiction handler. The procedure `ask-user-handler` calls `handle-one-contradiction` to remove the first contradiction (remember that one assumption retraction may remove all contradictions) and then calls `check-for-contradictions` again.

The procedure `handle-one-contradiction` finds the enabled assumptions underlying the well-founded explanation for the contradiction, prints them out, and allows the user to type at Common Lisp. If there are no enabled assumptions underlying the contradiction, an error is reported. Once the user has decided which assumption to retract, the procedure `tms-answer` returns control to the JTMS. Finally, the procedure `explore-network` is a higher-level interface to the preceding procedures for exploring the dependency network.

---

1. Since list structures are unique, and the markers are checked by `eq`, no unmarking is required.

7.11 Exercises

1. ⋆ One might argue that the final case in `enable-assumption` is a mistake, on the grounds that a node that already has a supporting justification is more solid than something that is merely assumed. What is wrong with this argument?

2. ⋆⋆ If a node receives a justification with no antecedents, then that justification is made its supporting justification. Thus, it is easy to tell which nodes are premises. However, some nodes hold universally but are not premises (e.g., a node with a justification whose only antecedents are premises). It can be very useful to propagate "premise-hood" giving premise justifications to all nodes that hold universally. In search tasks this saves useless backtracks because there never will be assumptions supporting a universally held node. Modify the JTMS such that every node that holds universally receives a premise justification. What do we lose in this scheme?

3. ⋆⋆ In analogy to the previous exercise we can also propagate "contradiction-hood." For example, if a contradiction has a justification all but one of whose nodes is universally held, then the remaining node can be marked as a contradiction as well. Modify the JTMS to propagate contradictions. Notice that this feature is of marginal utility in our JTMS, as the presence of contradictions merely indicates that the inference engine should be signaled.

4. ⋆⋆ The JTMS procedure `assumptions-of-node` returns the enabled assumptions underlying the current well-founded support of the node. However, there might be an alternative well-founded support which doesn't include all the assumptions returned by `assumptions-of-node`.

   a. Show a sequence of JTMS calls which demonstrates this phenomenon.

   b. Write a procedure `minimal-assumptions-of-node` which returns a subset of the assumptions returned by the original call to `assumptions-of-node` which still supports the node, but which contains no proper subset which supports the node. Hint: Try to retract the assumptions returned by `assumptions-of-node` and see whether the node remains in.

c. Provide an example where there is more than one such smallest subset.

d. In what kinds of cases would it be useful for the inference engine to use `minimal-assumptions-of-node` instead `assumptions-of-node`?

5. ⋆⋆ When there are a large number of justifications, the cost of repeatedly checking whether a justification is satisfied becomes excessive. Modify our JTMS to keep a count with each justification indicating the number of antecedent nodes which are in. When the count becomes zero, the consequent node is supported. Be careful to avoid circularities.

6. ⋆⋆ Consider a backtracking search problem which is controlled by enabling and retracting assumptions. Our JTMS prevents useless inference engine work in contexts known to be inconsistent (Section 6.1.3). However, an analogous problem arises within the JTMS itself—the contradiction may be discovered after substantial relabeling work. Therefore it can be useful to expand the JTMS by explicitly recording every set of assumptions that is known to support a contradiction (such a set is called a *nogood* in later chapters). Then, whenever any assumption is enabled, before doing any relabeling, the new assumption set is immediately checked to see if it contains any known nogood; and if so, the relabeling is aborted and a contradiction is reported to the inference engine. Modify the JTMS to accomplish this. Explain why the implementation that just installs a contradictory justification for every contradicting set assumptions accomplishes very little.

7. ⋆⋆ Design a JTMS algorithm which records with each justification *one* node that is preventing it from becoming a supporting justification and with each node, the justifications it has blocked. Explain under what circumstances this implementation is more efficient.

8. ⋆⋆⋆ Design a justification-based TMS which, instead of propagating in and out labels through the network, records a derivation count

with each justification which is the maximum number of justifications between it and an assumption or premise (infinity, if the justification doesn't hold) and stores with each node the minimum derivation depth of the justifications that support it. Explain how you handle retraction with circularities present. What other uses can you think of for this derivation depth count?

8 Putting the JTMS to Work

We have seen that the justification-based truth maintenance system can provide valuable problem-solving services. But how should we organize our systems to best exploit this resource? This chapter examines the issues involved in linking a TMS to an inference engine. We illustrate the general issues in the inference engine/TMS interface discussed in the previous chapter via JTRE, a version of the Tiny Rule Engine that incorporates the JTMS. Section 8.1 begins by outlining the issues involved in interfacing the FTRE inference engine to the JTMS. Section 8.2 describes the design of JTRE and how it addresses these issues. Section 8.3 goes over the code, showing how FTRE was changed to produce JTRE. The rest of the chapter illustrates how the JTMS enables us to build better problem solvers. Section 8.4 explores *dependency-directed search*, using the simple N-queens puzzle as an illustration. Section 8.5 shows how JTRE can be used to partially reconstruct SAINT, a classic AI program which first demonstrated that indefinite integration could be done via computer. SAINT was capable of solving most of the integration problems on a calculus final examination used at MIT. Our reconstruction will not be nearly so powerful. However, we include capabilities not found in Slagle's original program: Our version, JSAINT, is organized around the JTMS, which it uses to record both control and data dependencies. This allows JSAINT to explain its answers and operations. JSAINT provides a substantial example of problem-solver design.

8.1 Interfacing a JTMS to an inference engine: Issues

In Chapter 6 we introduced a view of problem-solver architecture where a problem solver consists of a combination of a truth maintenance system and an inference engine. Typically a TMS is viewed as a module used by the inference engine, rather than the other way around. This perspective suggests asking what services the TMS provides and figuring out how the inference engine can properly use them. In Chapter 6 we saw that the five basic actions of a TMS are:

1. Upon request, the TMS creates a node with the specified properties.
2. The TMS accepts records of inference engine deductions (as justifications).
3. The TMS computes the correct labels for nodes and supplies them on request.
4. When a contradiction is detected, the inference engine is signaled.

In addition to these four basic actions, there is yet one more:

5. The TMS accepts rules from the inference engine to be scheduled for execution when particular belief conditions are met.

This is an appropriate division of labor because the TMS is responsible for managing beliefs (i.e., updating the labels of the nodes in the dependency network).

Each of these TMS actions imposes constraints on the inference engine. Understanding these constraints is the first step in understanding the design of JTRE. The first action, creating nodes on request, suggests:

1. The inference engine must inform the TMS when a new node is needed, and ensure the appropriate connection is made between the new node and the assertion it corresponds to.
2. The inference engine must be able to retrieve the TMS node associated with any assertion.
3. The inference engine must provide an interface for marking assertions as premises or assumptions, and for enabling and retracting assumptions.

The second TMS action suggests:

4. The inference engine must provide facilities for representing justifications.

The third TMS action suggests:

5. The inference engine must provide facilities for inspecting node labels.

The fourth TMS action suggests:

6. The inference engine must provide a method for handling contradictions.

The fifth TMS action suggests:

7. The inference engine must provide facilities for including constraints on beliefs in the conditions for triggering rules.
8. The inference engine must ensure that rules are executed only when both the belief constraints and the syntactic matching constraints are satisfied.

Any inference engine that uses a TMS effectively must satisfy these eight constraints. There are a variety of designs that will work, depending on the particulars of the TMS and the inference engine. The next section explores one region of this design space by considering how to modify the FTRE inference engine of Chapter 5 by hooking up the JTMS of Chapter 7 to create a new system, JTRE.

8.2 The design of JTRE

Adding a TMS to an inference engine requires substantial changes in the inference engine's structures and operations. We can divide these changes into five categories:

1. Providing a mapping between inference engine structures and TMS structures (constraints 1 and 2).
2. Facilities for changing the system's beliefs and expressing dependency relationships (constraints 3 and 4).

3. Facilities for inspecting the system's beliefs (constraint 5).
4. Facilities for contradiction handling (constraint 6).
5. Methods for tying the execution of rules to belief states (constraints 7 and 8).

We examine each category in turn.

8.2.1 Mapping assertions to TMS nodes

In FTRE, an assertion is believed exactly when that assertion can be found in the database. The TMS now has the responsibility of representing belief states and tracking changes in them. Consequently, the appearance of an assertion A in the database only indicates that A was mentioned sometime in a previous computation. To establish whether or not an assertion is believed requires examining the label of the TMS node associated with it. To be effective, TMS nodes must have indefinite temporal extent, since the dependency network they participate in provides a cache for inference engine operations. Consequently, assertions should also have indefinite extent.

We must therefore distinguish the act of *mentioning* an assertion from the act of *believing* it. Mentioning an assertion causes it to be installed in the database and associated with a unique TMS node. Once mentioned, an assertion is never removed from the database. The inference engine's belief in that assertion may change, naturally. Finding the current belief status of an assertion requires querying the TMS node associated with it.

In FTRE the internal form of an assertion was simply the corresponding Lisp expression. In JTRE we want to associate more properties with an assertion, such as its TMS node and whether or not it corresponds to an enabled assumption. Consequently, we introduce a `datum` struct to serve as the internal representation of assertions. The mapping between TMS nodes and assertions can easily be implemented by having each TMS node point to its corresponding datum, and each datum in turn points back to its TMS node. To make the connection between a datum and its Lisp form we (a) store the Lisp expression as a property of the datum and (b) provide a table which associates Lisp forms with their datum. This design provides us with the ability to move from any perspective on an assertion (datum, Lisp expression, TMS node) to any other.

One implication of this decision is that we can no longer use the context mechanism of FTRE. The context mechanism operated by creating temporary databases in which assumptions could be made and conclusions drawn, such that all results were thrown away when it finished with that context. Since the TMS promotes efficiency by caching justifications, throwing away assertions would greatly reduce the value of a TMS. To reason by manipulating assumptions, we must use some mechanism that keeps track of what assumptions need to be made and "swaps" them in and out of the JTMS to figure out their consequences. A simple version is illustrated in Section 8.4.

8.2.2 Queries concerning belief states

In TRE and FTRE we could find out whether or not an assertion was believed by seeing if it was contained in the database. Since we have made the TMS the arbiter of beliefs and given assertions indefinite temporal extent, we must now look to the TMS for belief information. The simplest design is to provide procedures which, given an assertion, fetch the corresponding TMS node and check its label to return an answer. If an assertion is believed, we can also use the TMS node to look up its source of support, and trace backward to the underlying assumptions. There are procedures to support each of these operations in the JTMS, so all we have to do in JTRE is provide procedures which translate from assertions to TMS nodes and call the underlying JTMS primitives.

In addition to looking at information about current beliefs, problem solvers sometimes need to examine the structure of the dependency network itself. For instance, in figuring out how a particular assertion could be argued for, inspecting the justifications that could support it provides valuable information about what other assertions might be useful to assume. The same principle can be used for these queries as well: the JTRE-level code translates the assertions into TMS nodes, which are then passed to the appropriate JTMS procedure. If necessary, the TMS nodes returned from calls to the JTMS can be translated back to assertions using the `datum/tms-node` mapping described above.

8.2.3 Premises and assumptions

Recall that there are three ways to directly change the status of a TMS node: it can be made a premise, it can be assumed, or an assumed node may be retracted. Since the mapping between assertions and TMS nodes is one-to-one, we can apply the same distinctions to assertions. That is, we can speak of assertions being made premises, or being assumed, or being retracted, when those operations are performed on their corresponding TMS nodes.

8.2.4 Justifying assertions in terms of others

Clearly JTRE must provide a means of installing justifications in the JTMS. As before, whatever procedures we define for this task must translate the assertions they are given (i.e., the consequent and the list of antecedents) into TMS nodes and then call `justify-node` to do the TMS-level work.

Recall that justifications and premises are permanent additions to the TMS. Using the same interface procedure to do both jobs helps remind users of this fact. Furthermore, it simplifies the implementation, since the JTMS implements premises as nodes whose support is a justification without antecedents.

8.2.5 Tying rule execution to belief states

In FTRE, rules were executed when assertions matching their trigger pattern(s) appeared in the database. (An assertion that matches a rule's trigger patterns is called an *antecedent* of an instance of that rule.) The distinction between mentioning an assertion and believing it gives us a new set of events which can be used as conditions for triggering rules. In JTRE there are three events that can happen to an assertion:

1. The assertion appears in the database. This happens exactly once.
2. The assertion becomes believed (i.e., its TMS node gets the label `:IN`).
3. The assertion is retracted (i.e., its TMS node gets the label `:OUT`).

JTRE provides the corresponding three *belief conditions* on rule triggers:

`:INTERN` The rule should be executed for each assertion matching ⟨*pattern*⟩, independent of its belief state. (So named because it is analogous to the `intern` procedure of Common Lisp.)

`:IN` ⟨*pattern*⟩ should be believed before the rule is executed.

`:OUT` ⟨*pattern*⟩ should not be believed for the rule to be executed.

There are circumstances in which each of these trigger conditions is useful. The `:INTERN` condition will cause the rule to be executed as soon as a matching assertion is mentioned. This is useful for installing background constraints. For instance, if the assertions $X = 5$ and $X = 10$ are mentioned, many problem solvers immediately install a justification for a contradiction node, to ensure that inconsistent beliefs are detected quickly. The `:IN` condition corresponds to the antecedent being believed. This means we won't execute the rule on assertions that are mentioned but are currently out. This condition is useful if executing the rule could set into motion a substantial amount of work, or if it seems unlikely that the assertion will ever be believed. The `:OUT` condition is probably the least useful (and least used). One of the few uses of `:OUT` rules is to initiate attempts to justify particularly important kinds of facts when they are mentioned but not yet believed.

Efficiently linking the triggering of rules in the inference engine to changes in the labels of TMS nodes is a crucial job of the TMS/inference engine interface. Conceptually there are two ways this can be accomplished. First, the queuing system in the inference engine could probe the TMS for each rule instantiation, and only execute the rule when the appropriate belief conditions are met. This has the disadvantage of placing the burden of monitoring on the inference engine. The second strategy is to pass rule instantiations into the TMS and allow it to schedule their execution. We call rule instantiations which have been passed into the TMS *consumers*. This strategy is simpler because consumers can be stored with the TMS nodes corresponding to the rule antecedents. Thus the algorithms which incrementally update the TMS's belief state (i.e., `make-node-in`, `make-node-out` in our JTMS implementation) can queue consumers up as part of their normal operations. This consumer strategy is very common, and is what we shall use in JTRE.

Most rules have more than one trigger. The interpretation of multiple triggers in FTRE was conjunctive, that is, all antecedents had to be believed before the rule would execute. There is a subtle distinction lurking here, however. Do we demand that the conjuncts all be believed at some point in time, or must they all be believed at the same time before the rule is executed? The former definition is easier to implement, because it requires only tests on individual antecedents, but has the drawback that it might execute a rule on a combination of assertions that actually are not simultaneously believed. The latter definition more accurately captures the intuition of conjunctive triggers, but requires a slightly more sophisticated implementation. We choose the simpler specification for JTRE, and leave implementing the more sophisticated specification for Exercise 3.

Now that we have specified the belief conditions that may be placed on triggers and what conjunctive triggers mean, we need to choose a syntax for expressing them. There are several alternatives we might use. For instance, we can simply add more information to each trigger. Instead of a trigger being a pattern, we might change the syntax of triggers to be:

(⟨*condition*⟩ ⟨*pattern*⟩ ⟨*options*⟩)

where ⟨*pattern*⟩ is simply the trigger pattern, as before, ⟨*condition*⟩ is one of `:INTERN`, `:IN`, or `:OUT`, and ⟨*options*⟩ are the `:VAR` and `:TEST` keywords described in Chapter 5. Another alternative is to restrict the triggers to a single condition, and make the condition part of the syntax of the rule outside the triggers. Thus we might replace the syntax of FTRE rules by

(`rule` ⟨*condition*⟩ ⟨*triggers*⟩ . ⟨*body*⟩)

where ⟨*condition*⟩ is the same as before, and ⟨*triggers*⟩ and ⟨*body*⟩ have the same definition as in FTRE. Each syntax has identical power, since a rule with multiple belief conditions can be expressed by nesting several rules in the "condition outside" syntax. The distinctions are more a matter of taste, so we use we use the "condition inside" syntax for JTRE and will use the "condition outside" syntax in Chapter 14.

It is extremely important to notice that we cannot use `:TEST` in quite the same way as we did in FTRE. In FTRE a common use of `:TEST` was to skip executing rules whose conclusions were currently known, by using `fetch` as part of a `:TEST` option. This worked because the same fact could be asserted over and over again in different contexts. This is not the case when a truth mainenance system is used, so using `:TEST` in this way is a terrible mistake. Remember that each rule is tested against each assertion exactly once. If the `:TEST` form rejects the match, that particular rule-assertion combination will never be tested again. This means that `:TEST` is safe only when the form is limited to examining the structure of the assertions themselves, using the pattern variables already bound in its lexical environment. It must not examine the state of the database in any other way. It must not use any global variables, and it must not examine the state of the TMS. Tests involving only structure will always return the same result because the structure of each assertion is fixed for all time. Deciding to reject a match based on some factor that can change over time is disastrous because there is no way to reconsider a rule-assertion combination when that external factor changes.

The nastiness of the bugs that can occur when `:TEST` is abused is one reason that some creators of problem-solving languages carefully restrict what can be put into them. A common strategy in constraint logic programming, for instance, is to define a sublanguage which is sufficiently restrictive to prevent such bugs. Such restrictions have other advantages, such as allowing the problem solver to be more easily implemented in a primitive host language (i.e., `ART-IM`'s use of C as a substrate) or providing leverage for correctness proofs or automatic reordering of rule triggers for efficiency. However, we opt here for simplicity (but see Exercise 1).

Now that we have pinned down the syntax of rules and the semantics of belief conditions on triggers, let us examine how they should be executed. Recall that we have extended the semantics of trigger conditions so that we can specify conditions on the beliefs of their triggers that must be satisfied before they are executed. In the discussion that follows, we assume single-trigger rules, since we have defined the semantics of triggers so that each trigger can be considered independently. Recall that the sequence of operations that occurred in FTRE when a rule or assertion is added was:

1. A rule's matcher is executed on an assertion to see if the assertion fits the trigger.
2. If the assertion doesn't fit, nothing happens. If the assertion fits, the rule's body procedure is queued along with the values of the variables it needs.

3. When the queue is serviced next, the rule is executed by applying the body procedure to the arguments queued with it.

While this sequence of operations is not implemented by any single procedure, it correctly describes what the system is doing.

This sequence of operations must be changed to take the belief conditions of triggers into account. The first thing to notice is that if all rule triggers used the `:INTERN` condition, the same sequence of operations would be appropriate. So if we can modify this sequence to take the testing of other trigger conditions into account we will have an appropriate design. Let us consider the trade-offs in modifying each of these steps in turn.

We could modify the first step in the execution sequence by changing matchers to first test for the assertion's belief condition and to carry out the pattern-matching test only if the belief condition is appropriate. This isn't a very good idea. An assertion's pattern is permanent, but unless it is a premise or a contradiction, the system's belief in it need not be. Thus if we put the belief test first we would have to go back and retest assertions that failed to match whenever their belief state changed. It is better to filter based on the assertion's structure, because an assertion that does not currently match the trigger will never do so, and that rule-assertion pair can be forever ignored.

What about modifying the second step? That is, once the assertion has been determined to match and the variables bound by the match are computed, check to see if the assertion's TMS label matches the condition. If it does, then queue the rule for execution. Otherwise, stash the body-pattern variables pair on the `in-rules` or `out-rules` of the TMS node corresponding to the assertion. Then, if we set up the TMS's queuing procedure correctly, when the node's label changes appropriately the rule would be queued for execution. This is a much better design. It still has one drawback: the label of the triggering assertion could change while the rule is waiting on the queue. Do we want to execute the rule anyway in that case? It could be argued in either direction, but we will presume that we want to delay execution in such cases until the triggering assertion again satisfies its belief condition. (The reason we prefer this choice is that many assertions can be believed once but are quickly found to be inconsistent. Building any justifications involving such assertions as antecedents adds irrelevant but permanent structures to the

TMS.) Restricting execution to environments where the trigger's belief conditions are currently met requires that we arrange to test those conditions again when the rule is executed. That, in turn, is equivalent to modifying the third step of our original sequence. Since modifying the third step of the original sequence suffices by itself to achieve our purposes (as we will show below), we rule out modifying the second step.

Since we have settled on modifying the third step, let us think about how to do it. Essentially, we can make the body procedure a bit smarter. If one of its arguments is the TMS node corresponding to the triggering assertion, we can write into the body procedure a test to ensure that this node satisfies the belief condition. If the condition is satisfied, the original body is then executed. If it is not satisfied, then the body procedure and its current arguments can be stored in the `in-rules` or `out-rules` of the input TMS node as appropriate. Again, assuming we have set up the TMS's queuing procedure correctly, a change in belief state will cause the reconsideration of the assertion-rule pair.

Let's step back and examine whether or not we are satisfied with our design for the rule system. Consider, for instance, the following rule:

```
(rule ((:IN (Foo ?x) :VAR ?f1)
       (:IN (Bar ?y) :VAR ?f2))
  (rassert! (Foo-Bar ?x ?y)
            (:RANDOM-COMBO ?f1 ?f2)))
```

Suppose we assume `(Foo a)` and then `(Bar b)`. When `(Foo a)` is installed in the database, the outer rule will be triggered and a consumer will be installed on the node for `(Foo a)`. Since that fact is believed, the rule will be executed, thus spawning a rule which looks for instances of `(Bar ?y)`. When `(Bar b)` is assumed, this newly spawned rule will be triggered. It in turn will justify `(Foo-Bar a b)` on the basis of these two facts. Notice that if we merely mention `(Bar b)` (by using `referent`, defined in Section 8.3.2) the consumer will trigger, but instead of executing the original rule body it will requeue itself to wait for `(Bar b)` to become in. If `(Bar b)` is ever believed, either as an assumption or because of some other justification, the consumer will execute the original rule body and our conclusion will be drawn.

So far, so good. But is it? What happens if `(Foo a)` is retracted between the time `(Bar b)` is mentioned and believed? As written, the code will execute, installing the assertion corresponding to the conclusion in the TMS. This conclusion will not be believed, of course, until both antecedents are. But if we never believe (Foo a) again, then we have created a useless node and justification. This is especially true if it happens that (Foo a) and (Bar b) are, due to the structure of the dependency network, contradictory.

Our intuition in writing this rule was very likely that both triggers should be believed *simultaneously* before the rule is executed. That is not, however, what we settled on in our specification or our design. Instead we demanded only that each trigger's belief conditions must be satisfied in order to execute that rule's body. We knew abstractly that the sort of problem just raised could happen, but seeing a concrete example of such a potential inefficiency might cause us to think twice. To keep things simple we stick with this design, because if all justifications are correctly written this implementation will never lead to incorrect beliefs. The only drawback with our current design is that the dependency network may, in the worst case, be festooned with useless nodes and justifications. Whether or not this drawback is serious depends on the particular problem solver. We have found that in most situations it does not matter, and our simple design suffices. Ensuring simultaneous satisfaction of belief conditions is not much more complicated if that proves desirable (see Exercise 3).

8.2.6 Handling contradictions

JTRE requires two capabilities to process contradictions effectively. The first is a method of declaring particular nodes to be contradictory. Inconsistencies can then be recorded by justifications of contradiction nodes. The second capability is rebinding the TMS's contradiction handler. Each task that makes assumptions carries with it the responsibility for processing contradictions, so rebinding the contradiction handler allows JTRE to install the appropriate task-specific procedure. Fortunately, these capabilities are already provided by the JTMS implementation. We can wrap code that translates from assertions to TMS nodes and then calls the TMS procedure make-contradiction to declare an assertion to be contradictory. The inference engine can supply new handlers through the JTMS macro with-contradiction-handler, and contradiction checking can be turned off or on as desired using macros supplied with the TMS.

This completes the design of JTRE. We turn now to describing an implementation of this design.

8.3 Implementing JTRE

Now that we have the design of JTRE firmly in mind, let us go over an implementation of it. We describe each file in turn, paralleling the structure of FTRE to highlight the differences between FTRE and JTRE due to the introduction of the TMS.

8.3.1 The JTRE interface (jinter.lisp)

The `jtre` struct differs in several respects from the `ftre` struct. First, all the fields for caching local rules and data are gone, since the stack-oriented context mechanism of FTRE no longer makes sense with a JTMS. Similarly, the two queues have been re-merged into one, since assumption making is not an activity typically done via pattern-directed rules in a JTMS-based system. The `jtre` struct also has several new fields not found in FTRE:

`jtms` Holds the JTMS associated with this JTRE.

`datum-counter` Provides a unique identifier for structs used to implement assertions.

`rule-counter` Provides a unique identifier for structs used to implement rules.

The purpose of the `jtms` field is obvious: a common operation involving a JTRE is mapping JTRE-level constructs to TMS-level constructs, so rapid access to the JTMS associated with a JTRE is important. The `-counter` fields are used to provide integer identifiers for assertions and structs, as described in Section 4.3.3. We follow the convention of using a single global variable to refer to an instance of a JTRE. The following procedures create and manipulate JTREs:

`(create-jtre` ⟨*title*⟩ `&key` ⟨*debugging*⟩`)` Creates a new JTRE whose printing name is ⟨*title*⟩. When ⟨*debugging*⟩ is non-`nil`, information about internal operations will be printed.

`(in-JTRE ⟨jtre⟩)` Resets the global variable `*jtre*` to the JTRE ⟨*jtre*⟩.

`(with-JTRE ⟨jtre⟩ &rest ⟨forms⟩)` Evaluates ⟨*forms*⟩ within ⟨*jtre*⟩, that is, in an environment where `*jtre*` is bound to ⟨*jtre*⟩.

`(change-jtre ⟨jtre⟩ &key ⟨debugging⟩)` Changes the amount of internal information printed out in ⟨*jtre*⟩'s operations: If ⟨*debugging*⟩ is not `nil`, internal debugging information will be printed, and if `nil`, internal information is not printed.

The interface procedures for running a JTRE are similar to those of FTRE. In particular, `run`, `run-forms`, and `show` are basically the same as their FTRE cousins, but with `*jtre*` instead of `*ftre*`. The only new wrinkles are the procedures `uassert!` and `uassume!`, which simplify interactive dialogs with a JTRE. They operate by first performing the appropriate activity and then executing all the rules queued by that activity. Often this manner of interaction is preferable to a driver loop like `run`.

8.3.2 The JTRE database (jdata.lisp)

The JTRE database follows the same implementation strategy as the FTRE database. The major differences are

1. Each assertion is now implemented as a `datum` struct instead of its Lisp form.
2. New interface procedures are added for installing justifications and manipulating assumptions.
3. The set of interrogatives is expanded to take into account the TMS's role in tracking belief states.

Let us start with the `datum` struct. It has the following fields:

`id` Integer identifier, unique within the JTRE, for easy reference.

`jtre` Pointer to the JTRE it belongs to.

`lisp-form` The list structure comprising the form of the assertion.

`tms-node` Pointer to the corresponding node in the TMS.

`dbclass` Pointer to the database class it belongs to.

`assumption?` Indicates whether or not the assertion is an enabled assumption. If non-`nil`, it is an enabled assumption, with the specific value being the informant.

`plist` A property list for the datum. Handy in certain mark-sweep algorithms and as a place for external systems to record information.

The interface procedures can be divided into several parts. First are the procedures that introduce new entities into the database and the TMS:

`assert!` Makes permanent changes to the TMS. Its calling pattern expresses a justification, i.e.,
`(assert!` ⟨*consequent*⟩ `(` ⟨*informant*⟩ ⟨*ante1*⟩ `...` ⟨*anten*⟩`))`
where ⟨*consequent*⟩ is the assertion being justified, ⟨*ante1*⟩ . . . ⟨*anten*⟩ are the antecedents, and ⟨*informant*⟩ indicates the source. If the list of antecedents is `nil` or the second argument is simply an informant, the effect of `assert!` is to make ⟨*consequent*⟩ into a premise.

`rassert!` Like `assert!`, but treats its arguments as expressions into which the values of pattern variables are to be substituted rather than as expressions to be evaluated.

`quiet-assert!` Like `assert!`, but suppresses contradiction handling. Useful for asserting a set of constraints without interruption.

`assume!` Converts an assertion into an enabled assumption, if it is not already one. Takes two arguments, ⟨*fact*⟩ which is the assertion to be assumed, and ⟨*reason*⟩, a symbol indicating why it is being assumed.

`already-assumed?` Returns non-`nil` if its argument is already an enabled assumption.

`retract!` Retracts an enabled assumption. The optional argument ⟨*just*⟩ is a reason for retraction. If the reason for retraction is not the same as the reason for making the assumption, the retraction does not occur.

`rretract!` Is to `retract!` what `rassert!` is to `assert!`.

`contradiction` Marks the TMS node corresponding to the given assertion as a contradiction. Any attempt to support this assertion will thus result in the invocation of contradiction processing.

As with FTRE, all of these procedures have an optional argument of `*jtre*`, the default JTRE. This has the dual effect of allowing the user to not refer to the JTRE if that variable is already bound in the operating environment, and also ensures that `*jtre*` is bound for any calls internal to these interface procedures. The same convention is used in other interface procedures without comment.

The pattern seen in these procedures is characteristic of all inference engine/TMS interfaces. That is, the inference engine data is mapped into TMS nodes (via `get-tms-node` or its equivalent) and the corresponding TMS operations are then performed on these nodes.

Notice that `assume!` keeps track of the informant for the assumption at the level of the inference engine, by the equality test on the ⟨*reason*⟩ argument. It is important for `assume!` to check whether or not an assertion is already assumed to prevent programs from stepping on each other's toes. Consider a problem solver used as part of an engineering design system. One task is to estimate the parts cost of a particular design, which may involve making assumptions about what material the parts are made of if this is not already known. Typically, by the time cost estimations are made, many of the materials are already known due to other assumptions in the design process. The problem solver must keep track of which assumptions are made by each task, so that a task does not retract assumptions it was not responsible for. This same constraint is enforced in the implementation of `retract!` by carefully checking to see whether the assertion is an enabled assumption and whether it has the same source of support as was given as the reason for enabling it.

The next set of interface procedures can be used to interrogate the database and the TMS:

`in?` Returns non-`nil` exactly if the given assertion is in.

`out?` Returns non-`nil` exactly if the given assertion is out.

`why?` Describes the immediate support for an assertion.

`assumptions-of` Produces a list of the assumptions underlying the belief in an assertion.

`wfs` Displays the well-founded support for belief in an assertion (see Chapter 7).

`show-justifications` Displays the justifications in the TMS which can lead to belief in the given assertion.

`fetch` Returns a list of the assertions matching a given pattern.

`show-data` Prints the contents of the database.

Obviously `show-data` is useful only for small databases. Again, all of these procedures are implemented as per our design. That is, we first translate from Lisp forms to database items, then access the corresponding TMS node to gather the appropriate information about beliefs, and finally translate the results back into assertions, if necessary.

In addition to the procedures above, there is a second tier of interface procedures which are often useful in debugging. They presume more familiarity with the internals of the system (e.g., the distinction between datums and nodes).

`referent` Returns the datum corresponding to the given Lisp expression, if it exists in the database. If the optional argument `virtual?` is non-`nil`, if a datum does not already appear in the database one is created. `referent` is useful for finding out if something has been mentioned at all, independently of its belief state.

`map-dbclass` Executes the given procedure on each database class. Useful for performing some test over all assertions and rules.

`get-tms-node` Returns the TMS node corresponding to the given fact, creating it if necessary.

`view-node` The inverse of `get-tms-node`.

`show-datum` Produces a user-interpretable string from the given datum.

`get-datum` Returns the datum whose identifier equals the given integer, if that datum exists, and `nil` otherwise.

`get-just` Returns the justification whose identifier equals the given integer, if that datum exists, and `nil` otherwise.

The ⟨*virtual?*⟩ flag in `referent` is useful because it is important to see whether or not an assertion has been mentioned at all, not just whether or not it is believed. (For instance, when debugging one may want to ask if a fact is not in the database without triggering any `:INTERN` rules which would be triggered if it is added.) Intuitively, an interrogative should not add structure to the database. We respect this intuition by using `referent` with ⟨*virtual?*⟩ set to `nil` in the interrogatives like `in?` and `out?`.

8.3.3 The JTRE rule system (jrules.lisp)

Conceptually the rule system in JTRE has three major differences from the rule system in FTRE:

1. Triggers must be parsed differently, to extract their belief condition (`:IN`, `:OUT`, and `:INTERN`)
2. Body procedures must be built differently, to take the belief conditions of the triggers into account.
3. The TMS must be brought into the process of scheduling rules when the triggers include `:IN` or `:OUT` belief conditions.

These three major changes result in many small changes in the implementation. Most of these small changes are fairly obvious consequences of a few key changes. Consequently, we focus on the key changes, and only sketch the small changes.

Implementing the first major change requires changing the procedure `parse-rule-trigger`. Since we specified that the belief condition will be the first element of the trigger, this change is straightforward. The caller of `parse-rule-trigger`, the procedure `build-rule`, must of course be prepared to receive this information and must pass it to the appropriate subroutines for building the body and matcher procedures.

The second major change requires more substantial modifications to `build-rule`. As before, the body procedure we build takes as input:

- The variables bound by the matches of triggers for all rules that the current rule is contained in.
- Any variables introduced by a `:VAR` option in the triggers of containing rules.

There is now potentially one more argument:

- The TMS node corresponding to the triggering assertion, if the trigger's belief condition is `:IN` or `:OUT`.

Since it is the matcher which provides the other arguments to the rule, we change the procedure `generate-match-procedure` so that it returns a third argument. The third argument indicates whether or not `try-rule-on` should add the TMS node for the matching assertion to the argument list it builds for body procedures. Once again we have moved most of the interpretation and analysis of a rule into a compilation process: At run time, `try-rule-on` just follows the instructions of the matcher, which has the right decision hard-wired into it.

(The astute reader might see several alternative implementations both for this choice and for others. For instance, we might have included a field in the `rule` struct that has a flag indicating whether or not a TMS node should be included in the arguments of the body procedure, analogous to our use of the `assumption?` field in FTRE's rule struct. Each rule instance consists of a distinct struct, so adding a field increases storage costs proportionately to the number of rule instances built. In contrast, the matcher is shared between all instances of a particular rule, so adding the information to it provides no additional storage charge per rule instance. Consequently we prefer to incorporate this information in the matcher. It also has other useful implications, as explored in Exercise 2.)

How should we bring the TMS into the scheduling process? When designing the rule system we decided that a rule's execution would be deferred if the trigger's belief condition was not satisfied. The easiest way to do this is to wrap a `cond` around the original body (see `generate-body-procedure`) which performs the appropriate test on the TMS node provided at run time. If the test succeeds, the original body is executed on the spot. Otherwise the procedure and all its arguments are stored with the TMS node, which will requeue them when the appropriate changes in its belief state occur.

8.3.4 Testing JTRE (jtest.lisp)

Part of putting a new ship in working order is taking it on a shakedown cruise, to make sure all the subsystems work and that everything operates smoothly together. The procedure `shakedown-jtre` serves an analogous purpose by running a set of standard examples and checking that their results at least crudely match with expectations. While it does not check every subsystem extensively, it is surprising just how sensitive such shakedown can be. `shakedown-jtre` is very useful when making sure that JTRE is running properly on a new system, or when you have made some change to its internals and you want to look for unanticipated effects.

8.4 Example: Dependency-directed search

The only good thing about repeating your mistakes is that you know when to cringe.
—from an AIX fortune file

In Chapter 5 we saw how the classic N-queens puzzle could be solved via chronological search. Chapter 6 pointed out the problems with chronological search, and outlined how truth maintenance systems could help. Recall that using a TMS can make search more efficient in two ways:

1. When an inconsistency is discovered, the assumptions underlying it can be tracked down. This capability supports more intelligent backtracking schemes.
2. Inconsistent combinations of assumptions (called *nogoods*) can be noted in the TMS so that they are never tried again. This capability allows a system to avoid making the same mistake twice.

Search strategies that exploit these two TMS capabilities are known as *dependency-directed search strategies*. Here we show one implementation of a dependency-directed search strategy in the context of the N-queens puzzle. Since this puzzle was used in Chapter 5 to illustrate chronological search, we can then analyze the performance of the FTRE and JTRE versions to get more insight into the trade-offs between these two families of strategies.

To facilitate the comparison, we keep the structure of the JTRE implementation as close as possible to the FTRE version. The principal design decisions in that system were:

1. Represent the placement of a queen on a chessboard by assertions of the form `(queen` ⟨*column*⟩ ⟨*row*⟩`)`.
2. Since there can be at most one queen per row, define the placement of a queen in each row as the collection of choice sets that spans the space of possible solutions.
3. Search the collection of choice sets via chrological backtracking to generate all solutions.

We need only to change the third design decision, by implementing a dependency-directed search strategy instead of chronlogical backtracking. Accordingly, most of the code in our new version of *N*-queens remains the same.

How should a dependency-directed search be organized? We might use chronological search as a starting point. Abstractly, chronological search was characterized in Chapter 5 as follows:

```
(defun Chrono (choice-sets)
 (if (null choice-sets) (record-solution)
     (dolist (choice (first choice-sets))
      (while-assuming choice
         (if (consistent?)
             (Chrono (rest choice-sets)))))))
```

In the FTRE version of *N*-queens, the parts of this abstract procedure were implemented as follows:

- `record-solution` was implemented by fetching the set of `queen` assertions and caching them in a global variable.
- `while-assuming` was implemented by a call to `try-in-context` which assumed the particular choice.
- `consistent?` was implemented by looking for the output of PDIS rules which detected captures in the beginning of `solve-queens`, triggered in response to the assumed placement made by the call to `try-in-context`

As a first approximation, dependency-directed search can be described abstractly as a variation of chronological search like this:

```
(defun DDS (choice-sets)
 (if (null choice-sets) (record-solution)
     (dolist (choice (first choice-sets))
      (unless (nogood? choice)
       (while-assuming choice
        (if (consistent?)
            (DDS (rest choice-sets))
            (record-nogood choice)))))))
```

The obvious changes are:

- `nogood?` checks to see if the choice is already known to be inconsistent with the rest of the dependency network. If so, there is no point in assuming it.

- `record-nogood` must use the information supplied by a contradiction handler to create a warning that `choice` is inconsistent under the assumptions that led to the contradiction. These assumptions need not include all the assumptions made by previous stages of the search, and could include assumptions that were made independently of the search.

The mechanics are slightly more complex, however, since we must arrange for making and retracting assumptions rather than just throwing away an inconsistent database.

To implement a dependency-directed search routine for N-queens, we can keep the same mechanism for contradiction detection (e.g., PDIS rules) and use the JTMS contradiction-handling mechanism to notify us immediately when a capture is detected. As with the FTRE version, the way we have organized the search means that the last assumption will always be implicated in any contradiction that is detected. This greatly simplifies matters. After making an assumption, all we must do is detect the difference between the database reaching quiescence naturally and having a contradiction occur.

The astute reader might also notice that, since the last assumption is always implicated in a contradiction, this example does not demonstrate the full potential benefit of dependency-directed search. One of the presumed advantages, after all, was being able to backtrack farther, past irrelevant choices. It is always advantageous to organize problem solving so that mistakes are found as quickly as possible.[1] The more complex, and the less understood, a problem is, the less likely it is that such organizations are possible, and hence the more beneficial dependency-directed search strategies are likely to be. The implementation of search routines to deal with multilevel backtracking are a bit more complex, and so we postpone discussion of them until Chapter 10.

We now understand, at least in outline, how to exploit the TMS's contradiction processing abilities to facilitate testing partial solutions for consistency. What about recording mistakes? Suppose we detect that a particular queen placement, say `(queen 3 8)`, is inconsistent with our

---

1. One engineer has remarked that a valuable property of modern CAD tools is that "they allow us to make more mistakes, more quickly."

previous choices (say (queen 1 1) and (queen 2 7)). The assumptions returned by the contradiction handler would be in this case

```
((queen 2 7) (queen 3 8))
```

Notice that (queen 1 1) was not implicated: although it was a choice made as part of the search, it did not participate in the current contradiction. We can record this mistake by creating a new justification whose antecedent is (queen 2 7), so that whenever we have chosen (queen 2 7) some warning would automatically become in. Then we can modify our search algorithm so that if a warning is spotted before a choice is made, we simply skip it. Thus we never have to make the same mistake twice.

An implementation of this design can be found in the file jqueens .lisp. Most of the file is the same as the FTRE version (called fqueens .lisp). The differences center around two changes:

- Since JTRE does not contain FTRE's try-in-context, we implement a new version of try-in-context which uses a contradiction handler to detect contradictions.
- solve-queens has been changed to create warnings when captures are detected and to use this information to avoid repeating mistakes.

Let us examine these procedures in more detail.

Comparing the two versions of try-in-context is illuminating because they are quite different. Recall that the FTRE version pushed and popped stacks of rules and assertions. This implementation strategy is not a viable option for JTRE because its assertions have indefinite temporal extent. Instead, we assume and retract assertions, carefully surrounding each JTMS transaction with forms that help ensure its integrity.

try-in-context begins by binding the contradiction handler to a closure including try-contradiction-handler as its procedural base. This handler detects when a contradiction involves the current assumption by encapsulating a marker (the value of try-marker) which is unique for each call to try-in-context. If the given assumption is already believed, thunk is evaluated without further ado. Otherwise, the assumption is enabled and the PDIS rules are executed (via run-rules) to figure out the consequences of this new assumption. The catchs are required because each of these steps could trigger a contradiction (do you see why?) that would result in `try-contradiction-handler` performing its `throw`. In each case, the `return-from` provides an answer from `try-in-context` that indicates the assumptions underlying the problem. Once `thunk` has been evaluated, the cleanup clause of the `unwind-protect` is invoked to retract the current assumption, and `try-in-context` returns.

`solve-queens-puzzle` orchestrates the use of `try-in-context`. In particular, before a choice is made, it checks to see if the negation of the choice is believed within the current JTRE. The negation of the choice being in indicates that we already know, from earlier in the search, that making this assumption would lead to a contradiction. Therefore we simply skip over this particular possible choice. If we do not know that the assumption will be inconsistent, we use `try-in-context` to test it and continue the search. Notice that we trap the contradiction coming back from `try-in-context`, and use the underlying assumptions to justify the negation of the choice just assumed. This provides the nogood information needed by the earlier portion of `solve-queens-puzzle`. The pattern of detecting and installing nogoods used in this procedure is found in all dependency-directed search strategies, although it is often distributed across several distinct procedures.

How does this dependency-directed backtracking version of N-queens compare with the chronological backtracking version of Chapter 5? Table 8.1 shows the data gathered using the `test-queens` procedure in `jqueens.lisp`, while Table 8.2 shows the data for `fqueens.lisp` (using FTRE) for the same problems. The data for the dependency-directed search version are plotted in Figure 8.1. Figures 8.2 and 8.3 compare FTRE's chronological search against JTRE's dependency-directed search. The lessons from computational experiments, like those from any other experiments, need to be extracted with care. In this case, the simple nature of the N-queens puzzle provides two advantages for chronological search that do not generalize to most situations. First, we know due to the way we structured the search space that the last assumption made is always the one to be retracted. Second, the amount of work involved in testing a combination of assumptions is quite small. Thus there is a smaller penalty for backing up in this puzzle than in most real-world problems. So this test is somewhat biased in favor of chronological search. And, as Figure 8.2 indicates, chronological search is actually faster from the perspective of measured run time. Is dependency-

Table 8.1
Performance of JTRE on N-queens. Using an IBM RT Model 125 with 16MB of RAM, running Lucid Common Lisp. Time is user run time, in seconds.

N	# Soln's	# Asns	Time
4	2	53	1.27
5	10	137	4.47
6	4	332	12.33
7	40	860	44.70
8	92	2554	153.48

Table 8.2
Performance of FTRE on N-queens. Using an IBM RT Model 125 with 16MB of RAM, running Lucid Common Lisp. Time is user run time, in seconds.

N	# Soln's	# Asns	Time
4	2	60	0.55
5	10	220	1.33
6	4	894	5.13
7	40	3,584	20.23
8	92	15,720	95.13

directed search a bad idea? Consider Figure 8.3, which compares these strategies with respect to the number of assumptions required. From this perspective there is a very clear advantage for dependency-directed search. In most real problems the overhead of testing assumptions is much larger, and often the problem space is not well enough understood to allow for optimal ordering of choice sets. In such cases dependency-directed search should show a run-time advantage as well. The crossover will occur when the effort saved by not repeating the same mistakes over and over again outweighs the extra mechanism of the JTMS.

There is no magic here—both search strategies are still exponential. Dependency-directed search only postpones the day of reckoning by increasing the range of problems that can be solved with a fixed computational resource.

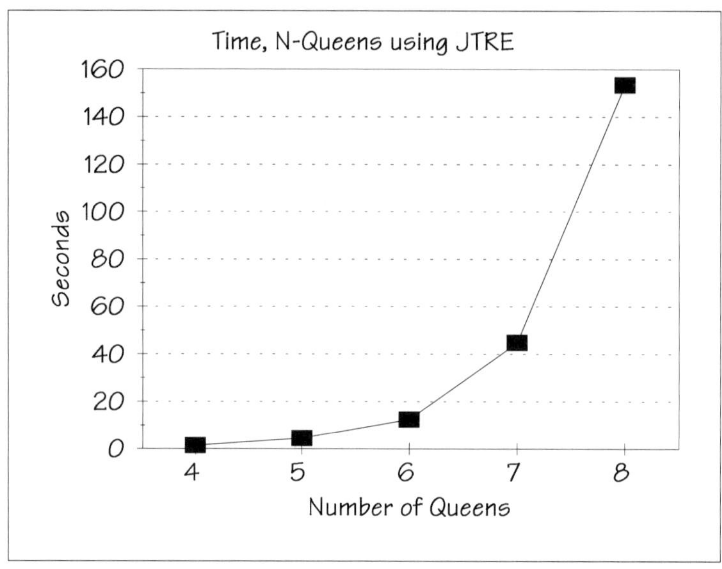

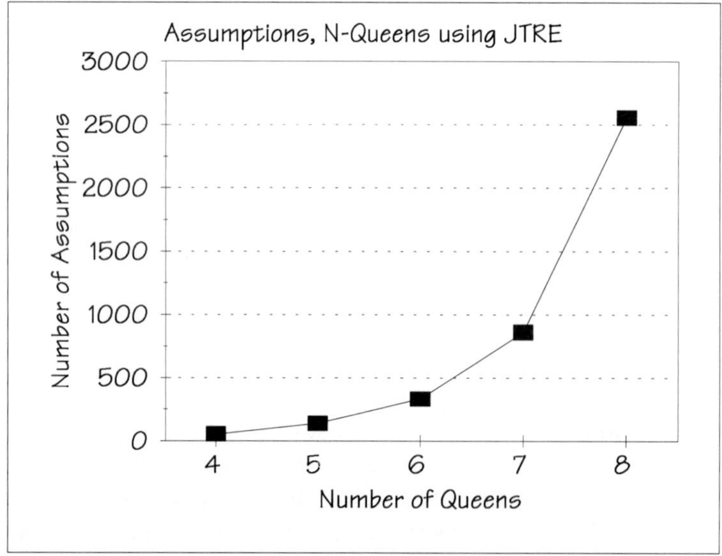

Figure 8.1 Dependency-directed search performance as *N* increases

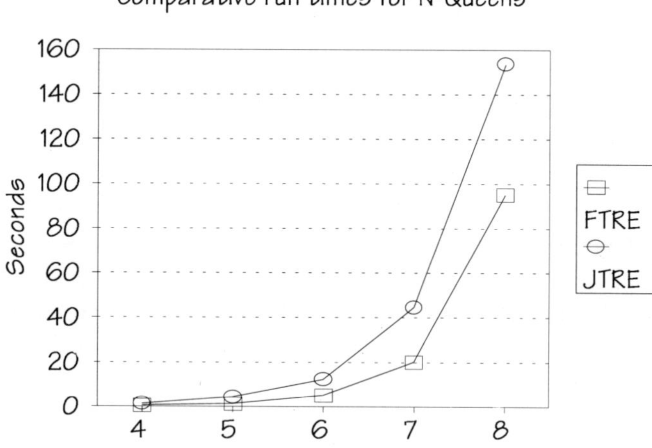

Figure 8.2 Run times for search strategies

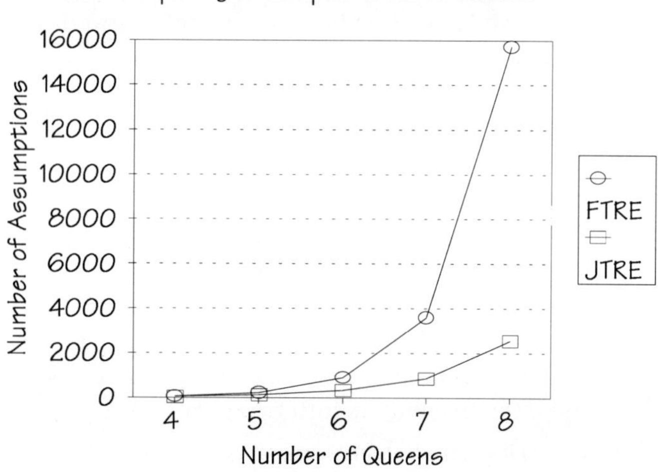

Figure 8.3 Number of assumptions by search strategy. In both cases the number of assumptions rises exponentially, but dependency-directed search makes many fewer assumptions.

8.5 Example: Reconstructing SAINT

Next we turn to a more substantial example. SAINT was one of the first AI programs. SAINT performed indefinite integration, and was able to solve most of the problems that appeared on an MIT calculus exam. As its author, Slagle, described it, "Let SAINT read in its card reader an IBM card containing (in a suitable notation) the symbolic integration problem $\int xe^{x^2}dx$. In less than a minute and a half, SAINT prints out the answer, $\frac{1}{2}e^{x^2}$. . . . After working for less than a minute on the problem $\int e^{x^2}dx$ (which cannot be integrated in elementary form) SAINT prints out that it cannot solve it" (page 191, [8]).

Here we partially reconstruct SAINT, using JTRE as a substrate. Obviously, our goal is not to imitate all aspects of the program. Card readers, after all, are rather hard to find these days. Instead, we replicate a subset of SAINT's functionality and methods of operation to illustrate some principles for designing problem solvers. These principles include:

1. *Explicit representation of control knowledge:* Representing "how" knowledge is often just as important as representing "what" knowledge. We have already seen a simple form of control knowledge, the `show` operator, in our implementation of KM* in Chapters 4 and 5. Here we describe a richer control vocabulary of problems, solutions, and relationships between them. This vocabulary allows us to record many control decisions in the database where they are thus interpretable by PDIS rules, rather than hiding them in procedures. By using the TMS to link these control statements into the dependency network, we can achieve better control of the reasoning process.
2. *Control via suggestions:* It is hard to avoid combinatorial explosions, or even infinite loops, in a purely antecedent reasoning system. One valuable technique for organizing problem solvers is to decompose the inference engine into two parts:
   - *PDIS:* The pattern-directed inference system, e.g., JTRE. It has the responsibility of maintaining the assertional database and drawing "obvious" conclusions. An important class of obvious conclusions are suggestions about how to solve particular subproblems.
   - *Controller:* The controller is responsible for guiding the problem-solving process. It detects when the problem is solved and when

resource allocations have been exceeded. It selects what problem(s) are currently to be worked on, based on suggestions from the PDIS.

This decomposition provides finer-grained control than any purely antecedent scheme, even given control assertions, can provide. Purely local rules have no hope of accurately detecting loops and combinatorial explosions. The controller provides a more global perspective that potentially can make more accurate decisions.

3. *Use of special-purpose higher-level languages:* The conceptual gap between our intuitions about problem solving and JTRE is smaller than the gap between our problem-solving intuitions and Lisp, but it can still be substantial. One way to narrow that gap is to design domain-specific representation (or programming) languages that capture exactly the right distinctions needed to solve particular classes of problems. Ideally, for instance, a mathematician extending JSAINT would not have to know how to write JTRE rules to debug or extend its knowledge of integration. A little extra code is often all it takes to achieve substantial improvements in ease of use.
4. *Explanation generation:* One motivation for using a TMS is to provide explanations. In JSAINT we show how the JTMS can be used to explore the rationale underlying a solution, including some of the control decisions which led to it. Since the reasons for failures are also recorded, we can also use the TMS to track down what JSAINT would need to know in order to solve a problem it failed on.

8.5.1 How SAINT worked

SAINT solved indefinite integration problems. For those whose calculus courses are but a distant memory (or a future plan, or something that is not to be), here is the essence of such problems. Given a mathematical expression one can do a variety of things—operations—to it. One of those operations is taking its *derivative* with respect to some variable. Finding an expression's derivative is interesting because it corresponds to the rate of change. For example, speed is the derivative of position: If you travel at 110 miles per hour for 20 minutes (without getting caught) you will have covered 33 miles. Integration is the *inverse operation* of taking a derivative. The calculation which netted us 33 miles of progress (or a speeding ticket) is a simple example of *definite integration*. What made it definite rather than indefinite was that we knew for how long we were going. Indefinite integration finds an expression representing the inverse of the derivative that is independent of any specific interval. Solving indefinite integrals is useful because the results can be used to easily solve a whole family of definite integration problems. (If you are not familiar with the mathematical notation for integration, this is the time to borrow a good calculus text and take a few minutes to brush up.)

Roughly, SAINT worked like this: Given an integral to solve, SAINT first attempted to match the integral to one of a set of *standard forms* whose solutions are immediately known. Here is a simple standard form:

$$\int v\,dv \longrightarrow \frac{1}{2}v^2$$

Given the problem $\int x\,dx$, this transformation rule tells us immediately that the answer is $\frac{1}{2}x^2$, by substituting x for v.

When a problem did not match a standard form, SAINT began applying *transformations* to decompose it into easier pieces. Three examples include:

$$\int c g(v)\,dv \longrightarrow c\int g(v)\,dv$$

where c is constant in v, and

$$\int \sum g_i(v)\,dv \longrightarrow \sum \int g_i(v)\,dv$$

and finally,

> *Let $g(v)$ be the integrand. For each nonconstant nonlinear subexpression $s(v)$ such that neither its main connective is minus nor is it a product with a common factor, and such that the number of nonconstant factors of the fraction $\frac{g(v)}{s'(v)}$ (after cancellation) is less than the number of factors of $g(v)$, try substituting $u = s(v)$. Thus, in xe^{x^2}, substitute $u = x^2$. (Page 197, [8])*

Unlike standard forms, which directly solve a problem, transformations define the solution of a problem in terms of new, presumably simpler, problems. If more than one transformation is applicable, both might be pursued. SAINT organized subproblems into an AND/OR tree, with the AND branches being the subproblems needed to solve a given

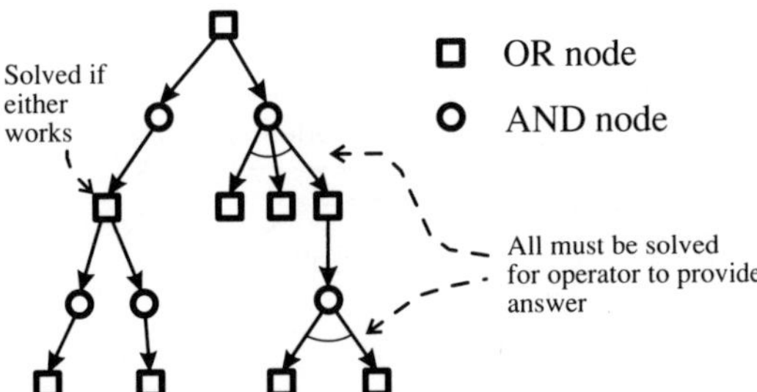

Figure 8.4 An AND/OR tree

problem and the OR branches being alternate methods to solve a given problem. Figure 8.4 illustrates.

SAINT included two kinds of transformations, *algorithm-like transformations* and *heuristic transformations*. Slagle defined an algorithm-like transformation to be one "which, when applicable, is always or almost always appropriate." Heuristic transformations are those which are much less likely to work. The first two transformations above are algorithm-like, and the third is heuristic. When deciding what to do, SAINT always preferred to try standard forms first, then algorithm-like transformations, and finally heuristic transformations.

To keep our program simple, JSAINT implements only a small fraction of SAINT's knowledge of integration. SAINT used 26 standard forms, 8 algorithm-like transformations, and 10 heuristic transformations. JSAINT includes only 20 operators. The exercises provide opportunities for extending JSAINT's knowledge.

8.5.2 The design of JSAINT

In designing anything, it makes sense to start with "the big picture" to see what parts are needed and roughly how they fit together. Based on this global perspective, we can then design the pieces so that they fit together to instantiate our original picture. In designing problem solvers this typically means starting with the system's architecture. Thus we begin by outlining JSAINT's architecture, and proceed to describe the design of each component in more detail. The description of the implementation itself begins in Section 8.5.3.

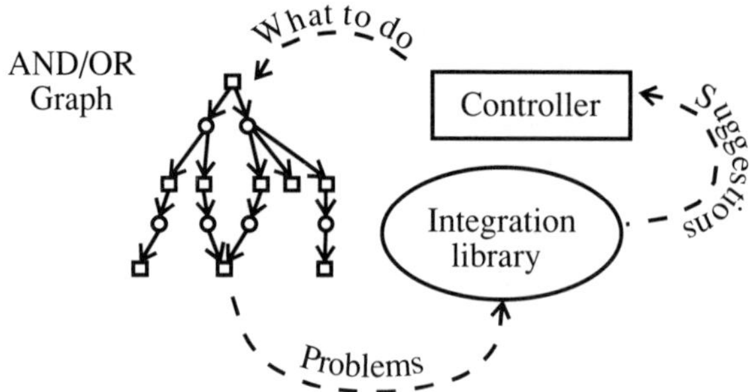

Figure 8.5 JSAINT architecture

8.5.2.1 The architecture of JSAINT

Figure 8.5 shows the architecture of JSAINT. It has three main parts, each with the following responsibilities:

1. *Central controller:*
   - Gathering suggestions from the Integration Library about how to proceed.
   - Choosing what subproblem(s) to work on.
   - Ensuring that resource limitations are not exceeded.
2. *AND/OR graph:*
   - Maintains status of progress on problems and subproblems.
   - Detects when problems have been solved or when they cannot be solved.
3. *Integration Library:*
   - Provides direct solutions to simple problems (e.g., SAINT's standard forms).
   - Makes suggestions for how to decompose complex problems (e.g., SAINT's transformations).

Abstractly, the basic cycle of this architecture is:

1. If the original problem has been solved or clearly cannot be solved, or if resource bounds have been reached, quit.
2. Select best subproblem P to work on.

3. If P can be directly solved, do it.
4. Otherwise, gather suggestions for how to solve P and extend the AND/OR graph accordingly.

In SAINT, working on a subproblem consists of applying a standard form to solve it directly or applying a transformation to decompose it into simpler problems. The same will be true of JSAINT, except that the standard terminology for both kinds of knowledge is now *operators*, so we call them that for convenience.

The basic JSAINT cycle is analogous to the discipline of `show` assertions used in Chapters 4 and 5. Recall that an assertion `(show` $\langle G \rangle$`)` was an expression of interest in proving the statement $\langle G \rangle$. In effect, the pattern-directed database broadcasts an appeal for other rules to pitch in. A crucial limitation of this scheme is that the connection between the act of recognizing an operation as potentially relevant and performing that operation is a bit too direct. Rules that respond to `show` assertions directly by doing something often lead to inefficiencies. For instance, close metering of our implementation of KM* indicates that it can waste time finding alternative proofs for a proposition which had already been demonstrated or which was no longer relevant.

In JSAINT, the connection between proposing an action and carrying out that action is much less direct. The Integration Library makes suggestions, but it is the controller that decides what to do about them. Dividing the process in this way adds some overhead, to be sure. However, overall efficiency improves because better control can be achieved than would otherwise be possible.

To gain maximum advantage from JTRE, JSAINT uses its database as much as possible to store both domain and control information. For example, JSAINT's AND/OR graph is implemented as a set of assertions in the dependency network. The Integration Library is implemented as PDIS rules. This design choice, along with our reuse of the simplifier program of Chapter 3, allows the JSAINT code itself to be surprisingly compact.

We begin by examining the control vocabulary JSAINT uses, and then describe the design of the AND/OR graph. Next we look at how operators work, and then we examine the central controller in more detail. Once the design is firmly understood, the fine points of the implementation are explored in Section 8.5.3.

8.5.2.2 A control vocabulary

Some problem-solver designers treat representation almost as an afterthought. We believe this is a horrible mistake. Representation is *always* a central factor in any AI system. As problem-solver designers we must strive to develop representations that promote coherence and efficiency. In JSAINT we have two representation problems. The first, how to represent mathematical expressions in Lisp, has already been solved for us by the convention of prefix notation. The second is how to represent control information. This is harder, and there is much less agreement about what the optimal conventions are.

The first issue is how we should represent the idea of a problem itself. One obvious, but suboptimal, solution is not to talk about them. That is, suppose we represent the mathematical expression

$$\int (x + 5) dx$$

as

```
(integral (+ x 5) x)
```

We could simply let this `integral` statement stand for both the mathematical expression and the problem of finding an equivalent expression without an occurrence of `integral`. This is inadequate because in a larger system, one could easily imagine knowing certain integral expressions without having the slightest urge to act upon them. Therefore, just as we used `show` assertions in natural deduction to express interest in providing a proposition, we use `integrate` as a predicate to express interest in finding the solution to the integral that is its argument. Thus, the problem above would be posed to JSAINT as

```
(integrate (integral (+ x 5) x))
```

Another reason to use `integrate` explicitly is that a problem solver often faces more than one kind of problem. Suppose we were building JSAINT as the first component of a more general mathematical reasoning system. We might have another set of rules for solving systems of equations, for example, in which definite integrals must be solved as subproblems. In this case the form of the algebraic expression isn't enough to signify what needs to be done to an expression.

The ideas of goal and problem are closely linked. Often goals have the form "solve this problem," and so we could just as easily think of `integrate` expressions as goals. Similarly, we could treat "achieve this goal" as a problem to be solved. Consequently we sometimes use the two terms interchangeably here, even though in general they are not identical.

The conceptual distinction between goals and problems raises an important issue: should our representation include predicates like `problem`, `goal`, and `task`? Our answer is no, unless the system actually needs these distinctions to operate. One can easily imagine tasks that would require these distinctions, and indeed, others. Suppose for instance that we had some very powerful problem-solving methods that were applicable to several kinds of goals or problems. In that case, predicates like `goal` and `problem` would be necessary to help express when such methods are applicable. Or suppose we were developing a program to pose mathematical problems rather than solve them (e.g., one that postulates interesting conjectures for mathematics or develops quizzes to test a student's knowledge of what it just explained). If this level of generality is needed, one might be better off having yet another element in the control vocabulary, say, `solve`, which indicates the goal of solving a particular problem (specified by an `integrate` or similar expression). We leave such possibilities for the reader to explore, since for JSAINT's simple control structure those particular predicates would be a frill.

In JSAINT, the only kind of goal is to try a particular method. This will be expressed as:

```
(try (integral-of-sum (integral (+ x 5) x)))
```

where `integral-of-sum` is the name of one of JSAINT's transformations and the `integral` statement is what it is being applied to.

Problems are sometimes solved and sometimes not. Sometimes we lose interest in a problem, perhaps because it is no longer relevant or because we have no more time to spend in on it. The problem solver needs a vocabulary for expressing the status of its subproblems and goals. The necessary vocabulary is surprisingly subtle. The most obvious distinction to draw is whether or not a problem has been solved. JSAINT uses the predicates `solved` and `failed` for this purpose. Given a problem P,

`(solved` $\langle P \rangle$`)` is believed exactly when P has been successfully solved.

`(failed ⟨P⟩)` is believed exactly when P cannot be solved by JSAINT as constituted.

Obviously `(solved ⟨p⟩)` and `(failed ⟨p⟩)` are mutually inconsistent.

Typically in a mathematics problem, knowing that the problem has been solved isn't enough—one wants to know what the solution actually is.[2] The problem solver needs a way to link the solution of a problem to the problem itself. We use the relation `solution-of` as follows:

`(solution-of ⟨P⟩ ⟨A⟩)` holds exactly when ⟨A⟩ is the result of solving problem ⟨P⟩.

Sometimes the same goal or subproblem arises more than once. For example, in calculus problems it is common to find the same subexpression cropping up again and again when performing an indefinite integration. It is important to recognize such cases so that we don't waste time starting a new effort to solve a goal when there is already an attempt underway. Representing problems and goals as assertions makes recognition trivial, since identical problems will be identical assertions. There is still the problem of recognizing that we have started to work on a goal already. The traditional term for setting to work on a subproblem or subgoal is to *expand* it [1], so we include the predicate `expanded` in JSAINT's vocabulary:

`(expanded ⟨PG⟩)` is true exactly when JSAINT has begun working on problem or goal ⟨PG⟩.

An aside: Notice that our choice of representation for problems and goals forces us to diverge slightly from SAINT's organization: SAINT used an AND/OR tree, while JSAINT uses an AND/OR graph. If we wanted to implement an AND/OR tree via assertions we still could, by reifying problems and goals. Each problem or goal could be given a unique name (say, `GOAL86`) and described via assertions like these:

```
(goal GOAL86)
(GOAL86 form-of
 (try (risch-algorithm (integrate
                         (integral (hairy-fun x) x)))))
(GOAL86 difficulty 500)
```

2. But sometimes it is, e.g., when trying to prove that a problem is decidable.

This convention makes recognition more difficult, of course.

Let us return to the status of problems and goals. So far we have chosen representations for saying when a problem is solved and when we have started to work on something. Once JSAINT has started working on a problem, it also needs to know when to stop working on it. There are two reasons to stop working on a problem:

1. The problem has been solved, or it has become clear that no solution is possible.
2. The problem or goal doesn't matter anymore.

The first case can be detected when either `solved` or `failed` is believed about a problem. Traditionally, a node in an AND/OR graph (or other search tree) which has been expanded but whose fate has not yet been resolved is said to be *open*. Once its fate is resolved it is said to be *closed*. For reasons that will become clear later, `JSAINT` only needs `open`:

`(open` ⟨*P*⟩`)` is believed exactly when problem ⟨*P*⟩ has been expanded but is not yet solved or known to be unsolvable.

`(open` ⟨*G*⟩`)` is believed exactly when goal ⟨*G*⟩ has been expanded but is not yet achieved or known to be unachievable.

The second case, when a problem becomes moot, is more subtle. Suppose JSAINT was working on a problem P because P was a subproblem raised by solving some larger problem $\hat{P}$. If $\hat{P}$ is solved by some other method that does not require solving P, then P is moot and no further effort should be expended on it. JSAINT uses the predicate `relevant` to make this distinction:

`(relevant` ⟨*PG*⟩`)` holds exactly when goal or problem ⟨*PG*⟩ is still potentially relevant to solving the original problem.

The vocabulary for the status of problems and goals may seem a bit complex, but it is necessary to capture the distinctions JSAINT needs. Figure 8.6 illustrates how these statements capture the possible time histories of subproblems and goals.

With the basic control vocabulary understood, we can proceed to consider the design of the AND/OR graph.

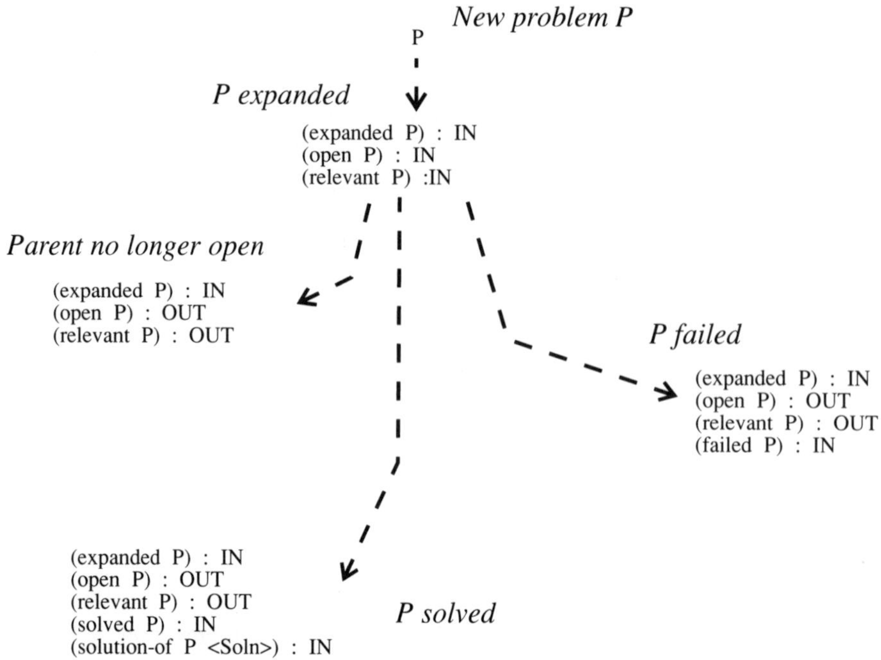

Figure 8.6 The control vocabulary describes progress on problems and goals

8.5.2.3 The design of the AND/OR graph

The AND/OR graph represents the relationships between the various subproblems and goals explored during problem solving. Subproblems and goals arise for two reasons:

1. Several operators might be suggested to solve a particular problem.
2. Many operators work by decomposing a problem into subproblems which, if solved, can be combined to form a solution to the original problem.

The appropriate relationship in the first case is disjunctive, since if any of the suggested operators works the problem is solved. The appropriate relationship in the second case is conjunctive, since typically all the subproblems need to be solved in order form the solution to the original problem. (If this were not the case, the operator might best be broken up into several operators.)

Given our suggestions architecture, the structure of an AND/OR graph consists of alternating layers of suggested operators (corresponding to *or-nodes*) and subproblems whose solutions are needed to apply an operator (corresponding to *and-nodes*). It is convenient to use the parent-child metaphor to describe the immediate relationships between nodes. An and-node will always be a `try` goal and its children will always be `integrate` problems. An or-node will always be an `integrate` problem, and its children will always be `try` goals.

In SAINT and other early problem solvers, AND/OR graphs were implemented via special-purpose datastructures and procedures. In JSAINT we implement AND/OR graphs as collections of assertions, woven together via justifications in the problem solver's dependency network. The advantage of this tactic is that it allows us to make more of the problem solver's operation explicit, with less hidden inside primitive procedures. Specifically, we can define the semantics of our control vocabulary and the relationships within the AND/OR graphs via PDIS rules. The TMS thus takes over a substantial portion of the bookkeeping and provides the grist for explaining what happened during problem solving and why.

To define the semantics of the control vocabulary, we start by considering the relationship of the success and failure of a node's children to the success and failure of its parent(s). This will pin down most of the relationships. We then explore the consequences in the other direction, to show how the predicate `relevant` works.

Consider and-nodes first. Suppose ⟨*P1*⟩ . . . ⟨*Pn*⟩ are conjunctive subproblems of the goal of the and-node ⟨*Gp*⟩. Failure of any ⟨*Pi*⟩ means failure of ⟨*Gp*⟩. In other words,

```
(failed ⟨P1⟩ ) ⇒ (failed ⟨Gp⟩ )
.
.
.
(failed ⟨Pn⟩ ) ⇒ (failed ⟨Gp⟩ )
```

This statement about the semantics of failure can be turned into a Horn clause appropriate for the JTMS by making `(failed ⟨Gp⟩)` the consequence of a justification which includes `(failed ⟨Pi⟩)` as one of its antecedents. There should be at least one other antecedent as well to indicate that ⟨*Pi*⟩ is one of the children of ⟨*Gp*⟩. The exact form of this statement will depend on the details of the representation we implement. Its purpose is to ensure that all of the structure of the AND/OR graph is explicit in the TMS, so that explanations can take it into account.

At first glance the success of an and-node seems easy to express: it succeeds exactly if all of its children succeed. This is indeed the semantics used in JSAINT, but we would be remiss if we did not raise a potential problem with this definition. In general, it is possible that even if all the subproblems of an and-node are successfully solved, the particular solutions they yield may not permit themselves to be combined into a successful global solution. Consider designing an airplane, where there is a fixed upper bound on weight. Typically there is no purely local criteria which lets one say that a part is "light enough," since this decision must be based on considering the other parts constituting the aircraft. This problem cannot arise in JSAINT, given the limited amount of expressive power it gives the authors of operators (described below).

DeMorgan's law leads one to expect that or-nodes will be the dual of and-nodes, and this is indeed the case. That is, if a single child of an or-node succeeds then the or-node is solved, and if all the children of an or-node fail, then the or-node fails to be solved. This raises an interesting design issue. Should JSAINT be organized so that the complete set of relevant suggestions is available by essentially an atomic operation, or should we allow new suggestions to be added incrementally? For instance, since only one successful or-node is needed, it might be more efficient to generate them incrementally. At first glance this may seem like a control issue and not a vocabulary issue. But our choice on this issue has a substantial impact on the representation. As explained later, we organized JSAINT to presume that the set of suggestions it gathers when it first expands a goal is complete, and do not process solutions added later. This choice allows us to represent the parental relationships of or-nodes quite simply, by creating an assertion that explicitly lists the disjuncts:

```
(or-subgoals ⟨Gp⟩ (⟨G1⟩ ... ⟨Gn⟩))
```

Furthermore, it means that once a node has failed, it remains failed forever. This would not be the case if new suggestions could be added incrementally (say, by a user adding an operator as the result of a JSAINT failing to solve its problem). Assertions that list a complete set of options would still be highly desirable in a more general setting, but our control language must be enriched to handle such possibilities. For example, in Chapter 10 we show how explict *closed-world assumptions* can be used to achieve this kind of incrementality. But for JSAINT we stipulate that all suggestions are gathered up once when the goal is expanded, and that no suggestions appearing afterwards for that goal shall be entertained.

Now that we understand how the status of a parent node is affected by its children, let us consider the converse: how should the parent's status affect that of its children? If we restrict ourselves to AND/OR trees rather than AND/OR graphs, so that each node has a single parent, the constraints imposed by parenthood are quite strong. For example, if the parent succeeds or fails, we should stop working on any children not yet processed, since they are now irrelevant. The situation in JSAINT is a bit more complicated because a node can have multiple parents, and furthermore the graph is generated incrementally, so we cannot guarantee that a node will not receive new parents later on.[3] So in expressing the impact of the parent's status on the status of its children we must be careful to ensure that our method allows for reinstatement of nodes as relevant when appropriate.

Recall that we used the predicate `open` to indicate that we have not yet solved or failed to solve (alternatively, achieved or failed to achieve) a goal or problem, and `relevant` to indicate that a goal or problem potentially had a role in solving the original problem. A child node $\langle C \rangle$ is relevant only if it has a open parent $\langle P \rangle$, because if all of its parents are closed, any work done on that node is moot. If for each parent $\langle P \rangle$ we install the Horn clause equivalent of

(open $\langle P \rangle$) $\Rightarrow$ (relevant $\langle C \rangle$)

then we have captured the relationship. This method is incremental in exactly the right way, since each parent can be added independently, and any open parent ensures the relevance of the child. (The root of the AND/OR graph will have to be automatically assumed to be relevant.)

3. This unbiological situation demonstrates a limit of the parent-child metaphor. The inquiring reader might ponder whether or not the root of the graph can gain parents, and if so, under what circumstances.

With the conventions of the AND/OR graph understood, we can turn to the design of operators.

8.5.2.4 Defining operators

Now let us examine how operators should work. First we must consider the *protocol* that operators must adhere to in order to interact appropriately with the control vocabulary described above. Then we must consider how they should be structured.

We already described how the output of operators is expressed, so let us begin our examination of the operator protocol there. Recall that we defined (`solution-of` $\langle P \rangle$ $\langle A \rangle$) to mean "the solution of problem $\langle P \rangle$ is the expression $\langle A \rangle$." To ensure valid explanations, every `solution-of` statement must be appropriately justified in terms of the solutions of subproblems (if any) and the operator used. If $\langle Pp \rangle$ is the problem the operator instance $\langle OpInst \rangle$ was successfully applied to, then we would expect to see in the JTMS a justification corresponding to the logical expression:

$$
\begin{aligned}
&(\texttt{solution-of}\ \langle P_1\rangle\ \langle A_1\rangle)\\
&\vdots\\
&\quad \wedge\ (\texttt{solution-of}\ \langle P_i\rangle\ \langle A_i\rangle)\\
&\vdots\\
&\quad \wedge\ (\texttt{solution-of}\ \langle P_n\rangle\ \langle A_n\rangle)\\
&\quad \wedge\ (\texttt{operator-instance}\ \langle OpInst\rangle) \Rightarrow (\texttt{solution-of}\ \langle P_p\rangle\ \langle A_p\rangle)
\end{aligned}
$$

The other three tasks the operator protocol must perform are:

1. An operator must find out about problems it should look at, and see if it is applicable.
2. An operator must be able to signal the controller that it is relevant to a particular problem (i.e., suggest itself as the solution).
3. An operator must apply itself when the controller selects it.

The first task is carried out by making operators look for `expanded` assertions, since such assertions are the first indication that a node is being worked on. The second task is carried out by making operators create new assertions that represent suggestions. Suggestions have the form:

(suggest-for ⟨*P*⟩ ⟨*OpInst*⟩)

where ⟨*P*⟩ is the problem that would be solved by the successful application of operator instance ⟨*OpInst*⟩. The third task, of applying itself on demand, is accomplished by looking for an `expanded` statement for the goal of (try ⟨*OpInst*⟩).

One might suspect, given that JTRE is our substrate, that operators will be implemented by a collection of PDIS rules (and that would be correct), but it is important to understand the protocol independently of how operators are implemented. An example will help make it concrete. Suppose we had an operator `integral-of-sum` which decomposed the integral of the sum of two terms into the sum of the integrals of the terms. Then when the controller starts to work on the problem

```
(integrate (integral (+ 1 (sqr x)) x))
```

it signals the operators via an assertion of the form

```
(expanded (integrate (integral (+ 1 (sqr x)) x)))
```

To indicate that it might be able to solve the problem, the `integral-of-sum` operator uses an assertion of the form

```
(suggest-for (integrate (integral (+ 1 (sqr x)) x))
             (try (integral-of-sum (integral (+ 1 (sqr x)) x))))
```

When the central controller wishes to take up this suggestion it adds an assertion of the form

```
(expanded (try (integral-of-sum (integral (+ 1 (sqr x)) x))))
```

to the database, which causes the operator instance to propose two new subproblems (e.g., integrating X^2 and 1 seperately) which, if solved, will allow it to solve the original problem.

With the operator's protocol now clear, let us examine their structure. The expression of integration laws in calculus textbooks only provides part of the story. For concreteness, here are two integration laws, expressed in standard mathematical notation:

$$\int cg(v)dv \longrightarrow c\int g(v)dv$$

where c is constant in v, and

$$\int \sum g_i(v)dv \longrightarrow \sum \int g_i(v)dv$$

Representing these operators in a form JSAINT can use requires adding additional information. First, we must encode the conditions under which the operator is applicable. This includes the left-hand side of the rule, plus any statements made about it, such as "where c is constant in v" above. Second, there must be some way to extract subproblems from the right-hand side of the rule (i.e., $\int g(v)dv$) and specify how their combination results in the solution to the original problem. Third, it is useful for explanation and debugging purposes to give names to the operators.

An inevitable tension in designing problem solvers comes from the gap between the constructs in which one prefers to think and the primitives supplied by the language in which the system is to be implemented. A mathematician would be happy with the integration laws as described above, but these descriptions are too vague for JSAINT to use. The obvious implementation of operators is to use a set of PDIS rules for each operator—one rule per step of the protocol above. But these implementation decisions must remain hidden as much as possible, since the mathematical knowledge of integration is completely independent of the operator protocol, much less of its implementation.

In the least abstracted implementation, we would force users to write explicit JTRE rules, or even Lisp code, to implement operators. In the most abstracted implementation, we would implement a parser (or actually, several parsers) to process mathematical statements in the notation that the particular user community was most comfortable with, extract extra conditions on applicability and subproblems automatically, and so forth. In JSAINT we choose a middle ground, selecting a set of conventions that is very easy to implement yet still shields users from most of the internals of the system. In particular, we require the author of an operator to name it and to explicitly identify subproblems and applicability conditions. Operators are defined by the form `defIntegration`. Its syntax is:

```
(defIntegration ⟨name⟩ ⟨pattern⟩ ⟨stuff⟩)
```

where ⟨*name*⟩ is a symbol naming the operator, ⟨*pattern*⟩ is the left-hand side of the operator, expressed in the usual Lisp notation for mathematical expressions, and ⟨*stuff*⟩ is a list of keywords and their arguments. The valid keywords are:

`:TEST` Optional. Extra applicability conditions applied to the pattern. Any pattern variables appearing in ⟨*pattern*⟩ may be used.

`:SUBPROBLEMS` Optional. The list of subproblems which must be solved before the operator can provide a result. Each subgoal is given a pattern variable as its name.

`:RESULT` Required. The right-hand side of the rule. Any pattern variables used in ⟨*pattern*⟩ or the subgoals may be used here.

Here is how the first integration operator mentioned previously would be implemented using these conventions:

```
(defIntegration Move-Constant-outside
  (Integral (* ?const ?nonconst) ?var)
  :TEST (and (not (occurs-in? ?var ?const))
             (occurs-in? ?var ?nonconst))
  :SUBPROBLEMS ((?int (Integrate (Integral ?nonconst ?var))))
  :result (* ?const ?int))
```

The basic idea is that to integrate an expression which is the product of a constant term and a term containing the variable of integration, one can simply take the product of the constant term and the integral of the non-constant term. Thus this operator would be applicable to

```
(integral (integrate (* 5 y)))
```

but not to

```
(integral (integrate (* (sin x) x) x))
```

The mathematical user, then, is asked to learn several things. They still have to use a prefix syntax for mathematical expressions, and need to know when (and what) subgoals the system needs to have identified for it. However, they no longer have to know about the internal control vocabulary or the detailed syntax of JTRE, which is a blessing both for them and for the implementers who would otherwise be forced to explain it to them.

8.5.2.5 *The design of* JSAINT*'s controller*

The controller's job is to orchestrate the operation of the other parts. It must

- Initialize the AND/OR graph.
- Select what subproblem or goal to work on.
- Extend the AND/OR graph with suggestions and subproblems as appropriate.
- Detect when the original problem is solved.
- Detect when resource bounds have been exceeded.

JSAINT's controller is organized around an *agenda*, which holds the subproblems and goals that have not yet been expanded. Notice that this is very different from the queues in the TREs, where the intent is that every queued item eventually will be executed. Each agenda item includes an estimate of its difficulty, to allow JSAINT to select the least difficult task to try next. If the difficulty estimate is even roughly accurate, this organization increases the chances of finding a less expensive solution before an expensive one.

Abstractly, the controller algorithm is:

1. Check the original problem.
   1.1 if `SOLVED`, then halt and report success.
   1.2 if `FAILED`, then halt and report failure.
2. If the agenda is empty, then halt and report failure.
3. If the resource allocation has been exceeded, report failure.
4. Select the simplest subproblem on the agenda and work on it.
5. Return to step 1.

The purpose of the first two steps should be obvious. Notice that the status of the original problem is checked each time through the loop. This detects cases where a critical subgoal may have failed, making further effort pointless. The resource bound provides a safety valve, just like FTRE, by providing an arbitrary bound on how much work JSAINT is willing to put in on solving the problem it is given. In practice, several kinds of resource bounds can be useful. Implementation-dependent bounds include CPU time and memory used. Implementation-independent bounds include upper bounds on the length of a derivation or the size and complexity of subproblems considered. JSAINT uses the simple but effective strategy of placing an upper bound on the number of subproblems it explores.

Step 4 raises most of the remaining issues. For instance, how should we estimate the difficulty of problems? Obviously the difficulty depends on the complexity of the expression being integrated—a polynomial with 100 terms takes more work to solve than a polynomial with two terms. Depending on one's perspective, the difficulty also depends on the path (or paths) between the subproblem and the original problem. Considering that JSAINT allows a subproblem to have multiple parents, we choose to ignore properties of the derivation path and base our estimates of difficulty solely on the structural properties of the subproblem or goal itself.[4]

What does processing a subproblem entail? The control statements associated with setting up a problem ⟨*P*⟩ act in part as signals used by the rules that implement operators. The process starts by asserting `(expanded ⟨P⟩)` and assuming `(open ⟨P⟩)`. Notice that we assert `expanded` because a problem can be expanded at most once during the course of problem solving, but we assume `open` because a solved (or failed) problem is no longer open, so we must be able to retract `open` statements.

Once `expanded` and `open` are believed, JSAINT runs the JTRE queues to completion in order to find applicable operators and their results. As noted above, if we find a `solution-of` statement for ⟨*P*⟩, we are finished with it. (The bookkeeping for this can be handled by a pattern-directed rule, as with the rest of the protocol.) If no solution has been found then we have to look for suggestions. Recall that suggestions have the form:

```
(suggest-for ⟨P⟩ ⟨OpInst⟩)
```

So by fetching `suggest-of` statements we have a set of operator instances that are applicable. A `try` goal must be added to the agenda for

4. Notice that we are also implicitly assuming something important about our problem-solving abilities: Our ability to solve a subproblem is independent of when we tackle it in the course of solving a larger problem. This would not be true for learning systems: see for example the literature on *explanation-based learning* [3] and the notion of *Socratic completeness* [2]).

each such instance. The set of suggestions themselves is recorded in the database by an `or-subgoals` assertion. Should there fail to be suggestions, then we assert that ⟨P⟩ has failed, justifying this statement on the empty `or-subgoals` list.

An aside: Notice that we would get the same answers if we simply asserted the failure of ⟨P⟩ as a premise in the circumstances just outlined. However, justifying it on the basis of the `or-subgoals` statement, which itself is a premise, provides an extra level of information about why the failure occurred. Intuitively, the reason for the failure is, "There was nothing which seemed relevant to solve the problem." For problem solvers that have several stores of knowledge to draw on, or have an associated learning or knowledge-acquisition system, such statements should be assumptions rather than premises, since there is the possibility that knowledge added later could provide new prospects for solving ⟨P⟩.

One question that may be bothering the alert reader at this stage is what should happen to the `(open ⟨P⟩)` assumption if we solve ⟨P⟩. We have been presuming it will be retracted, but how? Since solutions are detected locally and asynchronously by pattern-directed rules, we would like a similar, distributed solution. Two such solutions are:

1. Add a rule that explicitly retracts a problem's `open` statement when it is either solved or failed.
2. Install a nogood between `open` and `solved` and between `open` and `failed`, and ensure that the contradiction handler will retract the appropriate `open` statement in such conflicts.

The second solution is the most general and is typically preferable, since it allows a problem to become open again if we find out that our solution was inappropriate or if we gain new knowledge that lets us succeed where we failed previously. Its only disadvantage is that it sets up additional justifications in the JTMS, which are of course permanent. Given the way we have set up our problem solver such justifications would be used at most once. In these special circumstances, explicit retraction is more efficient. Since we presume here that our information about `solved` and `failed` is unretractable, our implementation uses the simpler method.

```
(rule ((:IN (AND-SUBGOALS ?parent ?children) :VAR ?def))
      (dolist (child ?children)
       (rlet ((?child (:EVAL child)))
              (rassert! (PARENT-OF ?child ?parent :AND)
                        (:DEF-OF-AND ?def))
              (rule ((:IN (failed ?child) :VAR ?delinquent))
                    (rassert! (failed ?parent)
                              (:AND-FAILURE ?def ?delinquent)))))
      (assert! '(solved ,?parent)
                '(:AND-SUCCESS ,?def
                  ,@ (mapcar #'(lambda (child)
                                 '(SOLVED ,child))
                             ?children))))

(rule ((:IN (OR-SUBGOALS ?parent ?children) :VAR ?def
            :TEST ?children))
      (dolist (child ?children)
        (rlet ((?child (:EVAL child)))
              (rassert! (PARENT-OF ?child ?parent :OR)
                        (:DEF-OF-OR ?def))
              (rule ((:IN (SOLVED ?child) :VAR ?winner))
                    (rassert! (SOLVED ?parent)
                              (:OR-SUCCESS ?winner ?def)))))
      (assert! '(FAILED ,?parent)
               '(:OR-FAILURE ,?def
                             ,@ (mapcar #'(lambda (child)
                                            '(FAILED ,child))
                                        ?children))))
```

Figure 8.7 PDIS rules for implementing AND/OR graph relationships

8.5.3 The JSAINT implementation

Now that we have seen how JSAINT is organized, it is time to explore how it is implemented. We will step through `jsrules.lisp` first, then go through `jsaint.lisp`, and end by examining `jsops.lisp`, a sample set of integration operators.

8.5.3.1 The bookkeeping rules jsrules.lisp

The rules in this file provide most of the enforcement of the semantics of the control vocabulary. The first two rules are reproduced in Figure 8.7.

The first rule implements the relationships between an and-node and its children, while the second rule implements the relationships between an or-node and its children. Notice that an equivalent form (the `parent-of` assertion) is produced by both rules to provide a pattern for retrieval and for rules common to both types of node. The only other feature of note is the use of `rlet` to bind `?child` inside these rules so that the rules spawned to detect success and failure will have the appropriate environment.

Since there are very few rules, we describe each of the rest of them in turn.

```
(rule ((:IN (PARENT-OF ?child ?parent ?type) :VAR ?lineage))
      (rassert! (RELEVANT ?child)
                (:STILL-WORKING-ON (OPEN ?parent) ?lineage)))
```

This rule defines `relevant` for a child in terms of `open` on its parent(s), as outlined in the design. (We recommend long informant names (e.g., `:STILL-WORKING-ON`) as a matter of style: they make tracking down bugs much easier.)

```
(rule ((:IN (SOLUTION-OF ?problem ?answer) :VAR ?found))
      (rassert! (SOLVED ?problem) (:FOUND-ANSWER ?found)))
```

This rule notes that a problem is solved once its solution has been found.

```
(rule ((:IN (OR-SUBGOALS (Integrate ?expr) NIL) :VAR ?no-ideas))
      (rassert! (FAILED (Integrate ?expr)) (:NO-METHODS ?no-ideas)))
```

This trigger can only occur when no suggestions have been made for the problem of integrating `?expr`. (The controller is careful to avoid asserting `or-subgoals` if the problem has already been solved.) Since no suggestions means that none of the system's knowledge is appropriate, failure is the only recourse.

```
(rule ((:IN (SOLVED ?problem))) ;; Can only happen once
      (retract! `(OPEN ,?problem) :EXPAND-AGENDA-ITEM t))

(rule ((:IN (FAILED ?problem)))
      (retract! `(OPEN ,?problem) :EXPAND-AGENDA-ITEM t))
```

These rules decomission work on `?problem`, since retracting its `open` statement will render its children irrelevant. Using retraction inside PDIS rules is generally unwise, and should only be done under special circumstances. Here it is safe only because we know what program made the assumptions (e.g., we know the informant is `:EXPAND-AGENDA-ITEM`) and we know that once retracted, an `open` statement will never be reassumed.

8.5.3.2 The JSAINT *main code*

As with the TREs, JSAINT uses a struct to define the collection of parameters associated with a copy of it instantiated for solving a particular problem. A JSAINT has its own JTRE and agenda, as well as the usual title, debugging flags, statistics counters, and so forth. The rest of the first page simply implements the same conventions we have used in other programs for creating and referring to copies of a system. Notice that we presume that no contradictions ever occur, so we make the contradiction handler be a call to `error`.

The second page describes the basic interface. `solve-integral` creates and runs a copy of JSAINT in order to solve a given integration problem. `explain-result` uses information cached in the JSAINT struct to explain what happened, using the JTMS routine `explore-network` as a subroutine.

The third page implements the central controller outlined earlier. `run-jsaint` provides the main loop, while most of the inferential work is performed within `process-subproblem`. The test for an `expanded` statement prevents duplication of effort, while the creation of the `or-subgoals` statement is in effect a higher-order inference: it makes an assertion about the global state of the database, something which cannot be done by any single PDIS rule.

The next page contains the procedure `queue-problem`, which adds items to the agenda, and ancillary procedures which calculate a heuristic estimate of complexity to order problems. JSAINT uses the sum of the maximum depth of the problem expression plus the number of symbols in it as its estimate of difficulty, since larger problems typically require more work to decompose into directly solvable pieces. Given a problem, `fetch-solution` simply returns the answer by looking for an in `solution-of` assertion.

The code for defining operators is next. This is the most difficult part of the system, since it must turn the reasonably civilized `defIntegration` statements into the appropriate pattern-directed inference rules.

```
(defIntegration Integral-of-Sum
  (Integral (+ ?t1 ?t2) ?var)
  :SUBPROBLEMS ((?int1 (Integrate (Integral ?t1 ?var)))
                (?int2 (Integrate (Integral ?t2 ?var))))
  :result (+ ?int1 ?int2))
```

Figure 8.8 A sample integration operator. This operator expresses the idea that the sum of two terms can be integrated by taking the sum of the integrals for the two individual terms.

Examining a simple operator will help focus our discussion. Figure 8.8 states that the problem of integrating the sum of two terms can be solved by integrating each term individually and then adding their result together. What must we do to implement this operator? First, we must be able to recognize situations in which it is applicable. Second, when it is applicable, we either use it to compute a result directly or suggest it as something to try, depending on whether or not it requires additional problems to be solved first. Finally, if the required subproblems have been solved, the solution to the original problem must be asserted (if feasible, given the particular solutions found to the subproblems).

We can implement this operator in JTRE by means of a pattern-directed rule, and write `defIntegration` as a macro which writes such rules. The outermost trigger must establish the potential applicability of the rule. Then, if there are no subproblems, the `:RESULT` field should be installed as the solution to the triggered problem. If there are subproblems, then the suggestion of `integral-of-sum` must be made and another rule spawned to look for this suggestion being taken up. If that rule ever fires, the subproblems must be queued and yet another rule spawned to look for their solutions. Once these solutions are found, the solution to the original problem can then be asserted in terms of the solution to the subproblems. Figure 8.9 illustrates this structure for the operator defined in Figure 8.8, as computed by `defintegration`.

It is worth studying this expanded rule closely, since it reveals several important implementation principles for systems of this kind. First, we have taken steps to keep both the generated rule and its results readable by automatically introducing intermediate variables via `rlet` and by using `keywordize` to introduce recognizable informants. This both simplifies `defintegration` and makes the expansion of the rules easier to understand (and, if necessary, easier to debug and extend). Second, we

```
(rule ((:IN (expanded (integrate (integral (+ ?t1 ?t2) ?var)))
            :VAR ?starter))
 (rlet ((?integral (integral (+ ?t1 ?t2) ?var))
        (?problem (integrate (integral (+ ?t1 ?t2) ?var))))
  (rlet ((?op-instance (integral-of-sum ?integral)))
    (rassert! (operator-instance ?op-instance)
              :OP-INSTANCE-DEFINITION)
    (rassert! (suggest-for ?problem ?op-instance)
              (:INTOPEXPANDER ?starter))
    (rule ((:IN (expanded (try ?op-instance)) :VAR ?trying))
      (rlet ((?goal0 (integrate (integral (:EVAL (simplify ?t1))
                                          ?var)))
             (?goal1 (integrate (integral (:EVAL (simplify ?t2))
                                          ?var))))
            (queue-problem ?goal0 ?problem)
            (queue-problem ?goal1 ?problem)
            (rassert! (and-subgoals (try ?op-instance)
                                    (?goal0 ?goal1))
                      (:INTEGRAL-OF-SUM-DEF ?trying))
            (rule ((:IN (solution-of ?goal0 ?int1) :VAR ?result0)
                   (:IN (solution-of ?goal1 ?int2) :VAR ?result1))
             (rlet ((?solution (:EVAL (simplify '(+ ,?int1 ,?in2)))))
              (rassert! (solution-of ?problem ?solution)
                 (:INTEGRAL-OF-SUM (operator-instance ?op-instance)
                                   ?result0 ?result1)))))))))
```

Figure 8.9 How an integration operator is implemented. Here is the JTRE rule built by `defintegration` to implement the integration rule of Figure 8.8.

have kept all control and data dependencies separate. All control statements are justified in terms of `expanded` statements, while the only data justification (the `solution-of` conclusion) is justified strictly in terms of `operator-instance` and other `solution-of` statements. This separation reflects the fact that, while it is important to record dependencies for both results and how they are obtained, the actual result in this case does not depend on the detailed sequence of control decisions made in deriving it. Both parts of the dependency network are useful for different purposes. When explaining the solution the data dependencies are the most important. When figuring out why JSAINT failed on a problem, the control justifications become more relevant.

`defintegration` itself uses several helpers to accomplish its mission. The principal helper is our old friend `simplify` (see Chapter 3), which is used to massage both subproblems and solutions into more reasonable forms. The procedure `calculate-subproblem-list` introduces the `?GOAL` variables for referring to subproblems. `simplifying-form-of` generates a call to `simplify` which is used at run time to simplify subgoals. And finally, `calculate-solution-rule-parts` uses the list of subgoals and result variables to create the triggers and antecedents for the rule that gathers the subproblem solutions and constructs the original problem solution from them.

The end of the file includes some interrogatives and debugging facilities. `show-problem` summarizes what is known about a particular problem or subproblem, while `show-ao-graph` provides a report describing the entire AND/OR graph. `try-jsaint` provides a handy way to try new problems, and `jfetch` provides a simple method for making ad hoc queries about the results. A small suite of sample problems, all of which JSAINT can solve, is also included.

8.5.3.3 The sample operator library jsops.lisp

The integration operators provide a good starting point for building up a library of integration laws. It begins with some standard forms for degenerate cases, namely

```
(defIntegration Integral-of-Constant ;; ∫ k dx → kx
  (Integral ?t ?var)
  :TEST (not (occurs-in? ?var ?t))
  :result (* ?t ?var))

(defIntegration Integral-of-Self ;; ∫ x dx → x^2/2
  (Integral ?exp ?exp)
  :result (/ (expt ?exp 2) 2))
```

The simplest transformation is next,

```
(defIntegration Move-Constant-outside ;; ∫ c f(x) dx → c ∫ f(x) dx
  (Integral (* ?const ?nonconst) ?var)
  :TEST (and (not (occurs-in? ?var ?const))
             (occurs-in? ?var ?nonconst))
  :SUBPROBLEMS ((?int (Integrate (Integral ?nonconst ?var))))
  :result (* ?const ?int))
```

which moves a constant outside the integration sign.

The rest of the file can be divided up according to the kind of operators it concerns. Figure 8.10 illustrates the operators that handle sums and polynomials. Notice that n-ary sums are handled in `Integral-of-Nary-sum` by decomposing them into the integral of the first, second, and rest. Operators involving exponentials, logarithms, and trigonometric functions are shown in Figure 8.11.

```
(defIntegration Integral-of-Sum
  (Integral (+ ?t1 ?t2) ?var)
  :SUBPROBLEMS ((?int1 (Integrate (Integral ?t1 ?var)))
                (?int2 (Integrate (Integral ?t2 ?var))))
  :result (+ ?int1 ?int2))

(defIntegration Integral-of-Nary-sum
  (Integral (+ ?t1 ?t2 . ?trest) ?var)
  :SUBPROBLEMS ((?int1 (Integrate (Integral ?t1 ?var)))
                (?int2 (Integrate (Integral ?t2 ?var)))
                (?intr (Integrate (Integral (+ . ?trest) ?var))))
  :TEST (not (null ?trest))
  :result (+ ?int1 ?int2 ?intr))

(defIntegration Integral-of-uminus
  (Integral (- ?term) ?var)
  :SUBPROBLEMS ((?int (Integrate (Integral ?term ?var))))
  :result (- ?int))

(defIntegration Integral-of-minus
  (Integral (- ?t1 ?t2) ?var)
  :SUBPROBLEMS ((?int1 (Integrate (Integral ?t1 ?var)))
                (?int2 (Integrate (Integral ?t2 ?var))))
  :result (- ?int1 ?int2))

(defIntegration Integral-of-SQR
  (Integral (sqr ?var) ?var)
  :result (/ (expt ?var 3) 3))

(defIntegration Integral-of-polyterm
  (Integral (expt ?var ?n) ?var)
  :TEST (not (same-constant? ?n -1))
  :result (/ (expt ?var (+ 1 ?n)) (+ 1 ?n)))
```

Figure 8.10 Operators involving summation and polynomials

```
(defIntegration Simple-e-integral
  (Integral (expt %e ?var) ?var)
  :result (expt %e ?var))

(defIntegration e-integral
  (Integral (expt %e (* ?a ?var)) ?var)
  :TEST (not (occurs-in? ?var ?a))
  :result (/ (expt %e (* ?a ?var)) ?a))

(defIntegration non-e-power-integral
  (Integral (expt ?b (* ?a ?var)) ?var)
  :TEST (and (not (occurs-in? ?var ?a))
             (not (occurs-in? ?var ?b)))
  :result (/ (expt ?b (* ?a ?var)) (* ?a (log ?b %e))))

(defIntegration Log-Integral
  (Integral (log ?var %e) ?var)
  :result (- (* ?var (log ?var %e)) ?var))

(defIntegration sin-integral
  (Integral (sin (* ?a ?var)) ?var)
  :TEST (not (occurs-in? ?var ?a))
  :result (- (/ (cos (* ?a ?var)) ?a)))

(defIntegration cos-integral
  (Integral (cos (* ?a ?var)) ?var)
  :TEST (not (occurs-in? ?var ?a))
  :result (/ (sin (* ?a ?var)) ?a))

(defIntegration sin-sqr-integral
  (Integral (sqr (sin ?var)) ?var)
  :result (- (/ ?var 2) (/ (sin (* 2 ?var)) 4)))

(defIntegration cos-sqr-integral
  (Integral (sqr (cos ?var)) ?var)
  :result (+ (/ ?var 2) (/ (sin (* 2 ?var)) 4)))
```

Figure 8.11 Operators involving exponentials, logs, and trig

One limitation of our implementation language for operators can be seen by the substitution operators at the end of `jsops.lisp`, reproduced in Figure 8.12. These operators implement the following substitutions:

`SinToCosSqrSub` $\sin(x) \longrightarrow \sqrt{1 - \cos^2(x)}$
`CosToSinSqrSub` $\cos(x) \longrightarrow \sqrt{1 - \sin^2(x)}$
`SinSqrToTanCosSub` $\sin(x) \longrightarrow \tan^2(x) \times \cos^2(x)$

```
(defIntegration SinToCosSqrSub
  (Integral ?exp ?var)
  :TEST (and (occurs-in? ?var ?exp)
             (occurs-in? '(sin ,?var) ?exp))
  :SUBPROBLEMS
  ((?Int (Integrate (Integral
                     (:EVAL (subst '(sqrt (- 1 (expt (cos ,?var) 2)))
                                   '(sin ,?var)
                                   ?exp :TEST 'equal)) ?var))))
  :result ?Int)

(defIntegration CosToSinSqrSub
  (Integral ?exp ?var)
  :TEST (and (occurs-in? ?var ?exp)
             (occurs-in? '(cos ,?var) ?exp))
  :SUBPROBLEMS
  ((?Int (Integrate (Integral
                     (:EVAL (subst '(sqrt (- 1 (expt (sin ,?var) 2)))
                                   '(cos ,?var)
                                   ?exp :TEST 'equal)) ?var))))
  :result ?Int)

(defIntegration SinSqrToTanCosSub
  (Integral ?exp ?var)
  :TEST (and (occurs-in? ?var ?exp)
             (occurs-in? '(sin ,?var) ?exp))
  :SUBPROBLEMS
   ((?int (Integrate (Integral
                      (:EVAL (subst '(* (sqr (tan ,?var))
                                          (sqr (cos ,?var)))
                                     '(sin ,?var)
                                     ?exp :TEST 'equal))))))
  :result ?Int)
```

Figure 8.12 JSAINT's language is clumsy for certain substitutions

These are what in SAINT would be heuristic transformations—on certain problems they are very useful, but on others they will propose subproblems that are more complex than what they started with.

8.5.4 Exploring JSAINT's operation

Running JSAINT on the suite of sample problems provides some interesting insights into its operation. Figure 8.13 illustrates in detail what JSAINT produces for `problem2` from the example suite. By using `explain-result` we can explore the argument for the answer as well as the answer itself. The ability to explore the reasons for a failure is illustrated in Figure 8.14, where the impasse can be traced to the system's lack of knowledge about hyperbolic functions.

```
> (try-jsaint problem2)
(+ (* 5 X) (/ (SQR X) 2))
<Agenda JSAINT Test>
> (explain-result)

 Solved the problem:
(SOLUTION-OF (INTEGRATE (INTEGRAL (+ 5 X) X)) (+ (* 5 X) (/ (SQR X) 2)))
 is IN via INTEGRAL-OF-SUM on
  (SOLUTION-OF (INTEGRATE (INTEGRAL 5 X)) (* 5 X))
  (SOLUTION-OF (INTEGRATE (INTEGRAL X X)) (/ (SQR X) 2))
>>>1

(SOLUTION-OF (INTEGRATE (INTEGRAL 5 X)) (* 5 X))
 is IN via INTEGRAL-OF-CONSTANT on
  (OPERATOR-INSTANCE (INTEGRAL-OF-CONSTANT (INTEGRAL 5 X)))
>>>0

(SOLUTION-OF (INTEGRATE (INTEGRAL (+ 5 X) X)) (+ (* 5 X) (/ (SQR X) 2)))
 is IN via INTEGRAL-OF-SUM on
  (SOLUTION-OF (INTEGRATE (INTEGRAL 5 X)) (* 5 X))
  (SOLUTION-OF (INTEGRATE (INTEGRAL X X)) (/ (SQR X) 2))
>>>2

(SOLUTION-OF (INTEGRATE (INTEGRAL X X)) (/ (SQR X) 2))
 is IN via INTEGRAL-OF-SELF on
  (OPERATOR-INSTANCE (INTEGRAL-OF-SELF (INTEGRAL X X)))
>>>q
#<Node: (SOLUTION-OF (INTEGRATE (INTEGRAL X X)) (/ (SQR X) 2))>
```

Figure 8.13 JSAINT solving an integral

```
> (try-jsaint '(integrate (integral (+ (* 3 x) (cosh x)) x)))
:FAILED-EMPTY
<Agenda JSAINT Test>
> (explain-result)

 Ran out of things to do.
(FAILED (INTEGRATE (INTEGRAL (+ (* 3 X) (COSH X)) X)))
 is IN via OR-FAILURE on
  (OR-SUBGOALS (INTEGRATE (INTEGRAL (+ (* 3 X) (COSH X)) X))
             ((TRY (INTEGRAL-OF-SUM (INTEGRAL (+ (* 3 X) (COSH X)) X)))))
  (FAILED (TRY (INTEGRAL-OF-SUM (INTEGRAL (+ (* 3 X) (COSH X)) X))))
>>>2

(FAILED (TRY (INTEGRAL-OF-SUM (INTEGRAL (+ (* 3 X) (COSH X)) X))))
 is IN via AND-FAILURE on
  (AND-SUBGOALS (TRY (INTEGRAL-OF-SUM (INTEGRAL (+ (* 3 X) (COSH X)) X)))
               ((INTEGRATE (INTEGRAL (* 3 X) X))
                (INTEGRATE (INTEGRAL (COSH X) X))))
  (FAILED (INTEGRATE (INTEGRAL (COSH X) X)))
>>>2

(FAILED (INTEGRATE (INTEGRAL (COSH X) X)))
 is IN via NO-METHODS on
  (OR-SUBGOALS (INTEGRATE (INTEGRAL (COSH X) X)) NIL)
>>>1

(OR-SUBGOALS (INTEGRATE (INTEGRAL (COSH X) X)) NIL)
 is IN via OR-SUBGOALS on
>>>q
#<Node: (OR-SUBGOALS (INTEGRATE (INTEGRAL (COSH X) X)) NIL)>
```

Figure 8.14 JSAINT failing to solve an integral

Solving $\int(sin^2(x) - 1)dx$ provides a good example of how the controller allows JSAINT to stop working as soon as it finds a solution. Figure 8.15 depicts the AND/OR graph for this problem. In addition to the solution shown, there is an alternative solution which first uses `integral-of-sum` to split the terms, `integral-of-constant` to handle the -1, and `sin-sqr-integral` to handle the $sin^2(x)$ term. (To verify this, try running this example with `SinToCosSQRSub` commented out.) Notice that the node for the instance of `Integral-of-Sum` is not even opened, so no work was wasted finding an alternate solution.

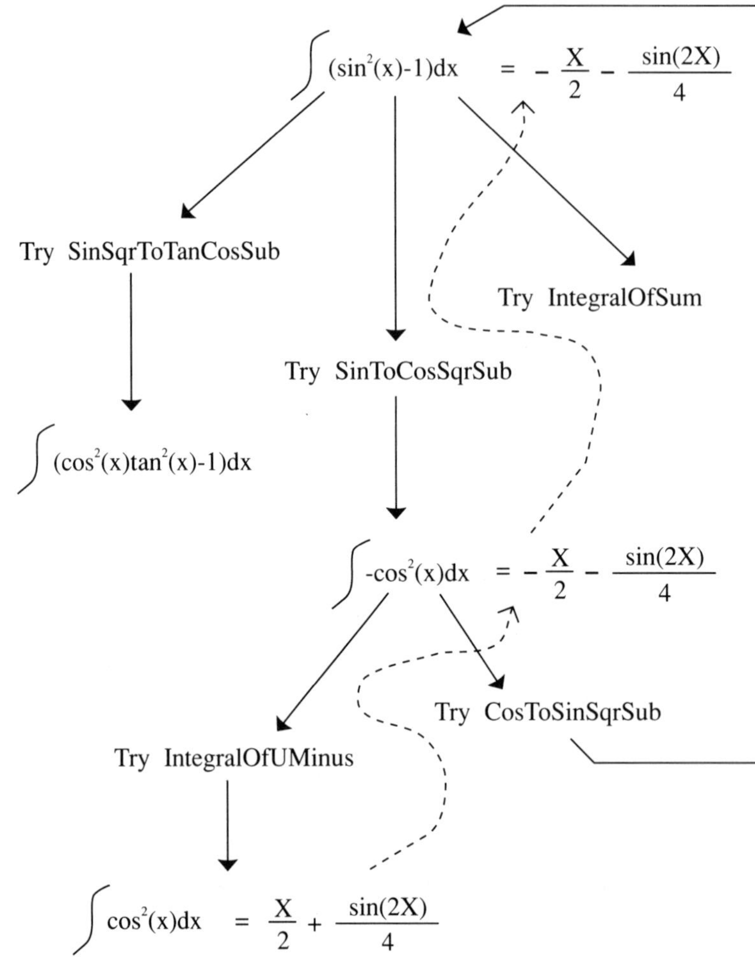

Figure 8.15 JSAINT avoids finding redundant solutions. The solid lines indicate parent relationships, the dashed lines indicates how the solution of subgoals propagates back to become the solution of the original problem.

8.6 Summary

In this chapter we have seen how a JTMS can be exploited in problem solving. The issues involved in the inference engine/TMS interface have been explored by building JTRE, a version of FTRE which uses the JTMS. In the N-queens example, we saw how dependency-directed search works, and that it could potentially increase efficiency considerably. In JSAINT, we saw how a problem solver could be built that both exhibits interesting performance and provides (at least rudimentary) explanations of its results.

The increased power we gained by using a TMS raises an interesting question: Could a more powerful TMS allow us to build even more powerful problem solvers? The answer is yes, within certain boundaries. The exact nature and shape of these boundaries is still very much an area of active research at this writing. For example, in the next chapter we show how a logic-based TMS can make most propositional reasoning occur automatically and efficiently. But if one tries to make this new TMS powerful enough to be complete, we give the exponential a new toehold in our programs. The next five chapters provide some useful data points, both positive and negative, reflecting the field's current understanding of the matter.

These systems also illustrate another central design principle. The inference engine used by the problem solvers in this chapter were divided into two parts: the pattern-directed inference system and a control scheme which made global decisions based on the state of the JTRE database. No single module should be expected to do everything. Divide-and-conquer is as crucial a technique for designers of problem solvers as it is for the problem solvers themselves.

8.7 Backpointers

The technique of control via suggestions is an abstraction of common practice in many AI communities, including many builders of blackboard systems and production-rule systems [1, 5].

Much has been learned about indefinite integration since Slagle's pioneering work. For example, there is an algorithm for indefinite integration (the *Risch algorithm*) which covers the analytic functions, and hence, in principle, most search is unnecessary. However, the Risch algorithm produces results that are hard to simplify, and so most fielded symbolic algebra systems rely on search techniques descended from SAINT. The early history of automatic symbolic integration techniques is described in [7]. A good introduction to the state of the art in symbolic algebra is provided by [5].

8.8 Exercises

1. One problem with :TEST is that it can give naive users a bit too much rope with which to hang themselves. In this problem we examine this issue more closely.

   a. ⋆ What two disasters can occur with the following rule? Illustrate with specific examples.

```
(rule ((:IN (prime-number ?n) :VAR ?f0
            :TEST (fetch '(Using trap-door-code))))
 (rassert! (suggest-code-key ?n) (:PRIMES-NEEDED-FOR-KEY ?f0)))
```

   b. ⋆ Select a subset of Common Lisp that provides a safe language for writing tests. That is, if every :TEST is written in this subset, the problems identified previously cannot occur.

   c. ⋆⋆ Extend `junify.lsp` to enforce the use of your sublanguage in :TEST options.

   d. ⋆⋆ Evaluate your sublanguage by finding examples of tests which might be both plausible and useful, but cannot be expressed in your sublanguage.

2. ⋆⋆ Consider again the `rule` struct. Since any rule is stored under some class, we do not really need to keep either the JTRE or the `class` backpointers. After all, given the rule and a JTRE struct, we could always search its classes to see if the rule was there. Similarly, the `counter` field is only for debugging purposes. Write a version of `jrules.lsp` that uses a single cons cell to store a rule, rather than a rule struct. How much harder would it be to debug this version? Is it worth it? How could you get the best of both worlds?

3. ⋆⋆ Change `jrules.lisp` so that rules are only executed when all of the belief conditions of the triggers hold simultaneously.

4. ⋆⋆ Consider the following rule:

```
(rule ((:IN (foo ?x) :VAR ?f1)
       (:IN (bar ?x) :VAR ?f2))
 (rassert! (mumble ?x)
           (:GRUMBLE ?f1 ?f2)))
```

   If (FOO A) is asserted, eventually a rule struct is created to look for a matching occurrence of BAR. Notice that only one fact (i.e., (BAR A)) can ever successfully match against this rule struct. Ideally, once a successful match has occurred the rule struct should be removed, since any further attempts to match against it will be fruitless. Modify JTRE to detect such rules and remove them once they have been used.

5. ⋆⋆ The version of TRY-IN-CONTEXT in jqueens.lisp is not as general as it should be. In particular, it can fail to perform properly when used in a problem solver that caches previous partial solutions as well as nogoods. Devise an example which illustrates this problem, and rewrite TRY-IN-CONTEXT so that it handles such cases successfully.

6. Notice that the mathematical law

$$\int u^n du \longrightarrow \frac{u^{n+1}}{n+1}$$

   where $n \neq -1$, is implemented by two defintegration operators, namely Integral-of-SQR and Integral-of-Polyterm. A similar situation occurs with simple-e-integral and e-integral.

   a. ⋆ Explain what feature(s) of JSAINT make this necessary.

   b. ⋆ Propose two ways that JSAINT might be extended so that this mathematical fact could be represented via a single operator.

7. ⋆ What is the logical status of control terms such as integrate? Is it best viewed as a standard predicate, a modal operator, or a connective? Discuss the trade-offs of each point of view.

8. ⋆⋆ Implicit in our design of integration operators is the assumption that if we can solve the subgoals proposed by the method, then those results can always be combined to form the solution to the original problem. Are there operators for which this is not true? That

is, are there integration techniques whose applicability cannot be determined until after the subgoals are solved? If not, explain why not. If so, design an extension to `defIntegration` that allows such techniques to be implemented.

9. ⋆⋆ The resource bounds currently incorporated in JSAINT focus on internal measures. Add bounds on run time and storage utilization, to ensure that only a limited amount of computation is used on problems beyond the system's capabilities.

10. There are several ways in which JSAINT's algorithms for estimating difficulty and for selecting what problem to work on next could be improved.

    a. ⋆⋆ Discuss the trade-offs in making JSAINT's difficulty estimation algorithm depend on its connection(s) to the original problem.

    b. ⋆⋆ Some operators work better than others. Revise the JSAINT difficulty estimation algorithm to take the kind of problem and/or operator into account.

    c. ⋆⋆ One complaint raised against programs like JSAINT which base their activities on unstructured agendas is that their behavior can appear incoherent. For example, if two subproblems $P1$ and $P2$ locally appear equally hard, but $P1$ is the last subproblem out of 12 in one approach to solving the original integral, while $P2$ is the first subproblem of 48 to be tackled in a completely different approach, most people would choose to work on $P1$ rather than $P2$. Can you devise a scheme that will increase JSAINT's coherence?

11. One facility SAINT had which JSAINT lacks is the ability to suggest more complex substitutions. For example, given the problem

    $$\int \ln(3x)dx$$

    a human mathematician might transform this into a simpler problem by using the substitution

    $$u = 3x; du = 3dx$$

    because it turns the original problem into

$$\frac{1}{3}\int \ln(u)du$$

which can be solved by first using a standard form and then substituting back to get rid of u. In this problem we examine what is needed to implement this *u-substitution method.*

a. ⋆⋆ This method requires the ability to take derivatives. Write a set of rules using `match.lisp` to provide a simple symbolic differentiation system.

b. ⋆⋆ The ability to make useful suggestions is critical to this method's success. What sources of knowledge should be tapped to make suggestions?

c. ⋆⋆⋆ Implement a facility for defining substitution methods.

12. Like SAINT, JSAINT does not perform integration by parts. The rule of integration by parts says

$$\int udv \longrightarrow uv \int vdu$$

a. ⋆ What problems would we encounter in implementing this rule? (Hint: Consider $\int x \ln(x)dx$.)

b. ⋆⋆⋆ Extend JSAINT to implement integration by parts.

13. ⋆⋆⋆ While the rewrite rules in `simplify.lisp` are elegant, they are less than optimal computationally. Consider the rule

```
((+ (?? pre) (* (? f1) (? thing)) (?? mid) (? thing) (?? post))
 (+ (?? pre) (* (+ 1 (? f1)) (? thing)) (?? mid) (?? post)))
```

which combines like terms (i.e., $3x + x \longrightarrow 4x$). What this rule says intuitively is that if you have `thing` occurring by itself and you already have a term in the sum which is the product of `thing` and something else, you might as well merge the two `thing` terms. `simplify` gets this effect in a most inefficient way, which includes trying all possible bindings for `(?? pred)` even if the sum involves no products at all.

A more efficient method might be to follow our intuitions more closely. That is, in looking over an expression one might scan for common subexpressions, and use their relative placement in the expression's structure to suggest both what simplification rules might be relevant and what bindings they should have. Implement such a scheme and compare its performance to the current simplifier.

14. ⋆⋆⋆ The kind of problem mentioned in the previous exercise in fact permeates many pattern-directed systems. For example, in the `move-constant-outside` rule on page 241, we had the trigger condition

```
(* ?const ?nonconst)
```

which would match expressions like

```
(* 5 (log x))
```

but not expressions like

```
(* 5 Cp (expt x t))
```

or even

```
(* (log x) 5)
```

Write a higher-order language for patterns that allows one to state concisely ideas like "If the expression is a product which has a non-trivial subset of constant terms, the integral is the result of taking the product of the constant terms with the integral of the product of the non-constant terms." Incorporate this language into JSAINT.

15. ⋆⋆⋆⋆ Using the results of the previous exercises, extend JSAINT to be able to solve at least the same range of problems as SAINT.

16. ⋆⋆⋆⋆ Using JSAINT as a starting point, reconstruct the LEX learning system developed by Mitchell, Utgoff, and Banerji [6].

8.9 Bibliography

[1] Barr, A., and Feigenbaum, E., *The Handbook of Artificial Intelligence*, Morgan-Kaufmann, 1981.

[2] Crawford, J., and Kuipers, B., "Towards a theory of access-limited logic for knowledge representation," *Proceedings of the first international conference on principles of knowledge representation and reasoning*, Morgan-Kaufmann, 1989.

[3] DeJong, G., "An introduction to explanation-based learning," in Shrobe, H. and the AAAI (eds.), *Exploring Artificial Intelligence*, Morgan-Kaufmann, 1988.

[4] Engelmore, R., and Morgan, T. (eds.) *Blackboard Systems* Addison-Wesley, 1988.

[5] Geddes, K., Czapor, S., and Labahn, G., *Algorithms for Computer Algebra*, Kluwer, 1992.

[6] Mitchell, T., Utgoff, P., and Banerji, R., "Learning by experimentation: Acquiring and refining problem-solving heuristics," in Michalski, R., Carbonell, J., and Mitchell, T. (eds.), *Machine Learning: An Artificial Intelligence Approach*, Tioga Press, 1983.

[7] Moses, J., "Symbolic Integration: The stormy decade," *CACM*, 14(1971) 548–560.

[8] Slagle, J., "A heuristic program that solves symbolic integration problems in freshman calculus," in Feigenbaum, E. and Feldman, J. (eds.), *Computers and Thought*, McGraw-Hill, 1963.

[9] Slagle, J., "A computer program for solving problems in freshman calculus (SAINT)," Ph.D. dissertation, Massachusetts Institute of Technology, 1961. (Available through National Technical Information Service.)

9 Logic-Based Truth Maintenance Systems

The justifications which the JTMS accepts as input are very limited in expressive power. Logically, JTMS justifications are simply definite clauses (i.e., formulas of the form $x_1 \wedge \cdots \wedge x_n \Rightarrow c$ where x_i and c are all TMS nodes). Many applications need to express more than just definite clauses. For example, they may need to say things like: if x is true, then y is false. Although, as we shall see, arbitrary clauses can be partially encoded in the JTMS by various encoding tricks, these encodings can be quite cumbersome. Logic-based truth maintenance systems (LTMSs) [5, 6, 7, 8] were invented to overcome this limitation. The LTMS generalizes the JTMS to allow any propositional clause as input (see Figure 9.1). This enables the inference engine to express logical relationships involving the negations of nodes as well, and therefore to express every possible logical relationship among nodes.

9.1 Why reasoning about negation is important

It is instructive to look first at some of the problems resulting from the logical weakness of the JTMS. This will illustrate that developing a TMS which accepts any propositional clause would provide a significant problem-solving advantage.

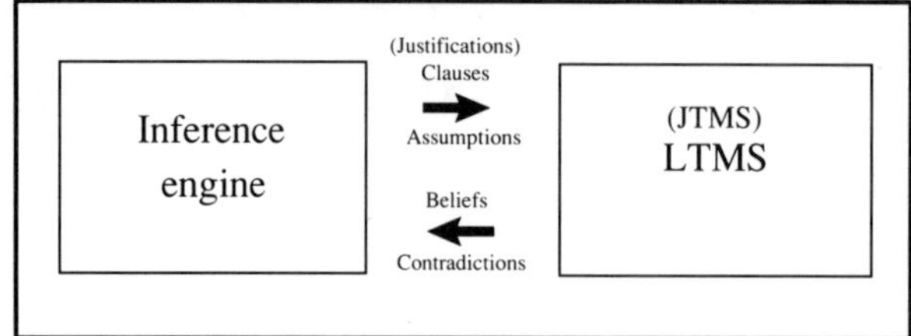

Figure 9.1 The change from JTMSs to LTMSs. The inference engine now supplies the TMS arbitrary clauses instead of definite clause justifications.

9.1.1 Representing clauses approximately in the JTMS

The JTMS can only represent definite clauses. Nevertheless, we can "approximately" encode arbitrary clauses as definite clauses via a set of encoding tricks. Consider the following:

$$A \vee B \vee C.$$

From this clause we should be able to derive A if B and C are false. Although the JTMS cannot directly represent "B is false," it can be approximated by creating another node $\overline{B}$ which is in when B is false. To prevent B from being both true and false simultaneously we have to signal a contradiction when both are in:

$$B \wedge \overline{B} \Rightarrow \bot.$$

If we encode C similarly, then the derivation we desire can be achieved by the justification:

$$\overline{B} \wedge \overline{C} \Rightarrow A.$$

In general, a JTMS can encode arbitrary clauses by constructing distinct nodes for negations, adding justifications contradicting every node with its negation, and adding justifications to encode all the ways the clause can be used to infer nodes and their negations. The entire set of justifications needed to encode $A \vee B \vee C$ is:

$$A \wedge \overline{A} \Rightarrow \bot \qquad \overline{A} \wedge \overline{B} \Rightarrow C$$
$$B \wedge \overline{B} \Rightarrow \bot \qquad \overline{B} \wedge \overline{C} \Rightarrow A$$
$$C \wedge \overline{C} \Rightarrow \bot \qquad \overline{C} \wedge \overline{A} \Rightarrow B$$

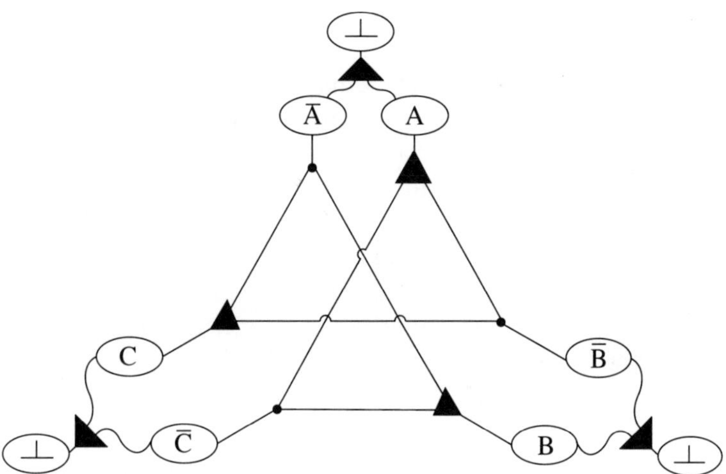

Figure 9.2 Encoding $A \vee B \vee C$ for the JTMS

Figure 9.2 shows the resultant dependency network consisting of six nodes and six justifications. Within the LTMS formulation, $A \vee B \vee C$ is simply represented by three nodes and one propositional clause—a significant savings in complexity and space over the JTMS formulation.

It is important to note that *all* clauses, not just non-definite clauses, must be encoded in this way in the JTMS. For example, it does not suffice to encode the material implication $A \rightarrow B$ as simply the justification $A \Rightarrow B$. We must also add the contrapositive as a justification: $\overline{B} \Rightarrow \overline{A}$. This second justification ensures that if B becomes false, A will become labeled false—the JTMS cannot make this inference without this second justification (except perhaps through contradiction handling).

9.1.2 Importance of negation for guiding backtracking

In Chapter 7 we saw that one of the major advantages of a TMS is that it aids backtracking by helping recognize previously encountered contradictions. If the inference engine enables a set of assumptions that produces a contradiction, then the JTMS signals a contradiction before any more inference engine operations take place. In the JTMS architecture, choosing which assumption(s) to retract given a contradiction is solely the responsibility of the inference engine's contradiction handler.

Unfortunately, there is nothing in this scheme to ensure that the same contradiction will not occur repeatedly so that the contradiction handler may have to make the same retraction decision over and over again.

Consider a typical scenario resulting from the JTMS signaling the inference engine about a contradiction. The inference engine asks the JTMS for the set of assumptions underlying a well-founded explanation for the contradiction and then chooses one of those assumptions to retract. But what mechanism ensures that the very same contradiction with the same assumptions will not happen again? Suppose that JTMS assumptions $A_1, \ldots, A_n$ underlie a contradiction. The JTMS, in effect, has inferred the formula:

$$\neg(A_1 \wedge \cdots \wedge A_n),$$

which is equivalent to the clause (called a *nogood*),

$$\neg A_1 \vee \cdots \vee \neg A_n,$$

but the JTMS cannot directly represent or use this. Suppose that $A_1, \ldots,$ $A_{m-1}, A_{m+1}, \ldots, A_n$ hold. Then the JTMS cannot deduce $\neg A_m$ directly without reinvoking contradiction handling or encoding the nogood using the encoding scheme of the previous section.

If the search order through assumptions is fixed and A_n is the last assumption, then it is only necessary to install a fraction of the cumbersome encoding:

$$A_1 \wedge \cdots \wedge A_{n-1} \Rightarrow \overline{A_n},$$

$$A_n \wedge \overline{A_n} \Rightarrow \bot.$$

This technique was used in the N-queens example in Section 8.4 (in which the pairwise nogoods were obeyed by the search order and thus not explicitly represented in the TMS). Whether backtracking uses a fixed order or not, reasoning with negations has another advantage which improves the performance of backtrack search. Suppose we are at a point in a search where we have discovered the nogoods,

$$\neg Q \vee \neg B,$$

$$\neg Q \vee \neg A,$$

we just determined Q, and we have a future choice of $\{A, B, C\}$. Given Q, we should be able to immediately infer C, thus the backtracker no longer has to make a future choice at $\{A, B, C\}$. This could have been achieved with an JTMS by fully encoding the clause, $A \vee B \vee C$. In this and all the examples of this section, the JTMS could represent nogood clauses using the encoding of the previous section. However, search usually generates a large number of nogood clauses, and the overhead of the cumbersome encoding will quickly consume too many computational resources.

9.1.3 LTMS intuitions

Consider an analogy. We could represent floating-point numbers as strings of characters, and write code that ensures that these strings are manipulated to satisfy the laws of floating-point numbers. However, it is far more efficient to implement floating-point operations directly, since there are special properties that can be exploited in hardware that way. So it is with the LTMS versus the JTMS: one can obtain much of the logical power of the LTMS by using the JTMS with an appropriate encoding procedure, but this procedure is very clumsy and the dependency network it produces is inefficient.

The shift from the JTMS to the LTMS is also a shift of point of view: from regarding the TMS as a simple device for recording the inference engine's computations, to seeing it as a device for carrying a substantial inferential burden itself. If the TMS is to be a central component of the inferential system, it pays to make it more and more powerful. The LTMS method of encoding clauses directly reduces the amount of work the inference engine must do in encoding formulas, and provides a more efficient implementation of the same logical structures.

9.2 LTMS basics

9.2.1 LTMS labels

Most of the functionality of the LTMS is very similar to the JTMS. As in the the JTMS, every problem-solver datum is assigned a distinct node.

Unlike in the JTMS, a distinct node *need not* be created for negations of data. Since the LTMS accepts propositional clauses, we do not need to define a special syntax for LTMS inputs (in contrast to JTMS justifications).

The JTMS permits only two labels: `:IN` and `:OUT`. Given a set of justifications $\mathcal{J}$ and set of enabled assumptions $\mathcal{A}$, node x is labeled `:IN` if it logically follows from $\mathcal{J} \cup \mathcal{A}$ and `:OUT` otherwise. Labeling a node `:OUT` can either mean that its negation is derivable or that there isn't enough information to tell whether x or its negation is derivable. As negations of nodes are important in the LTMS, the label set is expanded. `:IN` becomes `:TRUE` and `:OUT` becomes `:FALSE` when the negation of the node is derivable; the node becomes `:UNKNOWN` otherwise. We use C to represent the set of clauses supplied by the inference engine.

- A node is labeled `:TRUE` if it is derivable from C and the enabled assumptions.
- A node is labeled `:FALSE` if its negation is derivable from C and the enabled assumptions.
- A node is labeled `:UNKNOWN` otherwise.

(In the case where the clauses combined with the enabled assumptions are logically inconsistent, namely when both a node *and* its negation are derivable, then a node's label is (almost) arbitrary. We discuss this situation later.)

We saw that negation could be encoded in a JTMS by creating nodes to represent the negations. Using the encoding convention of the previous section, Figure 9.3 illustrates the mapping between the different labels: (1) P and $\overline{P}$ `:IN` cannot happen in the LTMS; (2) P `:IN` and $\overline{P}$ `:OUT` corresponds to P `:TRUE`; (3) $\overline{P}$ `:OUT` and P `:IN` corresponds to P `:FALSE`; and (4) P and $\overline{P}$ `:OUT` corresponds to P `:UNKNOWN`.

At first it might seem that the only advantage left to the JTMS is that it allows reasoning in contradictory situations where both P and its negation $\overline{P}$ hold (i.e., when the pairwise contradiction is not installed). Even this advantage is illusory. This same effect can be accomplished in the LTMS in exactly the same way. Instead of treating P and $\neg P$ as negations of each other, the inference engine can instruct the LTMS to construct distinct unrelated nodes for each of P and $\overline{P}$.

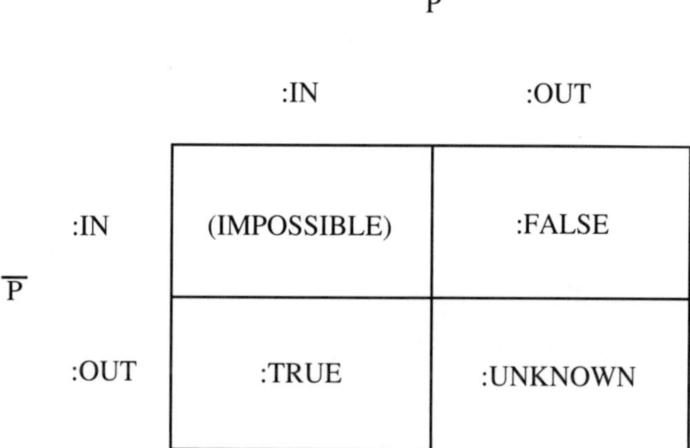

Figure 9.3 Mapping the JTMS labels for P and $\overline{P}$ to the LTMS label for P

9.2.2 LTMS nodes

A TMS distinguishes three node properties: a node can be a premise, a contradiction, or an assumption. These properties are treated in an LTMS as follows:

- The LTMS does not require an explicit *premise* property: a node is regarded as a premise if it is the only node in some inference engine-supplied clause.
- The LTMS has no notion of a *contradiction* node.
- An *assumption* is a node whose belief may be later changed by an explicit inference engine operation. An assumption is *enabled* if the inference engine has signaled the LTMS that it chooses to label it `:TRUE` or `:FALSE`. A retracted assumption is treated as any other node.

The fact that the LTMS does not require a notion of a contradiction node bears examination. In the JTMS, the fact that a node is a contradiction has no direct bearing on JTMS labels. Marking the node as contradiction merely informs the JTMS that when this node comes `:IN`, the JTMS should signal the inference engine, whose responsibility it is to retract assumptions (or do whatever is necessary) to make the contradiction node `:OUT`. This complex sequence of interactions is often unnecessary with the LTMS. For example, consider the JTMS justification,

$$A \wedge B \Rightarrow \bot.$$

If A and B are enabled assumptions, then this would invoke contradiction handling, which would probably (depending on the inference engine) retract A or B. In the LTMS, the clausal equivalent is simply:

$$\neg A \vee \neg B \vee \bot,$$

which is the same as

$$\neg A \vee \neg B.$$

If assumption A is enabled to `:TRUE`, then the LTMS immediately labels B `:FALSE`. Thus, the LTMS is logically stronger and consequently can avoid some backtracking for inference engines that use this technique.

Of course, contradiction handling is still required because the LTMS may discover that the current labeling violates some clause. This would happen in the previous example if A and B were both enabled assumptions and then the clause $\neg A \vee \neg B$ were added. Contradiction handling is unavoidable because the inference engine must decide whether to retract A or B. This is discussed in more detail later.

9.2.3 Logical specification for an LTMS

We can specify the LTMS just has we have the JTMS (see Section 7.2). The LTMS nodes define a set of propositional symbols S. A subset of those symbols are marked as assumptions which can be enabled by initially setting them to `:TRUE` or `:FALSE`. We define $\mathcal{A}$ to be a set of assumption literals. $x \in \mathcal{A}$ if assumption x is initially labeled `:TRUE` and $\neg x \in \mathcal{A}$ if assumption x is initially labeled `:FALSE`. A clause is a disjunction of literals with no repeated or complementary literals. Let C be the set of clauses, defined over S, the inference engine has supplied. The reason for distinguishing $\mathcal{A}$ from C is that C is guaranteed to grow monotonically, while assumptions may be added and retracted from $\mathcal{A}$ at any time.

The LTMS has three fundamental tasks: (1) to provide labels for nodes, (2) to detect contradictions, and (3) to provide explanations for the labels.

Consider the first task. Given a query about some symbol s, the LTMS answers as follows: If there exists a $\mathcal{E} \subset \mathcal{A} \cup C$ such that $\mathcal{E}$ is satisfiable and s follows propositionally from $\mathcal{E}$, then the LTMS answers `:TRUE` for s. If there exists a $\mathcal{E} \subset \mathcal{A} \cup C$ such that $\mathcal{E}$ is satisfiable and $\neg s$ follows propositionally from $\mathcal{E}$, then the LTMS answers `:FALSE` for s. Otherwise the label for s is `:UNKNOWN`. If $\mathcal{A} \cup C$ is satisfiable, then it is sufficient that $\mathcal{E} = \mathcal{A} \cup C$. However, we want the LTMS to provide useful answers to queries even when $\mathcal{A} \cup C$ is not satisfiable. In that case, the LTMS may arbitrarily provide either `:TRUE` or `:FALSE`, but it must provide the corresponding explanation as well.

The second LTMS task is to detect contradictions. Whenever $\mathcal{A} \cup C$ is unsatisfiable, then the LTMS is expected to signal the inference engine to this effect. Note that the LTMS is still expected to provide labels and their explanations even if $\mathcal{A} \cup C$ is unsatisfiable.

The third LTMS task is to provide explanations, even in circumstances where the $\mathcal{A} \cup C$ is not satisfiable. (Otherwise, for example, the inference engine has no way to track down which assumption to retract in response to a contradiction.) The explanation must at least be a logical proof using $\mathcal{E}$ for the label that the LTMS provided for the node. Generally its form depends on the precise rules used by the implementation, so we return to the details later.

9.3 Boolean constraint propagation

The logical specification of an LTMS can be implemented in a variety of ways. A particularly useful algorithm for implementing an LTMS is Boolean constraint propagation (BCP). While logically incomplete with respect to the propositional calculus, BCP is efficient and sound. We begin by describing the essence of BCP, and later we examine different ways to overcome its logical incompleteness.

BCP labels every symbol `:TRUE`, `:FALSE`, or `:UNKNOWN`. BCP is provided with an initial labeling of assumptions $\mathcal{A}$. All remaining symbols are initially labeled `:UNKNOWN`. The LTMS algorithm labels symbols (represented by nodes), not literals. However, to describe the algorithm it will be convenient to define the label of literal x to be the label of the symbol x and the label of literal $\neg x$ to be `:FALSE`, `:TRUE`, or `:UNKNOWN`, depending on whether the label of x is :TRUE, :FALSE, or :UNKNOWN. Given a labeling, every clause $C \in C$ is either:

1. *Satisfied.* Some literal of C is labeled :TRUE. For example, x being labeled :TRUE satisfies the clause $x \vee y$.
2. *Violated.* Every literal of C is labeled :FALSE. Given the clause $x \vee y$, the labeling where both x and y are :FALSE violates the clause.
3. *Unit open.* One literal is labeled :UNKNOWN, and the remainder are labeled :FALSE. This allows BCP to force the label of the :UNKNOWN literal to be :TRUE. Given the labeling where x is :TRUE and y is :UNKNOWN, the clause $\neg x \vee y$ is unit open.
4. *Non-unit open.* More than one literal is labeled :UNKNOWN and the remainder are labeled :FALSE.

The BCP algorithm is very straightforward. BCP maintains a pending stack S of clauses to examine. In addition, BCP maintains a set of violated clauses V which it uses in signaling the inference engine about the contradiction. BCP processes the clauses on the stack one at a time, relabeling :UNKNOWN nodes to be :TRUE or :FALSE if possible. The behavior of BCP depends on the condition the clause is in as follows:

Algorithm 9.1 **(BCP)**

1. Repeat until S is empty.
2. Pop clause c off of S.
3. If c is unit open, then compute the label of the :UNKNOWN literal l which will satisfy c. Call **SET**(l).
4. Otherwise, do nothing.

Step 3 is the key step. For example, given the unit open clause $\neg x \vee y$ where x is labeled :TRUE, the label of y is forced to be :TRUE.

Algorithm 9.2 **(SET(l))**

1. Set the label of the node of l to make the literal l :TRUE.
2. Push every unit open clause which contains $\neg l$ on to S.
3. Push every violated clause which contains $\neg l$ on to V.

When the inference engine adds a clause, the following procedure is invoked:

Algorithm 9.3 **(ADD(c))**

1. Add c to C.
2. If c is violated, then push c on to V and signal the inference engine that a contradiction has occurred.
3. If c is unit open, then push c on to S.
4. Call **BCP**.
5. If V is not empty, then signal the inference engine that a contradiction has occurred.

Assumptions are enabled by:

Algorithm 9.4 **(ENABLE-ASSUMPTION(l))**

1. Call **SET**(l)
2. Call **BCP**
3. If V is not empty, then signal the inference engine that a contradiction has occurred.

Consider the following sequence of LTMS inputs. The LTMS receives the following clause set via calls to **ADD**. None of these clauses provide any node labels.

$$y \vee s \vee z, \tag{1}$$

$$\neg y \vee q \vee r, \tag{2}$$

$$x \vee \neg y, \tag{3}$$

$$r \vee \neg s, \tag{4}$$

$$r \vee z, \tag{5}$$

Now consider the following sequence of events.

1. **ENABLE-ASSUMPTION**($\neg x$).
   a. Set x's label to `:FALSE`.
   b. Clause (3) is now unit open, so $S = \{3\}$.
   c. Processing S, BCP determines that clause (3) forces y's label to be `:FALSE`. None of the clauses mentioning y are now unit open, so BCP halts.

2. **ENABLE-ASSUMPTION**($\neg r$).
   a. Set r's label to `:FALSE`.
   b. Clauses (4) and (5) are now unit open, so $S = \{4, 5\}$.
   c. Processing S, BCP determines that clause (4) forces s's label to be `:FALSE`. Clause (1) is now unit open, so $S = \{1, 5\}$.
   d. Processing S, BCP determines that clause (1) forces z's label to be `:TRUE`. Now $S = \{5\}$
   e. Processing S, BCP determines that clause (5) is now satisfied so BCP halts.

This process makes it very clear that BCP is a simple forward propagation engine. Our BCP is depth first, but we can easily make it breadth first by changing S from a stack to a queue.

BCP on clauses is equivalent to the circuit value problem which is P-complete (see also [3]). BCP's worst-case complexity is the number of literals in the clauses. One can see this intuitively because it examines every clause at most once for every literal it contains.

9.3.1 Well-founded explanations

The BCP-based LTMS can produce *well-founded explanations* (in analogy to JTMS well-founded explanations—see Section 7.3) for its conclusions. A well-founded explanation for a node c's label consists of a sequence of steps $S_1, \ldots, S_k$ each step consists of a 4-tuple written as:

n ⟨*conclusion*⟩ ⟨*antecedents*⟩ ⟨*reason*⟩

- n is an integer, so this step can be referred to in later steps.
- ⟨*conclusion*⟩ is a literal. A symbol (or its negation) can be in the conclusion of at most one step.
- ⟨*antecedents*⟩ is a (possibly empty) set of integers corresponding to steps earlier in the sequence.
- ⟨*reason*⟩ is either an inference engine-supplied clause or the word "Assumption."

The conclusion of the final step S_k must correspond to the label of node c.

There are two kinds of steps, *assumption steps* and *derivation steps*. An assumption step takes the form:

n	⟨*conclusion*⟩	⟨*antecedents*⟩	⟨*reason*⟩
n	x	{}	Assumption

where x is a literal corresponding to an enabled assumption.

A derivation step is of the form

n	⟨*conclusion*⟩	⟨*antecedents*⟩	⟨*reason*⟩
n	x	A	C

where x is any literal, A is a set of antecedent steps, and x follows from clause C and the consequences of the steps mentioned in A.

Consider the clauses:

$x \vee y,$

$\neg y \vee z,$

$\neg z \vee r.$

If x is assumed to be `:FALSE`, then a well-founded explanation for r is:

n	⟨*conclusion*⟩	⟨*antecedents*⟩	⟨*reason*⟩
1	$\neg x$	{}	Assumption
2	y	{1}	$x \vee y$
3	z	{2}	$\neg y \vee z$
4	r	{3}	$\neg z \vee r$

It is crucial to note that the notion of well-founded explanation is useful even if the database is inconsistent. When the database is inconsistent, the labels of nodes are arbitrary except that the LTMS must be able to provide well-founded explanations for the labels it chooses. The well-founded explanation is very important, as it identifies the assumptions underlying a contradiction.

As a node can appear in several clauses, there can be a large number of well-founded explanations for any particular node. The LTMS is obligated to find only one of them. The BCP-based LTMS achieves this by identifying a single supporting implication for each node. This implication consists of a single clause and the set of antecedent nodes that are sufficient to force the conclusion (i.e., a derivation step in a well-founded explanation) using this clause. The set of implications forms a directed acyclic graph. A well-founded explanation for any node can then be found by traversing this digraph backward from consequences to antecedents.

9.4 Encoding propositional formulas as clauses

Although our BCP algorithm is restricted to clauses, any propositional formula can be converted into a logically equivalent set of clauses. Permitting the inference engine to supply propositional formulas is so convenient that our LTMS implementation includes a facility to convert formulas into clauses. We use the following conventions for expressing formulas:

- A node is a formula.
- If x is a formula, then so is $\neg x$ (in our Common Lisp implementation, negation is indicated by `:NOT`).
- If x and y are formulas, then so is $x \Rightarrow y$ (in our Common Lisp implementation, implication is indicated by `:IMPLIES`).
- If x and y are formulas, then so is $x \equiv y$ (in our Common Lisp implementation, equivalence is indicated by `:IFF`).
- If $x_1, \ldots, x_n$ are formulas, then so is $x_1 \vee \cdots \vee x_n$ (in our Common Lisp implementation, disjunction is indicated by `:OR`).
- If $x_1, \ldots, x_n$ are formulas, then so is $x_1 \wedge \cdots \wedge x_n$ (in our Common Lisp implementation, conjunction is indicated by `:AND`).
- If $x_1, \ldots, x_n$ are formulas, then so is the formula requiring exactly one of them to hold (in our Common Lisp implementation, such taxonomic formulas are indicated by `:TAXONOMY`).

To convert a propositional formula into an equivalent set of clauses, we employ a technique widely used in theorem proving [1, 4]. We convert the formula into conjunctive normal form and every resulting conjunct is then added to the database as a clause. The conversion is as follows: (x, y, and the x_i are formulas):

- Eliminate equivalences by replacing all occurrences of $x \equiv y$ with $(x \Rightarrow y) \wedge (y \Rightarrow x)$.

- Eliminate implications by replacing all occurrences of $x \Rightarrow y$ with $\neg x \vee y$.
- Eliminate all taxonomic formulas on $x_1, \ldots, x_k$ by replacing them with the conjunction of $x_1 \vee \cdots \vee x_k$ and for all $i \neq j$, $\neg(x_i \wedge x_j)$.
- Repeatedly use the rule $\neg\neg x \rightarrow x$ and DeMorgan's laws,

  $$\neg(x_1 \vee \cdots \vee x_k) \rightarrow \neg x_1 \wedge \cdots \wedge \neg x_k,$$

  $$\neg(x_1 \wedge \cdots \wedge x_k) \rightarrow \neg x_1 \vee \cdots \vee \neg x_k,$$

  to bring negations just before nodes.
- Repeatedly use distributivity, associativity, and commutativity to produce a conjunction of disjunctions.

For example, consider the formula,

$$(r \wedge (s \Rightarrow t)) \Rightarrow u.$$

Removing implications we obtain:

$$\neg(r \wedge (\neg s \vee t)) \vee u.$$

Applying DeMorgan's law twice we obtain:

$$(\neg r \vee (\neg\neg s \wedge \neg t)) \vee u.$$

Removing the double negation we obtain:

$$(\neg r \vee (s \wedge \neg t)) \vee u.$$

By associativity (and using commutativity) we obtain:

$$u \vee \neg r \vee (s \wedge \neg t).$$

By associativity and distributivity we obtain the conjunctive normal form:

$$(u \vee \neg r \vee s) \wedge (u \vee \neg r \vee \neg t).$$

From the conjunctive normal form we obtain two clauses:

$$u \vee \neg r \vee s,$$

$$u \vee \neg r \vee \neg t.$$

The ability to automatically encode arbitrary formulas provides the inference engine a convenient mechanism to add formulas which only hold under certain conditions. For example, if the above formula only holds if z holds, then the inference engine can supply the formula:

$$z \Rightarrow [(r \wedge (s \Rightarrow t)) \Rightarrow u].$$

Also, if the inference engine wishes to refer to the label of an entire formula, then it can use $\equiv$:

$$z \equiv [(r \wedge (s \Rightarrow t)) \Rightarrow u].$$

The formula now holds exactly when z holds.

9.5 The logical properties of BCP

Although BCP is an attractive algorithm, it does not fully meet the logical specifications laid out in Section 9.2.3. To effectively use a BCP-based LTMS we must analyze its logical properties in more detail.

BCP is sound. The BCP never labels a node `:TRUE` or `:FALSE` when it shouldn't, nor does it signal a contradiction when there isn't one.

Unfortunately, BCP is not logically complete. Given the fact that the set of tasks BCP can solve is P-complete, this should not be surprising. After all, propositional satisfiability is known to be NP-complete. We analyze two distinct manifestations of logical incompleteness because each has different consequences for problem solving.

BCP is logically incomplete in that it sometimes fails to do so label a node `:TRUE` or `:FALSE` when it should. We call this *literal incompleteness.* Consider the following two clauses when all labels are `:UNKNOWN`:

$$x \vee \neg y,$$

$$x \vee y.$$

From these two clauses, x should be labeled `:TRUE`, but BCP fails to do so because x does not follow from either one of the two clauses alone.

BCP is also logically incomplete in that it sometimes fails to detect contradictions. We call this *refutation incompleteness.* Consider the following four clauses when all labels are `:UNKNOWN`:

$x \vee y,$

$x \vee \neg y,$

$\neg x \vee \neg y,$

$\neg x \vee y.$

There is no :TRUE/:FALSE labeling which satisfies these four clauses, but BCP does not detect this and therefore fails to signal the inference engine about the contradiction.

It might seem that, since BCP is so widely used, someone would have managed to precisely characterize those circumstances under which BCP is logically complete. Unfortunately, to date, no crisp characterization exists. BCP is equivalent to finding all unit clauses using unit resolution alone. Unfortunately, the theorem-proving literature does not tell us under precisely what circumstances unit resolution is logically complete.

If the clause set is Horn, then BCP is known to be refutation-complete and literal-complete for *positive literals* only. Hence, BCP is literal-complete for the JTMS definite clauses. In practice, BCP is useful for non-Horn clause sets, but we do not know how to formally characterize those adequately. (See Chapter 13 for further discussion of the logical properties of BCP.)

9.5.1 When to use a BCP-based LTMS versus a JTMS

A central motivation for using an LTMS over a JTMS is its expressive power. But how does the logically incomplete LTMS stack up against the JTMS? If the application only generates definite clauses and :TRUE initial labels, then the performance of the JTMS is identical to the BCP-based LTMS. No node will ever be labeled :FALSE, because given a set of definite clauses it is never possible to infer the negation of a node. Therefore, the JTMS :IN corresponds to the LTMS :TRUE, and the JTMS :OUT corresponds to the LTMS :UNKNOWN. The computational complexity of the LTMS and JTMS is the same in this case. Therefore, there is no important reason to use a JTMS over an LTMS other than it being a bit simpler.

What happens when we use the encoding of Section 9.1.1 to represent arbitrary clauses? Using this encoding, and interpreting labels as shown in Figure 9.3, the JTMS and the BCP-based LTMS produce the same result.

But in this case BCP is more efficient. The complexity of both BCP and our JTMS algorithm is the number of literal occurrences in the database (i.e., in C for BCP and $\mathcal{J}$ for the JTMS). Since the encoding converts a single LTMS clause into multiple JTMS justifications, the same literal will occur more often in the equivalent justification structures $\mathcal{J}$ than in the original clauses C . Hence, the BCP-based LTMS is more efficient.

9.6 Search

In Chapter 13 we show how to augment BCP to be logically complete. Achieving full logical completeness is inherently extremely expensive. Most LTMS-based problem solvers rely solely on BCP and accommodate the resulting logical incompleteness in some other (non-TMS) way. One method to accommodate the logical incompleteness is to use search. However, before we address search, we will consider the situations under which logical incompleteness poses a problem.

Just having some node labeled `:UNKNOWN` is not necessarily a symptom of BCP's logical incompleteness—the inference engine may not have supplied enough information to logically determine the labels of all nodes. In general, BCP cannot distinguish between its own logical incompleteness and simply having insufficient information. However, in some cases we can make some headway. If every clause in C is satisfied by the node labels, then no more nodes can be determined. We can be guaranteed that there are no contradictions and, in addition, that relabeling any `:UNKNOWN` node to be `:TRUE` or `:FALSE` will still satisfy all the clauses. Thus, search is called for only if some clauses remain (non-unit) open.

The exact form of the search depends on the application and is implemented by the inference engine. One simple strategy uses a fixed clause and node ordering and systematically attempts to relabel the first `:UNKNOWN` node of the first open clause. Then when a contradiction occurs, the nodes underlying the contradiction are examined to determine the appropriate backtrack point.

Backtrack search can be excruciatingly expensive, and unless organized properly, the search may encounter the same contradiction repeatedly (see Section 9.1.2). Therefore it is often useful to explicitly cache the information discovered during backtracking. Unlike the JTMS, the LTMS has sufficient expressive power to easily represent the results of contradiction handling. When a contradiction is signaled, the contradiction handler should identify the enabled assumptions underlying the violated clause(s). Let $A_1, \ldots, A_n$ be the literals corresponding to these assumptions. The contradiction indicates that

$$A_1 \wedge \cdots \wedge A_n,$$

cannot hold and therefore its negation,

$$\neg(A_1 \wedge \cdots \wedge A_n),$$

must hold which is clause

$$\neg A_1 \vee \cdots \vee \neg A_n.$$

Although BCP does not explicitly construct this clause, the search procedure (part of the inference engine) can add it to the database. Notice that although assumptions were used in the construction of the nogood, the nogood depends on no underlying assumptions. The derivation of the nogood corresponds to employing reductio ad absurdum (RAA) in a natural deduction system—if, assuming the negation of the desired result produces a contradiction, we can derive the result.

A clause that logically follows from a set of clauses C is called an *implicate* of C. Adding implicates of C to itself can never cause any logical difficulties because everything that follows from C and its implicates must necessarily follow from C alone (see Chapter 13 for more discussion of this point).

Adding the nogood clause to C helps avoid the recurrence of this contradiction and therefore saves subsequent backtracking. Consider a situation in which the search did not add this nogood and now $A_1, \ldots, A_{m-1}, A_{m+1}, \ldots, A_n$ holds. Presuming the database hasn't changed in the meantime to label A_m :TRUE/FALSE, the search would assume A_m :TRUE which would provoke contradiction handling and backtracking to label A_m :FALSE. With the nogood clause present, the LTMS labels A_m :FALSE without contradiction handling or backtracking. In general, if all nogoods are present in C, then it is easily shown (the argument is left as an exercise) that the search for a consistent labeling never backtracks.

Consider a concrete example. Consider 4 clauses of some larger LTMS database:

$\neg a \vee b,$

$\neg c \vee d,$

$\neg c \vee e,$

$\neg b \vee \neg d \vee \neg e,$

where all nodes are assumptions and are initially labeled `:UNKNOWN`. Suppose that the search labels a `:TRUE`. That is not enough for BCP to label c. However, labeling c `:TRUE` provokes a contradiction, forcing backtracking to label it `:FALSE`. The fact that labeling a and c `:TRUE` provokes a contradiction is recorded as the nogood clause,

$\neg a \vee \neg c.$

Because of the presence of this new clause, if a is later retracted and then labeled `:TRUE` again, then c will immediately be labeled `:FALSE` without invoking contradiction handling or backtracking.

Thus, we see that adding implicates (e.g., nogoods) of C to itself both reduces backtracking and improves the logical completeness of the LTMS by enabling BCP to make more nodes known. If the nogood clause $\neg a \vee \neg c$ could have been inferred in some more direct way, then we would have been able to infer a label for c directly without backtracking. In the Chapter 13 we develop a general method for constructing implicates.

This kind of search is useful for some applications. However, although BCP is linear, this search is exponential. The reason for this is that the backtracking can add an exponential number of many additional clauses for BCP to consider. Thus for many applications, the number of nogood clauses added to C is so great that it is counterproductive to record nogood clauses at all. Chapter 13 explores various examples which have an exponential number of nogoods.

9.7 The LTMS interface

Before analyzing the Common Lisp implementation of our LTMS in detail, we present interface to our implementation. Here are the primary procedures and accessors that the inference engine should reference:

add-clause	retract-assumption
add-formula	satisfied-clause?
add-nogood	support-for-node
assumptions-of-clause	tms-create-node
assumptions-of-node	tms-node-datum
change-ltms	tms-node-false-rules
clause-informant	tms-node-true-rules
compile-formula	true-node?
create-ltms	unknown-node?
enable-assumption	violated-clause?
false-node?	with-assumptions
find-node	with-contradiction-check
known-node?	with-contradiction-handler
ltms-pending-contradictions	without-contradiction-check

```
(create-ltms title &key (title nil)
                        (node-string 'default-node-string)
                        (debugging nil)
                        (checking-contradictions t)
                        (contradiction-handler 'ask-user-handler)
                        (enqueue-procedure nil)
                        (complete nil)
                        (delay-sat t))
```

`create-ltms` returns a datastructure which contains the entire state of the LTMS. The keyword arguments are similar to the those of a JTMS with some slight differences:

`contradiction-handler` This specifies a procedure to call when the LTMS detects a contradiction. During problem solving there can be a stack of contradiction handlers. Upon encountering a contradiction, the LTMS will unwind the contradiction handler stack until a handler returns a non-`nil` result indicating it has handled the contradiction. The procedure supplied to the original call to `create-ltms` will be the last contradiction handler tried.

`enqueue-procedure` This procedure is called when a node becomes labeled `:TRUE` or `:FALSE`. It should not do any LTMS operations.

`complete` Discussed in Chapter 13.

`delay-sat` Discussed in Chapter 13.

```
(change-ltms ltms &key node-string
                       debugging checking-contradictions
                       contradiction-handler enqueue-procedure)
```

This allows the inference engine to change the initial settings provided to `create-ltms`. Changing `contradiction-handler` has the effect of resetting the contradiction handler stack to a stack of depth one, containing the supplied procedure.

```
(tms-create-node ltms datum &key assumptionp)
```

The inference engine creates a LTMS node with this procedure call specifying the datum for the node and whether it is an assumption or not. This is identical to the JTMS call (except that the LTMS does not have contradiction nodes). The LTMS node is used to represent both the positive and negative instances of a datum. Most problem solvers adopt the convention of using `:NOT` to refer to the negation of a node. For example, if the datum of some node is `(MORTAL SOCRATES)`, then its negation is represented as `(:NOT (MORAL SOCRATES))`. But this detail is irrelevant to the LTMS. The inference engine must indicate to which LTMS the node is to be added. A node can be in only one LTMS, and every node keeps track of the LTMS it belongs to. Hence, most LTMS procedures need not be supplied with the explicit LTMS argument.

```
(find-node ltms datum)
```

This finds a node in the `ltms` whose datum is equal to `datum`. This is very convenient for implementing simple examples and debugging.

```
(tms-node-true-rules node)
(tms-node-false-rules node)
```

The inference engine can push Common Lisp objects (usually problem-solving rules) on the node slots `tms-node-true-rules` and `tms-node-false-rules`. When a node becomes known, the LTMS calls the `enqueue-procedure` of the LTMS on each of the objects on the appropriate rule list.

```
(enable-assumption node label)
(retract-assumption node)
```

If a node is created with the assumption property, then the assumption is initially disabled. These are procedures to enable and retract an assumption. Notice that, unlike the equivalent JTMS procedure, the LTMS procedure to enable assumptions must indicate which label, `:TRUE` or `:FALSE`, to assign the node. This procedure will cause an error if the assumption is already known and has a label different than the one supplied.

As the LTMS permits more labels, it supplies a variety of procedures (all returning `t` or `nil`) to make various queries of the nodes:

```
(unknown-node? node)
```

Checks whether the node is labeled `:UNKNOWN`.

```
(known-node? node)
```

Checks whether the node is not labeled `:UNKNOWN`.

```
(true-node? node)
```

Checks whether the node is labeled `:TRUE`.

```
(false-node? node)
```

Checks whether the node is labeled `:FALSE`.

```
(satisfied-clause? node)
```

Checks whether the current node labels satisfy a clause. This is often used within search-based inference engines.

```
(add-formula ltms formula &optional informant)
```

This is the main procedure to add formulas to the LTMS. The formulas must be expressed using the conventions of Section 9.4 but be stated in conventional Common Lisp prefix notation. For example the formula,

$$(r \wedge (s \Rightarrow t)) \Rightarrow u,$$

in Common Lisp notation is:

```
(:IMPLIES (:AND r (:IMPLIES s t)) u)
```

Symbols in formulas can be represented in two different ways. Most commonly `r, s, t`, and `u` are all LTMS nodes. However, if a subexpression does not follow logical syntax and is not a node, then `add-formula` will find (and construct if necessary) a node whose datum is equal to the subexpression. This latter convention makes it very convenient to experiment with simple examples.

```
(add-clause true-nodes false-nodes &optional informant)
```

This adds the clause with positive literals `true-nodes` and negative literals `false-nodes`. The preferred procedure for adding formulas is `add-formula`. `add-clause` is intended primarily for internal use. The caller should ensure that the clause is not a tautology and does not contain repeated literals.

```
(compile-formula ltms formula &optional informant)
```

One difficulty with `add-formula` is that the expansion of its argument to conjunctive normal form takes place at execution time. In many cases, the entire formula is already known at compile time. The macro `compile-formula` is given a formula and expands it into conjunctive normal form at *compile* time to improve run-time efficiency. Under most situations, calls to `add-formula` can be directly replaced with calls to `compile-formula`. For example,

```
(compile-formula *ltms*
     '(:IMPLIES (:AND ,r (:IMPLIES ,s ,x)) u)),
```

will compile the formula into its equivalent clauses assuming that `r, s, t` are bound to nodes at run time, and that `u` will be looked up at run time:

```
(let ((#:u (find-node tms 'u)))
  (add-clause '(,#:u ,s) '(,r) nil)
  (add-clause '(,#:u) '(,x ,r) nil))
```

Our `compile-formula` is relatively simple and makes two important presuppositions. First, it assumes that the structure of the entire formula is available at compile time. Second, it assumes that different Common Lisp variables always refer to different nodes. It does not check if these conditions actually hold, and if they do not, then either Common Lisp errors or incorrect node labels will result. For example,

```
(compile-formula ltms '(:OR .,x) &optional informant)
```

gets an error at compile time because our macro cannot analyze the value of x. On the other hand,

```
(compile-formula ltms '(:OR ,x ,y) &optional informant)
```

is perfectly analyzable. However, x and y will be presumed to refer to distinct nodes such that if at run time x and y refer to the same node, then the LTMS will fail to determine that this node is :TRUE.

```
(supporting-clause-for-node node)
(assumptions-of-node node)
(assumptions-of-clause node)
```

The LTMS records enough information to construct a well-founded explanation for every node label. There are three basic procedures to explore this graph: supporting-clause-for-node and assumptions-of-node and assumptions-of-clause.

```
(support-for-node node)
```

This procedure either returns a description of the formula which forced node's label, :ENABLED-ASSUMPTION, or nil. The description consists of two values. The first value is a list of the antecedent nodes that the formula used to force node's label. The second value is the informant. If the node's label was determined by a clause directly added via add-clause, then informant is whatever the inference engine supplied in that call. If the formula was added by add-formula, then informant is a list of three values. If the first element is the symbol :IMPLIED-BY, then the second and third elements of the list are the arguments to the original call to add-formula: the original formula and its informant.

```
(assumptions-of-node node)
```

As with the JTMS, the most common reason for exploring the well-founded explanation for a node is to identify the enabled assumptions which underlie it. The procedure `assumptions-of-node` returns the set of enabled assumptions underlying the well-founded explanation for a node.

```
(assumptions-of-clause clause)
```

As there are no contradiction nodes in the LTMS the `assumptions-of-node` procedure is of limited value for contradiction handling. Instead the LTMS provides this more complex procedure. `assumptions-of-clause` only makes sense if every node in the clause is known (and hence the clause is either satisfied or violated), otherwise it reports an error. The result of `assumptions-of-clause` is a set of enabled assumptions constructed by finding the assumptions underlying each node of the clause whose label contradicts its sign in the clause. For example, if a node is labeled `:TRUE`, then its assumptions will be included only if it is one of the negative literals of the clause. The assumption set returned by `assumptions-of-clause` can be used for many purposes.

If the clause is violated, then the result of `assumptions-of-clause` is the set of assumptions underlying the well-founded explanations for all of the nodes of the clause. (Here we rely again on the property that well-founded explanations make sense in the presence of logical inconsistency.) As contradiction handling is always invoked on an offending clause, `assumptions-of-clause` plays a major role in processing contradictions. If the clause is satisfied by it forcing a particular node label, then the result of `assumptions-of-clause` is the set of enabled assumptions underlying the well-founded explanation for the forced node. If the clause is satisfied, but the clause itself was never used to force a node's label, then the result of `assumptions-of-clause` has limited utility.

When the LTMS detects that the current database is inconsistent, it calls the inference engine-supplied contradiction handler with two arguments: the list of contradictions (as violated clauses) and the current LTMS. As contradiction handling is invoked as the last operation of any LTMS procedure that can provoke a contradiction, the contradiction handler can `throw` out. However, when the contradiction handler `throws` out without removing the contradictions, the LTMS database will be logically inconsistent, although the internal LTMS datastructures will be reasonable and the LTMS will still correctly label nodes according to the specifications of Section 9.2.3. If the contradiction handler returns a `nil` result, then the next contradiction handler up the stack is invoked. If every contradiction handler returns a non-`nil` result, then the LTMS operation will leave the LTMS database logically inconsistent as just described.

Three LTMS procedures play major roles within contradiction handlers: `assumptions-of-clause`, `violated-clause?` and `add-nogood`. The procedure just discussed, `assumptions-of-clause`, returns the set of enabled assumptions underlying the well-founded explanations for all the nodes of the violated clause.

```
(violated-clause? clause)
```

This macro checks whether `clause` is still violated. This is important because as the contradiction handler processes multiple contradictions at a time, resolving earlier contradictions in the list may automatically resolve others. There is little point in attempting to avoid a non-contradiction.

```
(add-nogood culprit sign assumptions)
```

This provides a mechanism for the contradiction handler to record the contradiction (see Section 9.6). Typically the sequence of events for processing a contradiction is:

1. Check whether the contradiction is still a problem with `violated-clause?`.
2. Find all the enabled assumptions underlying the contradiction.
3. Pick one assumption, the culprit, to retract via `retract-assumption`.
4. Record the contradiction by adding a clause consisting of the negations of all the assumptions.

It is important not to put step 4 before step 3 because if the clause is added before this particular contradiction is removed, then adding the nogood clause would immediately cause another contradiction resulting in infinite recursion. Instead the contradiction must first be removed by `retract-assumption`. If step 4 did occur before step 3, then the procedure `add-nogood` would only need to have one argument: `assumptions`. However, when it is called, one of the assumptions no longer has a label (i.e., `culprit`) because it was retracted to remove the contradiction in the first place. Therefore, `culprit` is the one assumption in `assumptions` which is no longer known; its new label is provided by the argument `sign`. The argument `culprit` is logically unnecessary because `add-nogood` should easily be able to identify the one unknown assumption. However, contradiction handling is a common source of bugs and therefore the extra checking is done.

`tms-node-datum` is the datum of a node. Changing the contents of the datum will almost always lead to serious confusions. The inference engine can also request the informant of a clause via `clause-informant`.

The remaining interface procedures `with-contradiction-check`, `without-contradiction-check`, `ltms-pending-contradictions`, `with-contradiction-handler`, and `with-assumptions` are designed for sophisticated problem solvers, and their use is described later.

9.8 A simple example of LTMS usage

The following simple sequence of top-level Common Lisp procedure calls produces the BCP database and well-founded explanation of Section 9.3.1. First we must create a fresh LTMS for our example (recall that we distinguish user input by prefixing the expressions with >):

```
>    (setq *ltms* (create-ltms "Simple Example"))
```

Then we must create the four nodes (one of which is an assumption):

```
>         (setq x (tms-create-node *ltms* "x" :ASSUMPTIONP t)
                y (tms-create-node *ltms* "y")
                z (tms-create-node *ltms* "z")
                r (tms-create-node *ltms* "r"))
```

Then we introduce the three clauses:

```
>      (add-formula *ltms* '(:OR ,x ,y))
>      (add-formula *ltms* '(:OR (:NOT ,y) ,z))
>      (add-formula *ltms* '(:OR (:NOT ,z) ,r))
```

Enabling the assumption provokes BCP to label all the nodes:

```
>      (enable-assumption x :FALSE)
```

We can ask for a well-founded explanation for `r` and we obtain:

```
>       (explain-node r)

 1         (:NOT x)          ()    Assumption
 2                y          (1)   (:OR x y)
 3                z          (2)   (:OR (:NOT y z)
 4                r          (3)   (:OR (:NOT z r)
```

9.9 The BCP algorithm

The actual propagation phase of the clausal BCP has the same central concerns as the JTMS: enabling assumptions, retracting assumptions, and adding formulas. The algorithmic concerns for avoiding circularities and ensuring well-founded support are nearly identical to those we studied for a JTMS.

The BCP algorithm we describe here is cleverer than the one we discussed in Section 9.3. It never needs to examine the original form of clauses. Instead it creates auxiliary datastructures so that BCP can be implemented by just incrementing and decrementing counters. The node datastructure includes two lists: the clauses in which the nodes appear positively, and the clauses in which the nodes appear negatively. The clause datastructure includes a counter of the number of nodes in the clause which can potentially help violate it. Maintaining these counts is key to BCP. Remember that a clause will be violated if all of its literals become false. Consider the clause

$x \vee \neg y.$

If all nodes are unknown, this clause has two potential violators: x labeled `:FALSE` and y labeled `:TRUE`. If the x becomes labeled `:FALSE`, then it cannot satisfy the clause and the count is reduced to one. If x becomes labeled `:TRUE`, then the clause is satisfied. A simple BCP might discard the clause at this point, but our more complex algorithm keeps on maintaining the counts because x's label might later be retracted; thus, the count remains two.

The algorithm for enabling an assumption is very simple.

1. If the node receives the label `:TRUE`, then find all clauses in which it appears negatively and decrement their counts. Schedule any clause whose count drops below two for processing in step 3.
2. If the node receives the label `:FALSE`, then find all clauses in which it appears positively and decrement their counts. Schedule any clause whose count drops below two for processing in step 3.
3. Check each of the clauses whose count has been decremented. If the count becomes zero, then the clause has been violated and a contradiction should be indicated. If the clause has one potential violator, then the clause forces a node's label. Unless that node has already been set to `:TRUE` or `:FALSE`, set that node label and recursively apply this algorithm. If the clause is responsible for labeling a node, then the node is stored in the clause datastructure to aid possible future retractions.

The algorithm for retracting an assumption is similar and obeys the same key constraint as the JTMS assumption retraction algorithm. That is, before alternative support for labels is looked for, all the consequences of the retraction must be completed in the first phase:

1. If the node was labeled `:TRUE`, then find all clauses in which it appears negatively and increment their counts. Schedule clauses whose count increases above one for processing in step 3.
2. If the node was labeled `:FALSE`, then find all clauses in which it appears positively and increment their counts. Schedule clauses whose count increases above one for processing in step 3.
3. Check each of the clauses whose count has been incremented. If the count has become greater than one (the usual case), then the node whose label may have been forced by this clause loses support. If a node has lost support, recursively apply this algorithm.

The second phase attempts to find alternative support for any of the nodes that became labeled `:UNKNOWN`, in the first phase. For each node just marked `:UNKNOWN` examine all the clauses that mention it. If any clause's count is one, then set the node's label (unless some other clause has just relabeled it) and propagate this value just as in the case of the enabled assumption.

Adding a new clause is very straightforward. BCP simply computes the correct initial count for that clause. If it is zero, then it signals a contradiction. If it is one, then it sets that node's label and propagates that node's value just as in the case of an enabled assumption.

9.10 The LTMS code

The code in `ltms.lisp` is a simple logic-based truth maintenance system. In reading the code you will notice a few additional hooks to allow systems like TRE to interface with it. Otherwise the algorithms are precisely as presented so far. Chapter 13 presents a set of additional procedures to be added to `ltms.lisp` to ensure the LTMS is logically complete. In order to avoid redefining common procedures and datastructures, `ltms.lisp` includes some hooks which are only explained in the later chapter.

As with the JTMS, LTMS operations cannot be safely aborted, nor can one LTMS operation be safely invoked before another is finished (except as specified in the interface), nor can multiple processes safely access the same LTMS simultaneously.

9.10.1 Overview

The program is divided into eight parts:

1. *Definitions.* The datastructures and initialization procedures.
2. *Basic inference engine interface.* Interfaces for programs that use the LTMS.
3. *Adding formulas.* Sets up the internal LTMS datastructures representing the input formulas.
4. *BCP.* The guts of the Boolean constraint propagation algorithm.
5. *Retraction.* Making sure all the consequences of a retracted assumption are removed, and looking for alternative support for such nodes.
6. *Contradiction handling interface.* For signaling contradictions to the inference engine.

7. *Well-founded support.* Procedures for inquiring about the well-founded support of nodes and their underlying assumptions.
8. *Simple user interface.* Some basic procedures that allow the LTMS to be used alone. Any serious problem solver will replace or encapsulate most of these with more sophisticated procedures.

9.10.2 Definitions

Like the JTMS code, we use an LTMS datastructure, thereby allowing for multiple LTMS instances within a single problem solver. The `ltms` datastructure contains the following fields:

`title` Ignored by the LTMS but useful for debugging.

`node-counter` Provides a unique name for nodes.

`clause-counter` Provides a unique name for clauses.

`nodes` A hash table of all the nodes created, keyed by their data. Two nodes are considered the same if their data are equal. Mainly used for simple examples, debugging, and printing out the state of the LTMS database.

`clauses` List of all clauses either directly supplied by the inference engine or inferred from the formulas it has supplied. Currently used only for debugging.

`debugging` A debugging flag to trace the internals of LTMS operation.

`checking-contradiction` This flag defaults to `t`. It allows advanced programs to turn off contradiction checking temporarily.

`node-string` An inference engine-supplied procedure which should return a descriptive string for a node. The LTMS supplies a default.

`contradiction-handlers` A stack of inference-engine supplied contradiction handlers. See Section 9.7 for more details. The file `ltms.lisp` supplies two default contradiction handlers for stand-alone operation. Any real problem solver should supply a better one.

`pending-contradictions` A list of violated clauses upon which contradiction handling will be invoked at the conclusion of the current LTMS operation.

`enqueue-procedure` A user-supplied procedure which should be called if a node with true-rules is labeled `:TRUE` or a node with false-rules is labeled `:FALSE`. Rules are explained later.

`complete` This flag indicates whether the LTMS ensures logical completeness. For the basic LTMS it is always `nil`. See Chapter 13.

`violated-clauses` The BCP algorithms detect violated clauses while propagating labels through the database. At the point a violated clause is detected, the database state is inconsistent and no new LTMS operations should be commenced before it terminates. Therefore, BCP accumulates all the violated clauses here and checks them at the conclusion of any LTMS operation.

`queue` See Chapter 13.

`conses` See Chapter 13.

`delay-sat` See Chapter 13.

`cons-size` See Chapter 13.

Two defstructs are introduced to implement LTMS nodes and justifications. The fields of the `TMS-NODE` defstruct have the following interpretation:

`index` Integer serving as unique name for this node.

`datum` The (positive) datum supplied by the inference engine.

`label` Represents current belief status of the node. `:TRUE` indicates the node is true, `:FALSE` indicates that the node is false, and the node is labeled `:UNKNOWN` otherwise.

`support` This field is `nil` if the node is unknown. If the node is an enabled assumption, this field contains the symbol `:ENABLED-ASSUMPTION`. Otherwise this field contains the clause which BCP used to force the node's label.

`true-clauses` This and the next field are the generalization of the JTMS justifications and consequences. This field is a list of clauses in which this node occurs positively.

`false-clauses` This field is a list of the clauses in which the node occurs negatively.

`mark` Holds a marker for the sweep algorithm used in finding the assumptions underlying a node.

`assumption?` If non-`nil`, this field indicates that this node should be treated as an assumption whose belief can be explicitly enabled and retracted by the inference engine.

`true-rules` Rules that should be run when the node becomes labeled `:TRUE`. If this LTMS is being used without an external system, this field should be `nil`. The LTMS enqueue procedure is called on each element of this field if it is non-`nil`. The queue is then cleared.

`false-rules` Like `true-rules`, but these rules are queued when the node is labeled `:FALSE`.

`ltms` The LTMS instance to which this node belongs.

`true` This contains a single Common Lisp `cons` cell whose `car` is the node itself and whose `cdr` is `:TRUE`. This is the way the LTMS represents the positive literal. Every instance of this literal must be represented by this `cons` cell. This ensures that two literals are the same exactly when they are Common Lisp `eq`. This makes certain operations more efficient and saves a little bit of memory.

`false` The dual to the previous field.

The `clause` defstruct encodes clauses. The fields are:

`index` Integer for unique name.

`informant` A description of the clause. If the clause was added by the procedure `add-clause`, then it is supplied by the inference engine. If the clause is a result of calling the procedure `add-formula`, then it consists of a three-element list of `:IMPLIED-BY` and the two original arguments to `add-formula`. While this information is preserved within the LTMS, it is not used by any of the algorithms.

`literals` A description of the literals appearing in the clause. It consists of a list of node-label pairs. For example, the clause,

$x \vee \neg y$,

is represented as,

```
((x . :TRUE) (y . :FALSE))
```

`pvs` This counter is central to making BCP efficient. It is a count of the number of nodes which, if relabeled, might violate the clause (`pvs` comes from potential violators). Thus it counts the number of literals which are either :UNKNOWN or :TRUE. BCP maintains these counters incrementally. Initially, pvs is the number of nodes in the clause. If pvs is reduced to one, then the clause forces the label of the single remaining node. If pvs is reduced to zero, then the clause is violated and a contradiction is signaled.

length This contains the number of literals in the clause. This could be computed by just calling length on the literals slot. This is used primarily in Chapter 13.

sats This is a counter of the number of literals currently satisfying the clause. If this counter is greater than zero, then this clause is satisfied. This can be used by the inference engine to quickly test whether a clause is satisfied. It is also extensively used in Chapter 13.

status See Chapter 13.

The procedures node-string, debugging-ltms, ltms-error, and default-node-string are nearly identical to their JTMS counterparts. satisfied-clause? returns t if the clause is satisfied. walk-clauses is a macro which calls a procedure on every clause in the database. This is a distinct macro because the datastructure for ltms-clauses is different in Chapter 13.

9.10.3 Basic inference engine interface

The procedures create-ltms and change-ltms behave as do their JTMS counterparts. The procedures unknown-node?, known-node?, true-node?, and false-node? simply query the label of the node. The procedure tms-create-node creates a node.

The procedure enable-assumption sets an assumption node :TRUE or :FALSE. This procedure simply does some initial checking, and if any actual BCP work is needed, it calls top-set-truth.

The procedure convert-to-assumption is an unadvertised procedure to convert a non-assumption node into an assumption. Be warned that this must be used with great care. If a node is converted to an assumption after it has contributed to a contradiction, then it will be missing from any nogoods that that may have been constructed by the inference engine to record that contradiction. This may lead to unexpected logical incompleteness.

The procedure retract-assumption removes an assumption's label. It first calls propagate-unknownness to label it and all its consequences :UNKNOWN. propagate-unknownness returns a list of all the nodes which just became labeled :UNKNOWN. The procedure find-alternative-support is called with this list and attempts to find alternative well-founded support for all the nodes that were just labeled :UNKNOWN.

9.10.4 Adding formulas to the LTMS

The code in this section first converts any inference engine-supplied formula into conjunctive normal form, then identifies the clauses of the formula, and finally, adds these clauses to the LTMS database.

The procedure add-formula is the top-level procedure for adding formulas. add-formula first converts the formula into conjunctive normal form using the procedure normalize. The set of clauses from the conjunctive normal form of the formula is then added to the LTMS.

The procedure simplify-clause removes duplicate literals and detects tautologies (clauses that contain both a node and its negation). To achieve this, it calls sort-clause to order all the literals by increasing tms-node-index. This ensures that duplicate and complementary literals will be adjacent. In Chapter 13 we will exploit the fact that sort-clause also puts the clause literals into a canonical form.

The procedure normalize converts an expression into conjunctive normal form exploiting the rules described in Section 9.4. In order to avoid including an extra ltms argument in all the recursive calls to convert a formula, it is bound to the dynamic variable *ltms*. The auxiliary procedure normalize-1 does all the work. Its second argument is t or nil, depending on whether the resulting formula is negated. With the inclusion of such an extra negate argument, DeMorgan's laws can be obeyed while the clauses representing the formula are built up, and no additional distinct rewrite rule is required. The auxiliary functions normalize-tax, normalize-conjunction, normalize-iff, normalize-disjunction, and disjoin normalize the different syntactic possibilities. Every one of these functions returns a CNF expression represented as a list of lists of literals.

The code has to be careful in handling degenerate formulas. The disjunction of zero literals (i.e., (:OR)) is false, while the conjunction of zero literals (i.e., (:AND)) is true. The various normalizing procedures all return expressions in CNF (with operators removed). Therefore, false is represented simply by `(nil)` (i.e., `(:AND (:OR))` and true is represented by `nil` (i.e., `(:AND)`).

The procedure `find-node` uses a simple hash table to look up nodes by their datum. Notice that this presumes that if an implementation uses `find-node` (which it need not), then every node should have a unique datum. `find-node` can be called in three different contexts: (1) by the inference engine directly, (2) when `add-formula` finds an operand atom in a formula which is not a node, and (3) from `compile-formula`.

The macro `compile-formula` is like `add-formula` except that it attempts to expand its formula argument at compile time. It achieves this by first analyzing its formula argument via the procedures `expand-formula` and `partial`. Then it creates an LTMS instance at compile time to facilitate the conversion process and translates the clauses from this temporary LTMS into calls to `add-clause` at run time. The procedure `expand-formula` partially evaluates the formula argument, constructing what the formula would look like at run time. When `quote` is found, partial evaluation is no longer necessary to construct the run-time formula, although any atoms in the argument need cleaning up. This is achieved by `partial`.

9.10.5 Adding clauses

The procedure `add-clause` adds a clause to the LTMS. It is called with two lists of the positive and negative literals of the clause; it simply converts these to the standard LTMS representation for clauses and calls `add-clause-internal`.

In the basic LTMS, the procedure `add-clause-internal` immediately calls `bcp-add-clause` as the `:COMPLETE` flag (see Chapter 13) is always `nil`.

The procedure `bcp-add-clause` indexes the clause; it initializes the clause counts. At its conclusion it calls `check-clause`, which invokes BCP. In the CLTMS (see Chapter 13), `bcp-add-clause` is sometimes requested to create the clause without indexing it. This is indicated by an optional fourth argument which is always `t` in the LTMS.

The procedure `add-nogood` is a variant of `add-clause` that is useful during contradiction handling. It simply adds the clause corresponding to the current labels of the assumptions and the culprit.

9.10.6 Boolean constraint propagation

The BCP algorithm uses the single dynamically bound special variable `*clauses-to-check*` to enumerate the clauses that BCP needs to check. This variable is bound only within internal LTMS operations, so there is no possibility of it conflicting with other LTMS instances.

`check-clauses` is the top-level invocation of BCP. It repeatedly pops a pending clause and calls the procedure `check-clause` on it.

The procedure `check-clause` first checks whether the clause is violated, and if so, schedules it for later contradiction handling. Otherwise, it checks whether the clause forces a node's label. Unless that node's label has been set by another clause, it calls `set-truth` to propagate the label. `find-unknown-pair` is called as an auxiliary procedure to find that node whose label might be forced.

The procedure `top-set-truth` is a top-level way to call `set-truth`. After calling `set-truth` it calls `check-clauses` to propagate the changed label (if any) and then performs contradiction handling if needed.

The procedure `set-truth` is the main workhorse of BCP. Whenever a node's label is set to `:TRUE` or `:FALSE` it immediately signals the inference engine. Notice that the inference engine is signaled in the middle of LTMS operations and hence the inference engine should not make any changes at all to the LTMS at this point. Neither should it do a `throw`. Then `set-truth` updates the counts of all clauses that mention the node. If the node becomes labeled `:TRUE`, then all the clauses in which it appears negatively should have their count decremented. Conversely, if the node becomes labeled `:FALSE`, then all the clauses in which it appears positively should have their count decremented.

9.10.7 Retracting an assumption

Retracting an LTMS assumption is very similar to retracting a JTMS assumption. First, the node and all its consequences are marked `:UNKNOWN`. Only when this concludes may the algorithm attempt to establish alternative support for each node just marked `:UNKNOWN`.

The procedure `propagate-unknownness` performs the first phase of retraction. For every node that becomes labeled `:UNKNOWN`, every clause it participates in is checked to see whether that clause forced the label of some other node. If so, that other node is labeled :UNKNOWN as well. The auxiliary procedure clause-consequent takes a clause and returns the node (if any) whose label it has forced. We could include this node in the clause datastructure, but that would be just one more piece of datastructure BCP would have to update.

The procedure find-alternative-support's main purpose is to attempt to find alternative support for the nodes labeled :UNKNOWN by propagate-unknownness.

9.10.8 Contradiction-handling interface

At the conclusion of every LTMS operation that may add :TRUE/:FALSE labels, the LTMS invokes the procedure check-for-contradictions. check-for-contradictions first checks whether any violated clauses detected during the LTMS operations are still violated. If so, it invokes contradiction-handler on the entire set of violated clauses.

LTMS contradiction handling is affected by two fields of the LTMS datastructure: contradiction-checking and contradiction-handlers. If contradiction-checking is nil, then the violated clauses are placed on the LTMS slot ltms-pending-contradictions in case the inference engine might later want to examine the violated clauses. Otherwise contradiction-handler unwinds the contradiction-handler stack until one returns a non-nil result, which indicates that the contradictions have been dealt with. Algorithmically, the contradiction handler can throw out, or return a non-nil result even if violated clauses remain. Although this is useful for some purposes, it can leave the database in a logical mess which the inference engine will have to clean up.

For some types of problem-solving operations it is useful to temporarily turn contradiction handling on and off. The macros without-contradiction-check and with-contradiction-check, and the auxiliary procedure contradiction-check accomplish this. It is up to the inference engine to dequeue any violated clauses that may have accumulated on ltms-pending-contradictions while contradiction checking is disabled.

The macro with-contradiction-handler allows the inference engine to temporarily and cleanly install a contradiction handler during some fragment of problem solving.

The macro with-assumptions allows the inference engine to temporarily and cleanly enable some assumptions.

9.10.9 Inquiring about well-founded support

The procedures support-for-node, assumptions-of-node, and assumptions-of-clause allow the inference engine to explore well-founded explanations for nodes.

The procedure support-for-node returns the clause that forces the node if there is one, otherwise it returns :ENABLED-ASSUMPTION or nil. The inference engine can walk through the well-founded explanation for a node by repeatedly calling support-for-node. The procedure assumptions-for-node returns the set of all enabled assumptions underlying the current well-founded support for the node. (Note that there may be many—the LTMS only finds one.) It operates by walking through the acyclic graph representing the well-founded explanation for nodes.

9.10.10 Simple user interface

The remaining set of procedures in ltms.lisp allows the LTMS to be used in a stand-alone mode without any inference engine. Most real problem solvers will have their own versions of these procedures or call them as subprocedures from a more user-friendly front end.

ask-user-handler, handle-one-contradiction, print-contra-list and tms-answer are nearly identical to their JTMS counterparts. The procedure avoid-all is an alternative contradiction handler. If this is used as the final contradiction handler, it will remove all contradictions (if it is possible to do so) by retracting assumptions and then installing nogoods to prevent them from reoccurring. One design strategy is to make this the contradiction handler of last resort and ask-user-handler the handler of next-to-last resort such that if the user does not specify which assumption to retract, the LTMS will do so automatically.

The procedures clause-antecedents, signed-node-string, and node-consequences are three auxiliary procedures used in the explanation-generating code that follows. The procedure clause-antecedents returns a list of the nodes of a clause which are currently antecedent to that clause. signed-node-string returns a string describing that node, taking into account its current label. node-consequences returns a list of all clauses a node currently affects.

why-node and why-nodes behave much like their JTMS counterparts. The procedure explain-node prints a well-founded explanation for a node. It calls the recursive procedure explain-node-1 to actually construct the explanation. The procedures pretty-print-clauses and pretty-print-clause print out clauses in a logical syntax. The procedure show-node-consequences prints out the current consequences of a node. The procedure node-show-clauses prints out all the clauses a node appears in. Finally, the procedure explore-network is a higher-level interface to the preceding procedures for exploring the dependency network.

9.11 Exercises

1. ⋆ In the encoding of the clause $A \vee B \vee C$ in Section 9.1.1 we did not add a justification $\overline{A} \wedge \overline{B} \wedge \overline{C} \Rightarrow \bot$. Why not?

2. ⋆ In Section 9.6 we stated that if all nogoods were present, search would be backtrack-free. Provide an argument or proof.

3. ⋆ Calculate how many clauses the following call to add-formula creates. Is this reasonable?

```
(add-formula *ltms*
 '(:OR
 (:AND (= ?a ok) (= ?b in) (= ?c low) (= ?d low) )
 (:AND (= ?a ok) (= ?b in) (= ?c normal) (= ?d normal) )
 (:AND (= ?a ok) (= ?b in) (= ?c high) (= ?d high) )
 (:AND (= ?a ok) (= ?b out) (= ?c low) (= ?d low) )
 (:AND (= ?a ok) (= ?b out) (= ?c normal) (= ?d low) )
 (:AND (= ?a ok) (= ?b out) (= ?c high) (= ?d low) )
 (:AND (= ?c none) (= ?d none) )
 (:AND (= ?a stuck_open) (= ?c low) (= ?d low) )
 (:AND (= ?a stuck_open) (= ?c normal) (= ?d normal) )
 (:AND (= ?a stuck_open) (= ?c high) (= ?d high) )
 (:AND (= ?a stuck_closed) (= ?c low) (= ?d low) )
 (:AND (= ?a stuck_closed) (= ?c normal) (= ?d low) )
 (:AND (= ?a stuck_closed) (= ?c high) (= ?d low) )
 ))
```

4. ⋆⋆ Consider the a :TAXONOMY formula on n nodes. How many conjuncts does it have when expanded into conjunctive normal form?

5. ⋆ Prove that if all the implicates are added to the LTMS database, BCP is logically complete.

6. ⋆⋆ Modify our LTMS to allow the user to justify, enable, and retract clauses.

7. Our LTMS implementation finds all violated clauses. In many cases it is sufficient to find only one, thereby improving the overall efficiency of the problem solver.

   a. ⋆ What problem would occur if our implementation stopped checking clauses when encountering the first violated clause?

   b. ⋆⋆⋆ Redesign our BCP implementation so that it works correctly and stops when encountering the first violated clause. Hint: This will require adding a new field to the LTMS defstruct.

   c. ⋆⋆ Our BCP implementation wastes a lot of storage consing to queue of clauses to check. Redesign the datastructures to avoid all such consing.

8. ⋆⋆⋆ Our BCP operates by expanding formulas into conjunctive normal form. This can often generate a very large number of clauses. For example, consider your answer to Exercise 4. Build a BCP that does not expand formulas into clauses. Hint: Substitute :TRUE and :FALSE for known literals occurring in formulas and then simplify.

9. ⋆⋆ It can often be useful to determine whether the label of a node is permanent or can be changed by future assumption retractions. Implement a version of the LTMS that keeps track of whether the label is fixed or variable and prefers the fixed label over a variable label.

10. ⋆⋆ Some applications generate an extremely large number of clauses. It is possible to garbage-collect clauses if they become permanently satisfied, that is, if one of their literals is permanently true (i.e., its well-founded explanation has no enabled assumptions). Write an LTMS that constantly checks for such clauses and discards them.

11. ⋆⋆ Section 9.1.1 describes a way of encoding LTMS clauses for a JTMS. Write a LTMS that functions this way.

12. ⋆⋆⋆⋆ Write a full LTMS that does not expand formulas into clauses.

9.12 Bibliography

[1] Chang, C., and Lee R.C., *Symbolic Logic and Mechanical Theorem Proving*, Academic Press, 1973.

[2] de Kleer, J., "A practical clause management system," Xerox PARC Technical Report, 1988.

[3] Dowling, W.F. and Gallier, J.H., "Linear time algorithms for testing the satisfiability of propositional horn formulae," *Journal of Logic Programming* 3 (1984): 267–284.

[4] Genesereth, M.R., and Nilsson, N.J., *Logical Foundations for Artificial Intelligence*, Morgan Kaufmann, 1987.

[5] McAllester, D., "A three-valued truth maintenance system," S.B. thesis, Department of Electrical Engineering, Massachusetts Institute of Technology, 1978.

[6] McAllester, D., "An outlook on truth maintenance," MIT AI Lab, AIM-551, 1980.

[7] McAllester, D., "Reasoning utility package user's manual," MIT AI Lab, AIM-667, 1982.

[8] McAllester, D., "Truth Maintenance," in *Proceedings of AAAI-90*, 1990, 1109–1116.

10 Putting an LTMS to Work

As Chapter 9 demonstrated, the LTMS provides greater expressiveness than the JTMS. While in principle the encoding tricks of Section 9.1.1 can be used to express arbitrary clauses in a JTMS, in practice using an LTMS can greatly simplify programs. Because the LTMS accepts arbitrary propositional formulas (by translating them to logically equivalent sets of clauses), developing computational renderings of axiomatic theories becomes much easier.

The LTMS moves the dividing line of responsibility between the TMS and the inference engine. Consider the natural deduction system KM* implemented in Chapters 4 and 5. In those systems KM* was implemented entirely in the inference engine, which performed propositional reasoning via handcrafted pattern-directed inference rules. The burden of propositional reasoning is shifted from the inference engine to the TMS in an LTMS-based problem solver. The inference engine is still responsible for instantiating knowledge and global control (cf. JSAINT in Chapter 8), but now it can rely on the LTMS's Boolean constraint propagation algorithm to draw a reasonable set of propositional inferences automatically and efficiently. To draw an analogy with logic, the LTMS performs the propositional reasoning while the inference engine performs universal instantiation. This chapter shows how to incorporate the LTMS into a pattern-directed inference system, called LTRE (for Logic-based Tiny Rule Engine). LTRE mostly follows the structure of JTRE, but includes changes designed to maximally exploit the LTMS.

Earlier chapters explored a variety of important problem-solving techniques including the use of control knowledge, context manipulation via stacks, and the suggestions architecture. These are powerful techniques, but additional advanced techniques are needed for many problems.

Realistic problems are often ill-structured, in the sense that the dependencies between different aspects of the problem can be complicated and often not apparent in advance. In designing a complex artifact, for example, the decisions made about one subsystem often impact the decisions made about another subsystem. Adding more slots to a computer design, for instance, may require resizing the power supply, which may require revising the cooling system, which may in turn affect where the expansion slots should be placed. Moreover, realistic tasks often involve incomplete knowledge. Examples include diagnosis, where a program might not have complete knowledge of the values of measurements or the possible failure modes of a artifact's components, or even a complete understanding of what components constitute the artifact (try fixing a car with electronic ignition sometime). This chapter describes advanced inference techniques which address these problems. Some of these techniques can be implemented with simpler TMSs, but using an LTMS greatly simplifies their exposition as well as their operation.

We begin by describing the design of LTRE, focusing on the changes in knowledge model motivated by using the LTMS and a more powerful discipline for contradiction handling. The implementation of LTRE is briefly outlined next. The rest of the chapter focuses on advanced inference techniques. Section 10.3 shows how indirect proof can be implemented elegantly to overcome the incompleteness of Boolean constraint propagation in a focused manner. Section 10.4 describes a mechanism for using *closed-world assumptions* to help overcome limitations imposed by incomplete knowledge. Finally, Section 10.5 illustrates the design and construction of a generic dependency-directed search facility suitable for problems with complex interdependencies.

This chapter uses very simple examples to illustrate these reasoning techniques. In the next chapter we show how these techniques can be used to build a substantial problem solver—a qualitative reasoning system.

10.1 The design of LTRE

We have already discussed the issues involved in interfacing a TMS with an inference engine in Chapter 8. Most of the design decisions for JTRE are still valid when using an LTMS (e.g., the extent of assertions, the design of the database and mappings between Lisp forms, assertions, and TMS nodes, etc.). Consequently, we focus on two issues here. The first is a change in how assertions are interpreted, and is motivated by the character of the LTMS. The second is a change in how contradiction handling works, motivated by the consideration of more realistic problem domains. We examine each in turn.

10.1.1 Consequences of a propositional knowledge model

So far we have seen two models of belief in pattern-directed inference systems:

- TRE/FTRE*:* If the assertion F is found in the database, the system is said to believe F. If F is not found in the database, then the system cannot be said to believe F.
- JTRE*:* If the assertion F is found in the database and its corresponding JTMS node has the label `:IN`, then the system is said to believe F. Otherwise, the system cannot be said to believe F.

Neither model makes any assumptions about the form of F. Generally, assertions are viewed as propositions, in the usual sense of propositional logic. But nothing so far in our PDIS model has enforced this perspective. As Section 4.1 explained, assertions are typically list structures but in principle could be anything. For instance, the following could in these systems legitimately be assertions:

- `3`
- `(integral (sqr (sin x)) x)`
- a bitmap

The problem with using these entities as assertions is that it isn't clear what it means to believe in them. "Believing in 3" has a distinctly metaphysical ring to it. Since bitmaps can be pictures of physical objects, it might seem easier to establish a consistent interpretation of them as assertions. But it is not as easy as it looks. Suppose bitmap B is in. There are several ways to interpret this:

1. B depicts the image currently captured by the camera attached to the problem solver containing the TMS.

2. B depicts a state of affairs that represents the problem solver's interpretation of what is currently happening in the world around it.
3. B depicts a state of affairs that the robot intends to bring about.
4. B is a drawing that the problem solver has decided should be presented using its graphics facilities.

Extending any of these intuitions into a full semantics is difficult. For instance, the consequences of two bitmaps being in is different for each interpretation. Almost always, problem-solver designers tend to eschew special-purpose semantics, relying on the well-developed (some might say well-worn) semantics provided by logic. That is, assertions in the database are always treated as logical propositions. Naturally this does not mean that bitmaps and other entities cannot appear as objects to be reasoned about (e.g. `(integrate (integral (sqr (sin x)) x))`). It is simply that, in keeping with the conventions of logic, objects are not themselves propositions.[1]

By agreeing to keep to a strict propositional interpretation of assertions we can gain additional efficiencies from the LTMS. First, with a JTMS we had to have both P and $\neg P$ in the database. (Recall from Chapter 6 that P is true exactly when P is IN and $\neg P$ is OUT, and false when P is OUT and $\neg P$ is IN.) Using an LTMS, to determine if P is true or false we need only look at the label for the corresponding TMS node. The assertion $\neg P$ is redundant.

What are the consequences of deciding not to store the negation of assertions? In a PDIS, an assertion P is referred to for one of four reasons:

1. Inquiring as to the belief in P
2. Making P (or $\neg P$) a premise.
3. Assuming P (or $\neg P$).
4. Asserting a constraint on P (or $\neg P$).

Each of these still requires some way to refer to $\neg P$. Following our earlier conventions, in LTRE the negation of a proposition P is referred to via

1. Certain sophisticated readers may be reminded of reifying propositions as objects in order to keep higher-order reasoning strictly first-order. We are ignoring such refinements here.

`(:NOT P)`. Excluding the assertion of constraints, propositions of the form `(:NOT P)` will be interpreted by LTRE in the following ways:

- During queries, if the query concerns `(:NOT P)` the answer returned will be the inverse of the label found for *P*. That is,

  `:TRUE` ⟶ `:FALSE`

  `:FALSE` ⟶ `:TRUE`

  `:UNKNOWN` ⟶ `:UNKNOWN`

- When asserting `(:NOT P)` as a premise, *P* will be made a premise with the label `:FALSE`.
- When assuming `(:NOT P)`, *P* will be assumed with the label `:FALSE`.

This same convention is often used in logic programming, where negation is viewed as "the sign of" a proposition. Unnegated propositions are positive literals, and negated propositions are negative literals.

What about installing constraints? In JTRE the only constraints which could be added were Horn clauses, since that was all that the JTMS could accept. Chapter 9 showed that arbitrary propositional statements could be translated into sets of clauses (e.g., the algorithm used by `add-formula`) which the LTMS could then reason with. Consequently, LTRE should allow the assertion of arbitrary propositional statements, in order to gain the maximum benefit from the LTMS. There are two ways this might be accomplished:

Multilevel expansion: Given a compound statement, install each propositional subexpression in the database as an explicit assertion. For each propositional subexpression, install clauses which implement just that subexpression, treating its arguments as atomic propositions.

Direct translation: Given a compound statement, translate it into a set of clauses involving atomic propositions and install those clauses directly into the LTMS.

To see the differences between these two strategies, consider the statement

```
(:IFF (:IMPLIES (:OR a b) (:NOT (:AND c d))
      (:TAXONOMY e f g))
```

Asserting this statement under either implementation strategy will result in the propositions a, b, c, d, e, f, and g appearing in the database, if they aren't there already. Under the multilevel expansion strategy, the following propositions also will be added to the database

```
(:IFF (:IMPLIES (:OR a b) (:NOT (:AND c d))
      (:TAXONOMY e f g))
(:IMPLIES (:OR a b) (:NOT (:AND c d))
(:OR a b)
(:AND c d)
(:TAXONOMY e f g)
```

The clauses added to the LTMS database under the multilevel expansion strategy include compound propositions such as (:OR a b) and (:NOT (:AND c d)), whereas the clauses added under the direct translation strategy are all in terms of the atomic propositions (e.g., a, b, and so on). The attraction of the multilevel expansion strategy is that the structure of the explanations produced by the LTMS directly reflects the structure of the knowledge entered into the system. This can make explanations easier to understand. Suppose we ask why f is believed to be true. Under the multilevel expansion strategy, inspecting the dependencies might show us that f is true because e and g are false and the three propositions are linked by a :TAXONOMY statement, which is true because the :IMPLIES is true, which in turn is true because both a and b are false. Under the direct translation strategy, the reason for f being true would be that a, b, e, and g are all false. The attraction of the direct translation strategy is efficiency. Clearly, fewer propositions will be needed to encode a particular piece of knowledge, and perhaps even fewer clauses.

Which strategy is preferable? Let us look at efficiency first, by looking more closely at the example above. Under the direct translation strategy, seven TMS nodes are required, one for each atomic proposition. In the multilevel expansion strategy, an additional five nodes are needed, one for the original expression and four more for the subexpressions. What about clauses? Using the LTMS algorithms, it is easy to confirm that under multilevel expansion, 25 new clauses would be added to the TMS, while under direct translation 24 would be added. To summarize:

Strategy	# Assertions	# Clauses
Multilevel expansion	12	25
Direct translation	7	24

The direct translation strategy comes out slightly better in terms of clauses required to encode our example proposition, and substantially better in terms of the number of assertions required. Building and indexing assertions and their corresponding TMS nodes takes more space and time than building clauses, so the tradeoff in assertions required is the critical one. Clearly, the efficiency advantage goes to direct translation.

What about clarity of explanation? In the multilevel expansion strategy, some of the intermediate nodes in explanations are propositions which are recognizably something asserted by the user (e.g., `(:TAXONOMY e f g)`), thus making it easier to track down the source of a bug. We can get the same effect in the direct translation scheme by adding an informant which encapsulates the original propositional constraint. In particular, recall that the LTMS procedure `add-formula` calculates a new informant based on the formula and informant it is given as inputs. This feature can be exploited by allowing `assert!` to include an informant as well as a constraint. Thus the call

```
(assert! '(:IMPLIES (human robbie) (mortal robbie)) :SAD-FACT)
```

leads to the following clause being installed in the LTMS:

```
((<#NODE: (HUMAN ROBBIE)> . :FALSE)
 (<#NODE: (MORTAL ROBBIE)> . :TRUE))
```

with the informant of this statement being

```
(:IMPLIED-BY (:IMPLIES <#NODE: (HUMAN ROBBIE)>
                       <#NODE: (MORTAL ROBBIE)>)
             :SAD-FACT)
```

Thus by including informants in the explanation, an LTMS-based system using the direct translation strategy can achieve the same degree of clarity as a system using multilevel expansion.

We have built inference engines using both strategies, and our experience confirms what these examples suggest: that the direct translation strategy tends to work better in practice. Empirically, we have found the explanations given by direct translation schemes to be easier to use than than explanations given by multilevel expansion schemes. Explanations given by the latter tend to be boring, since they step through each intermediate connective. Consequently, LTRE uses the direct translation strategy.

10.1.2 Contradiction handling for flexible problem solving

A primary function of truth maintenance systems is the detection and processing of contradictions. What should be done when a contradiction occurs depends on the nature of the computation. Suppose a problem solver is checking the consistency of a user's assumptions. It might do this by calculating the set of consequences entailed by those assumptions plus its other knowledge using Boolean constraint propagation. In this case a contradiction probably would be handled by offering up the offending assumptions for inspection and retraction. Suppose a problem solver is performing an indirect proof, and the contradiction detected includes the assumption to be denied. In this case the method has succeeded and the original hypothesis can be marked as proven, based on the other assumptions involved in the contradiction. Suppose a problem solver is performing a dependency-directed search. In this case a contradiction involving one of the search assumptions indicates that backtracking is required. The commonality underlying each of these examples is that the problem solver is engaged in an *assumption-manipulating operation*. Each type of assumption-manipulating operation requires a particular contradiction-handling strategy.

Realistic problem solvers are often engaged in several assumption-manipulating operations at once. In confirming a user's assumptions about a malfunction, for instance, a dependency-directed search might be undertaken to see if the assumptions can lead to a consistent explanation of the observed symptoms. Conversely, an interactive design system might, in the midst of a dependency-directed search through a space of possible designs, ask its user for sample component values, which it must check for reasonableness before proceeding. As the state of the art progresses, the kinds of interactions between such operations will become even more complex: a fault-management system that collaborated with human operators in diagnosing malfunctions in, say, a space station, and helped design work-arounds to allow continued station operations would require interleaving troubleshooting and design activities. Clearly no single contradiction-handling procedure will suffice. What we need is a method for orchestrating multiple contradiction handlers.

The implementation of contradiction handlers in the JTMS, explained in Chapter 7, provided only a partial solution. Recall that a default contradiction handler could be provided with a JTMS, and that a macro `with-contradiction-handler` allowed a program to rebind this handler temporarily during a computation. The utility of this mechanism was illustrated in Chapter 8 by the implementation of a simple dependency-directed search algorithm for the *N*-queens puzzle. But, as noted in Section 8.4, we had carefully arranged the search so that the last assumption was always what should be retracted. In general this cannot be done. To see this, imagine a problem solver based on JTRE was carrying out a dependency-directed search involving three choice sets:

A_1, A_2, A_3

B_1, B_2, B_3

C_1, C_2, C_3

Like `n-queens`, each phase of the search rebinds the JTRE's contradiction handler to catch contradictions involving its assumptions (see Figure 10.1). Suppose the problem solver is exploring A_2, B_2, C_2, and uncovers a contradiction depending only upon A_2, B_2. The contradiction handler for the *C* choice set cannot deal with this contradiction. The handler for the *B* choice set could, but it has been hidden by the rebinding of the contradiction handler during the search process.

One can imagine case-specific patches, of course. However, as noted above, to build flexible problem solvers we should be able to interleave assumption-manipulating operations arbitrarily. This means introducing a protocol that allows locally defined contradiction handlers to be combined appropriately. Let us first examine the design assumptions underlying the JTMS/JTRE implementation of contradiction handlers, in order to understand what must be changed and why.

A single contradiction handler which can be rebound is adequate only under the following three restrictions:

1. All assumption-manipulating operations must be identified, and an appropriate contradiction handler must be provided for each.
2. Assumption-manipulating operations must proceed depth first.
3. *Relative closure:* Every consequence that holds for the current set of assumptions and which might lead to a contradiction must be computed before making more assumptions.

The relative closure restriction is clearly problematic. Strictly speaking it is impossible to satisfy, since (a) the set of consequences can be infinite,

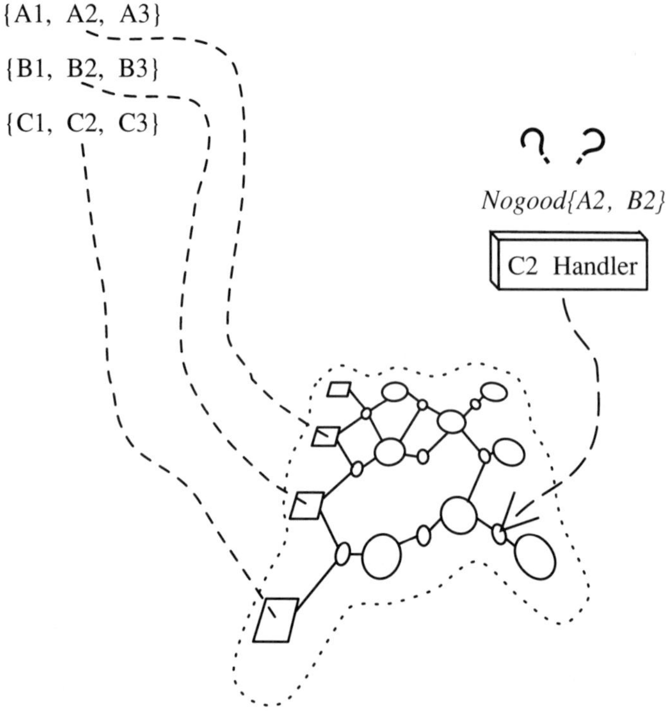

Figure 10.1 Multi-level backup requires visible handlers

and (b) in developing our reasoning algorithms we have eschewed completeness in favor of efficiency. But even restricted versions, i.e., those in which every consequence of the current assumptions is derivable via Boolean constraint propagation, are unrealistic.

The purpose of assuming relative closure is the same as the requirement in FTRE (Section 5.1.3) that all rules that do not require assumptions be executed before any rules that do. Recall that the FTRE discipline was motivated by the use of a stack for making temporary additions to the database. It was important to ensure that conclusions were based on as few assumptions as possible—otherwise, they would be inappropriately retracted when the stack was popped and never rederived in that manner within that context or any future subcontext of it.

Here the problem was not losing derivations. The problem was that the appropriate handler for a contradiction may be shadowed. In the case of the dependency-directed search above, one might argue that it is the search itself that should be better organized, as we did with N-queens. For many searches that may be possible. However, it is not possible for arbitrary combinations of assumption-manipulating operations. Consider a JTRE-based problem solver whose job is to ask a user for a set of assumptions, check them for consistency (using contradiction handler `H1` to complain about mistakes), and then perform a dependency-directed search based on choice sets derived from those assumptions (using handler `H2` to backtrack as needed). Now suppose we give this program some assumptions, but interrupt its computation of their consequences. The initial assumptions may be contradictory, and worse yet, our collection of choice sets might be incomplete at this point. Now we let the program proceed with the search, without letting it finish these updates. (If this malevolence seems unfair, imagine that this problem solver is implemented in a distributed processing environment where tasks are carried out in parallel in order to maximize average throughput.) Starting the search means `H2` now shadows `H1`. If the rules triggered by the initial assumptions are then allowed to run, any contradiction involving the initial assumptions will be seen by `H2` but not by `H1`. There is absolutely no guarantee that `H2` will do anything sensible in this case. And we cannot rewrite `H2` to include `H1` as a subcase, since that would violate modularity and thereby restrict our ability to compose assumption-manipulating operations.

Importantly, interruptions are not the only way to violate the relative closure assumption. Any situation where the order in which information is obtained cannot be fixed in advance can cause trouble. Consider a troubleshooter working on a computer network, for instance, who is trying to pin down what machine is clogging the network with excess packets. If she finds that the subnet in question has an extra machine that she didn't know about, then any processes of elimination underway may need substantial revision. Or consider a designer who on Tuesday settles on CMOS as the technology for a peripheral controller, but on Wednesday management changes the speed specifications so that only GaAs will do. In this situation, most of the choices defining the design space are now different. Or consider a researcher who finds out that a piece of plotting software is buggy, so that the conclusions drawn from the pilot data are incorrect and the follow-on experiments must be redesigned. Typically the world does not provide us with enough order;

we have to impose the order we need when we can, and be ready to respond when the world signals us that our choices won't work.

The relative closure restriction can sometimes be lived with for simple problems, with careful planning. But for most problems it is too confining. Consequently, in LTRE we drop the relative closure assumption. The other design assumptions remain the same, though. Clearly, every assumption-manipulating operation must still provide a handler which carries out the appropriate action when one of its assumptions is implicated in a contradiction. It may not be so clear that assumption-manipulating operations must still proceed depth first. The reason is that context within the LTMS is global: we cannot explore two mutually inconsistent sets of assumptions in parallel without causing a contradiction. (Overcoming this limitation is one of the primary reasons for using an ATMS, as explored in later chapters.) This does not mean that all computations within a particular assumption-manipulating operation must proceed depth first, naturally.

The LTMS presented in Chapter 9 provided a simple stack mechanism for contradiction handlers which overcomes the need for the relative closure restriction. As before, each assumption-manipulating operation must have an associated contradiction handler. The new handler is pushed onto the stack, but this does not block access to previous handlers. When a contradiction (or set of contradictions) occurs, each handler is executed in turn. A handler returns `nil` to indicate that it did not fully resolve the current set of contradictions. A non-`nil` result indicates that all contradictions are now cleared, and processing may proceed. (See the procedure `contradiction-handler` in `ltms.lisp` for details.)

10.2 The implementation of LTRE

LTRE consists of the following files:

`linter.lisp` Datastructures and interface.

`ldata.lisp` Database system.

`lrules.lisp` Rule system.

`unify.lisp` Unifier. Identical to FTRE version.

`funify.lisp` Open-coding unification. Identical to FTRE version.

`indirect.lisp` Indirect proof mechanism. Explained in Section 10.3.

`cwa.lisp` Closed-world assumption mechanism. Explained in Section 10.4.

`dds.lisp` Dependency-directed search mechanism. Explained in Section 10.5.

We describe how `linter.lisp`, `ldata.lisp`, and `lrules.lisp` differ from their JTRE equivalents in this section. The design and implementation of the advanced inference mechanisms occurs in the later sections, as noted above.

10.2.1 Summary of the LTRE interface (linter.lisp)

Almost all of the changes in `linter.lisp` are renamings, using `LTRE` where `JTRE` appeared in `jinter.lisp`. The only additions are some debugging utilities:

`show-by-informant` Prints all clauses in the LTMS whose informant is associated with the symbol provided as input. Very handy for debugging complex systems.

`view-clause` Given an LTMS clause, substitutes the Lisp forms corresponding to its TMS nodes to produce a readable expression. Used by `show-by-informant` and other debugging utilities.

10.2.2 Summary of the LTRE database (ldata.lisp)

This file contains most of the substantial changes in LTRE. As Section 10.1.1 described, LTRE translates logical constraints directly into clauses. To implement this design it must be able to figure out whether or not the functor of a proposition is a connective. The variable `*connective-list*` indicates what connectives are known to the LTMS (i.e., `:NOT`, `:AND`, `:OR`, `:IMPLIES`, `:IFF`, and `:TAXONOMY`). The procedure `simple-proposition?` returns non-`nil` exactly when a proposition should be treated as a literal by the TMS. Since determining the sign of a proposition is a common operation, the procedure `negated-proposition?` returns non-`nil` when a proposition is negative, and `nil` otherwise.

Except for the ability to take arbitrary propositional statements, the database interface is the same as JTRE. The strategy is the same: When given a proposition to assert or assume, translate it into a form the TMS can process and make the appropriate TMS call. In LTRE this job is handled by the procedure `build-tms-formula`. `build-tms-formula` creates a new expression with TMS nodes substituted for all simple propositions. It creates assertions for simple propositions as needed (e.g., the call to `referent`, which plays the same role in LTRE as it did in JTRE).

As with JTRE, `assert!` causes permanent changes to the dependency network. Notice that it does not actually build a node corresponding to the input formula, unless that formula is a ground term.

The definition of `assume!` is similar to `assert!`, with one crucial difference. Since an assumption can be retracted, we must take care to ensure that any clauses we add to the LTMS can be decommissioned if the assumption is disabled. (Deleting clauses is still not an option, of course, because it would reduce the utility of the dependency network to serve as a cache.) To do this, `assume!` builds an explicit node corresponding to the input formula and then asserts that this node implies the original formula. That is, given input formula F, it generates a TMS node N_F and asserts the constraint `(:IMPLIES` N_F $\langle F \rangle$`)`
Thus all the usual clauses will be created for F, except they also will depend on N_F. The clauses which implement F can be decommissioned by disabling the TMS node N_F. Suppose for example we call `assume!` as follows:

```
(assume! (:IMPLIES (human robbie) (mortal robbie)) :STILL-SAD)
```

Three TMS nodes would be created, as well as the clause

```
((#<NODE (:IMPLIES (HUMAN ROBBIE) (MORTAL ROBBIE))> . :FALSE)
 (#<NODE (HUMAN ROBBIE)> . :FALSE)
 (#<NODE (MORTAL ROBBIE)> . :TRUE))
```

In addition to these changes, the procedure `contradiction` must change in meaning because, unlike the JTMS, there are no contradiction nodes in the LTMS. The LTRE procedure `contradiction` builds a clause indicating that the given nodes cannot have their current labelings. Also, the macro `assuming` is provided as a convenience for systems which must assume several facts at once. It basically provides an LTRE-level interface to the LTMS macro `with-assumptions`.

The rest of the changes are all minor:

- `get-dbclass` must now know about negated propositions, since a form whose `car` is `:NOT` must be interpreted as a signed statement rather than as the form of a fact itself. Similar changes are made in `referent1` and `insert`.
- The set of interrogatives has been changed to reflect the new set of possible labels. The procedures `true?`, `false?`, `known?`, and `unknown?` test the belief in a proposition, while `label-of` returns the label itself. Notice that these procedures, too, must treat `:NOT` properly as a signed statement.
- The procedures `why?`, `assumptions-of`, `consequences`, and `explore` provide LTRE-level interfaces to the LTMS procedures `why-node`, `assumptions-of-node`, `show-node-consequences`, and `explore-network`, respectively.
- The procedure `fetch-global` provides a new debugging feature. Recall that the TRE database organization requires the leftmost symbol of a pattern to be known. That is, one cannot make queries of the form `(?n1 <= ?n2)` if `?n1` is free, since we must know the database class of the leftmost symbol to find out what subset of the database to look at. `fetch-global` gets around this problem by mapping over the entire database, using `unify` to perform the necessary matching. The `status` argument provides filtering, ensuring that `fetch-global` only returns facts with a particular label.

10.2.3 Summary of the LTRE rule system (lrules.lisp)

The changes to this file are straightforward: The trigger conditions for rules are now `:TRUE`, `:FALSE`, and `:INTERN`, to reflect the labels supported by TMS nodes. LTRE does not support `:UNKNOWN` as a trigger condition, which would be the analog of `:OUT` rules, since they will not be needed by the systems we build on top of LTRE.

Now let us turn to the new, more advanced features of LTRE.

10.3 An indirect proof mechanism

The incompleteness of Boolean constraint propagation generally is not a problem: empirically, the set of inferences it draws does a good job at covering the "obvious" conclusions that should be made given a set of assumptions and clauses. There are plenty of exceptions, however. As Section 9.5 described, Boolean constraint propagation is both literal-incomplete and refutation-incomplete. A common source of literal incompleteness is disjunction. For instance, given

```
(:OR P Q)
(:IMPLIES P R)
(:IMPLIES Q R)
```

R must hold, but the LTMS does not derive this. One well-known strategy for overcoming such problems is indirect proof. In Chapter 5, indirect proof was implemented using a stack-based context mechanism. We can achieve the same effect in LTRE through its contradiction-handling mechanism.

The essence of indirect proof is to assume the negation of the fact F to be shown and derive a contradiction. Once a contradiction has been derived, F can be justified based on the assumptions underlying the contradiction, minus the assumption $\neg F$. The procedure `try-indirect-proof` in Figure 10.2 provides a simple implementation. (This procedure is from the file `indirect.lisp` in the listings.)

`try-indirect-proof` works like this. The initial `unless` test filters out situations where the proposition to be shown (`fact`) is already known. Since its goal is to provoke a contradiction, it first pushes a contradiction handler on the stack for the current LTMS (via `with-contradiction-handler`) which provides an appropriate response. That is, if the contradiction detected involves F, the assumption it made is retracted and a clause is created (via `add-nogood`) to record the reasons for believing F. To provoke the contradiction, $\neg F$ is assumed (via the call to `assuming`) and any rules triggered by this action are executed. If a contradiction occurs the handler just described takes care of it. If no contradiction occurs, then F doesn't in fact follow. In that case, the assumption is automatically retracted when `assuming` finishes, returning the database to its original state (modulo some rule firings). The upshot of the proof attempt is reported by the final call to `known?`.

The operation of `try-indirect-proof` is illustrated in Figure 10.3. (Improving the quality of the explanation given is the subject of Exercise 4.)

```
(defun try-indirect-proof (fact &optional (*LTRE* *LTRE*))
  (unless (known? fact)
    (with-contradiction-handler (ltre-ltms *ltre*)
      #'(lambda (contradictions ltms &aux assumptions)
          (setq assumptions
                (assumptions-of-clause
                 (car contradictions)))
          (let ((the-node ;; Is the assumption a culprit?
                 (find (datum-tms-node (referent fact T))
                       assumptions)))
            (when the-node
              (let ((status (tms-node-label the-node)))
                (retract-assumption the-node)
                (add-nogood the-node status
                            assumptions)))))
      ;; Assume the negation
       (assuming '((:NOT ,fact)) *LTRE*
                 (run-rules)))
   (known? fact)))
```

Figure 10.2 An indirect proof mechanism for LTRE

```
> (in-ltre (create-ltre "Indirect Proof Example"))
<LTRE: Indirect Proof Example>
> (assert! '(:OR p q) :disjunction)
NIL
> (assert! '(:IMPLIES p r) :p-case)
NIL
> (assert! '(:IMPLIES q r) :q-case)
NIL
> (known? 'r)
NIL
> (try-indirect-proof 'r)
T
> (why? 'r)

R is TRUE via NOGOOD on
#<NODE: R>
```

Figure 10.3 The indirect proof mechanism in operation

10.4 Closed-world assumptions

Problem solvers often must operate with incomplete information. Typically, AI programs are written under the presumption that all relevant information of some type is known. A scheduling algorithm might be written to assume that the resources it knows about are the only ones available. A troubleshooter might be written to assume that the components it knows about in an artifact are the only ones it has. An intelligent tutoring system might be written to presume that it knows the important facts about a country's climate, so that if a student asks if a country has high rainfall and the system doesn't know or cannot infer that it does, it will tell the student that the rainfall isn't high. Such assumptions are called *closed-world assumptions* [1, 3, 6].

Often such closed-world assumptions are implicit in the structure of the program. Simple planners, for instance, often have wired into them the presumption that they know all the objects in the problem and that they are the only actor which can affect that world. More realistic problem solving requires making such closed-world assumptions explicit, so they may be reasoned about in the face of changing information and requirements. A scheduler, for instance, might be able to request more resources if it cannot generate an acceptable course of action. A troubleshooter might suspect that there is more to the malfunctioning system than meets the eye if all known parts are exonerated. And a tutoring system may have to revise its maps and population charts to reflect political upheavals and demographic trends.

From the standpoint of problem-solver design, there are several advantages to making closed-world assumptions explicit. Explicit closed-world assumptions can participate in dependencies, thus indicating which conclusions rely on incomplete information. The problem solver can then figure out what needs to be rederived as new information is obtained or derived, or if old information turns out to be invalid. This section describes a simple but effective mechanism for closed-world assumptions. Section 10.4.1 describes the design and Section 10.4.2 describes its implementation.

10.4.1 Defining set construals via closed-world assumptions

Many important kinds of information can be expressed as sets.[2] For example, a scheduler might know the set of resources it has available, a troubleshooter might know the set of components which comprise the malfunctioning artifact and the set of failure modes for each type of component, and a tutoring system might know the set of facts it has about a country's climate. A program's knowledge may be partial, of course. There might be resources the schedule doesn't know about, components the troubleshooter isn't aware of, and climatic data that is unavailable to the tutoring system. Furthermore, each of these sets can change over time: an intelligent tutoring system whose subject matter was Eastern European political history, for instance, would have required almost daily updates to its knowledge base during the early 1990s.

In each of the above cases, we can easily provide an intensional description of a set of knowledge relevant to the problem solver (e.g., "the set of components comprising the artifact"). To be useful, the problem solver's knowledge must concern the extension of these sets (e.g., the troubleshooter actually needs a list of the artifact's components, not just the knowledge that the set exists). Since the problem solver's knowledge can be incomplete and incorrect, we must introduce a way of describing the problem solver's current state of knowledge regarding the extension of a set. We define the *construal* of a set to be the hypothesis that the members of a set known to the problem solver are indeed the only members of that set (i.e., that they comprise its extension). In other words, if the problem solver knew

$$m_1 \in S$$

$$m_2 \in S$$

$$\neg \exists m_3 s.t. m_3 \in S,$$

the hypothesis that $S = \{m_1, m_2\}$ would be a construal of S.

2. Readers with a particularly formal bent might think this tautological, because set theory provides an axiomatic basis for mathematics and hence in some sense everything can be represented as sets. This is not what we mean. In this discussion, that perspective is about as valuable as using Turing machines for practical programming problems.

Construals must be updated when new information appears about what a set contains. Usually, but not always, this means abandoning the processing based on the old construal. Consider for example how one might build a hydrostatics troubleshooter. A simple diagnostic strategy is to create, for each component, a choice set consisting of its normal model and its failure models. Dependency-directed search over these choice sets, ruling out combinations whose predictions did not fit observations, would yield candidate explanations for a malfunction. Part of the knowledge base of a hydrostatics troubleshooter must then include failure models for components. Suppose that for valves it had two failure models, `StuckOpen` and `StuckClosed`. To create the choice sets necessary to execute the diagnostic algorithm just outlined, the system must first create a construal for the set of components in the plumbing system (perhaps by assuming that the parts shown on its blueprint are the only ones) and then must create for each component a construal for its set of failure models. If a new part is discovered (i.e., a modification made during construction, a common occurrence) or a new failure model is discovered (e.g., that valves can leak), the appropriate construals must be retracted and the search reorganized. Furthermore, if the troubleshooter failed to find an explanation for the malfunction, it must be the case that either (a) the plumbing system has parts that were not taken into account or (b) the components of the system have models that were not taken into account.

Construals rest on closed-world assumptions. That is, the justification for the conjecture $S = \{m_1, m_2\}$ must rely on more than just the membership statements $m_1 \in S$ and $m_2 \in S$. When construals are made an explicit statement, called the *closed-world assumption* for that set, is also made. This assumption must be retracted when the information about the extension of the set changes. We turn next to the design of the representations and processes to carry this out.

10.4.1.1 Gedanken example: The logic of drawing-room mysteries

The design issues in creating reasoning mechanisms to support closed-world assumptions are surprisingly subtle. Consequently, we use a more detailed hypothetical example to illustrate them. We call this a gedanken example because, like gedanken experiments in physics, it would be infeasible to actually build such a problem solver given the field's current state of knowledge and resources.

Suppose we are writing a problem solver that reads and understands drawing-room mystery novels. In such novels a murder is invariably the engine that drives the plot. The grisly details of an actual murder are suppressed, and the whole affair is treated as a puzzle. A premise of the genre is that the author will "play fair," and include enough clues in the story that the astute reader can solve the puzzle before the detective reveals the solution. Obviously, building such a program is well beyond the state of the art in AI. It would involve huge advances in natural language understanding and common sense reasoning, for instance. But it provides an instructive example for thinking about closed-world assumptions and set construals.

The classic formula for convicting a murderer is to show that he or she had motive, means, and opportunity, and that furthermore, no one else had all three. We can recast this structure in terms of sets and their construals as follows:

- Given a murder `M`, the set `(whodunit M)` is the list of suspects who had motive, means, and opportunity.
- The mystery is solved when |`(whodunitM)`| = 1. The murderer is the sole element of `(whodunit M)`.
- To be in `(whodunit M)`, a suspect must be in all three of the following sets:

  `(motivated M)` The set of suspects motivated to perform the murder.

  `(had-means M)` The set of suspects who could have carried out the actions involved in the murder, if the circumstances were right.

  `(had-chance M)` The set of suspects who were in the right circumstances to carry out the murder.

Our hypothetical problem solver's job, in reading a murder mystery, is to interpret the text as information about the constituents of these sets and thus solve the murder. When halfway through a particular mystery (say `Murder32`), our program might have the following construals:

(Had – Chance Murder32) = {LadyDrinkwater}

(Motivated Murder32) = {Butler LadyDrinkwater LordLayabout}

(Had – Means Murder32) = {Butler LordLayabout}

(Had – Chance Murder32) = {Butler LadyDrinkwater}

Whatever their motives, we might have eliminated LadyDrinkwater from having the means to carry out the murder if the victim, DukeEarl, died of a bullet fired from a long distance and her preferred hunting technique involved shotguns. Similarly, we might have eliminated LordLayabout from having the opportunity to commit the murder if he was seen at a fox hunt far away from HysteriaLodge, the site of the murder, when it occurred. Although by a strict definition we have enough information to identify a murderer, let us assume the program is sophisticated enough to know that in a well-written mystery these construals will change substantially as it reads further.

10.4.1.2 Representing sets

It is time to delve into the reasoning in more detail, so we need some conventions for describing sets in a computer-friendly form:

(⟨*Set*⟩ has-member ⟨*m*⟩) is true exactly when ⟨*m*⟩ ∈ ⟨*Set*⟩ .

(⟨*Set*⟩ members M) is true exactly when the problem solver believes ⟨*Set*⟩ = ⟨*M*⟩ .

For instance, the following statements would be true given the construals above:

```
((Had-Means Murder32) has-member Butler)
((Had-Means Murder32) has-member LordLayabout)
((Had-Means Murder32) members (Butler LordLayabout))
```

This particular implementation of the representation is chosen for two reasons. First, we assume there may be many sets, so indexing via members and has-member would be inefficient. Second, this implementation simplifies fetching all the relevant information about a particular set.

10.4.1.3 Closing sets

Constructals are created by *closing* a set. Conceptually, closing a set entails

1. Fetching what is known about what are members of the set.
2. Creating a closed-world assumption (CWA for short) for that set and list of members.
3. Justifying the construal based on the known members and the CWA.

We examine each of these steps in turn.

The first step, fetching what is known about what are members of the set, looks easy enough: Given a set ⟨*S*⟩, simply fetch all assertions of the form

```
( ⟨S⟩ has-member ?el)
```

and filter out those whose belief status is not `:TRUE`. Unfortunately this process is a little too simple. Suppose the assertions whose database class is `(had-means Murder32)` consists of

Assertion	Belief
`((had-means Murder32) has-member Butler)`	`:TRUE`
`((had-means Murder32) has-member LadyDrinkWater)`	`:FALSE`
`((had-means Murder32) has-member LordLayabout)`	`:TRUE`

Our mechanical reader ruled out `LadyDrinkWater` because of an inference as to her sharpshooting skills. But characters in murder mysteries often lie. If the set `(whodunit Murder32)` becomes empty, the program must be able to use the TMS to find the assumptions to be reanalyzed with greater skepticism. Consequently, our justification for the construal of `(had-means Murder32)` should include the `has-member` statement involving `LadyDrinkWater`, since that is part of what we know about the extension of `(had-means Murder32)`.

More generally, the justification of a construal must include all `has-member` statements known to be either true or false *at the time the set is closed*. The temporal distinction is important, because closing a set should (and in our implementation, will) make unknown `has-member` statements false. After all, anything not listed in the extension of a set must not be in that set, by definition. Ensuring that these justifications fully reflect the system's knowledge is very important. Failure to include information about negative `has-member` statements can result in entire subspaces being skipped in searches. In the example above, not including our conjecture about `LadyDrinkWater` having the means to commit `Murder32` might have led to exonerating her inappropriately.

The second step, creating the closed-world assumption, has several related requirements:

- *Informative:* The closed-world assumption must accurately summarize the information that went into the construal.
- *Defeasible:* When information changes, the closed-world assumption must be retractable.
- *Isolatable:* Closed-world assumptions that are no longer relevant must not interfere with further processing.

The form of the CWA statement must be unique for each distinct construal. Otherwise it would be neither informative nor defeasible. For instance, assertions of the form

(CWA ⟨*S*⟩)

are useless, since this single assumption would not provide a means of selecting between alternate construals. The form of the CWA must include, in addition to the name of the set being closed, at least the list of items known to be members when it was closed.

We noted above that negative `has-members` statements should be included in the justifications for a construal. Should the CWA include a list of "known not to be members" as well? We have chosen not to include this information because it will always be available in the justifications that use the closed-world assumption. Including the negative information would simplify gathering information, at the cost of creating distinct assertions for every combination of positive and negative information. Since construals are independent of the negative information (although their justifications are not!), leaving the negative information out of the CWA seems more appropriate.

The format we use for CWA statements is

(⟨*Set*⟩ CWA ⟨*KnownMembers*⟩)

where ⟨*KnownMembers*⟩ is a list of the known members of the set ⟨*Set*⟩ when it was closed. Given any LTRE database, we can construct the appropriate CWA statement by fetching the positive `has-member` statements.

Defeasibility is easy to achieve by making the CWA statement be an enabled assumption. When the problem solver's beliefs change in such a way that the CWA becomes false, it can be retracted.

Isolation is provided in two ways. First, we avoid installing any clauses that would allow the positive derivation of a closed-world assumption. Such derivations are always a mistake, given the non-monotonic nature of this reasoning. Consider the set (had-means Murder32). Suppose for instance we had constructed a clause which could support a closed-world assumption being true based on the suspect list being Butler, LadyDrinkWater, and LordLayAbout. Suppose the author now stirs DukeEarl's American cousin, ChesterDrawers, into the plot. Any justification that forced a positive derivation of a closed-world assumption based on the previous suspect list could still do so again, which could in turn cause an incomplete members statement to be believed.

The second way isolation is provided is by limiting the temporal extent of closed-world assumptions. Prior to closing a set, we retract the previous closed-world assumption explicitly, rather than counting on the contradiction mechanism to do so automatically. Since the only clauses that mention previous closed-world assumptions include them as negative literals, they can only be derived as false.

The final step, constructing the justification, is simplicity itself. We simply assert that the combination of known has-member statements, together with the closed-world assumption, implies a particular construal of the set. Returning to our previous example, the justification would be

```
(:IMPLIES
 (:AND ((had-means murder32) has-member Butler)
       (:NOT ((had-means murder32) has-member LadyDrinkWater))
       ((had-means murder32) has-member LordLayAbout)
       ((had-means murder32) CWA (Butler LordLayAbout)))
 ((had-means murder32) members (Butler LordLayAbout)))
```

10.4.1.4 Orchestrating the use of closed-world assumptions

Now that the representations for sets and the method for closing sets is understood, we can consider how construals should be updated when the state of the database changes. To exploit the contradiction-handling mechanism outlined previously, we must:

- Ensure that relevant new information is detected as soon as possible.
- Install a contradiction handler for each set when it is closed.

These goals are easy to achieve, given the infrastructure provided by LTRE. An LTRE rule can detect conflicting information about set construals. There are two forms of conflict: (1) A `has-member` statement conflicts with every `members` that does not mention its element and (2) Any `members` statements representing non-identical construals conflict. The contradiction handling can be accomplished by pushing a handler that looks for a closed-world assumption about the set in the ground support underlying a contradiction. If such an assumption is found, it can be checked against the database for validity by fetching the `has-member` statements for that set. If invalid, the closed-world assumption can then be retracted, and processing proceeds accordingly.

10.4.2 Implementing the set construal mechanism

The set construal mechanism is implemented in two files. The first, `setrule.lisp`, contains an LTRE rule which enforces the semantics of `has-member` and `members` statements, as outlined above. Figure 10.4 illustrates. The `alphalessp` test[3] prevents the installation of redundant construal uniqueness constraints.

The bulk of the code is in the file `cwa.lisp`. The primary interface procedures are:

`set-members` Given the name of a set, returns its current construal if any. The closed-world assumption underlying the construal is returned as a second value.

`close-set-if-needed` Closes a set if it isn't already closed.

`close-set` Closes a set.

`with-closed-set` Takes two arguments, the name of a set and a list of forms. The forms are executed in a logical environment which includes

---

3. `alphalessp`, a refugee from Maclisp, provides an ordering on any two arguments by translating them into strings and using `string<`. It is defined in `ldata.lisp`.

```
(rule ((:TRUE (set ?name) :VAR ?f1))
  (rule ((:INTERN (?name members ?construal1) :VAR ?f2))
    (rule ((:INTERN (?name has-member ?new) :VAR ?f3
                    :TEST (not (member ?new ?construal1
                                       :TEST #'equal))))
          (rassert! (:IMPLIES (:AND ?f1 ?f2) (:NOT ?f3))
                    :NOT-IN-SET))
    (rule ((:INTERN (?name MEMBERS ?construal2) :VAR ?f3
                :TEST (and (alphalessp ?construal1 ?construal2)
                           (set-exclusive-or ?construal1
                                             ?construal2
                                             :TEST 'equal))))
          (rassert! (:NOT (:AND ?f1 ?f2 ?f3))
                    :CONSTRUAL-UNIQUENESS))))
```

Figure 10.4 Enforcing the semantics of set relationships

the current environment plus the current construal of the set it was given.

These procedures are shown in Figure 10.5. We focus only on the highlights of these programs, since they are fairly straightforward.

The procedure `close-set` begins by gathering the current `has-member` statements, using the procedure `get-set-information`, and uses that information to build the appropriate `members` and `CWA` assertions. Next, any existing closed-world assumptions for that set are retracted by `retract-cwas`. Then the closed-world assumption is enabled (by the call to `assume-cwa-if-needed`) and the justification for the `members` statement is created in terms of the positive and negative `has-member` statements and the closed-world assumption (via `justify-cwa-if-needed`).

Notice that `close-set` and its utilities are written very defensively. For instance, `retract-cwas` iterates over every every `CWA` assertion for the given set, retracting every one that is an enabled assumption. But if our design has been followed rigorously, there can be at most one such assumption. It would therefore be more efficient to return once any assumption had been found. Similarly, in `assume-cwa-if-needed`, the `false?` test should only be needed if some closed-world assumption statement has been left in place. In our experience, bugs involving closed-world assumptions can be extremely subtle, and defensive programming here is very important.

```
(defun set-members (set-name &optional (*LTRE* *LTRE*)
                             &aux m-s)
  (dolist (mform (fetch '(,set-name MEMBERS ?elements)))
          (if (true? mform) (return (setq m-s mform))))
  (cond (m-s (values (third m-s) (find-cwa-for-set m-s)))
        (t nil)))

(defun close-set-if-needed (set-name
                            &optional (*LTRE* *LTRE*))
  (multiple-value-bind (construal cwa)
                       (set-members set-name)
  (cond (cwa (values construal cwa nil))
        (t (close-set set-name)))))

(defun close-set (set-name &optional (*LTRE* *LTRE*))
  (multiple-value-bind (known-members known-not)
   (get-set-information set-name)
   (let ((cwa-form (make-cwa-form set-name known-members))
         (members-form
          '(,set-name MEMBERS ,known-members)))
     (retract-CWAs set-name)
     (assume-cwa-if-needed cwa-form)
     (justify-cwa-if-needed set-name known-members known-not
                            cwa-form members-form)
   (values known-members cwa-form t))))

(defmacro With-Closed-Set (set-name &rest body)
  '(multiple-value-bind (members cwa)
       (close-set-if-needed ,set-name *LTRE*)
      (With-Contradiction-Handler (ltre-ltms *LTRE*)
       #'(lambda (clauses ltms)
           (set-cwa-handler clauses ltms ,set-name
                            cwa ':LOST-CWA))
       (let ((answer (catch cwa ,@ body)))
         (cond ((eq answer ':LOST-CWA) (values nil nil))
               (t (values t members)))))))
```

Figure 10.5 The set construal interface procedures

```
> (cwa-interactive-test)
;;; Loading binary file "/u/bps/code/ltms/setrule.bbin"

 Parts are: (PUMP METER VALVE)
>(assume! '((parts system) has-member sensor) :SAW-IT)

<Datum 7>
 Parts are: (SENSOR PUMP METER VALVE)
>(assume! '((parts system) has-member motor) :SAW-IT)

<Datum 10>
 Parts are: (MOTOR SENSOR PUMP METER VALVE)
>(assume! '((parts system) has-member heat-exchanger) :SAW-IT)

<Datum 13>
 Parts are: (HEAT-EXCHANGER MOTOR SENSOR PUMP METER VALVE)
>(retract! '((parts system) has-member motor) :SAW-IT)

#<NODE: ((PARTS SYSTEM) HAS-MEMBER MOTOR)>
 Parts are: (HEAT-EXCHANGER SENSOR PUMP METER VALVE)
>quit
NIL
```

Figure 10.6 The closed-world mechanism can track changing information

The procedure `justify-cwa-if-needed` has one wrinkle necessitated by our choice of the direct translation strategy for turning logical constraints into clauses. The problem with turning constraints directly into clauses is that there is no record of constraints in the `LTRE` database. Consequently, unlike simple propositions, asserting the same constraint multiple times can lead to redundant information in the dependency network. Our strategy to overcome this is to cache in the `datum-plist` of the assertion corresponding to the closed-world assumption a record of what justifications have been created already. This allows the system to avoid creating redundant clauses when reexploring a particular construal of a set.

The end of `cwa.lisp` contains two debugging utilities. The first is `interactive-cwa-test`, which maintains a construal of `(parts system)` through user-supplied additions and deletions. Figure 10.6 shows a sample interaction with that procedure. The second is `cwa-shakedown`, which automatically tests the set construal implementation for problems.

10.5 A dependency-directed search facility

In Chapter 8 we saw how dependency-directed search could be used to greatly improve search efficiency in the N-queens puzzle. Here we apply the lessons learned in that program to create a general-purpose dependency-directed search facility. As with the rest of LTRE, we presume a stack-oriented model for global control. That is, our mechanism allows searches and other assumption-making activities to be nested in arbitrary combinations, but we will not be able to switch back and forth between two parallel searches, neither of which occurs in the context of the other. This restriction is a direct consequence of the stack discipline used for contradiction handlers and of the global nature of the LTMS dependency network.

Recall that in Chapter 8 we characterized dependency-directed search by the following abstract procedure:

```
(defun DDS (choice-sets)
 (if (null choice-sets) (record-solution)
     (dolist (choice (first choice-sets))
      (unless (nogood? choice)
       (while-assuming choice
        (if (consistent?)
            (DDS (rest choice-sets))
            (record-nogood choice)))))))
```

where

`record-solution` did whatever was needed to store the solution just found,

`nogood?` checked to see if a warning about the current choice was already in as a consequence of dependencies recorded earlier,

`while-assuming` enabled the choice as an assumption,

`consistent?` looked for contradictions, and

`record-nogood` installed a warning about the current choice if it turned out to be contradictory.

The abstract procedure `dds` can be used as a skeleton for an executable procedure, given the infrastructure provided by LTRE. The procedure `dd-search`, shown in Figure 10.7, is one such implementation. This pro-

```
(defun DD-Search (choice-sets end &aux answer marker choices)
  (when (null choice-sets)
    (debug-dds "~%    DDS: Found solution.")
    (eval end)
    (return-from DD-Search nil))
  (setq marker (list 'DDS (car choice-sets)))
  (setq choices (car choice-sets))
  (dolist (choice choices)
    (debug-dds "~%    DDS: Considering ~A..." choice)
    (cond ((false? choice) ;skip if known loser
           (debug-dds "~%    DDS: ~A already known nogood." choice))
          ((true? choice) ;skip useless if known
           (debug-dds "~%    DDS: ~A true by implication." choice)
           (DD-Search (cdr choice-sets) end)
           (return nil))
          (t (debug-dds "~%    DDS: Assuming ~A." choice)
             (with-Contradiction-Handler (ltre-ltms *ltre*)
               #'(lambda (clauses ltms &aux asns)
                   (debug-dds
                     "~%    DDS: Entering handler for ~A with ~A~A."
                         choice clauses
                         (mapcar #'violated-clause? clauses))
                   (dolist (cl clauses)
                     (setq asns (assumptions-of-clause cl))
                     (debug-dds "~%    DDS: Assumptions are: ~A"
                                (mapcar #'view-node asns))
                     (dolist (asn asns)
                       (when (or (equal choice (view-node asn))
                                 (and (listp choice) (eq (car choice) ':NOT)
                                      (equal (cadr choice)
                                             (view-node asn))))
                         (throw marker
                           (cons :LOSERS (delete asn asns)))))))
               (setq answer (catch marker
                              (Assuming (list choice) *ltre*
                                (run-rules *ltre*) ;run tests incrementally
                                (DD-Search (cdr choice-sets) end))))
               (when (and (listp answer)
                          (eq (car answer) ':LOSERS))
                 (debug-dds "~%    DDS: ~A inconsistent with ~A."
                            choice (mapcar #'view-node (cdr answer)))
                 (assert! `(not (and ,choice
                                     ,@ (mapcar #'view-node (cdr answer))))
                          ':DD-SEARCH-NOGOOD)))))))
```

Figure 10.7 Implementation of a dependency-directed search facility

```
(defun Test-DD-search (&optional (debugging? t))
  (in-LTRE (create-ltre "DDS Test" :DEBUGGING debugging?))
  (eval '(rule ((:TRUE A) (:TRUE C))
             (rassert! (:NOT (:AND A C)) :DOMAIN-NOGOOD)))
  (eval '(rule ((:TRUE B) (:TRUE E))
             (rassert! (:NOT (:AND B E)) :DOMAIN-NOGOOD)))
  (DD-Search '((A B) (C D) (E F))
           '(show-DD-test-solution)))

(defun show-DD-test-solution (&aux result)
  (dolist (var '(F E D C B A))
    (when (true? var *ltre*) (push var result)))
  (format t "~% Consistent solution: (~A)." result))

> (test-dd-search nil)

 Consistent solution: ((A D E)).
 Consistent solution: ((A D F)).
 Consistent solution: ((B C F)).
 Consistent solution: ((B D F)).
NIL
```

Figure 10.8 A simple dependency-directed search example

cedure is not much more complex than the abstract version. The sources of complexity are:

- The decomposition of `while-assuming` and `consistent?` is easy to understand, but does not accurately reflect the asynchronous nature of contradiction processing in the LTMS. These operations could be decomposed by turning off contradiction processing while making assumptions and then looking for contradictions afterwards as a distinct operation. We prefer to interleave them because it allows the system to backtrack as quickly as possible, which can increase efficiency.
- There are two kinds of information gleaned from earlier parts of the search which are useful: Choices can be ruled out (i.e., be labeled `:FALSE`) or be forced as a consequence of earlier decisions (i.e., be labeled `:TRUE`). Exploiting the second is as important as the first, since in that case we know (because choice sets are mutually exclusive) that all remaining choices in the current choice set are irrelevant.

- We have added reporting facilities, using a macro `debug-dds`, for printing extra information about the search on demand.

Unlike the dependency-directed search procedure for N-queens, `DD-Search` supports multilevel backup. Notice that the search through the choice sets is depth first, so that the contradiction handlers will appear on the LTMS's contradiction-handling stack with the most recent at the top of the stack. When a contradiction occurs, the search is unwound back to the last relevant assumption. Ergo `dd-search` implements chronological search *within the set of relevant choices.*

Figure 10.8 shows `DD-Search` tested on a familiar example. More complex examples of `DD-Search` in action are postponed until the next chapter (and, of course, the exercises).

10.6 Backpointers

The `try-indirect-proof` procedure and example of Figure 10.2 is adapted from [4]. The stack-oriented contradiction handler and closed-world assumption mechanism in this chapter are modern versions of similar mechanisms first used in the `DEBACLE` inference engine [2]. An interesting variation on this scheme is used in McAllester's `ONTIC` [5], which maintains a stack of binding assumptions that link logical variables to constants as part of a virtual copy mechanism.

10.7 Exercises

1. ⋆ Why won't the following rule work?

```
(rule ((:TRUE (:NOT ?x))) (format t "~% ~A is false."))
```

2. ⋆⋆ Add the logical connective `:XOR` (i.e., exclusive or) to LTRE.

3. ⋆⋆ Sometimes one wonders why a particular fact is not yet believed. It would be very handy in such cases to be able to find out what other assumptions could be enabled to support a particular potential belief. Making such information available to programs would, for instance, allow LTMS clauses to be used for back-chaining and abduction.

a. ⋆⋆ Write a procedure `NEEDS` that, when given a fact and a truth value, returns a list of sets of facts which, if known, would result in the conclusion that the given fact had the desired truth value.

b. ⋆⋆ Not all facts are created equal. Sometimes we can only supply certain kinds of facts. For example, we might ask a program to tell us what sets of observations we could make that would tell us whether or not a particular component was behaving normally in the context of a larger system. Extend `NEEDS` by adding an optional third argument, consisting of a list of patterns that comprise forms of facts that we are willing to assume.

c. ⋆⋆ There can be many possible ways to support a desired belief. A common constraint in abduction is to pick a *minimal cost explanation*. A simple model of costs for explanations is to assign a cost to each class of allowed assumption, and let the cost of the explanation be the sum of the costs of the assumptions made to support it. Write `LABDUCE`, which takes an unknown fact and an alist of allowable assumption forms and costs, and uses the LTMS database to construct a minimal-cost explanation.

4. ⋆⋆ The `try-indirect-proof` procedure gives correct results, but they are not as informative as they might be (see Figure 10.3). Change `try-indirect-proof` to produce more informative answers, without introducing any new TMS nodes or clauses.

5. ⋆ A problem you may have noticed with the `close-set` procedure is that it violates the basic handler discipline, which calls for pushing a contradiction handler whenever an assumption (or set of related assumptions) is made. Invoking `close-set` indirectly via the `With-Closed-Set` macro is an improvement, but a lingering CWA can still cause contradictions even after the body has terminated. Add one line to `With-Closed-Set` that will prevent this bug.

6. ⋆⋆⋆ A more subtle problem with the closed-world assumption mechanism is that it fails to detect when "the dog doesn't bark"—that is, the current mechanism correctly detects when we have *gained* information about the constituents of a set, but not when we have *lost* information about it. Suggest an additional discipline that an LTRE programmer could use to avoid this problem.

7. Used in moderation, puzzles can provide a good source of examples for understanding the search aspects of reasoning techniques.
   a. ⋆ Use DD-Search to write a procedure that solves the N-queens puzzle.
   b. ⋆⋆ Use DD-Search to write a cryptarithmetic puzzle solver.
8. Examples of a more difficult class of puzzle are what some call "logic puzzles." These can be found on many newsstands, especially in airports and train stations. They fall somewhere between cryptarithmetic problems and drawing-room murder mysteries in difficulty. Each puzzle contains a scenario, a set of clues, and a list of questions to be answered by reasoning using the clues. A scenario might involve three people who play in a jazz group, each having different phobias, with the goal being to find out who plays what instrument. The collection of clues might include statements like
   - The guitarist is afraid of heights.
   - The spouse of the drummer lives on the twenty-seventh floor.

   from which the reader should infer that the guitarist and drummer aren't married. Solving such puzzles involves extracting information from clues and reasoning by a process of elimination, much like our gedanken program for understanding drawing-room mysteries. Suppose we wanted to build a program that automatically solved such puzzles.
   a. ⋆ Explain why this problem is much simpler than understanding drawing-room murder mysteries.
   b. ⋆ Explain why this problem is far more difficult than cryptarithmetic problems.
   c. ⋆⋆ Outline how the mechanisms of this chapter could be used in a puzzle solver for this class of problems. How would you decompose the problem, and what would the interface between the parts look like?
   d. ⋆⋆ Implement the parts of your design from the previous problem that rely only on techniques from this chapter.
   e. ⋆⋆⋆⋆⋆ Write a program that can take as input the natural-language description of logic puzzles from magazines and solve them with reasonable success.

9. ⋆⋆ The LTMS only maintains a single derivation for any supported node. As we have seen, procedural methods for non-monotonic reasoning, such as the closed-world assumption mechanism for set construals, do not guarantee that the LTMS derivations exploit the best available information. In fact, such guarantees don't hold for the purely monotonic case either, given the existence of alternate derivations. Suppose we set out to write a procedure `RECLOSE` which, given a contradiction, recomputes the construals of any sets that were closed by assumption in order to increase the amount of independent information included in the set of support underlying the contradiction. What problems are involved in writing such a procedure? How efficient can such a procedure be? How efficient can it be if it must guarantee that the amount of independent information used is maximized?

10. In outlining our gedanken program for understanding murder mysteries, we ignored the problem of building and maintaining the overall list of suspects. An implicit assumption of most reasoning in detective novels is that all characters are suspects until cleared. Suppose our system used the predicate `Player` to indicate that a person should be considered a character major enough to be thought of as a suspect. That is,

    ```
    (Player LadyDrinkwater)
    ```

    would be true while

    ```
    (Player TelevisionAnnouncer)
    ```

    would be false.

    a. ⋆ Write an LTRE rule that ensures that a character mentioned as a player will be included in the construal of `WhoDunIt`, ignoring anything else known about that character.

    b. ⋆⋆ Other mechanisms are needed to support this variety of default inference. To figure out what they are, analyze the kinds of transactions that can occur between LTRE and the rest of the story-understanding system. For instance, one important situation to consider is what must be done when a character is removed from a construal due to information which may itself later be retracted (e.g., someone's testimony). Describe the kinds of transactions that would be needed, and outline mechanisms sufficient to handle them.

c. ⋆⋆ Implement the mechanisms outlined in your previous answer, and test them on several examples.

11. ⋆⋆⋆ Using your favorite technology (e.g., CLOS), turn the `DD-Search` program into a generator. The generator should support at least the following operations:

    `reset` Retracts all existing assumptions, makes ready to begin the search from the beginning.

    `try-next` Causes the generator to search for the next consistent solution, if any.

    `winning?` Returns non-`nil` only when the search is underway and the generator has settled on a consistent solution.

    `choices` Returns the current set of choices.

12. Scheduling problems often involve complex constraints, and thus are good candidates for dependency-directed search. Typically the major problem is developing a language in which to express the constraints, with the search for a solution being relatively straightforward after that.

    a. ⋆⋆⋆⋆ Develop a set of relationships to express the scheduling constraints a typical professional might have when planning an average workday. These relationships should include demands for certain amounts of particular activities each day (or each week) as well as ways to specify appointments. An important class of relationships are *preferences*: One person may prefer their isolated work time to be in the morning with meetings absorbing the afternoon, while another might prefer the opposite.

    b. ⋆⋆⋆ Using this language, try generating a schedule using dependency-directed search.[4]

---

4. Warning: Typically one does not want to generate all consistent solutions to scheduling problems. Using a very simple scheduling program, Forbus once found out that there were 2,880 consistent ways to schedule appointments with eight graduate students in an afternoon, even with many constraints imposed by courses and other scheduled meetings.

c. ⋆⋆⋆⋆ While generating truly optimal schedules can be extremely expensive, it is often possible to generate very good schedules with little work. Using preference information, develop a scheduler that starts with inconsistent schedules that maximize everyone's preferences and performs local perturbations to achieve a consistent schedule. (Such an algorithm is analogous to simulated annealing—how does the dependency system help?)

10.8 Bibliography

[1] Collins, A., Warnock, E., Aiello, N. and Miller, M., "Reasoning from incomplete knowledge," in Bobrow, D., and Collins, A. (eds.), *Representation and Understanding*, Academic Press, 1975.

[2] Forbus, K.,"Qualitative Process Theory," MIT AI Lab Technical Report No. 789, 1984.

[3] Gentner, D. and Collins, A., "Studies of inference from lack of knowledge," *Memory & Cognition*, 9(1981):434-443.

[4] McAllester, D., "An outlook on truth maintenance," MIT AI Lab, AIM-551, 1980.

[5] McAllester, D., *ONTIC: A Knowledge Representation System for Mathematics*, MIT Press, 1989.

[6] Reiter, R., "A logic for default reasoning," *Artificial Intelligence*, 13(1980): 81–132.

11 Implementing Qualitative Process Theory

This chapter shows how LTRE can be used to implement a subset of Qualitative Process (QP) theory [10]. The system we present here, TGIZMO[1], uses common sense knowledge to figure out what might be causing changes observed in simple physical situations. TGIZMO is substantially more complex than the programs exhibited in previous chapters. We believe it is important to look at such larger-scale examples, because they better illustrate how the ideas we have presented can be combined to build powerful reasoning systems.

We begin by describing the class of problems TGIZMO is designed to solve. Section 11.2 briefly summarizes QP theory, highlighting those aspects of its representations and reasoning needed to understand TGIZMO. Section 11.3 describes TGIZMO's design, analyzing the critical issues and trade-offs and providing a global perspective on the system. Section 11.4 goes through the implementation, pointing out how the various LTRE inference mechanisms interact in problem solving. TGIZMO's performance on some examples is illustrated in Section 11.5.

11.1 A problem: Measurement interpretation

There are many ways in which qualitative knowledge is used in reasoning about the physical world. One important way is interpreting measure-

1. GIZMO was the first implementation of Qualitative Process theory. TGIZMO stands for "Tiny GIZMO."

Figure 11.1 A measurement interpretation example

ments. Measurement interpretation is the task of translating readings from an artifact's gauges and instruments into a conceptual understanding of what is occurring inside the artifact. This is a central task for operators of complex systems, such as power plants, since knowing what is happening inside an artifact is a prerequisite to controlling it or troubleshooting it.

Here we focus on an important subset of this problem. Real physical systems often have complicated dynamics, and measurement interpretation typically involves integrating measurements taken over spans of time. There has been solid progress on this problem in qualitative physics [5, 13], but here we presume that all our measurements are taken in a very brief interval, during which the system's behavior can be characterized by a single state of affairs. Furthermore, we restrict our input information to purely qualitative information about the parameters of the system. What does "purely qualitative" mean? Consider an example like the three-container situation in Figure 11.1. A purely qualitative measurement would be the information that the water level in G is falling and the level in H is rising, but without any knowledge of how fast they are rising or falling. This restriction lets us ignore the difficulties involved in translating uncertain, numerical data to qualitative values.[2]

Even with these restrictions, there is still some sophisticated reasoning to be performed. First, we must use knowledge of the kinds of things that can happen in the physical world to figure out the sorts of physical processes that might occur in this situation. We might rule out phase changes because we don't see any heat source to cause boiling, and we know that evaporation typically takes place very slowly, so that probably isn't causing visible changes in fluid levels. Liquid flows seem possible, because there are visible paths connecting the containers. So let

2. See [5] for one good solution to this problem.

us presume that the only kind of physical process that can occur in this scenario is liquid flow. (Of course, if we receive new information about the scenario we may have to change these assumptions.) Once we have figured out what kinds of processes can occur, we have another complicated task: figuring out what combination(s) of these processes could cause the given measurements. Suppose we detect that the level in G is falling while the level in H is rising. There are three possible interpretations for these measurements. It could be the case that the level in G is highest, and so water is flowing from G to both F and H. Or it could be the case that F has the most water in it, and there is a flow of water from F to G and from G to H, but the rate of flow between G and H is higher than the rate from F to G. Or, finally, the path between F and G might be blocked and the level in G is higher than the level in H, so there is only a flow from G to H and nothing is happening between F and G. Finally, if we need to distinguish between these interpretations, their observable consequences can be compared to make predictions. Here, measuring F would allow us to disambiguate the possibilities: F rising means the first possibility must hold, F falling implies the second, and F constant implies the third interpretation.

So far our explanations have been informal, drawing on our shared, common sense knowledge of the physical world. Let us explore next how such knowledge can be made precise, and how the reasoning outlined above can be automated.

11.2 A QP theory primer

Qualitative Process theory (QP theory for short) provides a formalism for encoding knowledge about the physical world and some methods for reasoning with that knowledge. Here we give only a brief overview, sufficient to motivate and support a simple—and partial—implementation. We begin by describing the ontological assumptions of the theory. Then we outline its qualitative mathematics in Section 11.2.2. The organization of domain theories is discussed in Section 11.2.3. Since representation without reasoning might be interesting philosophy, but certainly not AI, the basic inferences sanctioned by QP theory are outlined in Section 11.2.4.

11.2.1 The ontological assumptions of QP theory

Ontology is traditionally defined as the study of what kinds of things exist. Ontological commitments are crucial to representation, since knowledge is typically organized around various kinds of "things." QP theory takes a very simple perspective: many kinds of things in the world are *physical objects*. Examples of objects include cups, pieces of water, boilers, and so forth. Among the important properties of physical objects are *continuous properties*, like mass and temperature. Various kinds of relationships can hold between objects, such as contact and containment (e.g., a piece of water can be inside a cup).

Another category of things in the world are *physical processes*. Examples of physical processes include liquid flow, boiling, and motion. Occurrences of physical processes are just as real, physically, as cups and pieces of water. In basic QP theory, physical processes are viewed as the sole agents of change in the continuous aspects of the physical world. That is, no change in physical properties can occur without the agency of a physical process directly or indirectly causing it, and something isn't a physical process unless it can potentially cause such changes. Thus a cup isn't a process (although it can participate in processes, such as heat flow). Similarly, the flow of water from a (stoppered) leak in the radiator of my car is a physical process, even though it doesn't happen to be acting at this particular point in time.

The ideas of objects and physical processes expressed so far should seem very close to common sense, and that is by design. Processes are in a sense "nature's agents," how things get done in the continuous part of the world. Notice that this is subtly different from the definition of process sometimes found in philosophical writings, where a process is simply a named pattern of activity in the physical world. In QP theory, processes are *mechanisms* which cause such patterns of activity, rather than the patterns of activity themselves. The reason for making this distinction is composability. Suppose we defined liquid flow as the occurrence of the amount of liquid in a source container shrinking and the amount of liquid in a destination container rising. This definition ignores the possibility of interactions between processes. For instance, in the simple three-container measurement interpretation example, we saw that the effects of one process could be counterbalanced or even masked by those of another. Defining processes as the mechanisms of change, rather than patterns of changes themselves, allow us to more cleanly represent such interactions.

The assumption that physical processes are the only source of change in physical situations (called the *sole mechanism* assumption) provides several important advantages for representing and reasoning about physical domains. To explain a change, look for the process (or processes) that are causing it. To troubleshoot, figure out what processes are occurring instead of those intended, and change conditions so that the desired ones occur. To learn, figure out how the changes observed in the domain can be encoded as processes that are applicable across all of the relevant phenomena. QP theory does not specify the exact contents of any domain theory—one can for instance encode Newtonian, Aristotelian, or impetus theories of motion in it—but sets strict limits on the form of such theories. These constraints on form simplify the discovery and use of the appropriate contents. Thus a central part of a domain theory becomes its *process vocabulary*, the set of mechanisms which can be composed to generate any pattern of change that can occur.

A central claim of QP theory is that this view of physical processes is a good portrayal of a substantial part of human common-sense knowledge. This includes both the person on the street and those with professional knowledge, such as scientists and engineers. In many physical domains, such as hydraulics, thermodynamics, and chemistry, this notion of physical process is directly useful in encoding and organizing domain theories. There are of course other ways of looking at the world, like component-based ontologies [6], developed for important special cases like electronics, but these are relatively recent in human culture. The notion of physical process seems to be part of the conceptual stock-in-trade of every engineer, scientist, and person on the street.

11.2.2 The mathematics of QP theory

The qualitative aspect of QP theory comes from two things. The first is the explicit symbolic representation of entities such as physical objects. The second is the use of *qualitative mathematics* to represent partial knowledge about continuous properties and mathematical relationships. The necessity of qualitative mathematics should be obvious in the case of common-sense reasoning: people who have never in their life seen, much less solved, an equation manage to get around in the physical world perfectly well. Consequently, the traditional formalisms of physics and mathematics cannot be necessary prerequisites to physical reasoning. It may be more surprising to find that qualitative knowledge is also indispensable to many kinds of expert, professional reasoning about the physical world. Conceptual design, for instance, consists of the stages in engineering design occurring before precise details have been specified, and hence before techniques like numerical simulation can be applied. Qualitative knowledge is used in such tasks to formulate what the important questions are, so that they may be resolved with more specific information as needed. In monitoring, control, and diagnosis, precise mathematical models of failure modes and fault conditions often do not exist for systems of interest, requiring human operators and troubleshooters to operate with less detailed models.

Continuous properties, such as temperature and pressure, are modeled by *quantities*. A quantity consists of an amount and a derivative, each of which are functions whose range is the real numbers ($\Re$). The semantics of quantities are simply those of continuous functions of time on the real numbers, where the *amount* of a quantity denotes its value at any specific time, and the *derivative* of a quantity denotes the value of its temporal derivative at that time. The function `A` maps a quantity to its amount, and `D` maps a quantity to its derivative. Thus it is legitimate to say:

```
A[temperature(water)] > ZERO
D[temperature(water)] < ZERO
```

where `ZERO` is simply the real number 0. The sign and magnitude of a number, with their usual mathematical interpretation, are denoted by the functions `s` and `m` respectively. The sign of the derivative, denoted `Ds`, is particularly important because it represents the direction in which something is changing, and that is often about as much as one can observe (or can predict) about a situation. (In the case above, `Ds[temperature(water)] = -1`, that is, the water is cooling off.) It is also important because changes in numerical values can lead to changes in what physical processes are occurring: presumably if the water gets cold enough, it freezes.

The example of freezing water highlights a crucial problem in qualitative reasoning: How should we represent numerical values? If we have some water in a cup in front of us, we may not know its exact temperature. But we do know that if we make it cold enough it will freeze, and that if we make it hot enough it will boil. These phenomena are important enough that the temperatures at which they occur are given names in physics (i.e., the freezing point and boiling point). Knowing the relationship between the temperature of a piece of water and these two points suffices to determine that piece's phase. This example suggests that ordinal relationships—that is, information about whether one numerical value is greater than, less than, or equal to another—provide a useful foundation for qualitative reasoning.

Ordinal relationships are surprisingly powerful. For instance, flows occur when pressures (or their equivalents) are unequal, and the comings and goings of pieces of stuff can be tracked by noting how much of them there is. Comparisons form the minimum amount of information needed to track changes: knowing that the temperature of a piece of water is currently below its boiling temperature but that its temperature is rising suffices to conclude that, unless things change, the water will eventually boil.[3] Certainly knowing that the temperature of water is 35 degrees C and rising by 4 degrees per second would allow us to make the same conclusion. With that much information we might even be able to estimate how long it would take for the water to start boiling. But often such information isn't available. In fact, figuring out that we might want to make such measurements requires knowing that the water might boil!

Qualitatively, we know that if the temperature of the heat source is less than the boiling temperature, then the heat flow will stop before boiling can start. If we don't know the relative temperatures involved, the qualitative reasoning produces ambiguous results. This is not a bad thing: ambiguity of the right kind is crucial in formulating interesting questions about a system. In this example, the ambiguous result informs us that if we really need to know what will happen (say, we are cooking) then we have to make the appropriate measurements. This is an example of using qualitative physics to propose possible outcomes and using

---

3. This is an example of the *relevance principle* of qualitative physics: A representation must be capable of making relevant distinctions. Simple representations of value like `TEPID`, `WARM`, `HOT`, `VERY-HOT`, etc. tend not to have this property. Does water boil when it is hot, very hot, or very very hot? Only if we pin these labels down by defining them in terms of a physically meaningful comparison (e.g., the boiling point) can we make more interesting predictions.

other kinds of information to decide between them. (It also illustrates another important design criterion of qualitative representations: they must allow *graceful integration* of more detailed information.)

In QP theory the value of a number is defined by its *quantity space*, a collection of ordinal information relating it to other significant parameters. For instance, the quantity space for the temperature of a piece of water typically includes its relationship to its freezing point and boiling point. The other parameters to which the number is compared are called its *limit points*, since they delimit either the occurrence of physical properties or the existence of an object (more on that momentarily). Limit points need not be constant: for example, the boiling point of a body of water varies according to the substances dissolved in it and its pressure. The set of limit points for a number is determined automatically, by analyzing the physical processes the quantity is involved with and the other comparisons needed by the basic inferences (more on this in Section 11.2.4). As illustrated with the cooking example above, quantity spaces need not impose a total ordering on the numbers they relate: the ordering can be partial, to accurately reflect states of partial knowledge.

Sometimes it is convenient to give names to specific values of limit points, for example to track how a limit point changes over time. Such named values are called *landmark values* [22]. Limit points and landmarks are not the same: landmarks can be thought of as the points on a graph denoting the progress of a quantity through time, while limit points mark important boundary conditions on such progress. For any particular quantity there are only a finite number of limit points, but a potentially infinite number of landmark values. Consider for example a spring-block oscillator that is subject to friction. To figure out the force applied by the spring to the block, one limit point (the rest length of the spring) suffices. On the other hand, if we are analyzing the rate at which the oscillator is slowing down, we may need to describe the maximum position of the block on each particular oscillation with a distinct landmark value. Here we will be concerned only with limit points (but see Exercise 12).

From the standpoint of qualitative mathematics, an object can be thought of as a bundle of quantities. This perspective alone is insufficient to capture many of our important intuitions about the physical world. An important fact about physical objects is that they have finite temporal extent. That is, they can be created and destroyed. Coffee cups get filled with cappuccino, leading to a distinct physical entity whose existence is ended via consumption. Lakes can arise from blockages in rivers, and dry up when rainfall diminishes for several years. It does not make sense to talk about the temperature and pressure of a lake when all that is before you is a dry hole in the ground. Consequently, QP theory makes the existence of physical properties contingent on the existence of the physical object itself, and ordinal relationships involving a nonexistent individual are not defined. The expression of this in logical terms is described in Section 11.4.8.

In physics, equations provide the formalism for precisely describing detailed relationships between continuous parameters. Equations in physics are chosen to be as precise as possible, given what is known and the constraints on the modeling task. Very precise measurements and calculations are the norm, with accuracy of fit and ability to generate precise predictions as the principal evaluation criteria. After all, human scientists and engineers already have their common sense to generate rough predictions—the goal of their formalism is to go beyond their intuitions. On the other hand, the goal of qualitative physics is to formally capture their intuitions. That is, qualitative physics explores the representations required to operate under a different set of assumptions: Very little information, with simplicity of computation being more important than detailed answers. Thus the mathematics used in qualitative physics tends to be simpler. In QP theory, *qualitative proportionalities* provide the major building block for equations. "Q_1 is qualitatively proportional to Q_2" means that there is some function which (1) determines Q_1, (2) depends at least on Q_2, and (3) is increasing monotonic in its dependence on Q_2. (The idea of "inversely qualitatively proportional" is defined similarly, with the implicit function being decreasing monotonic.) For example, we might say:

```
(qprop (acceleration Block) (applied-force Block))
(qprop- (acceleration Block) (mass Block))
```

which is a qualitative rendering of Newton's second law, $F = m \times a$. What do these statements tell us? Suppose the mass is constant. Then if the applied force is increased, the acceleration will also increase, and if the applied force is decreased, then the acceleration will also decrease. In general, a qualitative proportionality tells us how changes in one parameter can cause changes in another, all else being equal. What we lose is the ability to figure out what happens if both the mass and the applied force are changing at once (as might happen if we are pushing against a car rolling downhill which is leaking brake fluid). The qualitative proportionalities above are just as valid for $F = m^5 \times a^3$ as for the correct form of Newton's second law. (Notice they would not be correct for $F = m^5 \times a^2$, since decreasing negative accelerations would lead to increased F, thus violating the monotonic relationship.)

QP theory allows more information to be specified about functions implied by qualitative proportionalities; for instance, we can pin down values at a finite number of points by *correspondences*, i.e.,

```
(Correspondence ((acceleration Block) ZERO)
                ((applied-force Block) ZERO))
```

which says that when the applied force is zero the acceleration is zero as well. (An important consequence of this statement and the sign of the qualitative proportionality between the two quantities is that the sign of the acceleration will always be the same as the sign of the applied force.) One can also name the function determining a quantity, which has the effect of allowing inequality information to be propagated across distinct individuals. However, for our purposes we will only use simple qualitative proportionalities (but see Exercise 16).

Qualitative proportionalities suffice to express ordinary equations, but to represent dynamics requires expressing differential equations, where constraints are placed on the derivative(s) of a quantity rather than on the quantity itself. In QP theory the notion of *direct influence* provides this representation. The relations `I+` and `I-` are defined as follows:

$$I+(Q_1\ Q_2) \Leftrightarrow \frac{dQ_1}{dt} = \cdots + Q_2 + \cdots$$
$$I-(Q_1\ Q_2) \Leftrightarrow \frac{dQ_1}{dt} = \cdots - Q_2 + \cdots$$

To express the direct effects of a heat flow `hf1` between a stove and a kettle, for instance, one might say

```
(I+ (heat Kettle) (flow-rate hf1))
(I- (heat stove) (flow-rate hf1))
```

There are two things to notice here. First, as with qualitative proportionalities, a single direct influence statement does not by itself determine how the parameter it constrains will change. Its effect on the parameter must be combined with all the other influences on that parameter to ascertain their net effect. For instance, if the stove is on there may also be some process such as combustion which is replenishing its internal energy (also known informally as heat). The operation of combining these effects is called *influence resolution*, and is one of the basic inferences sanctioned by QP theory. It will be described in detail shortly. From the standpoint of representation design, the importance of allowing partial information is that it supports *composability*, a desirable feature in any modeling language. Second, notice that we have specified more information about the relationship imposed by direct influences than by qualitative proportionalities. Direct influences combine via addition. If we know the relative magnitudes of the various effects (which, again, demonstrates the utility of the quantity space representation!) then we can often figure out how the influenced parameter will actually change. But given a set of qualitative proportionalities, we cannot tell what the result of conflicting inputs will be unless we know more about the underlying function they partially specify.[4]

The combination of qualitative proportionalities and direct influences as described so far gives us a language that is sufficiently powerful to express, albeit with less precision, any system of ordinary differential equations whose independent parameter is time.[5] A qualitative equation is an abstraction of an entire family of quantitative equations. But there is a second, equally important, role these primitives play: they also express the causality which holds between the parameters. Thus the expression of Newton's second law:

```
(qprop (acceleration Block) (applied-force Block))
(qprop- (acceleration Block) (mass Block))
```

---

4. This was a deliberate design choice in QP theory, trading off the need to handle common cases easily against the need to represent nonlinear equations.

5. In mathematics, ordinary differential equations are those where the only derivative terms are with respect to a single parameter. Partial differential equations are those which include derivatives taken with respect to several parameters.

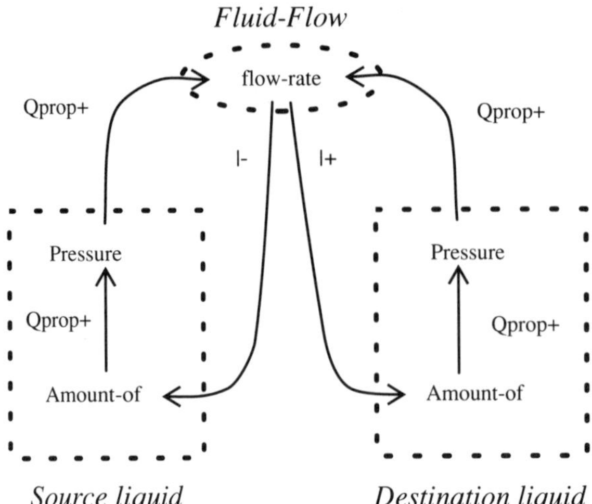

Figure 11.2 An example of the causal account of QP theory. Arrows indicate causal relationships. Qualitative proportionalities represent algebraic relationships, while direct influences represent integral connections.

tells us that a change in applied force causes a change in acceleration, rather than the other way around. Similarly, the direct influences

```
(I+ (heat Kettle) (flow-rate hf1))
(I- (heat stove) (flow-rate hf1))
```

tell us that the flow rate of the heat flow causes a change in the internal energies of the objects it happens between, rather than the other way around.

Here is the causal account provided by QP models. Physical processes are the root of all changes, acting to affect some parameters directly via their direct influences. These direct effects are propagated via qualitative proportionalities, thus providing for indirect effects (for this reason qualitative proportionalities are often called *indirect influences*. Figure 11.2 illustrates.

To keep its causal accounts coherent, QP theory places certain restrictions on models. First, direct influences can only be imposed by physical processes. This helps enforce the sole mechanism assumption introduced earlier. Second, consider the graph whose nodes are the quantities that exist during some interval and whose directed edges are the qualitative proportionalities that hold during that interval. QP theory stipulates that this graph must be free of cycles. For example, there can be no interval of time in which

```
(qprop (heat foo) (flow-rate hf1))
(qprop (temperature foo) (heat foo))
(qprop- (flow-rate hf1) (temperature foo))
```

all hold. There are two interrelated reasons why such combinations are disallowed. First, their solutions would give rise to changes without processes, thus violating the sole mechanism assumption. Second, computing a causal story for such sets of equations can be tricky. Mathematically, they correspond to simultaneous equations, and additional information is required to impose a causal ordering (see [6, 21]). Unless this additional information is chosen correctly, unintuitive causal arguments can be generated (i.e., "a rise in internal energy causes mass to increase, since temperature remains constant" [10]). Finally, QP theory stipulates that no quantity can be both directly influenced and indirectly influenced at the same time. This restriction, along with the other two, enforces the simple causal story described above.

The restrictions imposed by QP theory's causal interpretation are not without cost: they limit the expressive power of QP theory's qualitative mathematics. Instead of representing any system of ordinary differential equations whose independent parameter is time, we can only express such systems when they are free of simultaneities. This restriction is less onerous than it might at first seem. It is analogous to the state space formulation widely used in engineering modeling, where systems are decomposed into a set of state variables and dependent variables. In QP theory, directly influenced parameters play the role of state variables and indirectly influenced parameters play the role of dependent variables. This analogy also points out how QP theory deals with feedback. In a state space model, any loops in the graph of equations must have some *delay element*, usually expressed as a derivative or integration operator. Analogously, in a QP model any loop of influences must include at least one direct influence (by stipulations above), and that satisfies the state space definition of delay element. In essence, the direct influences "break the loop," using the physical processes to ground the causal account of the model.

The implication of QP theory's causal account for representing physical phenomena is that we must identify some physical process to be responsible for each direct influence. While perhaps annoying at first to someone used to jotting down third-order differential equations, this design choice makes the modeler be explicit in choices of ontology, and thus helps enforce the tight integration of mathematics with formal physical models.

Systems of influences are a useful representation, but they are only part of the story: Much of the leverage of qualitative physics comes from providing representations that allow simplifying assumptions and other modeling ideas to be formalized. We examine this aspect next.

11.2.3 Organizing domain theories

In any problem, there are some aspects that remain fixed. For instance, if we are thinking about what happens if we put a kettle of water onto a lit stove, we may have doubts about the lifespan of the water (and the kettle if we don't move quickly at some point), but we treat the stove as remaining a stove, even though it will someday be rust. Predicates and relations that remain fixed throughout an analysis can, for present purposes, be considered as input, and not treated further.[6] But some properties, like the existence or nonexistence of water or steam in the kettle, are of central concern. To define time-varying relationships, QP theory uses the notion of *individual view*, or just *view*.

A view is defined by four fields. The *individuals* field specifies what kinds of things the view holds between. The semantics of the individuals field is that of universal instantiation. That is, for each set of terms that satisfy the constraints of the individuals field, there is a corresponding instance of that view. The view is active (i.e., the relationship it expresses is true of its arguments) exactly when the statements in the *preconditions* and *quantity conditions* fields associated with the view hold. These two fields thus specify (along with the constraints in the individuals field) the

6. Of course, any good physical modeling language will include means of defining such predicates in terms of others, in addition to the constructs of QP theory, but QP theory per se makes no stipulation as to how one chooses to do this.

```
(defview (Contained-Stuff (C-S ?sub ?st ?can))
  :INDIVIDUALS ((?can (container ?can)
                      (substance ?sub)
                      (phase ?st)))
  :QUANTITY-CONDITIONS ((> (A ((amount-of ?sub ?st) ?can)) ZERO))
  :RELATIONS ((only-during (exists (C-S ?sub ?st ?can)))
              (contained-stuff (C-S ?sub ?st ?can))
              (quantity (TBoil (C-S ?sub ?st ?can)))
              (> (A (TBoil (C-S ?sub ?st ?can))) ZERO)))
```

Figure 11.3 A definition of contained stuff

necessary and sufficient conditions for the relationship to hold. Quantity conditions are either descriptions of ordinal relationships or whether or not other views (and/or processes) are active, while preconditions contain every other kind of statement. The fourth (and final) field of a view is its *relations*, which expresses the direct consequences of the view being active. The contents of the relations field can be any statement of the modeling language, such as qualitative proportionalities or inequalities. Even non-QP consequences are allowed, such as descriptions of appearances. The only kind of statement not allowed are direct influences: those are reserved for physical processes.

An example will make the idea of a view clearer. Figure 11.3 defines the basic notion of contained stuff. A contained stuff is whatever pieces of material happen to exist in a particular container consisting of a particular substance in a particular phase. Intuitively, this corresponds to the notion of "the water in the kettle" being a distinct, identifiable object, even though we can add water to it or remove water from it. The `Contained-Stuff` view, according the individuals field of this definition, exists for each combination of container, substance, and phase. Whether or not this view is active is a separate issue, determined by its preconditions and quantity conditions. Since there are no preconditions, the quantity condition alone defines the necessary and sufficient condition for this view to be active: that is, that there be some amount of stuff of the given substance in the given phase inside the container in question.

When the `Contained-Stuff` view is active, we believe that a contained stuff (denoted by the function `C-S`) exists, as indicated by the predicate `Exists`. The `Only-During` signals that this consequence is biconditional: that is, when the view is false, this consequence must also be false. Normally, statements in the relations field have the semantics of implication, i.e., are "unidirectional." Finally, the contained stuff has a continuous property, `TBoil`, which is always positive.

The definition of view differentiates between three aspects of a relationship: when it should be thought of as being applicable (the `individuals` field), when it actually holds (the *preconditions* and *quantity conditions* fields), and what are its direct consequences (the *relations* field). Preconditions and quantity conditions are differentiated because changes in quantity conditions are always predictable within the QP aspect of a model, while no such guarantee is made for preconditions. Logically, such descriptions are equivalent to first-order predicate calculus axioms (see [10] for a translation). The extra conceptual distinctions, as reflected by the additional syntax, are motivated by two purposes. First, a theory about how to represent a class of domains must, to have power, restrict the class of things that can be said. A theory which says, "The right way to represent the physical world is to write predicate calculus axioms" isn't much of a theory. It does not help us distinguish, of all the ways we might write axioms, which of them will correspond to satisfactory theories of the physical world. The second purpose is computational. The conceptual distinctions imposed by the theory have computational implications (e.g., distinguishing a subset of conditions as sufficient grounds for instantiation). Encoding these distinctions explicitly in our representation greatly facilitates developing good reasoning algorithms.

Physical processes are the keystone of QP theory. Fortunately, in terms of syntax, they are (as hinted above) very close to views. The syntax for physical processes is exactly that of individual views, with one addition. The `influences` field contains the set of direct influence statements that represent the direct effects of of a kind of process on quantities. To be a process, something must have at least one direct influence. And, as stated earlier, nothing but processes can have direct influences. Figure 11.4 shows an example, a simple definition of heat flow.

Let us go over the `heat-flow` definition. Heat flow, according to this definition, can potentially occur between any two objects (`?src` and

```
(defprocess (heat-flow ?src ?path ?dst)
  :INDIVIDUALS ((?src (Quantity (heat ?src)))
                (?path (Heat-Connection ?path ?src ?dst))
                (?dst (Quantity (heat ?dst))))
  :PRECONDITIONS ((Heat-Aligned ?path))
  :QUANTITY-CONDITIONS ((> (A (temperature ?src))
                           (A (temperature ?dst))))
  :RELATIONS ((Quantity (flow-rate ?self))
              (> (A (flow-rate ?self)) zero)
              (Qprop (flow-rate ?self) (temperature ?src))
              (Qprop- (flow-rate ?self) (temperature ?dst)))
  :INFLUENCES ((I- (heat ?src) (flow-rate ?self))
               (I+ (heat ?dst) (flow-rate ?self))))
```

Figure 11.4 A physical process

?dst) which have the quantity `heat` and are connected via a heat path (`?path`). The precondition for heat flow represents the requirement that the path must be able to conduct heat.[7] The quantity condition expresses the fact that a temperature difference must exist to drive the process. When a heat flow is occurring, one can speak of it having a flow rate (i.e., the introduction of the quantity `flow-rate`) which is positive and depends on both of the temperatures. The increasing monotonic dependence on the temperature of the source and the decreasing monotonic dependence on the temperature of the destination is a partial encoding of the fact that the flow rate depends on the difference in temperatures between the source and destination.[8]

Recall that in our ontology physical processes are *things*, just as real, in a physical sense, as cups and cars. More exactly, each instantiation

7. In engineering, especially marine engineering, when the physical connectivity of a fluid path is such that flow could occur, that path is said to be *aligned*. The predicate `Heat-Aligned` is an extension of this idea for modeling changes in connectivity.

8. In full QP implementations one can simply state

```
(Q= (flow-rate ?self) (- (temperature ?src) (temperature ?dst)))
```

This statement has the effect of the qualitative proportionalities shown here, but also establishes a correspondence between the parameters, which provides a complete qualitative description of subtraction. The qualitative implications of sums, products, and quotients can be defined similarly, as readers who complete Exercise 16 will discover.

of a process definition gives rise to an individual, whose existence requires the existence of the objects mentioned in its individuals specification. The encoding of this constraint in propositional logic is described later.

The ability to explicitly state when a description is applicable gives us considerable leverage in representing and reasoning about modeling assumptions. Suppose, for instance, that we include extra statements in the `individuals` specification that describe the modeling assumptions under which that class of view or process makes sense. For instance, we might want a specialization of heat flow that explicitly models the thermal conductance of the path. We might go back and change the definition of heat flow introduced earlier, but that has the disadvantage of forcing us to think about the thermal conductance of the path even when we don't need or want to. Instead, we can introduce a new definition to the domain theory which adds information about this new aspect of heat flow:

```
(defview (Heat-Flow-Thermal-Conductance ?hf)
 :INDIVIDUALS ((?hf (process-instance (heat-flow ?src ?path ?dst))
                    (Consider (Thermal-Conductance ?path))))
 :QUANTITY-CONDITIONS ((Active ?hf))
 :RELATIONS ((Qprop+ (flow-rate ?hf) (thermal-conductance ?path))))
```

This description exploits the compositionality in our qualitative mathematics to add new constraints to functional relationships. This is one example of a general modeling methodology called *compositional modeling*. The interested reader should see [7] for details, and Exercise 18 below.

11.2.4 Basic inferences in QP theory

Now we have the basics of QP theory's representations in hand. This section outlines in functional terms how such descriptions are put to work in the performance of various tasks. The basic inferences outlined here directly provide many useful kinds of conclusions. More complex tasks can be addressed by weaving these inferences together into larger structures.

These basic inferences build on each other, so we describe them in a typical sequence that might be used for analysis and simulation.

11.2.4.1 Finding view and process instances

Building a model is a central task in reasoning about the physical world. Given some situation to analyze, we must figure out what constructs from our theory of that domain are applicable to our current situation. In QP theory, the simplest version of this task is figuring out, for a fixed set of modeling assumptions, what views and processes from a domain theory can be instantiated in the current situation and instantiating them. This is the first basic inference of QP theory.

For simple situations and domain theories, instantiating every potentially applicable description suffices for model building. More realistic situations require additional reasoning, but some form of this operation is still a necessary step in these more complex inferential processes. For instance, the next level of complexity is formulating a set of modeling assumptions given the situation, task, and domain theory. Even more complex is debugging and extending the domain theory itself. There have been some progress on model composition and some exploratory forays into acquisition and learning of domain theories, but currently these are hot areas of research, and so we leave out further discussion of them here.

11.2.4.2 Determining activity

The initial step of model building can be thought of as establishing the groundwork for a task. Inferring from the given information what must be happening in the situation is the next step. That is, given information about what processes and views exist, figure out which of their preconditions and quantity conditions hold, and thus establish what collection of processes are active. The collection of physical processes active at any given time is the situation's *process structure*. Intuitively, the process structure is the answer to the question "what's happening right now?" in the system.

The basic version of this operation is inferring as much as possible about the process structure from a given set of facts. More complex versions of this operation blend into measurement interpretation and diagnosis, depending on one's perspective.[9] The simple version of measurement interpretation we implement below is an example of one solution to this more general task.

11.2.4.3 Influence resolution

Given a process structure, we know the direct influences on the situation. These direct effects must be combined to determine their actual impact. For instance, if we have water pouring into an operating boiler, the amount of the water in the boiler will be either increasing, decreasing, or constant depending on the relationship between the rate at which water is being pumped in and the rate at which steam is being produced from the water. The indirect effects of these changes must then be propagated through the indirect influences (i.e., the qualitative proportionalities) to ascertain how the other, dependent parameters will behave. For instance, the change in the amount of water in the boiler will lead to a corresponding change in its level. Thus, given the process structure, we have enough information to figure out (at least up to some ambiguity) the signs of derivatives for all the continuous parameters in the situation. Furthermore, the set of influences in a situation provides a crucial part of its causal structure. In fact, the influences provide a *causal ordering* (in the sense of [21]) for the parameters in the situation. The directly influenced parameters "ground" the changes in the action of physical processes, thus breaking feedback loops and allowing a consistent account of causal relationships between the parameters. Creating the causal account linking the parameters and computing their `Ds`'s is the operation of *influence resolution.*

Influence resolution can be divided into three cases, according to the kind of influence a quantity Q_1 is subject to. First, Q_1 may not have any

9. Collins [4] has observed that although we like to call machines broken, it is really our model of them which has become inaccurate. After all, the machine is still accurately following the laws of nature.

influences on it at all. In that case, by the sole mechanism assumption, `Ds[` Q_1 `]` $= 0$. Second, Q_1 might be directly influenced. Here we must divide the effects on it according to sign. If the signs of all the direct influences on Q_1 are the same, then that will be the value of `Ds[` Q_1 `]`. If there are opposing direct influences, then the outcome is ambiguous and we must either gather more information or branch, according to our purposes. Suppose for example we find that an object has two heat flows affecting it, one where heat flows in and the other where heat flows out. If we knew the relative rates for these flows we could figure out their net effect, since direct influences combine via addition. (Conversely, if we put a thermometer on the object and discover that its temperature is rising, we are justified in concluding that its net change in internal energy is increasing, and thus that the flow of heat in is greater than the flow of heat out.) Depending on our task, we might choose to gather more data, or try to infer their relative magnitudes from other information (such as relative temperature differences and differences in thermal conductance), or simply reason about both alternatives.

The third case is resolving indirect influences. (Remember that we stipulated that no quantity could be both directly and indirectly influenced in order to keep the causal structure intact, and hence other cases cannot arise.) If a quantity Q_1 has only one indirect influence, then `Ds[` Q_1 `]` will simply be the `Ds` value of the quantity which is constraining it, modulated by the sign of the qualitative proportionality. That is, if

`(Qprop+` Q_1 Q_2`)`

holds, then if `Ds[` Q_2 `]` $= 1$ then `Ds[` Q_1 `]` $= 1$ also. But if

`(Qprop-` Q_1 Q_2`)`

holds, then if `Ds[` Q_2 `]` $= 1$ then `Ds[` Q_1 `]` $= -1$.

What about conflicting indirect influences? Like direct influences, we must gather the `Ds` values for the quantities constraining Q_1, and sort them according to their net effect by taking the sign of the functional dependence into account. However, unlike direct influences, relative magnitude information does not suffice to resolve conflicting indirect influences. The reason is that knowing the partial functional dependencies between the parameters does not constrain the underlying function enough to fix how they combine. The underlying function might be a sum, but it might also be a product, or a complex trigonometric or exponential expression. Our choices are thus similar to the case of unresolvable direct influences: we may choose to explore different assumptions about the net result, we may choose to make observations to pin down the outcome, or we may look for more detailed specifications of the function determining Q_1. What choice is appropriate depends on the task.

11.2.4.4 Limit analysis

One kind of change in the physical world is the smooth evolution of continous parameters. Another is the abrupt change in qualitative structure of the behavior itself: a ball colliding with a wall, or water in a kettle beginning to boil. Detecting the possibility of such changes and reasoning about their effects is the operation of *limit analysis*. Limit analysis is important in a variety of tasks. For instance, qualitative changes in behavior often coincide with changes in what set of equations is appropriate to use in modeling a system's behavior. Building a quantitative mathematical model of a phenomenon or a numerical simulation program thus requires identifying such transitions and handling them appropriately[17, 18]. Figuring out the medium- and long-term effects of an action also requires the ability to detect such qualitative changes. For instance, a moment's thought is sufficient to convince us that a plan that includes putting a kettle full of water on a stove, turning the stove on full-tilt, and then returning in six months, is likely to have some undesirable side effects.

The ability to determine potential changes in the qualitative structure of behavior is made possible by the quantity space representation for numerical values. Suppose we have heat flowing from object `P` to object `Q`. Since heat is flowing, we know that the temperature of `P` is currently above that of `Q`. If we know further that the temperature of `P` is decreasing and the temperature of `Q` is increasing, we know that ultimately, if nothing intervenes (e.g., someone doesn't move them apart) eventually their temperatures will become equal. And at that point the heat flow will stop. In essence, limit analysis "closes the loop" by completing the set of inferences needed to predict temporally evolving behavior. The quantity spaces determine the process structure, and the process structure then determines the `Ds` values for the situation's quantities, which in turn determine possible changes in the quantity spaces.

Limit analysis is a basic operation in prediction, both for figuring out what kinds of things might happen next and for constructing longer-range predictions. To represent behaviors over time, QP theory uses Hayes's notion of *histories* [19]. Histories consist of four-dimensional pieces of space/time, bristling with properties. They are spatially bounded but temporally extended, unlike the situation calculus which is temporally bounded but spatially unbounded. Histories are divided up into episodes, according to some criteria. One simple criterion is to divide up a behavior into intervals over which the qualitative structure of the behavior is identical.[10] Thus possible histories may be generated by performing limit analysis repeatedly. (This is roughly what programs like `QSIM` [22] do.)

An interesting observation about histories is that the same pattern of qualitative behavior can occur over and over again. If we consider an undamped oscillator, for instance, it is clear that a particular pattern of behavior can occur an infinite number of times. Often it is useful to directly generate and reason with these general patterns of possible behaviors and relationships between them, without worrying about a specific history they appear in. Such patterns of behavior are called *qualitative states*. The collection of all possible qualitative states and the possible transitions between them is called an *envisionment*. Envisionments can be generated by repeated limit analysis on some initial situation (or set of initial situations). While they can be large, envisionments are always finite, because any system that consists of a finite number of physical and conceptual entities has only a finite number of distinct qualitative states. The relationship between histories and qualitative states is more formally defined in [14].

Because of space limitations, we will not implement limit analysis in TGIZMO, nor use it to build history generators or envisioners. The interested reader should see [10, 12, 15, 22] and Exercises 10—12.

---

10. The spatial extent of the occurrence of a physical process is simply the union of the extents of the individuals involved in it. This spatial boundedness can be used to predict limits on interactions between parts of complex systems; see [19, 10].

11.3 The design of TGIZMO

Although we have LTRE as our starting point, TGIZMO is still substantially more complex than our previous example systems. Consequently, we carefully explore the design trade-offs involved first, before considering the algorithms in detail. Given our focus on measurement interpretation, the major design issues are:

- How should we represent changes over time?
- What should the modeling language we implement look like?
- How should the instantiation of modeling language constructs be controlled?
- How should inequality reasoning be performed efficiently?
- How should the search for interpretations be organized?

We consider each in turn.

11.3.1 Temporal representations

We have restricted TGIZMO's scope to interpreting measurements taken during a single period of time. This restriction allows us to make a design choice that radically simplifies the program. That is, we can leave time implicit in our descriptions, since we never need to make statements involving two distinct times.

If we were to extend TGIZMO there are several reasonable choices, including modal operators (see [1, 23]) or Hayes's notion of slices (see [10, 20]). For some tasks, implicit temporal notations can still be used for efficient dynamical reasoning (see [15]).

11.3.2 Design of the modeling language

QP theory provides a basic ontology and vocabulary for representing physical domain theories. But it does not completely determine how these ideas must be cast into a specific modeling language (or languages). For simplicity we leave out of TGIZMO most of the qualitative mathematics of QP theory, focusing only on direct and indirect influences. Correspondences, descriptions of explicit functions, and other primitives will not be implemented (but see Exercise 16).

The interaction between quantities and existence means we must also be able to tell which arguments of a quantity correspond to individuals with potentially finite temporal extent as opposed to domain-specific constants which are presumed to always exist. An example of the former is "the water in the kettle," and an example of the latter is the term `liquid` which denotes the liquid phase itself. If the kettle is emptied, the conceptual entity "the water in the kettle" no longer exists, and hence it makes no sense to talk about how much of it there is or how hot it is. So given a term which denotes a quantity, the implementation must be able to recognize which of its constituents are individuals with potentially finite temporal extent, so that it may install the correct implications.

How can we distingish individuals in references to quantities? Quantities are referred to by functions, such as

```
(heat ⟨stuff⟩)
(distance ⟨point1⟩ ⟨point2⟩)
(pressure ⟨fluid⟩ ⟨Reference⟩)
(amount-of-in ⟨substance⟩ ⟨phase⟩ ⟨container⟩)
```

Some of these arguments are, under any reasonably intuitive interpretation of these functions, clearly going to be individuals. ⟨*fluid*⟩ and ⟨*container*⟩, for example, could be individuals with finite temporal extent. An example of ⟨*fluid*⟩ is the Mississippi River, and a styrofoam coffee cup is an example of ⟨*container*⟩. Similarly, some of these arguments clearly should be logical constants, whose existence is outside of time. For example, ⟨*substance*⟩ could be the token `water` representing the substance water, and and ⟨*phase*⟩ could be the token `gas` representing the gaseous phase of matter. (Thus `(amount-of-in water gas boiler)` refers to "the amount of steam in the boiler.") The logical status of other arguments is less clear. For example, ⟨*Reference*⟩ might be a constant like `:ABSOLUTE` when measuring certain pressures, but also could be the pressure of another fluid when describing relative pressures.

Most QP-based modeling languages force the modeler to declare which arguments refer to individuals and which do not. In TGIZMO we opt for simplicity, and stipulate that all functions denoting quantities take exactly one argument, and that argument is an individual. Functions which normally would take more arguments can be represented in two ways.

The first is to simply drop the extra arguments. For example, reference points are often left implicit in defining temperatures and pressures, hence we could denote the pressure of a fluid by the term

(pressure ⟨*fluid*⟩)

In cases where the other arguments cannot be dropped, we use an old representation trick introduced by Curry, a logician. Given the old predicate and extra arguments, we define a new unary predicate which includes the extra arguments as part of itself. Thus the `amount-of-in` term used above can be written as follows:

((amount-of-in ⟨*substance*⟩ ⟨*phase*⟩) ⟨*container*⟩)

The compound predicate (`amount-of-in` ⟨*substance*⟩ ⟨*phase*⟩) takes one argument, ⟨*container*⟩, which is of course an individual. This trick is called *currying*. Currying will only work in TGIZMO when the extra arguments are constants, not when they are individuals, since the compound predicate is not decomposed and analyzed. Such distinctions will simply be beyond this particular modeling language.

Another place where modeling languages vary is in the conditions for instantiating constructs. In our earlier examples using `defprocess` and `defview`, for instance, we implicitly assumed the following syntax for each item in the `individuals` field:

(⟨*variable*⟩ . ⟨*patterns*⟩)

where ⟨*patterns*⟩ is a list of patterns which contains at least one occurrence of ⟨*variable*⟩. This choice makes for a very simple implementation of instantiation: we simply transform the contents of the `:INDIVIDUALS` field into patterns for an LTRE rule, whose consequences are created from the contents of the other fields. Again, this is simpler than other QP-based modeling languages, which introduce more syntax to simplify the domain modeler's work (see Exercise 17).

In addition to `defview` and `defprocess`, there are three additional constructs that are useful to have even in a stripped-down modeling language. The first is a means of defining the direct consequences of new predicates. We use `defPredicate` for this purpose:

(defPredicate ⟨*form*⟩ . ⟨*Consequences*⟩)

where ⟨*form*⟩ is a pattern corresponding to the predicate being defined and ⟨*Consequences*⟩ are the direct implications of statements of that kind. (Such descriptions are implications and not biconditionals, and thus are not really definitions in the sense of "necessary and sufficient." More accurately, we should say that ⟨*form*⟩ is constrained by a `defPredicate` statement, since the number of models is reduced as the set of axioms involving a term grows.) `defEntity` is defined similarly, except that the predicate is constrained to be unary, and its argument is presumed to be an object that exists whenever this predication holds. The final kind of modeling primitive should provide a method for expressing the occasional pattern-directed rule that doesn't quite fit the other primitives. We use `defrule` for this, with the following syntax:

`(defrule` ⟨*name*⟩ ⟨*triggers*⟩ `.` ⟨*consequences*⟩`)`

where ⟨*triggers*⟩ will be intern triggers for a rule whose body will assert the conjunction of ⟨*consequences*⟩, justified by the conjunction of ⟨*triggers*⟩ using ⟨*name*⟩ as the informant.

11.3.3 Instantiation issues

In this implementation we take the simplest possible approach to figuring out which constructs of the domain theory to apply to a given scenario. That is, we instantiate everything possible. Instances of processes (and views) are created for every combination of individuals that match the individuals specification. This is legitimate but of course can be suboptimal in many circumstances. Here are three such conditions:

1. *Only a subset of the situation is relevant.* If you have already figured out that the problem with your car lies in the ignition system, then effort spent building models of the fuel and exhaust systems would be wasted.
2. *Only a subset of the domain theory is relevant.* Typically one knows far more about a domain than is relevant for the task at hand. In principle quantum mechanics is applicable to understanding a car's fuel system, but in practice it is irrelevant.
3. *The domain theory can introduce arbitrarily many individuals.* There are legal QP domain theories which simply cannot be instantiated

antecedently because even with a finite set of initial individuals in a scenario they imply the existence of an infinite number of additional individuals [16].

None of these conditions hold for our range of problems, since we will keep our scenarios and domain theories small and simple. As hinted earlier, this means we can implement the process of finding instances of views and processes by the usual pattern-matching process in LTRE rules. The way in which individuals are specified thus determines what the triggers of these rules will be. What should the body of these rules be? There are two issues involved: (1) how do we represent particular instances and (2) what form do the desired consequences take?

To refer to a specific instance, we use the pattern provided as part of the `defprocess` (and `defview`) statements. For instance, the pattern for heat flow was:

```
(heat-flow ?src ?path ?dst)
```

so any instance of heat flow can be referred to by instantiating this pattern. (We already made implicit use of this convention when illustrating how model fragments could be composed in modeling phenomena at different levels of detail with the thermal conductance example.) Again this is not the only possible choice, but it has the virtue of simplicity.

What about the direct consequences of a process (or view) instance? We can divide these into two parts: constraints on when the instance exists and is active, and what must hold as a consequence of it being active. Since the latter is easier we tackle it first. Essentially, what we want is for the statements in the `Relations` field (and `Influences` field, if a process) to hold whenever the instance is active. If we let $R_1, \ldots, R_n$ be the statements in these fields, then the axiom schemata,

$$\texttt{(Active ?I)} \Rightarrow \bigwedge_{i=1}^{n} R_i$$

crisply represents the desired semantics. As we shall see, this logic can be quite directly translated into LTMS terms with only a few modifications (such as arranging for `ONLY-DURING` and some error checking).

A similar arrangement is used to encode the semantics of the existence and activity of processes and views. Consider the following sets for a process (or view) instance P:

$i_1, \ldots, i_n$ = the set of individuals for an instance

$I_1, \ldots, I_m$ = the set of constraints from the individuals field

$A_1, \ldots, A_o$ = the union of the preconditions and quantity conditions

Then the following statements, expressed as axiom schemata, suffice to enforce the desired semantics:

1. The logical possibility of the instance depends on the conditions in the `individuals` field.

   $$\bigwedge_{j=1}^{m} I_j \Rightarrow \texttt{(ProcessInstance P)}$$

2. The process has physical existence only when all of the individuals it depends upon exist.

   $$\bigwedge_{j=1}^{n} \texttt{(Exists } i_j\texttt{)} \Rightarrow \texttt{(Exists P)}$$

3. The process (or view) is active exactly when it exists and when preconditions and quantity conditions hold.

   $$\left[\texttt{(Exists P)} \wedge \left(\bigwedge_{j=1}^{o} A_j\right)\right] \Rightarrow \texttt{(Active P)}$$

4. An active process must physically exist.

   `(Active P)` ⇒ `(Exists P)`

   (This rules out "ghosts.")

Section 11.4.2 shows how these axiom schemata are implemented.

11.3.4 Inequality reasoning

The central role played by the quantity space representations in QP theory means that inequality reasoning must be made as efficient as possible. There are many ways to implement such reasoning. Unfortunately, the easy methods tend to be hopelessly inefficient. For example, the observation that such inferences are transitive suggests using LTRE rules like the following:

```
(rule ((:TRUE (> ?N1 ?N2) :VAR ?>1))
      (rule ((:TRUE (> ?N2 ?N3) :VAR ?>2))
        (rassert! (:implies (:and ?>1 ?>2)
                            (> ?N1 ?N3))
                  :transitivity))
      (rule ((:TRUE (= ?N2 ?N3) :VAR ?=1))
        (rassert! (:implies (:and ?>1 ?=1)
                            (> ?N1 ?N3))
                  :transitivity)))
```

with similar rules covering the combination of <'s and ='s. Such rules certainly find all the transitivity consequences of a set of ordinal relationships. The problem is that most of the results they calculate are irrelevant. Suppose we had a sequence of numbers $N_1, N_2, \ldots, N_i$ such that $N_1 > N_2$, $N_1 > N_2$, and so on. Adding the N_{i+1}th number, where $N_i > N_{i+1}$, results in $i - 1$ new $>$ statements. If none of these results are ever needed, why compute them? Furthermore, we should avoid storing both $N_a < N_b$ and $N_b > N_a$, since they are redundant.

By considering what we need out of an inequality system, we can design a far more efficient reasoner. Any model for a specific scenario built from a QP domain theory will mention some (presumably finite) number of ordinal comparisons. It is only these relationships that TGIZMO cares about. Computing anything else is a waste of time. In some forms of reasoning, computing and storing intermediate results is critical for efficiency, but inequality reasoning is not one of those cases.

There are two key observations motivating the design of TGIZMO's inequality system. The first is that for any scenario model there will be a set of comparisons mentioned in the assertions and rules, and only these comparisons are relevant. This set can grow over the course of reasoning, as new conceptual entities are discovered and as new distinctions become needed (e.g., two rates need to be compared because they are conflicting direct influences). Once mentioned, a comparison is always of interest. The labels of comparison statements may change over time, but the set of those which are relevant never decreases in size.

The second observation is that if we view the set of mentioned comparisons as a graph, where the nodes are the numbers being compared and the edges are the set of ordinal statements that may hold between a pair of nodes, all transitivity inference occurs in this graph's cycles. Consider again the $N_1, \ldots, N_i$ example, assuming that initially only the comparisons between each successive pair were mentioned. In that case no cycles exist, and there is no reason to draw any additional conclusions. Now suppose we want to know the relationship between N_1 and N_i. That relationship can be deduced from the $i - 1$ others only if certain conditions are right (more on this momentarily). Computing intermediate results would provide nothing, since all the potentially relevant information is contained in the newly formed cycle already. Therefore analyzing cycles in the graph of ordinal relations suffices for transitivity reasoning.

These observations suggest a good design:

- Use an incremental algorithm to find cycles in the graph of ordinal comparisons as each is mentioned.
- Cache these cycles in a separate datastructure.
- Whenever the belief state of an ordinal relationship changes, check the cycles it is part of to see if any new conclusions can be derived.

We also have to select a representation for ordinal relationships. The simplest representation would be to use the standard relationships >, <, and =. But we can do better than this. Consider the relationship ≤, i.e., "less than or equal to." Using this single relationship we can encode others as follows:

$$Q < P \equiv Q \leq P \wedge \neg P \leq Q$$

$$Q = P \equiv Q \leq P \wedge P \leq Q$$

$$Q > P \equiv \neg Q \leq P \wedge P \leq Q$$

As we shall see, using ≤ internally as the only ordinal relationship greatly simplifies transitivity processing. Convenience should not be sacrificed to simplicity, of course, so we must allow modelers to freely use the standard ordinal relationships. Automatically translating these results is straightforward with pattern-directed rules. These rules, and the details of the transitivity processing, are detailed in Section 11.4.5.

11.3.5 Organizing the measurement interpretation search

We start by considering what a valid interpretation is. QP theory gives us a precise answer: An interpretation is a set of processes and assumptions about their combined effects that predicts the observed data. Thus we must search the space of process structures, looking for those whose influences can be resolved to explain the observations. (This assumes that observations concern Ds values. Observations can also include other predicates, such as ordinal relationships or predicates found in preconditions. The process structure at a given time must be consistent with such observations, but explaining them requires a sojourn into the history of the system.)

The fact that for Ds values the interpretation actually implies the observations suggests viewing this problem as a special case of abduction. This in turn suggests that we might consider putting an additional constraint on our search, namely that we want the *best* interpretation, for some definition of best. There are tasks for which this is indeed the best approach. Suppose for example that some action must be chosen immediately, without the benefit of other information. Then, any a priori information about likelihoods of processes and direness of consequences should be used to define a preference metric for interpretations, and our search should be organized to provide the optimal interpretation (or good approximations thereof) under these criteria. However, there are arguments against this strategy. Suppose for instance that the best interpretation counsels doing nothing but the second-best interpretation indicates that a disaster is brewing which requires immediate action. If the action recommended by the second-best interpretation does not adversely affect the operation of the system, it should probably be taken just in case. So even when no additional data is forthcoming, it can be useful to consider multiple interpretations. And, more generally, gathering information about a physical system is an interactive, iterative process, where the ambiguities in one's understanding of the system indicate what kinds of new information should be sought. In such circumstances, comparing the implications of distinct interpretations for measurements yet unmade provides a valuable diagnostic tool.

Since the problems we are dealing with are small, and any information about probabilities or utilities of states provided would be an arbitrary invention, we organize our search to find all valid interpretations of the given observations. Since we have already stipulated that all process and view instances will be constructed antecedently, the problem can be cast as generate-and-test, where we use dependency-directed search to generate legal process structures, and use influence resolution to ascertain if they provide a valid interpretation.

Let us consider the search space in more detail. The most straightforward way to organize the search for legal process structures is to use

`{ (Active P), (:NOT (Active P)) }` for all process and view instances *P* as the choice sets. This indeed is better than, say, using the preconditions and quantity conditions, since there can be many distinct combinations of them which all have the effect of making some instance inactive. To see if a legal process structure corresponds to a valid interpretation, we must check it against the observations. One way to do this is simply to make the observations into LTRE assumptions underlying the search. That way a process structure that blatantly violates the observations (i.e., requiring flow through a path whose valve is shut) will simply never be generated. Not all violations are easy to detect, however. Explaining observed changes in parameters (i.e., `Ds` values) requires performing influence resolution. Other kinds of observations can constrain `Ds` values as well. For example, if while cooking on a camping trip we see bubbles in the water in a kettle, that means the water is boiling, which in turn means there is heat flowing to the water, which means that the level in the fuel reservoir in our portable stove is falling. Consequently, it is typically worth completely resolving influences to ensure the validity of an interpretation.

11.4 The implementation of TGIZMO

Now that we have the overall plan of the implementation in mind, let us turn to the details.

11.4.1 Global organization and LTRE interface (defs.lisp)

As usual, we use a struct to centralize the information concerning a particular copy of TGIZMO. It includes the following fields:

`title` String for printing.

`measurements` Set of measurements to be explained.

`scenario` Name of file defining the current scenario

`ltre` The LTRE used by this TGIZMO

`debugging` A list of symbols indicating what kind of debugging information should be printed.

`quantities` The list of quantities found for the given scenario.

`comparisons` The set of ordinal comparisons mentioned in the scenario model.

`comp-cycles` The cycles of comparisons used to derive transitivity information.

`influence-order` The causal ordering derived for the set of influences

`update-ineqs?` When non-`nil`, indicates that a new label has been found for an ordinal relationship and transitivity processing should be invoked.

`nstates` Counter for giving states a unique identifier.

`states` List of states found during a search.

Those which are not obvious are explained in detail later.

The procedures for creating a copy of TGIZMO should by now be quite familiar. The default contradiction handler (`IR-CWA-Contradiction-Handler`) automatically retracts invalid closed-world assumptions from influence resolution, if any. An important change is in the debugging system. In smaller systems it sufficed to turn on debugging for the whole system. TGIZMO is complicated enough that it makes sense to provide finer control over how much information, and about what subsystem, gets printed. Consequently, the `debugging` field of a TGIZMO holds a list of flags. A debugging statement is only executed if the appropriate flag is set. Thus `debugging-tgizmo` now takes an extra flag argument. Furthermore, sometimes there are interesting computations that should be performed as part of debugging, so we include the ability to add such code with the new macro `when-debugging`.

The `state` struct provides a medium for taking "snapshots" of the LTRE database, so that different states of a search can be cached and later compared. Each field contains expressions of particular types whose labels were known at the time. In particular,

`individuals` Statements about individuals.

`view-structure` Set of active view instances.

`process-structure` Set of active process instances.

`comparisons` Set of ordinal relationships other than `Ds` values.

`Ds-values` Comparisons of derivatives with zero.

Thus we can compare what different states predict for specific `Ds` values, for example, without changing any assumptions. (We could reconstruct the state of a search in some sense by "reloading" the LTRE database with assumptions corresponding to the statements in a state struct. There are several interesting issues here—see Exercise 9b).

Since many TGIZMO operations are defined in terms of `LTRE` operations, we also provide a set of procedures that simplifies such interactions. The mnemonic we use is to prefix the name of an LTRE operation with "`tg-`" to indicate that it is taken with respect to the LTRE of the current TGIZMO. (Notice that we also provide the usual hooks to rebind `*tgizmo*` as needed.) These procedures are `tg-fetch`, `tg-true?`, `tg-false?`, `tg-false-forms?` (like `tg-false?`, but over a list of forms), and `tg-run-rules`.

As is often the case in artificial intelligence, explicit representations of even simple situations can require a large number of propositions. To make our database easier to understand, the rest of the file contains procedures that take common kinds of facts and produce printable forms that look more like what one sees in technical papers. These procedures (`number-string`, `Ds-string`, `Ds-value-string`, `ineq-string`) are self-explanatory.

11.4.2 Implementing the modeling language (mlang.lisp)

The main job of these procedures is translating theories expressed in a form congenial to domain modelers into something executable by LTRE. For `defrule` this is trivial, since all we have to do is wrap the condition (`:INTERN`) around the list of triggers and create an `rassert!` form which embodies the logic of the rule. `defPredicate` and `defEntity` are only a little more complicated. We allow the variable `?self` to be used freely within these statements, so we must make its binding available via `rlet`. The consequences require a bit more processing, though. This job is done by `translate-relations`, which is explained shortly.

Since processes and views are syntactically very similar, the internal structure of `defview` and `defprocess` are also quite similar. `parse-vp` does the requisite syntaxing, and `make-vp-rule` creates a rule that detects instances of that view or process and installs the appropriate consequences. `parse-vp` does some basic syntax tests to check for common errors made by domain modelers. For example, there must always be an `individuals` field, and there must be at least some preconditions or quantity conditions (otherwise, a `defPredicate` or `defEntity` statement would probably be more appropriate). `parse-vp` also ensures that processes have direct influences and views don't, and makes sure that no field contains free variables.

`make-vp-rule` uses the `individuals` specification to create a set of triggers for a pattern-directed rule for detecting instances of that process or view. Aside from some debugging information (i.e., printing notices about instances found when the current TGIZMO is operating with the appropriate debugging flags turned on), the bulk of the body of this rule implements the axiom schemata described earlier. The only new wrinkle is, again, `translate-relations`. Let us turn to it next.

A good modeling language hides irrelevant details from the model builder. Obviously, implementation details should be abstracted away as much as possible. In addition, if there are common patterns of usage, the language should allow these patterns to be stated concisely. By constructing rule triggers automatically from other information, we have insulated the modeler from many LTRE details. `translate-relations` does the same job for the consequences of the descriptions in our modeling language. For example, we mentioned earlier that the semantics of `only-during` were those of a biconditional. That is, the statement

```
(Only-During (Exists (C-S ?sub ?st ?can))
```

in the `relations` field of the `Contained-Stuff` view really meant

```
(:IFF (:AND (container ?can)
            (substance ?sub)
            (phase ?st)
            (> (A ((amount-of ?sub ?st) ?can)) ZERO))
      (Exists (C-S ?sub ?st ?can)))
```

By providing `Only-During` we simplify our modeler's job, since the antecedents are "obvious" from the logical environment of the `defview` description. There are several other, similar translations of consequences needed as well. For instance, it is important to distinguish influence statements according to their source in making closed-world assumptions. Thus when translating influence statements we add the source—the view, process, predicate, or entity definition—as a third argument to the relationship. Finally, quantities local to a process or view are considered to exist only when the view is active, so we must install a biconditional for them as well.

`translate-relations` takes a set of consequences, a defining context, the antecedents for that context, and an informant, and produces a list of executable statements to be used in the body of a rule. It operates by performing a case analysis on each consequent. It accumulates two kinds of results: the simple cases which are to be justified on the basis of the antecedents (stored in `explicit`) and the executable statements comprising the translation of the more complicated cases (stored in `implicit`). `translate-relation`, which performs the case analysis, thus returns two kinds of values. (In the simple modeling language defined here, `translate-relations` only returns one kind or the other. More complex modeling languages often use both kinds of consequences in implementing single statements.)

Figure 11.5 shows how these procedures transform the definition of heat flow from Figure 11.4 into an LTRE rule.

11.4.3 Searching for patterns of activity (psvs.lisp)

The procedures in this file orchestrate the creation of a scenario model and create the choice sets for view and process structures needed for the measurement interpretation search.

The construction of a scenario model is handled by `load-scenario`. We assume that the domain theory has already been loaded into the current TGIZMO, and that the argument file `sfile` is a sequence of `assert!` or `assume!` statements describing the structural description for the scenario to be analyzed. Loading the file into the current TGIZMO and running the pattern-directed rules it triggers causes the construction of the scenario model, thanks to our organization of the implementation of the modeling language. Since new comparisons are likely to be mentioned as relevant and the scenario may specify ordinal information, the inequality system is invoked (via the call to `use-transitivity`) to draw whatever new inferences can be made using transitivity.

Recall that the measurement interpretation search is defined in terms of the view and process structures of the situation. TGIZMO must first gather all view and process instances and then create the necessary

The rule below shows how the heat flow process definition of Figure 11.4 expands into an LTRE rule that instantiates the logic of the QP description.

```
(RULE
  ((:INTERN (QUANTITY (HEAT ?SRC)))
   (:INTERN (HEAT-CONNECTION ?PATH ?SRC ?DST))
   (:INTERN (QUANTITY (HEAT ?DST))))
  (RLET ((?SELF (HEAT-FLOW ?SRC ?PATH ?DST)))
   (DEBUGGING-TGIZMO :MODELING "~% Found ~A: ~A." "process" ?SELF)
   (RASSERT! (:IMPLIES (:AND (QUANTITY (HEAT ?SRC))
                             (HEAT-CONNECTION ?PATH ?SRC ?DST)
                             (QUANTITY (HEAT ?DST)))
                       (PROCESS-INSTANCE
                          (HEAT-FLOW ?SRC ?PATH ?DST)))
             :CDI-IMPLIED)
   (RASSERT! (:IMPLIES (:AND (EXISTS ?SRC) (EXISTS ?PATH)
                             (EXISTS ?DST))
                       (EXISTS (HEAT-FLOW ?SRC ?PATH ?DST)))
             :PROCESS-EXISTENCE)
   (RASSERT! (:IMPLIES (ACTIVE (HEAT-FLOW ?SRC ?PATH ?DST))
                       (EXISTS (HEAT-FLOW ?SRC ?PATH ?DST)))
             :NO-GHOSTS)
   (RASSERT! (:IFF (ACTIVE (HEAT-FLOW ?SRC ?PATH ?DST))
                   (:AND (HEAT-ALIGNED ?PATH)
                         (> (A (TEMPERATURE ?SRC))
                            (A (TEMPERATURE ?DST)))))
             :CDI-ACTIVE-CONSTRAINT)
   (RASSERT! (:IMPLIES (ACTIVE ?SELF)
                       (:AND (> (A (FLOW-RATE ?SELF))  ZERO)))
             :HEAT-FLOW)
   (RASSERT! (:IFF (ACTIVE ?SELF)
                   (QPROP- (FLOW-RATE ?SELF) (TEMPERATURE ?DST)
                           ?SELF))
             :HEAT-FLOW)
   (RASSERT! (:IFF (ACTIVE ?SELF)
                   (QPROP (FLOW-RATE ?SELF) (TEMPERATURE ?SRC)
                          ?SELF))
             :HEAT-FLOW)
  (RASSERT! (:IFF (ACTIVE ?SELF) (QUANTITY (FLOW-RATE ?SELF)))
            :HEAT-FLOW)
  (RASSERT! (:IFF (ACTIVE ?SELF)  (I+ (HEAT ?DST) (FLOW-RATE ?SELF)
                                      ?SELF))
                  :HEAT-FLOW)
  (RASSERT! (:IFF (ACTIVE ?SELF)  (I- (HEAT ?SRC) (FLOW-RATE ?SELF)
                                      ?SELF)
                  :HEAT-FLOW))))
```

Figure 11.5 How physical processes are implemented

choice sets. The procedure gather-vsps does the first job by fetching all things that can be active, which by definition can only be true of a view or process instance. The second job is carried out by psvs-choice-sets, which constructs choice sets that can be used by the LTRE dependency-directed search facility (DD-Search, defined in Section 10.5).

The procedure search-PSVS generates all consistent view and process structures. In doing so it executes the procedure it is given (thunk) in every logical environment corresponding to a consistent view and process structure. Notice that search-PSVS is instrumented to print each consistent state when the debugging flag :PSVS-DDS is part of the debugging list for its TGIZMO. (The procedure it uses, show-psvs, is defined at the end of the file.) Notice also that search-PSVS calls retract-IR-CWAs, in case influence resolution was performed as part of the execution of thunk. This should not be necessary, but is carried out as a bit of bulletproofing. Even though IR-CWA-Contradiction-Handler is always part of a TGIZMO's set of contradiction handlers, retracting these assumptions avoids unnecessary contradiction handling.

11.4.4 Implementing influence resolution (resolve.lisp)

Resolving influences is the trickiest part of this implementation. It requires making appropriate closed-world assumptions, ascribing causality, and squeezing as many inferences as possible out of minimal information. Influence resolution presumes that the view and process structures have been completely determined. The procedure resolve-influences is the entry point. The basic steps, and subroutines which implement them, are:

1. Find the current construal of the set of influences on each quantity by fetching the influences currently believed to be active and assuming these are the only ones (the bulk of setup-IR).
2. Use the influences to impose a causal ordering on the quantities (find-influence-ordering, which is called from setup-IR and whose results are cached in tgizmo-influence-order).
3. Attempt to resolve each quantity (resolve-influences-on). Record any ambiguous outcomes, and return this list as the result (unknowns).

This basic outline captures most of `resolve-influences`, but a few things still require explanation. The `unless` test on `Resolved` statements exploits the LTMS cache; if the particular pattern of influences on a quantity has been seen before, the results of this computation would already be available, and so executing `resolve-influences-on` would be needless work (and could create redundant justifications). Another important feature of this algorithm is the use of the causal ordering to establish an order of computation. We could, after all, simply use dependency-directed search to hypothesize consistent `Ds`'s for all quantities and use the influence information to prune inconsistent possibilities. The problem with this pure constraint-satisfaction approach is that it fails to exploit what are typically strong constraints between parameters. The causal ordering provides a framework for constraint propagation, so that the `Ds` of a quantity can often be deduced simply from the influences on it.

The main job of `setup-ir` is to create construals for the sets of influences on each quantity. It does this by first calling `tg-run-rules` to execute any pending pattern-directed rules, thus ensuring that all "obvious" conclusions have been drawn. Then it uses LTRE's closed-world set mechanism to create construals for the sets `DIs` and `IIs` for each quantity. The set `DIs` are the direct influences on a quantity and the set `IIs` are the indirect influences on a quantity. Again the queue is emptied to take care of any obvious consequences, including perhaps the discovery of contradictions. Finally, `find-influence-ordering` is called to compute the causal ordering for the current logical environment.[11]

Closed-world assumptions can lead to contradictions, and so `IR-CWA-contradiction-handler` is provided to detect and retract such problems. The procedure `retract-IR-CWAs` is also provided to "clear the decks" after an analysis, thus reducing the need for contradiction han-

11. In most QP domain theories written to date, the set of causal orderings for a situation are *unidirected*: i.e., if a quantity Q_1 is causally prior to quantity Q_2 in one situation, then it is never the case that Q_2 is causally prior to Q_1 in another situation. When this condition holds, a single global causal ordering can be computed for the whole situation using the set of all mentioned influence statements, and the causal ordering for a specific situation will always be a subset of this global causal ordering. However, there is no stipulation that domain theories must be unidirected, and so no implementation of QP theory should presume this.

dling. In general this is a good idea: contradiction handling is a crucial facility and adds substantial logical power to a system. However, since contradiction handling is inherently asynchronous, it can lead to subtle timing problems in algorithms. Therefore it is good engineering practice to not rely on it when simpler means will do.

`find-influence-ordering` constructs the causal ordering by a simple propagation algorithm. An initial ordering is provided by assigning a rank of zero to directly influenced parameters and a rank of −1 to indirectly influenced parameters. The procedure `update-influence-table-orderings` loops through the set of parameters, increasing the rank of a quantity to be the highest rank of its constrainers, plus one. Since a directly influenced parameter has no constrainers its rank remains zero, and the rank of any indirectly influenced parameter must converge because the set of qualitative proportionalities is loop-free.

`resolve-influences-on` dispatches to different procedures according to the kind of influence(s) a quantity is subject to. As noted in Section 11.2.4.3, direct and indirect influences operate under different constraints, so they are handled by different procedures (`resolve-dis-on` and `resolve-iis-on`, respectively). Pattern-directed rules handle the uninfluenced case and enforce the exclusion of mixed influence types (see Section 11.4.8). The procedures `direct-influences-on` and `indirect-influences-on` fetch the influences on a quantity by grabbing the contents of the sets `DIs` and `IIs`.

`resolve-dis-on` begins by sorting the rate parameters according to their sign. Figuring out the sign contribution of an influence requires modifying the sign of the constrainer by the sign of the influence statement itself, to ascertain the actual direction of effect. That is, a positive flow rate and an `I+` statement leads to a positive effect, while a positive flow rate and an `I-` statement leads to a negative effect. Notice that we store in each set both the name of the number and the antecedents corresponding to the sign determined for it. Storing the antecedents greatly simplifies computing justifications for the results. If a sign isn't known, no particular determination can be made, and so `resolve-dis-on` immediately returns, providing `:UNKNOWNS` as the reason for failure and the list of parameters whose signs were not established. Otherwise, `analyze-dis-on` is used to squeeze conclusions from the rate information. `analyze-dis-on` performs a case analysis on this information, deducing a `Ds` value when possible but also ruling out impossible values. For example, if all the rates are equal to zero, clearly the quantity is not changing. The fourth and fifth clauses of the `cond` handle the cases of only positive or only negative rates, where the result must be either positive or negative, respectively. The second and third clauses use the disjunctive information in ≤ and ≥ to exclude whatever case isn't covered (i.e., positive for ≤ and negative for ≥). Once again, the `unless` test prevents the installation of redundant justifications if the program has already figured out this subproblem.

The rest of `analyze-dis-on` handles the case where a quantity is influenced in both directions. It begins by looking for opposing direct influences which may be canceled, since direct influences combine by addition. It starts by looking for identical rate parameters (i.e., the calls to `cancel-via-identity`) and then looks for opposing parameters of equal magnitude (i.e., the calls to (`cancel-via-=`). If any cancellations are made, `analyze-dis-on` is called recursively to see if the simpler problem has an unambiguous solution. Otherwise, the fact that the direct influences are ambiguous is duly noted, by calling `justify-ir-ambig`. Since the justification procedures are shared by the direct and indirect influence code, we postpone their description until after delving into indirect influences.

The structure of `resolve-IIs-on` is analogous to that of `resolve-DIs-on`, but simpler. The sorting by signs of constrainers is identical to the sorting by signs of rate parameters, as is the necessity for abandoning the attempt if some constrainer's sign is unknown. And the unambiguous and disjunctive cases in `analyze-iis-on` have the same logic as their counterparts for direct influences. The major difference is in the final case in `analyze-iis-on`, corresponding to a clear ambiguity. Since we do not know how qualitative proportionalities combine, we cannot invoke cancellation or any other strategy which rests on more knowledge. Our only choice is to note the ambiguity, which is done by a call to `justify-ir-ambig`.

The procedures `justify-ir-ambig`, `justify-ir-result` and `exclude-ir-result` install the conclusions reached by the routines above. They share a common structure of antecedents, processed by the procedure `ir-antecedents`. Recall that the list `antes` starts out as the list of influence statements and is incremented with any information added by cancellation in the case of direct influences. The rest of the sets consist of the sign information for the "inputs" to that quantity, so the statements defining the ordinal information cached during the initial sorting by signs can be extracted. The procedure `justify-ir-ambig` signals that no sign could be computed by justifying an `Unresolved` statement for the given quantity. `justify-ir-result` justifies both the `Ds` and the statement `Resolved`, to indicate that influence resolution succeeded in figuring out a `Ds` value. `exclude-ir-result` produces a clause that forbids a specific `Ds` value.

Ambiguity in qualitative representations can be handled in several ways. If the ambiguity is irrelevant, nothing needs to be done. If more precise information is available, such as the exact nature of the function partially specified by a set of qualitative proportionalities, then the ambiguity can be resolved. For our present purposes, the most useful strategy is simply to branch—that is, to generate alternate states based on different possible `Ds` values. The procedure `resolve-completely` provides this option, by creating choice sets for the unknown `Ds` values returned by `resolve-influences` (using `make-Ds-choice-sets`) and performing a dependency-directed search. As with `search-psvs`, `resolve-completely` is given a procedure which is then executed for each consistent solution to the influences.

The last two procedures in the file are interrogatives for reporting and debugging purposes. `show-IR-CWAs` displays the influences on each quantity, and `show-ds-values` shows the signs of derivatives for each quantity.

11.4.5 Implementing inequality reasoning (ineqs.lisp)

As outlined in Section 11.3.4, the inequality system operates by a mixture of bottom-up local processing and central control. LTRE rules are used to

- Detect the addition of new comparisons.
- Install clauses that implement the basic semantics of comparisons.
- Signal the system that beliefs in comparisons have changed, and so checking for transitive inferences is worthwhile.

On the other hand, transitivity inferences are made via special-purpose procedures. These procedures are invoked explicitly by other TGIZMO procedures, thereby taking advantage of the global structure of the computation. The code in `ineqs.lisp` is the heart of the inequality reasoner, providing the procedures which the LTRE rules use to do their work, the transitivity inference procedures, and support code.

The file begins with support code and interfaces to the inequality subsystem used by other parts of TGIZMO. The procedure `num-order` provides a canonical ordering on numbers, so that we can quickly figure out how a comparison is cached when necessary. The procedures `individual-of` and `quantity-of` extract the individual owning a quantity and the quantity itself from terms denoting numbers or quantities.

The procedure `install-comparison-constraints-if-needed` is called whenever an ordinal statement is mentioned (i.e., interned in the LTRE database, independently of its belief state). It uses the canonical ordering defined by `num-order` to construct a key to see if a comparison between the two numbers has been mentioned previously. If so, nothing needs to be done. Otherwise, some basic consequences of comparisons are asserted by `install-comparison-constraints` and any cycles involving the new comparison and previously mentioned ones are found by `find-comparison-cycles-for`. If such cycles exist, this fact is recorded in the current TGIZMO structure to ensure that transitivity processing is eventually invoked. The reason for deferring transitivity reasoning is efficiency. `install-comparison-constraints` is typically called by LTRE rules which are triggered by comparisons being mentioned. Presumably there are other rules queued for execution as well. These rules may install yet more comparisons, so it will be more efficient to check the comparison cycles once, after the queue is emptied.

`install-comparison-constraints` has two jobs. First, it enforces the law that two numbers cannot have a valid comparison unless the quantities they are part of exist. If part of a model included a comparison between `(A (pressure F))` and `(A (pressure G))`, the link between the comparison and existence would be enforced by adding the constraint

```
(:IFF (:OR (:NOT (quantity (pressure F)))
           (:NOT (quantity (pressure G))))
      (:AND (:NOT ((A (pressure F)) <= (A (pressure G))))
            (:NOT ((A (pressure G)) <= (A (pressure F))))
```

to the TGIZMO's LTRE database. The procedure uses `if` statements to compute the appropriate first argument to the `:IFF` in the `assert!` to cover the possibility of constants, like `ZERO`, being one of the numbers in the comparison. Constants are always presumed to exist. `ZERO` is in fact the only constant, so the error checking provided in the `unless` is a bit paranoid. But only a bit—one would be surprised what authors of domain theories can unintentionally do. The other job of `install-comparison-constraints` is to add consumers to the LTMS nodes for the comparison, to ensure that new information about an inequality results in transitivity processing. The procedure `update-ineqs-as-needed` provides this service by setting the inequality flag for the current TGIZMO whenever its node gets a label, and requeuing itself for future service.

The use of `<=` as our sole internal ordinal relationship obliges us to provide some procedures to insulate the rest of the system from this choice. By encapsulating the translation from other ordinal relationships to `<=` in one place we thus simplify the whole system. The predicates `greater-than?`, `less-than?`, and `equal-to?` return non-`nil` if the corresponding relationship holds between their arguments. The procedure `rel-value` computes a keyword symbolizing the relationship between two numbers, whatever it happens to be. `rel-value-clause` computes a clause for whatever keyword it is given, to help build clauses involving ordinal relationships. The procedure `comparison?` provides an interface to the inequality system that does the necessary work to ensure that the comparison between the given numbers is added to the system if necessary, and then calls `rel-value` to provide information about the ordinal relationship.

The next suite of procedures provides assistance for asserting ordinal relationships. `greater-than!`, `less-than!`, and `equal-to!` label the `<=` statements necessary to assume the desired relationship. The procedures `lt-forms`, `eq-forms`, `gt-forms`, `lte-forms`, and `gte-forms` create clauses for the appropriate relationship.

The rest of the file is concerned with reasoning via transitivity. The entry point for updating given new information is the procedure `use-transitivity`. `use-transitivity` essentially calls `check-comp-cycle` repeatedly until no new ordinal relationships are computed. The convention is that whenever new ordinal information is found (either by transitivity or from external sources), the flag `tigzmo-update-ineqs?` is set. (This flag is not a global variable, of course, but a field of the TGIZMO struct, so that different copies of the system can be in use at once.) The procedure `check-comp-cycle` is used to look at each cycle of comparisons to see if more information can be derived from it. We return to `check-comp-cycle` after first considering how cycles get created.

As noted above, `find-comparison-cycles-for` is invoked whenever a comparison between two numbers N_1 and N_2 is mentioned (i.e., interned in the LTRE database) for the first time. The new comparison in effect adds an edge to the graph of comparisons, and this procedure finds all cycles containing this new edge. It operates by a breadth-first exploration of the comparison graph, starting from all other comparisons involving N_1. (`find-comparison-set` provides this service, filtering the results of a `fetch` to find the appropriate inequalities and extracting the other number.) Cycles not ending in N_2 are ignored, since they will have been found by previous invocations of this procedure. Each element on the queue is a list of numbers, to simplify cycle detection, but for further processing it is more convenient to represent cycles by a list of pairs of numbers. This format conversion is carried out by `make-comp-cycle`.

The extraction of new comparison information from cycles is carried out by `check-comp-cycle`. Its operation can be viewed by analogy with BCP on clauses. A clause has a labeling, given by the labels of the literals that participate in it. Some partial labelings allow new conclusions to be drawn. Some labelings are inconsistent. And so it is with comparison cycles. Since the set of ordinal relationships is larger than the set of labels for literals, one might expect the constraints on labels to be slightly more complicated, and indeed they are. There are three main cases:

1. *More than one comparison in the cycle is unknown.* Nothing can be inferred from this case.
2. *Something is known about all comparisons in the cycle.* Requires further analysis, since there may be violations of transitivity or opportunities to further constrain a comparison.
3. *Exactly one comparison in the cycle is unknown.* Requires further analysis, since a relationship for the unknown comparison may be derivable.

`check-comp-cycle` begins by sorting the comparisons of the cycle into six sets, each corresponding to a possible labeling of the relationship between a pair of numbers, in order to make this case analysis. The first

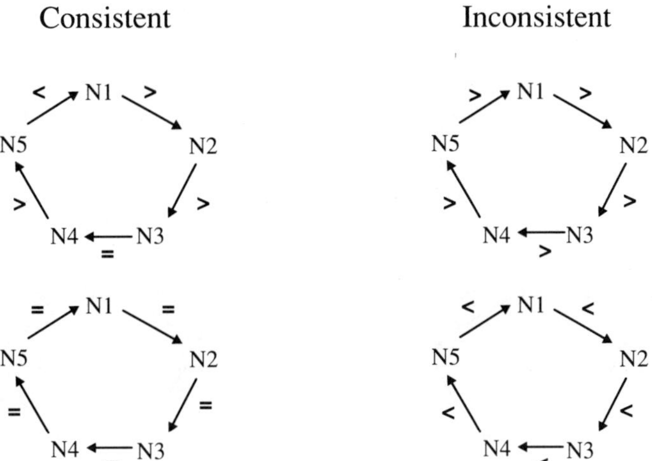

Figure 11.6 Inconsistent cases involving hard inequalities

determination is made on the basis of the set of unknowns (`unks`). The analyses of the second and third cases rest on the contents of the other sets.

When there are no unknowns, we may have a violation or the possibility of refining a comparison. Let us call the relationships $\leq$ and $\geq$ *soft* comparisons, since they contain a degree of ambiguity, and $>$, $=$, and $<$ *hard* comparisons. If all comparisons in a cycle are hard, then the only condition we must look for is inconsistency, since no ambiguity remains to be resolved. Such cycles are inconsistent if their net impact is to claim that a number is larger or smaller than itself. That is, either (1) one edge must be labeled $>$ and every other edge labeled either $>$ or $=$, or (2) one edge must be labeled $<$ and every other edge labeled either $<$ or $=$. Any other case involving all hard comparisons is consistent, since the existence of opposite ordinal relationships in the cycle provides a consistent model. Figure 11.6 illustrates. When one of the contradictory cases is found, the LTRE procedure `contradiction` is called with the list of nodes provided by the support procedure `find-cycle-support`. (`find-cycle-support` computes the antecedents for a cycle by including the `quantity` statements justifying the existence of the numbers involved in the comparisons and accumulating the `<=` statements involving the pairs

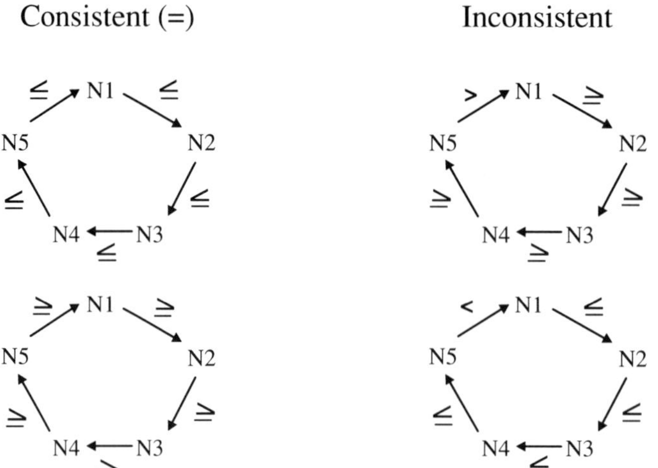

Figure 11.7 Inconsistent cases involving soft inequalities

of numbers in the cycle.) In the code, this case is noted using the informant `:NET-INEQ-CYCLE`.

The cases involving completely labeled cycles containing a mixture of hard and soft comparisons are a bit more complicated, because we may be able to "harden" the cycle if the conditions are right. The inconsistent cases for the pure hard case can be generalized by noting that if there are no comparisons in a particular direction (i.e., no ≤'s and no <'s, or no ≥'s and no >'s) and at least one hard comparison in the opposite direction (i.e., one > or one <, respectively) then we must have a contradiction, because no matter how the soft comparisons are hardened, they would end up corresponding to one of the contradictory cases for purely hard comparisons defined above. (In the code, these cases are indicated with the informant `:NET->-CYCLE and :NET-<-CYCLE`.) This observation also reveals where our opportunity for hardening comparisons comes from: if we have a cycle of all ≤ or all ≥ comparisons, the only possible consistent labeling for the individual comparisons is =. (These cases are noted in the code by the informant `:HARDENING->=` and `:HARDENING->=`. Also, see Figure 11.7.)

The final case, where there is exactly one unknown comparison, is most like the case of one unknown label in Boolean constraint propagation. Let us first consider what can be concluded when hard comparisons are present. When a cycle already has at least one comparison labeled >

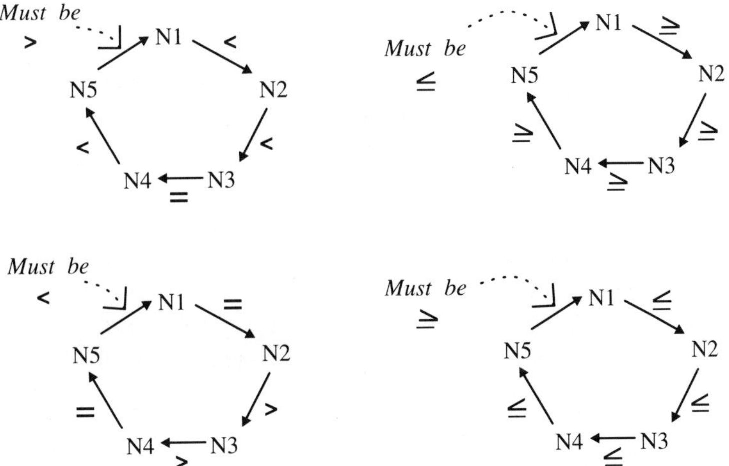

Figure 11.8 Inferences are possible with one unknown comparison

and one labeled $<$, nothing new can be concluded because the cycle will be consistent for any labeling of the unknown relationship. If there are $<$'s and no $>$'s or $\geq$'s, then the last comparison must be $>$ to avoid inconsistency. Similarly, if there are $>$'s and no $<$'s or $\leq$'s, then the last comparison must be $<$. Furthermore, if there are only $=$'s, then the only possibility for the last comparison is $=$. If no hard comparisons are present, similar but weaker conclusions can be drawn about the soft inequalities. That is, if there are $\leq$'s but no $\geq$'s, then the last relationship must be $\geq$. It will turn out to be $>$ if any of the $\leq$'s "harden" into $<$, but will become $=$ if they all become $=$. The same is true for labeling with $\leq$'s but no $\geq$'s. As before, `find-cycle-support` and `rel-value-clause` are used in building the appropriate LTMS clause. Figure 11.8 illustrates.

The end of the file contains some debugging utilities. The procedure `show-ineqs` prints the current belief state for every comparison in the given TGIZMO, and `show-comp-cycles` displays the cycles relating these comparisons.

11.4.6 Caching solutions (states.lisp)

When a consistent state has been generated, the labels of the statements in the LTRE database reflect the propositions of that state. Typically there is more than one state consistent with a set of measurements. Consequently, TGIZMO requires the ability to make a "snapshot" of the database which records the essential information about the state. These recorded states can be compared with regard to their predictions and plausibility as needed. The procedure `snapshot` provides this ability. It builds a `state` struct filled with the essential information about the current state, as represented in the LTRE database. For our purposes it is sufficient to store the existence statements, the view and process structures, and the set of beliefs about comparisons. Notice that the set of comparisons is divided into `Ds` values and other kinds of inequalities, since the former sometimes correspond to observable changes.

The rest of the file is concerned with manipulating state structures. The procedure `get-state` retrieves a state from a given TGIZMO based on its number. The procedure `show-state` provides a more easily readable description of a state. `report-states` produces an ASCII file for the states associated with a given TGIZMO.

The procedure `make-state-index` is another useful tool for understanding the relationship between interpretations. It builds a set of nested alists, discriminating according to the different fields of states. It can also be used for retrieving states. `summarize-state-index` produces a readable summary of an index, providing a good overview of a set of states.

The rest of the file contains procedures for carrying out more detailed comparisons of states. For example, one might run two TGIZMOs on a particular problem with different assumptions or domain theories and want to compare their results. `same-state?` returns non-`nil` if the states given as arguments differ in some way, and `find-corresponding-states` produces an alist of equivalent states, given two TGIZMOs. Sometimes an interpretation includes several states with identical (or nearly so) process structures, so that highlighting the differences in their `Ds` values becomes important to understanding them. Given a list of states, `summarize-Ds-differences` reports on what `Ds` values they have in common and highlights their differences.

11.4.7 The core measurement interpretation algorithm (mi.lisp)

One sign that a design has worked out well is that the code concerned with global issues and control turns out to be very simple. The TGIZMO measurement interpretation algorithm is simplicity itself, as Figure 11.9 shows. The procedure `find-states` computes all qualitative states consistent with the assumptions in force within the TGIZMO provided. It uses `search-psvs` to calculate the set of consistent view and process structures. For each such combination, `resolve-completely` generates the set of complete states by finding what changes in parameters can be caused by the active processes. Each complete state is recorded in the `tgizmo-states` field using `snapshot`.

```
(defvar *laws-file* "/u/bps/code/tgizmo/laws.lisp")
(defvar *domain-file* "/u/bps/code/tgizmo/tnst.lisp")

(defun mi (scenario measurements
                   &key (debugging nil)
                   (debugging-dds nil)
                   (title nil)
                   (domain *domain-file*))
  (with-tgizmo
   (setq *tgizmo*
   (create-tgizmo
    (if title title (format nil "MI of ~A" scenario))
    :DEBUGGING debugging :SCENARIO scenario
    :MEASUREMENTS measurements))
   (with-LTRE (tgizmo-ltre *tgizmo*)
    (load *set-rule-file*)
    (setq *debug-dds* debugging-dds)
    (load *laws-file*)
    (load domain)
    (load-scenario scenario)
    (dolist (d measurements)
            (assume! d ':MEASURED))
    (find-states *tgizmo*))
   (values *tgizmo* (length (tgizmo-states *tgizmo*)))))

(defun find-states (&optional (*tgizmo* *tgizmo*))
  (setf (tgizmo-nstates *tgizmo*) 0)
  (setf (tgizmo-states *tgizmo*) nil)
  (Search-PSVS '(Resolve-Completely
                '(push (snapshot (incf (tgizmo-nstates *tgizmo*)))
                       (tgizmo-states *tgizmo*)))))
```

Figure 11.9 The TGIZMO measurement interpretation procedure

To gain additional insight into the system, or to evaluate changes in models or in the system itself, it is often useful to provide additional hooks into the interpretation process. The procedure `debug-find-states` does this by executing a user-specified thunk for each consistent state.

11.4.8 Implementing other laws of QP theory (laws.lisp)

This file contains pattern-directed rules which encode the constraints of QP theory that do not appear elsewhere. Essentially, these rules provide either (1) clauses which are always appropriate whenever particular terms are mentioned in the database or (2) local constraints appropriate to particular belief states.

The first set of rules (Figure 11.10) installs the basic constraints of quantities. The first rule installs the basic constraint that having a continuous property means that the underlying object exists, notes that the quantity has sets of direct and indirect influences (whose construals are computed as part of influence resolution), and records the quantity in the current TGIZMO. The next five rules translate ordinal statements in the standard Lisp prefix form into the internal form used by the inequality system, and calls `install-comparison-constraints-if-needed` to carry out transitivity processing.

The next set of rules (Figure 11.11) provides the information needed to compute the view and process structures. Knowing whether or not a view or process is active determines whether or not it is a member of the view or process structure. These `has-member` statements could then used by the closed-world assumption mechanism to compute the construals of the sets `VS` and `PS` (see Exercise 18).

Basic constraints on influences are instantiated by the next set of rules (Figure 11.12). The first rule asserts several basic facts. While laws concerning individual influences suffice to infer that something is directly (or indirectly) influenced, only knowing that the set of influences is empty allows one to infer that a quantity is not directly (or indirectly) influenced. It enforces the constraint that no quantity can be both directly and indirectly influenced at the same time. And finally, it installs the constraint that an uninfluenced quantity cannot be changing. The next four rules install the direct consequences of influence statements.

```
(rule ((:INTERN (Quantity (?qtype ?individual)) :VAR ?qdecl))
      ;; Greatly restricted
      (rassert! (:IMPLIES ?qdecl (Exists ?individual))
                :QUANTITY-EXISTENCE)
      (rassert! (set (DIs (?qtype ?individual))) :DIS-DEF)
      (rassert! (set (IIs (?qtype ?individual))) :IIS-DEF)
      (push (list ?qtype ?individual) (tgizmo-quantities *tgizmo*)))

;;; In the next five rules,
;;;   ?n1, ?n2 = (<A or D> (?qtype ?individual)) | <constant>

(rule ((:INTERN (> ?n1 ?n2) :VAR ?gt))
      (install-comparison-constraints-if-needed ?n1 ?n2)
      (rassert! (:IFF ?gt (:AND (?n2 <= ?n1)
                                (:NOT (?n1 <= ?n2))))
                :>-DEF))

(rule ((:INTERN (< ?n1 ?n2) :VAR ?lt))
      (install-comparison-constraints-if-needed ?n1 ?n2)
      (rassert! (:IFF ?lt (:AND (?n1 <= ?n2)
                                (:NOT (?n2 <= ?n1))))
                :<-DEF))

(rule ((:INTERN (= ?n1 ?n2) :VAR ?eq))
      (install-comparison-constraints-if-needed ?n1 ?n2)
      (rassert! (:IFF ?eq (:AND (?n1 <= ?n2)
                                (?n2 <= ?n1)))
                :=-DEF))

(rule ((:INTERN (>= ?n1 ?n2) :VAR ?gte))
      (install-comparison-constraints-if-needed ?n1 ?n2)
      (rassert! (:IFF ?gte (?n2 <= ?n1)) :>=-DEF))

(rule ((:INTERN (<= ?n1 ?n2) :VAR ?lte))
      (install-comparison-constraints-if-needed ?n1 ?n2)
      (rassert! (:IFF ?lte (?n1 <= ?n2)) :<=-DEF))
```

Figure 11.10 Basic rules concerning comparisons

```
(rule ((:TRUE (Active ?p) :VAR ?aform))
      ;; If active, it's in there.
      (rule ((:TRUE (Process-instance ?p) :VAR ?pform))
            (rassert! (:IMPLIES (:AND ?pform ?aform)
                                (PS has-member ?p))
                      :PS-MEMBER))
      (rule ((:TRUE (View-instance ?p) :VAR ?pform))
            (rassert! (:IMPLIES (:AND ?pform ?aform)
                                (VS has-member ?p))
                      :VS-MEMBER)))

(rule ((:FALSE (Active ?p) :VAR ?aform))
      ;; If inactive, it's known to not be in there.
      (rule ((:TRUE (Process-instance ?p) :VAR ?pform))
            (rassert! (:IMPLIES (:AND ?pform (:NOT ?aform))
                                (:NOT (PS has-member ?p)))
                      :NOT-PS-MEMBER))
      (rule ((:TRUE (View-instance ?p) :VAR ?pform))
            (rassert! (:IMPLIES (:AND ?pform (:NOT ?aform))
                                (:NOT (VS has-member ?p)))
                      :NOT-VS-MEMBER)))
```

Figure 11.11 Rules supplying constraints on views and processes

That is, each influence statement contributes a member to the direct or indirect influences on a quantity.

11.4.9 Debugging utilities (debug.lisp)

This file contains some debugging utilities. The procedure `new` sets up a TGIZMO with the given scenario file, using the simple test domain theory described in Section 11.4.10. The calls to `in-tgizmo` and `in-ltre` ensure that the global variables `*tgizmo*` and `*ltre*` are bound to the newly created system. The first load statement provides the antecedent rules for enforcing QP theory constraints described previously, and the second load statement provides the default domain theory for testing. Loading the scenario completes the process. The procedures `test-ex1`, `test-ex2`, `test-ex3`, and `test-ex3-2` use `new` to provide some simple examples of state generation. The procedure `tgizmo-shakedown` runs a set of standard examples and checks that their overall results match the correct answers. Like our other shakedown procedures, `tgizmo-shakedown`

```
(rule ((:INTERN (Quantity ?q) :VAR ?qform))
      (rassert! (:IFF (:OR (:NOT ?qform) ((DIs ?q) members nil))
                      (:NOT (Directly-Influenced ?q)))
                :DIS-DEFINITION)
      (rassert! (:IFF (:OR (:NOT ?qform) ((IIs ?q) members nil))
                      (:NOT (Indirectly-Influenced ?q)))
                :IIS-DEFINITION)
      (rassert! (:NOT (:AND ?qform
                            (Directly-Influenced ?q)
                            (Indirectly-Influenced ?q)))
                :QP-CONSISTENCY-LAW)
      (rassert! (:IMPLIES (:AND ?qform
                                (:NOT (Directly-Influenced ?q))
                                (:NOT (Indirectly-Influenced ?q)))
                          (= (D ?q) ZERO))
                :UNINFLUENCED-DEFINITION))

(rule ((:TRUE (I+ ?influenced ?influencer ?source) :VAR ?Is))
      (rassert! (:IMPLIES ?Is (Directly-Influenced ?influenced))
                :DIS-DEFINITION)
      (rassert! (:IFF ?Is ((DIs ?influenced) has-member ?Is))
                :DIS-DEFINITION))

(rule ((:TRUE (I- ?influenced ?influencer ?source) :VAR ?Is))
      (rassert! (:IMPLIES ?Is (Directly-Influenced ?influenced))
                :DIS-DEFINITION)
      (rassert! (:IFF ?Is ((DIs ?influenced) has-member ?Is))
                :DIS-DEFINITION))

(rule ((:TRUE (Qprop ?influenced ?influencer ?source) :VAR ?Is))
      (rassert! (:IMPLIES ?Is (Indirectly-Influenced ?influenced))
                :IIS-DEFINITION)
      (rassert! (:IFF ?Is ((IIs ?influenced) has-member ?Is))
                :IIS-DEFINITION))

(rule ((:TRUE (Qprop- ?influenced ?influencer ?source) :VAR ?Is))
      (rassert! (:IMPLIES ?Is (Indirectly-Influenced ?influenced))
                :IIS-DEFINITION)
      (rassert! (:IFF ?Is ((IIs ?influenced) has-member ?Is))
                :IIS-DEFINITION))
```

Figure 11.12 Implementing basic constraints on influences

```
(defentity (Container ?can)
  (quantity (pressure ?can))) ;; at bottom

(defentity (fluid-path ?path))
(defentity (heat-path ?path))

(defentity (Physob ?phob)
  (quantity (heat ?phob))
  (quantity (temperature ?phob))
  (> (A (heat ?phob)) ZERO)
  (> (A (temperature ?phob)) ZERO)
  (qprop (temperature ?phob) (heat ?phob)))

(defentity (Temperature-Source ?phob)
  (quantity (heat ?phob))
  (quantity (temperature ?phob))
  (> (A (heat ?phob)) ZERO)
  (> (A (temperature ?phob)) ZERO))
```

Figure 11.13 Some basic types of entities

can be very useful in finding out whether a port of TGIZMO to a new environment is working correctly and assessing the impacts of changes to the system.

11.4.10 A sample domain theory (tnst.lisp)

This file describes *tiny naive steam theory*, a simple theory of fluids and heat. It is very naive, but provides a good illustration of how interesting conclusions can often be drawn from weak initial information. It begins by defining some basic objects, then defines some flow processes, and finally defines a simple theory of boiling. Let us consider each in turn.

Recall that `defentity` is used to introduce new classes of objects. Figure 11.13 shows how we define containers, paths, physobs, and temperature sources as basic kinds of objects. A *container* has a pressure, taken to be the pressure measured at the lowest point inside it. Here we take fluid paths and heat paths to be objects about which nothing particularly interesting is said, save that they connect objects to each other in ways that enable particular kinds of flows. A *physob* is a generic physical object. It has the thermal properties `heat` and `temperature`, both of

```
(defrule Contained-Stuff-Existence
  ((Container ?can)(Phase ?st)(Substance ?sub))
  ;; Assume that every kind of substance can exist in
  ;; in every phase inside every container.
  (quantity ((amount-of ?sub ?st) ?can))
  (>= (A ((amount-of ?sub ?st) ?can)) ZERO))

(defview (Contained-Stuff (C-S ?sub ?st ?can))
  :INDIVIDUALS ((?can (container ?can)
                      (substance ?sub)
                      (phase ?st)))
  :QUANTITY-CONDITIONS ((> (A ((amount-of ?sub ?st) ?can)) ZERO))
  :RELATIONS ((Only-During (Exists (C-S ?sub ?st ?can)))
              (Contained-stuff (C-S ?sub ?st ?can))
              (quantity (TBoil (C-S ?sub ?st ?can)))
              (> (A (TBoil (C-S ?sub ?st ?can))) ZERO)))
```

Figure 11.14 Defining contained stuffs

which are presumed to be greater than zero. Temperature is considered to be qualitatively proportional to the heat of the physob. A temperature source also has heat and temperature, but no functional relationship is presumed between them. Since no processes directly influence temperature, and temperature in the heat source is unconstrained by qualitative proportionalities, this means the temperature of a heat source will be constant no matter how much heat is added to or withdrawn from it.

Contained stuffs are a more complicated kind of object (see Figure 11.14). A contained stuff consists of all the substance in a particular phase inside a given container. Thus "the coffee in my cup" and "the water in the riverbed" and "the steam in the kettle" are all individuals of this type. The rule `contained-stuff-existence` asserts that for every combination of phase and substance and container, there is a quantity denoting the amount of that substance in that phase inside that container, and furthermore that amount can never be negative. (In a more sophisticated theory one might filter more, for instance noting that a copper cup won't hold concentrated acid for very long.)

The existence of a contained stuff is predicated on the amount of it there is: if one drinks all the coffee in a cup it is gone, and if the riverbed has no water we say the river has disappeared. This fact is captured by the view `contained-stuff`, which uses the function `C-S` to denote a

```
(defentity (Contained-Stuff (C-S ?sub liquid ?can))
  (Contained-Liquid (C-S ?sub liquid ?can)))

(defentity (Contained-Liquid (C-S ?sub liquid ?can))
  (physob (C-S ?sub liquid ?can))
  (quantity (level (C-S ?sub liquid ?can)))
  (qprop (level (C-S ?sub liquid ?can))
         ((Amount-of ?sub liquid) ?can))
  (qprop (pressure ?can) (level (C-S ?sub liquid ?can))))

(defentity (Contained-Stuff (C-S ?sub gas ?can))
  (Contained-gas (C-S ?sub gas ?can)))

(defentity (Contained-Gas (C-S ?sub gas ?can))
  (physob (C-S ?sub gas ?can))
  (qprop (pressure ?can)
         (temperature (C-S ?sub gas ?can)))
  (qprop (pressure ?can)
         ((amount-of ?sub gas) ?can)))
```

Figure 11.15 Representing some differences between liquids and gases

contained stuff. When the amount of a substance in a particular phase inside a container is greater than zero, we then say that the appropriate contained stuff exists. The `only-during` statement asserts, more strongly, that the stuff exists if and only if the conditions of this view are met. Contained stuffs are also presumed to have a boiling point (`tboil`), which is presumed to be greater than zero.

The differences between liquids and gases are captured by the `defentity` statements defining the predicates `contained-liquid` and `contained-gas` (see Figure 11.15). Both are physobs. A liquid has the additional parameter `level`, which is qualitatively proportional to the amount of stuff, and in turn helps determine the pressure of its container. A gas has no additional quantities, but contributes to the pressure inside the container differently than liquids. Specifically, the pressure of the can will tend to rise and fall as the amount of the gas and its temperature are increased and decreased, respectively. (Notice that if we have both a gas and a liquid in the same container, they jointly determine the container's pressure.) The two `defentity` statements for `Contained-Stuff` with constant arguments basically connect a particular contained stuff with its appropriate type.

```
(defprocess (heat-flow ?src ?path ?dst)
  :INDIVIDUALS ((?src (Quantity (heat ?src)))
               (?path (Heat-Connection ?path ?src ?dst))
               (?dst (Quantity (heat ?dst))))
  :PRECONDITIONS ((Heat-Aligned ?path))
  :QUANTITY-CONDITIONS ((> (A (temperature ?src))
                           (A (temperature ?dst))))
  :RELATIONS ((Quantity (flow-rate ?self))
              (> (A (flow-rate ?self)) zero)
              (Qprop (flow-rate ?self) (temperature ?src))
              (Qprop- (flow-rate ?self) (temperature ?dst)))
  :INFLUENCES ((I- (heat ?src) (flow-rate ?self))
               (I+ (heat ?dst) (flow-rate ?self))))

(defprocess (fluid-flow (C-S ?sub ?st ?src) ?path ?dst)
  :INDIVIDUALS ((?src (container ?src)
                      (substance ?sub) (phase ?st))
               (?path (fluid-Connection ?path ?src ?dst))
               (?dst (container ?dst)))
  :PRECONDITIONS ((Aligned ?path))
  :QUANTITY-CONDITIONS ((> (A ((amount-of ?sub ?st) ?src)) ZERO)
                        (> (A (pressure ?src)) (A (pressure ?dst))))
  :RELATIONS ((Quantity (flow-rate ?self))
              (> (A (flow-rate ?self)) zero)
              (Qprop (flow-rate ?self) (pressure ?src))
              (Qprop- (flow-rate ?self) (pressure ?dst)))
  :INFLUENCES ((I- ((amount-of ?sub ?st) ?src) (flow-rate ?self))
               (I+ ((amount-of ?sub ?st) ?dst) (flow-rate ?self))))
```

Figure 11.16 Simple flow processes

This theory has two flow processes, `heat-flow` and `fluid-flow` (see Figure 11.16). Heat flow is simpler, in that the source (`?src`) and destination (`?dst`) only have to have the quantity `heat` and be connected by a heat path (`?path`). When an instance of heat flow is active, there is a quantity of type `flow-rate` associated with the process, which is positive and is increasing monotonic in its dependence on the source temperature and decreasing monotonic in its dependence on the destination temperature. This is a qualitative encoding of the fact that the flow rate is proportional to the temperature difference driving the flow; see Exercise 16 for a more detailed qualitative rendering. Finally, the direct influences act to decrease the heat in the source and increase the heat

```
(defprocess (boiling (C-S ?sub liquid ?can)
                     (heat-flow ?ht-src ?hpath
                                (C-S ?sub liquid ?can)))
  :INDIVIDUALS ((?sub (substance ?sub))
                (?can (container ?can)
                      (Contained-Liquid (C-S ?sub liquid ?can)))
                (?hpath (heat-path ?hpath))
                (?ht-src (heat-connection ?hpath ?ht-src
                                (C-S ?sub liquid ?can))))
  :QUANTITY-CONDITIONS ((> (A ((amount-of ?sub liquid) ?can)) zero)
                        (Active (heat-flow ?ht-src ?hpath
                                           (C-S ?sub liquid ?can)))
                        (>= (A (temperature (C-S ?sub liquid ?can)))
                            (A (tboil (C-S ?sub liquid ?can)))))
  :RELATIONS ((quantity (generation-rate ?self))
              (:IMPLIES (Exists (C-S ?sub gas ?can))
                        (= (A (temperature (C-S ?sub gas ?can)))
                           (A (temperature (C-S ?sub liquid ?can)))))
              (> (A (generation-rate ?self)) zero))
  :INFLUENCES ((I+ ((amount-of ?sub gas) ?can)
                   (generation-rate ?self))
               (I- ((amount-of ?sub liquid) ?can)
                   (generation-rate ?self))
               (I- (heat (C-S ?sub liquid ?can))
                   (flow-rate (heat-flow ?ht-src ?hpath
                                         (C-S ?sub liquid ?can))))))
```

Figure 11.17 A simple representation of boiling

in the destination, by the amount of the flow rate. `fluid-flow` is very similar.

The only phase change included in this theory is boiling (see Figure 11.17), which happens for a contained liquid that has a heat path. It occurs when there is water in the container whose temperature is not less than the boiling point of the contained stuff and is being heated. There is a non-zero generation rate, and when there is steam in the container, it is at the same temperature as the water it came from. The direct influences on amounts are fairly obvious: the identical flow rates conserve matter, just as in the case of heat flow identical rates conserve energy. The flow rate of the heat flow is subtracted from the temperature of the water, to model the fact that the heat coming into the water is being used to change its phase rather than its temperature.

There are many flaws in this simple domain theory. We have not incorporated detailed container geometry, nor path conductances, nor the possible interactions between different substances. However, this simple theory suffices to exercise our system.

11.5 Examples

Let us examine the results of running TGIZMO on several examples.

11.5.1 Two containers

This simple example is useful for becoming familiar with the basics of TGIZMO and domain theories. The file `ex1.lisp` describes two containers, connected by a fluid path. The only declared phase is liquid, hence gases are not considered.[12] The procedure `test-ex1` in the file `debug.lisp` was used to generate all states for this scenario using the domain theory in `tnst.lisp`, making no additional assumptions about measurements. Notice that the scenario file does not itself directly specify the existence of physical processes, or even all the individuals implied by these circumstances. Inferring the existence of such individuals is one of TGIZMO's tasks.

Figure 11.18 summarizes the states computed for this scenario by using the state index computed from the results of `find-states`. Two views were created, corresponding to the possibility of contained liquid in each container. Two fluid-flow processes were created, thus modeling the possibility of flow in each direction across the path. There are eight states in all. The first cluster of three states corresponds to both `F` and `G` containing liquid, as indicated by both `contained-stuff` views being active. Depending on the relationship between the pressures in the containers (and whether or not the path is aligned, see Exercise a), either there will be a flow from `F` to `G`, a flow from `G` to `H`, or no flow at all. The cases where there is just water in `F` or just water in `G` are symmetric:

12. More general ways to modulate what aspects of a domain theory are used in modeling a specific situation can be found in [2, 7].

```
;;;; State index for Example 1, no constraints
;;;; Dumped 10/29/91, by KDF
 (EXISTS P1)
 (EXISTS G)
 (EXISTS (C-S WATER LIQUID G))
 (EXISTS F)
 (EXISTS (FLUID-FLOW (C-S WATER LIQUID G) P1 F))
 (EXISTS (C-S WATER LIQUID F))
 (EXISTS (FLUID-FLOW (C-S WATER LIQUID F) P1 G))
   (ACTIVE (CONTAINED-STUFF (C-S WATER LIQUID G)))
   (ACTIVE (CONTAINED-STUFF (C-S WATER LIQUID F)))
     (ACTIVE (FLUID-FLOW (C-S WATER LIQUID G) P1 F))
     (NOT (ACTIVE (FLUID-FLOW (C-S WATER LIQUID F) P1 G)))
       1 states.
     (NOT (ACTIVE (FLUID-FLOW (C-S WATER LIQUID G) P1 F)))
     (ACTIVE (FLUID-FLOW (C-S WATER LIQUID F) P1 G))
       1 states.
     (NOT (ACTIVE (FLUID-FLOW (C-S WATER LIQUID G) P1 F)))
     (NOT (ACTIVE (FLUID-FLOW (C-S WATER LIQUID F) P1 G)))
       1 states.
 (EXISTS P1)
 (EXISTS G)
 (EXISTS (C-S WATER LIQUID G))
 (EXISTS F)
 (EXISTS (FLUID-FLOW (C-S WATER LIQUID G) P1 F))
 (NOT (EXISTS (C-S WATER LIQUID F)))
 (EXISTS (FLUID-FLOW (C-S WATER LIQUID F) P1 G))
   (ACTIVE (CONTAINED-STUFF (C-S WATER LIQUID G)))
   (NOT (ACTIVE (CONTAINED-STUFF (C-S WATER LIQUID F))))
     (ACTIVE (FLUID-FLOW (C-S WATER LIQUID G) P1 F))
     (NOT (ACTIVE (FLUID-FLOW (C-S WATER LIQUID F) P1 G)))
       1 states.
     (NOT (ACTIVE (FLUID-FLOW (C-S WATER LIQUID G) P1 F)))
     (NOT (ACTIVE (FLUID-FLOW (C-S WATER LIQUID F) P1 G)))
       1 states.
 (EXISTS P1)
 (EXISTS G)
 (NOT (EXISTS (C-S WATER LIQUID G)))
 (EXISTS F)
 (EXISTS (FLUID-FLOW (C-S WATER LIQUID G) P1 F))
 (EXISTS (C-S WATER LIQUID F))
```

```
(EXISTS (FLUID-FLOW (C-S WATER LIQUID F) P1 G))
  (NOT (ACTIVE (CONTAINED-STUFF (C-S WATER LIQUID G))))
  (ACTIVE (CONTAINED-STUFF (C-S WATER LIQUID F)))
    (NOT (ACTIVE (FLUID-FLOW (C-S WATER LIQUID G) P1 F)))
    (ACTIVE (FLUID-FLOW (C-S WATER LIQUID F) P1 G))
      1 states.
    (NOT (ACTIVE (FLUID-FLOW (C-S WATER LIQUID G) P1 F)))
    (NOT (ACTIVE (FLUID-FLOW (C-S WATER LIQUID F) P1 G)))
      1 states.
(EXISTS P1)
(EXISTS G)
(NOT (EXISTS (C-S WATER LIQUID G)))
(EXISTS F)
(EXISTS (FLUID-FLOW (C-S WATER LIQUID G) P1 F))
(NOT (EXISTS (C-S WATER LIQUID F)))
(EXISTS (FLUID-FLOW (C-S WATER LIQUID F) P1 G))
  (NOT (ACTIVE (CONTAINED-STUFF (C-S WATER LIQUID G))))
  (NOT (ACTIVE (CONTAINED-STUFF (C-S WATER LIQUID F))))
    (NOT (ACTIVE (FLUID-FLOW (C-S WATER LIQUID G) P1 F)))
    (NOT (ACTIVE (FLUID-FLOW (C-S WATER LIQUID F) P1 G)))
      1 states.
```

Figure 11.18 Summary of states found for Two Containers example

each has two states, one corresponding to the possibility of water flowing from the container that has it into the container that doesn't, and the other state corresponding to no flow. The last state represents the possibility of both containers being empty, in which nothing at all can happen.

Let us look at a more complex example next, to see how the measurement interpretation operates.

11.5.2 Three containers

Consider again the scenario illustrated in Figure 11.1, now formally modeled in the scenario file `ex3.lisp`. What can we infer about the situation if we observe the level of water in `G` to be falling? Running the procedure `MI` on this problem yields nine states, as illustrated in Figure 11.19. Viewed in terms of process structures, these states can be divided into five equivalence classes (see Figure 11.20). This summarization is useful

```
(mi *ex3* *ex3-measurements* :DEBUGGING *default-debugging* :TITLE "Ex3 test")
;;; Loading source file "/u/bps/code/tgizmo/laws.lisp"
;;; Loading source file "/u/bps/code/tgizmo/tnst.lisp"
;;; Loading source file "/u/bps/code/tgizmo/ex3.lisp"
<TGizmo Ex3 test>
9
> (summarize-state-index (make-state-index *tgizmo*))

 (EXISTS P2)
 (EXISTS P1)
 (EXISTS H)
 (EXISTS (C-S WATER LIQUID H))
 (EXISTS G)
 (EXISTS (FLUID-FLOW (C-S WATER LIQUID H) P2 G))
 (EXISTS (C-S WATER LIQUID G))
 (EXISTS F)
 (EXISTS (FLUID-FLOW (C-S WATER LIQUID G) P1 F))
 (EXISTS (FLUID-FLOW (C-S WATER LIQUID G) P2 H))
 (EXISTS (C-S WATER LIQUID F))
 (EXISTS (FLUID-FLOW (C-S WATER LIQUID F) P1 G))
   (ACTIVE (CONTAINED-STUFF (C-S WATER LIQUID H)))
   (ACTIVE (CONTAINED-STUFF (C-S WATER LIQUID G)))
   (ACTIVE (CONTAINED-STUFF (C-S WATER LIQUID F)))
     (ACTIVE (FLUID-FLOW (C-S WATER LIQUID H) P2 G))
     (ACTIVE (FLUID-FLOW (C-S WATER LIQUID G) P1 F))
     (NOT (ACTIVE (FLUID-FLOW (C-S WATER LIQUID G) P2 H)))
     (NOT (ACTIVE (FLUID-FLOW (C-S WATER LIQUID F) P1 G)))
       3 states.
     (NOT (ACTIVE (FLUID-FLOW (C-S WATER LIQUID H) P2 G)))
     (ACTIVE (FLUID-FLOW (C-S WATER LIQUID G) P1 F))
     (ACTIVE (FLUID-FLOW (C-S WATER LIQUID G) P2 H))
     (NOT (ACTIVE (FLUID-FLOW (C-S WATER LIQUID F) P1 G)))
       1 states.
     (NOT (ACTIVE (FLUID-FLOW (C-S WATER LIQUID H) P2 G)))
     (ACTIVE (FLUID-FLOW (C-S WATER LIQUID G) P1 F))
     (NOT (ACTIVE (FLUID-FLOW (C-S WATER LIQUID G) P2 H)))
     (NOT (ACTIVE (FLUID-FLOW (C-S WATER LIQUID F) P1 G)))
       1 states.
     (NOT (ACTIVE (FLUID-FLOW (C-S WATER LIQUID H) P2 G)))
     (NOT (ACTIVE (FLUID-FLOW (C-S WATER LIQUID G) P1 F)))
     (ACTIVE (FLUID-FLOW (C-S WATER LIQUID G) P2 H))
     (ACTIVE (FLUID-FLOW (C-S WATER LIQUID F) P1 G))
       3 states.
```

```
    (NOT (ACTIVE (FLUID-FLOW (C-S WATER LIQUID H) P2 G)))
    (NOT (ACTIVE (FLUID-FLOW (C-S WATER LIQUID G) P1 F)))
    (ACTIVE (FLUID-FLOW (C-S WATER LIQUID G) P2 H))
    (NOT (ACTIVE (FLUID-FLOW (C-S WATER LIQUID F) P1 G)))
      1 states.
NIL
```

Figure 11.19 What can be happening when G is dropping?

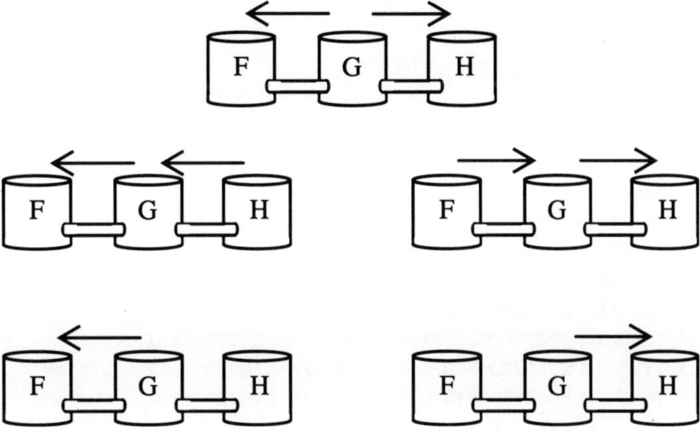

Figure 11.20 Possible interpretations for level in G dropping. Here is a graphical interpretation of the results in Figure 11.19.

because the process structure tends to be sufficient to determine what corrective action is needed, if any.

Suppose we need to pin down what is happening in the system more precisely. If we think about the possibilities shown in Figure 11.20, they differ in what they predict for the levels of F and H. If we measure F and find it decreasing, only one process structure is possible. There are three states corresponding to this process structure, because in our domain theory we have only very weak constraints on how the flow rate of fluid flow depends on the pressures in the source and destination. The results are illustrated in Figure 11.21.

```
(time (mi *ex3* *ex3-extra-measurements* :DEBUGGING nil  :TITLE "Ex3 test -- More
data"))
;;; Loading source file "/u/bps/code/tgizmo/laws.lisp"
;;; Loading source file "/u/bps/code/tgizmo/tnst.lisp"
;;; Loading source file "/u/bps/code/tgizmo/ex3.lisp"
<TGizmo Ex3 test -- More data>
3
> (summarize-state-index (make-state-index))

 (EXISTS P2)
 (EXISTS P1)
 (EXISTS H)
 (EXISTS (C-S WATER LIQUID H))
 (EXISTS G)
 (EXISTS (FLUID-FLOW (C-S WATER LIQUID H) P2 G))
 (EXISTS (C-S WATER LIQUID G))
 (EXISTS F)
 (EXISTS (FLUID-FLOW (C-S WATER LIQUID G) P1 F))
 (EXISTS (FLUID-FLOW (C-S WATER LIQUID G) P2 H))
 (EXISTS (C-S WATER LIQUID F))
 (EXISTS (FLUID-FLOW (C-S WATER LIQUID F) P1 G))
   (ACTIVE (CONTAINED-STUFF (C-S WATER LIQUID H)))
   (ACTIVE (CONTAINED-STUFF (C-S WATER LIQUID G)))
   (ACTIVE (CONTAINED-STUFF (C-S WATER LIQUID F)))
     (NOT (ACTIVE (FLUID-FLOW (C-S WATER LIQUID H) P2 G)))
     (NOT (ACTIVE (FLUID-FLOW (C-S WATER LIQUID G) P1 F)))
     (ACTIVE (FLUID-FLOW (C-S WATER LIQUID G) P2 H))
     (ACTIVE (FLUID-FLOW (C-S WATER LIQUID F) P1 G))
       3 states.
NIL
> (summarize-Ds-differences (tgizmo-states *tgizmo*))

 Common Ds values:
   Ds[PRESSURE(H)]=1
   Ds[(AMOUNT-OF WATER LIQUID)(H)]=1
   Ds[TBOIL((C-S WATER LIQUID H))]=0
   Ds[HEAT((C-S WATER LIQUID H))]=0
   Ds[TEMPERATURE((C-S WATER LIQUID H))]=0
   Ds[LEVEL((C-S WATER LIQUID H))]=1
   Ds[PRESSURE(G)]=-1
   Ds[(AMOUNT-OF WATER LIQUID)(G)]=-1
```

```
Ds[TBOIL((C-S WATER LIQUID G))]=0
Ds[HEAT((C-S WATER LIQUID G))]=0
Ds[TEMPERATURE((C-S WATER LIQUID G))]=0
Ds[LEVEL((C-S WATER LIQUID G))]=-1
Ds[PRESSURE(F)]=-1
Ds[FLOW-RATE((FLUID-FLOW (C-S WATER LIQUID G) P2 H))]=-1
Ds[(AMOUNT-OF WATER LIQUID)(F)]=-1
Ds[TBOIL((C-S WATER LIQUID F))]=0
Ds[HEAT((C-S WATER LIQUID F))]=0
Ds[TEMPERATURE((C-S WATER LIQUID F))]=0
Ds[LEVEL((C-S WATER LIQUID F))]=-1
For <State 3>:
  Ds[FLOW-RATE((FLUID-FLOW (C-S WATER LIQUID F) P1 G))]=-1
For <State 2>:
  Ds[FLOW-RATE((FLUID-FLOW (C-S WATER LIQUID F) P1 G))]=0
For <State 1>:
  Ds[FLOW-RATE((FLUID-FLOW (C-S WATER LIQUID F) P1 G))]=1
```

Figure 11.21 Interpretations for the case of G and F dropping

11.5.3 Analysis of the implementation

While TGIZMO lacks many features required of a full implementation of QP theory, it illustrates how many of the ideas described in this book can be combined to build powerful reasoning systems. It is large enough that some common features of "industrial-strength" reasoning systems begin to emerge, so it is worth remarking on them.

The first observation is that while attempts to formalize non-monotonic reasoning in logical terms are proceeding steadily but slowly, that does not mean that one cannot perform quite sophisticated non-monotonic reasoning in practice. For example, a thorny problem for logical formulations of change is the *qualification problem*, that is, stating kinds of things can affect a situation. The stance taken in QP theory is that such problems are best addressed at the level of theories that exploit properties of classes of domains. By defining processes as the sources of change, and using explicit closed-world assumptions to indicate what aspects of the world are being considered, we have the information needed both to sanction inferences and to figure out what to retract if those inferences turn out to be incorrect. The simple set-based closed-world assumption mechanism introduced in Chapter 10, when used correctly, produces exactly the results one would expect.

The second observation concerns an inevitable trade-off in building pattern-directed inference systems: How much work should be done by rules versus some other mechanism(s)? While rules as a procedure model have the advantages of explicitness and modularity, we have already seen that the necessity of making some decisions on global criteria means they cannot by themselves be sufficient. Here, the use of closed-world assumptions forced us to put certain operations in Lisp code. The decision to close a set is a global decision that cannot be made by any local antecedent rule. This is not to say that one cannot do better than Lisp code: one might for example describe meta-rules that trigger on global features of the database and specify what actions to perform based on global criteria. But figuring out the right vocabulary of global features, and the appropriate control strategy for such rules, is still very much an open problem.

The third observation concerns the other role for special-purpose programs in reasoning systems: efficiency. In TGIZMO we put responsibility for several aspects of qualitative reasoning, which could easily have been implemented via pattern-directed rules, into Lisp code. The unambiguous cases of influence resolution, for instance, can easily be specified as pattern-directed rules once the appropriate closed-world assumptions have been made. But since the laws of influence resolution are both fixed and central to the operation of the system, we decided to make them as fast as possible. This is the natural migration path when building systems to operate on problems that live near the edge of one's computing technology. Prototype using pattern-directed rules, by all means. But if performance becomes a problem, start examining what core operations can be moved into "hard-wired" procedures.

The final observation concerns building habitable systems. While interfaces are natural time-sinks, providing some basic facilities is always a good idea. For instance, expecting users to write Lisp code to describe a domain theory would be completely inappropriate. After all, the whole point of identifying a particular kind of reasoning and supporting it through a modeling language is to raise the level of abstraction closer to human intuitions. As systems grow larger, specialized display routines and debugging tools become indispensable. The file `states.lisp`, for instance, consists mostly of procedures that display information about states and produce reports. Such routines aren't very intellectually interesting. But then again, neither are low-level device drivers, even though they are essential to a computer's operations. As one moves from simple, knowledge-poor prototype systems to systems that know more, such utilities become even more essential. TGIZMO gets about as complicated to debug as one would like without having a powerful graphical user interface.

11.6 Backpointers

The algorithms in TGIZMO are mostly simplified and modernized versions of those found in GIZMO [9], the first implementation of QP theory, which also used a logic-based TMS as a substrate. The major exception is the idea of reasoning with soft inequalities, which is based on unpublished work by John Collins and Dennis DeCoste on IQE, an incremental qualitative simulator for QP theory.

A good starting point to learn more about qualitative physics is [24], which provides a broad overview, and [8, 1], which provide samples of recent research.

11.7 Exercises

1. ⋆ In Figure 11.16 the quantity conditions for fluid flow were given as

```
((> (A ((amount-of ?sub ?st) ?src)) ZERO)
 (> (A (pressure ?src)) (A (pressure ?dst))))
```

   Is the first conjunct necessary? Why or why not?

2. ⋆ What would happen when TGIZMO tried to instantiate the following description:

```
(defprocess (Zorch-it ?foo)
 :INDIVIDUALS ((?foo (physob ?foo)))
 :QUANTITY-CONDITIONS ((< (A (strength ?foo))
                          (A (strength ?bar))))
 :RELATIONS ((Quantity (grump ?self))
             (Qprop (grump ?self) (strength ?bar)))
 :INFLUENCES ((I+ (strength ?foo) (grump ?self))))
```

3. ⋆ Why does `resolve-influences` check for a `Resolved` statement rather than just looking to see if the `Ds` value for that quantity is known?

4. ⋆ Recall that the intimate relationship between an object and its continuous properties means that no ordinal relationship involving a number N_1 and any other number can hold when the object N_1 belongs to does not exist. That is, for all N_2,

   $\neg[N_1 \leq N_2] \wedge \neg[N_2 \leq N_1]$

   Why doesn't `check-comp-cycle` look for this case explicitly?

5. ⋆ In Figure 11.18, there is only one state for the circumstance where neither flow is active. Yet there are two reasons that the flow might not occur: (1) the pressures might be equal, or (2) the path might be blocked, modeled by `(aligned path)` being false. Why, then, is there only one state?

6. This problem concerns the implementation of the notion of magnitude (that is, the logical function `m`) in TGIZMO.

   a. ⋆ In what circumstances would `m` be useful?

   b. ⋆ Which TGIZMO procedures and rules would have to be modified to fully implement `m`?

   c. ⋆⋆ Extend the qualitative mathematics in TGIZMO to allow the use of `m`.

7. ⋆⋆ Profile the performance of TGIZMO on several examples and figure out which subsystem(s) are using the most resources. Make three suggestions for speeding up the most critical subsystem(s).

8. Suppose we have some way of marking particular parameters whose `Ds` values can be measured.

   a. ⋆⋆ Write a procedure `predictions` that figures out what additional measurements would discriminate between multiple interpretations suggested by existing measurements.

   b. ⋆⋆ If we run the measurement interpretation algorithm without any measurements to explain, it will generate the entire set of possible states for the scenario. Use this fact to write a system which, given a scenario and domain theory, compiles a discrimination tree that can provide the same results as the MI algorithm for any data, but without doing any qualitative reasoning on-line.

9. Ideally, the information stored in a `state` struct is sufficient to reconstruct the contents and labels of the LTRE database from which it was formed.

   a. ⋆ Is the information stored by `snapshot` really sufficient to allow the reconstruction of the original LTRE database? If not, specify what is missing and what other information should be stored to allow the reconstruction.

   b. ⋆⋆ Write a procedure `reconsider`, which takes a state and a TGIZMO (and perhaps some other information, if needed) and reproduces the given state in that TGIZMO.

10. ⋆⋆⋆ Extend TGIZMO to perform limit analysis.

11. ⋆⋆⋆ Use TGIZMO augmented with limit analysis to implement an envisioner.

12. ⋆⋆⋆ Use TGIZMO augmented with limit analysis to implement a history generator.

13. It is inevitable that interpretation of a situation always depends on the domain theory and what is known about the scenario.

   a. ⋆ What should the MI algorithm produce if we provide as inputs the domain theory `tnst` and the scenario `ex2`, and stipulate that the level of water in the can is dropping? Does it produce the answer you expect?

   b. ⋆⋆⋆ Extend the `tnst` domain theory to include evaporation and condensation. What sorts of results does the MI algorithm produce now for the scenarios `ex1`, `ex2`, and `ex3`?

14. Often other kinds of knowledge are available to reduce the number of possible interpretations for a set of measurements.

   a. ⋆ List three kinds of information that might reduce the number of interpretations of a set of measurements.

   b. ⋆⋆⋆ Extend TGIZMO to incorporate at least one of the kinds of knowledge from your answer for part (a). Test your extension on a variety of examples.

15. This exercise explores trade-offs in the organization of the search in the measurement interpretation algorithm.

    a. ⋆ Suppose we organized our measurement interpretation search around whether or not the union of all preconditions and quantity conditions were true or false, rather than basing it on what processes and views are active. How would this affect (1) the number of interpretations produced, (2) the amount of information in each interpretation, and (3) the efficiency of the reasoning?

    b. ⋆⋆ Suppose we don't want any more detail in our interpretations than the process structure. In that case, the current MI algorithm does more work than necessary. Rewrite it so that it does as little computation as possible to establish that a process structure provides a valid interpretation for a set of measurements.

    c. ⋆⋆⋆ For really large problems (e.g., troubleshooting an automobile engine or a process plant) even computing the entire process structure involves too much irrelevant work. Develop a backward chaining version of the MI algorithm that instantiates only the potentially relevant aspects of a domain theory in a scenario, and searches this more restricted space.

16. The modeling language used in TGIZMO supports only a subset of the qualitative mathematics defined in QP theory. This problem extends the modeling language in several directions, to allow more detailed qualitative models to be expressed.

    a. ⋆⋆ One useful primitive is `Correspondence`, which propagates ordinal information across qualitative proportionalities. For example, we might say:

```
(Correspondence ((Level (C-S ?sub ?ph ?can)) (Bottom ?can))
                ((Amount-of-in ?sub ?ph ?can) zero))
```

    which says that the level of water in a can is equal to the bottom (height) of the can when the amount of water in the can is equal to zero. If we know

```
(qprop (Level (C-S ?sub ?ph ?can)) (amount-of-in ?sub ?ph ?can))
```

    then the correspondence allows us to conclude that when the amount of water is greater than zero the level will be above the bottom of the can. Write an LTRE rule which implements `Correspondence`. Your rule must allow quantities to have multiple indirect influences, and must take the signs of the qualitative proportionalities into account.

b. ⋆⋆ A basic property of functions is that they are single-valued. For instance, we know that if we have two identical drinking glasses, and put more water in one than the other, then the level in the glass with more water will be higher than the level in the other. To draw conclusions like this requires surprisingly little: we only need to know that the functions are the same, not precisely what they are. The primitive `Function-Spec` provides this service. For instance,

```
(defentity (Contained-Liquid ?cl)
    (Function-Spec P-L-Function
       (Qprop (Pressure ?cl) (Level ?cl))))
```

indicates that the same function (`P-L-Function`) determines pressure as a function of level for all containers. (QP theory also defines other primitives for specifying functional dependencies involving things other than quantities, but we ignore this possibility here.) Essentially, `Function-Spec` provides a way to propagate ordinal information across objects. Write an LTRE rule that enforces the semantics of `Function-Spec`. (Hint: Your solution to implementing `Correspondence` will be very useful.)

c. ⋆⋆ Symbolic algebra can be computationally complicated, and hence tends to be avoided in most qualitative simulation algorithms. This does not mean that allowing more complex mathematical connectives is undesirable, however, even for simple qualitative models. For instance, we would really prefer to define the flow rate of heat flow as:

```
(= (flow-rate ?self) (- (temperature ?src)
                        (temperature ?dst)))
```

since for positive temperatures this forces the flow rate to be positive when the heat flow process is active. Write an LTRE rule that transforms = statements constraining a quantity by binary sums and products into the appropriate qualitative proportionalities and correspondences.

d. ⋆⋆ Products and ratios are also important in building domain theories. For instance,

```
(= (temperature ?stuff) (/ (heat ?stuff)
                           (amount-of ?stuff)))
```

is a more accurate definition of temperature, and

```
(= (flow-rate ?self) (* (thermal-conductance ?path)
                        (- (temperature ?src)
                           (temperature ?dst))))
```

is a more accurate definition of how the thermal conductance of a path affects rates of heat flow. Implement products and quotients in terms of qualitative proportionalities and correspondences.

e. ⋆⋆⋆ Ideally we would like to do as much expanding of rule information as possible when a rule is compiled. Applying this principle to domain theories suggests that instead of implementing the mathematical primitives in the previous subproblems as LTRE rules, we should instead move them into `translate-relations`, and figure out the "right" set of clauses to be instantiated at compile time. Extend `translate-relations` to perform these tasks.

17. A friendly modeling language should provide syntactic support for common patterns of usage. While the format of the individuals field in TGIZMO's modeling language is simple to implement, it could be easier to use. For instance, the pattern

```
(?sub (substance ?sub))
```

indicates that `?sub` is of type `substance`. Since this pattern is common, it can simplify a modeler's job if we allow the introduction of a keyword `:TYPE`, so that

```
(?sub :TYPE substance)
```

means the same thing. The ability to add additional statements after the initial specification can be recaptured by adding the keyword `:CONDITIONS`, i.e.,

```
(?gas :TYPE Contained-Gas
      :CONDITIONS (Consider (Gas :system)))
```

Another handy feature is the ability to perform procedural tests on the arguments bound so far, to filter out clearly unproductive possibilities. So, for example, before installing a view representing the existence of a reaction force, we might check to see if the force we are looking at is already a reaction to some external force, since in that case installing yet another reaction force will lead to an infinite regress. We could add a keyword :TEST for this, just as we added procedural tests to our TREs:

```
(?force :TYPE force :TEST (not (reaction-force? ?force)))
```

Finally, it is sometimes useful to allow abbreviations to be introduced for compound terms, like

```
(?dst-cl :BIND (C-S ?sub ?st ?dst))
```

which says that in the rest of the process (or view) description, the variable ?dst-cl (probably the "contained liquid in the destination") is shorthand for (C-S ?sub ?st ?dst), where ?sub, ?st, and ?dst are variables bound by earlier entries in the individuals field.

a. ⋆⋆ Extend mlang.lisp to allow :TYPE, :CONDITIONS, :TEST, and :BIND specifications in individuals fields.

b. ⋆ Some would argue on aesthetic grounds that we should also include a keyword :ASSUMPTIONS to indicate what subset of the individuals field consists of modeling assumptions. Present arguments for and against the inclusion of :ASSUMPTIONS.

c. ⋆⋆ An unfortunate consequence of our decision to use the simplest possible mapping between statements in the individuals field and LTRE rules is that someone writing a domain model must know more than they should about TGIZMO's internals to optimize their theories. For instance, a very natural way to write the individuals for heat flow is

```
:INDIVIDUALS ((?src (Quantity (heat ?src)))
              (?dst (Quantity (heat ?dst))))
              (?path (Heat-Connection ?path ?src ?dst))
```

since the source and destination are typically the primary focus of our analysis (unless we are thermal engineers). But the most efficient way to write this description is

```
:INDIVIDUALS ((?path (Heat-Connection ?path ?src ?dst))
              (?src (Quantity (heat ?src)))
              (?dst (Quantity (heat ?dst))))
```

since the first way looks at every pair of objects with heat, while the second exploits the fact that (at least in this domain theory) every heat path connects exactly two objects and thus once we know the path we know the source and destination, and if there is no path the whole issue of heat flow is moot anyway. Change `mlang.lisp` to automatically optimize the pattern-matching carried out in `individuals` specifications. What additional knowledge of the predicates do you need in order to get the most improvement, and how might you simplify the specification of such knowledge for domain modelers?

18. A useful technique in building domain theories is to add additional antecedents in the `individuals` field that describe the assumptions under which a particular fragment of that theory makes sense. We used this in modeling thermal conductance:

```
(defview (Heat-Flow-Thermal-Conductance ?hf)
 :INDIVIDUALS ((?hf (process-instance (heat-flow ?src ?path ?dst))
                    (Consider (Thermal-Conductance ?path))))
 :QUANTITY-CONDITIONS ((Active ?hf))
 :RELATIONS ((Qprop+ (flow-rate ?hf) (thermal-conductance ?path))))
```

That is, this view will only be applicable when

```
(Consider (Thermal-Conductance ?path))
```

holds. This technique can be used to encode multiple, and even contradictory, perspectives about a phenomenon in the same domain theory. Then, by changing the modeling assumptions, we can select which aspects of a domain theory to apply for a given analysis. This is useful because typically only a subset of one's knowledge is relevant to any particular task.

a. ⋆⋆ Add notions of fluid conductance and path conductance to the Tiny Naive Steam theory, scoped with the appropriate modeling assumptions.

b. ⋆⋆ Modify the evaporation and phase change processes you developed for Exercise b to include explicit simplifying assumptions.

c. ⋆⋆ Write a procedure `considerations` which, given a fact, produces the list of `Consider` assumptions it rests upon.

d. ⋆⋆⋆ Use the results of the previous parts of this exercise and your work from Exercise a to build a more efficient measurement interpretation system that first determines whether a very restricted set of the domain theory can account for what is seen, and widens the search to include more phenomena only when the most obvious candidates cannot by themselves explain what is happening.

11.8 Bibliography

[1] de Kleer, J., and Williams, B. (Eds.), "Special Volume: Qualitative Reasoning about physical systems II," *Artificial Intelligence*, 51(1991).

[2] Addanki, S., Cremonini, R. and Penberthy, S., "Graphs of models," *Artificial Intelligence*, 51(1991):145-177.

[3] Allen, J., "Towards a general model of action and time," *Artificial Intelligence* 23(1984): 123-154.

[4] Collins, J., "Diagnosis as failure understanding," Technical Report No. UIUCDCS-R-91-1699, Department of Computer Science, University of Illinois at Urbana-Champaign, 1991.

[5] Decoste, D., "Dynamic across-time measurement interpretation," *Artificial Intelligence*, 51(1991):273–341.

[6] de Kleer, J., and Brown, J., "A qualitative physics based on confluences," *Artificial Intelligence* 24(1984):7-83.

[7] Falkenhainer, B., and Forbus, K., "Compositional Modeling: Finding the Right Model for the Job," *Artificial Intelligence*, 51(1991):95–143.

[8] Faltings, B., and Struss, P. (Eds.), *Recent Advances in Qualitative Physics*, MIT Press, 1992.

[9] Forbus, K., "Qualitative process theory," Technical Report No. 789, MIT AI Lab, 1984.

[10] Forbus, K., "Qualitative process theory," *Artificial Intelligence* 24(1984): 85-168.

[11] Forbus, K., "Measurement interpretation in qualitative process theory," *Proceedings of IJCAI-83*, pp 315–320.

[12] Forbus, K., "The problem of existence," *Proceedings of the Seventh annual meeting of the Cognitive Science Society*, 1985, pp 272–276.

[13] Forbus, K., "Interpreting observations of physical systems," *IEEE Transactions on Systems, Man, and Cybernetics*, vol. SMC-17, no. 3, May/June 1987, pp 113–117.

[14] Forbus, K., "The logic of occurrence," *Proceedings of IJCAI-87*, 1987, pp 409–415.

[15] Forbus, K., "The Qualitative Process Engine," in Weld, D., and de Kleer, J., (eds.) *Readings in Qualitative Reasoning about Physical Systems*, Morgan-Kaufmann, 1990, pp 220–235.

[16] Forbus, K. "Pushing the edge of the (QP) envelope,", in Faltings, B. and Struss, P. (Eds.), *Recent Progress in Qualitative Physics*, MIT Press, 1992.

[17] Forbus, K. and Falkenhainer, B. "Self-Explanatory Simulations: An integration of qualitative and quantitative knowledge," *Proceedings of AAAI-90*, 1990,

[18] Forbus, K. and Falkenhainer, B. "Self-explanatory simulators: Scaling up to larger models," *Proceedings of AAAI-92*, 1992.

[19] Hayes, P., "The naive physics manifesto," in Michie, D. (Ed.), *Expert systems in the micro-electronic age*, Edinburgh University Press, 1979, pp 242–270.

[20] Hayes, P., "Naive Physics 1: Ontology for Liquids", in Hobbs, J., and Moore, R. (eds.), *Formal Theories of the Commonsense World*, Ablex, 1985, pp 71-90.

[21] Iwasaki, I., and Simon, H., "Causality in device behavior," *Artificial Intelligence*29(1986):3–32.

[22] Kuipers, B., "Qualitative Simulation," *Artificial Intelligence* 29(1986):289–338.

[23] McDermott, D., "A temporal logic for reasoning about processes and plans," *Cognitive Science* 6(1982):101–155.

[24] Weld, D., and de Kleer, J., (eds.) *Readings in Qualitative Reasoning about Physical Systems*, Morgan-Kaufmann, 1990.

12 Assumption-Based Truth Maintenance Systems

Many problem-solving tasks require the inference engine to rapidly switch among contexts or to work in multiple contexts at once. Two such tasks are qualitative reasoning and diagnosis. An inference engine can change the current JTMS or LTMS context by enabling and retracting assumptions. However, each assumption change reinvokes the TMS relabeling algorithms. Thus, if the rate of such assumption changes is high compared to the number of queries about whether a node is in or out, then most of the time is spent relabeling nodes that will never be examined by the inference engine. An assumption-based truth maintenance system (ATMS) [1] is very much like a JTMS, except that it avoids such relabeling.

At the level of the TMS interface, the ATMS has no procedures for enabling or retracting assumptions because its design does not depend on these concepts. Instead, ATMS interface procedures require an additional argument: the set of assumptions with respect to which the query is to be answered. For example, the ATMS procedure `in-node?` takes this additional argument. This procedure returns `t` only if the node would be in if we took a JTMS with the same set of justifications and enabled the assumptions of this second argument. ATMS context switches are free because they simply require choosing a different second argument. In addition, an inference engine can now work in multiple contexts at once.

The ATMS achieves its functionality by precomputing a complex label for each TMS node. Instead of labeling a node `:IN` or `:OUT`, the ATMS labels every node with the consistent sets of assumptions under which the node is in. The ATMS answers queries by checking this complex label. In making the choice of whether to use a JTMS or an ATMS it is important to keep this distinction in mind. In a JTMS one incurs the cost of context switching when the actual context switches are made. In the ATMS one incurs the cost up front. Therefore, if there are relatively few context switches, the JTMS will be more efficient, and if there are many context switches, the ATMS will be. (Of course, there are other reasons for choosing between the ATMS and the JTMS, which we discuss in this chapter).

As we saw with the JTMSs and LTMSs, each type of truth maintenance system engenders a unique style of problem-solving architecture. Compared to the transition from JTMSs to LTMSs, the transition to ATMSs requires a more radical shift in problem-solver design. In an ATMS-based problem solver, the implementor must break free of the "single current context" mentality and design the inference engine to operate in all contexts at once. This is often not an easy transition. In a subsequent chapter we examine, in detail, a diagnostic application that exploits this property of the ATMS. In performing differential diagnosis, a diagnostician must identify potential differences between different diagnostic hypotheses in order to decide what measurement to do next. Each diagnostic hypothesis is represented by a distinct context.

12.1 ATMS basics

12.1.1 ATMS nodes and justifications

ATMS nodes and justifications are nearly identical to their JTMS counterparts. Our ATMS architecture represents the three generic TMS node properties as follows:

- A node is a *premise* if the inference engine has provided it with a justification with no antecedents. Premises are therefore not distinguished from other nodes in the architecture.
- A node is a *contradiction* if the inference engine has indicated that it can never hold. Recall that in the JTMS, if a contradiction node becomes believed, the inference engine is signaled (presumably to retract some assumption to remove the contradiction). The ATMS, which has no notion of current context that might be inconsistent,

treats contradictions somewhat differently. The ATMS does not signal the inference engine when it detects a contradiction. Instead, the ATMS ensures that no node will be considered to follow from a set of assumptions (i.e., by the operation `in-node?`) if a contradiction node also follows from that set of assumptions. Unlike with the JTMS and LTMS, contradiction handling is not necessary. The more contradictions the better, because they reduce the number of sets of assumptions the ATMS might have to consider.

- A node is an *assumption* if the inference engine wishes to use it in the second argument to `in-node?`. The ATMS will then build the appropriate datastructures to make it easy to test whether a node follows from an arbitrary set of assumptions. In the JTMS or LTMS, making all nodes assumptions incurs little overhead. However, marking a node as an assumption tells the ATMS that the node can appear in the second argument of inquiries, and consequently label size can grow exponentially in the number of possible assumptions. Thus it is incumbent on the inference engine to introduce as few assumptions as possible.

ATMS justifications have the identical syntax as JTMS justifications: a justification consists of a *consequent* which follows from *antecedents* accompanied by an *informant* describing the deduction (which the ATMS never looks at).

12.1.2 The intuitions behind ATMS labels

Unlike the JTMS and LTMS, an ATMS label is a complex datastructure. The label is longer a single atom such as `:IN` or `:OUT`, because those only make sense with respect to some current context. Intuitively, the ATMS label consists of a parsimonious description of the consistent contexts in which the node holds. Consider the JTMS dependency network, illustrated in Figure 12.1. In this network assumptions A, B, D, and E are enabled, and node h is `:IN`. If we retracted assumptions A and E, node h would still hold (see Figure 12.2).

Repeating this process, we would discover that h holds under the following sets of enabled assumptions:

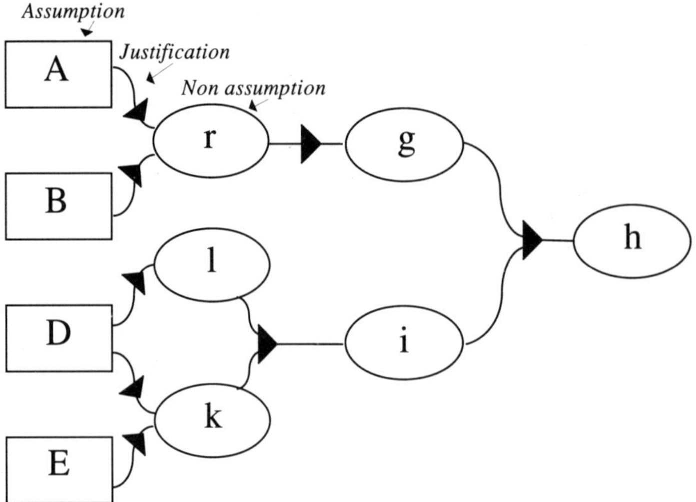

Figure 12.1 h follows from $\{A, B, D, E\}$

$\{A, D\}$

$\{A, B, D\}$

$\{A, D, E\}$

$\{A, B, D, E\}$

$\{B, D\}$

$\{B, D, E\}$.

We define an *environment* to be a set of assumptions. A node holds in an environment if, when all the assumptions of the environment are enabled in a JTMS, the node is labeled `:IN`. Thus, in the previous example, node h holds in 6 environments. A *nogood* is an environment in which some contradiction holds. A *consistent* environment is one which is not nogood. A *context* of an environment is the set of nodes that hold in the environment.

One way to answer queries about whether a node holds in some environment is to record in the label all the consistent environments in which a node holds. Unfortunately, this can be extremely inefficient. For example, if a node holds universally, its label might contain 2^n environments where n is the number of assumptions. However, two important obser-

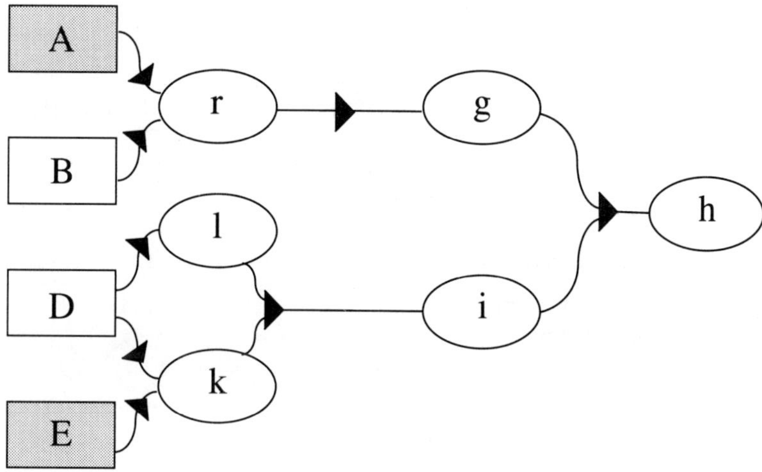

Figure 12.2 h follows from {B,D}

vations turn this idea into a usable one. First, we exploit monotonicity: if a node follows from an environment, then it follows from any superset of the environment, and hence it is unnecessary to represent the supersets in the label. Hence the label for node h is $\{\{A,D\}\{B,D\}\}$, which we notate as:

$$\langle h, \{\{A,D\}\{B,D\}\}\rangle.$$

Figure 12.3 indicates all the labels for the dependency network we have been considering. Second, there is no point in including nogoods in labels, as such contexts are of no interest. Consider the example of Figure 12.4 where z's label is:

$$\langle z, \{\{S,T\}\}\rangle.$$

Although the environment $\{R,S\}$ seems to support node z, it is not included in the label because it is nogood.

There are two important labels which play a major role. The first is the empty label, for example:

$$\langle d, \{\}\rangle.$$

A label is empty if either the dependency network contains no pathway from the assumptions to the node, or if all potential label environments

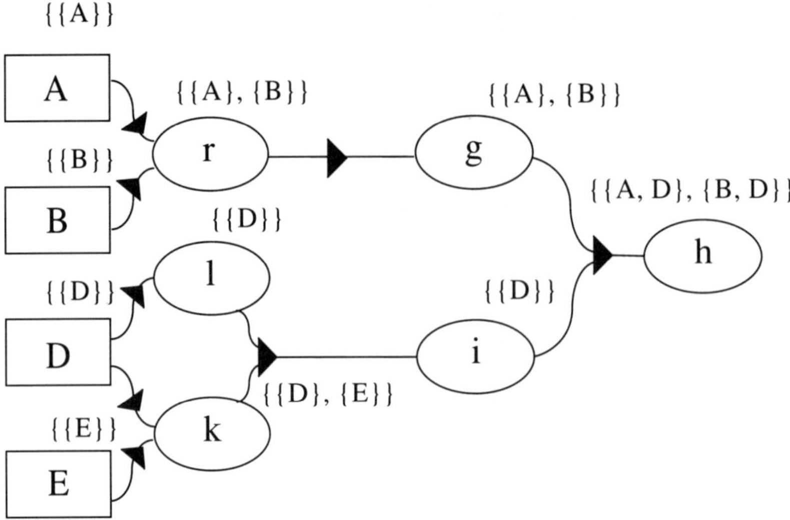

Figure 12.3 Labels

are nogood. Thus, an empty label indicates that the node holds in no consistent environment. The fact that the label is empty does not mean that its negation holds in every environment. Nor does it mean that d is a contradiction (although the labels of all contradictions are necessarily empty because nogoods do not appear in node labels).

The second important label contains only the empty environment, for example:

$\langle p, \{\{\}\}\rangle$.

All premises have a label consisting of the empty environment. The empty environment in the label indicates that the node holds in every environment, as every environment is a superset of the empty one. Note that non-premise nodes can hold in empty environments if they ultimately depend only on premises.

In the JTMS and the LTMS, the main purpose of contradiction handlers is to remove inconsistencies to ensure that the derivations of the TMS make sense. As the ATMS simply removes inconsistent environments from node labels, contradiction handling is not necessary for this purpose. However, contradiction handling also plays a less obvious role—it serves to signal the inference engine that a set of choices it has made are

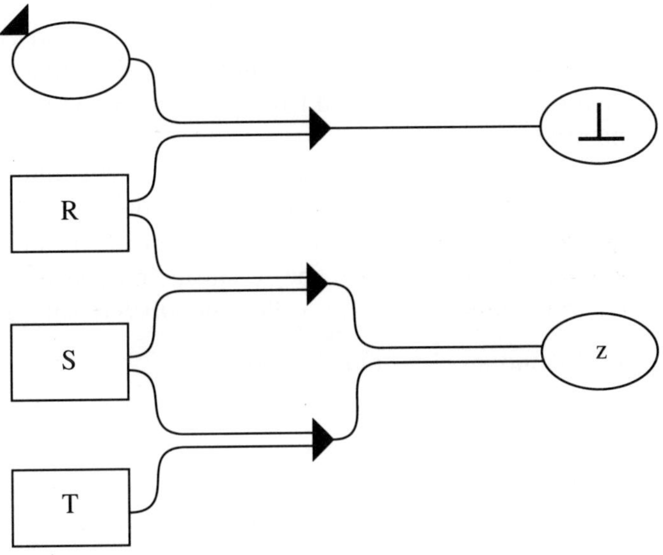

Figure 12.4 $\langle z, \{\{S, T\}\}\rangle$

inconsistent. This latter role is still important for the ATMS. Therefore, the ATMS implementation has the ability to attach rules to environments, such that when that environment becomes inconsistent an inference engine procedure is invoked. This gives the ATMS-based inference engine very fine control because it can specify precisely which of the myriad of possible environments it cares about.

12.1.3 Logical specification for an ATMS

The set of ATMS nodes defines a set of propositional symbols S. A subset of those symbols are marked as assumptions: $\mathcal{A} \subset S$. As with the JTMS, every ATMS justification is directly encoded as a definite clause. For every contradiction node n, we add a unit clause

$\neg n,$

to indicate that n does not hold. Let C be the set of clauses obtained. We presume C is consistent. An environment E is a subset of the assumptions, $E \subset \mathcal{A}$.

A node n is said to hold in environment E if n can be propositionally derived from the union of E with C. A nogood N is an environment consisting purely of assumption literals such that the empty clause can be propositionally derived from $N \cup C$. A nogood is *minimal* if it contains no other as a subset.

The ATMS is incremental, receiving a constant stream of additional nodes, additional assumptions, additional justifications, and various queries concerning the environments in which nodes hold. To facilitate answering these queries the ATMS maintains for each node n a set of environments $\{E_1, \ldots, E_k\}$ (called the *label*) having the four properties:

1. [Soundness.] n holds in each E_i.
2. [Consistency.] $\perp$ cannot be derived from any E_i (given C).
3. [Completeness.] Every consistent environment E in which n holds is a superset of some E_i.
4. [Minimality.] No E_i is a proper subset of any other.

Given this label datastructure, the ATMS can efficiently answer the query whether n holds in a consistent environment E by checking whether E is a superset of some E_i. To easily enforce the consistency property, the ATMS also maintains a database of unsubsumed nogoods.

12.2 ATMS algorithms

Like all TMS algorithms, the ATMS algorithm is incremental, taking a correct set of node labels and computing the incremental changes caused by adding a justification. The algorithm operates by making labels locally correct and propagating label changes until labels become globally correct. Note that assumptions are created with labels containing the single environment containing themselves, and all other nodes are created with empty labels.

The ATMS label update algorithm operates by repetitively ensuring that each node's label is locally correct. The locally correct label for node n could be computed as follows: Let L_{ik} be the label of the ith node of the kth justification for some node n.

1. Compute a tentative label

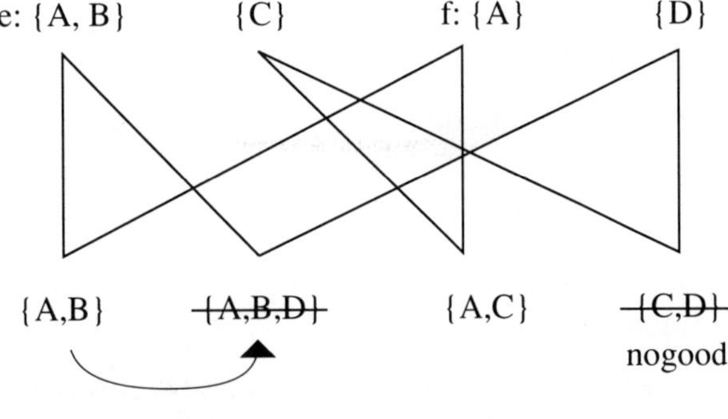

Figure 12.5 Given $e \wedge f \Rightarrow g$, compute g's label

$$L' = \{\bigcup_i e_i \mid e_i \in L_{ik}\}.$$

2. Remove from L' all nogoods and environments subsumed by others in L'.

Consider a simple example. Suppose we knew

$\langle e, \{\{A,B\}\{C\}\}\rangle$,

$\langle f, \{\{A\}\{D\}\}\rangle$,

$nogood\{C,D\}$,

and we just created a new node g with a single justification,

$e \wedge f \Rightarrow g$.

Computing the new label for g is illustrated in Figure 12.5. $L_{11} = \{\{A,B\}\ \{C\}\}, L_{21} = \{\{A\}\{D\}\}$, so step 1 computes,

$L' = \{\{A,B\}\{A,B,D\}\{A,C\}\{C,D\}\}$.

Step 2 removes the nogood $\{C,D\}$ and the subsumed $\{A,B,D\}$. The correct label for g is:

$\langle g, \{\{A,B\}\{A,C\}\}\rangle$.

The following is a simple algorithm which propagates label changes throughout the dependency network.

1. To update node n, compute its new label L' as just described.
2. If the label has not changed, then return.
3. If n is a contradiction node:
   a. Mark all the environments of L' nogood.
   b. Remove all new nogoods from every node label.
4. If n is not a contradiction node, then recursively update all the consequences of n.

This algorithm is guaranteed to terminate with correct labels.

Although this algorithm is easy to understand, it is inefficient, as it repeatedly recomputes node labels in step 1. A more efficient version of this algorithm only propagates incremental changes to node labels. The following algorithm is used in the ATMS code we present later as well as in most actual ATMS implementations.

When a new justification J is supplied, the ATMS calls **PROPAGATE** $(J, \phi, \{\{\}\})$. The two other arguments are present because **PROPAGATE** can be invoked recursively. The arguments to procedure **PROPAGATE** are a justification, an optional antecedent node a (absence is indicated by ϕ), and I a set of environments just added to the label of a. The intuition behind the algorithm is that it assumes that node labels are correct before the introduction of the new justification and therefore only propagates the incremental changes caused by a new justification.

Algorithm 12.1 **(PROPAGATE**$((x_1 \wedge \cdots \wedge x_k \Rightarrow n), a, I)$**)**

1. [Compute the incremental label update.] $L =$ **WEAVE**$(a, I, \{x_1, \ldots, x_k\})$. If L is empty, return.
2. [Update label and recur.] **UPDATE**(L, n).

UPDATE adds a set of new potential label environments L to node n.

Algorithm 12.2 **(UPDATE**(L, n)**)**

1. [Detect nogoods.] If $n = \bot$, then call **NOGOOD**(E) on each environment $E \in L$ and return.
2. [Update n's label, ensuring minimality.]
   a. Delete every environment from L which is a superset of some label environment of n.

   b. Delete every environment from the label of n which is a superset of some element of L.

   c. Add every remaining environment of L to the label of n.

3. For every justification J in which n is mentioned as an antecedent:

   a. [Propagate the incremental change to n's label to its consequences.] Invoke **PROPAGATE**(J, n, L).

   b. [Remove subsumed and inconsistent environments from L.] Remove from L all environments no longer in n's label.

   c. [Early termination.] If $L = \{\}$, return.

WEAVE does the basic work sketched in steps 1 and 2 at the beginning of this section. It attempts to save work by only computing the incremental update produced when adding environments I to node a for a single justification with antecedents X.

Algorithm 12.3 **(WEAVE**(a, I, X)**)**

1. [Iterate over antecedent nodes.] Repeat the following steps for each $h \neq a$ in X and then return I.

2. [Incrementally construct the incremental label.] Let I' be the set of all environments formed by computing the union of an environment of I and an environment of h's label.

3. [Ensure that I' is minimal and contains no known inconsistency.] Remove from I' all duplicates and nogoods, as well as any environment subsumed by any other. Set I to I'.

NOGOOD is called whenever an environment E is newly discovered to be nogood by the propagation algorithm. It then removes all nogood environments from all labels.

Algorithm 12.4 **(NOGOOD**(E)**)**

1. Mark E as nogood.

2. Remove E and any superset from every node label.

This label propagation algorithm is easily shown to terminate, and through careful choice of datastructures, can be made very efficient.

12.3 Constructing solutions

The exact definition of a solution is task-specific and is determined by the inference engine. However, in practice, when using a single-context TMS, a solution to a problem-solving task is usually just a contradiction-free context for which no inference engine rules can be executed. We can read off the solution by examining what nodes hold in the current context. Of course, this kind of answer is meaningless for an ATMS. In this section we examine two techniques for identifying solutions.

12.3.1 Using a goal symbol

Many problem-solving tasks are reducible to the following simple model: There are a set of choice sets (characterized in terms of assumptions), and any solution must pick one choice from each set. Through a judicious addition of nodes and justifications, we can read off the solutions to the task from the label of one *goal* node. This is easily demonstrated through an example.

Consider a task which has 7 assumptions: A, B, C, D, E, F, G; where every solution must pick one of $\{A, B\}$, $\{E, F\}$, and $\{C, D, G\}$ respectively. All the additional nodes and justifications that make up the dependency network can be ignored. For each choice set we create a node A_i. A justification is added from each assumption to the nodes representing the choice set(s) it is in. Finally, we create a node $GOAL$ which has the single justification with all the A_i as antecedents. Figure 12.6 represents the resulting dependency network.

The label for the node $GOAL$ will contain all the solutions to the problem-solving task. Suppose we ignore all the task-specific justifications. In that case, the label for $GOAL$ consists of all twelve combinations of choices: $\{A, E, C\}, \{A, E, D\}, \ldots$. As problem solving proceeds, more nogoods are discovered, and these eliminate many of the environments in $GOAL$'s label. For example, the nogood $\{A, E\}$ eliminates three environments from $GOAL$'s label: $\{A, E, C\}, \{A, E, D\}$, and $\{A, E, G\}$, corresponding to three solutions that have become ruled out.

Although using labels to represent solutions is elegant, it leads to efficiency problems on larger tasks. Therefore, numerous techniques have been developed in the ATMS literature to improve efficiency when using

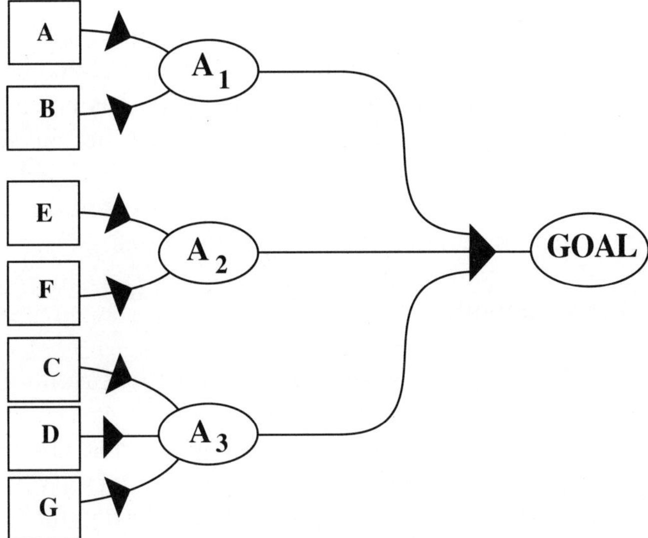

Figure 12.6 Constructing solutions by labeling *GOAL*

this technique. If the *GOAL* node and its justifications are created initially, then its label will be exponential in the size of the choice sets. This can be avoided by creating *GOAL* and its nodes after many or most nogoods have been discovered. This solution also deals with the difficulty that the choice sets defining the task may not be known at the outset of problem solving. Unfortunately, this approach raises a chicken-and-egg problem: to know whether problem solving is complete requires constructing the solutions, but constructing the solutions requires knowing that problem solving is complete. This issue is addressed by creating a sequence of *GOAL* nodes, each depending on the previous *GOAL* node and the new choice set. The labels of the intermediate *GOAL* nodes represent solutions at intermediate stages of problem solving.

12.3.2 Constructing solutions directly

The approach to constructing solutions outlined in the previous section has two major drawbacks. The first is that it relies on a general label updating algorithm, while the justification structure is very stylized. The second is that during problem solving many intermediate goals might be constructed and discarded, leaving large labels which are never looked at again but occupy a significant portion of available memory. Therefore, most ATMS implementations include a specialized solution construction procedure, called `interpretations`, which is given a set of choice sets and returns a set of environments representing the solutions. The result returned by this procedure is identical to the label of the *GOAL* node, except that it is achieved more efficiently and without the permanent introduction of new nodes and justifications.

12.3.3 Defaults

One of goals of TMSs is to support default reasoning (see Section 6.1.5). Although the ATMS itself is monotonic, it can support default reasoning. Defaults are widespread in AI applications, and many ATMS applications use them extensively. To implement defaults in an ATMS, one uses assumptions to represent points at which default inferences are introduced.

Consider the following example of default reasoning. Suppose we've heard a rumor of some person Nixon who is both a Quaker and a Republican, and we know that Quakers typically are pacifists, and that Republicans typically are not. We can frame this problem by creating three assumptions to represent the three defaults in this example: that Nixon exists, that a Quaker is a pacifist, and that a Republican is not a pacifist. Figure 12.7 illustrates a dependency network that encodes this.

A solution to a default reasoning task must be defined entirely differently. A solution is defined to be a consistent set of assumptions to which no other assumption can be added without introducing an inconsistency. Such solutions are sometimes referred to as *extensions* or *maximally consistent environments*. The dependency network of Figure 12.7 leads to one nogood:

{*Person-Nixon, Normal-Quaker, Normal-Republican*}.

Therefore, there are three solutions:

{*Person-Nixon, Normal-Quaker*},

{*Person-Nixon, Normal-Republican*},

{*Normal-Quaker, Normal-Republican*}.

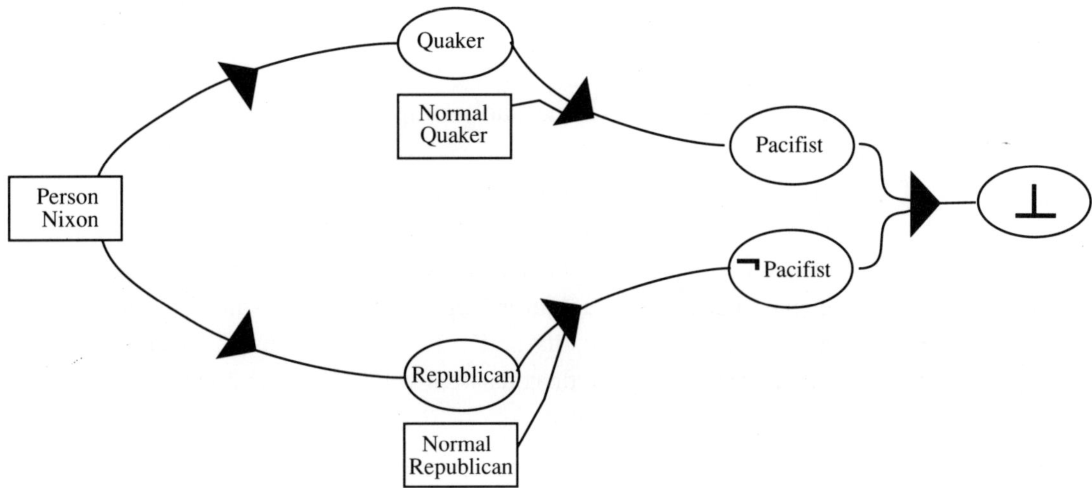

Figure 12.7 Who and what is Nixon?

Intuitively, these solutions correspond to the three possibilities: either Nixon is not a normal Quaker, or he is not a normal Republican, or he is not a real person. Notice that the semantics of default do not sanction the possibility that Nixon is neither a real person nor a normal Republican, because we can consistently add the assumption that he is a normal republican or a real person. The solution that he is a real person, *and* is both a normal Quaker and a normal Republican leads to an impossible inconsistency.

To simultaneously support both the default and the choice set paradigms for defining solutions, the ATMS `interpretations` procedure is supplied two arguments: the set of choice sets, and all the assumptions that are to be treated as defaults. This procedure returns solutions which have the property that they pick one choice from each choice set *and* that no default assumption can be added to them without introducing an inconsistency.

A construction analogous to that of Figure 12.6 is not possible for defaults. However, the basic ATMS can be extended to reason with defaults directly (see [2]).

12.4 The ATMS interface

The ATMS interface is remarkably simple.

change-atms	interpretations	remove-node
create-atms	just-antecedents	supporting-antecedent?
env-rules	just-consequence	tms-create-node
explain-node	just-informant	tms-node-datum
get-solutions	justify-node	tms-node-rules
in-antecedent?	node-consistent-with?	true-node?
in-node?	out-node?	

```
(create-atms title &key (node-string 'default-node-string)
                             (debugging nil)
                             (enqueue-procedure nil))
```

`create-atms` returns a datastructure that contains the entire state of an ATMS. Notice that there is no concept of contradiction handling.

An existing ATMS can be changed by `change-atms`, which takes the same keyword arguments as `create-atms`.

```
(true-node? node)
```

Returns `t` if the node holds universally, i.e., has a label consisting of the empty environment.

```
(in-node? node &optional env)
```

Returns `t` if the node holds in the consistent environment `env`. If `env` is not supplied, then `in-node?` returns `t` if the node holds in any environment.

```
(out-node? node env)
```

Returns `t` if the node does not hold in environment `env`.

```
(node-consistent-with? node env)
```

This returns `t` if there exists some consistent environment which is a superset of `env` in which the node holds. This effect could be achieved by creating two dummy nodes and a justification, but as this is such a common inference engine query, it is implemented more efficiently.

```
(tms-create-node atms datum &key assumptionp contradictoryp)
```

This is identical to the JTMS. A node can either have the assumption or contradictory property.

The inference engine can push Common Lisp objects (usually problem-solving rules) on the node slots `tms-node-rules`. When a new environment is subsequently added to the node's label, the ATMS calls `enqueue-procedure` of the ATMS on each of the objects on the rule list. Likewise the inference engine can push rules onto `env-rules`. Such rules are invoked when the environment becomes nogood.

```
(in-antecedent? antecedents)
```

This procedure is designed for more sophisticated inference engines that want to check whether the conjunction of a set of nodes has a non-empty label. This procedure can be used to check whether a given justification contributes to the label of some node.

```
(supporting-antecedent? nodes env)
```

This procedure is designed for more sophisticated inference engines. It checks whether the conjunction of the given set of nodes holds in the given environment.

```
(remove-node node)
```

This procedure is to be used with great care. It removes a node from the ATMS. However, this procedure will only work correctly if the given node does not itself appear in other justifications.

```
(justify-node informant consequent antecedents)
```

This is also identical to the JTMS.

```
(interpretations atms choice-sets &optional defaults)
```

`choice-sets` is a set of sets of assumptions. The ATMS returns a set of consistent environments in which at least one assumption from each set of `choice-sets` holds. This is the fundamental procedure for interpretation construction. `defaults` consists of a set of assumptions that will be interpreted as defaults for interpretation construction.

The contents of the `tms-node-datum` slot of a node is determined by the inference engine. To queue rules on nodes, the inference engine should place them on the `tms-node-rules` slot. The inference engine is also permitted to access the slots of a justification: `just-informant`, `just-antecedent`, and `just-consequence`.

```
(explain-node node env)
```

This returns an explanation for why `node` holds in environment `env`. `env` may be nogood. The explanation returned is a list of justifications or `(ASSUME ⟨assumption⟩))`.

Notice that the usual TMS procedures of `retract-assumption` and `enable-assumption` are irrelevant for an ATMS.

12.5 Simple example of ATMS usage

We illustrate the use of the ATMS on the example of Figure 6.9, which was analyzed by a JTMS in Section 7.9. First we must create a fresh ATMS for our example:

```
>   (setq *atms* (create-atms "Simple Example"))
```

Then we must create the initial three assumptions. Note that unlike the JTMS we do not need to enable these assumptions.

```
>   (setq assumption-a (tms-create-node *atms* "A" :ASSUMPTIONP t)
          assumption-c (tms-create-node *atms* "C" :ASSUMPTIONP t)
          assumption-e (tms-create-node *atms* "E" :ASSUMPTIONP t))
```

Then we introduce the node `h` and justify it:

```
>   (setq node-h (tms-create-node *atms* "h"))
>   (justify-node "R1" node-h (list assumption-c assumption-e))
```

We can look at the label of node node-h:

```
>   (why-node node-h)
<h,{{C, E}}>
```

Then we introduce node g, justify it, and then contradict it:

```
>   (setq node-g (tms-create-node *atms* "g"))
>   (justify-node "R2" node-g (list assumption-a assumption-c))
>   (setq contradiction (tms-create-node *atms* 'CONTRADICTION
                                                :CONTRADICTORYP t))
>   (justify-node "R3" contradiction (list node-g))
```

In a JTMS this last justification introduces a contradiction which invokes contradiction handling to retract one of A or C. However, here the ATMS simply records the new nogood {A,C} and removes it and its supersets from node labels. We can ask for the interpretations, assuming that all assumptions are defaults:

```
>   (mapc 'print-env (interpretations *atms* nil
                                        (atms-assumptions *atms*)))
```

The result is the two maximal interpretations:

```
E-8: A, E
E-5: C, E
```

12.5.1 The ATMS code

The code in `atms.lisp` is a simple assumption-based truth maintenance system. It is based on the algorithms presented earlier in this chapter. As with the previous JTMS and LTMS implementations, ATMS operations cannot be safely aborted, nor can one ATMS operation be safely invoked before another is finished, nor can multiple processes safely access the same ATMS simultaneously.

12.5.2 Overview

The program is divided into nine parts:

1. *Definitions.* The datastructures and initialization procedures.
2. *Common utilities.* Common macros and utility procedures used throughout the ATMS.
3. *Basic interface.* Interfaces for programs that use the ATMS.

4. *Label updating.* The core ATMS label update algorithm.
5. *Creating and extending environments.* Procedures to do simple manipulations on environments.
6. *Environment tables.* Algorithms for manipulating tables of environments.
7. *Processing nogoods.* Manipulation and recording of nogood environments.
8. *Interpretation construction.* Techniques for constructing interpretations.
9. *Printing.* Some simple procedures to allow the user to make queries of the ATMS database.

12.5.3 Definitions

Like the rest of our implementations, we use a single global ATMS datastructure instead of global variables, thereby allowing for multiple ATMS instances within a single problem solver. The `atms` datastructure contains the following fields:

`title` Ignored by the ATMS but useful for debugging.

`node-counter` Provides a unique name for nodes. Also is used to order the assumptions of an environment.

`just-counter` Provides a unique name for justifications.

`env-counter` Provides a unique name for environments.

`nodes` List of all nodes created. Used only for debugging.

`justs` List of all justifications supplied by the inference engine. Used only for debugging.

`contradictions` A list of all nodes which have been marked contradictory. Used only for debugging.

`assumptions` A list of all nodes which have been marked assumptions.

`debugging` A debugging flag to trace the internals of ATMS operations.

`nogood-table` An environment table containing all the unsubsumed nogoods.

`contra-node` An internal node created by the ATMS to encode contradictions.

`env-table` A table containing all the consistent environments that have ever been mentioned.

`empty-env` The empty environment consisting of no assumptions is commonly used.

`node-string` An inference engine-supplied procedure which should return a descriptive string for a node. The ATMS supplies a default.

`enqueue-procedure` This is a procedure that is called when a node becomes labeled `:IN`. This procedure should not do any ATMS operations itself, because it is called when the ATMS database is inconsistent.

The `tms-node` datastructure describes an ATMS node:

`index` Integer serving as unique name for this node.

`datum` Supplied by the inference engine. For simple demonstration systems, one should put something printable in here. For TRE-like system, a pointer to the assertion object goes here, as we will see later.

`label` A list of environments representing the set of minimal sets of assumptions that support belief in the node.

`justs` The set of justifications which could provide support for this node.

`consequences` The justifications which use this node as an antecedent.

`nogood?` If non-`nil`, this field indicates that belief in this node represents a contradiction. Note that any contradictory node will always have an empty label.

`assumption?` If non-`nil`, this field indicates that this node should be treated as an assumption. The initial label of an assumption node is the singleton environment mentioning itself.

`rules` Rules which should be run when the node's label receives an environment. The ATMS `enqueue-procedure` is called on each element of this field if it is non-`nil`. The queue is then cleared.

`atms` The ATMS instance to which this node belongs.

The ATMS justification `just` is identical to the JTMSs justification:

`index` Integer for unique name.

`informant` An inference engine-supplied description of the justification.

`consequence` The node which this justification can support.

`antecedents` The nodes that must be believed in order for this justification to provide support for its consequence.

The `env` datastructure represents ATMS environments:

`index` Integer for unique name.

`count` Number of assumptions in this environment.

`assumptions` The assumptions of the environment in sorted order.

`nodes` The nodes which have the environment in their labels.

`nogood?` This flag is non-`nil` when the environment is nogood. Note that if the environment is contradictory, it necessarily has no nodes.

`rules` Rules which are run when this environment becomes nogood.

Note that the fields `index`, `count`, and `assumptions` cannot change once the environment has been created.

12.5.4 Simple utilities

This section includes a set of utility procedures used throughout the ATMS implementation. `node-string`, `debugging`, and `default-node-string` play the same role as in the JTMS and LTMS implementation.

Often it is important to keep lists sorted. The procedure `ordered-insert` takes a `list` already in order and a new `item` to be added onto `list` and returns the new list (which shares structure with the input, but the original `list` is not side-effected). The argument `test` is the procedure which that orders list items. In this code, `test` is either the procedure `assumption-order` or `env-order`. The macro `ordered-push` provides a version of `ordered-insert` which stores the new list back to the variable.

12.5.5 Basic inference engine interface

The procedures `create-atms` and `change-atms` behave as their JTMS and LTMS counterparts. `true-node?`, `in-node?`, `out-node?`, and `node-consistent-with?` are 4 simple procedures to inquire about a node's label. `true-node?` returns `t` if the node holds in the empty environment (i.e., holds universally). `in-node?` returns `t` if the node holds in the environment supplied. These functions are usually intended to be supplied a consistent environment, but return useful results if supplied a nogood environment. For example, `in-node?` returns `t` if the node holds in some consistent environment which is a subset of the supplied environment. `out-node?` returns `t` if the node does not hold in the consistent environment supplied. `node-consistent-with?` holds if the node could hold in some consistent superset of the environment supplied. This is computed by checking if the union of some label environment with the supplied environment is consistent.

`tms-create-node` is exactly like its JTMS counterpart. Notice that it ensures that the initial label of an assumption is a singleton environment containing itself. `assume-node` changes a node from a non-assumption to an assumption. `make-contradiction` changes a node from a non-contradictory node to a contradiction. `justify-node` is exactly like its JTMS counterpart. The procedure `propagate` does all the label updating work. `contradiction` records the contradiction by simply justifying the known contradictory node with the nodes supplied.

12.5.6 Label updating

The guts of the label update algorithm are performed by the procedures of this section and the next. The procedures `propagate`, `weave`, and `update` perform exactly as outlined in Section 12.2. `update-label` is an auxiliary procedure to `update`. The procedure `update` includes additional functionality to maintain ATMS datastructures. It ensures that the `nodes` slot of all environments is always correct. If an environment is added to a node's label, then that node is also added to that environment's node list. Conversely, if an environment is removed from some node's label, that node is also removed from that environment's node list. Also, if an environment is added to any node, the `enqueue-procedure` is called on every element of its `rules` slot.

The procedure `in-antecedent?` uses `weave?` to check whether any union of antecedent environments is consistent. The procedure `supporting-antecedent?` uses `in-node?` to check whether each of the antecedent nodes holds in a given environment. The procedure `remove-node` removes nodes from the ATMS. It simply removes this node from all relevant datastructures. If this node appeared as an antecedent in any justification, then removing the node would require a complicated analysis of all affected nodes. Therefore this procedure only works in the case where the node appears in no other justifications. It should be used with great caution. It is used in ATCON (Chapter 16).

12.5.7 Creating and extending environments

The procedures in this section ensure that one unique instance of the `env` datastructure is assigned to every environment. This is important for quickly determining the consequences of a contradiction and streamlining ATMS operations. The most basic way to create a new `env` structure is `create-env`, which presumes that the set of assumptions supplied is properly sorted (via `assumption-order`) and that no datastructure has yet been created for this environment. It should only be called after failing to discover it in the environment tables (see next section). `union-env` returns the environment resulting from the union of its two arguments. `cons-env` returns the environment resulting from adding an assumption to an environment.

12.5.8 Env tables

The ATMS maintains two tables in identical formats. `atms-env-table` contains all environments created during ATMS processing. `atms-nogood-table` contains all unsubsumed nogoods discovered so far. The table groups environments by their size. The table consists of a set of buckets, each bucket consisting of an integer indicating the size of all environments in this bucket, followed by these environments. The table is kept sorted, so smaller environments come first. The procedure `insert-in-table` adds an environment to a table. The nogood table is used to check whether newly created environments are subsumed by known nogoods. The environment table is used to ensure that a single, unique datastructure is created for each distinct set of assumptions.

The procedure `lookup-env` sees whether an `env` structure has already been created for the environment specified by the assumptions. It presumes the assumptions are properly ordered. The procedure `subset-env?` checks whether the assumptions of `e1` are a subset of `e2`. Many ATMS procedures need to compare two environments. So `compare-env` returns `:EQ` if its two arguments are identical, `:S12` if the first is a proper subset of the second, and `:S21` if the second is a proper subset of the first.

12.5.9 Processing nogoods

`new-nogood` is called whenever the ATMS discovers that an environment, thus far presumed to be consistent, is nogood. It first removes the newly nogood environment from all the node labels it appears in by calling `remove-env-from-labels`. It then adds the new nogood to the nogood table. Then it removes any subsumed nogoods from the table. The nogood table is kept in minimal form because every new environment must be checked to see whether it is nogood by comparing it to every nogood in the nogood table. Finally, it checks all existing environments to see whether they are subsumed by the new nogood, and marks them nogood as well. These environments are removed from node labels as well. The procedure `set-env-contradictory` is called whenever a new `env` is created. If the newly created `env` is subsumed by some nogood in the nogood table, then the new environment is nogood as well. The procedure `remove-env-from-labels` is an auxiliary procedure to remove nogoods from labels.

12.5.10 Generating explanations

Constructing explanations for ATMS deductions is surprisingly subtle because the ATMS does not maintain a current context, nor keep track of which justifications are responsible for particular label environments. The procedure `explain-node` constructs an explanation for why `node` follows from the set of assumptions represented by `env`. It is important to note that the naive way of constructing explanations by just recursively identifying any justification that supports a label environment is not guaranteed to construct well-founded explanations if the dependency graph contains cycles. The only way to truly find a non-circular support is to ignore the node labels and trace back through the justifications.

12.5.11 Interpretation construction

`interpretations` is the basic procedure to create interpretations. The main work is done by two auxiliary procedures. `get-depth-solutions` constructs solutions by simple depth-first backtrack search. `extend-via-defaults` takes every interpretation that satisfies the `choice-sets` and adds as many defaults to it as possible. These two procedures are extremely primitive and inefficient.

12.5.12 Printing

The final procedures in the file `atms.lisp` provide convenient ways of printing and inspecting ATMS datastructures. Most of these functions are used for debugging only.

`why-node` prints out the label of a node. `why-nodes` prints out the labels of all ATMS nodes. `node-justifications` prints out the justifications for a node. `print-justification` prints out a single justification. `e` finds the environment with a specific index. `print-env` prints out an environment as a set of assumptions. `env-string` is a general procedure which returns a string describing an environment. `print-nogoods` prints out all current unsubsumed nogoods. `print-envs` prints out all environments in the environment table. `print-atms-statistics` prints out the sizes of two main ATMS tables.

12.6 Exercises

1. ⋆ The label for *GOAL* (see Figure 12.6) can also be constructed by a binary tree of justifications. Pick a slightly larger example and show how. What are the advantages and disadvantages of this?
2. ⋆⋆ Ignoring efficiency, implement the functionality of an ATMS with the JTMS.
3. ⋆⋆ Show a set of justifications which cause the number of environments the ATMS constructs to be exponential in the number of these justifications.

4. ⋆ Interpretation construction is in some sense a form of dependency-directed search, carried out with respect to the logical constraints that already exist in the ATMS justification database. Sometimes there are additional constraints that solutions must satisfy, and the results of `interpretations` will be filtered further. These constraints may be very expensive to apply, and hence they are not done antecedently. Yet there is a tradeoff, since intermediate interpretation bulge can bring one's machine to a crashing halt. Define a *filter procedure* as a procedure that takes an environment and returns non-`nil` if it satisfies the constraints of interest.

   a. Write a version of `interpretations` that invokes filter functions when it appears that intermediate interpretation bulge is occurring.

   b. The file `aqueens.lisp` solves the N-queens puzzle by antecedently installing nogoods. Rewrite this system to use filter procedures instead.

5. ⋆⋆⋆ Bit vectors are a more efficient representation of assumption sets, if the number of assumptions is not too large. Each bit position is assigned to a particular assumption. The bit is set to `1` if the assumption is in the set, and set to `0` if not. Rewrite `atms.lisp` to use bit vectors to represent assumption sets.

6. For many problems, not all logically consistent solutions are equal. People have preferences, and one can view solutions as being at least partially ordered by these preferences. Consider, for example, the problem of finding an assignment of groups in an organization to rooms and floors in a new building. While many consistent solutions exist, there is a wide variation in desirability. Some groups will benefit from close spatial contiguity with others. Some groups may prefer not to be near others. In some cases, special facilities needed by groups impose important constraints on location.

   a. ⋆⋆⋆ Develop a representation for the topological and spatial relationships between the different rooms of a building.

   b. ⋆⋆⋆ Develop a representation for preference criteria which uses the spatial vocabulary.

c. ⋆⋆⋆ Develop a program that uses these representations to produce reasonable solutions to this spatial planning problem.

d. ⋆⋆⋆⋆ Test this program on a real organization and a real building.

7. ⋆⋆ An intriguing possibility is to allow the ATMS to accept arbitrary clauses as input. Such a program might have the same advantages over the ATMS as the LTMS has over the JTMS. Using `atms.lisp` as a base, implement a simple version of such a TMS. How difficult will it be to ensure logical completeness?

8. ⋆⋆ Interpretation construction is just conventional backtrack search (assuming no defaults). Implement an interpretation constructor which uses the conventional techniques of forward checking and future variable reordering to improve search efficiency. Such an interpretation constructor dynamically reorders the choice sets by size (future variable reordering) and remove choices from as-yet-unconsidered choice sets which are guaranteed to be inconsistent with the solution constructed so far (forward checking).

9. ⋆⋆ A constraint satisfaction problem (CSP) is specified by a set of variables each having a domain set of possible variables and a set of constraints among subsets of the variables. A constraint can be specified by listing all the allowable combinations of variable values. We don't bother listing constraints that are universal. A solution is an assignment of values to variables which satisfies all the constraints. (We describe CSPs in more detail in Section 18.1.) A familiar CSP problem consists of three variables x, y, and z, with respective domains $D_x = \{a, b\}, D_y = \{e, f\}$, and $D_z = \{e, d, g\}$. The constraints are $C_{xy} = \{be, bf\}, C_{xz} = \{bc, bd, bg\}$, and $C_{yz} = \{ed, fg\}$. One solution is $x = b, y = e, z = d$. Using one of the two methods for constructing solutions, write a simple Common Lisp procedure for solving CSP problems. The example problem could be specified by:

```
(csp '((x a b)
       (y e f)
       (z c d g))
     '(((x y) (b e) (b f))
       ((x z) (b c) (b d) (b g))
       ((y z) (e d) (f g))))
```

What are the results of the following examples? Explain.

```
(csp '((n1 r g b)
       (n2 r g b)
       (n3 r g b))
     '(((n1 n2) (r g) (r b) (g r) (g b) (b r) (b g))
       ((n2 n3) (r g) (r b) (g r) (g b) (b r) (b g))
       ((n1 n3) (r g) (r b) (g r) (g b) (b r) (b g))))

(csp '((n1 r g b)
       (n2 r g b)
       (n3 r g b)
       (n4 r g b))
     '(((n1 n2) (r g) (r b) (g r) (g b) (b r) (b g))
       ((n2 n3) (r g) (r b) (g r) (g b) (b r) (b g))
       ((n1 n3) (r g) (r b) (g r) (g b) (b r) (b g))
       ((n1 n4) (r g) (r b) (g r) (g b) (b r) (b g))
       ((n2 n4) (r g) (r b) (g r) (g b) (b r) (b g))
       ((n3 n4) (r g) (r b) (g r) (g b) (b r) (b g))))
```

12.7 Bibliography

[1] de Kleer, J., "An assumption-based truth maintenance system," *Artificial Intelligence* 28 (1986): 127–162. Also in Ginsberg, M.L. (ed.), Morgan-Kaufmann, 280–297.

[2] Dressler, O., "Extending the basic ATMS, *Proceedings of ECAI-88*, 535–540.

13 Improving the Completeness of Truth Maintenance Systems

The LTMS implementation of Chapter 9 achieves a subtle balance between two tensions. On the one hand it has sufficient expressive power to represent arbitrary formulas. On the other hand it is based on an efficient but incomplete Boolean constraint propagation algorithm. On average, the BCP-based LTMS achieves an excellent balance between computational tractability and logical expressibility. However, the incompleteness of BCP means that sometimes we cannot obtain the inferences we desire. Although it is often better to leave the inference engine to deal with this incompleteness, sometimes it is useful to have a more complete LTMS. Analogously, the ATMS implementation of Chapter 12 accepts only Horn clause justifications. We would like to be able to generalize the ATMS to accept arbitrary clauses and formulas.

This chapter addresses a collection of techniques to improve the completeness of TMSs to varying degrees. It is important to realize at the outset of this chapter that any improved degree of completeness invariably comes at significant computational cost. Therefore, the techniques of this chapter are impractical for many problem-solving tasks. Nevertheless, they represent the logical generalization of TMS systems, and are extremely useful for some tasks.

Unlike the other TMS chapters, which follow a single line of development, this chapter presents a collection of ideas to extend the TMSs we have seen. However, the fundamental idea of *prime implicate* will underlie all of them. (Intuitively, a prime implicate is a minimal clause that follows logically from the information the inference engine has provided.) This chapter is organized as follows. First, we show how to extend a BCP-based LTMS to arbitrary formulas by exploiting prime implicates. Second, we show that through the use of prime implicates an LTMS can be made logically complete. Third, we briefly discuss a simple way of producing an ATMS that operates on formulas and is logically complete. Fourth, as prime implicate algorithms are typically extremely slow, we spend considerable effort analyzing how to make these algorithms more efficient. Finally, as in all the preceding chapters, we provide Common Lisp code to illustrate how these ideas can be implemented.

13.1 Extending BCP to formulas

The core idea of BCP is that of propagating labels through a dependency network of clauses. We can extend the BCP concept to propagate labels through networks of arbitrary formulas. In this generalized BCP, a label propagates through a formula in essentially the same way as through clauses: the known literals of the formula force some unknown literal of the formula. Such a BCP still propagates labels locally and therefore is relatively efficient, although still incomplete.

In Section 9.4 we examined a scheme for expanding any formula into a logically equivalent set of clauses. Why doesn't BCP on these clauses have the same results as BCP would produce on the original formulas? Consider a simple example:

$$(x \Rightarrow (y \vee z)) \wedge (x \vee y \vee z).$$

From y labeled `:FALSE` BCP concludes from this single formula that z is labeled `:TRUE`. One way to see this is to imagine what would be the case if x were known. If x were labeled `:TRUE`, then, by the implication in the first conjunct, z would have to be labeled `:TRUE`. If x were labeled `:FALSE`, then to satisfy the second conjunct, z would have to be labeled `:TRUE`. As x must be either true or false, z should be labeled `:TRUE`. Expanding the formula produces two clauses, one for each of the two cases. We can no longer draw the same conclusion, since it depended on the combination of the two cases:

$$\neg x \vee y \vee z,$$

$$x \vee y \vee z.$$

Running clausal-BCP on these two clauses does not label z `:TRUE`.

This example shows that the results of running BCP on a set of formulas does not produce the same results as running BCP on the clauses produced by converting those formulas to CNF. In general, BCP on the formulas is always stronger (i.e., labels more nodes `:TRUE`/`:FALSE` or detects more contradictions) than BCP on the corresponding clauses. Hence, we cannot directly use the efficient BCP algorithms that have been developed for clauses for arbitrary formulas, and no correspondingly efficient BCP algorithm is known for arbitrary formulas. When the dependency network consists solely of clauses, propagation can be made efficient because we just store a counter with each clause that is incremented and decremented as the labels of its literals change (see Section 9.9). We would like an analogously simple scheme for formulas, not just clauses. What we seek is a simple test which, given a current set of labels for symbols and a formula, determines whether the formula violates the labeling or forces additional symbols to be labeled `:TRUE`/`:FALSE`. Later we lay out a scheme that achieves this. The basic intuition is to encode every formula as a logically equivalent set of clauses, which includes logically redundant clauses which describe all the ways the formula can be violated or force a symbol's label. The encoding of Section 9.4 does not achieve this because although the CNF encoding is formally equivalent *given the complete inference rules of propositional logic* to the original formula, it is not equivalent given the incomplete unit resolution strategy clausal-BCP is based on. The key idea is that we can add additional clauses which produce an equivalent set of clauses given unit resolution. In order to do this we must go through some formal preliminaries.

13.1.1 Some basic formalities

Our formula-BCP algorithm is based on extending our encoding of formulas into clauses such that clausal-BCP on the resulting clauses produces the same labeling as formula-BCP on the original formulas. To achieve this we must define some basic terminology.

Definition 13.1

For every symbol s, s and $\neg s$ are complementary literals. A clause is a disjunction of literals with no literal repeated and no complementary literals.

Definition 13.2
An implicate of a formula or a set of formulas C is a clause entailed by C.

If we replace every formula with its entire set of implicates, then BCP on the resulting set of implicates produces the same result as BCP on the original formulas. Returning to our example, reducing

$$(x \Rightarrow (y \vee z)) \wedge (x \vee y \vee z), \tag{13.1}$$

to CNF produces two clauses:

$$\neg x \vee y \vee z, \qquad x \vee y \vee z.$$

However, the clause,

$$y \vee z,$$

is also an implicate of the formula. The addition of this clause allows clausal-BCP on the implicates to produce the same result as formula-BCP on the original formulas. In this example, adding this third implicate to the encoded formula was sufficient to achieve formula-BCP. In general, we may have to add a large number of such implicates.

Unfortunately, there may be a very large number of implicates, most of which are redundant. Suppose two implicates of a formula are:

$$a \vee b \vee c,$$

$$a \vee b.$$

The first clause $a \vee b \vee c$ is both logically redundant and has no value to BCP. There are only four ways BCP can use the clause $a \vee b \vee c$. If the clause is used to force b `:TRUE`, then a and c must have been `:FALSE` and the second clause will force b to be `:TRUE` also. The situation is identical for a. If the first clause is used to force c `:TRUE`, then both a and b must be `:FALSE` and the second clause is violated. Finally, if the first clause is violated, then the second clause is necessarily violated. Therefore, the clause $a \vee b \vee c$ can be safely removed. We say this clause is *subsumed* by the clause $a \vee b$.

Definition 13.3
Clause A subsumes clause B if all the literals of A appear in B.

Generalizing the preceding shows that:

Theorem 13.1
Suppose C is a set of clauses and $C' \subset C$ are the clauses of C not subsumed by any other. BCP on C produces the same labels as BCP on C'.

Notice that in formula 13.1, if we have the implicate $y \vee z$, it is unnecessary to have the two clauses:

$$\neg x \vee y \vee z,$$

$$x \vee y \vee z.$$

Definition 13.4
A prime implicate of a formula C is an implicate of C which is not subsumed by any other implicate of C.

Therefore it is sufficient to only use the prime implicates in our encoding. This greatly reduces the number of implicates needed to achieve formula-BCP.

Theorem 13.2
Given a set of formulas $\mathcal{F}$ and the union, $\mathcal{I}$, of the prime implicates of each individual formula of $\mathcal{F}$, then BCP on $\mathcal{F}$ produces the same labeling as BCP on $\mathcal{I}$.

Proof We presume BCP is sound. As each formula is individually replaced by its prime implicates, BCP on $\mathcal{I}$ cannot label any symbol that BCP on $\mathcal{F}$ does not. We do the reverse direction by proof by contradiction. Suppose BCP on formula $b \in \mathcal{F}$ labels symbol s while BCP on the prime implicates of b does not. If s is labeled `:TRUE` let x be the literal s, and if s is labeled `:FALSE` let x be the literal $\neg s$. Given BCP on b labels s it must be the case that,

$$A_1 \wedge \cdots \wedge A_n \wedge x_1 \wedge \cdots \wedge x_m \Rightarrow x$$

follows from b alone where the x_i are literals involving symbols of b, and A_i are assumption literals. Therefore, the clause

$$\neg A_1 \vee \cdots \vee \neg A_n \vee \neg x_1 \vee \cdots \vee \neg x_m \vee x$$

is an implicate of $\{b\}$ alone. Therefore, it either is or is subsumed by a prime implicate of $\{b\}$. As this prime implicate necessarily contains x, BCP on this implicate must have labeled x true. ∎

Returning to the example in Section 13.1, the formula

$$(x \Rightarrow (y \vee z)) \wedge (x \vee y \vee z), \tag{13.2}$$

has only one prime implicate:

$$y \vee z.$$

However, the CNF transformation of the formula produces the two clauses:

$$\neg x \vee y \vee z, \qquad x \vee y \vee z.$$

This example illustrates that there may be fewer prime implicates than conjunctions in the conventional CNF. Unfortunately, the reverse is usually the case. Consider the clause set:

$$\neg a \vee b,$$

$$\neg c \vee d,$$

$$\neg c \vee e,$$

$$\neg b \vee \neg d \vee \neg e.$$

All four are prime implicates, but there are three more:

$$\neg a \vee \neg d \vee \neg e,$$

$$\neg b \vee \neg c,$$

$$\neg a \vee \neg c.$$

13.1.2 A simple algorithm for constructing prime implicates

The key step in computing prime implicates consists of a resolution rule called consensus[4, 7, 8]. Given two clauses:

$$x \vee \beta,$$

$$\neg x \vee \gamma,$$

where x is a symbol and β and γ are (possibly empty) disjunctions of literals, the consensus of these two clauses with respect to x is the clause

$\beta \vee \gamma,$

with duplicate literals removed. If the two clauses have more than one pair of complementary literals, then the consensus would contain complementary literals and is discarded (since it is a logical tautology).

The consensus of any two clauses is necessarily an implicate of those two clauses. Intuitively this can be seen as follows. Consider any labeling satisfying all the clauses. If x is `:FALSE`, then one of the literals of β must be `:TRUE`. On the other hand if x is `:TRUE`, then one of the literals of γ must be true. As x must be `:TRUE` or `:FALSE`, one of the literals of β or γ must be `:TRUE`.

The prime implicates of a set of clauses can be computed by repeatedly adding the consensus of any pair of clauses to the set and continually removing all subsumed clauses (until no further consensus and subsumption is possible). In our simple example, this process was particularly simple:

$$(x \Rightarrow (y \vee z)) \wedge (x \vee y \vee z)$$

expands into two clauses,

$$\neg x \vee y \vee z, \qquad x \vee y \vee z,$$

which are reduced to one prime implicate:

$$y \vee z.$$

This prime implicate is the result of computing the consensus of the two CNF clauses:

$$\begin{array}{l} \neg x \vee y \vee z \\ x \vee y \vee z \\ \hline y \vee z. \end{array}$$

The result subsumes the two original clauses; therefore, this is the only prime implicate.

The following algorithm finds the prime implicates of an arbitrary formula:

***Algorithm 13.1* (BRUTE-FORCE)**

1. Let $\mathcal{P}$ (the result) be $\{\}$.

2. Let Q be the set of clauses obtained by converting the formula to CNF.
3. Take the first clause q off of Q. If none, we are done.
4. If q is subsumed by any clause of $\mathcal{P}$, then go back to step 3.
5. Remove all clauses of $\mathcal{P}$ that are subsumed by q.
6. Try to compute the consensus of q and every clause in $\mathcal{P}$. Whenever the consensus exists, add it to Q.
7. Add q to $\mathcal{P}$.
8. Go to step 3.

Suppose the formula expands into the following CNF clauses:

$$\neg a \vee b, \tag{1}$$

$$\neg c \vee d, \tag{2}$$

$$\neg c \vee e, \tag{3}$$

$$\neg b \vee \neg d \vee \neg e. \tag{4}$$

We start with clause 1, it is not subsumed, and as P is empty, we immediately move it to $\mathcal{P} = \{1\}$. Q is now $\{2, 3, 4\}$. Clause 2 is not subsumed by clause 1, nor does it resolve with it. Therefore $\mathcal{P} = \{1, 2\}$ and $Q = \{3, 4\}$. Similarly, after processing clause 3, $\mathcal{P} = \{1, 2, 3\}$ and $Q = \{4\}$. Clause 4 is not subsumed by any other in $\mathcal{P}$, therefore the algorithm continues to step 6 and it is resolved with every clause in $\mathcal{P}$. The consensus of clauses 1 and 4 is

$$\neg a \vee \neg d \vee \neg e. \tag{5}$$

The consensus of clauses 2 and 4 is

$$\neg b \vee \neg c \vee \neg e. \tag{6}$$

The consensus of clauses 3 and 4 is

$$\neg b \vee \neg c \vee \neg d. \tag{7}$$

Clause 4 is added to $\mathcal{P}$ and $Q = \{7, 6, 5\}$. Clause 7 is not subsumed by any other clause in $\mathcal{P}$ therefore, the algorithm continues to step 6 and it is resolved with every other clause in $\mathcal{P}$. The consensus of clauses 2 and 7 is

$$\neg b \vee \neg c. \tag{8}$$

The consensus of clauses 1 and 7 yields

$$\neg a \vee \neg c \vee \neg d. \tag{9}$$

Clause 7 is added to $\mathcal{P}$ and $Q = \{9, 8, 6, 5\}$. Clause 9 is not subsumed by any other clause in $\mathcal{P}$, therefore the algorithm continues to step 6 and it is resolved with every other clause in $\mathcal{P}$. The consensus of clauses 2 and 9 is

$$\neg a \vee \neg c. \tag{10}$$

Clause 9 is added to $\mathcal{P}$ and $Q = \{10, 8, 6, 5\}$. Clause 10 is not subsumed by any clause in $\mathcal{P}$. However, clause 9 is subsumed by clause 10 and is thus removed from $\mathcal{P}$. Resolving clause 10 with every other produces no new results. Clause 10 is then added to $\mathcal{P}$ (which now consists of the clauses $\{10, 7, 4, 3, 2, 1\}$) and the queue consists of $\{8, 6, 5\}$. Clause 8 is not subsumed by any clause in $\mathcal{P}$. However, clause 7 is subsumed by clause 8 and thus is removed from $\mathcal{P}$. The consensus of clauses 1 and 8 is

$$\neg a \vee \neg c. \tag{11}$$

Clause 8 is added to $\mathcal{P}$ (which now consists of $\{10, 8, 4, 3, 2, 1\}$) and $Q = \{11, 6, 5\}$. The next clause to process, 11, is the same as clause 10 (i.e., is subsumed) and is discarded. The queue now consists of clauses $\{6, 5\}$. Likewise, clause 6 is subsumed by clause 8 and is discarded, leaving $Q = \{5\}$. Clause 5 is not subsumed by any clause in $\mathcal{P}$. The consensus of clauses 3 and 5 is

$$\neg a \vee \neg c \vee \neg d. \tag{5'}$$

The consensus of clauses 2 and 5 is

$$\neg c \vee \neg e \vee \neg a.$$

Clause 5 is added to $\mathcal{P}$, producing $\{10, 8, 5, 4, 3, 2, 1\}$. Both the new clauses produced are subsumed by a clause in $\mathcal{P}$. Thus, these are the prime implicates of the clause set $\{1, 2, 3, 4\}$.

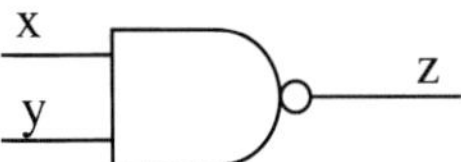

Figure 13.1 A NAND gate

Table 13.1
Truth table for NAND gate

x	y	z
:TRUE	:TRUE	:FALSE
:FALSE	:TRUE	:TRUE
:TRUE	:FALSE	:TRUE
:FALSE	:FALSE	:TRUE

13.1.3 The importance of formula-BCP

The basic advantage of formula-BCP is that it enhances the logical completeness of the LTMS without paying an excessive penalty in computational performance. Under what circumstances is this enhanced completeness useful? In this section we examine three examples in detail. The basic intuition behind the examples is that often it is more natural for an inference engine to operate with formulas (or sets of clauses considered as single units). For those cases, the prime implicate encoding of clauses provides the extra information BCP needs.

Suppose that we are building a reasoner for digital circuits. This reasoner should be able to predict circuit outputs from its inputs as well as inputs from outputs. Digital components are specified in terms of truth tables. The NAND gate of Figure 13.1 has the truth table illustrated in Table 13.1. One could encode this truth table for the LTMS as a conjunction of four implications corresponding to the four rows of the truth table:

$$x \wedge y \rightarrow \neg z,$$

$$\neg x \wedge y \rightarrow z,$$

$$x \wedge \neg y \rightarrow z,$$

$$\neg x \wedge \neg y \rightarrow z.$$

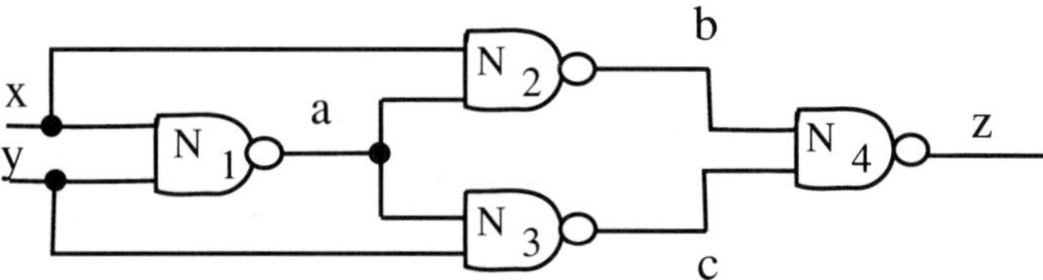

Figure 13.2 An XOR gate built up from NAND gates

Suppose we know that z is `:FALSE` but y is `:UNKNOWN`. In this case, x remains `:UNKNOWN` using BCP, which is not at all what we want. If instead we replace the formula with its prime implicates we get

$\neg x \vee \neg y \vee \neg z,$

$x \vee z,$

$y \vee z.$

Using BCP on the prime implicates, it is possible to make the desired inference: if z is `:FALSE`, BCP labels x `:TRUE` regardless of y's label.

Suppose we wish to model an exclusive or (XOR) gate built up out of four more primitive NAND gates as illustrated in Figure 13.2. If we describe each NAND gate by the three prime implicates just discussed, then we will not be able to infer from z `:TRUE` and y `:TRUE` that x must be `:FALSE`. Consider the prime implicates for the NAND gate N_4. As both b and c are `:UNKNOWN`, the fact that z and y are `:TRUE` does not force any other value. However, treating the conjunction of all four models as a single formula and expanding it to its prime implicates yields twenty-eight clauses. Only four of those prime implicates constrain the input-output variables x, y, and z:

$\neg x \vee \neg y \vee \neg z,$

$x \vee y \vee \neg z,$

$x \vee \neg y \vee z,$

$\neg x \vee y \vee z.$

From these prime implicates we can see that we can now infer that x must be `:FALSE` from z `:TRUE` and y `:TRUE`.

Suppose our task is to build a composite model of the two-pipe system shown in Figure 13.3 that characterizes how pressure varies with flow.

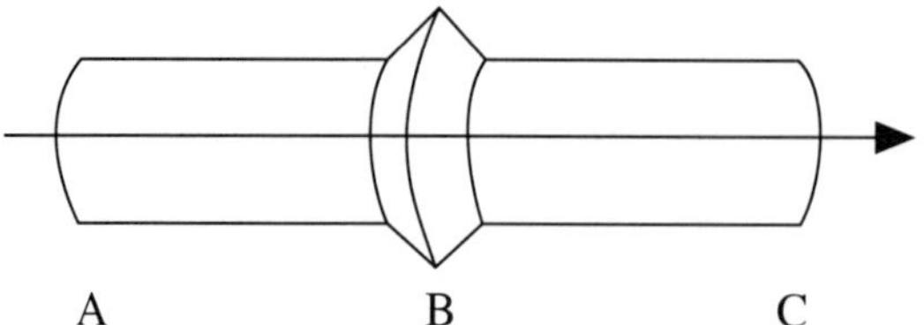

Figure 13.3 Building a model of two pipes

Each pipe is modeled by the qualitative equation (see [1]) $[dP_l] - [dP_r] = [dQ]$ where P_l is the pressure on the left, P_r is the pressure on the right, and Q is the flow from left to right. ($[dx]$ denotes the sign (+, 0, −) of $\frac{dx}{dt}$). Thus, the attached pipes are completely modeled by three qualitative equations:

$$[dP_A] - [dP_B] = [dQ_{AB}], \tag{13.3}$$

$$[dP_B] - [dP_C] = [dQ_{BC}], \tag{13.4}$$

$$[dQ_{AB}] = [dQ_{BC}]. \tag{13.5}$$

An inference engine can encode these equations as follows. Each qualitative variable x is encoded as a taxonomic formula:

$$tax(x = +, x = 0, x = -).$$

Each qualitative equation is expanded into a set of clauses listing all the combinations of values disallowed by qualitative addition. For example, $x + y = 0$ expands to:

$$\neg(x = +) \vee \neg(y = +),$$

$$\neg(x = +) \vee \neg(y = 0),$$

$$\neg(x = 0) \vee \neg(y = +),$$

$$\neg(x = 0) \vee \neg(y = -),$$

$$\neg(x = -) \vee (y = 0),$$

$$\neg(x = -) \vee \neg(y = -).$$

Suppose we know that the pressure is rising at A (i.e., $[dP_A] = +$) and the pressure is fixed at C (i.e., $[dP_C] = 0$). Applying BCP to the clause set does not produce any useful inferences. This can be seen directly from looking at the qualitative equations. Considering each component or qualitative equation individually, we cannot infer anything about the flows. We only know one of the three variables in the first and second qualitative equations, and none of the variables in third. Therefore, none of the equations, individually, can be used to infer a new variable value. The only way to determine the behavior is to somehow solve the equations—but that requires global reasoning over the entire set of equations.

If we compute the prime implicates of the conjunction of the entire set of clauses, they include the prime implicate:

$$\neg([dP_A] = +) \vee \neg([dP_C] = 0) \vee ([dQ_{AB}] = +).$$

Hence, BCP can infer that $[dQ_{AB}] = +$ and from this $[dQ_{BC}] = +$. This example illustrates that in the context of qualitative physics, compiling a model into its prime implicates allows simple propagation (BCP) to derive inputs from outputs and vice versa. Using qualitative algebra we can solve the qualitative equations to obtain:

$$[dP_A] - [dP_C] = [dQ_{AB}] = [dQ_{BC}].$$

If we reduce this qualitative equation to its prime implicates, we obtain the same result as before. As the combination of two pipes occurs commonly, we can compile these prime implicates and include them in a model library so that we need not repeatedly compute the prime implicates for every two-pipe combination.

13.2 A complete LTMS

Let us review (from Section 9.5) how clausal-BCP is incomplete. If clausal-BCP is given the two clauses

$$x \vee \neg y,$$

$$x \vee y,$$

it cannot determine that x should be labeled `:TRUE`. BCP fails to do this because x does not follow from either one of these two clauses alone.

If BCP is given the following four clauses:

$x \vee y$,

$x \vee \neg y$,

$\neg x \vee \neg y$,

$\neg x \vee y$,

it fails to detect that the database is contradictory.

BCP is refutation-complete and partially literal-complete for a broader range of clause types. In particular, BCP is refutation-complete for any clause set which, by substituting literals with their negations, can be put in Horn clause form (note that it is not necessary to actually do the substitution for BCP to work) [3, 5]. Analogously, BCP will be literal-complete for the positive literals in the substituted clause set.

There are, however, many trivial syntactic checks that sometimes indicate the existence of a substitution that can transform the clause set into Horn clauses. If a symbol only occurs negatively or positively (often called a *dangling literal*), then only clauses not mentioning that literal need be Horn for BCP to be complete. If a symbol occurs only once positively in a Horn clause and otherwise only occurs in negative clauses, then it can be replaced by its negation in an attempt to make more clauses Horn (this substitution must be applied sequentially). (In these conversions, any assumptions must be taken into account, as well, and can prevent a conversion from being of any use.)

13.2.1 An inefficient full LTMS

The prime implicate idea provides the conceptual basis for a logically complete LTMS for formulas. The intuition is basically that if we regard the database as a single formula (the conjunction of all its constituents), and replace this single formula with its prime implicates, then the resulting clausal-BCP is logically complete:

Theorem 13.3
Suppose that the set of clauses $\mathcal{I}$ is the set of prime implicates of some set of formulas. Then BCP on $\mathcal{I}$ is logically complete.

Proof We presume BCP is sound. We must show that the theorem holds for any initial set of assumptions $\mathcal{A}$. Suppose that literal x logically follows from $\mathcal{I}$ and assumptions $A_1, \ldots, A_n$ (possibly none). If x follows from $A_1, \ldots, A_n$, then the formula,

$$A_1 \wedge \cdots \wedge A_n \Rightarrow x,$$

which in clausal form is

$$\neg A_1 \vee \cdots \vee \neg A_n \vee x,$$

must be an implicate of $\mathcal{I}$ and thus subsumed by some clause of $\mathcal{I}$. In one step, BCP will deduce x is `:TRUE` from all the $\mathcal{A}$. ■

Unfortunately, the number of prime implicates of a set of formulas is often exponential in the size of the formula. Therefore, unless the formula representing the encoding of the entire database is small, this technique is somewhat impractical. Nevertheless, there is a class of circumstances where this can be the right thing to do. Suppose we are performing a qualitative simulation task and we want to analyze the same device over and over again with slightly different inputs. Suppose the device has n inputs, each of which can be one of $+$, 0, or $-$. By computing the prime implicates of the device it is now possible to instantly read off the outputs for any given set of inputs. In effect, we have cached 3^n simulations. Whether this is the right approach or not is a time-space tradeoff. For smaller devices, it may often be worth it. From the resulting database of prime implicates one can determine the inputs from the outputs just as easily as the outputs from the inputs. So the same database can be efficiently utilized for a variety of distinct tasks.

Consider the pressure regulator (Figure 13.4) as an example. One version of the pressure regulator is described by:

$$[dP_1] - [dP_2] - [dQ] = 0,$$

$$[dP_2] - [dP_3] - [dQ] + [dA] = 0,$$

$$[dP_3] - [dP_4] - [dQ] = 0,$$

$$[dP_4] - [dP_5] - [dQ] = 0,$$

$$[dP_4] + [dA] = 0.$$

Converting into formulas and providing no initial labels, the full LTMS yields 2,814 prime implicates. At first sight this seems like an awful lot

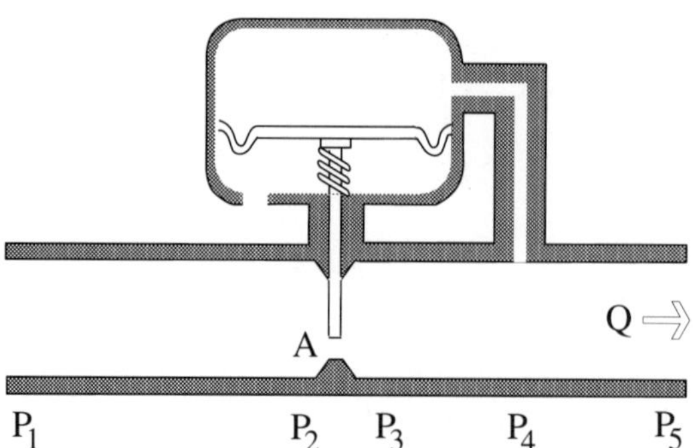

Figure 13.4 Constructing a composite model of the pressure regulator

of information, but these 2,814 prime implicates contain a very large amount of information for performing a variety of tasks on the device, and thus it makes sense to construct these implicates if we are repeatedly performing tasks on the same device. For example, many of the implicates are of the form

$$\neg([dP_1] = +) \wedge \neg([dP_5] = -) \Rightarrow \neg([dA] = +).$$

Often we are only interested in those values which follow from some other, and not such inequalities. Of the 2,814 prime implicates, 496 are such definite clauses. If we regard all except P_1, P_5 and Q as internal variables about which we will make no additional queries, there remain 21 prime implicates. Equivalently, of the 2,814 prime implicates, only 50 do not contain internal variables, and 21 of these are definite clauses. Thus we see that the input-output behavior of the pressure regulator can be compiled into relatively few very simple clauses.

13.2.2 A lazy full LTMS

The basic difficulty with the previous full LTMS is that it may be extremely difficult to construct the prime implicates, and there might well be an exponential number of them. Intuitively, computing all prime implicates is overkill if our goal is to make BCP complete. If we reduce the LTMS database to prime implicates, all BCP propagations are one step long and could just as well have been done by table look-up. For example, suppose A, B, and C are assumption literals which lead to the non-assumption conclusion d, given the current database. From this we immediately know that

$$\neg A \vee \neg B \vee \neg C \vee d$$

is either itself a prime implicate or has a subclause which is a prime implicate. Therefore, d can be concluded in one step.

In many cases it is sufficient to compute only a portion of the prime implicates. Consider the example we have been working with:

$$(x \Rightarrow (y \vee z)) \wedge (x \vee y \vee z). \tag{13.6}$$

A direct, easy conversion yields the clauses

$$\neg x \vee y \vee z, \qquad x \vee y \vee z.$$

Resolving these two clauses together produces one prime implicate:

$$y \vee z.$$

This prime implicate is needed to ensure completeness. But let us assume that x is labeled :TRUE by the inference engine. In this case, it is unnecessary to produce the prime implicate. If x is :TRUE as far as BCP is concerned, $\neg x \vee y \vee z$ and $y \vee z$ provide the same information and therefore the prime implicate is redundant. This idea leads to a variation of the full LTMS algorithm which computes prime implicates only when necessary. The general principle is that the consensus of a satisfied clause (i.e., a clause one of whose literals is labeled :TRUE) and any other necessarily produces a satisfied clause. Even though the satisfied clause produced is a prime implicate, it is unimportant to BCP.

This observation is central for producing a more efficient full LTMS, so it bears further analysis. Consider the consensus of two clauses:

$$x \vee \beta,$$
$$\neg x \vee \gamma,$$

where x is a symbol and β and γ are (possibly empty) disjunctions of literals. Then the consensus of these two clauses with respect to x (presuming there are no complementary literals) is the clause

$$\beta \vee \gamma,$$

with duplicate literals removed. Suppose x is unknown. If one of the antecedent clauses is satisfied, then one of the literals in β or γ is true. Hence, the consensus is satisfied. Otherwise, suppose x is known. If x is labeled :TRUE, then $x \vee \beta$ is satisfied, and to satisfy $\neg x \vee \gamma$ one of the literals of γ must be true. The consensus $\beta \vee \gamma$ therefore adds no useful information. The situation is analogous if x is labeled :FALSE. Therefore, it is unnecessary to compute the consensus of two clauses, one of which is satisfied.

A lazy full LTMS algorithm never computes the consensus of a satisfied clause. Instead, every such consensus calculation is delayed, and the satisfied clause is marked as dirty such that if it ever becomes non-unit open (see Section 9.3), consensus calculations will proceed. However, interspersed within the prime implicate algorithm are calls to BCP in order to avoid as many consensus calculations as possible.

Consider a simple example. Suppose the assumption x is enabled to be :TRUE and the LTMS receives the clauses

$$x \vee y,$$

$$\neg x \vee y.$$

The first clause is satisfied by x's label, so there is no point resolving the two clauses, but this clause is marked as dirty. BCP simply labels y :TRUE. However, if x's label is later retracted, then it becomes worthwhile resolving the two clauses to conclude the singleton clause y, and thus y would continue to be labeled :TRUE.

As a consequence of this efficiency consideration, the LTMS rarely actually computes the set of prime implicates. Instead it computes a set of unsubsumed implicates which are sufficient for BCP alone to achieve full completeness for the current assumption labels.

13.3 Application to ATMS

The ATMS of Chapter 12 is restricted to accepting only Horn clauses as input justifications. The prime implicate formulation we have been discussing provides a way of extending the ATMS to accept arbitrary clauses (and formulas) as input. Such a system is sometimes called a clause management system (CMS)[7].

Intuitively, the CMS accepts arbitrary clauses (or formulas converted into clauses) and computes ATMS labels for them. Consider a simple example. Suppose the CMS is given

$a \vee b \vee C,$

$a \rightarrow d,$

$b \rightarrow d,$

where a, b, and d are non-assumption nodes and C is an assumption. An ATMS cannot even accept the first clause (because it is non-Horn) and thus does not provide a label for d. On the other hand, a CMS gives d the label environment $\{\neg C\}$.

Given the terminology established by the ATMS, the CMS is very easy to define formally. The set of nodes defines a set of symbols S. A subset of those symbols are marked as assumptions: $\mathcal{A} \subset S$. Let C be the set of all clauses supplied by the inference engine (or obtained from converting formulas). An environment E is a subset of the set of assumptions, that is, $E \subset \mathcal{A}$.

What follows parallels the definition of the ATMS almost exactly, except that we must define labels of literals instead of nodes and the clauses are no longer restricted to being Horn. A literal l is said to hold in environment E if l can be derived from $E \cup C$. The notion of nogood is generalized to any environment N consisting purely of assumption literals such that the empty clause can be derived from $N \cup C$. A nogood is *minimal* if it contains no other as a subset. The CMS maintains for each literal l a set of environments $\{E_1, \ldots, E_k\}$ (called the *label*) having the four properties:

1. [Soundness.] l holds in each E_i.
2. [Consistency.] $\perp$ cannot be derived from any E_i (given C).
3. [Completeness.] Every consistent environment E in which l holds is a superset of some E_i.
4. [Minimality.] No E_i is a proper subset of any other.

The CMS label can be computed directly from the prime implicates of C which mention l. The label for a non-assumption literal l is constructed as follows. For every prime implicate of the form

$\neg\alpha_1 \vee \cdots \vee \neg\alpha_k \vee l$

where each of the α_i represent assumption literals, $\{\alpha_1, \ldots, \alpha_k\}$ is a label environment of l. The intuition behind this can be seen from the fact that the clauses that meet this pattern are equivalent to material implications of the form

$$\alpha_1 \wedge \cdots \wedge \alpha_k \Rightarrow l.$$

If l is an assumption literal, then in addition to the previous construction, the label also contains the singleton environment mentioning l itself.

Although the CMS is inefficient, it is extremely powerful. For example, many diagnostic tasks can be formulated directly within it (see Section 17.4.2 and Exercise 9). However, for most applications the full CMS is far too inefficient to be of much practical use. For some relatively simple tasks it might be just the right thing. One area in which the CMS can be useful is in abduction tasks. Suppose P, Q, and R are all assumptions and g is a non-assumption which represents some observation of the world. We have the following formulas:

$$P \wedge Q \wedge R \rightarrow g,$$

$$\neg P \wedge Q \rightarrow g,$$

$$\neg Q \wedge R \rightarrow g.$$

Suppose the inference engine is seeking the simplest explanations (i.e., an explanation not subsumed by another) for the observation g. g does not logically follow, and therefore is not explained. The inference engine seeks an explanation consisting of an hypothesis which, if added to the database, would cause g to logically follow. For this example, we can just read off three such explanations:

$$P \wedge Q \wedge R,$$

$$\neg P \wedge Q,$$

$$\neg Q \wedge R.$$

But these are not the simplest explanations. It is the job of a CMS to provide such simplest explanations. If the above three formulas are provided to a CMS, it finds the following environments for g:

$$\{\neg P, Q\},$$

$$\{R\}.$$

Thus, there are two simplest explanations for g, namely $\neg P \wedge Q$ and R. These are the simplest explanations that permit the derivation of g. Although this technique is very general, it tends to be exponential, and therefore for more complex abduction tasks more sophisticated techniques should be used.

13.4 Improving the efficiency of prime implicate construction

The algorithm presented in Section 13.1.2 is intuitively appealing but quite inefficient in practice. Constructing prime implicates is known to be NP-complete, and therefore it is unlikely that any really good algorithm exists. Nevertheless we can do dramatically better than the algorithm of Section 13.1.2. In this section we discuss two major improvements. First, through logical analysis we can eliminate a large number of the redundant consensus calculations. Second, we can redesign the datastructures to support addition and deletion of clauses relatively efficiently.

13.4.1 A more efficient consensus algorithm

When one observes the algorithm of Section 13.1.2 running, one sees that almost all the clauses produced by the consensus calculation are subsumed by others. One reason for this is somewhat obvious: the consensus operation is often commutative and associative. For example, if we have three clauses α, β and γ, typically $consensus(\alpha, consensus(\beta, \gamma)) = consensus(consensus(\alpha, \beta), \gamma))$. Unfortunately, the number of ways to derive a result grows exponentially in the number of clauses used to produce the final result.

Tison [4, 8] introduced the following key intuition which suppresses the majority of the consensus calculations. To compute the prime implicates of a set of clauses, place an ordering on the symbols, then iterate over these symbols in order, doing all consensus calculations with respect to that symbol only. Once all the consensus calculations for a symbol have been made *it is never necessary to do another consensus calculation with respect to that symbol, even for all the new consensus results*

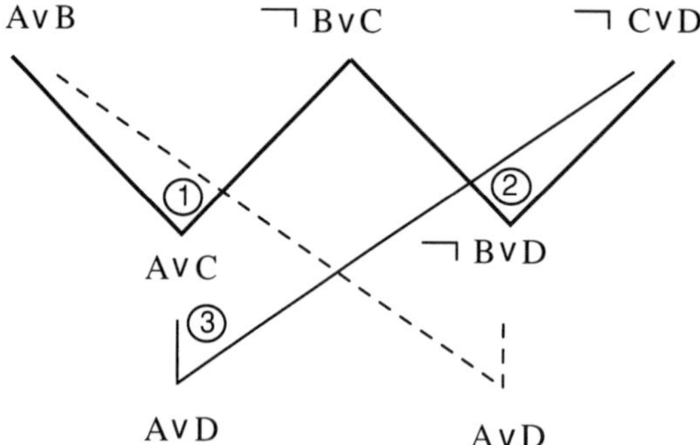

Figure 13.5 Tison's method

that are produced later (of course, when the inference engine incrementally supplies the next clause, the symbols must be reconsidered). Figure 13.5 provides a simple example. Suppose we are given clauses $A \vee B$, $\neg B \vee C$, and $\neg C \vee D$. The symbols are ordered: A, B, and C. There are no consensus calculations available for A. There is only one consensus calculation available for B (on the first and second clauses—at ① in the figure). Finally, when processing C there are two consensus calculations available (at ② and ③ in the figure). One of those consensus calculations produces $\neg B \vee D$. Although this resolves with the first original clause, Tison's method tells us that the result will be irrelevant because all the useful consensus calculations with respect to B have already been made.

The following algorithm incorporates his idea. The algorithm **IPIA** (this derives from the incremental Tison method presented and proved correct in [4]) takes a current set of prime implicates N and a set S of new clauses to add.

Algorithm 13.2 **(IPIA(N, S))**

1. Delete any $D \in N \cup S$ that is subsumed by another $D' \in N \cup S$.
2. Remove a smallest C clause from S. If none, return.
3. For each literal l of C, construct Π_l which contains all clauses of N that resolve successfully with C.
4. Let Σ be the set containing C.
5. Perform the following steps for each literal l of C.

a. For each clause in Σ which is still in N, compute the consensus of it and every clause in Π_l which is still in N.

b. For every new consensus, discard it if it has been subsumed by $N \cup S$. Otherwise, remove any clauses in $N \cup S$ subsumed by it. Add the clause to N and Σ.

Comparing this algorithm to the previous one, we see that a great many consensus computations are avoided:

- Consensus calculations with respect to a literal earlier in the order are ignored.
- Two clauses produced in the same main step (choice of C) are never resolved with each other.
- Consensus calculations with a D in the original N are ignored unless the consensus of D and C exists.

13.4.2 Implementing subsumption checking efficiently

Thus far we have been analyzing the logic of the prime implicate algorithms in order to improve their efficiency. However, all the algorithms we know of depend critically on subsumption checking, and unless that is properly implemented, all the CPU time will be spent checking subsumption. This section lays out some of the basic data structure considerations for performing subsumption checking efficiently.

A key observation is that we are maintaining a database of unsubsumed clauses. We need to implement 3 transactions with this database.

1. Check whether clause x is subsumed by some clause of the database.
2. Add clause x to the database.
3. Remove all clauses from the database which are subsumed by x.

To understand some of the complexities, consider the most obvious implementation: we could implement the subsumption check by the Common Lisp function `subsetp` and maintain the database as a simple list. This would be computationally disastrous for two independent reasons. First, using `subsetp` on two clauses of length n and m requires on the order of nm element comparisons. Second, using lists makes checking for subsumption of order the number of clauses, and thus the complexity of generating k prime implicates, at least k^2. Some of the problems we want to experiment with have 1,000,000 prime implicates, of average size 5, and it is clear that 25,000,000,000,000 of any fundamental operation is beyond the reach of most current computers.

Our implementation is based on an integration of two ideas. First, each clause is always represented in a canonical form. Second, the clause database is represented as a discrimination tree. To achieve a canonical form for clauses, we use the unique id assigned to it by the LTMS which is in `tms-node-index`. We order the literals of every clause in ascending order of `tms-node-index`. (Complementary literals have the same id, but they can never appear in the same clause, as this would produce a tautology.) This means that two sets of literals refer to the same clause if their respective `clause-literals` are Common Lisp `equal`. For example, given nodes A, B, and C with ids 1, 2, and 3, the clause,

$A \vee B \vee C$

is represented by the list

$[A, B, C]$.

The representation of clauses is very sensitive to the choice of ids. If the ids were 3, 1, 2 respectively, then the clause would be represented by the list,

$[B, C, A]$.

Recall that the basic LTMS also canonicalizes literals such that two literals are the same if and only if they are `eq`. This also makes it possible to test whether a clause of length n subsumes a clause of length m in at most $n + m$ `eq` comparisons. However, our algorithm never checks whether one clause subsumes another. Instead, our algorithm stores the canonical forms of clauses in a discrimination tree. By storing canonical forms in a discrimination tree, a single clause can be checked against all existing clauses in a single operation.

The discrimination tree for clauses is relatively simple. Conceptually, it is a tree, all of whose edges are literals and whose leaves are clauses. The edges below each node in the discrimination tree are ordered by the id of the literal. Suppose that A, B, C, D, and E are a sequence of nodes with ascending ids and the LTMS database contains the three clauses

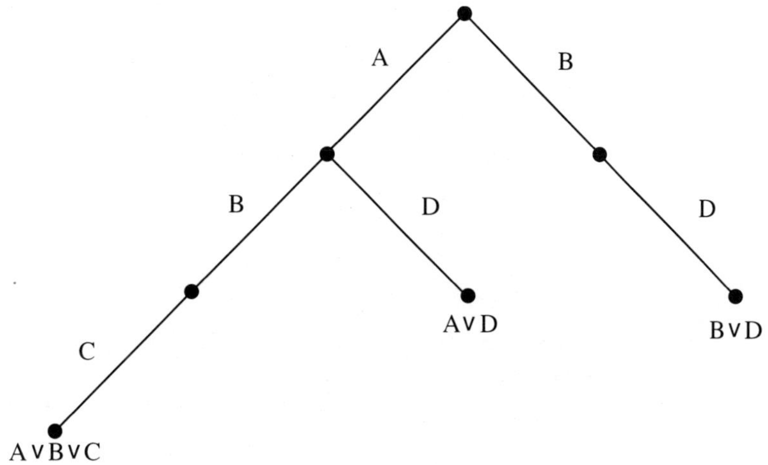

Figure 13.6 Database with 3 clauses

$A \vee B \vee C,$

$B \vee D,$

$A \vee D.$

The resulting tree is illustrated in Figure 13.6. Because clauses are canonically ordered, our discrimination trees have the important property that the id of any edge is less than the id of any edge appearing below it at any depth. This property is heavily exploited in the update algorithms that follow. This datastructure is called a *trie* [6], which has been explored extensively for representing dictionaries of words.

The most commonly called procedure checks whether a clause is subsumed by one in the database. Given an ordered set of literals, the recursive function **SUBSUMED?** checks whether the set of literals L is subsumed by trie N. The ordered literals are represented as an ordered list, and the trie by an ordered list of edges.

Algorithm 13.3 **(SUBSUMED?**(L, N)**)**

1. If N is a terminal clause, return success.
2. Remove literals from the front of L until the id of the first edge of N is greater than that of the first literal of L.

3. If no literals remain (L is empty), return failure.
4. For each literal l of L do the following until success, or until the id of the first edge of N is no longer greater than that of l.
   a. If the first literal of N is l, recursively invoke **SUBSUMED?** on the remaining literals and the edges below the first element of N.
   b. If the recursive call returns success, return success.
5. Remove the first element of N.
6. Go to step 2.

Suppose we want to check whether $D \vee E$ is subsumed by the database of Figure 13.6. The root of the trie has two outgoing edges, A and B. D has a larger id than the top two edges of the trie (A and B), therefore **SUBSUMED?** immediately reports failure. Suppose we want to check whether $A \vee B \vee D$ is subsumed by the trie. The first edge from the root matches the first literal, so the recursive call tries to determine whether the remaining subclause $B \vee D$ is subsumed by the trie rooted from the edge below A. Again B matches, but D does not match C, so the two recursive calls to **SUBSUMED?** fail. Finally, the top-level invocation of **SUBSUMED?** again recursively calls itself and finds a successful match.

Adding a clause to the database is very simple. Our algorithm exploits the fact that the clause to be added is not itself subsumed by some other clause, and that any clause it subsumes has been removed from the database.

Algorithm 13.4 **(ADD-TO-TRIE**(L, N)**)**

1. Remove edges of the front of N, until the id of the first edge of N is greater than or equal to the first literal of L.
2. If the label of the first edge of N is the first literal of L, then recursively call **ADD-TO-TRIE** with the remainder of L, the edges underneath the first edge of N, and return.
3. Construct the edges to represent the literals of L and return, and side-effect the trie such that it appears just before the current position N.

The potentially most expensive operation, and the one that requires the greatest care, is the third basic update on the trie. Here we are given

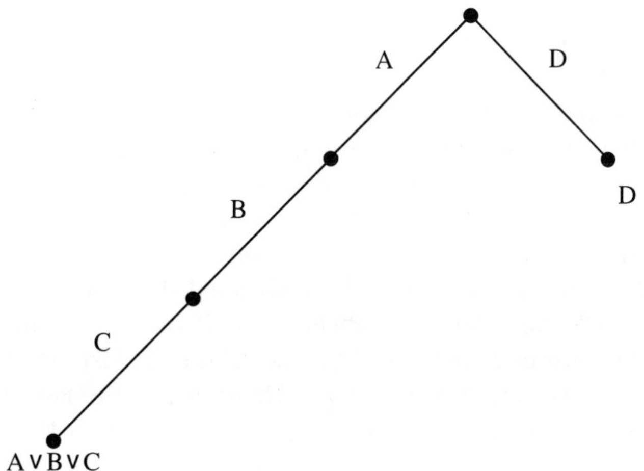

Figure 13.7 CLTMS database with two clauses

a clause not subsumed by the trie, and we must remove from the trie all clauses subsumed by it.

Algorithm 13.5 **(REMOVE-SUBSUMED(L, N))**

1. If there are no literals, delete the entire trie represented by N, and return.
2. If we are at a leaf of the trie, return.
3. For each edge e of N, do the following.
   a. If the label of e is the first literal of L, then recursively call **REMOVE-SUBSUMED** with the rest of the literals and the edges below e.
   b. If the label of e is lower than that of the first literal of L, then recursively call **REMOVE-SUBSUMED** on the *same* literals but the edges below e.

As an extreme case, suppose we want to remove all clauses subsumed by D from Figure 13.6. Because D is last in the ordering, the algorithm simply searches in left-to-right depth-first order removing all clauses containing D. After adding the clause D, the resulting trie is illustrated by Figure 13.7.

13.5 The full LTMS interface

The full LTMS is designed as an extension to the basic clausal LTMS. Therefore, the inference engine's interface to it is remarkably simple. One overall change is that the `informant` takes a more significant role in the CLTMS. In the other TMS implementations, informants were provided purely as a convenience to the inference engine (usually used to cache the name of the rule that constructed the justification). However, in the CLTMS they play a significant role. If the informants of two clauses (or two formulas) are non-`nil` and Common Lisp `eq`, the implementation will never attempt to resolve them (or, in the case of formulas, any of their constituent clauses) together. This allows the inference engine to indicate which resolutions need actually be performed.

```
(add-formula ltms formula &optional informant)
```

The procedure `add-formula` is redefined to add the prime implicates of the formula to the clause database. Therefore, the resulting LTMS labels will be the same as those a formula-BCP would find.

```
(create-ltms title &key (title nil)
                        (node-string 'default-node-string)
                        (debugging nil)
                        (checking-contradictions t)
                        (contradiction-handler 'ask-user-handler)
                        (enqueue-procedure nil)
                        (complete nil)
                        (delay-sat t))
```

The procedure to create an LTMS can be supplied a keyword `:COMPLETE` argument indicating whether it should be logically complete. There are three options for this keyword:

`nil` This indicates a conventional BCP will be used. If the inference engine only supplies clauses, then no resolutions will be performed.

`t` This indicates that a complete LTMS will be used.

`:DELAY` This is the typical way to use the CLTMS. The TMS will behave as a conventional BCP-based LTMS. However, enough datastructures will be accumulated so that the inference engine can later explicitly ask to produce the same database as would have resulted if this flag had been `t` initially. This is important because often the inference engine has a whole set of formulas to communicate to the CLTMS, and it would be futile for the CLTMS to compute prime implicates which would immediately be subsumed by additional inference engine clauses.

When the last keyword argument `delay-sat` is `t`, then the LTMS will delay consensus calculations of satisfied clauses. To use the CLTMS as a clause management system, this flag should be `nil`, otherwise it should be left at its default value.

```
(change-ltms ltms &key node-string
                       debugging checking-contradictions
                       contradiction-handler enqueue-procedure
                       complete delay-sat?)
```

The procedure `change-ltms` can change the type of LTMS used. The inference engine should use this judiciously, as the implementation does not try to change the results of previous LTMS operations accordingly.

```
(support-for-node node)
```

Some of the clauses used by the full LTMS are the result of resolution. Therefore, the procedure `support-for-node` is extended. If the first element of the informant is `RESOLVE`, then the second and third elements of the list are two clauses which resolve to produce this one. This informant is stored in the `clause-informant` slot of the clause currently supporting the node.

Notice that the LTMS procedure `set-truth` queues any nodes that receive new `:TRUE` or `:FALSE` labels for delayed consensus computations. New consensus computations are only called for when a retraction is done. Therefore, any call to `retract-assumption` eventually leads to a call to `ipia`, which either performs the delayed consensus computation or delays it again.

```
(complete-ltms ltms)
```

`complete-ltms` performs consensus computations which have been delayed because the `:COMPLETE` flag is set to `:DELAY`. It will have no effect if the `:COMPLETE` flag is `t` or `nil`.

13.6 A simple example of CLTMS usage

This simple example shows CLTMS behavior on the simple clauses that show BCP incompleteness.

```
>   (setq *ltms* (create-ltms "Simple Example" :COMPLETE :delay))
```

We add the two clauses (`compile-formula` is always the preferred method of adding to the CLTMS database):

```
>   (compile-formula *ltms* '(:OR x y))
>   (compile-formula *ltms* '(:OR x (:not y)))
```

We print out the clause database via

```
>   (pretty-print-clauses *ltms*)

(:OR Y X)
(:OR (:NOT Y) X)
```

We can print out the node labels via

```
>   (why-nodes *ltms*)

Y is unknown.
X is unknown.
```

After performing the delayed consensus calculation via,

```
(complete-ltms *ltms*)
```

we obtain

```
>   (pretty-print-clauses *ltms*)

(:OR X)
```

Notice that the two original clauses have been removed and replaced with a new singleton clause.

```
>   (why-nodes *ltms*)

Y is unknown.
X is TRUE ...
```

13.7 The full LTMS code

The code in `cltms.lisp` contains a set of procedures which must be combined with those in `ltms.lisp` in order to build a logically complete LTMS. Before studying the code in `cltms.lisp`, we should review some of the relevant hooks in `ltms.lisp`. The main LTMS datastructure `ltms` contains a field `clauses`. In the basic LTMS, this contains a list of the clauses the inference engine provided the LTMS. In the CLTMS, this contains the trie containing all the clauses of the LTMS database. The LTMS datastructure contains two additional fields used only in the CLTMS.

`queue` A queue of pending clauses that need to be resolved against other clauses in the database. This queue is organized for convenient insertion and removal of the shortest clause. It consists of a list of lists. Each component list consists of an integer length followed by clauses of that length. The top-level list is sorted on this integer length such that the list of shortest clauses always occurs first. Thus, an example queue value is:

```
((2 #<Clause 3> #<Clause 2)
 (4 #<Clause 5>)
 (7 #<Clause 9> #<Clause 101>))
```

`conses` A list of cons cells to be used as temporaries in the consensus algorithm.

`delay-sat` If this flag is `t`, then a satisfied clause should never be resolved with another.

`cons-size` The number of conses available in the `conses` slot.

The clause datastructure contains one additional field, `clause-status`, for use within the CLTMS. This field has four possible non-`nil` values:

`:SUBSUMED` This clause has been subsumed by some other in the database.

`:QUEUED` This clause is part of the database, but is queued for pending consensus calculations, i.e., it is a member of S in **IPIA**.

`:DIRTY` A consensus calculation of **IPIA** was blocked because this clause is satisfied. When this clause ceases to be satisfied, this clause must be requeued for further consensus calculations.

`:NOT-INDEXED` This clause has just been created in the inner loop of **IPIA** but has not yet been inserted into the connection graph.

There are three places in `ltms.lisp` which explicitly branch to code in `cltms.lisp`. The LTMS procedure `add-clause-internal` calls the CLTMS procedure `full-add-clause` instead of `bcp-add-clause`. `bcp-add-clause` does not perform any resolutions or subsumption tests. When the LTMS procedure `find-alternative-support` determines that a node becomes `:UNKNOWN`, it first tries to use simple BCP to determine its label, and if unsuccessful it invokes a procedure to compute additional implicates, which hopefully will constrain other node labels. The LTMS procedure `propagate-unknownness`, which is called when a node's label becomes `:UNKNOWN`, calls the CLTMS procedure `propagate-more-unknownness` to check whether some previously satisfied clauses need to be resolved with other clauses.

The LTMS procedure `tms-create-node` also maintains a sequence of temporary conses used by the consensus algorithm. As these conses are heavily used, it attempts to ensure that all these conses are localized in memory. Most Common Lisp implementations ensure that conses that are created at the same time are located in the same area of memory. In order to prevent creating a new sequence of conses every time a node is created, `tms-create-node` only recreates the sequence of conses every fiftieth node creation.

13.7.1 Adding formulas and clauses

The code in this section takes any inference engine-supplied formula, converts it into its prime implicates, and adds these to the clause database.

`add-formula` is the top-level procedure for adding formulas. Like the analogous LTMS procedure, it first converts the formula into conjunctive normal form (as explained in Section 9.4). However, there are some important improvements. The straightforward LTMS algorithm can produce an exponential number of clauses, most of which are ultimately removed by subsumption (see Exercise 3). Therefore the conversion code here performs subsumptions during the conversion to conjunctive normal form. In addition, it eliminates tautologies and duplicate literals as well as sorting the literals in canonical order during the conversion. These extensions yield dramatic performance improvements on many of the otherwise exponential cases. The procedures `normalize-disjunction`, `normalize-conjunction`, `disjoin-clauses`, and `subsumed-by?` combine with the procedures in `ltms.lisp` to perform this encoding. This first improvement simply depends on datastructure improvements to perform subsumption. It would be straightforward to extend the basic LTMS in the same way.

The second change to `add-formula` is that it converts the formula to its prime implicates. It achieves this by creating an instance of a complete LTMS, installing all the CNF clauses into it, converting these to prime implicates, and then copying these clauses back into the top-level LTMS. Although creating a temporary LTMS instance seems like overkill, this process has two important advantages. First, it is unnecessary to have a distinct algorithm to convert a formula to its prime implicates. Second, in the case where the database is expressed as a few very large formulas, the procedure exploits all the efficiency advantage of the main algorithm. In order to prevent two prime implicates of the same formula from being futilely resolved with each other, the consensus calculation refuses to process two clauses with the same informant. The inference engine can also exploit this property: individual clauses or formulas with the same informant will never be resolved with each other.

The procedure `compile-formula` functions identically to its LTMS counterparts. However, it transforms the formula at compile time. This improves execution time at the expense of compile time.

The macro `map-over` is used by `add-formula` to map the clauses from the main CLTMS to the temporary one and back again.

`add-clause` is almost identical to the basic LTMS version. Although the inference engine guarantees that there are no duplicate or complementary literals, every clause must be put in canonical form.

13.7.2 Consensus algorithm

The procedure `simplify-consensus` interleaves three primitive operations. First, it computes the consensus of two clauses with respect to a symbol. If the result would contain complementary literals, it fails. Second, it removes any duplicate literals that might appear in the result. Third, it ensures that the resulting literals are in canonical order. All three operations can be performed in one pass through the clauses, because the original clause literals are in canonical form to start with. To achieve this operation in one pass, it must construct the result clause as it goes—even though the partial result might be discarded if complementary literals are found.

Unless great care is taken, an exorbitant number of cons cells will be used inside this procedure. This is partially a consequence of the fact that in order to succeed in one pass, `simplify-consensus` may have to discard partially constructed results. But, more importantly, even with all the strategies we have discussed to reduce redundant consensus calculations, most consensus calculations remain redundant. Therefore, most of the clauses built by `simplify-consensus` are immediately discarded because they fail the subsequent subsumption check with respect to the database. Although Common Lisp's `cons` is relatively cheap, performing a great number of them in the inner loop of an algorithm significantly degrades performance and wastes storage. Therefore, our implementation uses an advanced Common Lisp programming idiom to save cons cells. When we initially create the `ltms` datastructure, we allocate a fixed number of cons cells. These cells are used repeatedly in consensus calculation. The body of the function `simplify-consensus` is written as if it were calling the usual `cons` procedure. However, the `macrolet` temporarily redefines Common Lisp's `push` within the body of the procedure such that all cons cells are allocated from the fixed set. Of course, `simplify-consensus` should not be called a second time until the results of the first call are copied or discarded. Otherwise the result of the first call will be changed as a consequence of the second.

The procedure `simplify-subsume-consensus` is called at the inner step of Tison's method. It first calls `simplify-consensus` to check whether a consensus exists, and if one does, it obtains the literal sequence. It then immediately checks whether the result is subsumed by the current database. Only if the clause is not subsumed does it copy the clause literals out of the temporary cons cells and install the clause in the database via a call to `process-clause`.

13.7.3 Maintaining the connection graph

In order to implement BCP efficiently, the basic LTMS maintains a list for each symbol containing the clauses in which it appears positively and negatively. This same datastructure plays a dual role in our consensus algorithm. When provided a new clause, we need to be able to quickly identify all the other clauses it can potentially resolve with. (In theorem proving, this datastructure is called a connection graph.) We have already seen in a number of places in this chapter that it is productive to find the shortest resolvents first. Therefore, we want to resolve the shortest clauses first. In order to facilitate this, the clauses in `tms-node-true-clauses` and `tms-node-false-clauses` are stored by descending length. The macro `insert-clause` achieves this and is used in the procedures `insert-true-clause` and `insert-false-clause`, which replace their LTMS counterparts.

The connection graph is not consulted in the inner loop of **IPIA** and many of the clauses constructed there are immediately subsumed. Therefore, the construction of the connection graph is delayed. The procedure `index-clause` inserts the clause into the connection graph when needed later—the indexing right after the clause is created in `bcp-add-clause` is suppressed. The procedure `literal-connections` is a handy function which returns the list of clauses in which the complement of a literal appears.

13.7.4 LTMS entry points

When the inference engine does a retraction, nodes may lose support. Whenever a node becomes `:UNKNOWN`, clauses which it previously satisfied may no longer be satisfied. If any clause becomes unsatisfied and **IPIA** was previously blocked from performing any resolutions with it, then the clause is queued for future consensus calculations. It is important to not immediately do the consensus calculations, as BCP may find alternative support for the node.

The procedure `full-add-clause` is called from the basic LTMS when a clause is added to a complete LTMS. It calls `install-clause` to add the clause to update the database. If the new clause is not subsumed by the database adds `install-clause` to the pending resolution queue.

Unless the CLTMS is run in delayed mode, it calls **IPIA** to perform all the necessary consensus calculations.

13.7.5 Implementing Tison's method

The next sequence of procedures implements Tison's method. This implementation combines all the different ideas discussed in this chapter plus a number of implementation strategies, and is therefore hard to follow. Experience has shown that it is preferable to always construct small resolvents first. Therefore, many of the internal lists are sorted by size (in the same format as `ltms-queue`). The first group of procedures and macros help Tison's algorithm maintain these lists. The macro `insert-list2` maintains a list in the form of `ltms-queue`. The procedure `insert-queue` uses this macro to insert clauses into `ltms-queue`. The procedure `insert-list-1` is simply the procedure version of the macro. The macro `insert-list` adds a clause to an arbitrary Common Lisp value using this format. The macro `delay-sat?` is used to delay consensus calculations involving satisfied clauses. If the LTMS is created with `:COMPLETE :DELAY`, then the inference engine should call `complete-ltms` to perform all pending consensus computations.

The heart of the prime implicate algorithm is the procedure `ipia`. It follows the outline of **IPIA**, but it is extended to block any consensus calculations with satisfied clauses. Also, it incorporates numerous local efficiency improvements.

13.7.6 Maintaining the discrimination tree

The next set of procedures implements the algorithms of Section 13.4.2. Note that the procedure `subsumed?` is actually less sophisticated than discussed there. This is because unless the problem is relatively large, the additional checking of the canonical order is not worth while. In particular, the `member` test which ignores the id order of literals, is almost always faster than a hand-coded search that does pay attention to the id order, simply because most Common Lisps implement `member` well. The procedure `add-to-trie` functions exactly as described in Section 13.4.2. It uses `build-trie` as an auxiliary procedure which consists of a fresh (sub)trie for a single (sub)clause.

The procedure `remove-subsumed` performs as described in Section 13.4.2. It uses `remove-subsumed-1` as an auxiliary. `walk-clauses` is a general auxiliary procedure used in a number of places. It invokes the procedure it is supplied as an argument on every clause in the LTMS. The procedure `collect` uses `walk-trie` to construct a list of all the clauses in the trie. The procedure `remove-clause` is designed to be called only from `remove-subsumed`. It removes the clause from the connection graph and updates the relevant BCP records. Note its use of the Common Lisp procedure `delete`. Even though a clause will appear only once in this list and one should think using `delete` with a keyword argument of `:COUNT 1` should be more efficient, most Common Lisps implement this operation poorly.

13.7.7 Processing clauses

The next two procedures do the top-level processing of new clauses and do all their work by calling other procedures. `install-clause` first checks whether the clause is subsumed by the current database, and if not, calls `process-clause`. `process-clause` first passes the clause to BCP, then removes all clauses it subsumes from the database, and finally adds it to the database.

The procedure `tms-env` is unrelated to the CLTMS, but provides a facility to implement a CMS. This procedure will take a node and a `:TRUE`/`:FALSE` label and return a set of literals (each indicated by a cons consisting of a node and its sign—`:TRUE`/`:FALSE`).

The procedure `pi` is included to support experimentation with prime implicates. It computes the prime implicates of a formula. It uses an heuristic to ensure that the initial trie is as small as possible. In many experiments this considerably improves the running time to compute the prime implicates.

13.8 Exercises

1. ⋆ Find a formula that has far more prime implicates than conjuncts in conjunctive normal form.

2. ⋆ Show three clauses that illustrate that the consensus calculation is not associative.

3. ⋆⋆ Modify our LTMS to allow the user to justify, enable, and retract formulas.

4. ⋆⋆ Consider a `TAXONOMY` formula on n nodes. How many prime implicates does it have?

5. ⋆⋆ Implement a version of `subsumed?` which does check ids. Does it make any difference in performance?

6. ⋆⋆ Write a procedure to convert qualitative equations to formulas and then reduce them to prime implicates.

7. ⋆⋆ Implement a version of the ATMS that is plug compatible-with our earlier implementation but which uses the CLTMS.

8. ⋆⋆ Our CLTMS datastructures for representing clauses are far more efficient for representing clauses than our ATMS nogood tables. Implement a more efficient ATMS which uses a trie to represent the nogoods.

9. ⋆⋆ Consider the following Common Lisp code:

```
(defun kean (m k &aux as)
  (setq *ltms* (create-ltms "Kean Problem" :COMPLETE t))
  (do ((i 1 (1+ i)))
      ((> i k) (add-formula *ltms* (cons :OR as)))
    (push `(:NOT (a ,i)) as)
    (do ((j 1 (1+ j)))
        ((> j m))
      (compile-formula *ltms* `(:OR (a ,i) (:NOT (s ,i ,j)))))))
```

   How many prime implicates are there for `(kean 3 6)`? How many for `(kean 5 10)`? Derive the formula for the number of prime implicates. Answer: `(kean 5 10)` has 60,466,236 prime implicates.

10. ⋆⋆⋆⋆ We discussed how computing prime implicates was overkill when using BCP. Our current algorithm is essentially post hoc, blocking consensus calculations when BCP satisfies clauses. Does it make sense to define the general notion of BCP-prime implicates which would be directly computable from a set of clauses and which en-

sured that BCP would be complete (with respect to the original clause set)?

11. ⋆ ⋆ ⋆ An implicant of a set of formulas Σ is a conjunction of literals π containing no pair of complementary literals. π is a prime implicant of Σ if no proper subconjunction of π is an implicant of Σ. Show that the prime implicants of Σ are the negations of the prime implicates of $\neg\Sigma$ (i.e., treating Σ as a conjunction of formulas). Using the CLTMS implementation as a base, write a Common Lisp procedure that returns the prime implicants of a set of formulas.

13.9 Bibliography

[1] de Kleer, J., and Brown, J.S., "A qualitative physics based on confluences," *Artificial Intelligence* 24 (1984): 7–83; also in Bobrow, D.G. (ed.), *Reasoning About Physical Systems*, MIT Press and North Holland, 1985, 7–83; also in Hobbs, J.R., and Moore, R.C. (eds.), *Formal Models of the Common-Sense World*, Ablex, 1985, 109–183; also in Weld, D.S., and de Kleer, J., (eds.), *Qualitative Reasoning about the Physical World*, Morgan-Kaufmann, 1990, 88–126.

[2] de Kleer, J., "Exploiting locality in a TMS," *Proceedings of AAAI-90,*, 1990 254–271.

[3] Henschen, L. and Wos, L., "Unit Refutations and Horn Sets," *JACM* 21 (1974): 590–605.

[4] Kean, A., and Tsiknis, G., "An incremental method for generating prime implicants/implicates," *Journal of Symbolics Computation* 9 (1990): 185–206.

[5] Lewis, H.R., "Renaming a Set of Clauses as a Horn Set," *JACM* 25 (1978): 134–135.

[6] Knuth, D.E., *The Art of Computer Programming* Addison-Wesley, 1972.

[7] Reiter, R., and de Kleer, J., "Foundations of assumption-based truth maintenance systems: Preliminary report," in *of Proceedings AAAI-87*, Seattle, 1987, 183–188.

[8] Tison, P., "Generalized consensus theory and application to the minimization of boolean functions," *IEEE Transactions on Electronic Computers* 4 (1967): 446–456.

14 Putting the ATMS to Work

The ideas of assumption-based truth maintenance introduced in Chapter 12 provide a new set of problem-solving capabilities. The compact encoding of contexts via environments makes it easy, in theory, for a problem solver to switch its focus (or foci) of attention. This should streamline searches and facilitate comparing alternatives. The association of complex labels with nodes and the maintenance of a global database of nogoods should simplify the propagation of results between different activities inside a problem solver.

This chapter explores how to organize problem solvers that capitalize on the strengths of the ATMS. To illustrate these ideas we present yet another variant of the Tiny Rule Engine, called ATRE. We begin by examining the issues involved in interfacing a rule engine to an ATMS. We outline two strategies (*many-worlds* and *focused*) for organizing ATMS-based problem solvers, followed by the design of ATRE which supports them. Section 14.2 then details how these design changes are reflected in ATRE's implementation. In Section 14.3, ATRE is used to build a simple planner. This system illustrates how to think about encoding domain rules in terms of restricting models. It also shows how an ATMS is used in *envisioning*, a reasoning technique briefly mentioned in Chapter 11. Envisioning, like other problem-solving techniques based on interpretation construction, works best for small problems or for small pieces of larger problems. In Section 14.4 we describe more focused ATMS-based problem-solving strategies, indicating how they can be more efficient in simple domains and can enable ATMS techniques to be used on much larger problems.

14.1 Interfacing to an ATMS

Although there are several important new issues raised by using an ATMS, many aspects of the TMS/inference engine interface remain the same. Like any other TMS, we expect that the inference engine (here, a version of FTRE) maintains the link between its data and the TMS. The format of ATMS justifications is identical to that of JTMS justifications, so we use the same conventions for assuming and justifying data. Like the JTMS, if we wish to adopt a strict propositional model for assertions, we shall have to enforce that explicitly in the inference engine. That is, distinct nodes for a proposition and its negation must be created, along with justifications that keep them from both being believed in any consistent environment, analogous to the justifications for contradiction nodes in JTRE which prevented a proposition and its negation from both being believed at the same time. Thus we shall see that many aspects of ATRE can be borrowed directly from JTRE. The reification of the notion of environment, however, gives us a new set of design choices for organizing problem solvers, which in turn affects how we should design our inference engine. Therefore we examine these organizations next.

14.1.1 Organizing ATMS-based problem solvers

Two strategies for organizing ATMS-based problem solvers can be characterized as follows:

Many-worlds Work in all consistent contexts at once; seek all possible solutions.

Focused Work in a single context (or small number of contexts) at a time to find a good solution. Switch contexts opportunistically.

In a design system, for instance, a context would include assumptions about the current state of the design and the specifications the artifact should satisfy. In a planner, the context would include a description of the plan generated so far. In an analysis system, the context would include information about the results achieved so far by a particular method. In all of these cases the context might also include control information (e.g., `show` assertions) describing the problem solver's goals and chosen methods.

The many-worlds strategy trusts in the "small infinity" effect [9] often found in artificial intelligence: while worst-case analyses look appalling, in realistic cases the amount of work or number of solutions is often small, due to the many constraints imposed by the world and due to the discovery of clever ways of carving up the problem. The use of envisioning in qualitative physics, and in the planner shown later, are examples of the many-worlds strategy. Efficient support for problem solvers using this strategy was the original motivation for developing assumption-based truth maintenance. "I will fear no exponentials" is the motto of the dedicated builder of many-worlds problem solvers.

The focused strategy is most like the strategy used in other TMS-based problem solvers. Here, a single environment is chosen to represent the problem solver's locus of effort. This environment is typically called the *focus environment* or *focus*. All queries are considered with respect to the focus, and activities irrelevant to the current focus are suspended. The leverage provided by the ATMS comes from the ease with which the focus can be changed. In a traditional TMS, changing assumptions requires retracting some subset of the old assumptions and enabling new ones, which can force label propagations through substantial portions of the dependency network. The ATMS extracts its price in advance, by making the initial propagation of an assumption more expensive (due to the need for label updating and maintaining the nogood database), but then switching becomes free. It is the expense of swapping sets of assumptions that forced JTRE and LTRE to use stack-oriented techniques for organizing searches and assumption-making operations. Freed of this expense, we can now explore more flexible problem-solver organizations.

It is important to realize that these strategies are extreme points in the design space of ATMS-based problem solvers. Many systems have been built using each strategy in its pure form. However, it is often more convenient and efficient to find an appropriate blend of them. Nevertheless, we continue to focus on the extreme cases below to simplify discussion.

Each strategy imposes different requirements on the inference engine and on the inference engine/ATMS interface. Specifically, we next examine how these choices impact the vocabulary of database queries, the control of rule execution, and contradiction handling.

14.1.2 Database queries

Under the focused strategy, the database can be treated as if it were a JTMS-based system. That is, a given statement is in if it is implied by the focus, and out otherwise. This can be implemented by a simple test to see if there is an environment in the label which is a subset of the focus environment. The many-worlds strategy requires a more catholic view of the database: a non-empty label may be sufficient reason for the problem solver to work on a given assertion. Thus, under the many-worlds strategy, we consider a node in if the label is non-empty, and out only if the label is empty.

The ATMS also facilitates queries about relative consistency. In the focused strategy, for example, it may be necessary for a problem solver to figure out how to extend its current focus to include some desirable consequence. (A designer, for instance, may need to extend the design of an aircraft by choosing a particular class of engine that will satisfy the aircraft's mission requirements.) In the many-worlds strategy, there may be several potential extensions to a partial solution, and the problem solver must filter out those which are inconsistent. (A logistics planner, for instance, may have several choices for routing a ship, each of which will allow the satisfaction of different goals.) In both cases the underlying ATMS operations are the same: if the given environment can be consistently combined with some environment in the statement's label, then the extension is consistent. In the focused problem solver, each such union is a candidate for its new focus, and in the many-worlds problem solver each union is a new (perhaps partial) solution.

The idea of computing relative consistency by unioning environments is commonly exploited in ATMS-based problem solvers. However, there are two caveats which must be kept in mind. First, nogoods discovered later on may render these new environments inconsistent. Second, these new environments are only complete relative to the set of assumptions in force when the label is examined. Adding new assumptions may enable yet more possible extensions. Minimizing the occurrence of these two situations is an important consideration in good problem-solver design. The first may be minimized by trying to discover nogoods as early as possible. The second may be minimized by structuring work so that, when possible, labels are used only when they are *maximal* (i.e., as large as they are going to get). Figuring out how to exploit the constraints of a domain to achieve these ends is an important part of the art of organizing ATMS-based problem solvers.

14.1.3 Rule execution strategies

The improved vocabulary for beliefs provides similar scope for improvement in controlling the execution of pattern-directed rules. Like the previous TMS/inference engine interfaces, we place the burden of finding matching sets of data on the inference engine, and delegate scheduling the execution of rules to the TMS. Let us consider what is needed to implement each ATMS strategy.

To implement many-worlds strategies, we need rules that operate as freely as possible. For instance, the notion of triggering rules when statements appear in the database, regardless of label, is especially useful when installing justifications which justify contradiction nodes. Consequently, we keep the `intern` triggering condition used in previous TMS-based inference engines. The definition of in used by many-worlds problem-solver queries can be turned into a trigger condition, by executing the body of a rule only when the triggers can be consistently believed together.

To implement focused strategies, we need tighter control over rule execution. The definition of in used in focused problem-solver queries naturally leads to the idea of executing a rule only when all of its triggers are implied by the current focus environment. We call this the *implied-by* strategy for rule execution.

The implied-by strategy for rule execution provides much tighter constraint than the intern or in strategies. Consider an intelligent design aid for VLSI. If the initial design called for CMOS, the program might begin elaborating and exploring the various alternatives under this assumption. If external factors force the design to use gallium arsenide instead, it should stop working on the CMOS version of the design. The CMOS design has not become inconsistent, it has simply become irrelevant (at least for the time being). Yet a program based on in or intern rules would continue to pursue both. Actually, the implied-by rule execution strategy is the ATMS analog to the label-sensitive strategies used in other TMSs—the problem of working on other possibilities simulaneously never arose in other TMSs due to their use of a single global context.

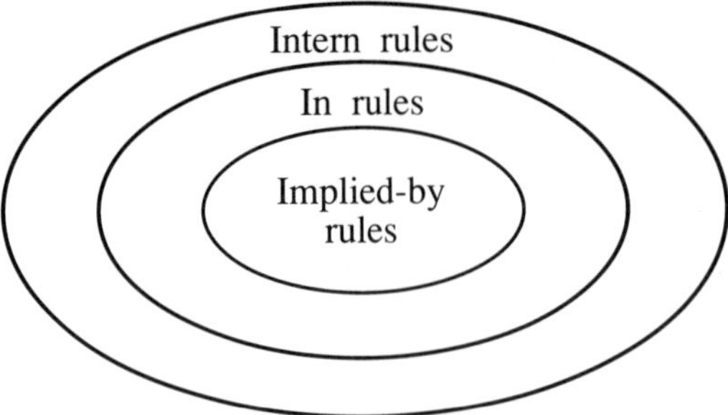

Figure 14.1 Applicability of rule execution strategies. This Venn diagram illustrates how the ATMS-based rule execution strategies compare in terms of their applicability to combinations of facts.

Figure 14.1 depicts the relative degree of control offered by each strategy. The intern strategy is the most profligate, since any combination of mentioned facts will do. The in strategy is more restrained, requiring that the combination of facts be mutually consistent. The implied-by strategy is the most restrictive, forcing the combination to be implied by the current focus, and hence presumably relevant to the problem solver's current activities. In all but a few cases, using some mixture of these strategies typically provides the most efficiency.

14.1.4 Contradiction handling

In non-ATMSs, the current context of the system is defined in terms of the belief states of the nodes in the dependency network. When context is implicitly represented by the global state of the TMS, contradiction handling must also be performed through a global mechanism. Every inference engine task must register its strategy for how contradictions involving its assumptions should be processed (e.g., the stack-oriented contradiction handling mechanism of Section 10.1.2). The explicit, distributed representation of context in the ATMS suggests using a different strategy. By associating contradiction handlers directly with environments, we can provide localized, distributed contradiction processing.

Let us see how this works. Consider first the focused problem solver. Suppose a task T has a procedure P that should be called if a contradiction relevant to T occurs. T always has some focus environment F

associated with it, corresponding to the assumptions under which that task makes sense to perform. (*F* may or may not be the focus of the problem solver at any particular time. It will be the problem solver's focus if the problem solver is working on *T* or some other task that shares *F* as its focus environment, and otherwise it won't be.) We can arrange the ATMS/inference engine combination so that the procedure *P* can be linked with *F*, so that *P* is executed exactly when *F* becomes contradictory. This can be done for each task independently. In other words, contradiction handlers are now indexed by environments.

Timing is always an important issue in processing contradictions. By decentralizing contradiction handling we cut what was a tight link between the processing of a task and the TMS operations associated with it. This leads to new constraints on representing tasks. The simplest case is that the focus environment *F* for task *T* is discovered to be contradictory while *T* is being processed. The simple non-local exit mechanism we used in most previous contradiction handlers would suffice for this case. But there is nothing that prevents *F* from being discovered as contradictory before or after *T* is processed. Good problem solver design can (and should) minimize this, of course, but sometimes it is inevitable. For instance, if we discover that we cannot actually afford to buy a new computer, then any tasks concerning which kind or configuration suddenly become irrelevant. Our new contradiction handling strategy forces us to represent tasks in such a way that we can mark them as irrelevant, even when they are not executing. There are a variety of ways to do this, some of which are considered in Section 14.4.

14.2 Implementing ATRE

ATRE is designed to support both the many-worlds and focused problem-solving strategies. Its organization follows that of the other TREs, with JTRE being the closest match. Let us consider each part of the system in turn.

14.2.1 The ATRE interface (ainter.lisp)

The code in this file defines four parts of the system:

1. The global structure of ATREs and manipulations on them.
2. The datastructures used by the other components.
3. The interface to the focus mechanism.
4. The implementation of contradiction handlers.

The first two parts are almost exactly like earlier TREs. The only new fields of the ATRE struct are:

`in-rules` Rules to be executed when their triggers are jointly believed.

`focus` An environment which is the current focal point of ATRE's processing.

`contradiction-rules` Contradiction handlers associated with particular environments.

`imp-rules` Rules to be executed when their triggers are implied by the current focus.

How these fields are used is explained below. The definition of rules has become more complex, with fields `in-nodes` and `imp-nodes` containing the lists of antecedent nodes that must be jointly believed and implied by the focus, respectively, before the rule is executed. The other new aspect in this part of the file is the procedure `solutions`, which provides an interface to the ATMS procedure `interpretations`.

The third part, focus manipulations, ensures that rule scheduling appropriately tracks changes in focus environments. The procedure `change-focus` does reality checks on the ATRE and the proposed focus environment, and if sound, makes the change. To support the implied by rule execution strategy, the vocabulary of trigger conditions is extended to include the keyword `:IMPLIED-BY`. The rules stored in the `atre-imp-rules` field are rules with `:IMPLIED-BY` triggers which were not executable under the previous focus. They may be implied by the new focus, though, so they are requeued for examination at the appropriate time. (If they still are not relevant they will be returned to `atre-imp-rules` later.) The procedure `focus-okay?` is provided for procedures using ATREs. Presumably, if the focus has failed, the control strategy must find a new task to work on. The macro `with-focus` encapsulates these mechanisms to simplify working with a focus temporarily.

The implementation of contradiction rules uses the ATMS to do the hard work. A contradiction rule is a procedure which takes one argument, the environment it is associated with. Contradiction rules are created by the procedure `contradiction-rule`. `contradiction-rule` operates by first seeing if the environment is already contradictory. If so, it queues the procedure for execution. Otherwise, it stashes the procedure and its argument on the environment's `env-rules` slot. If the environment ever becomes contradictory, the ATMS will call the enqueueing procedure given to it by ATRE, which ultimately will cause the procedure to be executed. (The procedure in the ATMS that services the `env-rules` field is `remove-env-from-labels`.)

14.2.2 The ATRE database (adata.lisp)

The basic structure of ATRE's database is the same as in the other TREs. The differences lie in the treatment of assumptions and the set of interrogatives provided.

Since assumptions are permanent in the ATMS, there is no distinct notion of enabling or disabling an assumption. Instead, `assume!` provides an interface to the ATMS procedure `assume-node`, which permanently makes the node associated with the fact into an assumption. (The procedures `already-assumed?` and `assume-if-needed` allow procedures to avoid mistakenly re-assuming facts.)

A common operation in ATMS-based problem solvers is stating that a combination of facts is mutually inconsistent. Thus we include the macro `rnogood!`, which allows us to state that a combination of facts taken together comprise a contradiction. (This is accomplished by providing a justification for `false`, the inference-engine statement whose node is the contradiction node for the ATRE's ATMS.) The syntax of `rnogood!` is close to what we have been using for Horn justifications, namely an informant followed by a list of antecedents. In an *N*-queens puzzle solver, for instance, the consistency rule might look like this:

```
(rule :IN ((Queen ?column1 ?row1) :VAR ?Q1
           (Queen ?column2 ?row2) :VAR ?Q2
           :TEST (not (or (= ?column1 ?column2)
                          (queens-okay? ?column1 ?row1
                                        ?column2 ?row2))))
     (rnogood! :DEATH ?Q1 ?Q2))
```

The set of interrogatives provide interfaces to the underlying ATMS procedures. `true?` is non-`nil` only when the fact holds in the empty environment, that is, is universally believed. As noted in Section 14.1.2, `in?` and `out?` play dual roles, according to whether or not they are given an environment to work with. Since environments are explicit objects to be reasoned with, procedures for constructing and dissecting environments are needed. The procedure `environment-of` produces the environment corresponding to a set of assumed facts, and the procedure `environment-cons` produces a new environment by adding an assumed fact to a given environment. The procedure `view-env` supports the dissection of environments by mapping their assumptions back into ATRE assertions.

The set of interrogatives for debugging has also expanded. `get-tms-node`, `show-data`, and `view-node` are defined as they were in previous systems. But the definition of `assumptions-of` has been simplified, from a search through the dependency graph to find the current set of assumptions supporting a fact to simply returning the fact's label. The procedures `the-e` and `get-just` provide methods for retrieving environments and justifications based on their index numbers, which is very useful in interactive debugging and instrumenting code. In addition to showing the whole database (`show-data`) and printing database statistics broken down by database class (`show-dclass`), the procedure `show-context` presents the subset of the database implied by the given environment.

14.2.3 The ATRE rule system (arules.lisp)

The major changes in the ATRE rule system stem from the need to keep track of the different trigger conditions during rule definition and execution. In defining rules, the global variables `*in-nodes*` and `*imp-nodes*` are used as registers to pass into a rule the nodes corresponding to the `:IN` and `:IMPLIED-BY` triggers accumulated from its surrounding environment. These are introduced into the form for defining nested rules by `build-rule`. In addition, the syntax for trigger conditions has been simplified by moving the trigger condition outside the list of antecedents. This change makes sense because most ATRE rules are written with a single trigger condition. No expressive power is lost by this change, since rules with different trigger conditions can be explicitly nested if required. Otherwise, the process of defining rules is directly analogous to JTRE.

Executing rules is a bit more complicated. Let us start by considering `try-rule-on`, which, as in previous systems, sees if a rule should be executed on a given datum. First, the rule's matcher is called on the form of the datum to see if it matches the trigger pattern. As before, the matcher returns the trigger condition of the rule as one of its results, and if the condition is other than `:INTERN`, the node is added to the list of bindings. When we queue the procedure, we have to keep track of two lists of nodes in addition to the bindings—the `:IN` nodes and `:IMPLIED-BY` nodes for that rule. Thus what we put on the queue has three parts: the procedure that is the body of the rule, the list of bindings, and the nodes that comprise the rest of the triggering environment for the rule. In `execute-rule`, this information is used to determine whether or not to actually run the rule. The globals `*in-nodes*` and `*imp-nodes*` are reset to reflect the control environment for the given rule, so that if the rule is executed, any new rules will receive this environment. If the nodes comprising the in triggers are jointly believable, and the nodes comprising the implied-by triggers are a consequence of the current focus, then the rule is executed. Otherwise, the rule is stored back in the ATRE for future consideration.

14.3 Building a planner

Planning is a good example of the need to construct and compare alternative solutions. We begin by examining how different world states can be compactly represented in an ATMS so that reasoning about changes in them becomes quite simple. The specific example we use is the classic Blocks World, but the lessons are applicable for a variety of more realistic domains as well. Then we explore the many-worlds problem-solving strategy by building an envisioner for Blocks World situations. Finally, we look at how the same world representations can be used in a more restrained planning strategy which can be applied to larger problems where envisioning would be inappropriate.

14.3.1 Representing worlds

There are many ways to represent states of affairs. As is often the case in knowledge representation, the properties of the content to be represented, while crucial, leave open a bewildering array of design choices. Considering how we wish to use that knowledge, however, can provide considerable constraint. If we are building a planner, then presumably we need to model actions and their effects. This requirement, combined with the computational properties of the ATMS, considerably narrows the range of sensible alternatives.

Here is the strategy we use. In any class of domain to be formalized, there is some set of actions which we want to reason about. We presume that actions directly change certain properties of the world. These direct changes may cause other properties to change in turn. For instance, if we are formalizing the Blocks World, the action of stacking block `A` on block `B` directly affects the position of `A` (that is, after the action `A` is on `B`) and whether `B`'s top is clear (it was before, but isn't afterwards). There are indirect effects as well: It is now the case that `A` is above `B`, and if `B` was the pinnacle of a large tower containing block `Z`, it is now the case that `A` is above `Z` as well.

Let us call statements that are directly affected by some action *causally primitive.* Let us further suppose that we can derive all other relevant statements in a world model from causally primitive statements, just as conclusions about whether one block is above another can be derived from statements about what blocks are directly atop other blocks. When true, these conditions allow us to closely align the representation of the world with the structure of the ATMS. That is, a compact way to represent a state of the world is to create an environment that consists of all causally primitive statements. The other statements which hold in a state of affairs are then the consequences of this environment. With this representation for states, actions can be represented as manipulations on environments of causally primitive statements.

This is not the only way to represent world states in an ATMS-based problem solver, but it is probably the most efficient and most useful. Let us see how this model can be applied to formalizing the Blocks World.

14.3.2 A simple Blocks World formalization

We use a standard set of simplifying assumptions in modeling the Blocks World. Specifically, we assume a table of indefinite extent and a collection of solid, rigid blocks. Blocks can neither be created nor destroyed. The set of blocks to be considered in a session of reasoning is fixed in advance. Each block is identified only by a unique name. Every block fits on the table, and the table has space for any number of blocks. Each block can have exactly one block stacked on top of it. We assume there is only one agent in this world, which has a single hand capable of gripping, lifting, and stacking any block, and a perceptual system that perfectly identifies blocks and their positions.

Here are the predicates used in this formalization, with their intuitive meanings:

`(on` ⟨*block*⟩ ⟨*thing*⟩`)` Holds if block ⟨*block*⟩ is on top of ⟨*thing*⟩, which can be another block or the table.

`(above` ⟨*thing1*⟩ ⟨*thing2*⟩`)` Holds if ⟨*thing1*⟩ is somewhere above ⟨*thing2*⟩.

`(clear` ⟨*thing*⟩`)` Holds if ⟨*thing*⟩ has space for a block on top of it.

`(holding` ⟨*thing*⟩`)` Holds if ⟨*thing*⟩ is being held aloft by our canonical agent.

`(hand-empty)` Holds if our canonical agent is not clasping a block.

The following actions can be taken by this world's agent:

`(pickup` ⟨*block*⟩`)` Grasps ⟨*block*⟩, which must not have anything on it, and hoists it high over the table, out of contact with any other block.

`(unstack` ⟨*block1*⟩ ⟨*block2*⟩`)` Like `pickup`, but ⟨*block1*⟩ is lifted from the top of ⟨*block2*⟩ instead of from the table.

`(putdown` ⟨*block*⟩`)` Places ⟨*block*⟩, which was being held, on the table.

`(stack` ⟨*block1*⟩ ⟨*block2*⟩`)` Like `putdown`, but ⟨*block1*⟩ is placed on top of ⟨*block2*⟩ instead of upon the table.

Given these actions, which predicates should count among the causally primitive? Clearly `holding` and `hand-empty` should be included, since these are the most direct effects of these actions. It is useful to keep the set of primitive predicates as small as possible, to shift the burden of bookkeeping from our action representation onto the inferential mechanisms. Can we avoid including other predicates? If we had exactly one block, then occurrences of `holding` and `hand-empty` would suffice to completely define the state of the world. If `hand-empty` were true, our block would be on the table, and if `holding` were true of our block, then we would know where it was. But in situations where there is more than one block, `on` statements must be treated as causally primitive, since they preserve world state beyond our agent's gripper.

What about `above`? We can prove that one block is above another by finding a chain of blocks, each of which is `on` the other, such that the blocks in question form the ends of the chain. (How to calculate `above` efficiently is described below.) Since occurrences of `above` can be derived from `on`, `above` does not need to be causally primitive. Actually, in our simple model we cannot treat `above` as causally primitive. If we pick up a block, we are making invalid an arbitrary number of `above` statements, since the block we grab could be the top block of an arbitrarily high tower. It is hard to see how to specify an action if we must take into account an arbitrary amount of the world surrounding the objects that the action is to directly affect. On the other hand, since a block is on top of exactly one other block, the action `unstack` need only specify two blocks, the one being hoisted and the one being relieved of its burden. The ability to derive the effects of this local change on its surroundings thus greatly simplifies the encoding of actions.

What about `clear`? The status of this predicate is less obvious at first glance. On one hand, `clear` statements are local effects of actions, given our simplifying assumptions. That is,

- If we `unstack`, then the block we freed of its burden becomes clear.
- If we `stack`, the recipient block is no longer clear.
- If we `stack` or `putdown`, the block just released is clear.

So we could easily include the bookkeeping to track changes in `clear` statements in the actions.

On the other hand, since `clear` statements are local effects of `on` statements, it might seem as though they should be easily derivable from `on` statements. The required inference runs something like this: Given a block `A`, `(clear A)` holds exactly when there is no other block `B` such that `(on B A)` holds. Since our set of blocks is finite, we could justify the nonexistence of a `B` for any given `A` by the disjunction of each consistent collection of `on` statements ascribing different locations to each of the other blocks. The inelegance of this "solution," let alone its combinatorics, make it too horrible to contemplate. What about establishing `clear` via default reasoning? That is, given a state resulting from an action, we could extend it incrementally by postulating `clear` for each block in turn, and backtracking when contradictions occur. This method would work correctly if the set of `on` descriptions in the state was sufficient to pin down every block's location (see Exercise 6). However, this computation of default extensions is still more work than putting the bookkeeping in the actions, and in this implementation we use the simpler technique.

The discussion of `clear` actually points out a subtle problem with our formalization of `above`. Certainly we can easily define positive instances of `above` using only positive `on` statements. Negative instances of `above`, that is, showing that a block is not above another, lead us to the same problems as trying to define `clear`. The most natural way to show that `A` is not above `B` is to show that `A` is not in the set of things above `B`. We could do this by calculating the set of things above `B` explicitly, using a closed-world representation for sets like that described in Chapter 10. Or we could use a form of negation by failure, presuming that if `(above A B)` isn't a consequence of our world's environment, then it isn't true. Or we could use the extension-by-defaults method suggested for `clear`, and try extending the state with negated `above` statements when relevant. For simple domains like the Blocks World, the differences between these alternatives are irrelevant. For more complex domains, the trade-offs are less clear, and have as much to do with the tasks to be performed as with the structure of the domain itself.

We now have an abstract design for our domain. Laying out a set of predicates and actions, and deciding which predicates will be causally primitive, was the first step. The next step is defining the laws of the domain, to more precisely determine the meanings of our predicates. (We use ATRE rules to encode them, naturally.) Then we define the actions for the domain, using a variation of the STRIPS formalism. With this design in hand, Section 14.3.4 shows how these ideas can be implemented.

14.3.2.1 The laws of blocks

Exactly what do we have to say in order to pin down the meanings of our predicates? A common problem in knowledge representation is knowing when to stop: Should we include weight, texture, or any of the myriad other properties we know about blocks? In this case clearly not: we have placed so many simplifying assumptions on our domain that predicates beyond our initial set are not required. But there is still the problem of determining when we have been precise enough about the relationships involving just the vocabulary we have chosen. In essence, we want to say enough about these predicates so that the states of affairs we generate are accurate. But how do we generate situations?

A useful way to think about situations is to find a collection of choice sets whose consistent combinations spans the collection of situations. The vocabulary used in these choice sets must be limited to the causally primitive predicates. Furthermore, all of the causally primitive predicates must participate in these choice sets. Otherwise, they would not adequately span the set of possible situations. What choice sets are appropriate for Blocks World situations? Three kinds of choice sets are needed:

1. For each block, what is it on top of?
2. For each block, what is on top of it?
3. What, if anything, is the gripper holding?

Clearly, having complete answers for each of these questions completely determines a Blocks World situation. Would less suffice? Consider a scenario involving just two blocks, `A` and `B`. The choice sets are:

1. `{(holding A), (on A B), (on A Table)}`
2. `{(holding A), (on B A), (clear A)}`
3. `{(holding B), (on B A), (on B Table)}`
4. `{(holding B), (on A B), (clear B)}`
5. `{(holding A), (holding B), (hand-empty)}`

The first two choice sets pin down the location of `A`, the third and fourth pin down the location of `B`, and the fifth determines the state of the gripper. Although there is redundancy, each choice set contains one unique element. Therefore any subset of them would fail to span the space of legal situations. Can they be merged? No, since each is a true set of exhaustive alternatives—merging any of them would again lead to a failure to span the space of legal situations. Such minimal collections of choice sets which span the situations implied by a scenario are called *generating sets* or *basis sets* (the latter by analogy with linear algebra).

So far we have focused on ensuring that the set of situations generated is large enough to contain all legal situations. But not all combinations of statements of a generating set are reasonable situations. For instance, the combination

```
(on B A),(on A B),(hand-empty)
```

violates our intuitions about physical blocks. Ruling out such combinations is the first constraint that must guide our formalization of the domain: the laws must suffice to rule out absurd situations. The second constraint is that all legitimate occurrences of statements from the non-causally primitive portion of the domain vocabulary are correctly inferred. Any formalization that satisfies these two constraints will be appropriate for our purposes.

We use ATRE rules as the medium for defining our laws. The first constraint to enforce is that a block cannot be in two places at once:

```
(rule :INTERN ((on ?obj ?s1) :VAR ?f1
               (on ?obj ?s2) :VAR ?f2
                 :TEST (not (equal ?s1 ?s2)))
      ;Something cannot be two places at once
      (rnogood! :PLACE-EXCLUSION ?f1 ?f2))
```

We use the intern condition to ensure that this constraint is imposed as quickly as possible. We use `rnogood!` to state that any collection of facts satisfying the triggers are mutually inconsistent, thus ensuring that no consistent global state will contain them together. Since we also stipulated that only one block could fit on top of another, we must enforce the uniqueness of `on` with respect to the other argument as well:

```
(rule :INTERN ((on ?obj1 ?s) :VAR ?f1
               (on ?obj2 ?s) :VAR ?f2
                 :TEST (and (not (equal ?obj1 ?obj2))
                            (not (equal ?s 'TABLE))))
      ;Only one thing can be on top of a block at any time.
      (rnogood! :TOP-EXCLUSION ?f1 ?f2))
```

The exception to this rule, as specified in the `:TEST`, is the table, which can have an arbitrary number of blocks on it.

One might expect that the relationship between `clear` and `on` is adequately expressed by the mutually exclusive nature of choice sets. That is, since `(clear A)` and `(on B A)` are in the same choice set, they would not end up in the same state, so we shouldn't have to rule out this possibility. Notice, however, that `(on B A)` will be in yet another choice set, the one constraining where `B` might be. This means that such combinations must be ruled out explicitly:

```
(rule :INTERN ((clear ?obj) :VAR ?f1
               (on ?other ?obj) :VAR ?f2)
      ;;Something cannot be clear if something else is on top of it.
      (rnogood! :TOP-CLEAR-EXCLUSION ?f1 ?f2))
```

A similar argument applies to the relationship between `holding` and `clear` and `on`. That is, if the gripper is holding a block then that block isn't clear, nor can something be on it, nor can it be on something else:

```
(rule :INTERN ((holding ?obj) :VAR ?f1
               (clear ?obj) :VAR ?f2)
      ;if you are holding it then it is not clear
      (rnogood! :CLEAR-HOLDING-EXCLUSION ?f1 ?f2))

(rule :INTERN ((holding ?obj) :VAR ?f1
               (on ?other ?obj) :VAR ?f2)
      ; You cannot hold a block that has something on it.
      (rnogood! :SINGLE-BLOCK-HOLDING ?f1 ?f2))

(rule :INTERN ((holding ?obj) :VAR ?f1
               (on ?obj ?other) :VAR ?f2)
       ;; When you are holding something, it is not on anything else.
      (rnogood! :HOLDING-IN-AIR ?f1 ?f2))
```

To finish defining `holding`, we must enforce the stipulation that the gripper can only hold one thing at a time, and enforce the obvious constraint that if something is being held then the hand isn't empty:

```
(rule :INTERN ((holding ?o1) :VAR ?f1
               (holding ?o2) :VAR ?f2
                :TEST (not (equal ?o1 ?o2)))
```

```
    ;; You can only hold one thing at a time
    (rnogood! :MULTIPLE-HOLD-EXCLUSION ?f1 ?f2))

(rule :INTERN ((hand-empty) :VAR ?f1
               (holding ?obj) :VAR ?f2)
    ;; Your hand isn't empty if it is holding something
    (rnogood! :EMPTY-HOLDING-MUTEX ?f1 ?f2))
```

Now we have completely pinned down the causally primitive predicates. What about `above`, the derivable predicate? The simplest case of `above` is `on`:

```
(rule :INTERN ((on ?a ?b) :VAR ?f1) ;; Base case for ABOVE
    (rassert! (above ?a ?b) (:ABOVE-BASE-CASE ?f1)))
```

We can use the fact that `above` is transitive to complete the definition:

```
(rule :INTERN ((above ?a ?b) :VAR ?f1
               (above ?b ?c) :VAR ?f2) ;; ABOVE is transitive
    (rassert! (above ?a ?c) (:ABOVE-TRANSITIVE ?f1 ?f2)))
```

The transitivity of `above` also suggests encoding other mathematical properties of it, namely that it is antireflexive and antisymmetric:

```
(rule :INTERN ((above ?a ?a) :VAR ?f1) ;; ABOVE is antireflexive
    (rnogood! :ABOVE-ANTIREFLEXIVE  ?f1))

(rule :INTERN ((above ?a ?b) :VAR ?f1
               (above ?b ?a) :VAR ?f2) ;; ABOVE is antisymmetric
    (rnogood! :ABOVE-ANTISYMMETRIC ?f1 ?f2))
```

These rules may be found in the file `blocks.lisp`. With our predicates defined, we turn to defining operators.

14.3.2.2 Defining actions

To define actions we adapt the STRIPS representation. That is, we view actions as *operators*, which transform one state into another. An operator has four parts:

Defining form. This form lists the name of the operator and the variables which must be defined for each instance of it. An example of a defining form is

```
(Pickup ?x)
```

Preconditions. A list of statements which must hold in a situation in order for the operator to be applicable to that situation. The preconditions for `Pickup`, for example, are

```
((on ?x Table) ;; The block ?x is on the table.
 (clear ?x)    ;; ?x has nothing on top of it.
 (hand-empty)) ;; Not holding anything already.
```

Delete-list. A list of statements believed in the situation before the action occurs that will no longer be true in the situation afterwards. The delete list for `Pickup` is

```
((on ?x Table) ;; Block ?x no longer on the table.
 (clear ?x)    ;; ?x no longer has space for a block.
 (hand-empty))  ;; The gripper is no longer empty
```

Add-list. A list of statements not believed in the situation before the action occurs, but true in the situation afterward because of the action. The add list for `Pickup` is

```
((holding ?x)) ;; The gripper is holding block ?x
```

Clearly, the functors of every member of the delete and add lists must be causally primitive predicates. The preconditions do not need to be causally primitive predicates, but often are.

Our syntax for operators follows the same pattern used in earlier systems. That is, we use the keyword `defoperator` to indicate that a form is defining an operator. The defining form is the next argument, and the rest are denoted via keywords. Thus the operators `Pickup` and `Putdown` can be encoded as follows:

```
(defoperator (Pickup ?x)
             :PRECONDITIONS ((on ?x Table)
                             (clear ?x)
                             (hand-empty))
```

```
              :DELETE-LIST  ((on ?x Table)
                             (clear ?x)
                             (hand-empty))
              :ADD-LIST ((holding ?x)))

(defoperator (Putdown ?x)
              :PRECONDITIONS ((holding ?x))
              :DELETE-LIST ((holding ?x))
              :ADD-LIST ((on ?x Table)
                         (clear ?x)
                         (hand-empty)))
```

Sometimes simple tests are needed to supplement the list of preconditions. For instance, the operators `stack` and `unstack` only make sense if the block being released or placed is on top of another block and not on the table. We allow an optional field `:TEST` to provide this capability. Thus the operators `stack` and `unstack` can be encoded as follows:

```
(defoperator (stack ?x ?y)
              :PRECONDITIONS ((holding ?x)
                              (clear ?y))
              :TEST (not (eq ?y 'TABLE))
              :DELETE-LIST ((holding ?x)
                            (clear ?y))
              :ADD-LIST ((hand-empty)
                         (on ?x ?y)
                         (clear ?x)))

(defoperator (unstack ?x ?y)
              :PRECONDITIONS ((hand-empty)
                              (clear ?x)
                              (on ?x ?y))
              :TEST (not (eq ?y 'TABLE))
              :DELETE-LIST ((hand-empty)
                            (clear ?x)
                            (on ?x ?y))
              :ADD-LIST ((holding ?x)
                         (clear ?y)))
```

There are two activities we must perform with operators. First, we must be able to ascertain what operator instances might be used in a given situation. Our convention is that if a statement of the form

(Applicable ⟨*Operator Instance*⟩)

holds in a situation, then ⟨*Operator Instance*⟩ may be legally applied in that situation to create a new situation.

The other activity involving operators is actually applying them to a situation. This involves performing surgery on the environment representing the situation, i.e., removing the facts in the delete list and adding facts in the add list in order to create (or retrieve) a situation representing the result of that action occurring. We explore next how both activities are performed when describing the implementation.

14.3.3 Implementing operators and planning domains

The listing `aplanr.lisp` provides an infrastructure for building ATMS-based planners. Although we use only the Blocks World as an example here, the code is designed to be quite general. The file contains three distinct parts:

1. A datastructure to organize the information about a particular planning problem.
2. The definition of operators and procedures for finding and applying them.
3. Procedures for finding states that satisfy particular criteria.

We examine each in turn.

The `plnpr` ("planning problem") struct provides the basics for describing any domain. Its fields are:

`title` String for printing.

`atre` The ATRE it is associated with.

`basis-set` The collection of choice sets which define the specific scenario.

`operators` The list of operators for the domain.

`plist` A property list for caching intermediate results.

The usual variables and procedures are supplied for operating within a particular planning problem (whose default name is `*plnpr*`).

The procedure `create-planning-problem` takes as input a title, an ATRE, and the basis set for a planning problem. Its main job is creating the ATRE which serves as the inferential scratch pad for planning. Since domain files are loaded by an external system, the operation ensuring that the statements in the basis set are all assumptions is part of a separate procedure, `setup-choice-sets`, which should be executed once the appropriate domain theory has been loaded into the ATRE.

We use a variation of the same strategy for implementing operators that was used in Chapter 8. That is, we define `defoperator` as a macro that produces a datastructure representing that operator. `defoperator` starts by extracting the possible fields from the given form, distributing this information appropriately among the fields of a new `operator` struct. It also creates an ATRE rule which detects combinations of the preconditions, and justifies the appropriate `applicable` assertion for each set of statements that satisfies the operator's preconditions. Figure 14.2 shows what `defoperator` produces for the `stack` operator defined previously.

The ATRE rule created by `defoperator` automatically detects combinations of facts satisfying an operator's preconditions. The procedure `find-applicable-operators` fetches those results of this rule that are relevant to a given situation. It accomplishes this by filtering `applicable` statements, requiring that they be implied by the state (i.e., environment) provided as input. Finally, the procedure `fetch-operator` retrieves the operator datastructure from the current planning problem, so that the information can be used in figuring out the effects of an operator instance.

The procedure `apply-operator` implements the semantics of action for STRIPS operators. It takes as input an environment representing a state and an operator instance that is applicable to that state, as provided by `find-applicable-operators`. It produces as output an environment corresponding to the state that results from the action represented by the operator instance occurring in the input state. The first step is to instantiate the add lists and delete lists for the operator with the specific bindings of the operator instance. We have arranged our definitions so that an association list of bindings can be built by associating the elements in the defining form with the description of the operator instance. The appropriate add and delete lists are then generated using `sublis`

```
(PROGN
  (LET ((ENTRY (ASSOC 'STACK
                      (PLNPR-OPERATORS *PLNPR*)))
        (OP
          (MAKE-OPERATOR :FORM
                         '(STACK ?X ?Y)
                         :PRECONDITIONS
                         '((HOLDING ?X) (CLEAR ?Y))
                         :ADD-LIST
                         '((HAND-EMPTY) (ON ?X ?Y) (CLEAR ?X))
                         :DELETE-LIST
                         '((HOLDING ?X) (CLEAR ?Y)))))
    (COND (ENTRY (SETF (CDR ENTRY) OP))
          (T (PUSH (CONS 'STACK OP)
                   (PLNPR-OPERATORS *PLNPR*)))))
  (RULE :INTERN
        ((HOLDING ?X) (CLEAR ?Y))
        (WHEN (NOT (EQ ?Y 'TABLE))
              (RASSERT! (APPLICABLE (STACK ?X ?Y))
                        (:OP-PCS-SATISFIED (HOLDING ?X) (CLEAR ?Y))))))
```

Figure 14.2 What `defOperator` produces

to make the substitutions of values for variables. The effect of the action is implemented by transforming the list of assumptions of the initial situation. First, the assumptions corresponding to the delete list are removed (in the `remove-if` statement). Next, assumptions corresponding to the add list are blended in (using `ordered-insert`). Finally, the environment corresponding to the transformed list of assumptions is found (or built, if necessary) by the ATMS primitive `find-or-make-env`. Figure 14.3 shows an example.

The final section of this file provides procedures which compute relationships between sets of statements and states. The procedure `fetch-states` finds all states that satisfy a ground partial description. This procedure is mainly useful for finding candidate initial states. It exploits the ATMS interpretation constructor by generating a list of redundant choice sets from input specification, in effect providing a "seed" environment around which states composed from the other choice sets can crystallize. Figure 14.4 shows an example of `fetch-states` in operation. In this case the input information can be satisfied by only a single state,

```
> (print-env (the-e 411))

E-411: (CLEAR A),(HOLDING C),(ON A B),(ON B TABLE)
NIL
> (apply-operator (the-e 411) '(stack c a))
E-192
> (print-env (the-e 192))

E-192: (CLEAR C),(HAND-EMPTY),(ON A B),(ON B TABLE),(ON C A)
NIL
```

Figure 14.3 Operators can be applied by manipulating environments

```
> (fetch-states '((on c b)(on b a)))
(E-216)
> (print-env (the-e 216))
E-216: (HAND-EMPTY), (CLEAR C), (ON C B), (ON B A), (ON A TABLE)
> (show-context (the-e 216))

(APPLICABLE (UNSTACK C B))
(BLOCK C)
(BLOCK B)
(BLOCK A)
(HAND-EMPTY)
(ABOVE C TABLE)
(ABOVE C A)
(ABOVE C B)
(ABOVE B TABLE)
(ABOVE B A)
(ABOVE A TABLE)
(CLEAR C)
(ON A TABLE)
(ON B A)
(ON C B)
15 facts total.
15
```

Figure 14.4 Contents of a sample state

represented by environment `E-216`. The assumptions in the environment itself show the causally primitive predicates which hold in it, and if we look at the statements implied by them (via `show-context`), we see that its implications are exactly what we can say about this situation, given our vocabulary of predicates.

The procedure `satisfies-goal?` determines whether or not a state can satisfy a list of statements. It searches through the potential unifications of the goal conjunction with the statements implied by the candidate solution state, returning `t` and a suitable set of bindings if it succeeds, and `nil` otherwise. Finally, the procedure `show-plan` prints an alternating list of states and operator instances in an easily digestible form.

14.3.4 An envisioner for the Blocks World

Small exponentials make nice pets.
—Anonymous

The idea of envisioning is very simple. The fact that we can define a basis set for Blocks World situations means that we can enumerate the possible states for any fixed collection of blocks. Moreover, we can generate the effects of every possible plan on a fixed collection of blocks by the following procedure:

1. Generate all legal situations for the given blocks.
2. For each state S,
    a. Find the applicable operator instances for S.
    b. For each operator instance O on S,
        i. Find the state T that results from applying O to S.
        ii. Install a pointer from S to T in a table of transitions.

This procedure is an example of envisioning. Its result, an *envisionment*, describes all possible situations that can occur for the given collection of individuals. These situations are linked by the actions that transform them from one to another. Given an envisionment, the problem of planning is reduced to graph search.

Envisioning is the prototypical many-worlds ATMS problem solving strategy. It works well for small problems, and can be very useful in gain-ing insight into the structure of a domain. However, it quickly becomes unmanageable. Clearly, games like chess and checkers are outside the scope of what can be explicitly generated, and even Blocks World scenarios can strain computational capacities, if enough blocks are considered. Nevertheless, its usefulness in understanding problem spaces and its simplicity make it a good place to start in understanding the use of ATMSs in planning.

The listing `plan-e.lisp` implements the procedure outlined above. It performs interpretation construction on the basis set to create the set of possible states, caching the result in the `:STATES` property of the planning problem's `plist`. It then iterates over the set of states, applying every operator in turn (by calling the procedure `apply-all-operators`), caching the result in the `:TRANSITIONS` property of the `plist`. These two properties comprise the envisionment for the planning problem. The procedure `show-envisionment` produces a report describing the envisionment.

The procedure `envis-find-plan` uses the envisionment to find a sequence of actions that transforms a state satisfying the given initial conditions to one satisfying the given goal conditions. There is a striking resemblance between this procedure and `bsolve` in CPS (Chapter 3). This should not be surprising upon reflection, since the compact representation of context provided by the ATMS provides a simple interface to the rest of the problem solver, just as our encapsulation of states in CPS did. The difference is that the knowledge of the domain (i.e., the laws and operators of the Blocks World) can be expressed in a more general, declarative fashion than in CPS.

Let us see how the envisioner works on some Blocks World examples. The procedures in the file `bcode.lisp` orchestrate the creation of Blocks World planning problems. Given a list of blocks, the procedure `build-blocks-problem` sets up a session of Blocks World problem solving. It creates a planning problem datastructure to orchestrate the information, and loads whatever file is specified by `*blocks-file*` to set up the appropriate laws and operators. (Recall that the file `blocks.lisp` contains this information.) It asserts the identity of the blocks in the ATRE, and calls `setup-choice-sets` to ensure that the basis set elements are all assumed.

Suppose we have three blocks, `A`, `B`, and `C`. Figure 14.5 shows the report generated about the envisionment for this scenario. The envisionment

```
22 states have been generated:

E-411: (HOLDING C), (ON A B), (ON B TABLE), (CLEAR A)
E-402: (HOLDING C), (CLEAR B), (ON B A), (ON A TABLE)
E-394: (HOLDING C), (CLEAR B), (ON B TABLE), (CLEAR A), (ON A TABLE)
E-376: (HOLDING B), (ON A C), (ON C TABLE), (CLEAR A)
E-364: (HOLDING B), (CLEAR C), (ON C A), (ON A TABLE)
E-350: (HOLDING B), (CLEAR C), (ON C TABLE), (CLEAR A), (ON A TABLE)
E-333: (HOLDING A), (ON B C), (ON C TABLE), (CLEAR B)
E-320: (HOLDING A), (CLEAR C), (ON C B), (ON B TABLE)
E-304: (HOLDING A), (CLEAR C), (ON C TABLE), (CLEAR B), (ON B TABLE)
E-293: (HAND-EMPTY), (ON B C), (ON C A), (CLEAR B), (ON A TABLE)
E-279: (HAND-EMPTY), (ON B C), (ON C TABLE), (ON A B), (CLEAR A)
E-270: (HAND-EMPTY), (ON B C), (ON C TABLE), (CLEAR B), (CLEAR A), (ON A TABLE)
E-251: (HAND-EMPTY), (ON A C), (ON C B), (ON B TABLE), (CLEAR A)
E-235: (HAND-EMPTY), (ON A C), (ON C TABLE), (CLEAR B), (ON B A)
E-229: (HAND-EMPTY), (ON A C), (ON C TABLE), (CLEAR B), (ON B TABLE), (CLEAR A)
E-216: (HAND-EMPTY), (CLEAR C), (ON C B), (ON B A), (ON A TABLE)
E-208: (HAND-EMPTY), (CLEAR C), (ON C B), (ON B TABLE), (CLEAR A), (ON A TABLE)
E-192: (HAND-EMPTY), (CLEAR C), (ON C A), (ON A B), (ON B TABLE)
E-185: (HAND-EMPTY), (CLEAR C), (ON C A), (CLEAR B), (ON B TABLE), (ON A TABLE)
E-169: (HAND-EMPTY), (CLEAR C), (ON C TABLE), (ON A B), (ON B TABLE), (CLEAR A)
E-160: (HAND-EMPTY), (CLEAR C), (ON C TABLE), (CLEAR B), (ON B A), (ON A TABLE)
E-152: (HAND-EMPTY), (CLEAR C), (ON C TABLE), (CLEAR B), (ON B TABLE), (CLEAR A), (ON A TABLE)
```

contains twenty-two states, with forty-two transitions between them. It is easy to inspect this table to see that each state and each transition makes sense. Confirming that these are the only legitimate possibilities takes more effort (see Exercise 2). Once the envisionment has been generated, however, planning is easy. Figure 14.6 provides an example. The initial state is a tower with C on top and A on the bottom, and the goal is a tower with the positions of A and C reversed. Since `find-plan` uses breadth-first search, we know this is no longer, in terms of operator applications, than any other plan for achieving the same goal.

14.3.5 Other ATMS-based planning strategies

Although envisioning is a natural way to use an ATMS, the same advantages accrue for most other planning strategies. For example, the file

```
Transition Table:
E-411:                 E-333:                  E-229:
(PUTDOWN C) -> E-169   (PUTDOWN A) -> E-270    (PICKUP B) -> E-376
(STACK C A) -> E-192   (STACK A B) -> E-279    (UNSTACK A C) -> E-304
E-402:                 E-320:                  E-216:
(PUTDOWN C) -> E-160   (PUTDOWN A) -> E-208    (UNSTACK C B) -> E-402
(STACK C B) -> E-216   (STACK A C) -> E-251    E-208:
E-394:                 E-304:                  (PICKUP A) -> E-320
(PUTDOWN C) -> E-152   (PUTDOWN A) -> E-152    (UNSTACK C B) -> E-394
(STACK C B) -> E-208   (STACK A C) -> E-229    E-192:
(STACK C A) -> E-185   (STACK A B) -> E-169    (UNSTACK C A) -> E-411
E-376:                 E-293:                  E-185:
(PUTDOWN B) -> E-229   (UNSTACK B C) -> E-364  (PICKUP B) -> E-364
(STACK B A) -> E-235   E-279:                  (UNSTACK C A) -> E-394
E-364:                 (UNSTACK A B) -> E-333  E-169:
(PUTDOWN B) -> E-185   E-270:                  (PICKUP C) -> E-411
(STACK B C) -> E-293   (PICKUP A) -> E-333     (UNSTACK A B) -> E-304
E-350:                 (UNSTACK B C) -> E-350  E-160:
(PUTDOWN B) -> E-152   E-251:                  (PICKUP C) -> E-402
(STACK B C) -> E-270   (UNSTACK A C) -> E-320  (UNSTACK B A) -> E-350
(STACK B A) -> E-160   E-235:                  E-152:
                       (UNSTACK B A) -> E-376  (PICKUP A) -> E-304
                                               (PICKUP B) -> E-350
                                               (PICKUP C) -> E-394
```

Figure 14.5 An envisionment for a three blocks problem

`plan-a.lisp` contains a forward-chaining search program that does not require an envisionment in order to operate. If we run it on the same problem we tested `find-plan` on, we get the following results:

```
(plan-a start '((on a b) (on b c)))
(E-279 (STACK A B) E-333 (PICKUP A) E-270 (STACK B C) E-350
 (UNSTACK B A) E-160 (PUTDOWN C) E-402 (UNSTACK C B) E-216)
15
```

The plan is the same, but seven fewer states (and their attendant transitions) needed to be examined. In this simple scenario we only cut the search space by 32 percent, but of course for larger problems the savings could be substantial. It is also straightforward to implement backward-chaining strategies and other more sophisticated problem-solving techniques using these state and operator representations. In other words,

```
(find-plan '((on C B) (on B A)) '((on A B) (on B C)))
(E-279 (STACK A B) E-333 (PICKUP A) E-270 (STACK B C) E-350
  (UNSTACK B A) E-160 (PUTDOWN C) E-402 (UNSTACK C B) E-216)
> (show-plan *)

E-216: (HAND-EMPTY), (CLEAR C), (ON C B), (ON B A), (ON A TABLE)
  then, by (UNSTACK C B),
E-402: (HOLDING C), (CLEAR B), (ON B A), (ON A TABLE)
  then, by (PUTDOWN C),
E-160: (HAND-EMPTY), (CLEAR C), (ON C TABLE), (CLEAR B), (ON B A), (ON A TABLE)
  then, by (UNSTACK B A),
E-350: (HOLDING B), (CLEAR C), (ON C TABLE), (CLEAR A), (ON A TABLE)
  then, by (STACK B C),
E-270: (HAND-EMPTY), (ON B C), (ON C TABLE), (CLEAR B), (CLEAR A), (ON A TABLE)
  then, by (PICKUP A),
E-333: (HOLDING A), (ON B C), (ON C TABLE), (CLEAR B)
  then, by (STACK A B),
E-279: (HAND-EMPTY), (ON B C), (ON C TABLE), (ON A B), (CLEAR A)

> (show-context (the-e 279))

(APPLICABLE (UNSTACK A B))
(BLOCK C)
(BLOCK B)
(BLOCK A)
(HAND-EMPTY)
(ABOVE A C)
(ABOVE B C)
(ABOVE C TABLE)
(ABOVE A B)
(ABOVE B TABLE)
(ABOVE A TABLE)
(CLEAR A)
(ON A B)
(ON C TABLE)
(ON B C)
15 facts total.
15
```

Figure 14.6 Finding plans using the envisionment

the ATMS is neutral with respect to the planning strategy employed. By propagating information across contexts easily, an ATMS provides a reasonably efficient system for world-modeling.

There are always trade-offs, naturally. The disadvantage of using an ATMS in planning is the cost of propagating complex labels versus repeatedly propagating simple labels. If backtracking is actually rare, or only a small fraction of the potential search space ends up being explored, then the extra inferential work involved in propagating complex labels is wasted. Worse yet, in some circumstances the size of labels can grow exponentially, making the ATMS itself a liability rather than an ally. Research on these trade-offs and how to extend the useful range of ATMS techniques continues (see [2, 4, 5]).

14.4 Using an ATMS in focused problem solving

While the many-worlds strategy can be surprisingly effective, it is clearly inappropriate for many kinds of problems. For many real problems, the full search space is vastly larger than the subset that needs to be explored to find an acceptable solution. Examples include engineering design, interpreting data from multiple sources, and solving textbook physics problems. Problem solvers for such domains must carefully shepherd their resources, narrowly focusing attention on only a small number of alternatives, while keeping track of the possibility that their current focus of attention could be wrong.

Section 14.1 outlined the mechanisms needed for such tight control: the encapsulation of locus of attention as *focus environments*, the *implied-by strategy* which only executes rules implied by the current focus, and *contradiction handlers*, which decentralize the choice of action to take when inconsistencies arise. This section examines how to arrange these mechanisms into coherent problem-solving strategies.

The easiest way to build a new problem solver is to adapt and generalize previous systems. Let us use the design of JSAINT from Chapter 8 as a starting point. The data, procedure, and reference models of JSAINT were based on JTRE. The global control structure was an AND/OR tree of tasks, built up from suggestions created by pattern-directed rules.

The first step in adapting the JSAINT organization to exploit the ATMS is to associate a focus environment with each task. Part of what it means for the problem solver to be working on a specific task is making the problem solver's focus be the environment of that task. This ensures that all pattern-directed rules implied by that environment will be executed. Like JSAINT, these rules will either solve the given subproblem directly or make suggestions about more expensive operations to try. If the initial problem remains unsolved, the leaves of the AND/OR tree will be examined and the most promising task scheduled for execution. This processing continues until either the initial problem is solved or there are no more tasks to try.

Let us examine more closely the impact of adding environments to tasks. The underlying logic of the relationships between tasks in the AND/OR tree (Section 8.5.2.3) would remain unchanged. However, we now have a new kind of event in our problem solver: the task's environment can become inconsistent. For most tasks, this indicates that the task is not worth trying, and should be marked as a failure. However, in some cases (i.e., indirect proofs) a contradiction is actively sought, and so for such cases a different contradiction handler should be supplied.

Although our goal is to design a general-purpose problem solver, it is useful to have some motivating examples in mind. We use natural deduction here, in order to draw on the reader's experience with the FTRE-based implementation of KM* from Chapter 5. In using our new problem solver to perform natural deduction, the initial task environment consists of the premises of the proof, and the goal condition is the existence of a proof for the given desideratum based only on the initial assumptions.

How different would the encoding of the knowledge of natural deduction be for this new system? Not very different, it turns out. The implementation of the laws of KM* could be adapted directly from **fnd.lisp**. Rules that do not make assumptions (e.g., Conditional Elimination) need only have their trigger syntax modified to fit the ATRE conventions and ensure that the appropriate justifications are created. For instance, the rule for Conditional Elimination becomes

```
(rule :IMPLIED-BY ((implies ?p ?q) ?p)
      (rassert! ?q (:CE (implies ?p ?q) ?p)))
```

More complex natural deduction rules can be implemented by a suggestions mechanism, analogous to that used in JSAINT. That is, part of the work of the pattern-directed rules implementing a natural deduction rule is to make a suggestion about some more complex problem-solving operation to perform. Suggestions for unsolved subproblems are then gathered up and used to extend the AND/OR graph. Some problem-solver operations, such as linking a goal to the solution of a conjunction or disjunction of subgoals, should be built in. For instance, the rule for AND INTRODUCTION must require both conjuncts to be proven before the conjunction may be asserted. If the `show-all` operation causes interest to be expressed in all of its arguments, and further ensures that if one subgoal fails the whole attempt fails, then we can write the rule for AND INTRODUCTION as follows:

```
(rule :IMPLIED-BY ((show (and ?a ?b)) :VAR ?f1)
      (rule :IMPLIED-BY (?a ?b)
            (rassert! (and ?a ?b) (:AI ?a ?b)))
      (rassert! (suggest-for ?f1
                  (show-all ?a ?b)) (:BC-AI ?f1)))
```

Similarly, the ability to handle disjunctive subgoals could be introduced by a `show-any` operation, which expresses interest in both of its subgoals, and succeeds if either of them does. Using this operation, we can write the rule for OR INTRODUCTION as follows:

```
(rule :IMPLIED-BY ((show (or ?p ?q)) :VAR ?f1)
      (rule :IMPLIED-BY (?p)
           (rassert! (or ?p ?q) (:OI ?p)))
      (rule :IMPLIED-BY (?q)
            (rassert! (or ?p ?q) (:OI ?q)))
      (rassert! (suggest-for ?f1
                  (show-any ?p ?q)) (:BC-OI ?f1)))
```

The operations `show-all` and `show-any` are likely to be useful in building a variety of problem solvers. A wise implementer, of course, will make the set of problem solver operations extensible to allow domain-specific constructs. In KM*, we saw that the ability to make local contexts was required by several of the inference rules. In the FTRE implementation, these rules called `seek-in-context`. We can replace them by rules that make suggestions about assumptions to try. For instance, the rules for CONDITIONAL INTRODUCTION and INDIRECT PROOF could be written as:

```
(rule :IMPLIED-BY ((show (implies ?p ?q)) :VAR ?f1)
 (rassert! (suggest-for ?f1
             (try-box ?p ?q (implies ?p ?q) CI))
           (:BC-CI ?f1)))

(rule :IMPLIED-BY ((show ?f) :VAR ?f1
           :TEST (not (and (listp ?f)
                           (member (car ?f)
                                   '(implies and iff not)))))
 (rassert! (suggest-for ?f1
              (try-box (not ?f) contradiction ?f IP))
           (:BC-IP ?f1)))
```

where `try-box` is a problem-solver operation whose arguments are something to be assumed (i.e., `?p`), something to be proved based on that assumption (i.e., `?q`), the conclusion to be drawn if the proof is successful (i.e., `(implies ?p ?q)`), and the informant to use in justifying the conclusion if successful (i.e., `CI`).

Although the necessary changes to the rules are syntactically small, their impact should not be underestimated. In the FTRE-based system, the use of a stack to manage assumptions forced us into a depth-first reasoning strategy. In that system, each new assumption had to be completely explored (within the given resource limitations) before exploring a different assumption. The reification of contexts as environments facilitates the use of other control strategies. For instance, the system can be biased toward shorter proofs by organizing the agenda of tasks to prefer those with smaller focus environments, resulting in a breadth-first search pattern.

When discussing contradiction handling previously, the issue of turning off tasks when they become irrelevant arose. The same vocabulary of control predicates (i.e., `open`, `solved`, and `failed`) used in JSAINT can be adapted to describe properties and relationships of tasks in the new system. That is, unless a contradiction is being sought, any task with a contradictory focus environment can be said to have failed. For tasks that seek contradictions (e.g., indirect proofs), a contradiction handler for the environment corresponding to the previous focus plus the disputed assumption can assert that the task has been solved should that environment become contradictory.

While this discussion is based on working systems we have built, we have not included an implementation of this design. Instead, in Exercises 12 through 14 we invite the reader to reconstruct a system like that of [7].

14.5 Backpointers

The particular Blocks World formalization used here is based on [8]. The model of actions and planning presented here corresponds to an early standard for AI research, the STRIPS model [6]. It is a very coarse approximation of the problems which originally motivated planning research. The real world in which human beings live is extremely complicated, with huge numbers of objects and many actions that can be taken with respect to them. Even more complexity arises from the fact that there are multiple agents and that nature itself does things. Predicting the distant future in such a complex world is a chancy enterprise, and even enumerating the indirect consequences of an action can be difficult. Much of the current research in the planning community, and on reasoning about actions in the knowledge representation community, is aimed at addressing these limitations. A good starting point from which to approach this literature is [1].

ATMSs were used commercially by both `KEE` (from IntelliCorp) and `ART` (from Inference Corporation). Their use of ATMSs to encode contexts rested on using assumptions as context markers. We believe that for most purposes the representation scheme described in this chapter is more efficient.

14.6 Exercises

1. ⋆ Remove the antisymmetric and antireflexive laws from the blocks formalization. Does `plan-e` generate any more states in the three-blocks case? If their condition was `:IN` instead of `:INTERN`, would they ever be executed?

2. ⋆⋆ Write a formula that predicts how many states there will be in an envisionment of N blocks and another formula that predicts how many transitions there will be in an envisionment of N blocks.

3. ⋆⋆ A handy debugging tool for problem solvers with other TMSs was `explore-network`. Write a version of `explore-network` for the ATMS which takes two additional arguments compared to the earlier versions. The first additional argument is an environment. The second additional argument is a keyword. If the keyword is `:IMPLIED-BY`, only nodes and justifications that are in under the given environment are shown. If the keyword is `:CONSISTENT`, only nodes and justifications whose labels are consistent with the given environment are shown.

4. ⋆⋆ Use the ATMS procedure `remove-node` to implement an efficient mechanism for executing rules with `:IN` triggers.

5. Suppose we wish to weaken the restriction that at most one block can be on top of another. In particular, let `straddles` be the set of things that a block is on, and let `straddlers` be the set of blocks on a given block.

   a. ⋆ Explain what extensions must be made to the STRIPS operators to correctly manipulate states defined using `straddles` and `straddlers` instead of `clear` and `on`.

   b. ⋆⋆ Define a new set of laws and operators for the Blocks World using `straddles` and `straddlers` as the causal primitives.

   c. ⋆⋆⋆ Implement your extended planner and new Blocks World formalization, and test it on several examples.

6. Suppose we wish to define `clear` as a default assumption. That is, a block will be presumed to be `clear` unless there is another block known to be on it.

   a. ⋆ What parts of the Blocks World implementation would become simpler and what parts would need to be more complicated if we make this change?

   b. ⋆⋆ Implement this change, and demonstrate that the examples in `plan-a` still operate correctly.

c. ⋆ Consider the operation of dropping a block. That is, before the `drop` operator occurs, the gripper is holding a block, and afterward it is not. Could we implement this operation in our original Blocks World formulation? Can we implement it with `clear` as a default?

d. ⋆⋆ Implement the `drop` operator. How does this new operator affect the envisionment for a three-blocks situation? For *N* blocks?

7. Given the extensions from previous problems, suppose we modeled a Casino Robot as follows: The action `grab-dice` causes the pair of dice lying on the table to be in the gripper and shaken. The action `shoot` spills the dice onto the table. For any situation, the predicate `(Score` ⟨*n*⟩`)` is true exactly if the sum of the faces showing on the dice is ⟨*n*⟩.

   a. ⋆⋆ Assuming fair dice, how would you use this formalization with this chapter's planning systems to compute the odds on various outcomes?

   b. ⋆⋆ Using whatever extensions you need from previous problems, implement the domain model for the Casino Robot.

8. Suppose we add another property to blocks, for example, color. Color can be changed by an operator `paint`, e.g.,

```
(paint A red)
```

would result in `A`'s color becoming `red`, no matter what it was before.

   a. ⋆ Write `paint` as a STRIPS operator.

   b. ⋆ What other changes must we make to the Blocks World domain to support the addition of color to the domain?

   c. ⋆ Suppose we further specify that painting is a very inexact operation, so that if we set out to paint a specific block, any other block resting on it also changes color. That is, applying `(paint B red)` to the situation

```
(On A table)
(On B A)
(On C B)
```

will result in all three blocks turning `red`. Why can't this version of `paint` be encoded in a standard STRIPS formulation?

d. ⋆⋆⋆ Extend the operator implementation to handle actions with partially specified add and delete lists, and demonstrate that your solution works by solving problems involving combinations of block movements and the extended `paint` operation.

9. The rule strategies described in Section 14.1.3 only partially span the space of possibilities. Here are two others:

   `:EACH-IN` The rule is queued for execution if each trigger is `:IN` by itself.

   `:CONSISTENT-WITH` The rule is queued only if the triggers are consistent with the current focus.

   a. ⋆ Do these strategies require an ATMS? Why or why not?

   b. ⋆ Explain whether or not these strategies are useful, including examples to support your argument.

   c. ⋆⋆ Implement the `:EACH-IN` strategy and evaluate its utility.

   d. ⋆⋆ Implement the `:CONSISTENT-WITH` strategy and evaluate its utility.

10. ⋆⋆⋆ Using `plan-a` as a model, implement a backward-chaining planner.

11. ⋆⋆⋆ Reimplement your favorite planning technique using ATRE as a world modeling system.

12. ⋆⋆⋆ Using the design in Section 14.4 as a starting point, implement a general-purpose ATMS-based problem solver that uses a focused control strategy in the suggestions architecture.

13. ⋆⋆⋆ Using your general-purpose problem solver from Exercise 12 as a module, implement a natural deduction reasoning system which solves propositional logic problems using KM*.

14. Focused ATMS-based problem-solving strategies are clearly the only viable candidates for very large problems. This question explores how useful they are for small puzzles, where the many-worlds strategy is often used.

a. ⋆⋆⋆ Using ATRE, implement a cryptarithmetic puzzle solver based on a many-worlds problem-solving strategy. Compare the efficiency, both in terms of run times and in terms of number of rules fired, of using `:INTERN` versus `:IN` rules.

b. ⋆⋆⋆ Using your general-purpose problem solver from Exercise 12, implement a focused cryptarithmetic puzzle solver. Compare the relative efficiency of breadth-first versus depth-first search, and variations in rule triggering strategies.

c. ⋆⋆⋆ Based on your analyses of the two cryptarithmetic systems, which strategy seems better for such puzzles? To what sorts of problems would you expect these results to generalize?

15. ⋆⋆⋆⋆⋆ While most ATMSs have been implemented on serial computers, the local nature of its computations suggests that parallel processing could be very effective. For example, a data-parallel ATMS has been implemented on Connection Machines [3]. Data-parallel machines are just one class of parallel machines, of course. How would you organize an ATMS to most efficiently operate in a scalable multiprocessor architecture, where there may be as few as two processors and as many as one hundred? Implement your scheme, and analyze its performance both theoretically and empirically.

16. ⋆⋆⋆⋆⋆ Two problems faced by teams of designers are (a) trying to keep their operations as coherent as possible and (b) encouraging the appropriate reuse of the products of their individual efforts, such as analyses, drawings, and so forth. For computer problem solvers implemented within a single address space, an ATMS provides considerable help in dealing with these difficulties. Can ATMS ideas be "turned inside out," to help solve these problems for other kinds of problem-solving systems? Consider how an ATMS-like system could be used as a component in a distributed computer system that supported a team of designers.

14.7 Bibliography

[1] Allen, J., Hendler, J., and Tate, A., *Readings in Planning*, Morgan-Kaufmann, 1990.

[2] Collins, J., and Decoste, D., "CATMS: An ATMS which avoids label explosions," *Proceedings of AAAI-91*, 1991.

[3] Dixon, M., and de Kleer, J., "Massively parallel assumption-based truth maintenance,", *Proceedings of AAAI-88*, 1988.

[4] de Kleer, J., "A hybrid truth maintenance system," Xerox PARC Technical Report.

[5] Dressler, O., and Farquhar, A., "Putting the problem solver back in the driver's seat: Contextual control of the ATMS," *Proceedings of the 2nd AAAI Workshop on Model-Based Reasoning*, 1990, 106-112.

[6] Fikes, R. E., Hart, P. E., and Nilsson, N. J. "STRIPS: A new approach to the application of theorem proving to problem solving," *Artificial Intelligence*, 2(3/4),189-208, 1971

[7] Forbus, K., and de Kleer, J., "Focusing the ATMS," *Proceedings of AAAI-88*, 1988.

[8] Nilsson, N. J., *Principles of Artificial Intelligence*, Morgan-Kaufmann, 1980.

[9] Winston, P. H., *Artificial Intelligence*, Addison-Wesley, 1984.

15 Antecedent Constraint Languages

A long-standing goal in artificial intelligence is to provide languages that automatically bridge the gap between "knowing what" and "knowing how." Existing languages tend to lie at one end or the other of a "what—how" spectrum. A traditional computer programming language is an example of the "how" extreme. Programs written in such languages focus on what to do, and when, while other kinds of knowledge are only embodied in the interpretation of opaque variable names and the ordering of conditional tests. An example of the "what" extreme, i.e., declarative languages, is traditional mathematics, where one can express constraints in the form of equations without formally specifying how and when these equations are to be used. This chapter examines a class of languages, *antecedent constraint languages*, which provides a model of computation that is much closer to the mathematical notion of constraint, while still providing an effective computational scheme. Today such constraint languages have found their way into spreadsheets, computer-aided design systems, and other computational aids to engineers.

We begin by describing the constraint network model in the abstract, and outlining what kinds of problems it is appropriate for. Then we "open the hood" and explore the implications of this abstract model for the choice of knowledge model, procedure model, and execution strategy for its implementations. Next we describe TCON, a simple constraint-network interpreter, and show how constraints can be used via two examples. First we show how constraint networks can be used as a scratch pad for using mathematical relationships in the course of problem solving. Second, we illustrate an important technique of model-based reasoning, called *constraint suspension*, which has been used in diagnosis tasks.

We end by describing several advanced topics involving antecedent constraint systems, including efficient implementation techniques, self-extending networks, and modeling changes over time.

15.1 The constraint model

Constraint languages are organized around the idea that the user (human or program) should express relationships between data declaratively. While computation must occur to determine and enforce the consequences of these relationships, the required computations should occur automatically, without special effort on the user's part.

Consider the equation $z = x + y$. To incorporate the knowledge expressed by this equation in a traditional, procedural computer language we might write

```
(setq z (+ x y))
```

which of course is interpreted as "find the value of the symbol x and the value of the symbol y, add them, and store the result as the value of the symbol z." This captures only part of the meaning of our original equation. For instance, given z and x, we can use subtraction to calculate y. Similarly, given z and y we could calculate the value of x. We could start to capture these two ways of using the equation by writing additional `setq` statements, but this requires additional code to describe the conditions under which each `setq` is appropriate. Writing such code on an ad hoc basis demands too much bookkeeping.

In the constraint metaphor, such bookkeeping occurs internally. We use a graphical notation for constraints, both to make the propagation of information among them clearer and to remove the potential ambiguity between declarative and imperative interpretations of equation-like statements. Figure 15.1 illustrates our conventions. To depict constraints we use icons similar to those used in diagrams of logic circuits in digital electronics. The boxes labeled x, y, and z are *cells*. The principal feature a cell has is its *value*. A cell also records several other pieces of information, including its relationships to the rest of the constraint network and how its value was supplied. All connections between constraints are

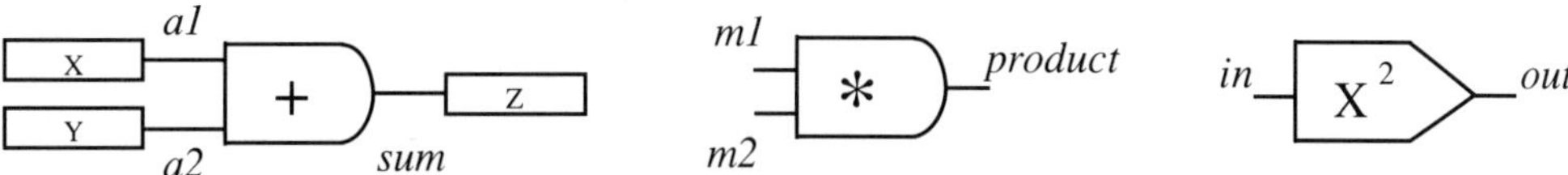

Figure 15.1 Graphical notation for constraints. Boxes indicate cells, which hold values. Icons similar to those used for logic circuitry are used to indicate constraints. The label indicates the type of constraint. Unlike logic circuits, it is assumed that information can flow in every direction. The cells which the constraint holds among are connected to it by lines. The constraint on the left is an adder constraint, the middle constraint is a multiplier, and the constraint on the right ensures that its `in` is the positive square root of its `out`.

made via cells. Such connections are depicted by lines running between the cells and the constraints.

An important difference to remember between constraints and logic circuits concerns the possible directions of information flow. Logic circuits have predefined inputs and outputs, and information only flows from inputs to outputs. In constraints, information can flow in any direction that makes sense, whenever possible. So, for example, if we knew

```
X = 2 ∧ Y = 3
```

then automatically the constraint should figure out that

```
Z = 5
```

while if

```
Y = 3 ∧ Z = 6
```

then automatically the constraint should figure out that

```
X = 3
```

From the perspective of a constraint, the cells it is connected to are its *terminals*. Each terminal has a name, corresponding to the particular role it plays in the constraint. (Even though information must be able to flow in every feasible direction between the terminals of a constraint, we still need to identify which terminal is which.) Terminals can be considered as the parts of a constraint that allow it to be connected to other things. (Other kinds of parts are discussed shortly.) In this adder constraint,

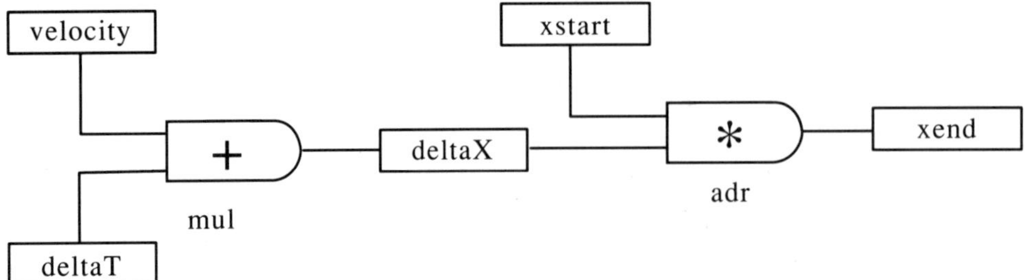

Figure 15.2 Constraint network for uniform motion. This network of constraints expresses the relationships which hold between the parameters of a body undergoing uniform motion in one dimension.

for instance, the terminals are `A1` (played by `x`), `A2` (played by `y`), and `SUM` (played by `z`). In this icon and many others, the form of the icon suffices to distinguish different terminals. Traditionally, the rounded end constitutes the result of the addition, and the connections on the flat end constitute the inputs to the addition. The distinction between `A1` and `A2` is moot in any correctly implemented adder constraint because addition is commutative. In cases where the part names are obvious or irrelevant, we leave them off to simplify diagrams, otherwise we label the wire leaving the constraint with the part name.

In problem solving, a *network* of constraints is built to model aspects of a problem or situation. The cells in the network correspond to aspects of the problem which can be thought of as having values. Like the constituents of assertions in the TREs, values can in principle be anything. However, constraint languages tend to be optimized around cells having values which are either numbers or uninterpreted symbols. The constraints in the network correspond to the relationships that hold in the situation. For example, Figure 15.2 shows a constraint network describing the mathematics of uniform one-dimensional motion. The cells `xs-tart`, `xend`, `velocity`, `deltaX`, and `deltat` describe the initial position, final position, velocity, distance traveled and time taken, respectively. Constraints communicate via shared cells. In this case, the cell `deltaX` is both the `A2` of an adder constraint and the product of a multiplier constraint. Suppose we provide numerical values for `xstart`, `velocity`, and `deltat`. As soon as `velocity` and `deltat` are known, the multiplier constraint can calculate a value for `deltaX`. This new value gives the adder constraint the information it needs to operate, since `xstart` is already known, and hence it computes `xend`. This flow of information through the network is an example of *propagation via constraints*.[1]

Continuing our example, suppose we now wish to use this network to calculate how long a moving object will take to reach a goal position, given the initial position and velocity. We must retract the value for `deltat`, which causes all values computed on the basis of it to be retracted in turn. In this case, `deltaX` and `xend` become unknown. Setting `xend` to be the goal position allows the adder constraint to calculate `deltaX`, which in turn allows the multiplier constraint to calculate `deltat`, which provides our answer.

As this example illustrates, we presume a built-in dependency mechanism to handle retraction and to provide explanations when required. An important role for constraint networks in problem solving is checking the consistency of proposed values: If our example network calculated a negative value for `deltat`, for instance, that might be a good signal to investigate different values for `velocity` (see Exercise 1). As later examples illustrate, contradictions can also arise because different parts of the network might compute two distinct values for a cell. We assume that each constraint network has a *coincidence handler* which judges whether or not two values should be considered distinct, and a *contradiction handler* that is executed whenever a contradiction is detected.

Powerful languages require a means of abstraction. For constraint languages, the means of abstraction is packaging up a network as a new primitive constraint. Since motion in different dimensions can be treated independently, if we treat the network of Figure 15.2 as a primitive `1D-uniform-motion` constraint, we can write a constraint for motion with uniform acceleration by using the uniform motion constraint with a constraint expressing the effects of acceleration (see Figure 15.3).

1. In the literature this is sometimes called propagation *of* constraints, which is a misnomer here because constraints are being applied rather than created. The term became popular because early systems would propagate algebraic expressions through the network, as outlined in Section 15.5.2. Propagation of constraints is also commonly used in frame systems, for example, in the inheritance of type or number restrictions in role fillers. If a neutral term covering both styles of computation is desired, we suggest "constraint propagation."

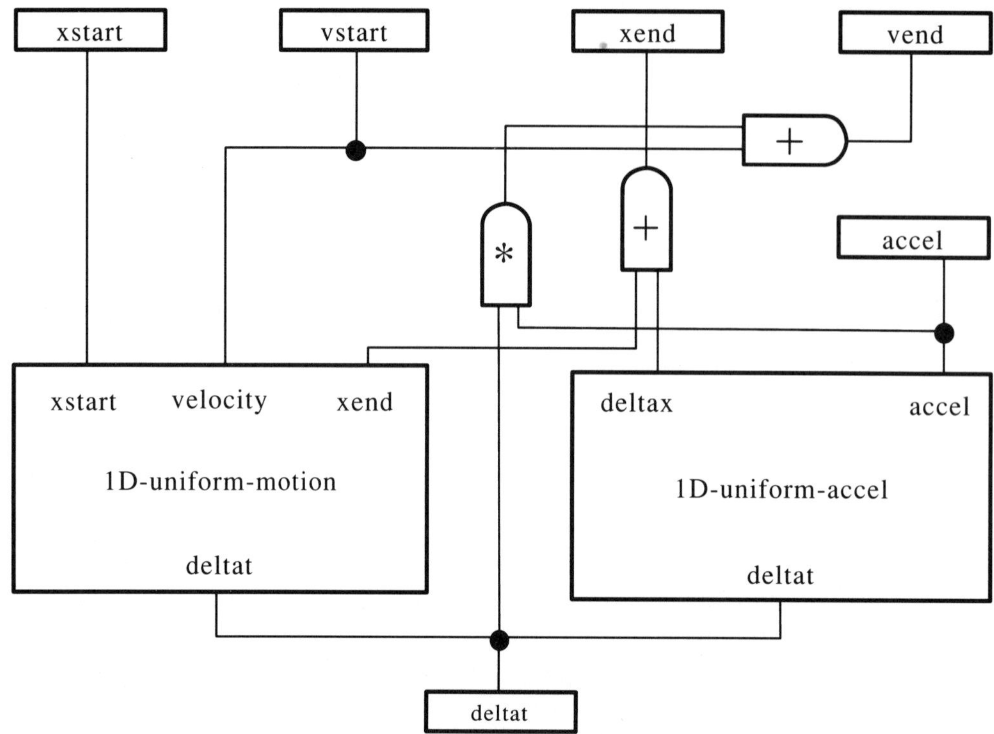

Figure 15.3 Networks can become higher-order primitives

15.1.1 Why use constraint languages?

The constraint metaphor just described has several attractive features, but why should we view it as the basis for a distinct class of languages for reasoning? After all, we could implement systems which use this metaphor via pattern-directed rules that would create the same external behaviors that we have described so far. Suppose, for example, we define the relationship `has-value` as relating a cell to its value, that is, believing

```
(has-value (>> a1 adder1) 2)
```

is tantamount to believing that the numerical value of `(>> a1 adder1)` equals 2. Constraints could be defined as predicates expressing laws that hold between cells, such as

```
(adder x y z)
```

We could then define rules for each such predicate that triggered on statements of constraints (e.g., `adder` statements) and values of its cells (e.g., `has-value` assertions concerning its parts), which would then compute the values of other cells by asserting more `has-value` statements. We must be sure to define enough rules, of course—ideally, given $n - 1$ cells of a constraint we should be able to compute the nth. (Not every relationship follows this pattern, as the definition of multiplication below illustrates.) The ability to inspect the rationale for all results would come from using a general-purpose TMS. We must also include a rule which states that any two sufficiently distinct `has-value` assertions for a cell are mutually contradictory (see Exercise 7).

Such PDIS-based systems can indeed implement the antecedent constraint model. But a PDIS implementation would ignore several simplifications allowed by the constraint network model which, if exploited correctly, can lead to important benefits. All the simplifications derive from the fact that the cell/constraint data model needs only local references. No pattern-matching is required, thus reducing overhead in both the database and the reference mechanism for procedures. Efficient datastructures can be built which "wire in" the connection between a cell and the procedures that use it. Furthermore, the rules associated with a constraint can be associated with a *prototype* constraint description and inherited by instances of that constraint. The PDIS overhead of building new rule instantiations for each combination of triggering data is thus avoided.

There are other efficiencies as well. Since the principal relationship is that of a cell having a value, we can leave that relationship implicit in the datastructure representing the constraint network. If the values of cells are assumed to be primitive data items, we do not need to cache values (assuming, of course, that rule executions are cheap). This means that we can simply store in some appropriate field the current value of a cell, and when we change the value, throw away the old one. Thus if we have n distinct values for a cell during the course of a computation, the cell at any time has stored with it at most one value and its associated dependency information. The PDIS version would require n distinct value assertions, with their associated TMS structures, and all the rule applications required to check for contradictions.

These efficiencies can be crucial for building large systems. Consider for example the construction of a VLSI design tool. A typical chip design might consist of hundreds of thousands of logic elements, which are implemented via millions of transistors. The laws of this domain are local, in that parts that are physically adjacent are the only parts that can interact.[2] This makes the domain a natural one for the antecendent constraint model. One function that a VLSI design tool provides is checking *design rules*: laws about allowable relationships between the parameters of parts (such as distance between two parts) which must hold for a circuit to work given a particular implementation technology. Implementing such a system in a PDIS is unlikely to work very well. However, such VLSI CAD systems have successfully been built using constraint languages. Moreover, ideas from constraint languages are finding their way into other design tools (e.g., mechanical CAD) as well.

15.2 The TCON constraint language

Here we outline a particular constraint language, TCON, which embodies the constraint metaphor. We begin by describing how primitive constraints are defined, and then describe how to link them into networks. Finally, we discuss how compound constraints can be defined in terms of primitive constraints, to provide the language with a means of abstraction. The implementation of `TCON` is described in Section 15.3.

15.2.1 Defining primitive constraints

Describing constraints and constraint networks requires a uniform convention for naming parts. We stipulate that every constraint has a name and a type. The function >> provides access to nested constraint structure. That is, the expression

```
(>> sum adder1)
```

2. Assuming we can ignore field effects, of course.

```
(constraint adder ((a1 cell) (a2 cell) (sum cell))
  (formulae (sum (a1 a2) (+ a1 a2))
            (a1 (sum a2) (- sum a2))
            (a2 (sum a1) (- sum a1))))
```

Figure 15.4 Definition of the `ADDER` constraint. Classes of TCON constraints are defined via prototypes, like the one above.

should be read "the `sum` of `adder1`". `>>` can take an arbitrary number of arguments, thus we can say

```
(>> x velocity ball32)
```

to mean "the `x` component of the `velocity` of `ball32`."

Each type of constraint is defined in terms of a *prototype*. The format of these definitions is

(constraint ⟨*name*⟩ ⟨*parts*⟩ . ⟨*body*⟩)

where ⟨*name*⟩ is the name of the class of constraint being defined. ⟨*parts*⟩ is a list of parts that each instance of the constraint must have. Each entry in ⟨*parts*⟩ takes the form

(⟨*PartName*⟩ ⟨*PartType*⟩)

where ⟨*PartName*⟩ is the name by which the part is refered to within ⟨*body*⟩. ⟨*PartType*⟩ is the kind of thing the part is, either a cell or another kind of constraint. (To start with, think of cells as the only kind of parts; Section 15.2.3 describes how compound constraints are built.) A constraint's cells are best interpreted as properties of the constraint itself. Figure 15.4 shows how the `adder` constraint used in Section 15.1 can be defined using this syntax. This definition specifies that adders have three parts, an `A1`, `A2`, and `SUM`, each of which are cells. The body of the adder constraint consists of a definition of `formulae`, which are rules that enforce the appropriate relationships between the values of these cells. Figure 15.5 depicts the relationships between the cells and rules.

Notice that in defining this constraint we have been forced to write rules that define what computation should occur for each combination of known inputs. What have we gained? First, we no longer must worry about when these rules are applied: the constraint interpreter handles that, ensuring that they are executed whenever relevant. Second, while

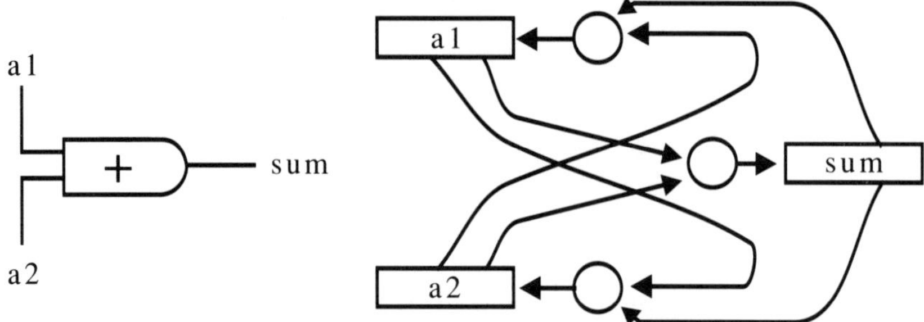

Figure 15.5 How an adder is implemented

primitive constraints require such rules, we shall see that once a primitive vocabulary of constraints is established we can write new, higher-order constraints solely in terms of primitive constraints.

The `formulae` declaration consists of a list of rules. Each rule computes a value for at most one cell, given the values for some other non-empty subset of the constraint's cells. The format of each rule is:

(⟨*sets*⟩ ⟨*uses*⟩ ⟨*RuleBody*⟩)

⟨*sets*⟩ is the cell for which the rule can provide a value. ⟨*uses*⟩ is a list of cells whose values must be known before the rule is executed. ⟨*RuleBody*⟩ is the procedure which is executed and whose result is the value for ⟨*sets*⟩. The first rule in the `adder` prototype, for example, specifies that when `a1` and `a2` are known, one can compute a value for `sum` by adding `a1` and `a2`. Similarly, the second rule specifies that if `sum` and `a1` are known, then `a2` can be computed by subtracting `a1` from `sum`, and so forth.

Formulae are interpreted antecedently. That is, whenever the values for the properties it uses are known, the rule is queued and eventually executed. Otherwise, no particular execution order is assumed between rules. In general, there may be multiple formulae which set any particular cell. And, of course, any cell may be used by multiple formulae. However, to ensure well-founded support, no ⟨*uses*⟩ of a rule can include the cell which it sets. When defining a primitive constraint, how do we know that the set of formulae is adequate? There have to be enough rules so that, given values for any subset of cells in the constraint, any other properties that follow from those values and the semantics of the relationship expressed by the constraint are calculated by the rules.[3]

Given a rule or cell, the constraint model provides concise ways of describing the potential dependency relationships between it and other constituents of the network. The following abstract procedures define these relationships. For rules:

`sets` The cell the rule provides a value for.

`uses` The set of cells which must be known before the rule can be executed.

For cells:

`Users` The set of rules which use the cell as an input.

`Suppliers` The set of rules which can provide a value for the cell.

To maintain the constraint model of computation, the code within the body of rules must follow certain guidelines:

1. A rule's body should only rely on the values of its `uses` cells.
2. All inferential work of a rule should occur via the result it returns.
3. A rule must refuse to return a value when only a subset of information from its `uses` cells suffices to obtain that value.
4. A rule must detect inconsistent data and signal the interpreter when it is found.

The first two guidelines are straightforward, and are analogous to similar limitations in PDIS systems. Drawing information from global variables which can change over the course of an analysis reduces the usefulness of the dependency system. Requiring side effects to carry out inferential work similarly prevents the model from providing maximal benefits. The second two guidelines are somewhat subtle and are best understood via example.

Figure 15.6 shows a definition of a multiplier constraint which illustrates the impact of the second two guidelines. Recall that the adder only

---

3. The analogous idea in propositional reasoning is the set of prime implicates of a theory. See Chapter 13.

```
(constraint multiplier ((m1 cell) (m2 cell) (product cell))
 (formulae (product (m1) (if (nearly-zero? m1) 0.0 :DISMISS))
           (product (m2) (if (nearly-zero? m2) 0.0 :DISMISS))
           (product (m1 m2) (if (or (nearly-zero? m1)
                                    (nearly-zero? m2))
                                   :DISMISS)
                                (* m1 m2))
           (m1 (product m2) (if (nearly-zero? m2)
                                (if (nearly-zero? product)
                                    :DISMISS
                                  :LOSE)
                              (/ product m2)))
           (m2 (product m1) (if (nearly-zero? m1)
                                (if (nearly-zero? product)
                                    :DISMISS
                                  :LOSE)
                              (/ product m1)))))

(defun nearly-zero? (m) (< (abs m) 1.0e-9))
```

Figure 15.6 Definition of a `multiplier` constraint. This multiplier constraint illustrates some subtleties involved in defining primitive constraints. To properly implement the constraint model requires paying careful attention to "squeezing out" as much information as possible from the properties of the relationship.

required three rules to enforce the relationship between its parts. Enforcing multiplication requires five rules because of special cases where certain values provide more or less information than normal. Suppose one of the inputs to the multiplier (e.g., `m1` or `m2`) is zero. In that case we know the output (e.g., `product`) must be zero no matter what the other input is. The first two rules in the `formulae` definition for the multiplier encode this fact. Of course, when their input isn't zero these rules cannot actually provide a value, even though their `uses` are completely known. Rules must return a special value, i.e., `:DISMISS`, in such circumstances. The TCON interpreter understands `:DISMISS` to mean "with the particular input values, this rule cannot produce an output."

The third rule of the multiplier encodes the usual definition of multiplication. The extra control structure is to comply with the third guideline. The TCON interpreter guarantees that every rule will be fired sometime after it has the data it needs to run, but places no guarantee on the order in which rules execute. This means that if the third rule can execute, so can the first two, but they may or may not have already run when the third rule is executed. The `if` tests to see if one of the first two rules is relevant, and if so, returns `:DISMISS` to allow the other rules to produce a zero value instead. Doing this may seem odd at first, since executing `*` would compute the correct value of zero if one of the inputs is zero. Recall, however, that TCON tracks dependency information. If we use the third rule to set the value of `product` to be zero, then we would record that this value depended on the conjunction of both inputs, whereas it actually only depended on one of them alone. If this result led to a contradiction, for instance, we might retract what we thought was a relevant value and find the contradiction still with us. Such pecularities in the relationship to be enforced must be kept in mind by the author of primitive constraints.

The last two rules in the multiplier constraint illustrate the fourth guideline. When appropriate, they use the value of the product and one input to compute a value for the other input. If the known input is zero, then these rules must dismiss themselves because in this case the other input could legitimately be anything. However, should the known input be zero and the product be something other than zero, we have a serious problem, since we know it must be zero. Clearly these data are contradictory, and the TCON interpreter needs to be informed about this discovery. Rules can signal such circumstances by returning the special value `:LOSE`, which declares the values for its `uses` cells to be contradictory. When a contradiction is detected, the TCON interpreter signals a contradiction handler which works exactly like contradiction handlers in truth maintenance systems. That is, it computes the set of assumptions underlying the contradiction and executes a user-supplied procedure to take care of the problem.

15.2.2 Creating networks of constraints

Problems are modeled by creating networks of constraints. Creating a constraint network requires building its parts and then wiring them together. Constraints are created by the procedure `create`, which takes two arguments, the name of the constraint being created, and the kind of constraint it is. For example, to create an adder called `foo` one says

```
(constraint 1D-uniform-motion ((xstart cell) (xend cell)
                               (velocity cell)(deltat cell)
                               (adr adder)(mul multiplier))
    (== (>> xstart) (>> a1 adr))
    (== (>> xend) (>> sum adr))
    (== (>> velocity) (>> m1 mul))
    (== (>> deltat) (>> m2 mul))
    (== (>> product mul) (>> a2 adr)))
```

Figure 15.7 Specifying the constraint `1D-Uniform-Motion`

```
(create 'foo 'adder)
```

Global properties can be represented by creating cells or constraints. If we were modeling an amplifier, for instance, a cell to represent the output voltage of the amplifier could be created by the call

```
(create 'output-voltage 'cell)
```

The primitive == provides the means to connect constraints to form networks. == takes two cells as input. Its result is a special constraint that propagates value information between the two cells. So for example, if we stated

```
(== output-voltage (>> sum foo))
```

then whenever a value was derived for the `sum` of `foo`, the value of `output-voltage` would be set to the same thing, giving the connection between the two cells as the reason. Naturally, the same thing would happen if we set `output-voltage`, since constraints are multidirectional. Equality links between cells can be broken by calling `un==`. `un==` retracts all values derived using the equality link as well as removing the equality constraint.

Figure 15.7 shows how these primitives can be combined to define the one-dimensional uniform motion constraint illustrated in Figure 15.2.

15.2.3 Defining compound constraints

Abstraction helps the vocabulary of a language keep pace with increased complexity. Abstraction in constraint languages is accomplished by

```
(constraint 3-adder ((a1 cell)(a2 cell)(a3 cell)(sum cell)
                     (add1 adder)(add2 adder))
 (== a1 (>> a1 add1))
 (== a2 (>> a2 add1))
 (== a3 (>> a1 add2))
 (== (>> sum add1) (>> a2 add2))
 (== sum (>> sum add2)))
```

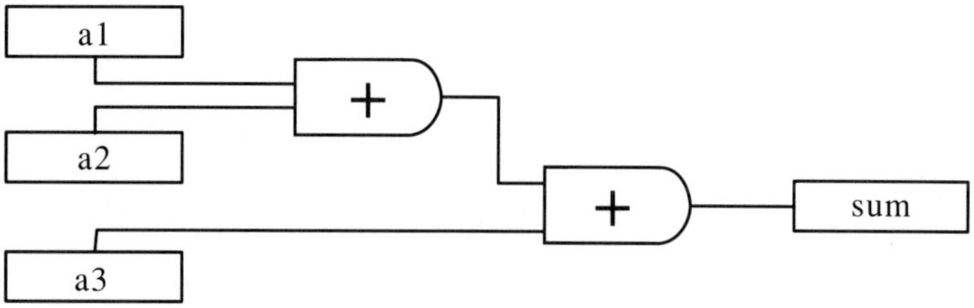

Figure 15.8 Definition of a three-input adder. By composing primitive constraints, more complex abstractions can often be built without resorting to defining new rules.

defining new constraints as networks of more primitive constraints. As Section 15.2.1 showed, TCON's syntax for defining constraints already allows parts to be other types of constraints as well as cells. The only restriction on this nesting is that constraints cannot be recursively defined. That is, the part relationship over types of constraints forms a lattice. The interconnections between the parts are define via ==, as introduced in Section 15.2.2. The three-input adder in Figure 15.8 illustrates how a new compound constraint can be defined in terms of primitive constraints, without the use of formulae.

Sometimes specific property values are part of the definition of a constraint; we use the form

`(constant` ⟨*Cell*⟩ ⟨*Value*⟩ `)`

to indicate that ⟨*Cell*⟩ always has the value ⟨*Value*⟩.

The ability to define hierarchical constraint networks provides an exciting ability: After defining a certain basic level of primitive constraints, we can often stay completely within a purely declarative style of computation.

15.3 Implementing TCON

The file `tcon.lisp` contains a complete implementation of TCON. We begin by outlining the interface procedures. We then describe in turn the data abstractions, the way networks, prototypes, and constraints are implemented, the rule system, the dependency system, and the interrogatives.

15.3.1 TCON's interface

New kinds of constraints are defined using the `Constraint` macro. A `Constraint` form has the syntax

`(Constraint` ⟨*name*⟩ ⟨*PartList*⟩ `.` ⟨*body*⟩`)`

⟨*name*⟩ is a symbol which is name of the kind of constraint being defined. ⟨*PartList*⟩ is a list of entries of the form (⟨*PartName*⟩ ⟨*PartType*⟩, where ⟨*PartName*⟩ is the name of the part (a symbol) and ⟨*PartType*⟩ is a type of constraint. ⟨*body*⟩ specifies rules and the forms that should be evaluated in order to create an instance of this constraint type.

A common statement in ⟨*body*⟩ is `formulae`:

`(formulae .` ⟨*ListOfRules*⟩`)`

where ⟨*ListOfRules*⟩ is a list of rules of the form

`(` ⟨*sets*⟩ ⟨*uses*⟩ ⟨*RuleBody*⟩`)`

⟨*sets*⟩ is the cell the rule sets and ⟨*uses*⟩ is a list of the cells whose values are required to execute ⟨*RuleBody*⟩, which is Lisp code. Both ⟨*sets*⟩ and ⟨*uses*⟩ must be cells defined in ⟨*PartList*⟩.

New constraints may be defined at any time. Typically, such definitions are accumulated in files which may then be loaded as part of an analysis.

As with previous systems, we use a global variable (here `*tcon*`) to simplify referring to the constraint network currently used. The following three procedures are included for creating constraint networks and modifying their global properties:

`(create-tcon title &key`*ellipses*`)` Builds a new constraint network with the name `title`. There are four keyword arguments:

`:DEBUGGING` When non-`nil`, prints information about internal TCON operations. The default is `nil`.

`:PROTOTYPE-FILE` A file name which specifies an initial set of constraint prototype definitions. The default is `nil`.

`:CONTRADICTION-HANDLER` Procedure to be called when a contradiction occurs. The default is `default-contradiction-handler`.

`:COINCIDENCE-HANDLER` Procedure used to compare values for a cell to determine if they are consistent or conflict. The default is `default-coincidence-handler`.

`(load-prototypes file-name &optional (tcon *tcon*))` Loads the constraints of file `file-name` into the specified constraint network, which defaults to the current one.

`(change-tcon tcon &key (debugging nil))` Provides a way to set the debugging flag associated with a network. The coincidence handler cannot be reset since there would be no guarantee that the state of the network would be consistent with the new criteria unless restarted from scratch.

The following procedures are used to create and examine the structure of constraint networks:

`(create name type &optional (tcon *tcon*))` Builds a constraint of type `type` called `name` in the constraint network `tcon`. Cells are created the same way by specifying the type `cell`.

`(>> &rest args)` Refers to a constraint or part of a constraint, using the names with respect to the current constraint network.

`(== first second)` Equates `first` and `second`.

The procedures for switching between constraint networks are

`(with-network tcon &rest forms)` Evaluates `forms` in the context of the constraint network `tcon`.

`(use-network tcon)` Makes the current constraint network be `tcon`.

The interrogatives used in TCON mirror those of pattern-directed inference systems in several ways, but the difference in data model allows some interesting variations. For instance, the constraints of a network are often aligned with natural structures in the domain being modeled, and thus provide a convenient way to package queries. Information about values in a constraint network can be gained using the following procedures:

`known?` Returns non-`nil` if the given cell has a known value.

`what-is` Prints the value of a cell.

`constraint-values` Prints the values of all cells in a constraint. With a non-`nil` second argument, does so recursively.

`show-network` Prints the value of every cell in the network, if known.

The dependency system is basically a stripped-down JTMS, so the kinds of information we can provide are similar to what we get in a stand-alone JTMS:

`why` Describes the informant for a value. This provides roughly the information that knowing the `support` would provide in a stand-alone JTMS.

`premises` Shows the list of ground values, similar to `assumptions-of-node`.

`needs` Describes what other cells might be given values in order to determine the value for a cell of interest.

Notice that the last procedure, `needs`, allows us to examine some information that is difficult to get in a PDIS. This works because the dependency system is more tightly coupled to the rule system. In JTRE an approximation of this information is available for nodes corresponding to the consequences of previously-executed rules, but finding out what might be derivable from rules that have not actually been executed is difficult, if not impossible.

Values can be set, retracted, or changed via the following procedures:

`set-parameter` sets a cell to a given value.

`forget-parameter` Retracts an assumed value.

`change-parameter` Changes the assumed value for a cell.

`constant` Provides a fixed value for a cell.

`tcon-answer` Tells the contradiction handler which assumption to retract given a contradiction.

Each procedure performs the appropriate local change and then propagates the effect of this change through the rest of the network. When called on a cell whose value was assumed, `change-parameter` retracts its value and does not attempt to find alternate support before assuming a new value for the cell. Typically this is more efficient than the composition of `forget-parameter` and `set-parameter`. Values provided using `constant` have the same status as premises in truth maintenance systems. That is, they cannot be retracted without violating the interface conventions. As with the JTMS, the macro `with-contradiction-handler` rebinds a network's contradiction handler during a computation.

Sme additional interface procedures for using TCON as part of a larger system are:

`known?` Predicate for determining if a cell has a value.

`enforce-constraints` Executes all pending rules for the given constraint network.

`cell-ground` Lists the cells providing ground support to the given cell.

15.3.2 Datastructures

The `tcon` struct provides a means of bundling up the properties of a particular constraint network. It has the following fields:

`title` String for printing.

`prototypes` List of prototypes associated with this network.

`cells` List of cells in the network.

`constraints` List of constraints in the network.

`beg-queue` Queue of cells to examine for alternate support.

`help-queue` Queue of rules ready for execution.

`coincidence-handler` Identity procedure for cell values

`contradiction-handler` User-supplied contradiction processor.

`debugging` Controls printing of information about internal operations.

The decision to store prototypes locally with a network allows us to explore the consequences of different definitions by building identical networks with different prototypes.

Prototypes have the following fields:

`name` A symbol.

`tcon` Network it is part of.

`parts` List of parts.

`creation-forms` Evaluated for each constraint of this type when created.

`cells` Information about its cells (`users` and `suppliers`).

`rules` Information about its rules (`sets` and `uses`).

The connections between cells and rules are made at the level of the prototype—these connections replace the pattern matching and indices used in pattern-directed inference systems. Since most of the information about a constraint is inherited from its prototype, the constraint datastructure itself is quite simple:

`name` A symbol.

`tcon` Network it is part of.

`owner` The constraint it belongs to. (If global, this is `:USER`.)

`parts` An alist of names and associated parts for this instance.

`prototype` Where to get information about rules and cells.

The datastructure for cells must support three functions. It must record the value for that cell, keep track of structural information so that the value is propagated appropriately, and keep track of dependency information so that explanations are accurate and retraction works properly. The `cell` structure has the following properties:

`name` A symbol.

`tcon` The network it belongs to.

`owner` The constraint it is part of. If global, this is `:USER`.

`value` The current value.

`informant` Either a rule, symbol (if ground support), or `nil` if the cell is unknown.

`roles` The parts the cell plays in various constraints. Used to find its `users` and `suppliers`.

`plist` Usual place to store extra information.

Aside from `*tcon*`, two other global variables are used by TCON. The variable `$self` is always bound to the cell or constraint currently being processed. This variable is rebound dynamically during the construction of hierarchical constraints. When no constraint is being processed, it is bound to `:USER`. The other global variable is `$informant`, which is bound internally to the current source of information. `$informant` is mainly useful for debugging.

15.3.3 Creating constraints, networks, and prototypes

The purpose of `create-tcon` and `change-tcon` and their inputs have already been described, so there are only a few more features to note. The special constraint prototype `==` must be included in every network, so it is added automatically by `create-tcon`. While the `:PROTOTYPE-FILE` keyword simplifies starting a network, new prototypes can be added at any time. Notice that `change-tcon` makes no provision for rebinding the coincidence handler. This is deliberate, because changing the criteria for judging two values to be the same could lead to previously consistent values being judged as contradictory. There would be no easy way to ensure the consistency of the network, short of recomputing every derived value in it.

The macro `Constraint` provides the syntactic sugar for defining prototypes. We presume `*tcon*` is dynamically bound, so that constraint definitions need not refer to a network explicitly. The bulk of its work is performed by `analyze-prototype-body`, which analyzes the body of the definition. `formulae` statements are passed on to `process-constraint-rules`, which will be described shortly. Within the body of a constraint definition, everything other than `formulae` statements are treated as forms which should be executed whenever an instance of that type of constraint is built. Examples of such statements are `==` and `constant`. All references (i.e., terms starting with `>>`) within a constraint must be local. Thus statements like

```
(== (>> sum adder1) (>> a1 adder2))
```

are converted into local statements by adding an indicator (`$self`) standing for the current constraint being built. TCON ensures that `$self` is always bound to the constraint currently being operated on. So if the

== statement above appeared in the scope of a constraint definition, it would automatically be transformed into

```
(== (>> sum adder1 $self) (>> a1 adder2 $self))
```

which places `$self` at the base of the reference chain. This job is done by the procedure `localize-references`.

The procedure `process-constraint-rules` analyzes the contents of a `formulae` statement. It builds up two alists, one describing rules and the other describing the cells referred to by the rules. These alists supply the dependency information that links rules and cells. The `sets` and `uses` of each rule are cached on the `rules` alist, and inverted to find the `Users` and `Suppliers` for each cell. For easy reference, rules are named by their order in the `formulae` statement.

The procedure `create` builds a constraint of a given type. It serves as an entry point, binding `$self` and `*tcon*` before calling `create1`, which does the real work. `create1` starts by building an instance of the constraint struct and fills its fields with information appropriate to its type. Next it recursively builds the constraint's parts, rebinding `$self` appropriately. Finally, the creation forms associated with the prototype are executed to finish setting up the interrelationships between the new constraint's parts. `create-cell` operates similarly, initializing the new cell's values and backpointers to weave it into the constraint and network.

An implementation of >> must allow for the fact that a chain of rferences can be arbitrarily long. The simplest way to support this is to define >> as a macro that alters its argument to simplify subsequent processing. Reversing the reference chain and stripping off the first element to identify the base of the chain turns the process into a simple iteration. This iteration is carried out by `nested-lookup`, which uses `lookup-global` to get the base of the chain and `lookup-part` to find the appropriate part from a constraint's list of parts. When the base is `$self`, `lookup-global` simply evaluates it, exploiting our convention of its dynamic binding, and otherwise looks up the constraint's name in the network.

References are inverted by the procedure `pretty-name`, which, given a constraint or cell, produces a reference chain that serves to specify the given object. `cell-pretty-name` and `constraint-pretty-name` are its helpers, doing the obvious recursive descent. These procedures are used in print routines found later in the file.

15.3.3.1 *Defining ==*

Recall that when `create` builds a new constraint, it also builds new constraints and cells to serve as its parts. This means that we cannot simply use `create` to build instances of `==`, for then it would not serve its purpose of establishing new connections between existing cells. Consequentlly, the macro `==` expands into a call to a new procedure, `process==`, instead of a call to `create` or `create1`. `process==` recursively walks through the structure of two constraints, equating each of their corresponding cells. The actual construction of `==` instances for cells is handled by `==cells`, which makes an instance of the `==` constraint with the argument cells as its parts, and increments their `roles` slots to indicate the additional part they play in the network. Since these cells may already have values, the rules of this constraint are queued to see what new conclusions can be drawn, if any, from this new connection.

15.3.4 The rule system

The implementations of the abstract functions `sets`, `uses`, `Users`, and `Suppliers` are the procedures `rule-sets`, `rule-uses`, `cell-users`, and `cell-suppliers`. Obviously, cell structs are the legal arguments for `cell-users` and `cell-suppliers`. The naming convention for rules is to use a pair whose `car` is the local name of the rule (as generated by `process-constraint-rules`) and whose `cdr` is the constraint struct the rule is defined in. All four procedures use the information cached with constraint prototypes to calculate their results. `rule-sets` and `rule-uses` are a simple nested lookup using `assoc` on the rule's prototype. `cell-users` and `cell-suppliers` are a bit more complicated because a cell can participate in multiple constraints. The `cell-roles` field specifies what these constraints are, and a nested lookup analogous to the procedures for finding rule information is performed on each constraint.

15.3.4.1 *Setting and propagating values*

The interface procedure `known?` is obvious—the special value `:UNKNOWN` is stored in a cell's `value` field to indicate that it currently is not known.

`set!` is the internal procedure that does the work involved in giving a value to a cell, including consistency checking and propagating the results. It begins by seeing if the cell is already known. If so, then if the newly computed value is not consistent with the previous value (i.e., `coincidence?` returns `nil`) contradiction handling is invoked. Otherwise, the cell's `value` and `informant` fields are updated to reflect the new value and its source. The `source` argument will always be either a pair indicating a specific rule (as noted previously) or a symbol, indicating ground support. Finally, `spread-results` propagates the effects of this new value by queuing for possible execution the rules which use the newly set cell.

The procedure `help!` is called internally to process items in a network's `help-queue`. It first tests whether the rule is executable by calling `runnable?`, which ensures that every cell in `uses` is known. It then executes the rule and examines the result. The special values `:DISMISS` and `:LOSE` are recognized here, and appropriate action is taken for each. Any other value is treated as a new value for the rule's `sets` cell, and so `set!` is called to store this value.

As with the PDIS rule system, much of the mechanism in defining TCON rules is designed to simplify the alignment of the procedure model with Lisp procedures. Specifically, the body of a rule is simply a procedure which is applied to the values of the cells the rule uses. In addition to rebinding the special variables `$self` and `*tcon*`, the global variable `$informant` is bound to the current rule for debugging purposes. A constraint author might, for instance, use these variables to print out more detailed information about the execution environment of a piece of code that appears in the body of several rules.

15.3.5 The dependency system

We have already seen how `set!` keeps track of informants as a means of caching dependency information. When assumed values are retracted, this information must of course be used to retract derived values. The procedure `forget!` carries this out by recursively retracting all the consequences of a given value. Two features are worth noting here. First, we must check to be sure that the informant sanctioning the retraction actually is the informant for the value. (It might not be, if some external system set a cell which already had a compatible value.) Second, we use an internal queue rather than syntactic recursion, since the number of cells traversed could be a substantial fraction of the network. The procedure `beg!` looks for alternate support (i.e., rederiving a new value for a cell) by queuing any executable suppliers for a newly forgotten cell.

The rest of the dependency system is concerned with detecting and processing contradictions. `default-coincidence-handler` provides a default test for equivalent values. `ground-justification` returns non-`nil` unless it is given a constraint rule. The procedures `cell-ground` and `rule-ground` return the set of cells whose assumed values form the set of support on which that cell or rule rests, respectively. `default-contradiction-handler` is a bit more complicated than some of the earlier TMS versions. The reason is that we have chosen to split the assumed values into three sets: those on which the old value relies, those on which the new value relies, and those which both values require. This provides users with a bit more information about what they might wish to retract.

15.4 Examples

We explore how constraints can be used in two kinds of problem solving. We start with a simple example to illustrate TCON in action. Section 15.4.2 illustrates the use of constraint networks as an inference facility in a larger system. Section 15.4.3 illustrates how constraint networks can be used in *constraint suspension*, a diagnosis technique developed by research in model-based reasoning.

15.4.1 A simple TCON example

Let us create an instance of the one-dimensional uniform motion constraint and examine how TCON computations work. First we need to build a network:

```
> (create-tcon "1D Motion" :prototype-file "/u/bps/code/tcon/motion.lisp")
;;; Loading source file "/u/bps/code/tcon/motion.lisp"
<TCON: 1D Motion>
> (create 'M '1d-uniform-motion)
<Constraint M>
```

Now the expression (>> M) refers to the constraint we just built, which instantiates the equations of uniform motion. Suppose we set an initial position and velocity of 0.0 and 3.2, respectively:

```
>(set-parameter (>> xstart m) 0.0)
4
0
>(set-parameter (>> velocity m) 3.2)
5
0
```

Do we know the final position yet? TCON says no:

```
>(known? (>> xend M))
NIL
```

Unlike a PDIS, where we do not know in advance what rule instances might be created that could provide a given assertion, in TCON we can actually find out, using `needs` or by examining what other cells of the constraint might be filled in:

```
>(constraint-values (>> m))

 (>> DELTAT M) is unknown.
 (>> VELOCITY M) = 3.2.
 (>> XEND M) is unknown.
 (>> XSTART M) = 0.0.
NIL
```

So by selecting a value for `deltat` we should be able to compute `(>> xend m)`. Suppose we let `deltat` be 24.0 seconds:

```
>(set-parameter (>> deltat m) 24.0)
15
0
>(what-is (>> xend m))

 (>> XEND M) = 76.8.
NIL
```

Now we have the value of the final position. We can also obtain details about the derivation of that value using `why` and find the assumptions underlying it with `premises`:

```
>(why (>>  xend m))

 (>> XEND M) = 76.8, via (RULE-1 . <Constraint 1<=>2>)
  and inputs:
     (>> SUM ADR M) = 76.8.
NIL
>(premises (>>  xend m))

 (>> XEND M) = 76.8, because:
      (>> deltat M) = 24.0, via USER.
      (>> VELOCITY M) = 3.2, via USER.
      (>> XSTART M) = 0.0, via USER.
NIL
```

Suppose we had a desired final position, say 5,000, and wanted to know how long it would take for the moving object to reach that position. By retracting `deltat` and setting `xfinal`, we can derive our answer:

```
>(forget-parameter (>>  deltat m))
1
6
>(set-parameter (>>  xend m) 5000)
15
0
>(what-is (>>  deltat m))

 (>> deltat M) = 1562.5.
NIL
```

Notice that we have succeeded in using the knowledge of arithmetic in a very declarative fashion. Once the problem solver has built a constraint network, it can be used to compute useful information in a variety of ways.

15.4.2 Using constraint networks as scratch pads

Many kinds of problems contain subproblems which involve solving mathematical equations. Often these problems involve not just computing numerical answers, but figuring out if the parameters of a situation or proposed solutions make sense. Suppose, for example, we are trying to destroy a falling satellite before it crashes into a populated area.

We may have several kinds of interceptor rockets at our disposal, and need to select one that is fast enough to reach the satellite's path before impact. Let us build a constraint network to evaluate the choice of interceptor.

We can model the satellite's motion as it approaches impact as if it were a projectile, falling under the Earth's gravitational field. If we assume that our interceptor rockets burn all their propellant extremely quickly, we can approximate their trajectory in the same way. The following variables are needed:

(X_S^i, Y_S^i) Initial position of the satellite
(X_S^f, Y_S^f) Final position of the satellite
(X_I^i, Y_I^i) Initial position of the interceptor
(X_I^f, Y_I^f) Final position of the interceptor
(VX_S^i, VY_S^i) Initial velocity of the satellite
(VX_S^f, VY_S^f) Final velocity of the satellite
(VX_I^i, VY_I^i) Initial velocity of the interceptor
(VX_I^f, VY_I^f) Final velocity of the interceptor
T_i Time taken to intercept
T_c Time until the satellite crashes

For the interception to succeed it must be the case that

$$X_S^f = X_P^f \wedge Y_S^f = Y_P^f$$

It is also desirable to have the collision take place as high as possible, so that the debris will be slowed down by air resistance and do less damage to the people and property below.

Let us build a constraint network to use as a scratch pad in solving this problem. That is, we can build a model of the situation by instantiating constraints to represent the trajectory of the satellite, the trajectory of the interceptor, and their intersection. By plugging numerical values into this network and evaluating the results, we can find a reasonable solution.

To model the trajectories of the satellite and interceptor we need a constraint which describes two-dimensional motion under the influence of gravity. One way to do this is to define a constraint which defines one-dimensional motion under acceleration and use two copies, one for X and one for Y. What should the $1D$ motion constraint contain? We can

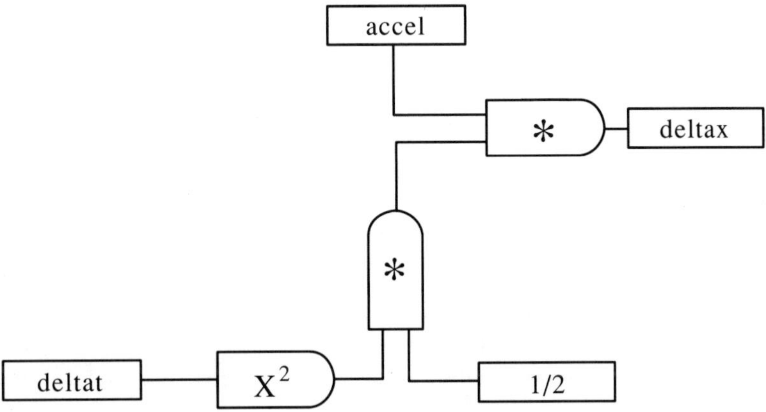

Figure 15.9 Constraint network for 1D uniform acceleration

use the $1D$ uniform motion constraint defined previously as a building block, but we must add a correction for the effects of acceleration. The equations for $1D$ motion under uniform acceleration are

$$S_f = S_i + V_i \Delta T + \frac{1}{2} a \Delta T^2$$

$$V_f = V_i + a \Delta T$$

where ΔT is the interval over which the motion occurs and a is the acceleration. Notice that the first two terms of the right-hand side of the first equation are exactly what is incorporated in the uniform motion constraint. To handle the effect of acceleration we must add a correction factor of $\frac{1}{2} a \Delta T^2$ to the uniform motion constraint, and add an equation defining the change in velocity as well. Figure 15.9 graphically depicts the `1D-uniform-acceleration` constraint; the file `motion.lisp` contains the TCON definition for this and the other constraints introduced in this example.

Our simplified problem presumes that all the momentum transfer occurs in a brief moment, and we also ignore air friction. Since rocket engines produce thrust in a particular direction, we need to know the required initial speed and heading for the interceptor. These parameters are comfortably expressed in polar coordinates. Of course, the constraint models for motion developed above are in terms of rectangular coordinates. We need to convert between the two; the `2D-vector` constraint shown in Figure 15.11 illustrates such a constraint. It is based directly upon the standard conversion formulas:

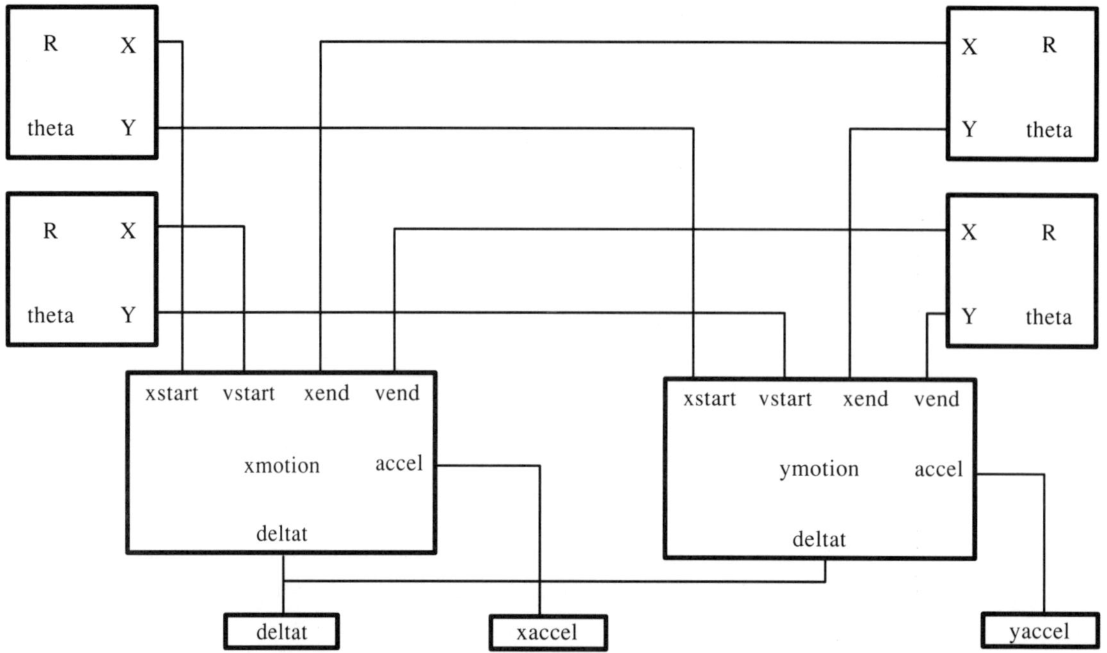

Figure 15.10 Representing two-dimensional motion

$$X = R \times cos(\theta) \wedge Y = R \times sin(\theta)$$

$$R = \sqrt{X^2 + Y^2} \wedge \theta = atan(\frac{Y}{X})$$

The procedural implications of these equations are worked out in the `formulae` statement. The code ensures that all angles are within the range $[0, 2\pi)$ and R is always non-negative, using `acos-corrected`, `asin-corrected`, and `atan-corrected` to transform the answers according to the quadrant the vector is in. (Exercise 14 explores an alternate organization.)

The constraint for two-dimensional motion (`2D-motion`) must include two copies of `1D-motion`, one for X and one for Y. The `2D-vector` constraint is used to translate between the polar coordinates desired for input and output and the rectangular coordinates used to model the motion. Figure 15.10 illustrates the constraint subnetwork for the `2D-motion` definition.

```
(constraint 2D-vector ((x cell)(y cell)
                       (signx cell) (signy cell)
                       (sgnx sign) (sgny sign)
                       (r cell)(theta cell)
                       (quadrant cell))
 (== (>> x) (>> in sgnx))
 (== (>> signx) (>> out sgnx))
 (== (>> y) (>> in sgny))
 (== (>> signy) (>> out sgny))
 (formulae (quadrant (signx signy)
                     (quadrant-from-signs signx signy))
           (signx (quadrant)
                  (multiple-value-bind (x-sign y-sign)
                    (signs-from-quadrant quadrant)
                    x-sign))
           (signy (quadrant)
                  (multiple-value-bind (x-sign y-sign)
                    (signs-from-quadrant quadrant)
                    y-sign))
           (theta (quadrant)
                  (angle-from-quadrant quadrant))
           (x (r theta) (if (nearly-zero? r) :DISMISS
                            (* r (cos theta))))
           (y (r theta) (if (nearly-zero? r) :DISMISS
                            (* r (sin theta))))
           (theta (r x quadrant)
                  (if (or (nearly-zero? r)
                          (not (simple-quadrant? quadrant))) :DISMISS
                    (acos-corrected (/ x r) quadrant)))
           (theta (r y quadrant)
                  (if (or (nearly-zero? r)
                          (not (simple-quadrant? quadrant))) :DISMISS
                          (asin-corrected (/ y r) quadrant)))
           (x (r) (if (nearly-zero? r) 0.0 :DISMISS))
           (y (r) (if (nearly-zero? r) 0.0 :DISMISS))
           (r (x y) (sqrt (+ (* x x) (* y y))))
           (theta (x y) (if (and (nearly-zero? x)
                                 (nearly-zero? y))
                            0.0 ;; By convention
                            (atan-corrected y x)))))

(constraint sign ((in cell) (out cell))
 (formulae (out (in) (if (nearly-zero? in) 0.0
                         (signum in)))
           (in (out) (if (= 0.0 out) 0.0 :DISMISS))))
```

Figure 15.11 Representing 2D vectors

Now let us begin to model the system. We can instantiate two copies of the `2D-motion` constraint, one for the satellite and one for the interceptor. Let us call these constraints `sat` and `int` respectively. Given our problem's assumptions, we must set the Y acceleration of both constraints to be $-9.98\frac{m}{s^2}$ (i.e., the acceleration of gravity in MKS units) and their X acceleration to zero. We can also encode the presumption of intersection by using `==` to equate the end points of the two trajectories.

Suppose we have the following initial data:

$$X_S^i = -1000m; Y_S^i = 1000m$$

$$X_I^i = 100m; Y_I^i = 0m$$

Let us set the parameters of the network to this data and see what happens:

```
>(create 'sat '2d-motion)
>(create 'int '2d-motion)
>(== (>>  deltat sat) (>>  deltat inf)) ;; equate intervals
>(set-parameter (>>  x start sat) -1000)
>(set-parameter (>>  y start sat) 1000)
>(set-parameter (>>  x start int) 100)
>(set-parameter (>>  y start int) 0)
```

Do we have enough to derive our answer? Not yet. Why? Examining the network closely (by using `constraint-values` on the parts of `sat` and `int`) will reveal that almost nothing has been computed about the constraints describing the end of the motions. Given even a smattering of information about the end state, the various motion constraints can start filling out the rest, but we must add some additional fact or stipulation for the system to get an answer. We should not have to add much information, and there are several natural choices. The desire to minimize damage on the ground suggests that we specify at what height the interception should take place. Let us be pessimistic about our rocket's power and try taking $Y_S^f = 100m$:

```
>(set-parameter (>>  y end sat) 100)
447
0
```

This single assumption lets us derive values for all of the relevant variables. By inspecting the (>> vstart int) constraint we can find out the necessary speed and heading for the rocket:

```
>(constraint-values (>>  vstart int))

 (>> X VSTART INT) = -63.30380008156704.
 (>> Y VSTART INT) = 48.45800007415186.
 (>> SIGNX VSTART INT) = -1.0.
 (>> SIGNY VSTART INT) = 1.0.
 (>> R VSTART INT) = 79.72169639410284.
 (>> THETA VSTART INT) = 2.48825566963078.
 (>> QUADRANT VSTART INT) = 2.
```

The initial speed needs to be roughly $80\frac{m}{s}$, at a heading of roughly 2.49 radians (≈ 142 degrees). We can perform sensitivity analyses by varying the desired interception height and seeing how the required speed varies. For example, if we want to intercept at a height of $200m$ we need an initial speed of roughly $102\frac{m}{s}$, and for $500m$ we need roughly $218\frac{m}{s}$.

15.4.3 Diagnosis via constraint suspension

Unfortunately, things break. Diagnosis is the process of figuring out what is wrong with a broken artifact or a malfunctioning system, be it a radio, a computer, a person, or an economy. The capabilities of constraint languages to model the behavior of some kinds of systems makes them natural candidates for thinking about diagnosis problems. This section describes a simple technique, called *constraint suspension*, which has been used in diagnostic systems. Another technique, called *GDE*, is described in Chapter 17.

Suppose the system to be diagnosed can be modeled as a set of interacting parts, in which all of the important relationships between the objects of the system are determined by the interconnections between the objects of the system. Systems that are naturally modeled this way include digitial logic circuits and many analog electronic circuits. (Systems that are not easily modeled this way include high-frequency electronic circuits, where geometric properties become important in determining

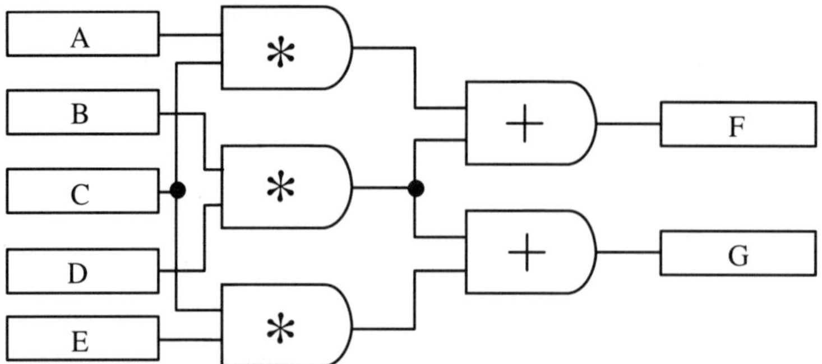

Figure 15.12 Polybox: A simple digital circuit

interactions, and spatially distributed systems like weather fronts.) Systems satisfying these assumptions can easily be modeled via constraint networks: each part is modeled by a constraint, and the constraints are linked together according to the relationships between the parts. For instance, in digital circuitry we might have integer adders and multipliers, which can be linked together to form a circuit as in Figure 15.12.

The task of diagnosis involves many subproblems. One important subproblem is generating candidate hypotheses of what is wrong with a system, given a set of observations of its behavior. Two common assumptions made in solving this subproblem are:

1. *Single-fault assumption:* At most one component of the system has failed.
2. *Non-intermittent failure assumption:* If a component is broken, it remains broken in the same manner while reasoning proceeds.

Even given these two assumptions, a component can break in many ways. A valve may be stuck open or stuck closed, for example, or clogged so that the maximum flow through it is below what it normally would be. One approach to diagnosis is to develop a library of fault models for each component, and use this library to construct explanations of the observed behavior. Each explanation thus identifies a possible faulted component. If there is only one explanation, then that component can be replaced. If there are multiple explanations, then more observations can be made to determine which explanation is correct.[4] One problem with this scheme is that libraries of fault models can be hard to generate, and if a problem arises that isn't covered by the library, the diagnostic algorithm will be in trouble. On the other hand, having a model of the correct behavior of a component is crucial to understanding the system's normal functioning. Constraint suspension exploits this fact. The key insight is that possible failures can be identified by retracting those parts of the normal explanation for behavior that result in discrepancies. Let us examine this idea in more detail.

Suppose that part of the definition of our system includes distinguishing a set of inputs and a set of outputs. In the circuit of Figure 15.12, the inputs are terminals `A`, `B`, `C`, `D`, and `E`, and the outputs are terminals `F` and `G`. By setting the input cells to the observed inputs, the normal constraint propagation mechanism will produce predictions for the values of the outputs. These predictions can then be compared against the observed values of the outputs. Suppose some of the observed outputs do not match the predicted values. Then we can use the dependency system to extract what constraints were used in the prediction of each questionable output value. The union of these sets of constraints represents the possible set of components which could explain the discrepancies. Since we are assuming single faults, we can further simplify our problem by taking the intersection of the constraints implicated by each discrepancy, since the same cause must explain them all.

Now we have a set of candidates. Each candidate is a constraint which participates in the explanation of the aspect of the normal behavior of the system contradicted by the discrepancies. Can we be certain that each candidate can explain the failure? Not yet. After all, the dependency system only maintains a single justification for any believed value. There might be alternative derivations which would still provide the predicted output values even if the constraint under suspicion weren't there. The only way to rule out this possibility is to *suspend* the constraint in question—in effect, unwire it from the network and make sure the values predicted for the questionable outputs are no longer believed. If this is

4. Or, in some circumstances, simply replace everything indicted by the explanations—a strategy sometimes favored by shady auto mechanics who would rather trade off your money against their CPU time.

```
(constraint polybox-example ((a cell)(b cell)(c cell)
                    (d cell)(e cell)(f cell)
                    (g cell) (x cell)(y cell)(z cell)
                    (add-1 adder)(add-2 adder)
                    (mult-1 multiplier)
                    (mult-2 multiplier)
                    (mult-3 multiplier))
  (== (>> a) (>> m1 mult-1))
  (== (>> b) (>> m1 mult-2))
  (== (>> c) (>> m2 mult-1))
  (== (>> c) (>> m1 mult-3))
  (== (>> d) (>> m2 mult-2))
  (== (>> e) (>> m2 mult-3))
  (== (>> f) (>> sum add-1))
  (== (>> g) (>> sum add-2))
  (== (>> x) (>> product mult-1))
  (== (>> x) (>> a1 add-1))
  (== (>> y) (>> product mult-2))
  (== (>> y) (>> a2 add-1))
  (== (>> y) (>> a1 add-2))
  (== (>> z) (>> product mult-3))
  (== (>> z) (>> a2 add-2)))
```

Figure 15.13 TCON formulation of the circuit example

the case, then the component represented by that constraint is a reasonable candidate to explain the failure. Furthermore, with the constraint unwired we can also get some additional leverage for comparing explanations. By propagating observations backward from the outputs, we can gain some predictions sanctioned by that explanation.

The candidate generation algorithm using constraint suspension we have just outlined can be summarized as:

1. Identify discrepancies by comparing observed outputs with predicted outputs derived via constraint propagation from observed inputs.
2. Compute the initial candidate set by intersecting the constraints involved in the explanation underlying each discrepancy.
3. Evaluate each candidate by suspending its corresponding constraint, and use constraint propagation to derive potential new observations from the observed output values.

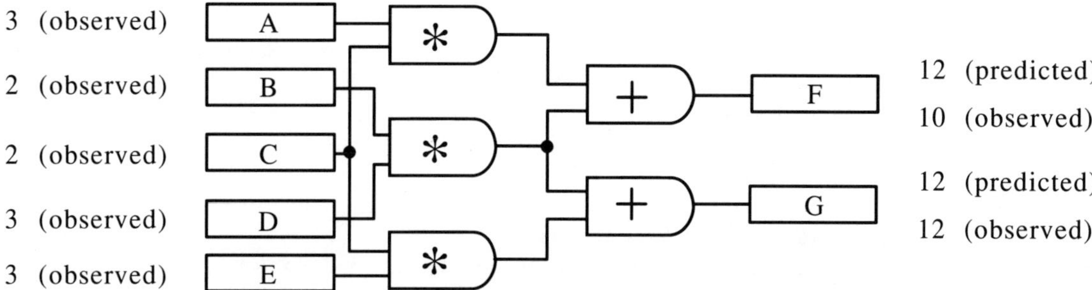

Figure 15.14 Simple test case for digital circuit diagnosis

The file `suspend.lisp` contains an implementation of this algorithm. The procedure `generate-candidates` organizes the computation. The first step is carried out by the sequence `setup-inputs` and `find-discrepancies`. The second step is carried out with the help of `find-contributors`, which itself is adapted from the procedure `rule-ground` in `tcon.lisp`. The third step is carried out by `evaluate-candidate`.

Now let us experiment with the example of Figure 15.12. For simplicity, we use the same adder and multiplier constraints as before. (Exercise 13 illustrates a useful variation.) Figure 15.13 shows the TCON definition of this example. Suppose we run `generate-candidates` on the combination of measurements and initial values shown in Figure 15.14.

```
> (create-tcon "Polybox Example" :debugging nil
               :PROTOTYPE-FILE *suspend-file*)
> (create 'ex 'polybox-Example)
> (generate-candidates *tcon*
      '((((>> a ex) . 3)((>> b ex) . 2)
        ((>> c ex) . 2)((>> d ex) . 3)((>> e ex) . 3))
      '(((>> f ex) . 10)((>> g ex) . 12))
      t)

;;; Loading source file "/u/bps/code/tcon/krd.lisp"

 1 discrepancies found.
  (>> F EX) was 12, should be 10.
 Contributors to (>> F EX) being 12 instead of 10:
    (<Constraint MULT-2> <Constraint MULT-1> <Constraint ADD-1>)
```

```
Candidates are (<Constraint MULT-2> <Constraint MULT-1>
                                    <Constraint ADD-1>).
Suspending <Constraint MULT-2>..
.. <Constraint MULT-2> exonerated.
Suspending <Constraint MULT-1>..
.. <Constraint MULT-1> possible.
Suspending <Constraint ADD-1>..
.. <Constraint ADD-1> possible.
((<Constraint ADD-1> (<Cell (>> SUM ADD-1 EX)> . 10)
                     (<Cell (>> A2 ADD-1 EX)> . 6)
                     (<Cell (>> A1 ADD-1 EX)> . 6))
 (<Constraint MULT-1> (<Cell (>> PRODUCT MULT-1 EX)> . 4)
                      (<Cell (>> M2 MULT-1 EX)> . 2)
                      (<Cell (>> M1 MULT-1 EX)> . 3)))
```

Predictions are easily generated by propagating the observed input values through the constraint network, and discrepancies can be identified by comparing the predicted values to the observations. The contributors are identified as the constraints "upstream" in the dependency trace for the predictions. With these observations there are two candidates, `add-1` and `mult-1`. Suppose the measured values were different. If for instance we measured both `f` and `g` to be 3, our algorithm produces the following analysis:

```
2 discrepancies found.
 (>> G EX) was 12, should be 3.
 (>> F EX) was 12, should be 3.
Contributors to (>> G EX) being 12 instead of 3:
   (<Constraint MULT-3> <Constraint MULT-2> <Constraint ADD-2>)
Contributors to (>> F EX) being 12 instead of 3:
   (<Constraint MULT-2> <Constraint MULT-1> <Constraint ADD-1>)
Candidates are (<Constraint MULT-2>).
Suspending <Constraint MULT-2>..
.. <Constraint MULT-2> possible.
((<Constraint MULT-2> (<Cell (>> PRODUCT MULT-2 EX)> . -3)
                      (<Cell (>> M2 MULT-2 EX)> . 3)
                      (<Cell (>> M1 MULT-2 EX)> . 2)))
```

Assuming only a single fault, there is just one candidate, `MULT-2`. Intuitively this makes sense, because both of the other inputs to `ADD-1` and

ADD-2 are identical, so if the same problem shows up at both of them, it must be due to the one component they have in common.

Constraint suspension has its limitations. Consider what must be wrong if we have the same inputs, but now f is measured to be 8 and g is measured to be 16. There is no single component failure that could explain this problem, and indeed the constraint suspension algorithm cannot find an explanation:

```
;;; Loading source file "/u/bps/code/tcon/krd.lisp"

 2 discrepancies found.
  (>> G EX) was 12, should be 16.
  (>> F EX) was 12, should be 8.
 Contributors to (>> G EX) being 12 instead of 16:
    (<Constraint MULT-3> <Constraint MULT-2> <Constraint ADD-2>)
 Contributors to (>> F EX) being 12 instead of 8:
    (<Constraint MULT-2> <Constraint MULT-1> <Constraint ADD-1>)
 Candidates are (<Constraint MULT-2>).
 Suspending <Constraint MULT-2>..
 .. <Constraint MULT-2> exonerated.
NIL
```

Since the problem affected both outputs, the intersection of the candidates lists yielded only MULT-2. But suspending MULT-2 and applying the output values to the network resulted in a contradiction, which means that the all of the remaining constraints cannot be correct and yet produce those outputs, given our particular inputs. From our perspective it is easy to see that something else must be broken. We explore a different algorithm which handles such cases in Chapter 17.

15.5 Extending the TCON model

TCON represents the simplest member of a family of languages that has been used to explore ideas in efficient reasoning about mathematical properties and engineered systems. For example, Chapter 16 shows how to hitch up an assumption-based truth maintenance system to TCON, leading to a system for easily implementing more sophisticated diagnosis systems. This section focuses on other extensions. First, we consider some implementation tricks for increasing efficiency and simplifying interactions with other reasoning facilities. Second, we outline several techniques for overcoming incompleteness in local propagation. Finally, we describe ways to use constraint languages in modeling dynamic systems.

15.5.1 Implementation techniques

To keep TCON simple, several standard implementation techniques for such languages were not incorporated, including *sharing structure, compilation, indirect cells,* and *removal rules.* We outline each in turn.

15.5.1.1 Sharing structure

Constraint languages permit efficient implementations in part by avoiding the overhead of pattern matching. The implementation of TCON described here does not fully exploit the possibilities for datastructure efficiency. Consider the role of == in defining a higher-order constraint (e.g., Figure 15.10. The parts equated will always be so, by the very definition of the constraint. Why, then, should two separate structures be built at all? For instance, if the definition of a constraint includes

```
(== (>> sum add1) (>> a2 add2))
```

then we could simply build a single cell to represent both `(>> sum add1)` and `(>> a2 add2)`. The savings in terms of cells may not seem very large, but if shared parts are themselves complex constraints, the savings can be considerable.

This strategy does not always make sense, of course. In defining a constraint network to model a specific system rather than a general class of constraints, the ability to undo connections is crucial. Consider, for instance,

```
(== (>> workstation port32 lan)
    (>> workstation Rm349 ILS))
```

i.e., that the workstation on port 32 of the LAN is the machine at Room 349 at ILS. Physically, of course, there is just one workstation, but nevertheless this equality may need to be broken if the machine is moved.

Implementing shared structure is not very difficult. Already, cells have the capability to support access of procedures from multiple sources, since that is how the special == constraints are implemented. Some careful analysis must be performed at the time of constraint definition, to identify which references resolve to the same entities. The only tricky part is that in creating a new constraint the code must become sensitive to what parts already exist, due to the context in which the constraint is being built (see Exercise 9). Implemented properly, sharing structure can typically cut the storage requirements of a constraint network by up to 50 percent.

15.5.1.2 Compilation opportunities

There are several opportunities for small speedups via compilation. First, the procedures that serve as the bodies of rules can be compiled. This compilation can be performed when the constraint prototype is loaded. Alternatively, techniques analogous to those in FTRE can be used to expand prototype definitions to include separate, named procedures, so that files of constraint prototypes can be compiled once and loaded as needed. The second opportunity for compilation is in creating instances of constraints. `create` analyzes each constraint prototype from scratch, every time something is created. It is more efficient to perform this analysis once and cache a special-purpose procedure for creating constraints of particular types. (This becomes even more useful as the analysis involved in processing a prototype definition becomes more complex, as in the structure-sharing technique described above.)

15.5.1.3 Indirect cells

A fundamental limitation of constraint networks as described so far is that they are not *metacircular*; that is, the act of building a constraint network is completely distinct from the the act of reasoning within a constraint network. This limitation is also a source of strength—limiting inference to be within the network makes it cheap, and thus simple antecedent control strategies suffice. Propagation via constraints cannot result in combinatorial explosions, and (given simple data) the amount of memory required is strictly bounded by the size of the network. Even so, the gains to be had by adding some rudimentary metacircular capabilities to constraint networks can be substantial.

Let us introduce a new class of cell, the *indirect* cell. The value of an indirect cell, if known, is always another constraint or cell. Indirect cells can participate in formulae statements just like any other. What does this mean? If an indirect cell is the `sets` of a rule, then that rule should produce a constraint which legitimately could play the role of the indirect cell. For example, suppose we are trying to figure out what a physical object, such as a ball, is doing at some particular time. If it is on a horizontal surface it is resting, on a steeply inclined surface it may be sliding, and if in midair it is falling. A constraint describing the state of the ball at a given time might have an indirect cell called `action`, which should be filled by a constraint which describes the ball's current activity.

Indirect cells can also particpate in *wiring rules*, a new kind of rule which specifies connections between the value of an indirect cell and the constraint of which it is a part. To continue the ball example, once a constraint for an action has been instantiated, it must be connected properly into the network. Wiring rules do this. For instance, to use the action constraints for simulation, the wiring rules must specify that the position and velocity of the ball should be equated with the initial position and velocity in the action description. In some constraint languages this is be stated in a form analgous to formulae:

```
(Wiring-Rules
 ((initial-state)
  (== (>> position initial-state) (>> initial-position))
  (== (>> velocity initial-state) (>> initial-velocity))
```

This rule is triggered when the `initial-state` cell receives a value, which must be a constraint. The `initial-position` and `initial-velocity` constraints of the action are then linked to the `position` and `velocity` parts of the constraint stored in `initial-state`. For instance, suppose we have a constraint `fly12` which describes the dynamics and kinematics of motion, and a constraint `ball-state17` which describes the state of a ball that is about to start flying through the air. Executing the statement

```
(set-parameter (>> initial-state fly12) (>> ball-state17))
```

has the identical effect to stating

```
(== (>> position ball-state17) (>> initial-position fly12))
(== (>> velocity ball-state17) (>> initial-velocity fly12))
```

The combination of indirect cells and wiring rules provides important modularity as well as shared structure. Suppose we have constraints describing a variety of physical systems, each of which involves different kinds of energy. If we stipulate that for any such system there will be a cell `energy` which is the sum of the kinds of energy involved in that system, then we can invoke conservation of energy through the following constraint:

```
(constraint Energy-Conservation ((before indirect)
                                 (after indirect))
 (wiring ((before after)
         (== (>> energy before) (>> energy after)))))
```

That is, no matter how the details of the system are transformed between its state as described by the network in `before` and the network described in `after`, the energy must be the same.

Increased expressiveness must always be used with caution. It should be obvious by now that the ability to have the constraint network extend itself can lead to combinatorial explosions and even runaway (see Exercise 11a).

15.5.1.4 Removal Rules

Interfacing constraint networks to other inferential facilities often requires using side effects. For instance, in building a VLSI design system, once the coordinates of a rectangle are known, a rule associated with the constraint describing that rectangle can call a graphics system to cause the rectangle to be displayed. But if a coordinate is retracted, we then want the rectangle to be erased. Such cleaning up can be handled by rules that are triggered when a cell's value is removed.

```
(constraint 1D-motion ((xstart cell)(xend cell)
                       (vstart cell)(vend cell)
                       (accel cell)(deltat cell)
                       (basic 1D-uniform-motion)
                       (fix 1D-uniform-accel)
                       (adr1 adder)(adr2 adder)
                       (mul multiplier))
 (== (>> deltat) (>> deltat basic))
 (== (>> deltat) (>> deltat fix))
 (== (>> deltat) (>> m1 mul))
 (== (>> xstart) (>> xstart basic))
 (== (>> xend) (>> sum adr1))
 (== (>> vstart) (>> velocity basic))
 (== (>> vstart) (>> a1 adr2))
 (== (>> vend) (>> sum adr2))
 (== (>> accel) (>> accel fix))
 (== (>> accel) (>> m2 mul))
 (== (>> xend basic) (>> a1 adr1))
 (== (>> deltax fix) (>> a2 adr1))
 (== (>> product mul) (>> a2 adr2))
 (formulae (deltat (xstart xend vstart accel)
            (if (nearly-zero? accel) :DISMISS
   (let* ((det (sqrt (- (* vstart vstart)
       (* 2.0 accel
  (- xstart xend)))))
  (ans1 (/ (- (- vstart) det) accel))
  (ans2 (/ (+ (- vstart) det) accel)))
     (if (< ans1 0.0)
 (if (< ans2 0.0) :DISMISS ans2)
       (if (< ans2 0.0) ans1
 :DISMISS)))))))
```

Figure 15.15 Constraints sometimes use formulae to overcome incompleteness. Most of the work in the constraint above is performed by more primitive constraints. Because of a loop in the constraints, however, `deltat` cannot be computed by these constraints in some circumstances where it can be figured out. The `formulae` statement defines a rule which performs this calculation as needed.

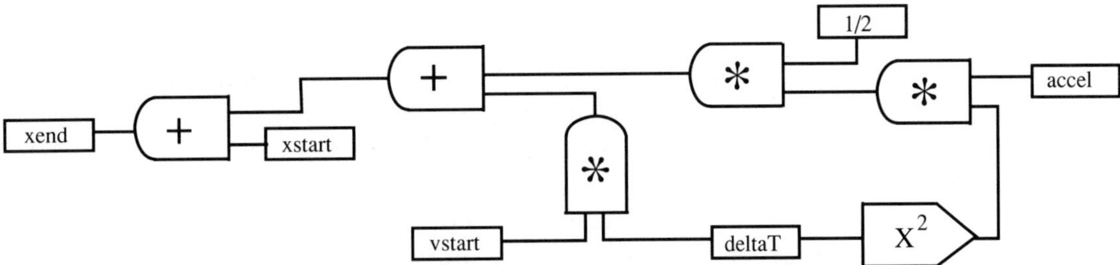

Figure 15.16 Loops in constraint networks lead to incompleteness

15.5.2 Overcoming the incompleteness of local propagation

Constraint propagation is very efficient, but as we have seen before, efficiency is typically purchased at the price of incompleteness. And indeed purely local propagation techniques on constraint networks are incomplete. We have already seen such an example in the relationships describing one-dimensional motion under uniform acceleration (see Figure 15.15). Suppose we represented the equation

$$\texttt{xend} = \texttt{xstart} + \texttt{vstart} \times \texttt{deltat} + \frac{\texttt{a} \times \texttt{deltat}^2}{2}$$

directly as a constraint network, as shown in Figure 15.16. If we knew `xstart`, `xend`, `vstart`, and `a`, then `deltat` can be determined by using the solution for quadratic equations, filtering out any negative solutions. Local propagation cannot derive this answer: it is stymied by the loop in the constraint network. The way we solved this problem previously was to add a special-purpose rule, using the `formulae` statement, in the `1D-motion` constraint which solved the quadratic equation for `deltat` when the right information became known.

The technique of introducing extra rules to break such loops is a good one, when there is some standard locality (e.g., higher-order constraint) in which to put such information. This is not always possible, since loops can arise within systems of constraints connected on an ad hoc basis. If the domain of the cells is a discrete set of values, dependency-directed search can be used to find possible solutions. If the domain of the network's cells are real numbers, non-local mathematical techniques can often be applied effectively to the constraint data model. The rest of this section examines two such techniques.

The first technique is to use numerical relaxation. Suppose we extended our constraint language so that every constraint included *error procedures* which estimated the degree to which its values violated the constraint and *change procedures* which suggested what parameters could be changed in which directions to reduce the error. Given a subnetwork that could not be solved via propagation, the local error procedures and change procedures could be assembled to produce a numerical optimization program that would iteratively find reasonable values for the subnetwork. This is essentially what Borning's THINGLAB [2] did. For drawing programs and other systems where constraints are viewed as advice about the structure of something, as opposed to hard statements which must be perfectly satisfied, this technique can be quite useful.

The second technique is to use the unsolved pieces of the constraint network to drive the formulation of equations which can then be solved via algebraic manipulation. This is essentially what was done by hand in defining the `1D-motion` constraint. Consider the unsolved portion of the network in Figure 15.16. Suppose we define primitive constraints so that if their cells that normally hold numbers are given symbols as a value, the constraint produces as output a symbolic expression which encodes the relationship it enforces. Then instead of placing a numerical guess in the network, as occurs with relaxation, we choose some variable to receive a symbolic value, which is then propagated through the system. (The act of giving a variable a symbolic value to allow the analysis to proceed is called *plunking the variable*, and the symbol given is called a *plunk*.) When a cell gets multiple symbolic values, it must be the case that each expression can be equated. Thus we can use local propagation to generate sets of equations to solve. This process is illustrated for the simple motion network in Figure 15.17.

The choice of cell to solve for strongly determines the efficiency of the solution process and, in some cases, even the form of the result, if solutions that contain symbolic parameters are satisfactory. There are several interesting issues in implementing system of this kind; see Exercise 12.

This algebraic propagation strategy is very powerful. It does have certain limitations. First, every constraint in the network must be translatable into an expression that can be manipulated symbolically. For mathematical constraints this is straightforward, but for many kinds of con-

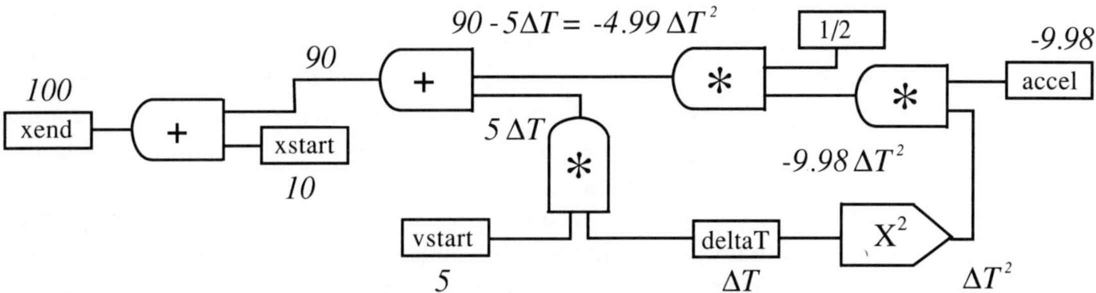

Figure 15.17 Loops can be broken by plunking

straints it is difficult. Second, these algorithms can waste much time generating and exploring redundant sets of equations (i.e., those which when solved yield such stunning insights as $1 = 1$). Such blunders can be minimized by careful algorithms, but can be hard to eliminate entirely.

15.5.3 Modeling dynamic systems

So far we have presumed in our modeling that time could be mostly factored out. For example, in discussing motion we relied on distinct named times (e.g., `xinitial` and `xfinal`) whose temporal relationship was only specified in relative terms (i.e., `deltat`). For many problems time must be represented more explicitly. There are two ways typically used to make time more explicit in constraint languages.

The first method is *network replication*. Suppose an object Obj with time-varying properties is described by a piece of constraint network N at a particular time t_1. To represent the properties of Obj at a new time t_2, we can simply build a copy of N, called, say, N'. Using constraints which describe classes of change (like the motion constraint described earlier), N' can be wired into the network. Then we can start using N' to reason about the properties of Obj at t_2, either using the values of N' found via propagation through the dynamics constraints, or setting values of N' and using propagation to see what that implies about Obj at t_1. This technique has the virtue of simplicity. Its disadvantage is that it seems to waste structure: only the cells of N' really need to be distinct, if the same relationships govern Obj at both t_1 and t_2.

The second technique can be thought of as *historical cells*. Suppose we represent Obj by a single subnetwork N for all time, but augment cells to allow multiple values with time stamps. Digital logic circuits, for example, typically use a global clock to keep the parts of the circuit operating in harmony, and the time of each discrete clock tick can be used to decompose time into distinct pieces. Thus the value of a cell might consist of entries that include a time stamp, a value, and an informant for that value at that time. Using historical cells with a discrete temporal ontology is fairly straightforward. Efficiently using historical cells with a continuous temporal ontology is still something of an open problem. Time is typically modeled as continuous when phenomena like feedback are crucial to model, which means that the value of a cell over an interval of time might depend on both the values of other cells and the value of the same cell at some earlier time.

15.6 Backpointers

TCON is based on CONLAN [9], which extended the language described in [16]. Carrying out the extensions suggested in Exercises 9, 10, and 11 will yield a modern implementation of CONLAN. [15] provides a good tutorial on implementation style.

In the early literature on using constraint propagation in engineering problem solving, the process of solving a network of constraints by picking a cell to solve for was called *plunking*, with the chosen variable called a *plunk* [6, 14].

The network replication technique for modeling dynamic systems was first used in FROB [8, 10]. Since constraint networks are most efficient for reasoning about systems that can be modeled as having fixed structure, historical cells have become the preferred technique for temporal reasoning. The technique of historical cells was first used in de Kleer's Ph.D. work [5], where timestamps consisted of ATMS-like assumptions. This technique has also been used by Davis's group at MIT in modeling digital logic circuits [3, 4]. Several ideas for reasoning with continuous temporal ontologies have been explored, including [1, 7]. An interesting proposal for maintaining appropriate justifications via concise intervals was made by Williams [17], but the computational complexity of such schemes is still an open question.

The idea of programming via constraints has taken several interesting turns. For example, [11] explores the declarative specification of new constraint languages, and [12, 13] extend the semantics of logic programming with mathematical constraints.

15.7 Exercises

1. Constraints can be used to perform various logical operations as well as numerical calculations.
   a. ⋆⋆ Implement a constraint `==?` that places `T` in its cell `output` when the values of its `in1` and `in2` cells are equal, in the sense of Lisp `equal`, and `nil` otherwise.
   b. ⋆⋆ Implement a constraint `comparator` that places a symbol in its `output` indicating what ordinal relationship holds between the values of its cells `in1` and `in2`.
   c. ⋆⋆ Using your constraints from the previous parts, implement the constraints `positive?`, `zero?`, and `negative?`, whose `output` cells are `T` exactly when the values in their `input` cells have the appropriate relationship with zero.
   d. ⋆⋆ Use your `positive?` constraint to enforce positive travel times in the uniform motion constraint.
   e. ⋆⋆ Implement a `relay` constraint that equates either `in1` or `in2` to `output` depending on whether or not its `coil` cell is `T` or `nil`.
   f. ⋆⋆ Use your `relay` constraint to implement a signed square root constraint: that is, if the input is non-negative the positive root is chosen, but if the input is negative, the negative root for the magnitude of the input is produced.
   g. ⋆ Physical relays can be connected together to make oscillators. Why doesn't this work with relays modeled as constraint networks?
2. ⋆ The definition of `process-constraint-rules` presumes that every constraint definition contains at most one `formulae` statement.

Explain why by describing a problem that would arise when two formulae statements are used in a single prototype.

3. ⋆ Why shouldn't constraints from two different networks be hooked up together via ==?

4. ⋆ What modifications are required to allow sets of symbols and numbers as the values of cells?

5. Given compatible values for a cell, the current implementation of `set!` keeps whichever value and informant came first.

   a. ⋆ One can imagine circumstances in which this is not the optimal behavior. Describe a set of interactions with TCON that could cause a problem due to this choice.

   b. ⋆ Modify `set!` so that ground values take precedence over derived values.

6. ⋆⋆ TCON requires authors of constraint formulae to ensure that every input is used in computing a value, so that the dependency records will be accurate. A different approach would be to require formulae to return, in addition to the value computed for the cell set by the rule, what subset of the input information was actually used in deriving that value. Modify TCON to use this approach, and analyze the trade-offs involved.

7. ⋆ Earlier we asserted that one could implement constraint languages using a pattern-directed inference system. Demonstrate that this is so, by writing a set of JTRE rules that implement an adder constraint, and a rule for detecting contradictory values.

8. ⋆ Consider again the three-input adder defined in Figure 15.8. Does it always accurately reflect the semantics of a three-input adder? If so, explain why. If not, explain how it might be fixed to do so.

9. ⋆⋆ Modify TCON to use shared structure in building constraints, as outlined in Section 15.5.1.1.

10. ⋆⋆ Modify TCON to allow removal rules, as described in Section 15.5.1.4.

11. This exercise explores the techniques outlined in 15.5.1.3.

a. ⋆ Describe how indirect cells and wiring rules permit constraint networks to exhibit uncontrolled growth. What limitations might be imposed to prevent this problem?

b. ⋆⋆ Extend TCON to support indirect cells and wiring rules.

c. ⋆⋆⋆ Test your extended TCON by building a constraint-based simulation that "grows" a description of behavior over time on demand.

12. This exercise explores the use of algebraic manipulation to overcome limitations in local propagation. Assume that the vocabulary of constraints consists entirely of algebraic relationships and analytic functions (e.g., *sin*, *cos*, ...).

a. ⋆⋆ Write a procedure `gather-equations` which, given as input a partially solved constraint network and a cell to solve for, uses the structure of the network to compute a set of equations concerning the value of that cell.

b. ⋆⋆ Hook up `gather-equations` to the algebraic manipulator of your choice, and explore the limitations of this combination using several examples.

c. ⋆⋆⋆ Rewrite TCON to support the generation of equations via propagation of symbolic values, as outlined in Section 15.5.2.

d. ⋆⋆⋆⋆ Using your extended TCON, reconstruct the `SYN` circuit synthesis program [6] or build a system for solving textbook algebra problems.

13. Many real devices can be approximated as having predefined inputs and outputs, with information always flowing from inputs to outputs. In [3], the formulae in a constraint were partitioned according to whether they represented simulation or inference; that is, whether they calculated outputs on the basis of inputs or inputs on the basis of outputs. This distinction is useful because the constraint propagation step of candidate generation can be used to provide predictions which can be tested by further measurements.

a. ⋆ Of the three calculated values returned by `generate-candidates` on the example in Section 15.4.3, which are legitimate predictions, and why?

b. ⋆⋆ One method for implementing the simulation/inference split is to divide constraints into two distinct components. Thus an adder might be defined in terms of an `adder-sim` constraint which incorporates the simulation rules for an adder and an `adder-inf` constraint which incorporates its inference rules. Using this scheme also requires associating two cells with each terminal, one to hold its inferred value and one to hold its simulated value. Thus we might set up our example by statements like

```
(set-parameter (>> sim a) 3)
(set-parameter (>> inf f) 10)
```

That is, we simulate from observed inputs and infer from observed outputs. Using this *dualist method*, write a set of constraints sufficient for this example.

c. ⋆⋆ Rewrite `suspend.lisp` to exploit the dualist method of constraint organization.

14. ⋆⋆ The definition of `2D-vector` (see Figure 15.11) is flat; that is, it uses a large number of rules to define the relationships between its cells directly, rather than expressing the interrelationships in terms of simpler constraints. Design a new version of `2D-vector` without a `formulae` statement whose meaning is derived from simpler constraints. (Hint: Several new types of constraints will be needed, and to use this constraint will require minor changes in `2D-motion`.)

15.8 Bibliography

[1] Allen, J., "Towards a general model of action and time," *Artificial Intelligence*, 23(1984):123–154.

[2] Borning, A., "THINGLAB: A constraint-oriented simulation laboratory," Report No. CS-79-746, Computer Science Department, Stanford University, 1979.

[3] Davis, R., "Diagnostic Reasoning based on structure and behavior," *Artificial Intelligence* 24(1984):347-410. Also in Hamscher, W., de Kleer, J., and Console, L., (eds.), *Readings in Model-Based Diagnosis*, Morgan-Kaufmann, 1992.

[4] Davis, R., and Hamscher, W., "Model-based reasoning: Troubleshooting", in Shrobe, H. and AAAI (eds.), *Exploring artificial intelligence*, Morgan-Kaufmann, 1988. Also in Hamscher, W., de Kleer, J., and Console, L., (eds.), *Readings in Model-Based Diagnosis*, Morgan-Kaufmann, 1992.

[5] de Kleer, J. "Causal and teleological reasoning in circuit recognition," MIT AI Lab Technical Report No. 529, 1979.

[6] de Kleer, J., and Sussman, G. J., "Propagation of constraints applied to circuit synthesis," *Circuit Theory and Applications* 8(1980):127–144.

[7] Dean, T., and McDermott, D., "Temporal data base management," *Artificial Intelligence*, 32(1987):1–56.

[8] Forbus, K., "Spatial and qualitative aspects of reasoning about motion," *Proceedings of the first annual conference of the American Association for Artificial Intelligence*, 1980.

[9] Forbus, K., "A CONLAN primer" Bolt, Beranek, and Newman Technical Report No. 4491, March 1981.

[10] Forbus, K., "Qualitative reasoning about space and motion" in Gentner, D., and Stevens, A. (eds.), *Mental Models*, Earlbaum, 1983.

[11] Leler, W., *Constraint Programming Languages: Their Specification and Generation*, Addison-Wesley, 1988.

[12] Jaffar, J., and Lassez, J. L., "Constraint logic programming," *Proceedings of the SIGACT-SIGPLAN Symposium on Principles of Programming Languages*, 1987, 111–119.

[13] Saraswat, Vijay A., "Concurrent constraint programming languages," Ph.D. dissertation, Carnegie-Mellon University, 1989.

[14] Stallman, R., and Sussman, G. J., "Forward reasoning and dependency-directed backtracking in a system for computer-aided circuit analysis," *Artificial Intelligence*, 9(1977):135–196.

[15] Steele, G. L., "The definition and implementation of a computer programming language based on constraints.", MIT AI Lab Technical report No. 595, 1980.

[16] Sussman, G. J. and Steele, G. L., "CONSTRAINTS: A language for expressing almost-hierarchical descriptions," *Artificial Intelligence*, 14(1980):1–39.

[17] Williams, B. C., "Doing time: Putting qualitative reasoning on firmer ground," *Proceedings of the National Conference on Artificial Intelligence*, 1986, 105–112.

16 Assumption-Based Constraint Languages

In the previous chapter we explored the simple antecedent constraint language TCON. Although TCON does not exploit a TMS directly, it incorporates many JTMS-like facilities. TCON could easily be adapted to use a full JTMS, which would significantly reduce the number of rule executions (see Section 16.2). Nevertheless, in this chapter we skip this intermediate step and develop ATCON—a tiny constraint language based upon an ATMS. For many applications, ATMS-like capabilities are far more appropriate. For example, the diagnostic application we discuss in the next chapter needs to analyze many alternatives simultaneously in order to perform differential diagnosis to identify which tests to make next. ATCON illustrates only a small fraction of the capabilities that are possible in connecting an ATMS to a constraint instead of a rule language. We primarily focus on a few capabilities which enable us to develop a very simple but surprisingly powerful architecture for model-based diagnosis.

Implementing ATCON requires extending TCON in two directions simultaneously. First, TCON must be adapted to work with a separate TMS module. Second, TCON, which takes a single context perspective, must be extended to operate in multiple contexts. Therefore, to successfully implement this desired functionality requires reexamining many of the issues we discussed in earlier chapters—this time in the context of a constraint language. Before we analyze implementations in detail, let us first consider what ATCON is supposed to do.

16.1 The ATCON language

16.1.1 The concept of cell in ATCON

In TCON a cell is a location which holds a value. Therefore, we write "$x = 1$" to indicate that cell x has the value 1. Using a TMS, each possible assignment of a value to a cell is represented as a TMS node. Thus, in ATCON, "$x = 1$" refers to a particular node representing the fact that cell x has the value 1. While each TCON cell could contain only one value at a time, when using a TMS, typically there will be multiple nodes associated with any particular cell. If we were using a single-context TMS such as an LTMS or a JTMS, at most one of the nodes associated with any cell should be believed at any given time. However, with an ATMS, each node of a cell simply has a distinct ATMS label representing the environments in which the cell has that value. No pair of cell nodes can simultaneously hold in any consistent environment.

16.1.2 Introducing assumptions in ATCON

The syntax of ATCON constraints is almost identical to that of TCON. For example, the following TCON constraint is also a perfectly valid ATCON constraint:

```
(constraint adder
         ((a1 cell) (a2 cell) (sum cell))
      (formulae (sum (a1 a2) (+ a1 a2))
                (a1 (sum a2) (- sum a2))
                (a2 (sum a1) (- sum a1))))
```

As ATCON includes a TMS, each conclusion of a constraint will now also have a justification. Let us reexamine the contents is of a constraint body. Each rule of a `formulae` of the form:

(⟨*Sets*⟩ ⟨*Uses*⟩ ⟨*RuleBody*⟩)

⟨*Sets*⟩ is a cell for which the rule can provide a value. ⟨*Uses*⟩ is a list of cells whose values must be known before the rule is executed. ⟨*RuleBody*⟩ is fragment of Common Lisp code which is executed and whose result is the value for ⟨*Sets*⟩ (unless this value is `:DISMISS` or

:LOSE). In ATCON, if ⟨*RuleBody*⟩ returns the value :DISMISS, then that rule execution is ignored. If the result is :LOSE, then the fact that the values in ⟨*Uses*⟩ are inconsistent is recorded via a call to the ATMS procedure nogood-nodes. In ATCON, a contradiction merely results in the introduction of a nogood; both ATCON and the underlying ATMS avoid working on values that do not hold in consistent environments. Therefore, all the contradiction-handling techniques of TCON are irrelevant here. Otherwise, the value produced by the rule is justified by the values in ⟨*Uses*⟩. For example, if we know that a1=1 and a2=1, then ATCON will deduce sum=2, justified by both a1=1 and a2=1.

The central change from TCON to ATCON is that both the constraint language and the ATMS operate in all contexts (i.e., all environments) at once. Environments and their contexts are built up out of assumptions, so we need some linguistic way of creating these assumptions.

ATCON has a new part-type assumption. Every time a new instance of a constraint is created, a new assumption is created for each one of its assumption parts (there need not be any, of course). For example, in the diagnostic task, one makes the default assumption that components are working correctly unless there is evidence to the contrary. Therefore, to describe an adder component one might write:

```
(constraint adder-component
        ((a1 cell) (a2 cell) (sum cell) (ok assumption))
     (formulae (sum (a1 a2 ok) (+ a1 a2))
               (a1 (sum a2 ok) (- sum a2))
               (a2 (sum a1 ok) (- sum a1))))
```

Note that we include ok in ⟨*Uses*⟩ even thought it is not referenced in any ⟨*RuleBody*⟩. The intention is that the adder component only propagates values under the assumption that the particular component in question is functioning correctly. Every conclusion produced by one of the rules of the constraint includes this assumption. For example:

```
>   (create 'add 'adder-component)
>   (set-parameter (>> a1 add) 1)
>   (set-parameter (>> a2 add) 2)
>   (what-is (>> sum add))
(>> SUM ADD) = [3,{{ADD}}]
```

(Notice that ATCON has been extended to print out values with their ATMS labels.) In other words, the output of the adder component is 3, assuming it is working correctly.

As this style of writing constraints occurs so commonly, ATCON provides a new primitive, assume-constraint, for it. The adder component constraint can be simply written equivalently as:

```
(assume-constraint adder-component ((a1 cell) (a2 cell) (sum cell))
            (formulae (sum (a1 a2) (+ a1 a2))
                      (a1 (sum a2) (- sum a2))
                      (a2 (sum a1) (- sum a1))))
```

For every instance of an assume-constraint, an ATMS assumption is created such that whenever any variable is set this assumption will be included as an antecedent.

16.1.3 Constraint programming style

In a more serious constraint language, one would like to be able to simply write the constraint as sum=a1+a2. In order to avoid symbolic algebra—which might be easy if the only operator was addition, but can get arbitrarily complicated otherwise—we must specify in our language how the constraint is to be implemented by a set of rules. There is therefore nothing in our language that would prevent one from writing a nonsensical constraint such as:

```
(assume-constraint adder-component ((a1 cell) (a2 cell) (sum cell))
            (formulae (sum (a1 a2) (+ a1 a2))
                      (a1 (sum a2) (+ sum a2))
                      (a2 (sum a1) (+ sum a1))))
```

This rule only makes sense if all the cells are 0. The consequences of writing such a rule are highly implementation- and context-dependent. For example, in our ATCON implementation, if a1=1 and a1=2, and we know nothing else, then sum=3 without any contradiction. The implementation doesn't bother checking whether the other two rules for adder-component are consistent with the first. If, however, sum=3 is discovered for some independent reason (in an environment different than the previous derivation of sum=3), then the other two rules are checked and the ATMS will discover a new nogood(s). Therefore, good constraint programming style demands that the rules of a constraint be consistent. Analogously, because ATCON will not run one rule of a constraint on the output of another, each rule of a constraint should make all the derivations that can be made from the inputs, given the conceptual constraint being implemented.

The ⟨*RuleBody*⟩ of a formulae can be an arbitrary fragment of Common Lisp code. This provides the programmer arbitrary power, but also opens the door to poor programming style. The basic conceptual style principle is that the Common Lisp code in ⟨*RuleBody*⟩s should be such that the results of an ATCON program are insensitive to the particular order in which the rules are executed. Some syntactic conventions which help ensure this are:

- ⟨*RuleBody*⟩s should not set the values of cells.
- ⟨*RuleBody*⟩s should not access cells other than those in ⟨*Uses*⟩.
- ⟨*RuleBody*⟩s should not perform any side effects on global datastructures or create state in any way.

16.1.4 Setting ATCON parameters

Consider the basic TCON interface for changing parameters: `set-parameter`, `forget-parameter` and `change-parameter`. In ATCON, `set-parameter` has a more rigid definition.

```
(set-parameter cell expression)
```

This permanently sets `cell` to `expression` by providing it an ATMS justification with no antecedents, i.e., it creates a premise. Thus, `cell` will be `expression` in all possible environments. There is no ATCON analog to TCON's `forget-parameter` and `change-parameter`—the analogous effects are now achieved through the introduction of ATMS assumptions. If a cell value may later be changed, one must use the new procedure `assume-parameter`.

```
(assume-parameter cell expression &optional string)
```

This assumes that `cell` is `expression` by making an ATMS assumption for the purpose. The optional `string` argument provides a pretty way to print out the ATMS assumption when it appears in environments.

Let us create an adder A and assume that its two inputs are 1 and 10 and that its sum is 100:

```
>   (create 'a 'adder)
>   (assume-parameter (>> a1 a) 1 "a1")
>   (assume-parameter (>> a2 a) 10 "a2")
>   (assume-parameter (>> sum a) 100 "sum")
>   (show-network *tcon*)
(>> SUM A) = [100,{{sum}}][11,{{a1,a2}}]
(>> A2 A) = [99,{{a1,sum}}][10,{{a2}}]
(>> A1 A) = [90,{{a2,sum}}][1,{{a1}}]
```

(`show-network` calls `what-is` on every cell in the network.) The final three lines are ATCON output. The first output line states that the output of the adder can have two possible values: 100 and and 11. The sum is 100 under the assumptions `sum` and `a1`. The interrogative `why` now prints out explanations for all environments:

```
>   (why (>> sum a) 11)
(>> SUM A) = 11 under environment {a1,a2}:
(>> SUM A) = 11 via <Constraint A> and inputs:
(>> A1 A) = 1
(>> A2 A) = 10.
Assuming that (>> A2 A) = 10.
Assuming that (>> A1 A) = 1.
```

16.1.5 Language extensions

TCON's primitive == for building composite constraints works in ATCON as well. Therefore, the following is a perfectly valid ATCON constraint.

```
(constraint 3-adder ((a1 cell)(a2 cell)(a3 cell)(sum cell)
                     (add1 adder)(add2 adder))
   (== (>> a1) (>> a1 add1))
   (== (>> a2) (>> a2 add1))
   (== (>> a3) (>> a1 add2))
   (== (>> sum add1) (>> a2 add2))
   (== (>> sum) (>> sum add2)))
```

ATCON will be used extensively in simulation and diagnostic tasks, and this syntactic convention becomes cumbersome for larger circuits. In addition, the == convention requires first creating cells and then equating them, which produces a larger number of redundant cells. In ATCON, the part-type can optionally be followed by a list which enumerates the type and some of the parts—when the part-type is created it will reuse parts that it is supplied. Thus, `3-adder` can be conveniently written as:

```
(constraint 3-adder ((a1 cell)(a2 cell)(a3 cell)(sum cell) (i cell)
                     (add1 adder a1 a2 i)
                     (add2 adder i a3 sum)))
```

This constraint specifies that a part of type `adder` should be created with name `add1`, but that it should not create instances of its first three parts (which are all of them), but instead reuse parts `a1` `a2` and `i` of its parent. The first definition of `3-adder` created ten distinct cells while this new definition requires only five. One difference is that internal cells (e.g., `i`) must now be given names. Notice that we can still access internal cells with the same accessors as before. For example, if we create an instance of `3-adder` called `3`, then the following all refer to the same cell:

```
(>> i 3)
(>> a1 add2 3)
(>> sum add1 3)
```

The previous version of `3-adder` required constructing three distinct cells for `i` and relating them with == constraints.

ATCON also allows a constraint to specify the values a cell can have. For example, if the adder can only add quantities between 0 and 3 (i.e., of two bits), this can be specified by enumerating the possible values to a cell part-type as follows:

```
(assume-constraint adder-component ((a1 cell 0 1 2 3)
                                    (a2 cell 0 1 2 3)
                                    (sum cell 0 1 2 3))
            (formulae (sum (a1 a2) (+ a1 a2))
                      (a1 (sum a2) (+ sum a2))
                      (a2 (sum a1) (+ sum a1))))
```

If a value is produced for `a1`, `a2` or `sum` which is not between 0 and 3, a contradiction is detected and an ATMS nogood(s) will be constructed.

The final extension from TCON to ATCON is the ability to add disjunctions of cell values. For example,

```
>   (disjunction ((>> sum a) 100) ((>> a1 a) 90))
```

states that either (>> sum a) must be 100 or (>> a1 a) must be 90. Disjunctions are not used in the constraint propagation phase, but are important when constructing solutions. This is the subject of the next section.

16.1.6 Finding solutions

ATCON continues propagating values through constraints until no more rules apply. Although this process determines all possible variable values in all possible environments, it does not explicitly identify overall solutions. Exactly what constitutes a solution is determined by the application. ATCON incorporates a simple interface to the two basic mechanisms the ATMS provides to specify the conditions a solution must meet. The ATCON procedure `solutions` provides access to the ATMS's interpretation constructor.

A very common use of assumptions is as representations of defaults (see Sections 12.3.3 and 6.1.5), i.e., a node whose belief is presumed unless there is evidence to the contrary. This notion of default is very common throughout artificial intelligence research. Under this definition, an interpretation is a consistent environment to which no other assumption can be added without making the environment nogood. ATCON presumes that every assumption is a default.

Consider the simple example we discussed earlier.

```
>    (create 'a 'adder)
>    (assume-parameter (>> a1 a) 1 "a1")
>    (assume-parameter (>> a2 a) 10 "a2")
>    (assume-parameter (>> sum a) 100 "sum")
>    (show-network *tcon*)
(>> SUM A) = [100,{{sum}}][11,{{a1,a2}}]
(>> A2 A) = [99,{{a1,sum}}][10,{{a2}}]
(>> A1 A) = [90,{{a2,sum}}][1,{{a1}}]
```

As there are three assumptions, there are eight environments, three of which are interpretations:

```
>    (solutions)
The solutions are:
  {a1,a2}
  {a1,sum}
  {a2,sum}
```

Consider the first solution `{a1 a2}`. It meets the two basic criteria for interpreting defaults. If the one remaining assumption `sum` is added to it, then the environment becomes nogood because $100 \neq 1 + 10$. Conversely, the consistent environment `{a1}` is not an interpretation because both the assumptions `a2` and `sum` can be added to it to yield another consistent environment.

The ATCON function `print-solutions` prints the values of all ATCON cells for each solution:

```
>   (print-solutions)
 .
 .
 .
 Cell values for solution {a1,a2}:
 (>> SUM A) = 11.
 (>> A2 A) = 10.
 (>> A1 A) = 1.
 Cell values for solution {a1,sum}:
 (>> SUM A) = 100.
 (>> A2 A) = 99.
 (>> A1 A) = 1.
 Cell values for solution {a2,sum}:
 (>> SUM A) = 100.
 (>> A2 A) = 10.
 (>> A1 A) = 90.
```

The ATMS allows an ATCON application to express very simple disjunctions. The ATCON function `disjunction` is provided a set of nodes, and the interpretation constructor ensures that every solution contains at least one node from each disjunction. Note that the only role disjunctions play is in constructing solutions, and they have no effect on the labels. ATCON (and the underlying ATMS) can clearly be extended to consider these disjunctions in the labeling algorithm itself, but this is beyond the scope of this book (see [1, 3]).

In the above example, after adding the disjunction:

```
>   (disjunction ((>> sum a) 100) ((>> a1 a) 90))
```

solution `{a1 a2}` is eliminated.

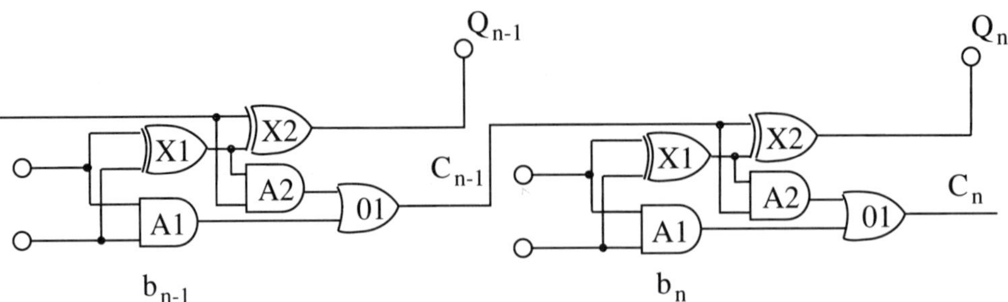

Figure 16.1 An n-bit ripple carry adder

16.1.7 Extended example

This section illustrates ATCON's functionality with an extended example. Suppose that we want to simulate and reason about a simple n-bit ripple carry adder such as that illustrated in Figure 16.1. Each bit of the ripple adder consists of a single full adder, and each full adder is built out of a combination of gates. We first must define the constraints for the three basic gates that comprise the full adder:

```
(constraint xor ((in1 cell 0 1) (in2 cell 0 1) (out cell 0 1))
          (formulae (out (in1 in2) (if (= in1 in2) 0 1))
                    (in1 (out in2) (if (= in2 out) 0 1))
                    (in2 (out in1) (if (= in1 out) 0 1))))

(constraint or ((in1 cell 0 1) (in2 cell 0 1) (out cell 0 1))
          (formulae (out (in1 in2) (if (and (= in1 0) (= in2 0)) 0 :DISMISS))
                    (out (in1) (if (= in1 1) 1 :DISMISS))
                    (out (in2) (if (= in2 1) 1 :DISMISS))
                    (in1 (out in2) (if (and (= out 1) (= in2 0)) 1 :DISMISS))
                    (in2 (out in1) (if (and (= out 1) (= in1 0)) 1 :DISMISS))
                    (in1 (out) (if (= out 0) 0 :DISMISS))
                    (in2 (out) (if (= out 0) 0 :DISMISS))))

(constraint and ((in1 cell 0 1) (in2 cell 0 1) (out cell 0 1))
          (formulae (out (in1 in2) (if (and (= in1 1) (= in2 1)) 1 :DISMISS))
                    (out (in1) (if (= in1 0) 0 :DISMISS))
                    (out (in2) (if (= in2 0) 0 :DISMISS))
                    (in1 (out) (if (= out 1) 1 :DISMISS))
                    (in2 (out) (if (= out 1) 1 :DISMISS))
```

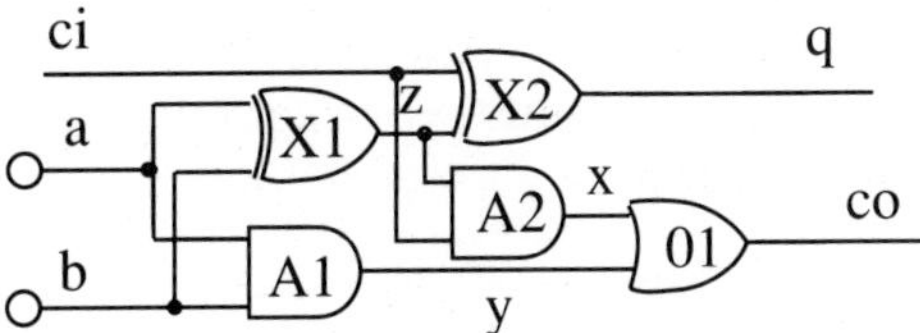

Figure 16.2 A Full adder

```
    (in1 (out in2) (if (and (= out 0) (= in2 1)) 0 :DISMISS))
    (in2 (out in1) (if (and (= out 0) (= in1 1)) 0 :DISMISS))))
```

Each full adder is built out of these gates as follows (see Figure 16.2).

```
(constraint full-adder ((co cell) (ci cell) (a cell) (b cell) (q cell)
                      (x cell) (y cell) (z cell)
                      (x1 xor a b z)
                      (a1 and a b y)
                      (x2 xor ci z q)
                      (a2 and ci z x)
                      (o1 or x y co)))
```

We can define a two-bit adder by:

```
(constraint 2-bit-adder ((ripple cell)
                         (bit0 full-adder ripple)
                         (bit1 full-adder () ripple)))
```

Notice that we need only create a cell for the intermediate carry because it is shared between the two full adders that comprise the two-bit adder.

Suppose we want to study the behavior of this adder under various inputs. We can do this by making every possible input an assumption:

```
>   (create 'add '2-bit-adder)
>   (assume-parameter (>> a bit0 add) 1 "a0=1")
>   (assume-parameter (>> a bit0 add) 0 "a0=0")
>   (assume-parameter (>> b bit0 add) 1 "b0=1")
>   (assume-parameter (>> b bit0 add) 0 "b0=0")
>   (assume-parameter (>> a bit1 add) 1 "a1=1")
>   (assume-parameter (>> a bit1 add) 0 "a1=0")
>   (assume-parameter (>> b bit1 add) 1 "b1=1")
>   (assume-parameter (>> b bit1 add) 0 "b1=0")
>   (assume-parameter (>> ci bit0 add) 1 "ci=1")
>   (assume-parameter (>> ci bit0 add) 0 "ci=0")
```

We can now look at the labels of the outputs to understand what inputs are responsible for what outputs. For example, we see that the label of the high-order output bit is:

```
(>> Q BIT1 ADD) = [1,{{a0=0,a1=0,b0=0,b1=1}
                     {a0=1,a1=1,b0=1,b1=1}
                     {a0=0,a1=1,b0=0,b1=0}
                     {a0=1,a1=0,b0=1,b1=0}
                     {a0=1,a1=1,b0=0,b1=1,ci=1}
                     {a0=1,a1=0,b0=0,b1=0,ci=1}
                     {a0=0,a1=1,b0=1,b1=1,ci=1}
                     {a0=0,a1=0,b0=1,b1=0,ci=1}
                     {a1=0,b0=0,b1=1,ci=0}
                     {a1=1,b0=0,b1=0,ci=0}
                     {a0=0,a1=0,b1=1,ci=0}
                     {a0=0,a1=1,b1=0,ci=0}}]
```

This label indicates all the patterns of inputs that force the high-order output bit. Note that in many cases one of the inputs is irrelevant to forcing this bit to 1. The ATMS only records the minimal sets of assumptions to produce a node's label, and therefore these are not included in the above list. The label for the high-order carry-out bit is:

```
(>> CO BIT1 ADD) = [1,{{a1=1,b1=1}
                      {a0=1,a1=0,b0=1,b1=1}
                      {a0=1,a1=1,b0=1,b1=0}
                      {a0=1,a1=0,b0=0,b1=1,ci=1}
                      {a0=1,a1=1,b0=0,b1=0,ci=1}
                      {a0=0,a1=0,b0=1,b1=1,ci=1}
                      {a0=0,a1=1,b0=1,b1=0,ci=1}}]
```

Let's use the same circuit for a slightly different example. Suppose we are faced with a diagnostic task in which the inputs to the two bit adder are all supposedly 1, but the carry out is observed to be 1. The task is to identify which inputs are not 1. We could set this up by:

```
>    (create 'add '2-bit-adder)
>    (assume-parameter (>> a bit0 add) 1 "a0=1")
>    (assume-parameter (>> b bit0 add) 1 "b0=1")
>    (assume-parameter (>> a bit1 add) 1 "a1=1")
>    (assume-parameter (>> b bit1 add) 1 "b1=1")
>    (assume-parameter (>> ci bit0 add) 1 "ci=1")
>    (set-parameter (>> co bit1 add) 0)
```

This results in the following ATMS interpretations:

```
{a0=1,a1=1}
{a1=1,b0=1}
{a0=1,b1=1}
{b0=1,b1=1}
{a0=1,b0=1,ci=1}
{a1=1,ci=1}
{b1=1,ci=1}
```

An ATMS interpretation lists only those assumptions which are true—all other assumptions are necessarily false. This result indicates that the order the observed carry out of 0 can only be caused by at least two and usually three inputs being 0 instead of 1.

16.2 Comparison of TCON and ATCON

One of the goals of the architecture of Figure 16.3 is to minimize the overall computational effort to perform a task. In particular, we would like the combined effort of using an inference engine and a TMS to be less than the effort of using some other inference engine without a TMS. Otherwise (assuming the other desiderata for using a TMS are not relevant) using a TMS just introduces a needless layer of bookkeeping. This figure illustrates a partitioning of concerns generically, but there are many different kinds of TMSs, and each leads to a somewhat different partitioning. The progression from TCON to ATCON provides an excellent case study.

Although TCON's dependency system is, in effect, a limited JTMS, it does not exhibit the familiar inference engine/TMS partitioning. TCON's dependency system performs three of the functions commonly associated with a TMS by: (1) identifying responsibility for conclusions (Section 6.1.1), (2) helping recover from inconsistencies (Section 6.1.2), and (3) guiding backtracking (Section 6.1.4). However, it does not maintain enough of a cache of inference engine deductions (Section 6.1.3) to be considered a JTMS. As a consequence, TCON may execute the same rules (i.e., the formulae which define constraints) repeatedly on the same antecedents as well as discover the same contradictions over and over again.

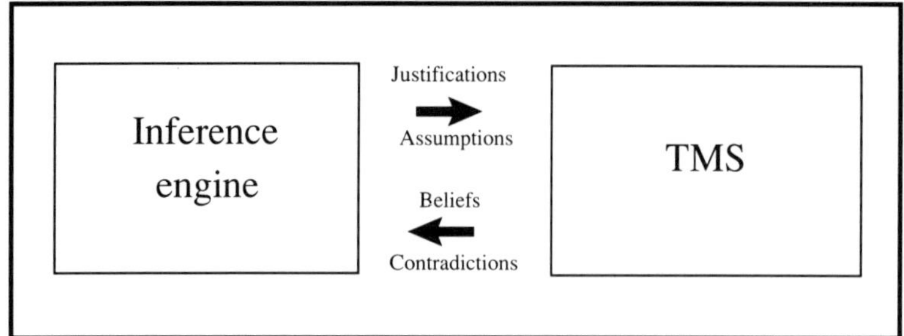

Figure 16.3 Problem solver = inference engine + TMS

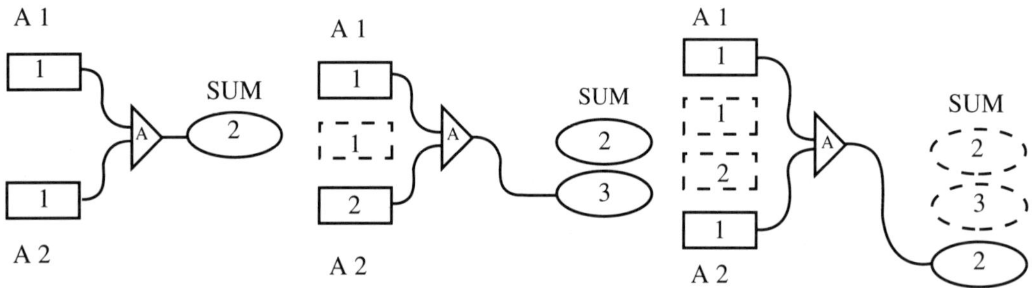

Figure 16.4 TCON's wasted effort

Let us first consider one of the kinds of troubles TCON gets into by not using a JTMS. Consider Figure 16.4. Adder A has inputs A1 and A2 and output SUM. If we set both A1 and A2 to 1, then TCON determines that SUM is 2 and records that SUM depends on A1 and A2. If we then change A2 to 2, then TCON determines that the SUM is 3. The old inference that SUM=2 follows from A1=1 and A2=1 is thrown away. Thus, if we subsequently change A2 back to 1, then TCON must redo the addition and set SUM to 2. Considering that SUM=2 might in turn trigger many other rules, one can easily see how not caching can lead to an exponential slowdown in performance.

If TCON had been hooked up to a TMS which cached all results, then the same addition need not be reexecuted. Figure 16.5 illustrates the justifications a TCON connected to a JTMS might produce. Initially, as TCON infers that SUM=2, it records a justification that SUM=2 follows

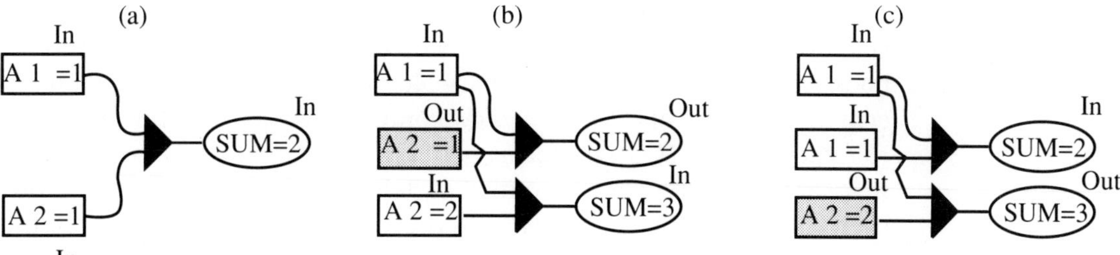

Figure 16.5 TCON with a JTMS

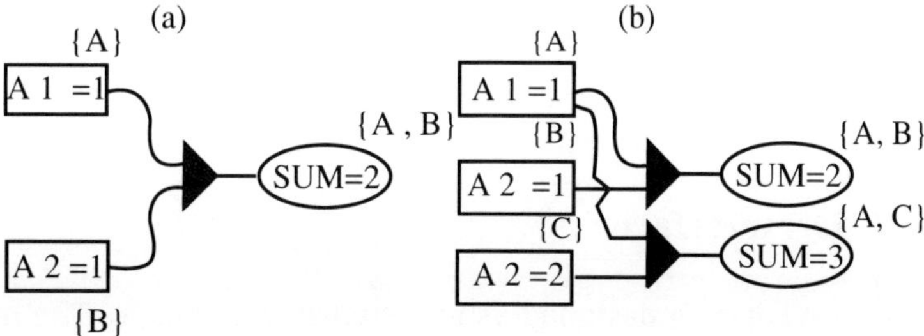

Figure 16.6 ATCON with an ATMS

from A1=1 and A2=1. Subsequently when A2 becomes 2, it records a justification that SUM=3. However, the original justification that SUM=2 follows from A1=1 and A2=1 is not discarded. Thus, when A2 is changed back to 1, the TMS can immediately infer that SUM=2, and the addition does not have to be repeated.

If we were using a single-context TMS, then every duplicate rule execution is replaced by a JTMS label propagation. In ATCON even this label propagation is avoided. For example, if A1=1 holds in environment {A} and A2=1 holds in environment {B}, then SUM=2 holds in environment {A,B}. If A2=2 is later introduced, then SUM=3 holds under environment {A,C} (see Figure 16.6). In ATCON there is no necessity to change values at all. To find the value of a cell in a context, one just looks at that node associated with the cell which has a label environment that is a subset of the context's environment. There will always be at most one such node.

The basic advantage of ATCON is that all of TCON's duplicate rule executions are avoided. On the other side of the balance is the additional bookkeeping cost. Which way this scale tips depends on the task. If execution is cheap, and there are few context switches (i.e., few duplicate rule executions), TCON performs better. If rule execution is expensive or there are a large number of context switches, ATCON will be better. However, seeing this tradeoff purely in terms of efficiency misses much of the picture. As context switching is truly free in ATCON (because it becomes an unnecessary operation), problem-solving tasks that would otherwise require a vast number of context switches become conceivable. One such example is discussed in the next chapter. (Of course, if the problem becomes large enough, the ATMS datastructures will exceed the available memory resources and performance will degrade, in which case TCON again will perform better.)

16.3 The ATCON interface

ATCON is designed as an extensible language. The most general definition of a constraint is:

`(constraint` ⟨*name*⟩ ⟨*parts*⟩ ⟨*body*⟩`)`

The ⟨*body*⟩ consists simply of a list of forms. These forms are evaluated by a very simple interpreter. We have already seen the `disjunction`, `formulae`, and `==` forms. However, the user can very easily define additional forms or just insert Common Lisp code in the ⟨*body*⟩. If the interpreter cannot identify the special form, then it analyzes the expression for all occurrences of `>>` and presumes they should all refer to the instance under creation. This interpreter is implemented via a set of Common Lisp macros, so the forms in a constraint body can be compiled by the conventional Common Lisp compiler.

ATCON is not a stand-alone problem-solving system. At a minimum, a user must make top-level Common Lisp calls to start an ATCON task, and for most tasks the user will write some additional Common Lisp procedures which function in tandem with ATCON. We see an extended example of this in the diagnostic task of the next chapter.

The following enumerates the main interface procedures. In this section we only discuss those procedures that have not already been adequately described.

`>>`	`fire-constraints`	`solutions`
`assume-parameter`	`nearly-equal?`	`what-is`
`cell-value-string`	`pretty-name`	`with-network`
`create`	`print-solutions`	
`create-atcon`	`show-network`	

Each constraint has a distinct global name. By loading a file, all the constraints defined therein become globally available in the Common Lisp environment. Files of constraints can also be compiled; however, any loading or compiling of constraint files can only be done after ATCON is loaded.

```
(create-atcon (title &key (nearly-equal 'default-nearly-equal)
                          (debugging nil)
                          (delay t))
```

`create-atcon` returns a datastructure which returns the entire state of the ATCON. This call will create an instance of the ATMS which ATCON will use. The meanings of the keyword arguments are as follows:

`nearly-equal` This is the procedure that ATCON should use to determine whether two values are equal. ATCON considers two values identical if they are `equal`, but many applications want to specify a level of precision within which two values are considered equal.

`debugging` If this flag is `t`, then ATCON will print out additional tracing information about its internal operations.

`delay` This flag defaults to `t`. If this flag is `nil`, then ATCON does not go to much effort to prevent the execution of rules that would produce useless results (see Section 16.4.8). When rule execution is cheap, the effort to prevent useless rule execution may outweigh the cost of the useless rule executions. Note that if the ATCON rules have any side effects or find any contradictions, the order of evaluation of constraint rules will vary. This may produce some unexpected effects.

Some ATCON procedures reference the variable `*atcon*` freely. The best way to bind this variable is to use the macro:

```
(with-network atcon &body forms)
```

The variable `atcon` must be bound to an ATCON instance. `forms` is a list of Common Lisp forms which reference this ATCON instance by default.

The user can create instances of ATCON constraints directly via:

```
(create name type &optional supplied-parts (atcon *atcon*))
```

This creates an instance of constraint `type` and gives it the name `name`. If there are `supplied-parts`, then these parts will be reused in the constraint instance just as in constraint definitions. If `atcon` is not supplied, then the current value of `*atcon*` is used, which can be bound with `with-network`.

The accessor >> can be used outside of `constraint` definitions:

```
(>> i1 ... in)
```

Note that `in` must be the name of a constraint (or cell) explicitly created by the user via `create`. However, when used within the body of a `constraint`, the current constraint is implicitly considered to be `in`.

The procedure `known?` is used to determine the value of a cell. The invocation:

```
(known? cell env)
```

finds the node (if any) associated with the cell that holds in a given environment. If `env` is not specified or `nil`, then `known?` returns a list of all the nodes which are known in any environment.

```
(nearly-equal? exp1 exp2 &optional atcon)
```

Returns `t` or `nil` depending on whether the equality checker of the current ATCON determines whether these two values should be considered identical.

```
(fire-constraints &optional (atcon *atcon*))
```

This instructs ATCON to run all the constraint rules that are currently pending and to continue doing so until no more new constraint rules are runnable.

```
(pretty-name thing)
```

This is the preferred procedure to obtain the name as a string of ATCON cells and constraints. The problem solver can use this string for any input-output with the user.

```
(cell-value-string node)
```

This procedure returns a string of the form ⟨*cell*⟩=⟨*value*⟩. This is how nodes print out by default.

```
(what-is cell &key env)
```

If `env` is not supplied, this procedure prints out a description of all its values and under which environments they hold. Otherwise, it prints out the values that hold in `env`.

16.4 The ATCON code

16.4.1 Overview

The ATCON program is divided into nine parts.

1. *Definitions and initialization.* The datastructures and initialization procedures.
2. *Defining prototypes.* The procedures for interpreting constraint definitions.
3. *Creating constraints.* The procedures for creating instances of constraints.
4. *Accessors.* Procedures for accessing constraints and their parts.
5. *Equality system.* This implements ==.
6. *Setting and accessing cell values.* The procedures for accessing and setting cell values.
7. *Rule execution.* Controls the scheduling and execution of ATCON rules.
8. *Constructing solutions.* Provides an interface to the ATMS interpretation constructor.

9. *Interrogatives.* A set of procedures for convenient printout of names and values.

16.4.2 Definitions and initialization

As with most of the systems we have seen in this book, we use a single global ATCON datastructure. The `atcon` datastructure contains the following fields:

`title` Ignored by ATCON but is useful for debugging. Used when printing out the ATCON defstruct.

`cells` A list of all cells in the ATCON network.

`queue` A list of all rule-node pairs waiting to be run by ATCON.

`constraints` A list of all the constraints in this ATCON.

`user-parts` A hash table of all the parts the user has created directly.

`atms` The ATMS instance this ATCON is associated with.

`nearly-equal` A procedure to be called to test whether two values are equal.

`disjunctions` A list of the disjunctions supplied by the user. ATCON does not do anything with this list itself. However, whenever it is necessary to call the ATMS interpretation constructor, it passes the list of disjunctions along to the ATMS.

`debugging` A debugging flag to trace the internals of ATCON operations.

`delay` A flag that controls to what degree ATCON tries to prevent the execution of useless rules. This flag is set in the call to `create-atcon`.

`executions` A simple debugging variable to keep count of how many rules have executed.

The primary repository for values in ATCON is the cell. The cell defstruct contains the following fields:

`atcon` The ATCON instance it is part of.

`name` The local, unqualified name of the cell it was given when created. Names are not unique. Different constraints may use the same variable names, and different instances of the same constraint will have different cells with the same name. Note that when the cell is reused in another constraint, this slot is unchanged. However, the ATCON look up mechanism can find this cell using either name.

`owner` The instance of the constraint that first created this cell. Note that the combination of the `name` and the `owner` slots is always unique. If the cell is used in later constraints, this slot will not be changed. If the cell is not part of any parent constraint, then this slot will contain the symbol `:USER`.

`nodes` The list of nodes associated with this cell.

`users` This describes all the rules that use this cell. For example, it might contain `((RULE-4 RULE-3 RULE-1) . <Constraint 01>) ((RULE-7 RULE-6 RULE-5 RULE-4) . <Constraint A1>`. The first element of this list states that `RULE-4`, `RULE-3`, and `RULE-1` of the constraint instance `<Constraint 01>` use this cell as an antecedent. Thus, when this cell receives a value, those rules should be checked to see whether they can be executed. (For brevity, this example named rules by integers. In the actual implementation, rules print out by listing the variables they use and set.)

`domain` A list of the allowable values a cell can have.

The ATMS `tms-node` defstruct contains only one slot, `tms-node-datum`, for use by the inference engine. Unfortunately, there are a number of distinct pieces of information that ATCON needs to associate with each datum. Therefore, ATCON has another distinct defstruct used store this additional information with each datum. Each node that ATCON creates will have an instance of the `value` defstruct as its datum. The `value` defstruct has the following fields:

`datum` The datum that we would normally have put into the TMS node datum directly. For example, in our digital circuit examples `datum` is typically 0 or 1.

`cell` A pointer back to the cell containing the node for which this value is the problem-solver datum.

`processed` A list of constraints which have looked at this value and processed it. This is used to prevent any rule from being executed more than once.

`string` A string, supplied by the user, which is only used to print cell values.

Each instance of a constraint is described by the `constraint` defstruct. Its fields are:

`atcon` The ATCON instance it is part of.

`name` The local, unqualified name of the constraint it was given when created. Names are not unique. Different constraints may use the same part names, and different instances of the same constraint will have different component constraints with the same name. Note that when a constraint is reused in another constraint, this slot is unchanged. However, the ATCON look up mechanism will find this constraint using either name.

`owner` The instance of the constraint that first created this component constraint. Note that the combination of the `name` and the `owner` slots is always unique. If the constraint is used in later constraints, this slot will not be changed. If the constraint is not part of any parent constraint, then this slot will contain the symbol `:USER`.

`parts` An alist that describes the parts which comprise the constraint. Each pair of the alist consists of the local name of the part and the actual part instance.

`prototype` The prototype this constraint is an instance of.

Each constraint definition is stored as an instance of the prototype datastructure. Its fields are:

`name` The constraint name. This name will be global, so ATCON records only one constraint prototype with every name.

`parts` The list of parts directly specified by the constraint definition.

`creation-form` Either an interpreted or compiled Common Lisp procedure which is invoked whenever an instance of this constraint is created.

`cells` An alist that describes all of the parts that can hold values (cells and assumptions). Each pair in the alist consists of the name of the cell followed by the actual rule instances which use that cell.

Each rule defined in a formulae of a constraint is described by an instance of the rule defstruct. Its fields come directly from the constraint definition:

`uses` A list of the names of the constraint cells upon which every conclusion of this rule depends. This list is stored in reverse order.

`sets` The name, if any, of the constraint cell which this rule can set.

`body` The body of the rule stored as a Common Lisp procedure. If the file containing the constraints is compiled, then this body is a compiled procedure.

The variable `*atcon*` is declared as a special variable. Some ATCON procedures refer to it freely. The macro `with-network` is the recommended way to bind `*atcon*`. All the constraint definitions (i.e., prototypes) are stored in a separate hash table `*prototypes*`. Notice that the same prototype definitions are then used for every ATCON instance. ATCON sometimes has to create temporary ATMS nodes in its internal operations. All such nodes with have as their datum the value of `*temporary-datum*`. The macro `debugging-atcon` is used throughout `atcon.lisp` to check whether the debugging flag is set for this ATCON instance. `create-atcon` simply creates an ATCON defstruct which references a newly created ATMS instance. `default-nearly-equal` is the equality checker that `create-atcon` uses if none is supplied by the problem solver. Most problem solvers will need to supply their own version of nearly equal. The default procedure is overly simplistic and presumes that two values are identical if they are equal or within .001 of each other. Although allowing the problem solver to supply its own equality checker helps with some problem-solving tasks, the notion of approximately equal is fraught with complexities outside the scope of this book.

16.4.3 Defining prototypes

This section consists of a set of macros and procedures to transform constraint definitions into Common Lisp code. If necessary, the resulting code can be compiled by the Common Lisp compiler to improve the efficiency of rule execution.

The macros constraint and assume-constraint are identical except that assume-constraint adds an ok assumption part. The procedure constraint-1 constructs the basic definition for a constraint. It calls the procedure analyze-prototype-body to analyze the body of a constraint. The procedure constraint-1 creates an instance of the prototype defstruct and binds it to the variable self. analyze-prototype-body generates Common Lisp code which modifies the prototype instance stored in self. In addition, the Common Lisp code is interpreted in a context where the macro >> is redefined (via macro-let) to refer to self. Notice that constraint-1 expands into code which finally adds the prototype to the *prototypes* hash table.

The procedure analyze-prototype-body examines every top-level form in the body. If the form is a formulae, then it invokes the procedure process-constraint-rules to analyze a formulae. All other forms in the body of a constraint are treated as conventional Common Lisp code which is evaluated in the context where self is bound to the current constraint and the macro >> is redefined to refer to this instance.

The procedure process-constraint-rules analyzes the rules of a formulae form. It generates Common Lisp code which first creates an instance of the rule datastructure for each rule of the form. This code also sets up the cells slot of prototype such that each cell name is listed with rules that use it. Notice that this code also creates all the Common Lisp procedures that implement the actual body for formulae. Since these are defined with function forms, by compiling a file of constraints one compiles the bodies of all the rules.

As the file atcon.lisp itself contains a constraint, some of the procedures that process constraints must be available at compile time. Therefore, three of the procedures of this section are embedded in eval-when declarations to ensure that this is the case.

16.4.4 Creating constraints

The procedure create is provided purely for the user. It immediately calls create1, which is the main procedure for creating constraint instances. create1 creates constraints. Notice that there are only two primitive constraint types: cell and assumption. All other constraints are treated identically. The procedure create-prototype creates all instances of defined constraints. It first finds the prototype of the constraint type. It creates an instance of that constraint, and then it in turn creates instances of all the parts of the constraint (unless these have been supplied). `create-cell` is the primitive for creating cells.

16.4.5 Accessors

The procedures of this section allow one to access cells, constraints, and their parts. The macro >> is used at top level. It presumes that the final indicator it is supplied refers to a global value, and therefore looks the object up in the global ATCON hash table. Note that >> is redefined within constraint bodies to refer to the current constraint. The procedure `nested-lookup` is used to look up parts for both definitions of >>. `nested-lookup` starts with the final indicator and works from back to front, repeatedly looking for a subpart with the given name. If the part is not found, it signals an error. `lookup-part` is a commonly used procedure to look up subparts, of a constraint. Notice that it is possible to attempt to reference a part of a cell. As cells have no parts this should produce a Common Lisp error.

16.4.6 Equality system

The procedures of this subsection implement ==. Notice that == is not treated as a special form when interpreting constraint bodies. Instead it is implemented as a simple set of Common Lisp procedures that could easily be separated from the rest of ATCON. It is an example for how to provide user-defined functionality within constraint bodies.

If both parts to a == are cells, then these cells are equated via the `==cells` procedure. If both parts are constraints having the same definition, then each part is equated recursively. This section also contains the definition of the == constraint itself. Thus, whenever ATCON is loaded, the prototype of the == constraint is available.

16.4.7 Setting and accessing cell values

The `cell` datastructure contains a slot `nodes` which lists all the nodes associated with the cell. Each node, in turn, points to an instance of the `value` datastructure which contains the value that the ATCON constraint body sees.

`set!` is the main procedure used for setting the value of a cell. It first invokes the the procedure `lookup-node` to find a node of the cell having that value. Then it calls the usual ATMS procedure `justify-node` to set the cell to that value under the appropriate contexts.

The procedure `lookup-node` does the main work. It first checks whether a node with the same (or approximately the same) value exists for that cell. To determine whether two values are approximately equal, ATCON uses a procedure `atcon-nearly-equal` which can be specified when the ATCON instance is first created. If the desired node is not found, then ATCON creates a new instance of a `value` and a `node` that refers to it. Then it enforces the condition that cells can have only one value by forcing every pair of nodes of a cell to be contradictory. Finally, it checks that the domain specification of the cell is not violated.

The remaining three procedures of this section are provided purely for the convenience of the problem solver. The procedure `known?` allows the problem solver to check whether a cell is known to have some value in some given environment. `assume-parameter` and `set-parameter` allow the problem solver to set the initial values of parameters, possibly under an assumption. Notice that both of these procedures call `fire-constraints`, which executes any rules that depend on the new values.

16.4.8 Rule execution

The next set of procedures controls the execution of ATCON rules. ATCON uses the ATMS-provided interface for scheduling execution. The `tms-node-rules` of every node contains a queue of ATCON rule objects which are to be executed when that node receives a non-empty label. Whenever the ATMS discovers a node to have a non-empty label it calls an inference engine-supplied procedure. When ATCON creates the ATMS instance it specifies `consider-node` to be this procedure. Since `consider-node` is called within ATMS operations, it cannot perform any ATMS operation recursively. Hence, ATCON maintains a queue of rules pending execution and runs these rules after the ATMS returns.

Creating an instance of a constraint will cause the creation of its subparts. Whenever a new cell is created, datastructures must be created to ensure that when this cell receives a value the rules which depend on that value are scheduled for execution. The code does not treat every individual rule of a constraint distinctly. Instead, if any of the rules of a constraint depend on a given cell, then ATCON creates a rule object that includes all the rules which use this cell and the the constraint itself. This rule object is then pushed on the `tms-node-rules` of the node. As add-role can be called when a node already has a value (this happens when a part is reused), add-role may call consider-node directly.

The procedure fire-constraints contains the main loop that executes rules. fire-constraints can be invoked by internal ATCON operations or by the problem solver directly. The inner loop of ATCON is like that of many inference engines that use the ATMS. fire-constraints repeatedly takes one of the queued rule objects on ATCON's queue. fire-constraints always runs the most recent rule object queued and hence executes in a LIFO order—however, that is relatively unimportant. A rule object appears on ATCON's queue only if its associated node had a non-empty label at the time. However, by the time fire-constraints is called and this rule object examined, this node may well have gone out. Therefore, ATCON first checks for this case, and if so, it simply requeues the rule object on the ATMS node.

Recall that ATCON has two execution modes. In the normal mode (where atcon-delay is t), ATCON prevents all unnecessary rule executions. However, when rule execution is cheap, the overhead of preventing all unnecessary rule executions is not worth the savings. In normal operation, fire-constraints performs an additional preliminary check to determine whether the rule object is executable. However, if atcon-delay is not set, then fire-constraints executes the rule(s) immediately without further checking. Notice that there are two distinct types of rule objects: (1) rule objects produced by add-role, and (2) rule objects created with the ATCON rule execution strategy—these rule objects have nodes whose datum is distinguished as containing the value of *temporary-datum*. These are explained later.

The two procedures that help prevent the execution of unnecessary rules are has-external-support and has-complete-external-support. These procedures are not intended to prevent the duplicate execution of rules—that is handled by rule-weave. Rather, these procedures are designed to help prevent the execution of rules when it is known, beforehand, that the resulting value will be useless. The most common case occurs when the output of one rule seems to trigger the input to some other rule of the same constraint. This is the case which has-external-support detects. It exploits the ATCON convention that the cdr of every informant is the constraint that derived the value. has-external-support exploits the ATMS primitive in-antecedent? to identify those justifications which support the node, and if any of those justifications derive from outside of the current constraint, then the rule object is considered executable.

While `has-external-support` performs this filtering action in the simple case involving a single node, the procedure `has-complete-external-support` performs the definitive test to determine whether a rule should be executed. `has-complete-external-support` is designed to be executed just before every rule of a constraint is executed. Note that `has-complete-external-support` is only invoked if all the antecedent nodes have non-empty labels and each of them has external support. However, the fact that each of the antecedent nodes is in and has external support, does not guarantee that the result of rule execution will hold in any consistent environment. The procedure `has-complete-external-support` ensures this by first computing the label that any result of a particular rule would have. If there are no such environments, then the rule is requeued (in the caller). Even if there are such environments, one must identify an environment within which all the inputs have external support. All the antecedent nodes may have external support, but this external support may all be in mutually inconsistent environments. In these cases, rule execution again should be suppressed.

The procedure `fire-constraint` executes conventional rule objects constructed by `add-role`. In this case, `rule-pair` is a pair consisting of the set of rules which use the cell and the constraint instance itself. `fire-constraints` is designed to prevent duplicate rule executions (as opposed to the two procedures just discussed, which prevent the first execution of a rule when the result is known to be without value). Consider the case of a rule with two antecedents, both of which simultaneously receive a value. In this case, ATCON will queue this rule for execution twice. The naive execution strategy would execute the rule twice: once for each value. However, `fire-constraint` only executes the rule once. It achieves this by associating a mark with each node (stored in the `processed` slot of the `value` defstruct in the node's datum) which indicates whether a constraint has processed a particular value. It only executes a rule if all of its antecedent nodes have been processed. So in our example where two antecedent cells receive values simultaneously, when `fire-constraint` is first called, it does nothing because the second value has not been marked as processed. Only when the second value is dequeued does `fire-constraint` execute this rule. Most of the work of avoiding this duplicate rule execution is done by the procedure `rule-weave`.

fire-constraint operates by calling rule-weave to determine all completely processed sets of antecedent cell values for each rule. As a final filter before executing the rule, it checks whether this combination of rules has external support via the procedure has-complete-external-support. If this combination of nodes does not yet have external support, then fire-constraint delays its execution. Of course, if atcon-delay is not set, then the rule is never delayed.

Delaying the execution of a rule is complex and resource-consuming. fire-constraint first creates a new, dummy ATMS node which is justified by the antecedents to the rule. This node is designed to be in only when the result holds in a consistent environment. Therefore, a special rule object is attached to this node so that a different execution procedure will be called if it ever comes in and has external support. Notice that at the very last, fire-constraint marks the new node it has processed by pushing the current constraint instance on the processed slot of the value of the current node.

The essential action of the procedure rule-weave has been described in the context of fire-constraint. rule-weave returns a list of lists of nodes, each of which can trigger the rule and include the newly discovered node.

16.4.9 Constructing solutions

The procedure solutions is the ATCON interface to the ATMS interpretation constructor. It will return a set of environments with every assumption interpreted as a default under the condition that all the interpretations must satisfy every disjunction. The disjunction macro provides a direct method for storing the disjunctions the ATMS interpretation constructor must satisfy.

16.4.10 Interrogatives

The final set of procedures provide facilities to nicely print ATCON datastructures and to make inquiries. pretty-name returns a string that describes the cell or constraint it is passed as an argument. It uses one of two subprocedures, depending on whether it is called with a constraint or a cell. cell-pretty-name first determines whether the cell has a constraint owner. If so, it constructs the descriptor that >> could use to access it. Otherwise, the cell is global and only this global name is returned. `constraint-pretty-name` constructs a descriptor that >> could use to find this constraint.

`label-string` is given a node and returns a string describing that node's ATMS label. `env-string` returns a single environment as a string.

The remaining procedures are primarily used as part of the interface and are intended for debugging. They are straightforward and most have been explained in Section 16.3. `constraint-parts` calls `what-is` on all the cells associated with a particular constraint. `print-solutions` is invoked with (usually) a set of interpretations and prints out the state of the network within each of those environments by calling `show-network`. Finally, `why` is like `what-is` except it exploits the ATMS explanation facility to construct an explanation for every particular value and environment of the cell.

16.5 Exercises

1. ⋆ Demonstrate an ATCON program whose performance significantly improves with `atcon-delay` set to `nil`. Demonstrate an ATCON program whose performance significantly degrades with `atcon-delay` set to `t`. Abstract the characteristics of the two programs that produce these results.

2. ⋆⋆ The JTMS can be modified to maintain an explicit nogood database (see Exercise 6) which is consulted before any assumption is enabled. Show a TCON program which manifests an exponential performance improvement using such nogoods.

16.6 Bibliography

[1] de Kleer, J., "Extending the ATMS," *Artificial Intelligence* 28 (1986): 163-196.

[2] de Kleer, J., "Problem solving with the ATMS," *Artificial Intelligence* 28 (1986): 197-224.

[3] de Kleer, J., "A general labeling algorithm for assumption-based truth maintenance," *Proceedings AAAI-88*, 1988, 188-192.

17 A Tiny Diagnosis Engine

In this chapter we use ATCON to build the Tiny General Diagnostic Engine or TGDE (a simplified version of GDE [2, 5]). Diagnosis is the task of identifying which components of a device are not functioning according to their behavioral specifications. Diagnosis is difficult because we almost never have direct evidence of the malfunctioning of any component. Components usually do not look faulted, and it typically is too expensive to remove all the components and check them individually. Instead, we only have indirect evidence from their behavior. The diagnostic process is characterized by hypothesizing faults which explain the observations and then determining what next measurement provides the most information to discriminate among those hypotheses. The ATMS is an ideal tool to implement a computer-based diagnostician because it can maintain multiple hypotheses simultaneously, quickly switch among them, and efficiently compare them.

TGDE is an example of the many-worlds strategy (Chapter 14) for building problem solvers. Although one can characterize what TGDE does in terms of the contexts representing hypotheses which explain the symptoms, the internal operations of TGDE pay almost no attention to them. Instead, TGDE works on all hypotheses simultaneously, using the ATMS to implicitly share results among them. In this kind of problem-solver design, once the designer has chosen the assumptions to be manipulated, no attention has to be paid to contexts, context-switching, backtracking, or contradiction handling. This leaves the designer free to focus on the issues that are specific to the task at hand.

Unlike most of the previous chapters, this chapter contains very little description of code. This is because the essence of TGDE can be implemented in a single page of Common Lisp code. Nevertheless, as it exhibits an important problem-solving paradigm which is of use for a variety of applications, this chapter lays out in detail the concepts of diagnosis and how ATCON and the ATMS are used to implement them. We also show how a formal analysis of the diagnosis task yields insights into the strengths and limitations of the implementation.

17.1 Example

Later in this chapter we give a precise formal characterization of the diagnostic task. But first we explore the concepts in terms of an extended example. The diagnosis task is initiated because of some discrepancy between an observation and an expectation. We presume the device has been correctly designed and thus the discrepancy is not due to a design error but rather to some component fault. Thus there is a discrepancy between what we predict a measurement outcome to be, given the design model of the device, and the actual observation. Consider the circuit of Figure 17.1. (This is the same circuit we studied in Section 15.4.3).

The circuit consists of three multipliers, M_1, M_2, and M_3, and two adders, A_1 and A_2. The inputs are known to be $A = 3$, $B = 2$, $C = 2$, $D = 3$, and $E = 3$. One output, F, has been measured to be $F = 10$. Is this a symptom? As the inputs to multiplier $M1$ are $A = 3$ and $C = 2$, X must be 6. As the inputs to multiplier $M2$ are $B = 2$ and $D = 3$, Y must be

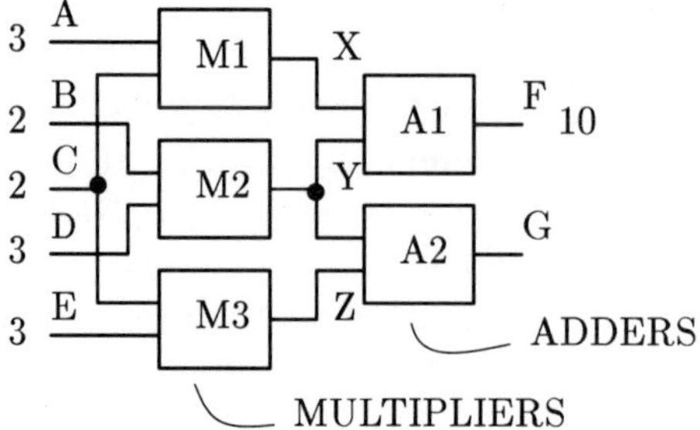

Figure 17.1 The polybox

6. Given these inputs to adder $A1$, F must be 12. However, F has been measured to be 10. Therefore, $F = 10$ is a symptom. As F is observed to be different from its predicted value, one of the components underlying this prediction must be faulted. In particular, one of the set $\{M1, M2, A1\}$ must be faulted—there may be other faulted components, but at least one of these must be malfunctioning to explain the symptom $F = 10$. We call such a set of components underlying a symptom a *conflict*.

We define a *diagnosis* to be a set of components whose malfunctioning can explain all the symptoms. Thus, $\{M1\}$, $\{M2\}$, and $\{A1\}$ are all diagnoses. As there may be other faulty components, the correct diagnosis may contain more components. However, the sets cannot be made smaller and still explain the conflict. Therefore, $\{M1\}$, $\{M2\}$, and $\{A1\}$ are all *minimal* diagnoses.

In order to discriminate among the diagnoses we need to obtain more observations. There are four possible places we can still measure: X, Y, Z, and G. To choose the best place to measure next, we have to analyze each possible measurement outcome and weigh the alternatives. Z is a very bad place to measure next because it provides no information about any of the three minimal diagnoses. X is a much better place: whatever the outcome, $\{M1\}$ or $\{A1\}$ (or possibly both) will be eliminated as a diagnosis. Analogously, whatever the outcome of measuring Y and G, $\{M2\}$ or $\{A1\}$ (possibly both) will be eliminated. Measuring G is best because it provides as much information about the minimal diagnoses as measuring either X or Y, but it also provides some weak information about $A2$ and $M3$. Suppose we measure G and observe that $G = 12$.

Is $G = 12$ a symptom? Multiplier $M2$ multiplies $B = 2$ and $D = 3$ to produce $Y = 6$. Multiplier $M3$ multiplies $C = 2$ and $E = 3$ to produce $Z = 6$. Adder $A2$ adds these two to produce $G = 12$. Even though this observation corroborates the prediction, it does not guarantee that $M2$, $A2$, and $M3$ are unfaulted. After all, $M3$ could be faulted adding a 1 to its output and $A2$ could be faulted subtracting a 1 from its output. Nevertheless, this observation has told us something very important about $M2$. Consider the diagnosis $\{M2\}$. If $M2$ is faulted, then Y must be 4 to ensure the observation $F = 10$. However, if $Y = 4$, then G must be 10. Therefore, surprisingly, $G = 12$ is a symptom. In particular, if $M1$, $A1$, $A2$, and $M3$ are working correctly, then G should be 10. Therefore, we have a new conflict: $\{M1, A1, A2, M3\}$. This means that $\{M2\}$ is no longer a minimal diagnosis—it is instead replaced by two minimal diagnoses:

$\{M2, A2\}$ and $\{M3, A2\}$. Put intuitively, $M2$ alone can no longer explain both observations: If $M2$ were faulted, contributing to $F = 12$, then one of $A2$ or $M3$ must also be faulted to cancel out the effect of $M2$'s fault to produce $G = 12$.

17.2 Implementation

We have just explored some of the basic concepts of model-based diagnosis through the use of an extended example. Now we describe an implementation which can perform this kind of reasoning.

We presume that we are given a description of how components are supposed to behave and how the constituent parts make up a specific device. Each component obeys particular behavioral rules. In the polybox example, the components are adders and multipliers whose behavior is to add and subtract. In digital circuits, we would be provided with models of `and`, `or`, and `not` gates and we would be given the schematic of any digital device we were requested to troubleshoot.

In Section 15.4.3 we presented a simple diagnostic algorithm which used the idea of constraint suspension in TCON to identify the diagnoses. That implementation used a single current context, which is awkward for diagnostic tasks. In contrast, TGDE uses an underlying multiple-context ATMS, which makes it easier to compare alternative diagnoses and directly choose which measurements to make next.

Each component is described by an ATCON constraint. Similarly, each composite device is described by an ATCON constraint. For every component that could possibly fault, we create a unique ATMS assumption which represents the presumption that it is working correctly. The following models suffice for describing the adder and multiplier. Recall that `assume-constraint` creates `ok` assumptions for each instance of `adder` and `multiplier` which is implicitly included in all the ⟨*Uses*⟩ of the `formulae`.

```
(assume-constraint adder ((a1 cell) (a2 cell) (sum cell))
          (formulae (sum (a1 a2) (+ a1 a2))
                    (a1 (sum a2) (- sum a2))
                    (a2 (sum a1) (- sum a1))))
```

```
(assume-constraint multiplier ((m1 cell) (m2 cell) (product cell))
          (formulae (product (m1) (if (= 0 m1) 0 :DISMISS))
                    (product (m2) (if (= 0 m2) 0 :DISMISS))
                    (product (m1 m2) (if (or (= 0 m1) (= 0 m2))
                                         :DISMISS
                                         (* m1 m2)))
                    (m1 (product m2) (if (= 0 m2) :DISMISS
                                         (/ product m2)))
                    (m2 (product m1) (if (= 0 m1) :DISMISS
                                        (/ product m1)))))
```

The polybox is described by:

```
(constraint poly ((a cell) (b cell) (c cell) (d cell) (e cell)
                  (x cell) (y cell) (z cell) (f cell) (g cell)
                  (m1 multiplier a c x)
                  (m2 multiplier b d y)
                  (m3 multiplier c e z)
                  (a1 adder x y f)
                  (a2 adder y z g)))
```

An instance of polybox with the given inputs can be created by:

```
>     (create 'p 'poly)
>     (set-parameter (>> a p) 3)
>     (set-parameter (>> b p) 2)
>     (set-parameter (>> c p) 2)
>     (set-parameter (>> d p) 3)
>     (set-parameter (>> e p) 3)
```

For simplicity we write each ok assumption created by **assume-constraint** as simply the name of the component itself. By default TGDE prints out OK assumptions by simply the name of the component. The contents of the ATMS label database are now as follows (see Figure 17.2):

$\langle A = 3, \{\{\}\}\rangle$ $\langle X = 6, \{\{M1\}\}\rangle$

$\langle B = 2, \{\{\}\}\rangle$ $\langle Y = 6, \{\{M2\}\}\rangle$

$\langle C = 2, \{\{\}\}\rangle$ $\langle Z = 6, \{\{M3\}\}\rangle$

$\langle D = 3, \{\{\}\}\rangle$ $\langle F = 12, \{\{A1, M1, M2\}\}\rangle$

$\langle E = 3, \{\{\}\}\rangle$ $\langle G = 12, \{\{A2, M2, M3\}\}\rangle$

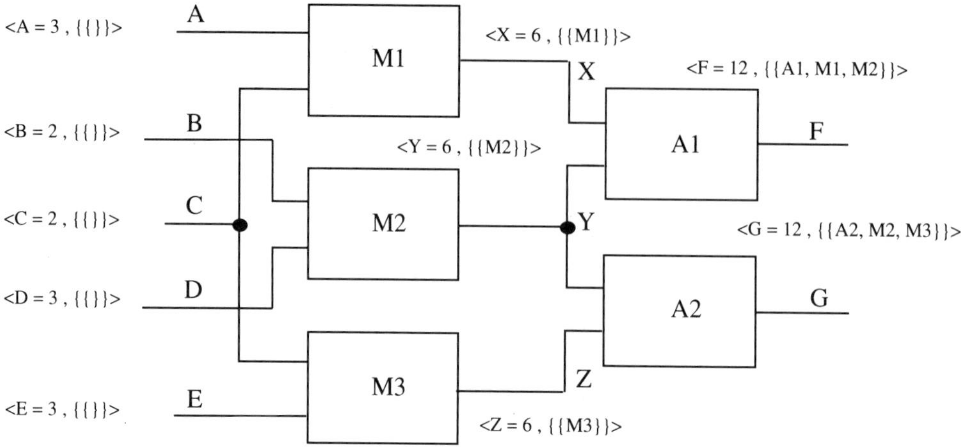

Figure 17.2 The polybox before any output observations

From the ATMS/ATCON point of view there is nothing unusual about this database. However, from a diagnosis point of view this database tells us a great deal. It lists every possible prediction that can be made from the inputs and the components, along with the minimal set of working components that ensure it. For example, we see that $F = 12$ follows from $\{A1, M1, M2\}$ all working correctly. As the ATMS label contains only minimal environments, we know that each set is minimal—removing any component from $\{A1, M1, M2\}$ will no longer guarantee that $F = 12$.

Suppose we now observe $F = 10$. This is achieved by:

```
(set-parameter (>> f p) 10)
```

As $\{A1, M1, M2\}$ supported $F = 12$, we immediately discover it to be nogood. Recall that a nogood is a set of assumptions at least one of which must not hold. Therefore, there is a direct one-to-one correspondence between those ATMS nogoods mentioning only OK assumptions and conflicts.

TGDE exploits the fact that ATCON makes all possible derivations from the information it is provided. Thus far all of ATCON's constraints have been run in the forward-going direction and the result was simply a causal simulation of the polybox from input to output. The consequences of $F = 10$ reveal that ATCON's analysis need not be purely causal. For example, given $F = 10$ and $X = 6$, the adder rule produces the ATMS justification:

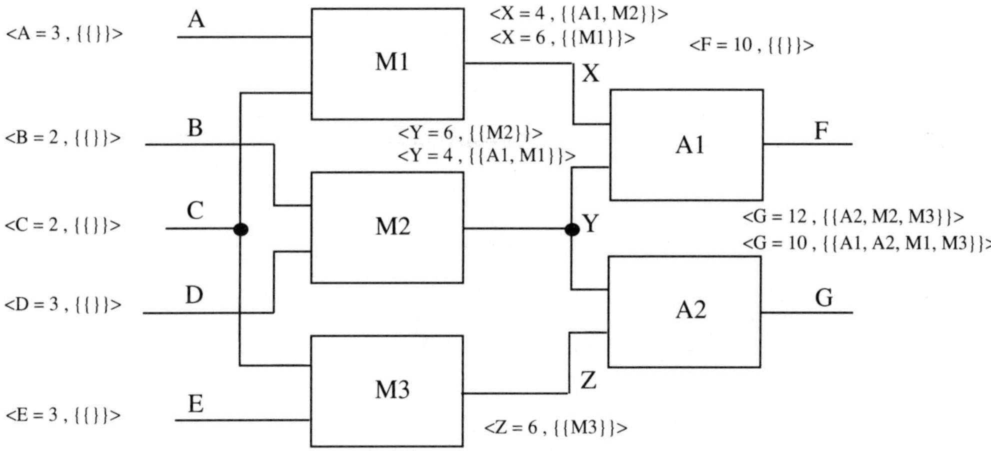

Figure 17.3 The polybox after $F = 10$

$F = 10 \wedge X = 6 \wedge A1 \Rightarrow Y = 4.$

This does not at all imply that the adder A1 causes $Y = 4$—correctly functioning digital adders cannot causally affect their inputs. Instead this justification should be read: If F is observed to be 10, the other input to the adder is 6, and the adder is functioning correctly, then it must be the case that some other component is forcing this input to be 4. The complete result is (see Figure 17.3):

$\langle A = 3, \{\{\}\}\rangle$ $\quad\langle Y = 4, \{\{A1, M1\}\}\rangle$

$\langle B = 2, \{\{\}\}\rangle$ $\quad\langle Y = 6, \{\{M2\}\}\rangle$

$\langle C = 2, \{\{\}\}\rangle$ $\quad\langle Z = 6, \{\{M3\}\}\rangle$

$\langle D = 3, \{\{\}\}\rangle$ $\quad\langle F = 10, \{\{\}\}\rangle$

$\langle E = 3, \{\{\}\}\rangle$ $\quad\langle G = 10, \{\{A1, A2, M1, M3\}\}\rangle$

$\langle X = 4, \{\{A1, M2\}\}\rangle$ $\quad\langle G = 12, \{\{A2, M2, M3\}\}\rangle$

$\langle X = 6, \{\{M1\}\}\rangle$

Note that data with empty labels have been deleted (e.g., $F = 12$).

Notice that ATCON derives two predictions for G. $G = 12$ follows from a straightforward causal simulation. $G = 10$ follows from $F = 10$ via $A1$, $A2$, $M1$, and $M3$. Therefore, when we measure $G = 12$, TGDE immediately discovers the new nogood: $\{A1, A2, M1, M3\}$.

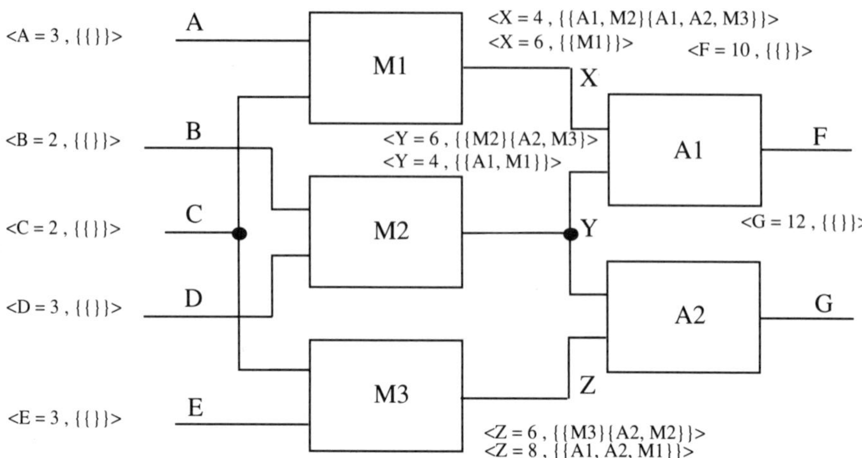

Figure 17.4 The polybox after $G = 12$

There are no other conflicts, and the final TGDE database is (see Figure 17.4):

$\langle A = 3, \{\{\}\}\rangle$

$\langle B = 2, \{\{\}\}\rangle$

$\langle C = 2, \{\{\}\}\rangle$

$\langle D = 3, \{\{\}\}\rangle$

$\langle E = 3, \{\{\}\}\rangle$

$\langle X = 4, \{\{A1, M2\}, \{A1, A2, M3\}\}\rangle$

$\langle X = 6, \{\{M1\}\}\rangle$

$\langle Y = 4, \{\{A1, M1\}\}\rangle$

$\langle Y = 6, \{\{M2\}, \{A2, M3\}\}\rangle$

$\langle Z = 6, \{\{M3\}, \{A2, M2\}\}\rangle$

$\langle Z = 8, \{\{A1, A2, M1\}\}\rangle$

$\langle F = 10, \{\{\}\}\rangle$

$\langle G = 12, \{\{\}\}\rangle$

17.2.1 Constructing minimal diagnoses

A diagnosis is represented by a set of failing components. If we presume the device contains a single fault, then all minimal diagnoses are singletons and can be constructed by intersecting all the conflicts. Our polybox example produced two conflicts: $\{A1, M1, M2\}$ and $\{A1, A2, M1, M3\}$. The intersection of those two sets is $\{A1, M1\}$, which contains the two single fault diagnoses $\{A1\}$ and $\{M1\}$. Early approaches to model-based diagnosis presumed that multiple faults could only arise out of combinations of single fault diagnoses. This is incorrect: the set $\{M2, M3\}$ is a perfectly good diagnosis which explains all the symptoms while neither

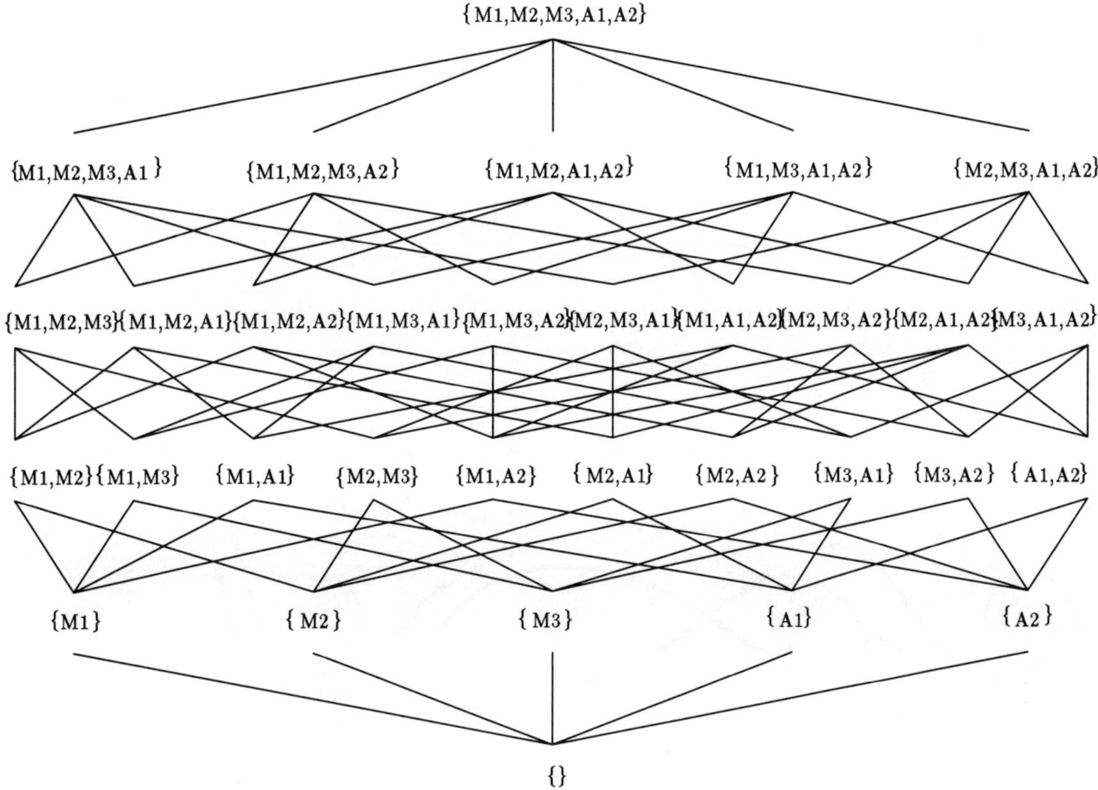

Figure 17.5 Diagnosis lattice

of *M*2 nor *M*3 is a single fault diagnosis. This is unfortunate, as set intersection is an extremely simple algorithm. Instead, the algorithm that generates minimal diagnoses must be more complicated.

The set of all diagnoses can be arranged as a lattice (see Figure 17.5). At the bottom of the lattice is the empty set, which represents the diagnosis in which nothing is faulted. At the top of the lattice is the diagnosis where all components are faulted. Every edge in the figure represents a link between a diagnosis and its immediate superset or subset. In order for a diagnosis to explain every symptom, the diagnosis must contain at least one component from every conflict. Initially, every set in the lattice (i.e., Figure 17.6) is a diagnosis. Every new conflict eliminates some diagnoses from the lattice. Since diagnoses include more and more failing components as we go upward in the lattice, each conflict can be viewed

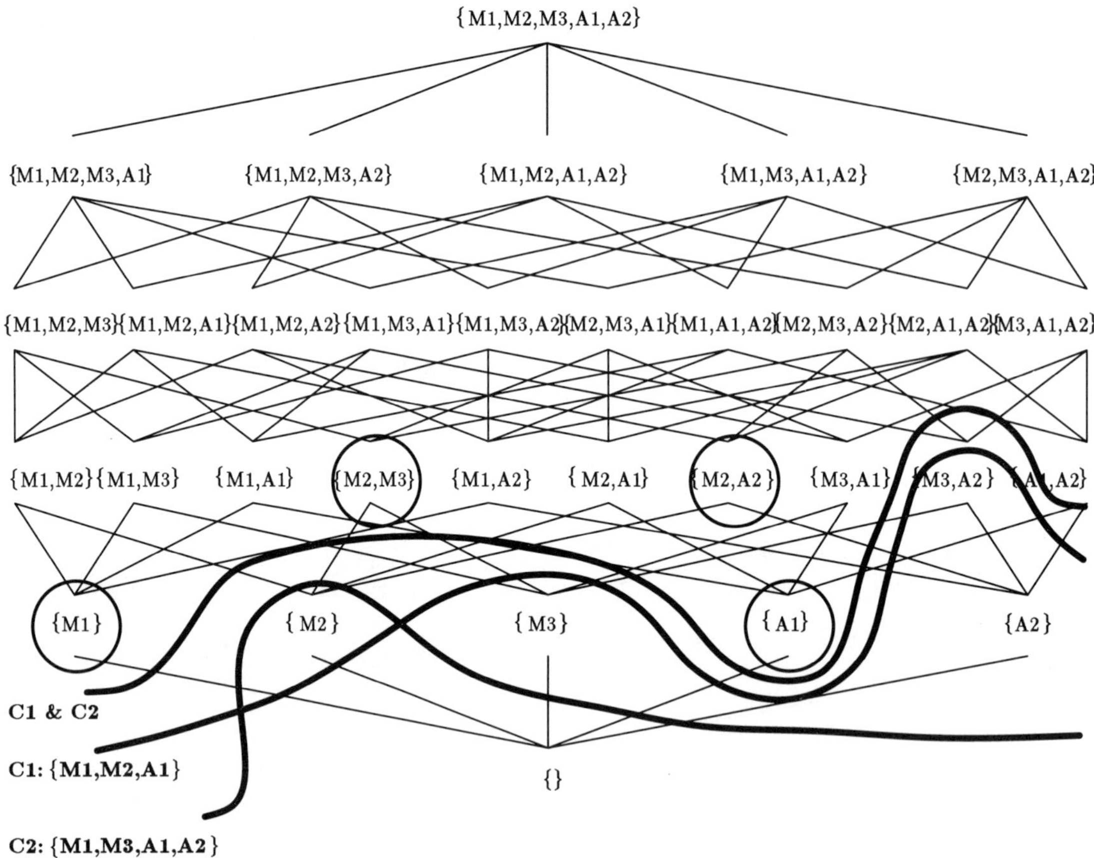

Figure 17.6 Diagnosis lattice with eliminated diagnoses removed

as a line drawn through the lattice which eliminates all diagnoses below the line. As conflicts accumulate, this line moves upwards through the lattice.

Figure 17.6 illustrates how conflicts affect the diagnosis lattice. The first conflict $\{A1, M1, M2\}$ eliminates all diagnoses that do not contain at least one of $A1$, $M1$, or $M2$. Thus, the diagnoses $\{\}$, $\{M3\}$, $\{A2\}$, and $\{M3, A2\}$ are eliminated. The second conflict eliminates only one additional diagnosis: $\{M2\}$.

Representing the entire lattice in TGDE is out of the question as this would requires exponential space. Fortunately, it is sufficient to identify only the minimal diagnoses. The minimal diagnoses are those which contain no other diagnoses as subsets. Thus the minimal diagnoses occur immediately above all those eliminated by the conflicts. All diagnoses in the lattice above the line (i.e., above the minimal diagnoses) are necessarily diagnoses. Therefore, to characterize all diagnoses, we simply need an algorithm that identifies the minimal diagnoses. The most straightforward algorithms to construct minimal diagnoses are set-covering algorithms [1]. Unfortunately, set covering is known to be NP-hard. The simplest algorithm for generating diagnoses is to perform a backtrack search that selects one component from each conflict, and then remove subsumed sets.

In TGDE, a diagnosis is a minimal set of assumptions which intersects every conflict. But we can view diagnoses from a complementary point of view. Consider the maximal sets of assumptions which do not intersect any conflict. For example, if there are no conflicts, then there is one such maximal set for the polybox: $\{A1, A2, M1, M2, M3\}$. In our example, there are two conflicts: $\{M1, M2, A1\}$ and $\{M1, M3, A1, A2\}$. There are thus four maximal sets of components: $\{M2, M3, A1, A2\}$, $\{M1, M2, M3, A2\}$, $\{M1, A1, A2\}$, and $\{M1, M3, A1\}$. These are the maximal sets of components which can all be OK but that do not support any prediction that conflicts with an observation. Such maximal sets clearly are in one-to-one correspondence with the diagnoses. Fortuitously, we already have an algorithm that constructs such sets. The ATMS interpretation construction algorithm, when directed to interpret each OK assumption as a default, identifies maximally consistent sets of defaults. Therefore, TGDE does not require a distinct algorithm to construct diagnoses—this work is done by the ATMS interpretation construction algorithm.

17.3 Sequential diagnosis

So far, TGDE merely produces a set of diagnoses which explain the symptoms. At the conclusion of the diagnostic task, we need to obtain a unique diagnosis that indicates which component(s) of the device must be replaced. TGDE usually produces multiple diagnoses. In some cases, one of the diagnoses is more likely than the others. In other cases, additional measurements are required to discriminate among the diagnoses. After every measurement, the diagnostician must decide whether to stop and replace the faulted components or continue to gather more evidence.

A general theory of diagnosis would take into account the failure probabilities of components, knowledge about dependent failures, costs of measurements, and the costs of misdiagnosis in order to make the economically optimal decision (see [2]). However, these issues raise complexities far beyond the scope of this book and are topics of current research in model-based diagnosis. Therefore, in TGDE we make a large number of simplifications.

We assume that every component fails with extremely small likelihood as well as independently (see [3]). Suppose every component fails with probability ϵ. Then the prior probability of some particular diagnosis D is:

$$p(D) = \epsilon^{|D|}(1 - \epsilon)^{n-|D|},$$

where n is the number of components in the device and $|D|$ is the number of faulted components in D. We assume that ϵ is very small and therefore

$$p_i = \epsilon^{|C_i|},$$

and only the smallest cardinality diagnoses are of interest. Therefore, the diagnostic process should continue until a single smallest cardinality diagnosis remains.

Every observation that is made can potentially shift the probabilities of diagnoses. We have already made the simplifying assumption that all components fail independently. We make the additional assumption that the models ensure that for whatever observation is actually made, every minimum cardinality diagnosis either predicts that new observation, or contradicts it (i.e., that no minimum cardinality diagnosis is agnostic about some observation). The combination of these two assumptions ensures that every observation divides the current set of minimal cardinality diagnoses into two sets: (1) the set inconsistent with the observation, and the posterior probability of each of these diagnoses becomes 0, and (2) the set which predicts (or should predict—see Section 17.4.2) the new observation, all of whose posterior probabilities remain identical. Under these assumptions, the probabilities of all minimal cardinality diagnoses, always remain equal and need not be recorded.

TGDE continues until one minimal cardinality diagnosis remains (we see an example later). If a new observation eliminates every one of the current minimal cardinality diagnoses then TGDE simply focuses on the minimal cardinality diagnoses remaining after taking into consideration the the new observation.

17.3.1 Choosing the best next measurement

If every device quantity were observable and measurements were free, then the best diagnostic strategy would be to measure everything. However, measuring is typically far more expensive than reasoning, as measuring requires a complex action in the world while the reasoning just requires computer time. Therefore, TGDE goes to considerable effort to plan the best measurement to make next. Depending on the method used to select measurement points, there can be dramatic differences in the average number of measurements required to isolate a fault. Imagine a very long chain of one thousand buffers (simple components whose outputs equal their inputs) in which one of the buffers is faulted. Initially there are one thousand possible single faults. We could first measure the input to the final buffer, trying to determine whether it was faulted. Continuing in this pattern, isolating the faulty buffer would take us, on average, five hundred measurements. On the other hand, if we first measured at the middle of the chain we could isolate the fault to one or the other subset of five hundred buffers. Repeating this process we would isolate any faulty buffer in no more than ten measurements. This simple example graphically illustrates that choosing measurement points carefully can have substantial payoff.

The process of choosing the best measurement to make next has two facets. First, we have to determine the possible outcomes of a measurement. Second, we have to weigh the different measurements to determine which set of outcomes is most informative.

Let us continue with the polybox example. Consider measuring Z. In the ATMS database we have the following information about Z:

$\langle Z = 6, \{\{M3\}, \{A2, M2\}\}\rangle$

$\langle Z = 8, \{\{A1, A2, M1\}\}\rangle$

Every diagnosis of Figure 17.6 provides a possible explanation for the symptoms $F = 10$ and $G = 12$. Therefore, we can examine each of these diagnoses and see what they say about Z. Consider the diagnosis $\{A1, A2\}$ in which $A1$ and $A2$ are faulted, and $M1$, $M2$, and $M3$ are functioning correctly. We can determine the predicted value of Z in $\{A1, A2\}$ by seeing what value of Z is supported by the environment

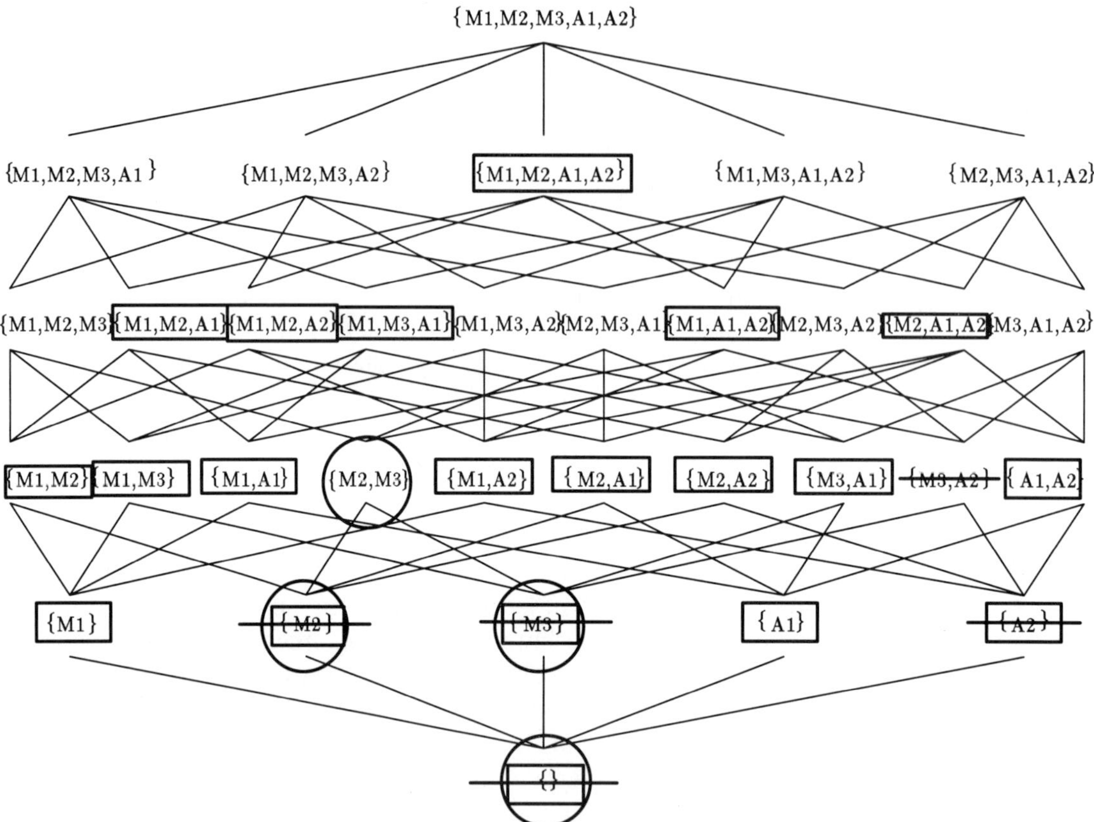

Figure 17.7 Diagnosis lattice. Rectangles indicate diagnoses where $Z = 6$. Circles indicate diagnoses where $Z = 8$.

$\{M1, M2, M3\}$. Thus, Z is 6 in $\{A1, A2\}$. Consider the diagnosis $\{M2, M3\}$. There Z is 8. Some diagnoses do not predict any value for Z at all. For example, the diagnosis $\{A1, A2, M3\}$ predicts no value for Z. Figure 17.7 summarizes the results. Impossible diagnoses have a line drawn through them. Diagnoses that predict $Z = 6$ are in rectangles and diagnoses that predict $Z = 8$ are in circles. Suppose we measure Z. For TGDE, there are three distinct possible outcomes. If Z is observed to be 6, then all the diagnoses in circles are eliminated. If Z is observed to be 8, then the diagnoses in rectangles are eliminated. If Z is observed to be neither 6 nor 8, then all diagnoses in circles or rectangles are eliminated.

Figure 17.7 gives us a clear picture of the logical outcomes of a measurement. We can construct a similar picture for each of the possible measurement points (X, Y, and Z in the case of the polybox). In order to weigh which is better we have to make some assumptions. In addition, we need an algorithm which does not have to construct the entire lattice to draw its conclusion, as this lattice is far too large for even moderately sized devices.

We assume that the cost of making every measurement is equal and therefore we do not have to be concerned with considering the differential costs among the measurement actions themselves. In particular, measuring X, Y, or Z has equal cost. We also make the simplifying assumption that we are only concerned with the minimum cardinality diagnoses. In the polybox example there remain only two minimum cardinality diagnoses: $\{A1\}$ and $\{M1\}$. In this case, it is pretty obvious that the only reasonable measurement to make is at X.

Hypothetical measurements could be evaluated by hypothesizing each possible outcome, simulating how it reduced the diagnoses, and repeating this process until one diagnosis remained. This is extremely expensive. Therefore, we evaluate measurements based with one-step lookahead alone. If we make the approximation that every measurement has k outcomes, then the smallest number of measurements required to discriminate among n diagnoses is $log_k n$ (in direct analogy to the number of probes required in a binary search where $k = 2$). Using this as an approximation, we can score every possible outcome as $log_k n$, where n is the number of diagnoses which would remain if that outcome were to occur. The likelihood that a particular outcome will occur is the fraction of diagnoses that predict that outcome. Therefore, a measurement can be scored by:

$$\sum \frac{c_i}{n} log_k c_i,$$

where c_i is the number diagnoses which predict the i'th outcome. As k and n are constants, the best measurement is the one that minimizes:

$$\sum c_i log\ c_i.$$

On occasion, some minimal cardinality diagnosis may not predict an outcome of a measurement. In such cases TGDE identifies (if possible) all consistent outcomes for the observation and assumes that each outcome

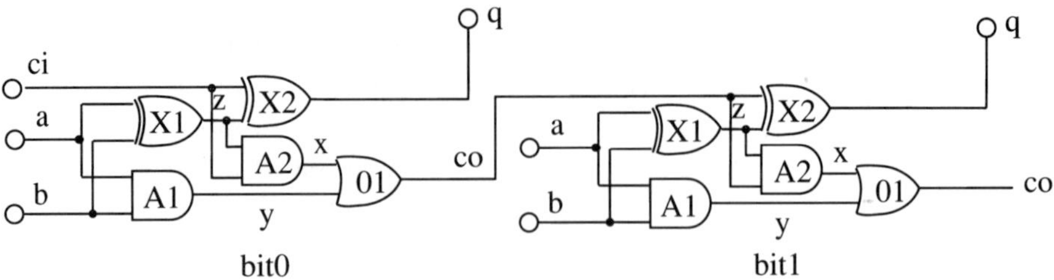

Figure 17.8 A two-bit ripple carry adder

is equally likely. For example, if there are m hypothetically possible values for a measurement outcome, then it adds $\frac{1}{m}$ to each c_i.

17.3.2 TGDE example

Consider the task of diagnosing the two-bit adder of Section 16.1.7 (see Figure 17.8). We use the same models as before, except that every component is modeled by an `assume-constraint` such that an OK assumption is created for every component. Given that all the inputs are 0, `(>> Q BIT1 ADD)` should be 0, but it is observed to be 1.

Invoking the TGDE procedure `diagnose` after the inputs and outputs have been applied results in the following (as there are multiple components with the same name, the node printer is modified to print out fully qualified names of assumptions):

```
There are 5 minimum cardinality diagnoses:
{(>> X2 BIT1 ADD)}
{(>> X1 BIT1 ADD)}
{(>> 01 BIT0 ADD)}
{(>> A2 BIT0 ADD)}
{(>> A1 BIT0 ADD)}
```

The five single faults that explain the observations are highlighted in Figure 17.9. Then TGDE prints out the scores for every measurement point:

```
Measuring <Cell (>> RIPPLE ADD)> has cost 6.7548876
Measuring <Cell (>> X BIT0 ADD)> has cost 8.0
Measuring <Cell (>> Y BIT0 ADD)> has cost 8.0
```

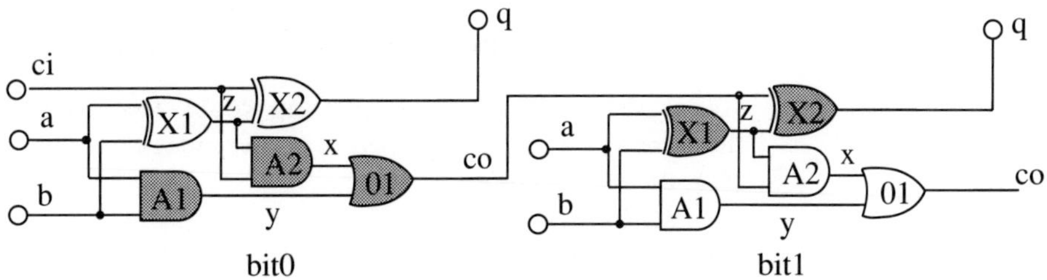

Figure 17.9 A full adder with single faults highlighted

```
Measuring <Cell (>> Z BIT1 ADD)> has cost 8.0
.
.
.
```

All the remaining measurement points provide no information. These scores arise because the possible measurement outcomes split the set of current diagnoses as follows:

Cell	Value	
	0	1
(>> Z BIT1 ADD)	4	1
(>> Y BIT1 ADD)	5	0
(>> X BIT1 ADD)	5	0
(>> Q BIT1 ADD)	0	5
(>> B BIT1 ADD)	5	0
(>> A BIT1 ADD)	5	0
(>> CO BIT1 ADD)	5	0
(>> Z BIT0 ADD)	5	0
(>> Y BIT0 ADD)	4	1
(>> X BIT0 ADD)	4	1
(>> Q BIT0 ADD)	5	0
(>> B BIT0 ADD)	5	0
(>> A BIT0 ADD)	5	0
(>> CI BIT0 ADD)	5	0
(>> RIPPLE ADD)	2	3

Thus measuring (>> RIPPLE ADD) is best. TGDE asks to make this measurement. Let us presume the fault lies in (>> A1 BITO ADD):

```
Please enter result of measuring <Cell (>> RIPPLE ADD)>:1
There are 3 minimum cardinality diagnoses:
{(>> O1 BITO ADD)}
{(>> A2 BITO ADD)}
{(>> A1 BITO ADD)}
 Measuring <Cell (>> X BITO ADD)> has cost 2.0
 Measuring <Cell (>> Y BITO ADD)> has cost 2.0
 .
 .
 .
```

Since there are only two places worthwhile to measure, and both provide equal information, TGDE asks which of these should be measured:

```
0 : <Cell (>> X BITO ADD)>
1 : <Cell (>> Y BITO ADD)>
Enter integer of point measured: 1
Please enter result of measuring <Cell (>> Y BITO ADD)>:1

Correct diagnosis is:
{(>> A1 BITO ADD)}
```

In this case TGDE has isolated the fault in only two measurements. If the fault lay elsewhere, then TGDE might take three measurements. In general, every single fault in the full adder can be isolated in three measurements or less.

17.4 A formalization of model-based diagnosis

So far we have defined the basic concepts of model-based diagnosis intuitively through examples, and then described an implementation embodying those concepts. Can the concepts be defined precisely? Is our implementation actually computing the right information? Are there important inferences we are missing? We can only begin to answer questions like this by developing a precise formal account of model-based diagnosis. A more extensive treatment of this material is found in [4, 6].

17.4.1 A theory of diagnosis

In the theory of diagnosis, the definition of a system incorporates all the information about the device we have available including observations, schematics, component models, etc.:

Definition 17.1
A system is a triple (SD,COMPS,OBS) where:

1. SD, the system description, is a set of first-order sentences.
2. COMPS, the system components, is a finite set of constants.
3. OBS, a set of observations, is a set of first-order sentences.

TGDE adopts the convention of specifying a diagnosis by a set of failing components, leaving implicit that the remaining components are OK. The theory generalizes this definition to make it possible for a diagnosis to leave the faultedness of a component unspecified. The definition of diagnosis is built up from the notion of abnormal. $AB(c)$ is a literal which holds when a component $c \in$COMPS is abnormal.

The system description for any device is relatively large because it must include axioms for equality, arithmetic, etc. The key sentences in SD describe the behavior of components. In the case of the polybox, SD contains the following two sentences (we presume all free variables are universally quantified) which describe the behavior of adders and multipliers.

$$\mathrm{ADDER}(x) \rightarrow [\neg AB(x) \rightarrow out(x) = in1(x) + in2(x)]$$

$$\mathrm{MULTIPLIER}(x) \rightarrow [\neg AB(x) \rightarrow out(x) = in1(x) \times in2(x)]$$

The first sentence can be read as: If x is an adder, then if x is not abnormal, then the output of the adder is the sum of its two inputs. We represent a diagnosis as a conjunction of AB-literals which indicates whether each component is normal or abnormal:

Definition 17.2
Given two sets of components Cp and Cn define $\mathcal{D}(Cp, Cn)$ to be the conjunction:

$$\left[\bigwedge_{c \in Cp} AB(c)\right] \wedge \left[\bigwedge_{c \in Cn} \neg AB(c)\right].$$

Definition 17.3
Let $\Delta \subseteq$COMPS. A diagnosis for (SD,COMPS,OBS) is $\mathcal{D}(\Delta, COMPS - \Delta)$ such that:

$$SD \cup OBS \cup \{\mathcal{D}(\Delta, COMPS - \Delta)\}$$

is satisfiable.

Thus in our polybox example, the TGDE diagnosis $\{M1\}$ represents the formal diagnosis $AB(M1) \wedge \neg AB(M2) \wedge \neg AB(M3) \wedge \neg AB(A1) \wedge \neg AB\ (A2)$ or $\mathcal{D}(\{M1\}, \{M2, M3, A1, A2\})$.

Unfortunately, there may be $2^{|COMPS|}$ diagnoses. The definition of minimal diagnosis derives from a desire to develop a more parsimonious characterization of the diagnoses of a system:

Definition 17.4
A diagnosis $\mathcal{D}(\Delta, COMPS - \Delta)$ is a minimal diagnosis iff for no proper subset Δ' of Δ is $\mathcal{D}(\Delta', COMPS - \Delta')$ a diagnosis.

Our implementation implicitly assumed that every TGDE diagnosis was a superset of some minimal TGDE diagnosis. This result can be proven from the preceding definitions.

Theorem 17.1
If $\mathcal{D}(\Delta, COMPS - \Delta)$ is a diagnosis, then there is a minimal diagnosis $\mathcal{D}(\Delta', COMPS - \Delta')$ such that $\Delta' \subseteq \Delta$.

More seriously, TGDE presumed that the converse held:

Hypothesis 17.1
(Minimal Diagnosis Hypothesis) If $\mathcal{D}(\Delta', COMPS - \Delta')$ is a minimal diagnosis and if $\Delta' \subseteq \Delta \subseteq COMPS$, then $\mathcal{D}(\Delta, COMPS - \Delta)$ is a diagnosis.

If this hypothesis holds, then every superset of a TGDE diagnosis would also be a TGDE diagnosis. Therefore, to completely characterize all the diagnoses of a system it is sufficient to identify only the minimal diagnoses, since all the possible diagnoses can be generated from them. Unfortunately, the minimal diagnosis hypothesis does not hold in general.

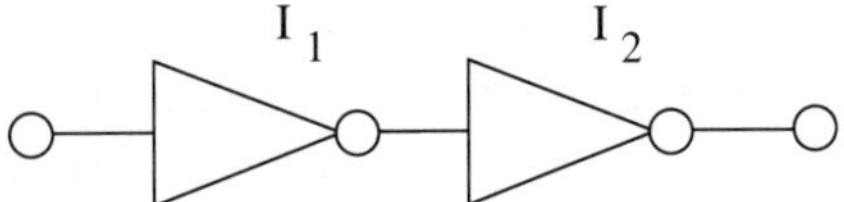

Figure 17.10 Two inverters

Consider the circuit of Figure 17.10. Suppose we know that the inverters we are using have only two failure modes: they short their output to their input or their output becomes stuck at 0. The model in SD for such an inverter is:

$$INVERTER(x) \rightarrow [\neg AB(x) \rightarrow [in(x) = 0 \equiv out(x) = 1]],$$

$$INVERTER(x) \wedge AB(x) \rightarrow [SA0(x) \vee SHORT(x)],$$

$$SA0(x) \rightarrow out(x) = 0,$$

$$SHORT(x) \rightarrow out(x) = in(x).$$

Suppose the input is 0 and the output is 1: $in(I_1) = 0, out(I_2) = 1$. There are two possible diagnoses:

$$AB(I_1) \wedge \neg AB(I_2),$$

$$\neg AB(I_1) \wedge AB(I_1).$$

However, the superset $AB(I_1) \wedge AB(I_2)$ is not a diagnosis. Intuitively, if I_2 is faulted and producing the observed 1, then it cannot be stuck at 0, and must have its input shorted to its output. But then I_1 must be outputting a 1 and there is no faulty behavior of I_1, which produces a 1 for an input of 0.

Fortunately, the preceding inverter model cannot easily be encoded as an ATCON constraint. It would be, however, possible to extend TGDE to be able to express fault models of this form. Diagnoses within this extended TGDE framework would violate the minimal diagnosis hypothesis. Fortunately, it is possible to show that the, unextended, TGDE model-writing conventions ensure that the minimal diagnosis hypothesis holds. If all the occurrences of *AB* occur as $\neg AB$ in antecedents when the system is viewed as implications, then the system is said to obey the *ignorance of abnormal behavior* (IAB) condition. If we use `assume-constraint` to model components, then OK assumptions only appear as antecedents to justifications and therefore *AB* only occurs negatively in antecedents. This means that TGDE's models obey the IAB condition. It is possible to prove that:

Theorem 17.2
If (SD,COMPS,OBS) satisfies the IAB condition, then the minimal diagnosis hypothesis holds for (SD,COMPS,OBS).

Finally, let us analyze TGDE's use of conflicts to construct diagnoses. First, we must make some definitions.

Definition 17.5
An *AB*-literal is $AB(c)$ or $\neg AB(c)$ for some c $\in$ COMPS. An *AB*-clause is a disjunction of *AB*-literals containing no complementary pair of *AB*-literals. A positive *AB*-clause is an *AB*-clause all of whose literals are positive.

Definition 17.6
A conflict of (SD,COMPS,OBS) is an *AB*-clause entailed by SD $\cup$ OBS. A positive conflict is a conflict all of whose literals are positive. A minimal conflict of (SD,COMPS,OBS) is a conflict no proper subclause of which is a conflict of (SD,COMPS,OBS).

Again TGDE's conflicts correspond one-to-one. For TGDE a conflict is represented as a set of components one of which is abnormal. The equivalent formal definition is a disjunction of *AB*-literals. For example, the TGDE conflict $\{M1, M2, A1\}$ represents the (positive) clause $AB(M1) \vee AB(M2) \vee AB(A1)$. As TGDE obeys the IAB condition, it can be easily shown that all minimal conflicts are positive. TGDE, through the use of the ATMS nogood database, only retains minimal conflicts. The motivation for only representing minimal conflicts is the same as for only representing minimal diagnoses—there typically are an exponential number of possible conflicts. Therefore, reducing the conflicts to a small set of those possible which is still sufficient to generate the minimal diagnoses is very important.

The key result which we are leading up to is that the minimal diagnoses can be generated from the minimal conflicts alone.

Definition 17.7
A conjunction C of literals covers a conjunction D of literals iff every literal of C occurs in D.

Definition 17.8
Suppose Σ is a set of propositional formulas. A conjunction of literals π containing no pair of complementary literals is an implicant of Σ iff π entails each formula in Σ. π is a prime implicant of Σ iff the only implicant of Σ covering π is π itself.

Theorem 17.3
(Characterization of minimal diagnoses) $\mathcal{D}(\Delta, COMPS - \Delta)$ is a minimal diagnosis of (SD,COMPS,OBS) iff $\bigwedge_{c \in \Delta} AB(c)$ is a prime implicant of the set of positive minimal conflicts of (SD,COMPS,OBS).

Our polybox example has two minimal conflicts:

$AB(A1) \vee AB(M1) \vee AB(M2),$

$AB(A1) \vee AB(M1) \vee AB(M3) \vee AB(A2).$

There are four prime implicants of these two clauses:

$AB(A_1),$

$AB(M_1),$

$AB(M_2) \wedge AB(M_3),$

$AB(M_2) \wedge AB(A_2).$

Each of these corresponds to a minimal diagnosis.

17.4.2 Consequences of incompleteness

In the previous section we saw that the notions of conflict and diagnosis and their interrelationships both make sense and can be precisely defined. We saw that there were potential pitfalls (such as the violation of the minimal diagnosis hypothesis) but, fortuitously, the limitations of TGDE avoided many of those pitfalls. In this section we take the precise specification developed in the previous section and examine TGDE more closely to see how faithful TGDE actually is to the basic definitions. We will discover numerous problems. Unfortunately, to fix many of these

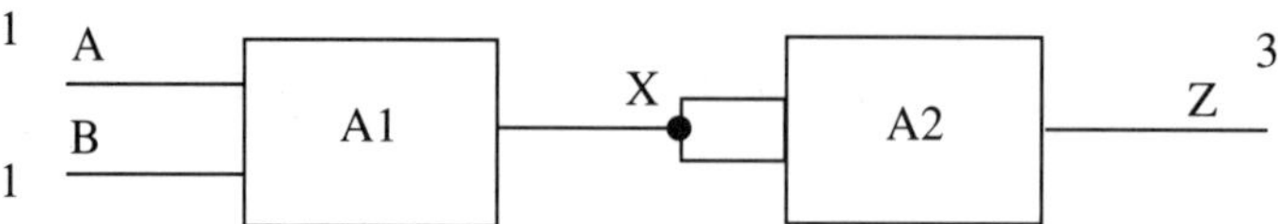

Figure 17.11 A simple two-adder device

problems we will be forced to generalize TGDE enough so that it falls victim to new difficulties.

One very obvious limitation of TGDE is that it cannot represent all possible models easily. As TGDE obeys IAB it is not possible to model faults as discussed for Figure 17.10. Generalizing TGDE to be able to represent such models is difficult and also leads to a violation of the minimal diagnosis hypothesis.

Another, less obvious, limitation is that the only information that TGDE can represent about a variable is that it is at a particular value. It cannot represent negations or disjunctions of assignments. This limits the kinds of observations that can be entered into the system as well as the kinds of inferences that are possible. For example, suppose we measure F and discover it to be 11 or 12. There is no convenient way to represent that. If we knew all the possible values for F, then we could contradict all values that were not 11 or 12. Suppose ATCON is not able to propagate this information. This problem arises even if observations are not disjunctive. Suppose we measure the output of a multiplier to be 1, but don't know any of its inputs. From this we can infer that neither input is 0. However, ATCON cannot use this information.

More generally, TGDE is incomplete. Consider the example of Figure 17.11. This circuit consists of a sequence of two adders which operate only on integers. Suppose that $A = 1$ and $B = 1$. From this, TGDE predicts that $Z = 4$. Suppose we observe Z to be 3. From this, TGDE gets the single conflict $\{A1, A2\}$ and two minimal diagnoses: $\{A1\}$ and $\{A2\}$. However, $\{A1\}$ is not a diagnosis according to our formal definition. There is no fault in $A1$ that could possibly cause Z to be 3. In general, Z has to be an even number if $A2$ is working. Thus, $\{A2\}$ is the only minimal conflict and $\{A2\}$ is the only minimal diagnosis.

Presuming we implemented TGDE correctly, it is sound. Therefore, all the nogoods TGDE finds correspond to real conflicts. The preceding example shows that minimal nogoods do not necessarily correspond to minimal conflicts. Due to its incompleteness, TGDE may not find all conflicts. Unfortunately, if TGDE cannot find all conflicts it may not eliminate enough diagnoses. As the example above showed, there are cases where TGDE returns diagnoses which, in fact, are not possible. As this weren't bad enough, this incompleteness degrades the quality of TGDE's measurement proposals. TGDE will propose measurements to discriminate among impossible diagnoses. In addition, since the set of predictions itself is incomplete, it may not realize that certain measurement points are of value and discriminate among important diagnoses.

At first blush these problems seem severe. Also, there is no general solution to all these difficulties. The literature contains numerous proposals which improve the completeness of representation and inferential mechanisms without incurring excessive computational overhead. Earlier, in Chapter 13, we presented a general propositional reasoner using prime implicates and prime implicants. Thus, if the problem can be represented propositionally (see Exercise 9), the CLTMS can be used to implement a completely general diagnostic procedure. In some cases this approach will be adequate, but for any large system the this approach is computationally unfeasible.

17.5 Exercises

1. ⋆ How many diagnoses can an n-component device have? What does this tell you about the size of the diagnosis lattice?

2. ⋆ Show that every minimal cardinality diagnosis is a minimal diagnosis.

3. ⋆ Why is there at most one predicted outcome for each measurement for any diagnosis? Consider the discussion of Section 17.3. Could Z ever have two values in some diagnosis?

4. ⋆ ⋆ The ATMS interpretation construction algorithm works best when interpretations contains relatively few assumptions. As there are usually only a few faults, the interpretations corresponding to diagnoses can become quite large, resulting in considerable inefficiency. Write an algorithm that computes minimal diagnoses directly and

thus manipulates small sets of faulted components instead of large sets of good components.

5. ⋆⋆ For most diagnostic tasks, TGDE spends most of its computational effort constructing minimal cardinality diagnoses. Rewrite `smallest-diagnoses` such that TGDE rarely spends much effort finding diagnoses.

6. ⋆⋆ Extend TGDE's modeling language to build hierarchical models. For example, the model for a full adder would call for a single assumption representing the fact that the adder is OK, and this same assumption would be passed along to all the rules which implement the behavior of the gates that comprise the full adder.

7. ⋆⋆ The measurements that best differentiate among the diagnoses of cardinality k may not be the best for differentiating among diagnoses of cardinality $k + 1$. Show an example where TGDE makes more measurements than necessary due to this horizon effect. Hint: Construct a multiple fault example for which the first few measurements eliminate all single faults.

8. ⋆ Show an example where TGDE produces a misdiagnosis which is not due to logical incompleteness (but due to its oversimplified notion of probability).

9. ⋆⋆⋆ The CLTMS provides a general-purpose propositional reasoner. Therefore, it is possible to implement a general diagnostic procedure that completely implements the formal definitions of diagnosis. Using the CLTMS, build a diagnostic algorithm that finds the minimal diagnoses of any propositional model. Try it on the polybox example. What are some of the disadvantages of this approach?

10. ⋆⋆⋆ TGDE is designed to determine the best measurement to make next. In some cases it may not be possible to make more measurements, but we can choose a different set of inputs and remeasure the outputs. Produce a version of TGDE which finds the best inputs to apply. Hint: Create an assumption for every possible value of every input cell. Try it on the full adder. Will your implementation work on the polybox example?

17.6 Bibliography

[1] Cormen, T.H., Leiserson, C.E., and Rivest, R.L., *Introduction to Algorithms*, MIT Press, 1990.

[2] de Kleer, J., and Williams, B.C., "Diagnosing multiple faults," *Artificial Intelligence* 32 (1987): 97–130. Also in [5].

[3] de Kleer, J., "Using crude probability estimates to guide diagnosis," *Artificial Intelligence* 45: (1990) 381-391. Also in [5].

[4] de Kleer, J., Mackworth A., and Reiter R., "Characterizing diagnoses and Systems," *Artificial Intelligence* 56 (1992): 197–222. Also in [5].

[5] Hamscher, W., Console, L., and de Kleer, J. (eds), *Readings in Model-Based Diagnosis*, Morgan-Kaufmann, 1992.

[6] Reiter, R., "A theory of diagnosis from first principles," *Artificial Intelligence* 32 (1987): 97–130. Also in [5].

18 Symbolic Relaxation Systems

Many search problems have a common structure. Each aspect of the problem can be represented as a set of alternatives or choice sets. Examples of choices include selecting the material to be used in an airplane wing or the value of a resistor in an electronic circuit. Selecting a consistent collection of alternatives, one from each choice set, yields a solution to the problem. In electrical circuit synthesis, for instance, a solution is a set of values for each component in the design so that the resulting circuit performs as desired.

Previous chapters have illustrated several general methods to solve such problems, including chronological and dependency-directed backtracking. In many cases the problems tackled with search techniques require exponential work. Sometimes, though, special characteristics of the problem allow more efficient solution methods to be applied. Exponential behavior arises from generating or examining combinations of solution fragments. If some fragments can be ruled out by an inexpensive local computation, the search space shrinks and the search becomes more efficient. In some circumstances search may not even be necessary, if local processing leaves only a single consistent alternative in each choice set. This is the intuition behind the method of *symbolic relaxation*, also known as *Waltz filtering*.

Symbolic relaxation is a commonly used and powerful AI technique. No discussion of building problem solvers would be complete without it. Furthermore, theoretical analyses of this technique have led to a new model of problem solving, *constraint satisfaction problems* (CSPs), which provides a formal method for describing and classifying certain kinds of problems. Such classifications provide insight as to how difficult particular classes of problems are, and what techniques are necessary to solve them.

This chapter examines symbolic relaxation. We begin by outlining the formal notion of constraint satisfaction problems. Next we explore how the structure of discrete CSPs can be exploited to implement very efficient problem solvers, using a variation of the constraint knowledge model introduced in Chapter 15. We describe the implementation of a specific symbolic relaxation system, WALTZER. The utility of symbolic relaxation is illustrated by using WALTZER to solve some classic AI problems, namely Blocks World scene analysis and reasoning about temporal relationships.

18.1 Constraint satisfaction problems

Formally, we can consider the collection of choice sets which define a problem to be *variables*, which take values from some specific domain. The domain can be finite, as in the search problems we have examined, or infinite, as in the antecedent constraint networks of Chapter 15. The connections between variables are described as *relations*. Relations define which assignments of values to variables are consistent. In this chapter we focus exclusively on cases where the domains are finite, since this class is important in practice and its theory is relatively self-contained.

Let us consider a simple puzzle to make these ideas concrete. Suppose we have the variables *pianist*, *harpist*, *talker*, *gambler*, *money*, and *animals*, all of which range over the domain *groucho*, *harpo*, *chico*. That is, the value for the variable *pianist* is the person who most likes to play piano, and is one of *groucho*, *harpo*, or *chico*. Puzzles include a variety of clues about the assignments of variables to values, such as:

1. The pianist, harpist, and talker are distinct brothers.
2. The brother who is fond of money is distinct from the one who is fond of gambling, who is also distinct from the one who is fond of animals.
3. The one who likes to talk doesn't like gambling.
4. The one who likes animals plays the harp.

5. Groucho hates animals.
6. Harpo is always silent.
7. Chico plays the piano.

Each clue can be construed as a relationship constraining assignments of values to the variables. For instance, the first clue can be formalized as a ternary relationship which forces assignments to the first three variables to be distinct. The third clue can be formalized as a binary relationship which ensures that the assignment for *talker* and *gambler* are distinct. The sixth and seventh clues can be formalized as unary relationships which force or forbid certain assignments to variables.

Suppose a problem P consists of the set of variables $v_1, v_2, \ldots, v_n$ and relations $R_1, R_2, \ldots, R_n$. Any collection of assignments of values to $v_1, v_2, \ldots, v_n$ which satisfies all of $R_1, R_2, \ldots, R_n$ is a solution to P.

A graph metaphor is often used to describe the collection of relationships. A graph can be defined as a set of nodes connected by a set of arcs. In thinking of a problem as a graph, the variables of the problem become the nodes of the graph, and the relationships between the variables become the arcs of the graph. (This is easy to visualize for unary and binary relationships, and a bit harder for relations involving more variables, but the principle and terminology are the same.) These formal definitions can thus be viewed as defining a constraint network, similar to those in Chapter 15. Both senses of constraint network encompass the notion of describing a situation declaratively using a vocabulary of relationships between the parts, and performing some automatic computation to fill in the details of the situation. The difference is in how the underlying computation is organized. In antecedent constraint networks specific value(s) for part of the network are computed on the basis of other known values. In symbolic relaxation networks, a process of elimination is used to filter out solution fragments that cannot be part of a global solution.

To understand this process of elimination requires defining local notions of consistency. Again the graph metaphor proves useful. The simplest version of consistency is to ensure that each node, taken individually, is consistent. A node is consistent when no unary constraint rules out any possible value for the variable represented by the node. Ensuring that each arc, taken individually, is consistent is one step more complex, since all the variables involved in the relationship must be considered. Even more complex is ensuring that each collection of paths through the constraint network is consistent, since combinations of relationships must be examined. In the literature these ideas are called *node consistency*, *arc consistency*, and *path consistency*, respectively.

Logically, node consistency means that each possible value for a variable satisfies the unary relationships on that variable. Suppose R_i were the only unary relation on the variable v_i, whose domain is D_i. Then node consistency holds exactly when the following formula is true:

$$\forall x \in D_i \; R_i(x)$$

Arc consistency ensures that each non-unary relation is individually consistent. That is, if R_j is a k-ary relation, it is arc consistent exactly when for each combination of values for $k - 1$ of the variables, there is a value for the kth which satisfies R_j. For binary relations, this constraint may be stated formally as:

$$\forall x \in D_i \; \exists y \in D_k \; R_j(x, y).$$

Given a constraint network, we can enforce node consistency by restricting the domain of each variable so as to satisfy the unary relations. In our puzzle above, the fifth, sixth, and seventh clues can be viewed as unary relationships on the variables $animals$, $talker$, and $pianist$, restricting their ranges to be

$$animals \in harpo, chico; \; talker \in groucho, chico; \; pianist \in chico;$$

Arc consistency can be enforced by further restricting the ranges of variables. That is, if a variable v_i participating in relationship R_i has a value V which is not consistent with the possible values for the other variables which participate in R_i, then V must be removed from the domain of v_i. In our example, the first clue is equivalent to three binary relations on the variables $pianist$, $harpist$, and $talker$ which enforce mutual exclusion between their values. To make the relation between $pianist$ and $harpist$ consistent we must remove $chico$ from the domain of $harpist$, since the only possible value for $pianist$ is now $chico$. Similarly, $chico$ must be removed from the domain of $harpist$ to make the relation between $pianist$ and $harpist$ arc consistent. After these restrictions, the domains become:

$$pianist \in chico; \; talker \in groucho; \; harpist \in groucho, harpo$$

To make the relationship between *talker* and *harpist* arc consistent, we must remove *groucho* from the domain of *harpist*, since *groucho* is now the only consistent value for *talker*. This leaves *harpo* as the only consistent value for *harpist*.

This example illustrates the power of symbolic relaxation: by simple, local operations, we are able to remove many possible solutions. If we started a standard backtracking search to find all consistent combinations of bindings to these six variables, we would search (in the worst case) 3^6, or 729 combinations. Using the results of the analysis so far, a backtracking search would only have to examine at most 27 more combinations. And sometimes (as in this example) arc consistency suffices to yield a unique solution, and no backtracking search is required at all.

As our examples later in this chapter illustrate, arc consistency is surprisingly powerful. It can also be enforced in linear time, making it quite efficient. As usual, efficiency is gained at the expense of completeness. In particular, a network being arc consistent does not even guarantee that a consistent solution exists, unless it produces a solution. (Conversely, if a network is not arc consistent then it has no consistent solution.)

Can a consistency-based formulation be generalized to gain completeness? Yes, but at the usual cost. The notion of *k-consistency* means that for any collection of $k - 1$ variables which satisfy all the constraints on them, any kth variable also can be bound such that the constraints on all k variables are satisfied. If a network contains n variables, then enforcing n-consistency yields a network that can be solved without backtracking. Unfortunately, the cost of enforcing k-consistency rises exponentially with increasing k. In practice, the best computational trade-off appears to be the combination of arc consistency followed by backtracking search [7, 8].

18.2 Constraint networks and finite CSPs

Many AI problems have aspects which can be viewed as finite constraint satisfaction problems. Recognizing them as such is useful for two reasons. First, complexity bounds can be applied to better analyze how well a problem solver can do. Second, there are simplified knowledge models and algorithms that can often be applied in such circumstances that lead to greater efficiency.

When does it make sense to cast a problem as a constraint network to be solved via symbolic relaxation? Two properties are important:

1. *Fixed choices:* The elements of each known choice set can be fully specified in advance.
2. *Fixed choice sets:* The set of choice sets itself can be fully specified in advance.

Having fixed choices means we can focus on reasoning by exclusion. Having fixed choice sets means we can use local knowledge and procedure models. In fact, we can adapt the nomenclature of constraint networks from Chapter 15. The variables of the CSP become *cells*, and the relationships are expressed as *constraints*. The set of constraints and cells that models a problem is called a *constraint network*. How these models differ is described next.

A cell might hold the interpretations of a line or a junction in Blocks World scene interpretation, the relationship between two intervals in a symbolic temporal logic, or the identity of the murderer in a drawing-room mystery. Each cell has a *domain*, consisting of a finite set of potential values. The values for a line might be its possible physical interpretations, the values for the relationship between two temporal intervals might include `Before`, `After`, and `During`, and the values for a role in a drawing-room mystery might be the named characters in the story. The *value* of a cell is the subset of possible values which are still possibilities. A cell is *determined* when it has exactly one value. By the end of a good drawing-room mystery, for example, the cell `murderer` is determined. A cell is *overconstrained* when the set of possible values becomes empty. Interpreting a "hard-boiled" detective novel as a drawing-room murder mystery can lead to such situations.

As before, *constraints* represent relationships between cells. Examples of constraints include the participation of a set of lines in a junction, the transitivity relationship between related pairs of temporal intervals, and the convention that neither the detective nor the murder victim are the murderer. Every constraint connects a fixed set of cells. These cells are the *parts* of the constraint. Unlike the previous constraint model, constraints in this model are never hierarchial—all their parts must be cells.

Now that we have our knowledge model specified, let us define the procedure model. There are two operations on cells:

exclude Takes two arguments, a cell and a value. Its effect is to remove that value from the list of possible values for that cell.

pick Takes two arguments, a cell and a value. Its effect is to force the given cell to have the given value.

Each constraint has an associated *update procedure*. The job of an update procedure is to enforce the semantics of the constraint, by seeing if the current possible values for its cells can be further restricted. There is only one operation on constraints:

update Takes a constraint as its argument. Its effect is to run the constraint's update procedure.

A constraint is updated whenever the value of one of its cells changes. We place no restrictions on how update procedures operate, except the following:

1. Each update procedure terminates in finite time.
2. The only information in the network an update procedure is allowed to draw upon are the values of the cells which are the parts of its associated constraint.
3. All effects on the constraint network occur through requests for `exclude` and `pick` operations.
4. Update procedures are deterministic; that is, given the same values for a constraint's cells, the update procedure always generates the same set of `exclude` and `pick` requests.

These operations are combined to enforce arc consistency as follows: When a constraint network is created, each constraint is queued for updating. Any `exclude` or `pick` operations suggested by a constraint are queued separately. The queue of cell operations is serviced with higher priority than the queue of constraint updates, since the more tightly restricted cells are, the more information each constraint update is likely to yield. Any change in a cell's value results in the constraints of which it is a part being requeued.

The algorithm just sketched is the symbolic relaxation method we implement below. Once started, it continues until either some cell becomes overconstrained or the queues become empty. Assuming the constraints are implemented as defined above, it must terminate. Why? An update operation can only lead to other updates if at least one cell loses at least one value, and we presume there are only a finite number of cells and values. A quiescent network can either be *determined*, meaning that every cell is determined, or *underdetermined*, if any cell is not determined. An underdetermined network can be further constrained by an external source (either the user or another module) picking or excluding some cell values. A CSP is solved when the network is determined. Each set of values which determines the network is a solution to the problem.

Sometimes an entire task can be cast as a CSP, but such circumstances are relatively rare. Typically it makes more sense to decompose a complex task into subproblems, some of which can naturally be formulated as CSPs (e.g., providing a restricted set of temporal inferences within a planner). In these cases symbolic relaxation provides a filter that can significantly speed up additional searches. This is yet another example of the divide-and-conquer approach to designing problem solvers.

18.3 The WALTZER constraint engine

This section describes a general-purpose symbolic relaxation engine, called WALTZER in honor of David Waltz, who pioneered this class of algorithms. The code described here is `waltzer.lisp` in the listings. It is divided into three major sections: constructing constraint networks, propagation, and interrogatives.

18.3.1 Datastructures and initialization

WALTZER uses three main datastructures: `network`, `cell`, and `constraint`, which implement constraint networks, cells, and constraints, respectively. The parts of a `network` constraint are:

`title` String for printing.

`cells` Alist linking cells to their names.

`constraints` Alist linking constraints to their names.

`name-test` Procedure to use in looking up names.

`equality-test` Procedure for comparing cell values.

`cell-queue` Queue of operations on cells.

`constraint-queue` Queue of constraints to update.

`timestamp` Global clock, useful in explanations.

`event-list` List of constraint updates, also useful in explanations.

`debug?` Controls printing of information about internal operations.

`status` One of `:NEW`, `:QUIESCENT`, `:IN-PROGRESS`, `:OVERCONSTRAINED`.

`contradiction-reason` If non-`nil`, a cell currently overconstrained.

`contradiction-hook` Procedure to call when overconstrained.

`plist` Cache for storing miscellaneous information about the network.

The procedure `create-network` builds constraint networks. The `name-test` and `equality-test` fields are provided to facilitate domain-specific naming conventions and allow flexibility in defining the domains of cells. The procedure `contradiction-hook` provides a signaling mechanism that external systems can use to receive notification of problems.

Cells have the following properties:

`name` Name used for indexing.

`network` The constraint network it belongs to.

`value` Current set of consistent values.

`constraints` Set of constraints it participates in.

`possible-values` Domain of the cell.

`out-reasons` Alist of reasons for each value excluded from the domain.

`plist` Cache for miscellaneous information about it.

The list of `out-reasons` provides a dependency record. If the entry for a value is `:IN`, it is believed to be consistent. Otherwise, the entry is a pair consisting of the constraint responsible for excluding the value and a time stamp indicating when in the propagation sequence the exclusion took place. As with antecedent constraint languages, a general-purpose TMS would not be appropriate for symbolic relaxation. In pattern-directed systems, the dependency network constructed by the rules is the only long-term expression of the relationships between facts. A constraint network itself plays that role, so the caching provided by the dependency network would be redundant. There is another reason as well: constructing reasonable and efficient justifications for this style of reasoning by exclusion is quite tricky (see Exercise 2).

Cells are created by the procedure `build-cell`, which expects a name, network, and list of values constituting the domain of that cell. How constraints are built depends on the specifics of the domain, so the procedure `add-constraint-cell` is provided for use by constraint constructors to ensure that the cell is updated appropriately.

Constraints have the following properties:

`name` Name used for indexing.

`network` Constraint network it belongs to.

`parts` Cells the constraint relates.

`update-procedure` Procedure to call to update it.

`queued?` If non-`nil`, already queued.

`plist` Cache for miscellaneous properties.

We place no restrictions on the format of the `parts` field of the constraint, so that domain-specific constructors can organize it as desired. We use the field `update-procedure` to hold the domain-specific procedure for accomplishing that constraint's update.

When a network is first built, it contains neither cells nor constraints. We assume external procedures call `build-cell` and `build-constraint` as necessary to create the constituents of the network. Since constraints do not hold changeable state aside from their cells in this model, `clear-network` simply initializes each cell, clears the event list, and zeros the time stamp. `clear-cell` refreshes the cell's `value` and `out-reasons` fields from its list of possible values.

Often, solving a network requires backtracking. WALTZER supports backtracking by caching on each cell's property list a stack of previous states. This is indicated by the property `:STACK`. Each entry on `:STACK` consists of a copy of the `value` and `out-reasons` for the cell. The procedure `push-network` causes each cell to push its state onto its local stack, and caches the network's current time stamp and event list under its own `:STACK` property. The procedure `pop-network` causes every cell to restore its state and restores the previous time stamp and event list.

18.3.2 The relaxation algorithm: Implementation

We begin with the operations on cells. The procedures are

(`exclude` ⟨*cell*⟩ ⟨*value*⟩ ⟨*informant*⟩)
(`pick` ⟨*cell*⟩ ⟨*value*⟩ ⟨*informant*⟩)

`exclude` rules out ⟨*value*⟩ as a possibility for ⟨*cell*⟩, citing the constraint ⟨*informant*⟩ as the source of this decision. Similarly, `pick` forces ⟨*value*⟩ to be the only possibility for ⟨*cell*⟩. Providing a symbol as the informant (e.g., the default `:USER`) allows the same procedures to be used as interfaces to external systems. `exclude` first checks to see if the value is still believed as a possibility, by fetching its entry on `cell-out-reasons` and testing whether `:IN` is listed as its state. If so, it starts the actual exclusion process. The first step is to update the `cell-out-reasons` entry, setting it to be the pair of the informant and network time stamp. This information aids in debugging and explanation. Second, the value is deleted from the list of possible values for the cell (i.e., `cell-value`). If that was the last possibility, `signal-contradiction` is called to mark the event. Finally, the constraints that use the newly restricted cell are queued to see if yet more restrictions can be applied.

`pick` operates via exclusion. That is, assuming the value selected is still in the running (as detected by `:IN` in its entry within the `cell-out-reasons` alist), `pick` simply calls `exclude` on every other value for that cell. Should the selected value have been ruled out for some reason, `signal-contradiction` is called to mark the event.

The procedure `update` is an internal procedure which runs the update procedure associated with a constraint. Since we treat constraint update procedures as black boxes, we call `constraint-update-procedure` on the constraint itself. This gives the procedure full access to any information stored in `constraint-parts` or `constraint-plist`.

Constraint update procedures should not call `pick` and `exclude` directly. Instead, the procedure `queue-cell` is provided which constructs the appropriate call to `exclude` or `pick`, placing it on the network's queue for cells.

The internal procedure `fire-constraints` services a constraint network's queues. It first checks to see whether the network is overconstrained and immediately halts if it is so. The reason is that an overconstrained cell will tend to wipe out the values for any cells connected to it, since the constraints attached to it cannot be satisfied. This is one reason why cell updates are queued rather than allowing constraint update procedures to directly call `exclude` and `pick`. Ideally one might insist that constraint update procedures avoid operating when their cells are overconstrained, but centralizing this test provides an additional level of safety.

If the network is not overconstrained, `fire-constraints` proceeds to empty the queues. It performs all cell updates before any constraint updates to ensure that the full consequences of each constraint are recorded before the next constraint is used. The global time stamp is incremented with each constraint update, since these are the major events in the system. When all the queues are empty, the network's status is set to `:QUIESCENT`. The network status `:IN-PROGRESS` indicates that there are still things to do on the queue; this flag is handy for detecting when a non-local exit has occurred.

Since cells can participate in multiple constraints, `queue-constraint` checks the `constraint-queued?` flag before doing anything, to avoid queuing something twice. (In correctly written update procedures executing a constraint redundantly will not cause errors, but it does waste time.)

The interface procedure `check-constraints` starts the whole process going by queueing all the constraints and running the network (by calling `fire-constraints`) until it becomes quiescent or a contradiction is uncovered.

`signal-contradiction` sets up the network for contradiction handling and calls the contradiction handler associated with the network. It starts by updating the network's `status` field and caches the overconstrained cell in the network's `contradiction-reason` field. A non-`nil` value in `network-contradiction-hook` is presumed to be a procedure for handling contradictions, which is executed with the constraint network itself as its sole argument.

18.3.3 Additional interface procedures

The procedures `lookup-cell` and `lookup-constraint` retrieve a named cell or constraint from a network.

The procedures `what-are`, `determined?`, and `to-plunk` interrogate the state of a constraint network. `what-are` prints the status of the network and the values remaining for each of its cells. `determined?` returns non-`nil` if the network has settled into a stable configuration where every cell has a unique value. `to-plunk` returns a list of cells which are not yet fully constrained.

The procedures `what-is`, `known?`, and `value` interrogate the state of a given cell. `what-is` prints the cell's remaining possible values. `known?` returns non-`nil` if the cell is determined (i.e., has exactly one possible value), and `value` returns that value.

Finally, the listing of WALTZER ends with a simple depth-first search routine, `search-network`. It takes two arguments: a procedure to execute when a consistent solution has been found, and a procedure to call whenever the network has become contradictory. The local procedure `search-thru-plunkable-cells` does the actual work. It is called with a list of underconstrained cells (found via the call to `to-plunk`) and a string. The string is for printing if the debugging flag is on, so that the depth in the search will be apparent.

The structure of `search-thru-plunkable-cells` is very similar to earlier search procedures. It starts by seeing if the network is overconstrained. If it is, the contradiction procedure given to `search-network` is executed. Next it checks to see if the network is fully determined. If it is, the procedure for consistent solutions (`consistent-proc`) is executed. In both of these cases, `search-thru-plunkable-cells` simply returns after executing the appropriate procedure because any backtracking is presumed to be handled by its caller. The third `cond` clause is an error check: given that `search-thru-plunkable-cells` is always called with the entire list of underconstrained cells, and each successive call selects a value for one of the cells, then the only way for the list of cells to be empty is for the network to be overconstrained or determined. Finally, it iterates over each value for the first underconstrained cell, trying each value in turn. It does this by saving the network state (via `push-`

network), selecting the current value (via pick), running the network (via fire-constraints), and recursing. No matter what the outcome, pop-network is executed to restore the network to its previous state so that the next value may be tried.

A simple example of how search-network can be used is provided by show-search, which uses say-solution and say-contradiction to display the progress and results of a search.

18.4 Example: Scene labeling

Vision is an extremely complex problem. It has been studied for hundreds of years by psychologists, philosophers, and other intellectuals. More recently, understanding vision has been a major focus of the computational models formulated in artificial intelligence and cognitive science. Nevertheless, the problem of how we come to know the world through our senses still retains an air of mystery.

As our understanding of vision grows, our perspectives on it change. For example, a popular decomposition in the late 1960s and early 1970s divided the problem of monocular vision into *line finding* and *scene analysis*. Line finding took as input an array of intensity data and found "significant" discontinuities, producing a result something like a line drawing of the objects in the visual scene. Scene analysis interpreted line drawings in terms of three-dimensional objects, dividing the lines and vertices into collections representing distinct objects. The responsibility for the signal-processing aspects resided in the line finders, and the responsibility for object semantics resided in the scene analysis module.

Something like this decomposition is still common in vision research today, since it seems that the nature of the physical world provides the dominant constraints on the signal-processing aspects of vision [10], while the uses to which vision is put provide the dominant constraints on semantic interpretations [3]. However, our example in this section is drawn from a simpler time. Consider the vision version of the Blocks World, where scenes consist entirely of a collection of toy blocks on a uniform surface. While camera angles can vary, we assume that the scene is lit so that there are no shadows, and that the blocks are perfect matte surfaces,[1] and we ignore clues from texture, stereo, and motion. These were common simplifying assumptions in the early 1970s. Furthermore, we will assume that our line finder produces "perfect" data—that is, descriptions delivered by the line finder consist entirely of connected straight lines and vertices, with no isolated blotches, no gaps in the lines, etc.

A theme of scene analysis during that period was identifying local properties of the scene which provided hints about the appropriate three-dimensional interpretation of the scene, and then combining these hints into a consistent global account which decomposed the regions of the image into objects. Guzman identified several local cues based on configural properties of vertices. Other researchers, including Huffman, Clowes, and Waltz, extended and systematized this approach into intricate and massive catalogs of knowledge that included aspects such as detailed geometry and lighting information. Delving into the details of these theories would take us too far afield, so we must content ourselves with a simplification, due to Winston [16].

Suppose we limit ourselves not just to blocks, but further assume trihedral vertices, that is, that no more than three physical surfaces ever come together at a point. Recall also that we are assuming uniform lighting, so there are no shadows, and that all surfaces are matte, ruling out highlights. Consider what a line in the scene might mean under these circumstances. It could be the boundary of an object. If it is, we still have to figure out which side of the line corresponds to the object and which side belongs to the background (i.e., which part is "figure" and which part "ground.") Another possible interpretation for the line is that it indicates a discontinuity between distinct surfaces of the same object. In that case the discontinuity could be either convex or concave. Each of these possible interpretations can be given a distinct label, as shown in Figure 4. Notice that the <, > labels give us the ability to identify a collection of lines as an object, by traversing the boundary and including all edges "inside" it. This means our representation is suitable for our needs, since finding objects is exactly what we wanted to do. But how do we compute these interpretations?

---

1. That is, there are no highlights or shiny parts. A layer or two of titanium dioxide paint implements this simplification quite nicely.

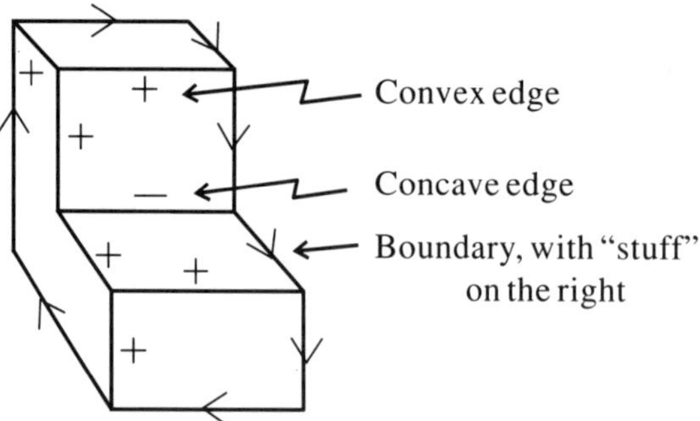

Figure 18.1 Semantics of line labels

The approach taken by Waltz was to analyze the physics of the domain, and construct a catalog of consistent possible interpretations for each type of junction. This catalog could then be used to interpret particular scenes by symbolic relaxation, using the fact that a line participates in two junctions to provide mutual constraint. (An important aspect of Waltz's work was that he tackled a much more complete version of the Blocks World, including cracks and shadows, but the simpler version suffices for our purposes.) Given the additional restrictions we have imposed, Figure 18.2, taken from [16], provides the appropriate junction catalog.

How can we now encode this problem in WALTZER? Clearly, lines will be represented by cells, whose possible values are +, −, <, and >. Junctions, too, must be represented as cells. The possible values of a junction cell are the elements corresponding to that type of junction in the junction catalog. We then need a type of constraint that links the cell representing a junction to the cells representing the participating lines. With these issues in mind, let us turn to the `scene.lisp` listing.

We begin by considering datastructures for scenes and junction catalogs. A scene is a WALTZER constraint network, stored as the value of the global variable `*scene*`. The global variable `*jlabel-table*` holds the junction catalog, and `*line-labels*` is a constant representing the possible interpretations of lines. The variables `*scene-file*` and `*jcatalog-file*` point to default examples. A driving routine is provided by `analyze-scene`, which takes a file containing a scene and a file containing a junction catalog, loads them, and analyzes them. The analysis is done by `interpret-scene`, which operates WALTZER on the

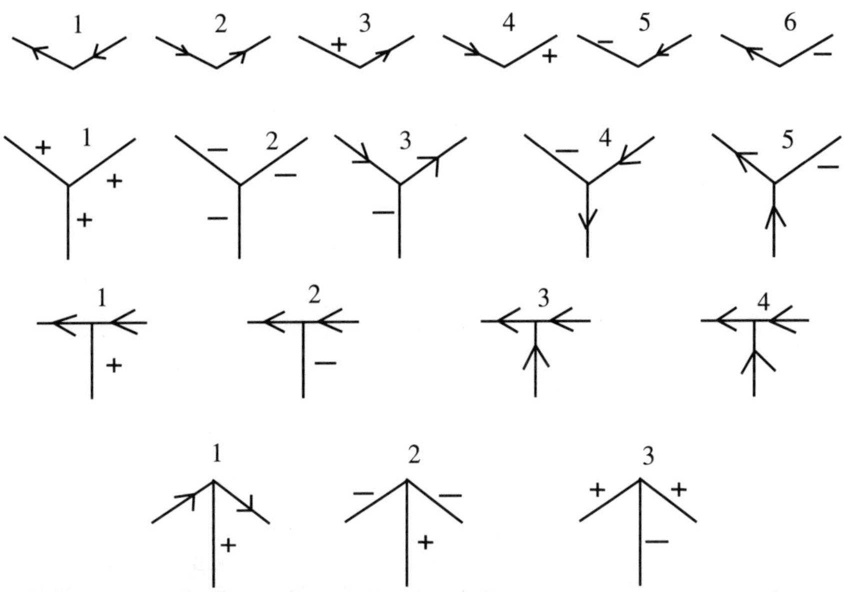

Figure 18.2 A junction catalog for the simple Blocks World. This catalog graphically depicts the possible junctions and their interpretations for a simplified Blocks World. (This figure is based on Figure 3-15, Page 55, of [16]).

constraint network. The procedure `show-scene` is essentially a variant of `what-are`, exploiting knowledge about the order of cell definition to present the results of these networks in a more intuitive manner.

The core of the junction catalog implementation is the `jlabel` struct. The `type` field refers to the geometric configuration of this junction. In our example vocabulary this field can be either `Ell`, `Fork`, `Tee`, or `Arrow`. The `name` field distinguishes different labels of the same type. We use integers for simplicity. The `lines` field describes the assignment of interpretations a catalog entry makes to its constituent lines. Each constituent line is given a unique name, such as `:LEFT`, `:RIGHT`, or `:BOTTOM`. These names are used as keys in an alist, linking the line to the interpretation forced by that junction label. The macro `junction-labeling` provides a simple way to enter elements of a junction catalog. Figure 18.3 shows how our junction catalog can be encoded in this way. The procedure `read-junction-catalog` assumes that the file it is given consists of calls to `junction-labeling`. It loads a new junction catalog by clearing the existing one and evaluating the forms in the file one by one.

```
(junction-labeling Ell 1 :LEFT < :RIGHT <)
(junction-labeling Ell 2 :LEFT > :RIGHT >)
(junction-labeling Ell 3 :LEFT + :RIGHT >)
(junction-labeling Ell 4 :LEFT > :RIGHT +)
(junction-labeling Ell 5 :LEFT - :RIGHT <)
(junction-labeling Ell 6 :LEFT < :RIGHT -)

(junction-labeling Fork 1 :LEFT + :RIGHT + :BOTTOM +)
(junction-labeling Fork 2 :LEFT - :RIGHT - :BOTTOM -)
(junction-labeling Fork 3 :LEFT > :RIGHT > :BOTTOM -)
(junction-labeling Fork 4 :LEFT - :RIGHT < :BOTTOM <)
(junction-labeling Fork 5 :LEFT < :RIGHT - :BOTTOM >)

(junction-labeling Tee 1 :LEFT < :RIGHT < :BOTTOM +)
(junction-labeling Tee 2 :LEFT < :RIGHT < :BOTTOM -)
(junction-labeling Tee 3 :LEFT < :RIGHT < :BOTTOM <)
(junction-labeling Tee 4 :LEFT < :RIGHT < :BOTTOM >)

(junction-labeling Arrow 1 :LEFT > :RIGHT > :BOTTOM +)
(junction-labeling Arrow 2 :LEFT - :RIGHT - :BOTTOM +)
(junction-labeling Arrow 3 :LEFT + :RIGHT + :BOTTOM -)
```

Figure 18.3 Implementing a junction catalog (`jcatalog.lisp`)

Next in the listing is the code for building a particular scene. As usual, we use macros to define a syntax that insulates users from the internals of the implementation.

The `Scene` macro creates a WALTZER constraint network. Any additional arguments are passed along under the assumption that they are keyword-value pairs recognized by `create-network`.

The `Line` macro creates a cell for a line in the scene, and the `Junction` macro creates a cell for a junction in the scene. We restrict line and junction names to be symbols, in order to simplify interacting with the program. The connections between lines and junctions are expressed via additional arguments to the `Junction` macro. The additional arguments are alternating keyword-value pairs, where the keywords are the named roles for the lines found in that type of junction. A constraint is created for each junction, with `constraint-parts` `setf`ed as needed and using `add-constraint-cell` to install the appropriate backpointers.

The only subtlety concerns `parse-junction-parts`, which checks the correctness of the format of a list of constituent lines. Such tests are necessary both in defining a junction catalog (so a vision catalog-builder won't include a sequence like `:LEFT :RIGHT`) and in reading a description of a specific junction. Although the actions to be taken for these purposes are different, the underlying logic of the traversal is the same. Consequently, we use a third argument, `to-do`, to provide an appropriate procedure to executed for each part name and role found.

Since constraints are associated with junctions, we name the constraint update procedure `update-junction`. We must do two things to correctly enforce the semantics of labels. First, we must see what labels are still possible for the junction based on the labels for its constituent lines. For example, if the `:BOTTOM` line of a `FORK` can only be either + or - , two possible labelings out of five for that junction can be ruled out as inconsistent. Once the set of consistent junction labels is computed, we can reverse this process to determine the implications of the new restricted set of junction labels for the labels of the constituent lines. In our `FORK` example, for instance, ruling out > and < for `:BOTTOM` means the only possible labels for `:LEFT` and `:RIGHT` are +, -, and > (see again Figure 18.3). While no more work can be done within this constraint (since we already know that the junction labels are consistent with the existing line labels), WALTZER queues the constraints corresponding to the other junction associated with each constituent line. This queuing ensures that the effects of these constraints will propagate.

The propagation step is carried out in `update-junction` as follows. The outermost `do` loops through the junction labels, ascertaining which are consistent. This test is made using `check-junction-label`, which returns `T` if the label is inconsistent. A call to `queue-cell` causes the failed label to be removed when the constraint is finished. Should the label be consistent, we cache the interpretations it assigns to the constituent lines in `possible-line-labels`. This variable accumulates the legal possibilities for each constituent line, and is used in the `dolist` in the exit form of the outermost `do` to exclude line labels which cannot satisfy the new set of junction labels. For debugging it is sometimes handy to examine the junction constraints in detail; `show-junction` and `show-junctions` simplify this.

The listings contain two examples, `cube.lisp` and `wedge.lisp`. Drawings corresponding to these descriptions are shown in Figure 18.4. Let us see how WALTZER does on these examples.

Figure 18.5 illustrates the results of the cube search. The drawing on the left shows what labelings are possible after symbolic relaxation.

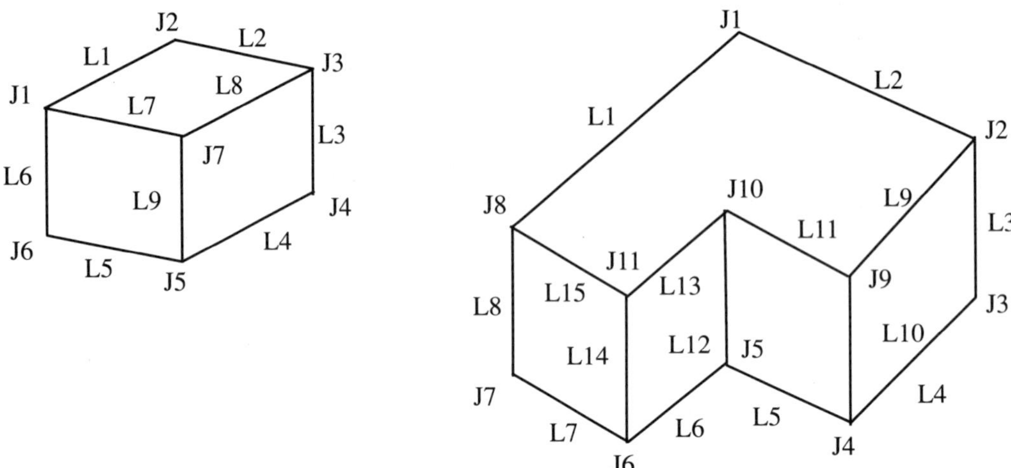

Figure 18.4 Two scene analysis examples. The scene described in `cube.lisp` is depicted on the left, and the scene described in `wedge.lisp` is depicted on the right.

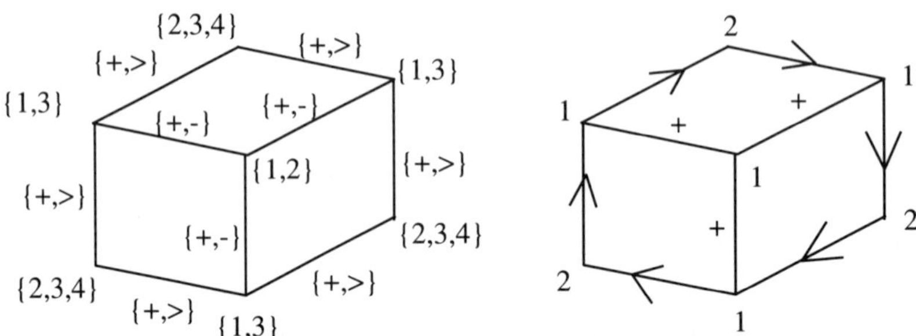

Figure 18.5 Analyzing the cube. On the left is the set of labels as pruned via symbolic relaxation, on the right is the sole consistent solution to the network, as found by a backtracking search on the pruned network. One additional choice sufficed to completely constrain the network.

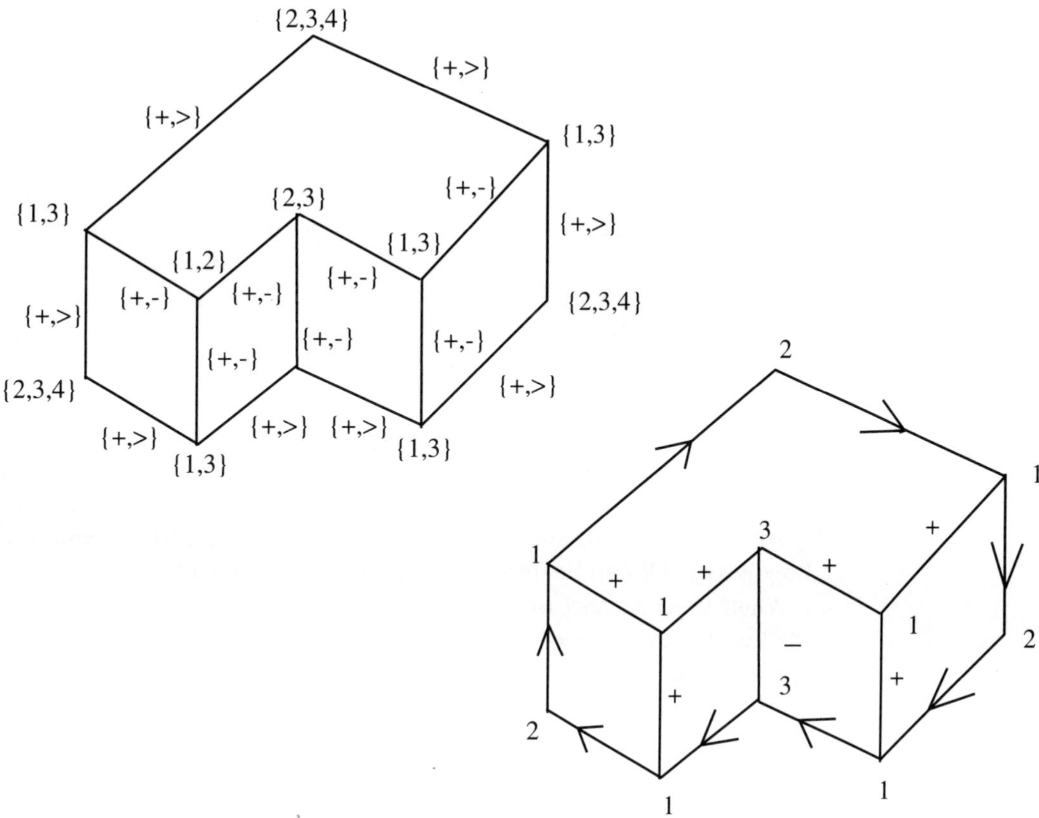

Figure 18.6 Analysis of the Wedge scene. The top drawing shows the possible labels computed via symbolic relaxation, the bottom shows the single consistent labeling found via backtracking search on the constrained network.

Local propagation has ruled out roughly half of the possible solutions, it seems. However, when the network is searched, only one consistent solution is found, namely the labeling shown on the right of Figure 18.5. A single plunk suffices to completely constrain the network.

The analysis for the wedge scene (`wedge.lisp`) is illustrated in Figure 18.6. Like the cube, symbolic relaxation does not provide a complete solution, but a single plunk suffices.

18.5 Example: Temporal reasoning

Serious AI research into temporal reasoning did not begin until the 1980s. One of the pioneers in this area was James Allen, whose interval-based temporal logic [1, 2] has had significant impact. Allen pointed out several important aspects of temporal reasoning. First, conclusions about temporal ordering often are drawn with very little information. For instance, if you knew that if Fred left the scene of a crime before Ricky arrived, and you also knew that Ricky and Ethel arrived together, then you would conclude that Fred also left before Ethel arrived. This obvious inference does not require specific dates, times, numerical estimates of duration, or other more detailed information. It follows solely from laws constraining the relationships between the intervals corresponding to the events "Fred left," "Ricky arrived," and "Ethel arrived." Allen identified a vocabulary of relationships that could hold between intervals and a set of laws expressing constraints between them. This section shows how WALTZER can be used to implement this logic of time.

When used as part of a larger inferential system, intervals are associated with facts or events. For our purposes, intervals are simply atomic entities. The relational vocabulary in Allen's logic consists of seven temporal relationships and their inverses:

`before(A,B)` A's entire temporal extent is earlier than B's. The inverse of `before` is `after`.

`during(A,B)` A's temporal extent lies completely within B's. The inverse of `during` is `contains`.

`equal(A,B)` A's temporal extent is exactly the same as B's. `equal` is its own inverse.

`overlaps(A,B)` B begins sometime in the middle of A, and ends sometime after A does. The inverse of `overlaps` is `overlapped-by`.

`meets(A,B)` A ends just before B begins, with no time "in between." The inverse of `meets` is `met-by`.

`starts(A,B)` A and B start at exactly the same time. The inverse of `starts` is `started-by`.

`finishes(A,B)` A and B end at exactly the same time. The inverse of `finishes` is `finished-by`.

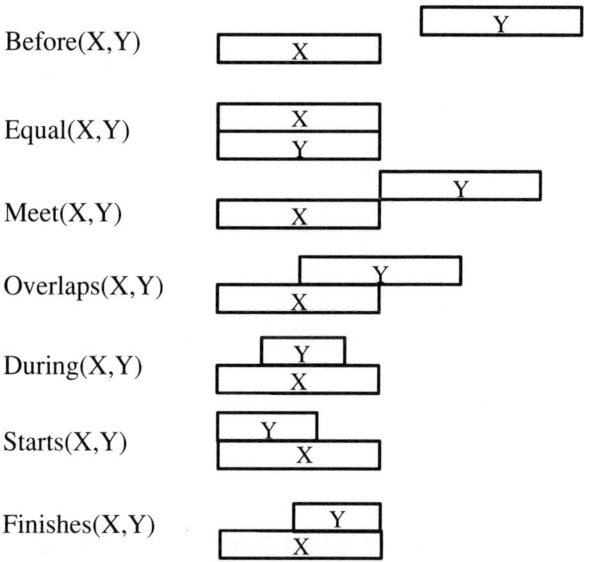

Figure 18.7 Allen's temporal logic, illustrated

These relationships are depicted graphically in Figure 18.7. They are mutually exclusive and exhaustive. In what follows it will prove convenient to introduce concise abbreviations for these relationships. From now on we use Allen's abbreviations, namely

```
< = before       > = after
d = during       di = contains
= = equal
o = overlaps     oi = overlapped-by
m = meets        mi = met-by
s = starts       si = started-by
f = finishes     fi = finished-by
```

Allen focused on cases involving partial information. Often, only disjunctive information is known. That is, we may know that only a subset of all of the possible relationships between two intervals may hold, but not know exactly which one. For simplicity in presentation, we use Allen's compact infix notation for stating such disjunctions. For instance,

```
A { <,> } B
```

indicates that [Before(A,B) ∨ After(A,B)] holds. If we know nothing about the relationship between A and B, we would write

```
A { <,>,d,di,=,o,oi,m,mi,s,si,f,fi } B
```

Already one can begin to see how to cast this logic as a symbolic relaxation problem: each possible relationship between pairs of intervals is a cell, whose domain is the set of legal temporal relationships. What are the constraints?

The example at the beginning of this section used the property of *transitivity*. Given that we knew something about the relationship between interval A and interval B and something about the relationship between B and another interval C, we could use those facts to restrict the possible temporal relationships between A and C. Allen derived a table that expresses, for each possible relationship between two pairs of intervals satisfying this pattern, the inferences one may draw through transitivity (see allen2.lisp). For example, if A meets B and B meets C, then clearly A is before B. On the other hand, if B is during C, then A either overlaps, starts, or is during C. Some combinations of relationships are more constraining than others.

The transitivity table can be used to restrict the possible relations between two intervals A, C as follows. For any intervals I_1, I_2, let $R(I_1,I_2)$ stand for the set of possible relationships between them. If we knew nothing about the relationship between I_1 and I_2 then

$$R(I_1,I_2) = \{<,>,d,di,=,o,oi,m,mi,s,si,f,fi\}$$

Suppose we have R(A,B), R(B,C), and R(A,C). Whatever we currently know about the relationship between A and C, it must be the case that it is consistent with the possibilities implied by transitivity. The possibilities for any particular pair of relationships drawn from R(A,B) and R(B,C) can be found by using the transitivity table. This means the entire set of possibilities can be found by taking the union of the transitivity results for each pair in the cross product of R(A,B) and R(B,C). Taking the intersection of this set with our previous value of R(A,C) provides a new value for R(A,C) that respects the constraints imposed by transitivity.

The simplest implementation of this scheme has some scary combinatorics. Suppose we have N intervals in our knowledge base. Potentially every interval could be related to every other interval, yielding N^2 intervals. Then, since each triple of intervals could in principle yield some constraints, we would end up installing N^3 constraints. If N is very large, such as the set of named times distinguished in a person's life, this scheme clearly breaks down. Allen proposed using *reference intervals* to structure one's times and thus reduce combinatorics. A reference interval is an interval which spans some substantial number of connected events, such as "being in college" or "living in Barstow." Reference intervals provide an index. Relationships between intervals stored under the same reference interval could be introduced at will, while relationships between intervals belonging to different reference intervals would be minimized. The challenge with reference intervals is to maintain expressiveness while preventing relationships from "leaking" between them. At this writing, ideas like reference intervals are still the subject of active research.

18.5.1 Design for a temporal database

A *temporal database* is a reasoning utility that maintains relationships between intervals. We can cast the algorithm above as a constraint satisfaction problem and thus provide a foundation for temporal databases. Cells in the constraint network represent the relationships between intervals. Constraints introduced for each "triangle" of relationships in the network enforce the consequences of transitivity. WALTZER's enforcement of arc consistency provides a good trade-off of efficiency versus completeness.

WALTZER provides most of the infrastructure we need to build a temporal database. We still need representations for intervals themselves, methods for incrementally building a constraint network, and procedures for constraint updating. Here we consider their design, leaving their implementation to the next section.

Typically an interval of time is distinguished from the rest of the continuum because it marks the temporal span of some event, object, or process. Two examples are the life span of the Golden Gate Bridge and the time it takes to read this sentence. The criteria for individuating intervals does not matter for our purposes, so it shall be left unspecified. To keep the design simple, the only non-temporal information specified about an interval will be its name. Some reference mechanism must be provided to make intervals accessible to external systems and to link them to a WALTZER network. We assume this job is done by the temporal database itself.

Since the temporal logic constrains relationships between intervals, some manner of asserting and recording such relationships is needed. Relating two intervals may also cause the temporal database to add new constraints, since new triangles may be formed. To keep the design simple, we install constraints for every triple of intervals that are mutually related and do not provide any representation for reference intervals.

A major job of the temporal database is setting up and running the WALTZER constraint network. As noted above, each relationship between intervals is represented in the constraint network as a cell, and each triple of relationships over which transitivity holds must have an associated constraint. Whenever information about the relationship between two intervals is given to the temporal database, it must:

1. Extend the network to include a cell for that relationship if it does not already exist.
2. Add the new information to whatever constraints have already been placed on that relationship.
3. Propagate this new constraint through the network to restrict other temporal relationships.

Previously determined restrictions must be respected for correct incremental operation. For instance, asserting that "Shakespeare did not live during the pre-Cambrian era" (i.e., every relationship except `d` is possible) adds no information if we already know that Shakespeare lived after the pre-Cambrian era.

Here is the outline of the interface we shall use.

`create-timedb` Creates a new temporal database.

`interval` Creates a new interval within the current temporal database.

`tassert` Places restrictions on the possible relationships between two intervals.

`what-time` Describes the possible relationships between two intervals.

We turn to the implementation to examine the details.

18.5.2 Implementation of a temporal database

The system consists of three files:

`timedb.lisp` Temporal database and definitions.

`allen.lisp` Definition of Allen's transitivity table.

`ttest.lisp` Simple test cases.

Since the transitivity table and test cases are straightforward, we only describe `timedb.lisp` in detail.

Temporal databases are implemented via the `timedb` struct. Many of this struct's fields should now be very familiar. It uses the usual method of introducing a global variable (in this case, `*timedb*`) as a register for simplifying reference to a current temporal database, with `in-timedb` and `with-timedb` providing global and local methods for changing what database is in use. The `intervals` field stores the intervals for the database, with `interval-id` providing a unique index for each such interval. The `relations` field holds the possible temporal relationships. This is made an explicit field of temporal databases rather than a global or a constant to support experimenting with alternative temporal vocabularies (see Exercise 7). The `transitivity-table` field holds tables in the form of nested alists. The `network` field holds the WALTZER constraint network associated with the database.

The `interval` struct provides the internal representation of intervals. The `name` field holds the name for this interval used by external systems. For simplicity, we assume that intervals are given names whose identity can be established by `eql` (i.e., typically symbols). To avoid the redundancy of building distinct cells for `R(A,B)` and `R(B,A)`, we impose a total ordering on intervals, and only create a relationship between two intervals in the canonical order. The procedure `interval-order` calculates the ordering of two intervals based on the information in the interval's `index` field. The `timedb` field points to the temporal database the interval is part of. The `relations` field of an interval is an index of relationships with other intervals. This index is an alist whose keys are other intervals and whose values are the constraint network cells corresponding to their relationship.

Relationships between intervals are accessed via `lookup-trel`, which uses `assoc` on the `interval-relations` fields. The `virtual?` argument forces the creation of a relationship if there isn't one already. New temporal relationships are created via `make-trel`, which builds a cell, indexes it under the `interval-relations` fields for its constituent intervals, and calls `find-transitive-relations` to figure out what new constraints, if any, should be created as a result.

`find-transitive-relations` begins by destructuring the cell's name to get the intervals of the newly created relationship. The `dolist` iterates over each relationship involving the first interval to find candidate third intervals to complete a triangle. The candidates are then tested by `assoc` to see if they are related to the second interval. The dispatch based on interval order when creating a transitivity constraint is due to the constraint update procedure expecting its arguments in a particular order, that is, `R(A,B)`, `R(B,C)`, `R(A,C)`. The actual constraint construction is carried out by `build-transitive-constraint`.

`update-trel-transitivity` provides the update procedure for constraints. It first computes `Possibles(A,C)` via `update-possible-trel-values`, and then finds what subset of `R(A,C)` is consequently forbidden (through the `set-difference` call). An `exclude` operation is queued for each forbidden value, thus enforcing the constraint. `update-possible-trel-values` is very simple, implementing the cross product by nested `dolists` and using `lookup-transitive-trels` to fetch the appropriate table entry. `lookup-transitive-trels`, in turn, consists of nested `assocs`.

The rest of the file `timedb.lisp` is concerned with interfaces. The macros `interval` and `tassert` provide constructors. `interval` creates a new interval within the current temporal database with its given name. `tassert` specifies that two intervals should be viewed as related. If the third argument to `tassert` is not provided, every relationship is viewed as possible. Otherwise, the third argument is interpreted as the list of possible relationships for that pair of intervals. (This interface is not bulletproof; see Exercise 5.)

The real work of `tassert` is carried out by the procedure `temporal-relations`, which does the appropriate error checking and transactions with the constraint network. Any relationships not consistent with the possibilities provided are ruled out (via the `exclude` call), and the consequences of these restrictions are propagated (via the call to `fire-constraints`).

The procedure `what-time` displays the possible relationships between two given intervals, and `what-times` summarizes the relationships for the whole temporal database. The subroutine `make-relations-string` provides the appropriate infix string for a list of relationships, allowing `what-time` (and hence `what-times`) to produce easily readable results.

The end of `timedb.lisp` contains two macros for defining temporal logics. Both operate with respect to the current temporal database. (Recall that `create-timedb` takes a file as an argument; these macros are used to define the contents of such files.) The macro `defTemporal-Relation` declares a symbol to be a temporal relationship. The macro `t-transitivity` defines an entry in a transitivity table. These macros substantially simplify entering large tables.

The file `ttest.lisp` contains some test cases.

18.6 Discussion

We have seen that sometimes problems, or pieces of them, can be cast as constraint satisfaction problems. The CSP formulation provides an alternative perspective on characterizing reasoning tasks. This perspective is useful in two ways. First, by recognizing that a task can be characterized as a particular form of CSP we then have solid bounds on how hard it is. Second, in some cases we can identify computational schemes with advantageous power-efficiency trade-offs (e.g., the use of arc consistency) and use off-the-shelf systems as modules (e.g., WALTZER).

There are limitations to this approach, however. Conclusions reached via arc consistency algorithms can be hard to explain, since chains of exclusion can be hard to follow (see Exercise 1). For most finite CSP tasks, the increased opacity is a small price to pay for the greatly reduced need for search.

Casting subproblems as CSPs allows specialized systems like WALTZER to shoulder part of the computational burden, but there are engineering tradeoffs which must be carefully examined when making such hybrid systems. Adding new possible values or removing constraints, for instance, typically requires reinitializing the entire network because of the difficulty of maintaining detailed dependencies. In architectures for solving complex problems, such as scheduling systems, the increased design effort to integrate disparate subsystems generally pays off.

18.7 Backpointers

There is a rapidly growing literature on constraint satisfaction problems. [12] provides a good survey, while [6, 11] explore the connections between CSP and logic. [5] focuses on the use of intervals. [13] explores a generalization of the notion of CSP to cover problems where the collection of relevant choice sets changes as a function of the choices that are made. Constraint satisfaction continues to be useful for scene analysis, interested readers may find [4, 9, 15] useful starting points into the literature.

18.8 Exercises

1. ⋆⋆ Often it is useful to understand why a specific value for a cell is ruled out or forced. Write a procedure `explain-exclusion` which generates a readable explanation of why a value was ruled out. In addition to taking as inputs a cell and a value, your procedure should also take an optional integer argument which limits how far back in the network's operation the explanation goes.

2. Suppose you wanted to incorporate a JTMS into WALTZER in order to provide a more detailed trace of its operation.

    a. ⋆⋆ Propose a set of conventions for assertions and justifications on them that would accurately express WALTZER's operation.

    b. ⋆⋆ Analyze the efficiency of your proposal, in terms of the number of justifications required as a function of the size of the network and the size of the domains of the cells.

3. A WALTZER constraint network can be thought of as a scratch pad to be used by other reasoning processes. Sometimes alternate interpretations must be explored in parallel. One way to do this is to create

duplicate constraint networks. Another way is to provide a facility for naming and saving states of the network. These saved states can be compared to facilitate the manipulation of alternate solutions.

a. ⋆ Change WALTZER to enable saving states of the network under particular names.

b. ⋆ Implement a procedure that compares two saved network states, indicating how they differ in a program-usable form.

c. ⋆⋆ Implement a version of `search-network` that explores completions of a constraint network breadth first, and analyze its performance by comparing it to `search-network` on several examples. Which works better, and why?

4. ⋆⋆ What do you expect to happen if the scene analysis system is given an impossible figure, such as the one below? What should happen? What actually happens?

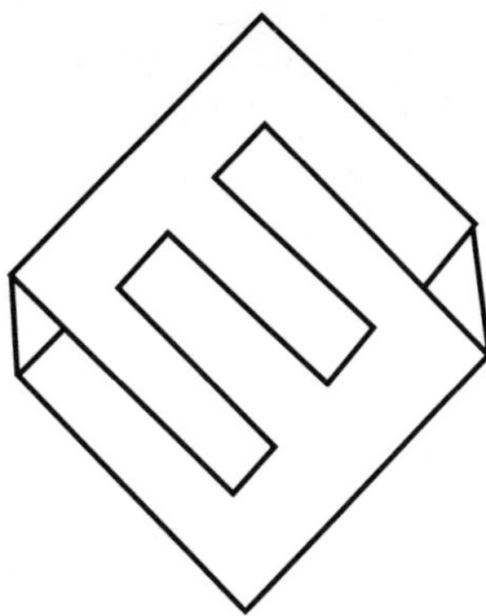

5. ⋆ The interface to the temporal database is not as robust as our earlier systems. Identify the major problems with `interval` and `tassert`, then write new versions that fix them.

6. ⋆⋆⋆ One service a temporal database can provide is scheduling rules for execution when particular temporal conditions hold. For instance, a scheduling program might need to detect when two manufacturing operations requiring the same piece of equipment might

overlap. Design and implement a system which allows users to specify rules to be executed when particular temporal conditions are satisfied in a WALTZER temporal constraint network.

7. ⋆⋆ Allen's logic, while very expressive, requires a large transitivity table. Suppose the relationships `starts`, `finishes`, and `during` were merged into one relationship, called `within`. What effect does this have on (a) the transitivity table and (b) the utility of the vocabulary for reasoning?

8. ⋆⋆⋆ There has been some progress on formalizing topology in ways analogous to Allen's formalization of time, particularly the work of Randell and Cohn [14]. Implement their spatial vocabulary using WALTZER, and test it on the examples from their papers.

9. ⋆⋆⋆⋆ Design a system for reference intervals that scales to very large temporal databases.

18.9 Bibliography

[1] Allen, J. F., "Maintaining knowledge about temporal intervals," *Comm. ACM*, 26(1983):832-843.

[2] Allen, J. F. "Towards a general model of action and time," *Artificial Intelligence*, 23(1984):123-154.

[3] Brady, J. M. (ed.), *Computer Vision*, North Holland, 1981.

[4] Cooper, P. R. "Structure recognition by connectionist relaxation: Formal analysis," *Computational Intelligence*, 8(1992):25–44.

[5] Davis, E. "Constraint propagation with interval labels," *Artificial Intelligence*, 32(1987):281-331.

[6] de Kleer, J., "A comparison of ATMS and CPS techniques," *Proceedings of IJCAI89*, 1989, 290–296.

[7] Dechter, R., and Meiri, I., "Experimental evaluation of preprocessing techniques in constraint satisfaction problems," *Proceedings of IJCAI-89*, 1989.

[8] Dechter, R. "Constraint networks: A survey," in S. Shapiro, (ed.), *The Encyclopedia of AI*, second edition, Wiley, 1991.

[9] Grimson, W. E. L., *Object Recognition by Computer: The Role of Geometric Constraints*, MIT Press, 1990.

[10] Horn, B. K. P., *Robot Vision*, MIT Press, 1986.

[11] Mackworth, A. K., "The logic of constraint satisfaction," *Artificial Intelligence*, 58(1992):3–20.

[12] Mackworth, A. K., "Constraint Satisfaction," in Shapiro, S. (ed.), *Encyclopedia of Artificial Intelligence*, vol. 1, 2nd edition, Wiley, 1990.

[13] Mittal, S. and Falkenhainer, B., "Dynamic Constraint Satisfaction Problems," *Proceedings of AAAI-90*, 1990, 25-32

[14] Randell, D., and Cohn, A. "Modelling Topological and Metrical Properties in Physical Processes," *Proceedings of KR-89*, 1989.

[15] Reiter, R. and Mackworth, A. K., "A logical framework for depiction and image interpretation," *Artificial Intelligence*, 41(1990):125–155.

[16] Winston, P. H., *Artificial Intelligence*, 2nd edition, Addison-Wesley, 1984.

19 Some Frontiers

In the rest of the book, we have taken you quite deeply into the art and science of building problem solvers. Problem solver design and construction is not a finished field, by any means. Each chapter has included signposts marking the borders of what is known in the areas that they cover. Here we take a more global view. This chapter highlights some issues and challenges for the design of reasoning systems that we think are especially promising and important.

19.1 Constraint logic programming

Over the last few years ideas from declarative representation, constraint satisfaction and concurrency have come together to create the new subdiscipline called *Constraint Programming* [21, 11, 23]. Constraint programming incorporates pieces of many of the concepts we have discussed in this book. For example, the programming language CHIP [23] incorporates many of the best CSP techniques within a declarative framework using backtracking to construct solutions. However, the ambition of constraint programming goes far beyond that of this book. Its objective is to provide a fundamentally new perspective on computation and what programming is and should be. This subdiscipline has become an exciting new research area of world-wide interest. Over this decade we expect substantial cross-fertilization and collaboration among researchers developing problem solving techniques with AI and those developing constraint programming.

19.2 Scaling up

Problems come in many shapes and sizes. The technologies described in this book have been extensively applied to problems with up to a few thousand facts. Many economically important and intellectually challenging problems lie in this range. But many interesting problems, such as designing, monitoring, or troubleshooting a large industrial plant, understanding a broad range of natural language, or building robots that can work effectively in relatively unconstrained environments will require harnessing much more knowledge. Ballpark estimates of the number of common sense facts a person knows range from 10^6 to 10^8 facts. Even with today's rapid progress in computer hardware, the raw memory and CPU capacity required for robust reasoning with such large knowledge bases seems daunting. Nevertheless, encouraging research now into understanding how to develop and use large knowledge bases seems like a wise investment, so that we may take advantage of new hardware capabilities as they become available.

Reasoning with such large knowledge bases raises many new challenges. For example, storage and indexing techniques that both permit the high capacities of today's database technologies and support efficient inference must be developed. Even the definition of what is efficient changes as a function of scale: Linear processes like boolean constraint propagation may be fine for small databases, but only sublinear processes will suffice for knowledge bases approaching the size of what any person on the street knows. Just as important is the discovery of techniques for accumulating, organizing, and maintaining large knowledge bases. It is a chicken-and-egg problem; without large knowledge bases to experiment with, development of reasoning strategies is hindered, and without useful reasoning strategies, the incentive to build large knowledge bases is diminished.

An important long-range goal of artificial intelligence is the creation of knowledge bases that capture broad aspects of human knowledge as well as narrow, specialized information. The normal process of knowledge engineering used in building expert systems, while useful for many applications, has not led to much progress towards this goal. The reason is that most expert system knowledge bases are too tightly focused. An expert system designed to diagnose problems with a printer, for example, has knowledge about diagnosis, printers in general, and the specific line of printers to be diagnosed tightly intertwined for efficient reasoning. But this means the same knowledge base is virtually useless for another task involving the same kind of printer, or for diagnosing a different kind of printer (c.f. [2]). Research in qualitative physics (e.g., Chapter 11) and model-based reasoning (e.g., Section 15.4.3 and Chapter 17) attempts to overcome this limitation by carefully distinguishing between the knowledge and reasoning required for particular tasks from the knowledge of particular domains. Such research proceeds in two ways. It develops *domain theories*, which can be thought of as knowledge bases that encode knowledge of a particular domain independently of whatever reasoning task or specific system is to be modeled. It also formulates theories of, and algorithms for, reasoning tasks that can be used in many domains. Thus instead of facing N^2 research problems (e.g., "diagnosis of analog electronic circuits," "monitoring of fluid/thermal systems", etc.), in this approach we only need to tackle $2 \times N$ research problems (e.g., "diagnosis" "domain theory for fluid/thermal systems"). We believe this decomposition is crucial for long-term enterprises such as the formalization of engineering problem solving [8].

The creation of large-scale knowledge bases, especially broad knowledge bases and domain theories, is a challenging problem. There are many obstacles to such an enterprise:

- *Shifting foundations:* Advances in representation and reasoning technology can make decisions based on an earlier state of the art seem unwise. Sometimes teams decide that it is better to start over than to try to convert existing knowledge bases.
- *Lack of infrastructure:* In part because of shifting foundations, there have been few tools or methodologies developed to help in the organization and accumulation of large, coherent knowledge bases.
- *No respect:* There is often little reward for developing domain theories. Currently papers about them are rarely deemed publishable, and any activity beyond what is needed to make a current application (or demo) work is rarely seen as a good investment towards future progress.

Despite the difficulties, these issues are receiving increasing attention in artificial intelligence. Some researchers are attempting to develop deep knowledge bases for particular domains, such as botany [20], electromechanical systems [22], and thermodynamics [8]. These projects tend to have a particulare suite of tasks in mind when developing their knowledge bases, and use these tasks to guide their efforts. A different approach is taken by the the CYC project [13], which is a frontal assault at developing a broad, common sense knowledge base. The CYC group has built the largest knowledge base to date, and thus has been directly confronting issues of scale in crafting and maintaining knowledge bases. There are many lessons yet to be learned.

19.3 Embedding

Of necessity, this book has focused on problem-solving systems that can stand on their own, and many real-world tasks have this character. But many do not. Let us call an *embedded problem solver* one where a reasoning system is integrated as a module into a larger system. Some examples of embedded problem solvers include the temporal reasoning component of a factory scheduling system, the abductive component of a natural language understanding system which uses world knowledge to disambiguate phrases, and the domain expert subsystem of an intelligent tutoring system. Embedded problem solvers can provide exciting capabilities for applications and fascinating technical challenges.

Designing embedded problem solvers involves a number of constraints which were ignored in this book. Here are three that seem particularly important:

- *Bounded-time response:* Many applications involving embedded problem solvers require interaction with people or the physical world. Thus the ability to produce results within a pre-determined span of time becomes important, even if the results are partial. For example, it is rarely wise to spend five hours figuring out the perfect response to the question "How are you?" Bounded-time response allows better management of computational resources and helps ensure that the results of reasoning remain relevant to the system's goals.
- *Interruptability:* An embedded problem solver may have to postpone completion of a task, perhaps indefinitely, when new information arrives or priorities change. For example, an intelligent tutoring system

which launches into long soliloquy while ignoring the student's questions will not be very successful.

- *Articulateness:* Dependency networks are an important tool in building problem solvers that can explain the reasons for their conclusions. Dependency networks are not the whole story, however. Dependency networks can provide too much information when they contain implementation-specific details that are unnecessary for purposes of the system, and can provide too little information when background knowledge that conclusions depend on are "compiled out" for efficiency. So although truth maintenance systems provide an excellent starting point for explanation generation, generally additional work is needed to produce appropriate explanations.

These issues are being addressed by the AI research community a in a variety of ways. For instance, bounded-time response and interruptability are key issues for work on blackboard systems [5], reactive systems [14, 3], and any-time algorithms [4]. Articulateness is a focus of work on using AI techniques to aid human-computer interaction, especially with regard to explanation generation [18, 15]

19.4 Integrated architectures

The long-term scientific goal of artificial intelligence is to understand minds well enough to build them. Typically this has involved two kinds of research: Understanding the computational nature of particular capabilities that seem likely to be part of minds (e.g., vision, language, reasoning, learning), and understanding how to put capabilities together to form mind-like systems, that is, architectures for intelligence. Understandably, research on particular capabilities tends to dominate the field, since progress on architectures relies critically on progress in understanding the capabilities that comprise them. An increasing number of AI researchers are now investigating ways to combine the capabilities the field has developed into mind-like systems.

Sometimes the phrase "intelligent architectures" is used to describe such experiments, but given that today's systems are nowhere close to human in intelligence, we forswear this term in favor of the more neutral *integrated architectures*. An integrated architecture is a system which is intended to be mind-like in some way, and is distinguished by three properties:

1. *Integration.* In addition to problem-solving, such systems must include several other parts. Typically these include a means for interacting with the world (e.g., language, graphics, vision, mechanical parts, or a combination of these) and some sort of learning compoment (i.e., chunking, explanation-based learning, or analogy). An integrated architecture will typically include one or more embedded problem solvers, as described above.
2. *Agency.* A characteristic feature of integrated architecture research is addressing the question of what it means for a computational process to be an agent, interacting with a world (either physical, social, or simulated), and having its own goals and purposes.
3. *Continuous, long-term operation.* Such systems are designed either as models of minds or to perform tasks which require minds, hence they must operate over extended periods of time, unlike, say, a spreadsheet. Ideally, such systems would never be turned off.

The technological payoffs from breakthroughs in this area are obvious, ranging from personal assistant software to smart cars and houses to the general-purpose robotic workers of science fiction. However, the state of the art in designing integrated architectures is far from such wonders, and in fact today is quite primitive.

Building an integrated architecture requires both good components and good ideas on how to put them together properly. Most progress in AI has centered on developing deep understandings of particular tasks (e.g., qualitative reasoning, object recognition, planning, etc.) in a narrow context, often driven by application needs. Such specialist accounts are useful for creating applications, but need to be broadened to serve as robust components in an architecture. There are deep conceptual questions as to how to organize integrated architectures. For instance, can a loose federation of modules, each with its own internal organization and representations, serve as a useful platform or does there need to be a uniform substrate within which all capabilities are implemented? And, of course, hardware limitations are still a serious problem: Despite dramatic improvements in computer technology, the amount of computer power on the desk of the typical AI researcher is still minute compared to the computer power between his or her own ears.

A good indication of the current state of the art can be seen in the fact that longevity is still an elusive goal for integrated architectures. Of the systems described in the 1991 AAAI Spring Symposium on Integrated Intelligent Architectures, for example, few if any survived for more than an hour of continuous operation.[1] The causes were manifold, ranging from getting stuck under furniture to battery exhaustion to memory overflow. Thus progress is needed along many fronts, such as more robust sensors and actuators and better strategies for managing computational resources.

Despite the current primitive state of the art, we find the progress that has been made in integrated architectures very heartening, and in hope of encouraging additional work in this area, we suggest two challenges:

The Day Barrier: Create an integrated agent that performs useful services, without interruption, for at least one day.

The Cockroach Challenge: Create an integrated agent that functions continuously and usefully for over a year, without the direct assistance of humans with detailed knowledge of its internal structure.

The definition of "useful" is of course subject to debate: we mean only that the agent should do something that others care about, and not simply brood in a corner. And perhaps it would make sense to allow a "sleep" period of up to eight hours per twenty-four hour period, for garbage collection and other self-maintenance chores. In any case, meeting either of these challenges would be a milestone in the design of integrated architectures for intelligence.

19.5 Cognitive modeling

The leading hypothesis about the nature of mind today is that it is a computational process. Artificial intelligence draws much of its inspiration about what intelligence is from human cognition. It should not be surprising that it, in turn, can be useful in the exploration of human cognition. *Cognitive science* is the growing multidisciplinary interaction between artificial intelligence, psychology, neurobiology, linguistics,

1. This refers to operation in the agent's time frame, since some of the software agents operated many times slower than real-time.

anthropology, and philosophy to understand the nature of the human mind. The goal of the artificial intelligence aspect of this enterprise is to better understand human minds by building computer models. Just as computer simulations are useful in other branches of science, *cognitive simulations* can provide insight into the possible computational structure of the human mind. Cognitive simulation provides a method to address questions that normally would be difficult or impossible by other means. For example, due to technological and ethical limitations, we cannot simply "clip out" a piece of knowledge or skill from a human subject to see how their performance changes.

Some identify cognitive modeling with *connectionism*, the study of the properties of neural-like computational systems. Connectionism is an important approach to cognitive modeling, but it is only one approach among many. One appealing aspect of connectionism is the hope that it can provide a description of how neural systems serve as a substrate for intelligence. But the structure and behavior of neurons is quite different from what is assumed by most connectionist models, so such hopes must be tempered with caution. A second problem is that many aspects of human cognition have not been successfully captured by connectionist models [19]. And finally, suppose that, someday, we succeed in creating an artificial brain, modeling the nuances of organic brains in all the relevant details. We would still have not succeeded in our quest for a scientific understanding of intelligence, for an account of the brain is not the same as an account of what intelligence is. Accounts of neural function are no more a satisfactory explanation of how the various capabilities of cognition work than a knowledge of VLSI circuitry provides a complete account of how and why operating systems work.[2] Thus modeling at the level of symbolic processing is an essential part of the cognitive modeling enterprise.

Most cognitive modeling focuses on phenomena at a fairly low level, the "assembly language" of cognition, so to speak. For instance, a model might be used to calculate reaction times, simulate learning curves, or produce other numerical measures that can be compared with human performance [1, 12]. Such process-oriented studies can provide valuable insights, but only provide part of the picture. An alternate approach is

2. See [16] for a good description of the levels involved in explanations of cognitive phenomena.

content-oriented cognitive modeling, where the focus is understanding the computational theory (in the sense of [16]) underlying a task or capability. Some examples of content-oriented studies are modeling how children learn subtraction [24], modeling the use and acquisition of mental models [9], and modeling analogical reasoning and learning [6, 7, 10]. Content-oriented studies tend to be more difficult for several reasons. First, they require taking knowledge representation seriously. Second, they often use psychological measures that are less easily quantifiable, such as protocol analysis.

The techniques in this book will, we hope, prove useful to cognitive modelers. We believe the systems described here can be used as modules in models that attempt to capture large-scale properties of human cognition, such as the ability to learn a semester-sized body of knowledge. This of course is a chancy enterprise, but one whose potential payoff is extraordinary: A deeper understanding of the workings of the human mind.

19.6 Bibliography

[1] Anderson, J. *The Architecture of Cognition*, Harvard University Press, 1983.

[2] Buchanan, B. and Shortliffe, E. (Eds.) *Rule-Based Expert Systems: The MYCIN experiments of the Stanford Heuristic Programming Project* Addison-Wesley, Reading, Mass. 1984.

[3] Chapman, D. *Vision, instruction, and action*, MIT Press, 1991.

[4] Dean, T. L., and Wellman, M. P., *Planning and Control*, Morgan Kaufmann, 1991.

[5] Engelmore, R., and Morgan, T. (eds.), *Blackboard Systems*, Addison-Wesley, 1988.

[6] Falkenhainer, B., "A unified approach to explanation and theory formation," in Shrager, J. and Langley, P. (Eds.)*Computational models of scientific discovery and theory formation*, Morgan-Kaufmann, 1990, pp 157–196.

[7] Falkenhainer, B., Forbus, K., Gentner, D. "The Structure-Mapping Engine: Algorithm and examples", *Artificial Intelligence*, 41(1989)1–63.

[8] Forbus, K. "Intelligent computer-aided engineering," *AI Magazine*, Fall, 1988, pp 23–36.

[9] Gentner, D. and Stevens, A. (Eds.), *Mental Models*, Erlbaum, 1983.

[10] Gentner, D., Rattermann, M. J., Kotovsky, L., and Markman, A. B., "The development of relational similarity," in Halford, G. and Simon, T. (Eds.), *Developing cognitive competence: New approaches to process modeling*, Erlbaum, 1993.

[11] Jaffar, J., Michaylov, S., Stuckey, P.J., and Yap, R.H.C., "The CLP(R) Language and System", *ACM Transactions on Programming Languages and Systems* 14 (1992): 339-395.

[12] Laird, J. E., Rosenbloom, P. S., and Newell, A., *Universal subgoaling and chunking: The automatic generation and learning of goal hierarchies*, Kluwer, 1986.

[13] Lenat, D. B. and Guha, R.V. *Building Large Knowledge-Based Systems*, Addison-Wesley, Reading, MA, 1990.

[14] Maes, P. (Ed.) *Designing Autonomous Agents: Theory and Practice from Biology to Engineering and Back*, MIT Press, 1991.

[15] Malin, J. T., Schreckenghost, D. L., Woods, D. A., Potter, S., Johannesen, L., Holloway, M., and Forbus, K. "Making intelligent systems team players: Case studies and design issues. Volume 1: Human-Computer Interaction Design," NASA Technical Memorandum 104738, September, 1991.

[16] Marr, D. *Vision*, W. H. Freeman, 1982.

[17] Newell, A. *Unified Theories of Cognition*, Harvard University Press, 1990.

[18] Paris, C. L., Swartout, W., and Mann, W. (Eds.), *Natural Language Generation in Artificial Intelligence and Computational Linguistics*, Kluwer, 1991.

[19] Pinker, S. and Mehler, J. (Eds.), *Connections and symbols*, MIT Press, 1988.

[20] Porter, B., Lester, J., Murray, K., Pittman, K., Souther, A., Acker, L., and Jones, T., "AI research in the context of a multifunctional knowledge base: The Botany Knowledge Base Project," Technical Report AI-TR-88-88, Department of Computer Sciences, University of Texas at Austin, 1988.

[21] Saraswat, V.A., *Concurrent constraint programming*, MIT Press, 1993.

[22] Fikes, R., Gruber, T., Iwasaki, Y., Levy, A. and Nayak, P. *How Things Work Project Overview Technical Report* KSL 91-70, Knowledge Systems Laboratory, Stanford University, 1991.

[23] Van Hentenryck, P., *Constraint satisfaction in logic programming*, MIT Press, 1989.

[24] VanLehn, K. *Mind bugs: the origins of procedural misconceptions*, MIT Press, 1989.

[25] VanLehn, K. (Ed.), *Architectures for Intelligence/The 22nd Carnegie Mellon Symposium on Cognition*, Erlbaum, 1991.

A Putting the Programs to Work

This appendix provides some tips for setting up and using the programs associated with this book.

A.1 Organizing the files

We assume many readers have internet access, and will prefer to obtain the programs via anonymous ftp. This procedure is described at the beginning of the book. Readers who do not have internet access should contact the MIT Press, as outlined in the beginning of the book, to get floppy disks appropriate to their system.

The ftp version of the code is in a tar file, which assumes a unix directory structure. This makes things very simple if you are using a unix system, of course. What about other systems? There are good shareware and freeware versions of tar that run on most microcomputers, so unpacking the files should not be too troublesome. (Remember to transfer them in binary mode!) The floppy version of the code will use a compression scheme appropriate to the kind of computer involved.

All file names were chosen to fit within the most restrictive conventions (i.e., MS-DOS), so those should not require changing. On an MS-DOS machine, the sources take up about 1.8MB of space.

The sources are grouped into subdirectories. These are:

`cps` Code for Chapter 3.

`tre` Code for Chapter 4.

`ftre` Code for Chapter 5.

`jtms` Code for Chapters 7 and 8.

`ltms` Code for Chapters 9, 10, and 13.

`tgizmo` Code for Chapter 11.

`atms` Code for Chapters 12 and 14.

`tcon` Code for Chapter 15.

`gde` Code for Chapters 16 and 17.

`relax` Code for Chapter 18.

`utils` Utility programs, described below.

For each system, the order in which files are mentioned in the corresponding chapter is an appropriate order for loading. Each system also includes a file which contains information which can be used with the loading utility described below.

A.2 A guide to the utility programs

The utility programs are contained in two files:

`loader.lisp`: Procedures for loading a collection of files.

`lst.lisp`: Procedures for making listings of code.

We describe them each in turn.

A.2.1 The loading programs (loader.lisp)

In using systems of programs it is typical to have files whose sole purpose is to orchestrate the loading and compilation of those files. The utilities in this file make the creation of such system files easier. The procedures are

`load-files` takes as input a list of file names and loads them. There are two optional arguments, the current file path and the default extension for files.

`compile-files` takes as input a list of file names and optionally, a file path. It compiles each file in turn.

`compile-load-files` takes as input a list of file names and optionally, a file path. It compiles and then loads each file in turn.

The optional argument information is drawn from the following global variables:

`*default-pathname*` is the file path used by default.

`*default-source-type*` is the file extension for Common Lisp sources, used by `compile-files`.

`*default-bin-type*` is the file extension for compiled Common Lisp files, used both by `load-files` and `compile-files`.

When you first set up the sources, you should edit the values of these variables to contain the values appropriate for your operating system and version of Common Lisp. (If you are using these files with more than one operating system or Common Lisp version, we highly recommend using the Common Lisp `#+` reader macros to allow the same file to be used across multiple environments. You will see examples of `#+` in the existing files.)

Each system includes a file which defines a list of other files and the file path for that system. When you begin to use a system, you should edit the file path variable to reflect where you put the code. To compile the programs, the procedure `compile-load-files` can be used. With some Common Lisp implementations it may be necessary to first load the sources (using `load-files` with the source extension as the file extension) and then call `compile-load-files`. We have attempted to minimize forward dependencies between files, but occasionally we allowed them if they optimized the readability of the code.

A.2.2 The listing program (lst.lisp)

Software documents are wonderful, but sometimes it is best to curl up with a good book or listing. The procedures in this file simplify the creation of readable listings. These procedures are part of the suite of programs that generated the companion Listings volume for this book. (If you intend to make many listings of programs from the book, we recommend instead buying the Listings volume—the MIT Press can probably print more cheaply than you can, and is selling them at cost.) The main procedures are

`lst` which takes as input the name of a file to print and produces as output a new file of some appropriate form. `lst` takes the following keyword arguments

- `:MODE` Determines the form of the output file. Must be one of `:LPT`, for pure ASCII files, `:EPSON`, for Epson FX-80 compatible printers, `:LATEX`, for producing stand-alone LaTeX source files, or `:BOOK`, for producing source files that can be inserted into other LaTeX files.
- `:OUTPUT` Name of the the file to be produced. If this argument is not supplied, the program makes its best guess.
- `:HEADER` A string inserted on the top of each page in the output file.

`lst-directory` runs `lst` on all the files in a given path.

`lst-files` runs `lst` on a list of files relative to a given path.

For LaTeX users: The `BPSCode` environment used by the LaTeX and book modes is illustrated below. The alltt.sty was written by Leslie Lamport, and is commonly available on LaTeX-related ftp sites.

```
\newenvironment{BPSCode}{
\packlines
\begin{small}
\begin{alltt}
}{
\end{alltt}
\end{small}
\unpacklines
}
```

Index

Artificial Intelligence
Patrick Henry Winston, founding editor
J. Michael Brady, Daniel G. Bobrow, and Randall Davis, current editors

Artificial Intelligence: An MIT Perspective, Volume I: Expert Problem Solving, Natural Language Understanding, Intelligent Computer Coaches, Representation and Learning, edited by Patrick Henry Winston and Richard Henry Brown, 1979

Artificial Intelligence: An MIT Perspective, Volume II: Understanding Vision, Manipulation, Computer Design, Symbol Manipulation, edited by Patrick Henry Winston and Richard Henry Brown, 1979

NETL: A System for Representing and Using Real-World Knowledge, Scott Fahlman, 1979

The Interpretation of Visual Motion, by Shimon Ullman, 1979

A Theory of Syntactic Recognition for Natural Language, Mitchell P. Marcus, 1980

Turtle Geometry: The Computer as a Medium for Exploring Mathematics, Harold Abelson and Andrea di Sessa, 1981

From Images to Surfaces: A Computational Study of the Human Visual System, William Eric Leifur Grimson, 1981

Robot Manipulators: Mathematics, Programming, and Control, Richard P. Paul, 1981

Computational Models of Discourse, edited by Michael Brady and Robert C. Berwick, 1982

Robot Motion: Planning and Control, edited by Michael Brady, John M. Hollerbach, Timothy Johnson, Tomás Lozano-Pérez, and Matthew T. Mason, 1982

In-Depth Understanding: A Computer Model of Integrated Processing for Narrative Comprehension, Michael G. Dyer, 1983

Robotic Research: The First International Symposium, edited by Hideo Hanafusa and Hirochika Inoue, 1985

Robot Hands and the Mechanics of Manipulation, Matthew T. Mason and J. Kenneth Salisbury, Jr., 1985

The Acquisition of Syntactic Knowledge, Robert C. Berwick, 1985

The Connection Machine, W. Daniel Hillis, 1985

Legged Robots that Balance, Marc H. Raibert, 1986

Robotics Research: The Third International Symposium, edited by O. D. Faugeras and Georges Giralt, 1986

Machine Interpretation of Line Drawings, Kokichi Sugihara, 1986

ACTORS: A Model of Concurrent Computation in Distributed Systems, Gul A. Agha, 1986

Knowledge-Based Tutoring: The GUIDON Program, William Clancey, 1987

AI in the 1980s and Beyond: An MIT Survey, edited by W. Eric L. Grimson and Ramesh S. Patil, 1987

Visual Reconstruction, Andrew Blake and Andrew Zisserman, 1987

Reasoning about Change: Time and Causation from the Standpoint of Artificial Intelligence, Yoav Shoham, 1988

Model-Based Control of a Robot Manipulator, Chae H. An, Christopher G. Atkeson, and John M. Hollerbach, 1988

A Robot Ping-Pong Player: Experiment in Real-Time Intelligent Control, Russell L. Andersson, 1988

Robotics Research: The Fourth International Symposium, edited by Robert C. Bolles and Bernard Roth, 1988

The Paralation Model: Architecture-Independent Parallel Programming, Gary Sabot, 1988

Concurrent System for Knowledge Processing: An Actor Perspective, edited by Carl Hewitt and Gul Agha, 1989

Automated Deduction in Nonclassical Logics: Efficient Matrix Proof Methods for Modal and Intuitionistic Logics, Lincoln Wallen, 1989

Shape from Shading, edited by Berthold K. P. Horn and Michael J. Brooks, 1989

Ontic: A Knowledge Representation System for Mathematics, David A. McAllester, 1989

Solid Shape, Jan J. Koenderink, 1990

Expert Systems: Human Issues, edited by Dianne Berry and Anna Hart, 1990

Artificial Intelligence: Concepts and Applications, edited by A. R. Mirzai, 1990

Robotics Research: The Fifth International Symposium, edited by Hirofumi Miura and Suguru Arimoto, 1990

Theories of Comparative Analysis, Daniel S. Weld, 1990

Artificial Intelligence at MIT: Expanding Frontiers, edited by Patrick Henry Winston and Sarah Alexandra Shellard, 1990

Vector Models for Data-Parallel Computing, Guy E. Blelloch, 1990

Experiments in the Machine Interpretation of Visual Motion, David W. Murray and Bernard F. Buxton, 1990

Object Recognition by Computer: The Role of Geometric Constraints, W. Eric L. Grimson, 1990

Representing and Reasoning With Probabilistic Knowledge: A Logical Approach to Probabilities, Fahiem Bacchus, 1990

3D Model Recognition from Stereoscopic Cues, edited by John E. W. Mayhew and John P. Frisby, 1991

Artificial Vision for Mobile Robots: Stereo Vision and Multisensory Perception, Nicholas Ayache, 1991

Truth and Modality for Knowledge Representation, Raymond Turner, 1991

Made-Up Minds: A Constructivist Approach to Artificial Intelligence, Gary L. Drescher, 1991

Vision, Instruction, and Action, David Chapman, 1991

Do the Right Thing: Studies in Limited Rationality, Stuart Russell and Eric Wefeld, 1991

KAM: A System for Intelligently Guiding Numerical Experimentation by Computer, Kenneth Man-Kam Yip, 1991

Solving Geometric Constraint Systems: A Case Study in Kinematics, Glenn A. Kramer, 1992

Geometric Invariants in Computer Vision, edited by Joseph Mundy and Andrew Zisserman, 1992

HANDEY: A Robot Task Planner, Tomás Lozano-Pérez, Joseph L. Jones, Emmanuel Mazer, and Patrick A. O'Donnell, 1992

Active Vision, edited by Andrew Blake and Alan Yuille, 1992

Recent Advances in Qualitative Physics, edited by Boi Faltings and Peter Struss, 1992

Machine Translation: A View from the Lexicon, Bonnie Jean Dorr, 1993

The Language Complexity Game, Eric Sven Ristad, 1993

The SOAR Papers: Research on Integrated Intelligence, edited by Paul S. Rosenbloom, John E. Laird, and Allen Newell, 1993

Three-Dimensional Computer Vision: A Geometric Viewpoint, Olivier Faugeras, 1993